Transitional Justice in Rwanda

Transitional Justice in Rwanda: Accountability for Atrocity comprehensively analyzes the full range of the transitional justice processes undertaken for the Rwandan genocide. Drawing on the author's extensive professional experience as the principal justice policy maker and the leading law enforcement officer in Rwanda from 1996–2003, the book provides an in-depth analysis of the social, political and legal challenges faced by Rwanda in the aftermath of the genocide and the aspirations and legacy of transitional justice. The book explores the role played by the accountability processes not just in pursuing accountability but also in shaping the reconstruction of Rwanda's institutions of democratic governance and political reconciliation. Central to this exploration will be the examination of whether or not transitional justice in Rwanda has contributed to a foundational rule of law reform process.

While recognizing the necessity of pursuing accountability for mass atrocity, the book argues that a maximal approach to accountability for genocide may undermine the promotion of core objectives of transitional justice. Taking on one of the key questions facing practitioners and scholars of transitional justice today, the book suggests that the pursuit of mass accountability, particularly where socio-economic resources and legal capacity is limited, may destabilize the process of rule of law reform, endangering core human rights norms. Moreover, the book suggests that pursuing a strategy of mass accountability may undermine the process of democratic transition, particularly in a context where impunity for crimes committed by the victors of armed conflicts persists. Highlighting the ongoing democratic deficit in Rwanda and resulting political instability in the Great Lakes region, the book argues that the effectiveness of transitional justice ultimately hinges on the nature and success of political transition.

Gerald Gahima was central to the rebuilding of Rwanda's justice system in the aftermath of the 1994 genocide, first as Deputy Minister of the Ministry of Justice from 1996–1999, and subsequently as the country's Attorney General from 1999–2003. He now works as an independent consultant to various organizations, including UN bodies, on issues relating to the rule of law and reconstruction of post-conflict countries.

Transitional Justice in Rwanda

Accountability for atrocity

Gerald Gahima

Routledge
Taylor & Francis Group
LONDON AND NEW YORK

First published 2013
by Routledge
2 Park Square, Milton Park, Abingdon, Oxon OX14 4RN

Simultaneously published in the USA and Canada
by Routledge
711 Third Avenue, New York, NY 10017

Routledge is an imprint of the Taylor & Francis Group, an informa business

British Library Cataloguing in Publication Data
A catalogue record for this book is available from the British Library

Library of Congress Cataloguing in Publication Data
A catalog record for this book has been requested

ISBN 978-0-415-52278-6 (hbk)
ISBN 978-0-415-52279-3 (pbk)
ISBN 978-0-203-07515-9 (ebk)

Typeset in Garamond
by Cenveo Publisher Services

Contents

Abbreviations

AfrCmHPR	Africa Commission on Human and Peoples' Rights
AI	Amnesty International
CERD	United Nations Committee on the Elimination of Racial Discrimination
DRC	Democratic Republic of Congo
ECHR	European Court of Human Rights
FAR	Forces Armées Rwandaises
FARG	Fonds National pour l'Assistance aux Rescapés du Génocide
HRC	Human Rights Committee
HRW	Human Rights Watch
I/ACtHR	Inter-American Court on Human Rights
ICC	International Criminal Court
ICJ	International Court of Justice
ICTR	International Criminal Tribunal for Rwanda
ICTY	International Criminal Tribunal for the Former Yugoslavia
ILC	International Law Commission
MDR	Mouvement Démocratique Républicain
MRND	Mouvement Révolutionnaire National pour le Développement
NRM	National Resistance Movement
OAU	Organisation of African Unity
RANU	Rwandese Alliance for National Union
RPA	Rwandese Patriotic Army
RPF	Rwandese Patriotic Front
UNAMIR	United Nations Assistance Mission in Rwanda
UNCHR	United Nations Commission on Human Rights
UNHCHR	United Nations High Commissioner for Human Rights
UNOHCHR	United Nations Office of the High Commissioner for Human Rights

Table of Legislation

Spain

United Kingdom

United States

Table of Cases

Documents of the International Criminal Tribunal for Rwanda, including indictments, minutes of proceedings and decisions are only published electronically, primarily on the tribunal's website: http://unictr.org. The tribunal also published its documents in CD-ROM form that are freely available to the public.

Table of International Instruments

Acknowledgements

The Rwanda genocide was a turning point in the history of accountability for atrocity. The manner in which the armed conflict of the 1990s was resolved made universal accountability for the genocide possible. The task of making justice a reality for the victims of the genocide was the work of hundreds of people across the justice sector, with a shared ambition to contribute to ending impunity in Rwanda. The difficult and often selfless service of many of these women and men was rarely appreciated, let alone commended, by a nation still deeply divided by its past and an outside world that did not adequately comprehend the challenges of their work. I would like to pay tribute to the dedication and hard work of many colleagues who played a role in Rwanda's attempt to deal with the legacy of the indescribable horror of genocide.

In the course of our efforts to craft and put into practice appropriate policy responses to the violence that our country experienced during the 1990s, we were over the years blessed with the help of a very large number of foreign professional colleagues who put their expertise in law, human rights, transitional justice and related disciplines at our nation's disposal. In the course of my work, I personally benefitted from the knowledge, expertise and advice of many such experts, including Professor William Schabas, Dr Moniker Klinger, Judge Karl Puszkajler, Andre Samson, Professor Madeleine Morris, Pierre St Hilaire, Neil Kritz, Michael Johnson, Onyen Yong, Roman Vichr and very many others, to all of whom I remain deeply grateful. I am particularly grateful to Professor Schabas, whose scholarship first awoke me to the need to always consider the human rights implications of my work. Professor Schabas also played a crucial role as a partner in our efforts to improve Rwanda's legal education system. He subsequently welcomed me as a student at the Irish Centre for Human Rights and also agreed to be the supervisor of my thesis that is the origin of this book.

Since leaving public service in Rwanda, I have had the privilege to work and collaborate with many distinguished scholars and practitioners in the fields of human rights, transitional justice and international development. Many of these have shared their insights, influenced my thinking and provided professional help in all kinds of forms, for which I am profoundly grateful. Among them, I particularly wish to thank Professor Siobhan Mullally. I would never be able to repay the debt I owe her for her guidance, friendship and inspiration.

Relations between the Rwanda government and the International Criminal Tribunal for Rwanda have been the subject of extensive journalistic reporting and significant academic writing. Much of this reporting and writing has focused on the relatively rare occasions of extreme tension between the tribunal and the Rwanda government. Contrary to prevailing misconceptions, the success of the tribunal in fulfilling its core mandate to bring perpetrators of the genocide to justice was always a key priority of the Rwanda government. My colleagues and I at all levels in government (with the exception of the military and security services) worked closely with officers and the management of the tribunal to facilitate its operations in Rwanda. I wish to thank Mohamed Othman, Bernard Muna and Adama Dieng for their collaboration during the difficult period of the tribunal's early years and the relations of mutual respect and trust that I believe made that collaboration possible.

Post-genocide Rwanda has attracted extraordinary research interest. My scholarship on Rwanda's transitional justice processes has introduced me to a very large number of scholars on Rwanda's reconstruction after war and genocide, a good number of whom have been helpful to me in my own work. Dr Susan Thomson, whose scholarship of citizens' engagement with the state in post-genocide Rwanda addresses some of the issues discussed in this book, deserves special mention. She has always generously shared her immense knowledge and insights of contemporary Rwanda.

This book, and the message that it conveys, would never have seen the light of day had the commissioning editors at Routledge not recognized the value of its worth and supported my desire to have it published. I am very grateful to Katherine Carpenter and Stephen Gutierrez of Routledge for their help in making the publication of this book a reality. I am also deeply indebted to Rebecca Wilson for her invaluable editorial assistance.

Last but not least, I would like to acknowledge the support of members of my family and friends that contributed immensely to making this work possible. My transition from policy maker to scholar occurred at a time when I was at a crossroads in my professional life and my personal engagement with public policy issues in Rwanda. This transition has not been without hardship and sacrifice, much of it shared, unfortunately, by those dear to me, especially my wife Anne, our children, my siblings and our mother. My family, both immediate and extended, has been a source of inspiration and fortitude during very trying times. A large number of friends have been an invaluable source of encouragement and support. I am grateful to all of them. I particularly wish to thank Michael Johnson, Roman Vichr, Peter Blunt, Dixean Walker and Tatek Zarou for their friendship and support over the past several years.

Much like Rwanda's wider post-genocide reconstruction, the processes of accountability for atrocity undertaken by Rwanda remain divisive. Needless to say, I alone bear responsibility for the views expressed in this work.

Olney, Maryland

Introduction

Rwanda has a long history of gross human rights abuses stretching back several decades (Rudasingwa 1994). The country experienced particularly catastrophic violence during the 1990s. The violence reached its peak in 1994, when the government of the day embarked upon a successful plan to carry out genocide against the Tutsi minority and to commit massacres of its Hutu opponents (Destexhe 1994; Des Forges 1999; African Rights 2000; Organization of African Unity 2000; Prunier 1995). A report of the government of Rwanda has indicated that the genocide claimed more than a million lives (Ministère de l'Administration Locale, de l'Information et des Affaires Sociales 2002).

The genocide occurred at a moment in history when the global fight against impunity for gross human rights violations had gained some momentum (Schabas 2003c, 2006). The human rights movement had managed to bring the issue of accountability for gross human rights abuses to the forefront of international relations. This momentum in the fight against impunity had recently culminated in the establishment of the International Criminal Tribunal for the Former Yugoslavia (ICTY).[1] Further, the enormity of the genocide and the shame of policy makers of the major world powers at having stood by, while hundreds of thousands of Rwandans were slaughtered, left the international community little choice but to take measures to bring at least some of the perpetrators of the genocide to justice.

Developments in Rwanda made prospects of justice for the genocide a foregone conclusion. The genocide was brought to an end by the military victory of the Rwandese Patriotic Army (RPA), a rebel army dominated by members of the Tutsi community. The defeat of the organizers of the genocide and the subsequent ascension to power of a Tutsi-dominated government ensured that justice for the genocide would be a reality (Scharf 1999: pp. 622–3). The manner in which the Rwandan genocide came to its end provided the first real opportunity in modern history to bring significant numbers of perpetrators of mass atrocity to justice.

Rwanda has undertaken what is arguably the most comprehensive attempt ever to bring perpetrators of mass atrocity to justice (Drumbl 2004: p. 44). The accountability processes that Rwanda has undertaken to address the atrocities that were committed during the 1990s include prosecutions through the formal domestic criminal justice system, trials by tribunals run by lay judges called *Gacaca*, international criminal justice administered by the International Criminal Tribunal for Rwanda (ICTR)[2] and trials by other states based on the principle of universal jurisdiction. Rwanda's domestic accountability mechanisms have been implemented against all odds. Law enforcement and judicial institutions ceased to function as a result of the war and genocide. The legal system that was tasked with dispensing justice for genocide lacked the financial and human resources to support law enforcement and judicial institutions of a normal, stable country, let alone one emerging from destruction caused by war and genocide. Rwanda remained deeply divided along ethnic lines.

The accountability processes that Rwanda has undertaken to bring perpetrators of the genocide to justice are positive developments in the fight against a culture of impunity for human rights abuses that has long been deeply entrenched in Rwandan society. These processes have, however, also been the subject of considerable criticism, especially on account of their failure to comply with applicable human rights standards and to address human rights violations alleged to have been committed by the victors (Cousineau 1997; Scharf 1999; Amnesty International 2000, 2004; Zorbas 2004; Waldorf 2006b). Much of the criticism is not without foundation. The mechanisms have certainly experienced certain shortcomings (International Crisis Group 1999; Amnesty International 2000; Oomen 2005, 2009; Human Rights Watch 2008, 2011). Nonetheless, in spite of the shortcomings, the accountability processes that Rwanda has attempted to carry out are not only significant within Rwanda, but should also be of interest to many beyond Rwanda's borders (Strain 2003: p. 123). Rwanda's judicial responses to the genocide are a landmark development in the global struggle against impunity for gross human rights violations in general and mass atrocity in particular.

Rwanda is not unique with regard to its experience of deadly conflict and violence, or even genocide. Genocide and mass atrocity have afflicted mankind throughout human history (Kiernan 2007). Nor is Rwanda's decision to respond to the violence that it experienced during the 1990s with justice out of character with practices in other post-conflict situations. Many other countries in or emerging from conflict, depending on their particular circumstances, undertake some form of transitional justice, a concept defined as the full range of processes and mechanisms associated with a society's attempts to come to terms with a legacy of large-scale past abuses, in order to ensure accountability, serve justice and achieve reconciliation (Kritz 1995; United Nations 2004). Rwanda's legal responses to genocide are, however, unique in at least one respect: the unprecedented lengths to which the state has gone to seek out and hold accountable, through criminal sanctions, each and every participant in crimes of mass atrocity. The central questions that this book seeks to explore are: What unique challenges does a society developing transitional justice policies to address a legacy of mass atrocity face? Are the mechanisms with which societies in political transition ordinarily reckon with legacies of past human abuses appropriate for situations of mass atrocity in general, and mass atrocity in which there has been large-scale participation in particular? Are legal responses that seek to enforce criminal sanctions against each and every perpetrator involved in mass atrocity, in which there has been popular participation, effective tools for promoting the goals of transitional justice in a post-conflict society? What transitional justice mechanisms, or combination of mechanisms, are appropriate for dealing with the aftermath of mass atrocity involving large-scale social participation? What lessons do the transitional justice processes that Rwanda has undertaken in response to the genocide have for other societies that have experienced or may experience mass violence and victimization?

This book explores whether the transitional justice processes that the post-genocide government of Rwanda adopted, which aimed at universal accountability for all crimes, were an appropriate response to the legacy of the 1990s or whether there were any viable alternatives to this approach. In investigating the question whether legal responses that seek to enforce criminal sanctions against each and every perpetrator involved in a mass atrocity in which there has been large-scale popular participation are effective tools for promoting the goals of transitional justice, the book considers whether the mechanisms of accountability that Rwanda chose to pursue have been effective in achieving the objectives that they were designed or intended to achieve. It explores the tentative lessons that may be drawn from Rwanda's experience with processes of accountability for mass atrocity and the potential implications of these lessons for other societies facing the challenge of reckoning with the violence of their past, particularly in situations of mass atrocity in which there has been large-scale participation by ordinary citizens. The book inquires about the ultimate legacy or lasting impact of Rwanda's mechanisms of accountability for atrocity.

This book seeks to advance the argument that while existing transitional justice theory provides a general framework to guide policy making on how societies that have experienced violent conflict can reckon with the violence of their past, situations of mass atrocity involving large-scale popular participation require a unique approach. The transitional justice processes of a society that has experienced mass atrocity must necessarily involve investigations and prosecution of serious human rights by domestic courts. International criminal justice is an indispensable part of the architecture for fighting impunity in such situations. However, the approach advocated by the human rights movement that all serious human rights violations must be investigated, prosecuted and punished cannot and should not be strictly applied to situations of mass atrocity in which there has been large-scale popular participation. Although criminal justice is a critical component of the architecture of transitional justice, a maximal approach to accountability, aiming at the indiscriminate pursuit of all suspected perpetrators in situations of mass atrocity in which there has been a high level of popular participation, is not likely to lead to realization of the goals of transitional justice, as established in existing scholarship. This approach leads to unfair trials that undermine efforts to promote a culture of respect for human rights and the rule of law. Large-scale prosecutions of crimes of mass atrocity also undermine efforts to promote reconciliation and are likely to fuel social divisions and lead to instability instead of advancing sustainable peace. The most appropriate policy response to a legacy of mass atrocity involving large-scale participation in atrocity is a blend of responses from within and beyond criminal justice that addresses the specific challenges that each of these societies faces. Alternatives to criminal prosecutions have a role to play in such situations. These alternatives may include mechanisms of conflict resolution based on custom or tradition. A society that has experienced mass atrocity involving large-scale popular participation must make difficult choices about what proportion of perpetrators should be tried by the courts and what proportion should be dealt with by the chosen alternatives. Neither criminal prosecutions nor any other alternatives are likely to help a post-conflict society achieve the objectives of transitional justice if the processes in question are not legitimate in the perception of the people. Transitional justice instruments and broader governance and democratization challenges appear to be intimately linked. Mechanisms of accountability for atrocity have little prospect of helping a post-conflict state to achieve the objectives of transitional justice if they are not part of a wider process of reforms that address the fundamental causes of conflict in the society in question.

The book is divided into 11 chapters.

Chapter 1 discusses the theoretical framework of the field of transitional justice that underpins the accountability processes that Rwanda has undertaken.

Chapter 2 provides the background context for the discussion of the mechanisms of accountability for atrocity that are the subject matter of the book. It discusses the broader historical background to the genocide and provides a brief history of the genocide itself. It also discusses a unique and defining character of the genocide of the Tutsi of Rwanda, namely the participation of a very large number of private citizens in committing atrocities.

Chapters 3–7 discuss the various accountability mechanisms with which Rwanda has responded to the legacy of the violence that the country experienced during the 1990s.

Chapter 3 discusses the recovery, reconstruction and development challenges that Rwanda faced in the aftermath of the genocide, the link between justice and national recovery and reconstruction, the policy development processes through which decisions on the accountability mechanisms that Rwanda adopted were made and the objectives of the mechanisms of accountability that the government of Rwanda chose to pursue.

Chapter 4 discusses the process of accountability for the Rwanda genocide through the ICTR. The chapter examines the background to the establishment of the tribunal, the issues that were in contention between the Rwandan government and the international community concerning the establishment of the tribunal, the objectives that the institution was established to promote, the performance of the tribunal since its establishment, and its relations with stakeholders in Rwanda. The chapter concludes with an examination of the tribunal's completion strategy and its impact and legacy.

Chapter 5 examines the genocide trials that have been undertaken by the formal criminal justice system of Rwanda since 1996. The chapter discusses the challenges and constraints that Rwanda's initial attempts to address the legacy of the genocide through domestic criminal prosecutions faced and the various strategies that the post-genocide government adopted to promote its transitional justice goals through domestic prosecutions. The chapter evaluates the impact that the domestic prosecutions that Rwanda's courts conducted had in advancing the government's transitional justice goals, the factors that account for the failure of these trials to achieve their original objectives, and the implications of the domestic prosecutions that Rwanda's courts have undertaken for the field of transitional justice. The chapter concludes with a discussion of the proceedings of the ICTR and courts of other states that have considered applications to transfer cases or to extradite genocide suspects for trial in Rwanda.

Chapter 6 discusses Gacaca, a modified version of a neo-traditional justice mechanism that Rwanda has adopted as its principal mechanism for reckoning with the legacy of the genocide. It then traces the implementation of the Gacaca process, evaluates its positive outcomes as well as the weaknesses, and explores the factors that have constrained Gacaca's potential to achieve intended objectives. The chapter concludes with a review of Phil Clark's work on Gacaca, especially the book *The Gacaca Courts, Post-Genocide Justice and Reconciliation in Rwanda – Justice without Lawyers* (Cambridge University Press, 2011), which challenged all previous scholarship on Gacaca as deeply flawed and reflects on Gacaca's lessons for transitional justice.

Chapter 7 discusses investigations and prosecutions of genocide and other serious crimes that were committed during the Rwanda genocide that have been undertaken by other states on the basis of the principle of universal jurisdiction. The chapter discusses the rationale and legal basis for the exercise of the principle of universal jurisdiction for international crimes and other gross human rights violations in general and in relation to the Rwanda genocide in particular, and provides an overview of the experiences of the various states in investigating and prosecuting crimes alleged to have been committed during the Rwanda genocide on the basis of universal jurisdiction.

Chapter 8 deals with issues relating to human rights violations alleged to have been committed by the victors. It discusses the human rights practices of the RPA and security services during and immediately after the genocide, and the extent to which Rwanda's accountability processes have addressed the human rights violations in question. The chapter explores the possible implications of failure to address the issue of the crimes that the victors are alleged to have committed and discusses whether lack of even-handedness negates the worth of transitional justice processes in general and in Rwanda in particular.

The final two chapters of the book explore the impact of the accountability mechanisms that Rwanda has experimented with and the tentative lessons that can be drawn from Rwanda's accountability experiences to date. Chapter 9 discusses the extent to which the accountability processes that Rwanda has undertaken have succeeded in achieving their intended objectives. The chapter focuses, in particular, on the impact of the accountability processes on Rwanda's post-genocide reconstruction and political transition, including the restoration of law and order, the eradication of impunity, the promotion of the rule of law and respect for human rights, and prevention of future conflict. The chapter includes a discussion of the role of the ICTR and its impact on Rwanda's reconstruction and political transition. Chapter 10 comprises a discussion on the tentative lesson or lessons that may be drawn from Rwanda's legal responses to genocide and other grave human rights abuses.

The book ends with a short conclusion that reflects on the future of transitional justice in Rwanda.

Justice after violent conflict is always a politically charged process. Justice after sectarian mass atrocity, rare as it is, is probably the most sensitive, difficult and divisive of the processes that a post-conflict society may ever have to undertake in the context of its state re-building agenda. The processes of transitional justice that this book discusses are no exception. The processes have been widely criticized within and outside Rwanda. Indeed, issues surrounding the mechanisms of accountability for atrocity that Rwanda has undertaken still deeply divide Rwandan society. In view of the competing points of views and deep passions that still surround the subject of accountability for the human rights violations that were committed in Rwanda during the 1990s conflict, it is only appropriate that I should at the outset indicate my intimate personal involvement in the events, issues and processes that this book discusses.

I had the privilege to serve in senior level positions in the Rwanda government after the 1994 genocide. My time of service in the government coincided with the process of reconstruction that followed the genocide and the development and implementation of policies to address the legacy of the violence that the country had recently experienced. As a lawyer and fairly senior member of the Rwandese Patriotic Front (RPF), I played a very active role in the development of the government's policies on accountability for the genocide from the very beginning.

I was the principal policy maker on issues relating to accountability for genocide and justice sector reform, and the face and voice of Rwanda's justice system, during the first ten years after the genocide. As Deputy Minister, I led the rebuilding of Rwanda's justice sector institutions in the aftermath of the war and genocide and was intimately involved in the day-to-day management of the many challenges that Rwanda's justice system faced at the time, and instrumental in the implementation of policies and strategies that we adopted to address those challenges. I played a key role in the formulation and implementation of policies relating to and the establishment of mechanisms of accountability for genocide and other grave violations of human rights. I served as the principal liaison between the government of Rwanda and the ICTR. As Prosecutor General, I had the enormous challenge of overseeing the investigation and prosecution of the crimes that had been committed by civilians in the context of the genocide, the largest number of prosecutions of genocide since the adoption of the genocide Convention. While I was an early and frequent critic of the tribunal, I also played a crucial role in providing support to the investigative work of the Office of the Prosecutor. I also participated in the development and establishment of the institution of Gacaca.

Post-genocide Rwanda and Rwanda's transitional justice processes have been the subject of exceptional research interest. Until now, much of the scholarship on the subject has been undertaken by foreigners. This book seeks to add to knowledge of Rwanda's transitional justice processes by rendering an account of the processes from an insider perspective. How were the policies on Rwanda's transitional justice processes developed? Which stakeholders were represented in the relevant policy discussions? What proposals or views did each of the groups involved push for? What motivated the various stakeholders to advocate the approaches? Why did we make the choices we finally made? What were our goals? And to what extent have the policies that Rwanda has pursued in response to the legacy of the genocide achieved the goals of transitional justice?

1 Theoretical Framework of Transitional Justice

This chapter discusses certain aspects of transitional justice in Rwanda in the aftermath of the 1994 genocide. It sets out the theoretical framework in which the subject discussed by the book is situated.

1.1 Defining Transitional Justice

The term 'transitional justice' is of relatively recent origins. Ruti Teitel writes that she first coined the phrase in a 1991 paper entitled 'Transitional Justice: A Bridge between Regimes' (Teitel 2010). The term was subsequently popularized by the publication of *Transitional Justice: How Emerging Democracies Reckon with Former Regimes* in 1995 (Kritz 1995). In *Transitional Justice*, Teitel defines the term as 'the conception of justice associated with a period of political change, characterized by legal responses to confront the wrongdoing of repressive predecessor regimes' (2003a: p. 69). This early definition appears to have been influenced by scholarship on political transition of the time, which assumed that transition from authoritarian rule would necessarily lead to the establishment of democracy and the rule of law. Experience has since taught us regime change does not necessarily set a society on an inevitable path to democracy and the rule of law. Yet, even regimes in states whose political transitions are unsuccessful often attempt to undertake some processes of reckoning with past abuses. Hence, the definition of transitional justice needs to be framed in terms that include situations of failed or stalled political transition. Some scholars have equated transitional justice with post-conflict justice (Bassiouni 2002), but the two are not synonymous. Transitional justice today plays a growing role even in situations where violent conflict is still ongoing. There is, as yet, no universally accepted definition of the concept. Roht-Arriaza has defined transitional justice as the 'set of practices, mechanisms, and concerns that are aimed at confronting and dealing with the legacies of past violations of human rights and humanitarian law' (Van der Merwe *et al.* 2009: p. vii). In the 2004 United Nations report on transitional justice and the rule of law, then Secretary General Kofi Annan defined transitional justice as 'the full range of processes and mechanisms associated with a society's attempts to come to terms with a legacy of large-scale past abuses, in order to ensure accountability, serve justice and achieve reconciliation' (United Nations 2004: p. 4). Vandegiste (2009: p. 22) perhaps provides the most inclusive definition of the subject, as 'the process through which states and societies deal with a legacy of large-scale human rights abuses in the context of a change of political regime.'

Transitional justice is an ever-evolving subject. There is a consensus, however, about its core elements. Transitional justice may be broadly defined as the policies, practices and mechanisms with which societies seek to confront and deal with legacies of past violations of human rights and humanitarian law in the context of political transition with a view to restoring or establishing social cohesion and securing durable peace.

1.2 Transitional Justice in Historical Perspective

Although the term 'transitional justice' is a recent phenomenon, the question of how to respond to mass atrocity and gross human rights abuses has long been an issue of international concern (Neier 1998). Historically, mass atrocity and other appalling human rights violations have generally gone unpunished (Akhavan 1996). In practice, the norm was effective immunity from prosecution under domestic law for officials carrying out the government's acts, even in cases involving the gravest crimes. Turkey got away with the genocide of the Armenians, the first of the genocides of the twentieth century. The victors of World World I tried, unsuccessfully, to have Germans account for atrocities for which they were responsible (Heberer and Matthäus 2008).

The Nuremberg and Tokyo tribunals represented a watershed moment in the struggle against impunity for gross human rights abuses. The trials of the two tribunals established several key principles relating to accountability for atrocity, including the principles that the human rights of individuals or groups are a matter of international concern; that the international community's interest in preventing or punishing offences against humanity committed within states overrules any concept of national sovereignty; that not just states but individuals can be held accountable for their role in committing atrocities; and that officials who order or commit such abuses can and must be held accountable (Kritz 1996b: p. 22; Ratner, Abrams and Bischoff 2009).

The relative success of the Nuremberg and Tokyo tribunals prompted initiatives to establish a permanent international criminal court (Schabas 2006: p. 11). The optimism about prospects for future enforcement of international law against perpetrators of atrocity that the Nuremberg and Tokyo trials had raised was soon dashed by the advent of the Cold War. Cold War tensions made progress towards establishment of the proposed court impossible (Schabas 2006: p. 3). In 1954, the General Assembly suspended the mandates of both the Committee and International Law Commission to prepare a statute for a permanent international criminal court.[1] Impunity for grave human rights abuses again became the norm, rather than the exception (Mutua 1997). Human rights issues became subordinate to the geopolitical considerations of states.[2] Governments generally avoided addressing human rights practices of other states, particularly allies.

The modern concept of transitional justice emerged in the 1970s and 1980s when countries in Latin America, Central and Eastern Europe and South Africa experienced transitions from authoritarian rule (Kamminga *et al.* 2009). The transitions of these states from autocratic rule to democracy encouraged demands for accountability for past human rights abuses. These demands compelled new governments to devise strategies for coming to terms with the abuses of prior regimes, and in some cases, guerrilla opposition groups (Ratner, Abrams and Bischoff 2009: p. 2). The end of Cold War rivalries led to the creation of an environment that was more conducive to multilateral cooperation in dealing with situations of conflict involving extensive human rights abuses. The declining imperative for global powers to assert hegemony in global conflicts reduced their inclination to condone or justify violations of human rights committed by their allies. This new environment in international relations deprived repressive regimes of powerful political support and opened space for creative strategies for the global human rights movement to scrutinize and hold governments accountable for their conduct. The significant and growing influence of the human rights movement generated pressure not simply for confronting past abuses, but for doing so through criminal trials. Still, prosecutions of perpetrators remained the exception rather than the norm, as perpetrators in many democratizing countries retained significant influence and were able to negotiate amnesties or to compel new regimes to choose mechanisms such as truth commissions as the price for peace and transition to democracy.

Beginning in the late 1980s, the globalization of communications increased the volume of reporting on human rights issues, as well as the speed at which egregious rights violations were drawn to international attention. The intrusive real-time availability of information on atrocities eventually made it difficult for policy makers to avoid addressing the need for accountability for gross human rights abuses. Kritz (2002a: p. 26) and Mutua (1997: p. 174) articulate a widely held view that the mobilization of shame by non-governmental organizations through exploitation of media reporting on atrocities (rather than the commitment of policy makers in powerful states to the intrinsic value of punishment or the rule of law per se) should be credited for the progress of the international community in establishing mechanisms for holding perpetrators of atrocity accountable, beginning with the decision to set up the United Nations ad hoc tribunals of Rwanda and the former Yugoslavia.

In an era of instant communications across the world, press coverage of the atrocities that were committed in Bosnia eventually made it imperative for the major world powers to adopt measures to bring perpetrators of the atrocities to account, through the establishment of the International Criminal Tribunal for the Former Yugoslavia (ICTY) (Schabas 2006: p. 3). The establishment of the Yugoslav tribunal in turn set a precedent for the establishment of the

International Criminal Tribunal for Rwanda (ICTR). Most observers agree that it is most unlikely that the Security Council would have set up the Rwanda Tribunal had the Council not set a precedent by the earlier decision to establish the ICTY (Mutua 2000). While the two tribunals have been criticized for a variety of shortcomings, their work has had a huge impact in changing norms on how the international community deals with egregious human rights violations.

Developments in the human rights field since the early 1980s have given rise to emerging norms in international law that place obligations on states undergoing transitions from dictatorship to democracy or from conflict to peace, as they confront change while having to reckon with legacies of mass atrocity. Under these normative principles, states have affirmative obligations: 1) to facilitate truth-telling in order to create an authoritative account of the history of the conflict and of its attendant human rights violations; 2) to investigate, prosecute and punish those responsible for the violations; 3) to offer reparations to the victims; and 4) to conduct institutional reform to dismantle extant systems which promote the perpetration of abuse (Méndez 1997). The climax of the evolution of the role of international law in ensuring accountability for human rights and promoting peace was the adoption of the Rome Statute for an International Criminal Court (ICC).

The changes in attitudes, policies and practices about how societies deal with gross human rights abuses that have taken place over the last 30 years are phenomenal. From a time when individuals were barely 'subjects' of international law, governments now have an affirmative obligation toward all persons within and without their territory, during war and peace, and the importance of those obligations has served to raise the violation of some of them to include criminal responsibility for the offenders (Ratner, Abrams and Bischoff 2009: p. 9). The shield of sovereignty which previously protected states from scrutiny of their human rights practices has largely been torn away. The immunity from being held accountable which leaders previously enjoyed is shrinking. It is now widely accepted that there exists a duty to prosecute, whether at the international or national level, genocide, crimes against humanity, war crimes and torture (Orentlicher 1991; Bassiouni 2002). There is an almost universal consensus that at least persons who bear the greatest responsibility for atrocities have to be held accountable through criminal prosecution. Men who once wielded unimaginable power in the former Yugoslavia, Liberia and Rwanda are currently on trial or have already been sentenced to imprisonment for the greater part of if not all their remaining lives.

The changes in values, legal norms and state practices relating to human rights in general and accountability for the most serious human rights abuses in particular that the world has experienced during the last three decades has led to extraordinary developments in the discipline of transitional justice. The international community has developed a legal framework, established institutional mechanisms and provided extensive financial and material assistance to support transitional justice processes. Almost every regime change of modern times goes hand in hand with accompanying processes addressing abuses of prior regimes. Transitional justice has become an expansive, multidisciplinary field of scholarly research.

1.3 Objectives of Transitional Justice

Transitional justice processes are often tasked with a wide range of responsibilities and vested with many expectations, some explicit and others implicit. The four core objectives that all transitional justice processes seeking to address the aftermath of large-scale human rights abuses, especially mass atrocity and genocide, have in common are the following.

1.3.1 Establishing the truth

Foremost, transitional justice processes aim to establish the truth about the past. Transitional justice scholars and practitioners (Crocker 1999; Vandegiste 2009) have identified different levels or kinds of truth that transitional justice processes aspire to establish. These include: 1) 'forensic truth' or 'hard facts', being factual, corroborated information obtained through objective and impartial procedures concerning the violation of moral or legal rights by whom, how and when; 2) 'emotional truth' also called 'personal or narrative truth', which is knowledge concerning the psychological impact on victims and victims' families from the rights abuses or the threat of such abuses and involves establishment of victims' perceptions of experiences of victimization; and 3)'general truth', such as the plausible causes of the abuses. The Truth and Reconciliation Commission of South Africa also identified two other categories of truth that it called 'social truth', a reference to truth that emerges from dialogue between parties with different views about the past; and 'healing or restorative truth', that is the 'kind of truth that places facts and what they mean within the context of human relations – both among citizens and between citizens and the state' (Truth and Reconciliation Commission 1998: p. 114).

Establishment of the truth about past abuses is the most critical aspect of every transitional justice process. Establishing an accurate historical record, a 'collective memory', of past human rights abuses is also considered to be an important goal because without reasonably complete truth with respect to the past, none of the other goals of transitional justice, including accountability, reparation and reconciliation are likely to be achieved (Crocker 1998: p. 496). Truth, it is often argued, is a precondition for reconciliation, which is considered to be a prerequisite for sustainable peace. Truth-telling is assumed to encourage social healing and reconciliation, promote or sometimes replace justice, allow for the establishment of an official historical record, serve a public education function, aid institutional reform, help promote democracy and pre-empt as well as deter future atrocities (Skaar 2011: p. 7).

However, truth may be only one of many possible strategies for the pursuit of reconciliation. While the view that truth is necessary to advance reconciliation has strong support, truth may not necessarily be the most critical prerequisite for reconciliation. Freeman and Hayner (2008: p. 122) argue that reconciliation may be more affected by factors other than knowing or acknowledging the truth about past wrongs, including a perception of a clear end to the threat of further violence, acknowledgement by the state or by perpetrators of the injuries suffered, a reparation programme for those injured, attention to structural inequalities and the basic material needs of victimized communities, the existence of natural linkages in society that bring formerly opposing parties together, or, most simply, the passage of time. Thus, truth may be only one of many possible elements in the pursuit of reconciliation. Transitions in places such as Spain and Mozambique suggest that a substantial degree of national reconciliation can sometimes occur even in the absence of a formal truth-seeking process.

Truth may, in some circumstances, even have harmful effects. Some truth may deepen hostility between victims, rather than foster reconciliation. Satisfying victims' need to know may incite violence. Apparently justified needs to limit the pursuit or disclosure of the truth imply the need to balance the truth against other goals of transitional justice (Crocker 1999).

1.3.2 Accountability

Another objective of transitional justice is accountability. Populations in states that have experienced authoritarian rule, internal armed conflict or trans-boundary conflict, or some combination of the three, will generally also have experienced significant human rights abuses or violations of international humanitarian law. Violations may include persecution, arbitrary arrests and detention, torture, extrajudicial execution, disappearances, war crimes, crimes against humanity, forced labour or enslavements, and genocide. These abuses may have been committed by state security forces, rebel groups, militias, corporations and private persons, many of whom may retain significant military, political or economic power. Accountability in the transitional justice context means determination and apportionment of the responsibility of individuals, organizations and states for past wrongs and of sanctions appropriate to such wrongs. Transitional justice helps to identify architects of past violence and to shame, punish, diminish and exclude them on account of their offences. A fair ascription to individuals and groups of responsibility for past abuses and the meting out of appropriate sanctions is considered to be a legal obligation of successor regimes and a moral and legal right of the victims. The concept of accountability ought to be understood in terms that go beyond criminal justice to include civil suits and administrative and political measures (Vandegiste 2009: pp. 27–30).

Proponents of accountability attribute a wide range of potential benefits to the process. Accountability is seen as the appropriate response to the legitimate cry of victims for recognition and justice. Accountability, it is contended, deters future violations, while impunity constitutes an invitation to repetition. Accountability processes in general, and criminal trials in particular, are said to provide a 'higher' degree of truth, focusing not only on events, but also incontestably identifying who bears personal responsibility for abuses. It is argued that the absence of accountability runs against the rule of law and therefore undermines one of the fundamental pillars of a more democratic regime, whereas accountability enhances the legitimacy of the new regime. Accountability prevents perpetrators from reclaiming power again through violence. It may help a new regime rid the armed and security forces of their worst elements and to create a better climate to foster respect for human rights. Holding perpetrators accountable prevents acts of vengeance, vigilante justice and cyclical patterns of reciprocal violations. Accountability individualizes guilt, helping to absolve groups or entire communities of the stigma of collective responsibility. Variations of accountability processes allow for a differentiation of sanctions, in response to different degrees of accountability (Vandegiste 2009: p. 30).

While the principle of accountability for past wrongs has broad if not universal support, its implementation in practice is difficult. For example, is it morally justifiable or legally acceptable to hold people accountable for acts that were not illegal at the time that they were committed? How should 'sins of commission' be morally compared to 'sins of omission'? Is the requirement of accountability absolute, or should it be balanced with other objectives of post-conflict reconstruction, such as ensuring peace and stability? Should, for example, perpetrators of human rights abuses be permitted to participate in peace negotiations and transition governments, or should institutions and policy makers promoting negotiated settlements of conflict insist on excluding them from both at the risk of prolonging conflict and prolonging the suffering of the victims of war?

Demands for justice are particularly compelling when the crimes to which victims have been subjected are grave (such as genocide or crimes against humanity) or the victimization has extended over a long period of time, as was the case in Rwanda (Organisation of African Unity 2000: Chapters 2, 3, 4). Justice is often the minimum condition that victims of atrocity seek as the price for peaceful coexistence with their victimizers. It is also often argued that victims of human rights abuses also need justice to be able to come to terms with their suffering, reach closure and move on with their lives (Minow 1999). The process of trying and punishing perpetrators of atrocities is an important and legitimate goal of transitional justice (Crocker 1999; Bass 2000: pp. 284–330; Drumbl 2007: pp. 149–80).

1.3.3 Reconciliation

Transitional justice also aims to promote reconciliation through addressing the divisions that arise in society as a result of human rights violations.

Reconciliation is considered to be the ultimate objective of all policies and practices of transitional justice as well as their legitimizing norms (Zalaquett 1990). The rendering of justice to the victims helps to establish the truth about the violence of the past, and the acknowledgement of the abuses of the past, it is argued, helps to diffuse hatred and animosity between individuals and communities, and in so doing, enables members of a society to live together non-violently and to begin a journey of reconciliation and healing (Crocker 1998: p. 496).

There is no 'universally applicable, perfect reconciliation model' (Bloomfield, Barnes and Huyse 2003: p. 17). What reconciliation entails may vary according to circumstances. In its most basic sense, reconciliation can be seen as the decision 'to defer the right to retribution to the extent that retribution would obstruct peace' (Daly 2002b: p. 87). This is a 'negative' definition of reconciliation, which does not necessarily include individual reconciliation, public apologies, or a quest for the truth. 'Negative' reconciliation prevents renewed conflict based on past abuses and creates a culture of minimum tolerance and acceptance necessary for democratic institutions to function.

'Positive' reconciliation, on the other hand, may include 'the personal healing of survivors, the reparation of past injustices, the building or rebuilding of non-violent relationships between individuals and communities, and the acceptance by former parties to a conflict of a common vision and understanding of the past' (Bloomfield *et al.* 2003: p. 19). In the broadest sense, reconciliation involves the rebuilding of fractured individual and communal relationships after conflict, with a view toward encouraging meaningful interaction and cooperation between former antagonists (Clark 2007: p. 770). Positive reconciliation is complex and long-term, and not every post-conflict society may be able to achieve it. The most basic precondition to reconciliation is a cessation of violence and restoration of a safe environment. In addition, the parties themselves must actually *want* reconciliation. Several other state-level preconditions may be necessary, if not sufficient, for reconciliation to occur. They include democratization and the development of civil society; political restructuring; economic processes such as a growing economy and the redistribution of land or wealth; and the establishment of policies or mechanisms to ensure justice (Clark 2007: pp. 791–2). The most lasting impediment to state-level reconciliation would be the inability to establish or sustain the 'essential codes of democracy' (Bloomfield *et al.* 2003: p. 21). The achievement of 'reconciliation' is a process, rather than an outcome, and may take place over a long period of time and in several different stages.

1.3.4 Reparation

Another major objective of transitional justice is the recognition and vindication of the victims (de Greiff 2009: pp. 57–8). Transitional justice provides victims and their families with a platform to disseminate information about their victimization, to explain their suffering and to articulate their expectation of justice. The public acknowledgement of the suffering of the victims serves to restore their dignity and to promote their psychological healing. Transitional justice also provides opportunity for victims to receive reparations to make up for the wrong that they have suffered.

The rationale for reparations is to repair, to the extent possible, the harm that the victim has suffered as a result of the violation of his or her human rights.[3] Reparation is a public acknowledgement of the violation of the rights of victims, of the suffering the victims have been subjected to as a result of such abuses, and of acceptance by the state of its responsibility in law for breaches of legal obligations attributable to previous regimes (Hamber 2000). Public recognition of the victimization and suffering of the victims, it is contended, meets the victims' deep desire for justice by raising public awareness about the harms that they have suffered, serving to expose their grievances, helping to restore their dignity and status as equal human beings, and redirecting blame towards those who are truly responsible for past wrongs. Reparation, it is often asserted, may both help victims to reach closure and facilitate coexistence and possibly reconciliation between previously antagonistic individuals, groups and communities. Reparation helps victims to manage the material aspect of their losses (Kritz 1996c: p. 599). The public acknowledgement of the wrongs that victims may have suffered can contribute to the reintegration of victims into society and to reduce the likelihood of renewed violent confrontation (Theissen 2004: p. 8). Reparation serves to demonstrate a successor regime's commitment to respect for human rights. Reparation serves to promote and protect human rights. By publicly recognizing the harms victims have suffered, reparation seeks not only to ensure accountability for past wrongs, but also to prevent the reoccurrence of such acts in the future (van Boven 1995: p. 509).

Reparation, in the context of political transition, acts as a bridge between the past and the future. It combines the backward-looking objective of compensating victims with the forward-looking objectives of political reform. Thus, it also helps the new state in reconciling itself with its past. Reparations may also serve as an indispensable alternative to criminal prosecutions of perpetrators of gross human rights abuses, where prosecution is not possible because the perpetrators have died or fled and prosecutions are not possible (due to the very large number of perpetrators) or are not considered appropriate because it may threaten political stability and undermine democratic consolidation (Vandegiste 2003a: pp. 147–8).

While the right of victims to reparations is a widely accepted principle, implementation of reparation programmes, especially programmes involving monetary compensation, often raises difficult dilemmas and challenges. Is it justifiable to impose an onerous financial burden on contemporary society to pay reparations for crimes that may have been committed by a relatively small part of the population of previous generations? Is it fair to tax innocent citizens to pay reparations, when most citizens were not responsible for the violations that victims were subjected to? Is it fair to spend substantial state resources on reparations that exclusively benefit victims of past abuses in societies where the majority of the populations are very poor people? Where, as in Rwanda, the majority of perpetrators of human rights violations are poor people, is it morally justifiable to take away their few assets (such as land) at the risk of further impoverishment of their families? Where individuals are required to pay compensation for their crimes, can the requirement to pay reparations be reconciled with the overriding goal of reconciliation? Is it justifiable to provide reparations to victims of the vanquished in armed conflicts brought to an end by the outright military victory of one side, while withholding reparations from victims of abuses of the victors, who may not be willing to accept the moral stigma and political costs that accepting responsibility for grave human rights abuses may entail? Rwanda's transitional justice processes have faced most of these dilemmas.

1.3.5 The aspirational or 'end goals' of transitional justice

Accountability, reconciliation, truth telling and reparation, the core objectives of transitional justice processes which Huyse and Salter (2008) categorize as instrumental objectives, are not the only objectives of transitional justice. Transitional justice processes have more general goals or broader ambitions.

Transitional justice processes aim, for example, to reduce or eliminate impunity and to promote respect for human rights in society. Transitional justice processes also aim to deter future violence or other human rights abuses. The theory of deterrence in transitional justice is extrapolated from the field of criminal justice. Proponents of the theory of deterrence argue that holding individuals, organizations and states accountable for rights abuses deters repetition in the future. Deterrence may be specific to individual offenders or generally to the community of potential offenders. Transitional justice processes help to educate the population about the past and the undesirable aspects of its violence. These processes, especially truth commissions, make recommendations on ways to deter future violations and atrocities. Accountability, it is argued, sends a message that the new political order is determined to break with a culture of impunity.

While there are anecdotal reports that suggest that potential perpetrators of international crime are deterred by the trial and punishment of others, there is no systematized or conclusive evidence that criminal trials deter the commission of international crimes (Minow 1998). According to Drumbl (2007: p. 169–73), the deterrent effect of criminal justice is undermined by a host of factors. Participants in atrocity may well believe that they are acting for the benefit of the collective, not their personal gain, and that their actions are morally justified or even necessary. The majority of participants in atrocity are never apprehended and brought to justice. The arrest and prosecution of persons suspected of being responsible for gross human rights abuses does not guarantee conviction. Drumbl argues that by overlooking the responsibility of the masses or broad public whose support and acquiescence is the singular prerequisite for mass atrocity and focusing exclusively on individual offenders, criminal justice does little to deter violence.

Transitional societies not only claim to commit themselves to the rule of law but also claim that the implementation of transitional justice measures is both an expression of that commitment and a means to strengthen the rule of law. On how transitional justice promotes democracy and the rule of law, de Greiff (2009: p. 59) writes that:

> The various transitional justice measures contribute to strengthening the rule of law as follows: criminal trials that offer sound procedural guarantees and that do not exempt from the reach of justice those who wield power illustrate nicely the generality of law; truth-telling exercises that contribute to understanding the many ways in which legal systems failed to protect the rights of citizens provide the basis on which, *a contrario*, legal systems can behave in the future; reparations programs that try to redress the violation of rights serve to exemplify, even if it is ex post facto, the commitment to the notion that legal norms matter; and, finally, institutional reform measures, even those that screen out those who abused their positions, help to make rule of law systems operative, prospectively at least.

De Greiff (2009: p. 61) adds that:

> The commitment to the rule of law that underlies transitional justice is one that points in the direction of democracy ... in claiming that transitional justice has as one of its 'final goals' the promotion of democracy, the argument is not merely that democracy is a desirable goal, but that it is closely connected with justice. The democratic rule of law is both a precondition and a consequence of justice; the possibilities of achieving justice overall and of attaining its full effects usually depend on the possibility of establishing democratic participatory practices. At the same time, these practices and rights are enabled by giving everyone grounds for thinking of themselves as fairly treated by the institutions under which they live.

Transitional justice measures, it is claimed, also aim to promote sustainable peace and stability. Indeed, transitional justice processes are now considered to be an integral part of the peace-building strategies of post-conflict states (United Nations 2004). Transitional justice is considered to be an essential building block for peace building because if a society leaves the legacies of mass atrocities and abuse unaddressed, or deals with them insufficiently, sustainable peaceful coexistence may remain elusive (Bloomfield, Barnes and Huyse 2003; United Nations 2004; Lenzen 2009).

Transitional justice measures can contribute to peace in a variety of ways. Holding perpetrators of human rights abuses accountable by removing them from office or imprisoning them deprives them of the capacity to continue to commit abuses, to destabilize the new regime, or to resume or continue to wage war. Effective peace-building strategies require identification of the root causes of conflict in a society. Transitional justice processes (especially truth commissions) contribute to the identification of these root causes of conflict and make recommendations on reforms of policies and institutions that are required to consolidate peace. Transitional justice mechanisms promote peace by allowing victims space to articulate safely their grievances and anger, by facilitating public acknowledgement of their suffering and reducing their desire for revenge, by providing reparation for their victimization and by helping them to repair their relations with the rest of society, especially the perpetrators. Transitional justice processes may also promote peace by supporting reforms of the security sector's institutions responsible for past abuses by exposing the role of these institutions, and making recommendations on how these institutions should be reformed. Last but not least, transitional justice promotes peace by supporting the democratic rule of law, which enables a society to manage its conflict in constructive and peaceful ways (Sriram *et al.* 2009).

Promoters of transitional justice also argue that transitional justice mechanisms have potential to promote national reconstruction and development. It is not in dispute that transitional justice and development have close links. The conflicts that give rise to the human rights violations that transitional justice seeks to address often have root causes grounded in structural conditions of poverty and inequality. It is argued that legacies of gross human rights violations, especially those that remain unaddressed, have a negative impact on development. Four key conditions – political and social stability; safety, security and access to justice; conflict prevention; and social and economic justice – that can foster development may be facilitated by transitional justice objectives, such as addressing grievances, reconciling groups and restoring trust in institutions (de Greiff and Duthie 2009). A stable, peaceful and democratic order empowers a society to meet challenges of national reconstruction and development (Stromseth 2003: pp. 7–13). Transitional justice processes serve to create a political and social environment conducive to just national reconstruction and development (Crocker 1998: p. 496). It is widely believed that the rule of law has implications for economic growth and its absence hinders economic and business development (Kaufman 2001).

According to de Greiff (de Greiff and Duthie 2009: pp. 28–75), transitional justice measures are norm affirming, and as such provide recognition to victims, promote civic trust, and make a contribution to the democratic rule of law. In these ways, transitional justice measures help redress some of the obstacles to development left by human rights abuses, obstacles that include 'adverse terms of recognition', weak bonds of trust, and fragile or non-existent regimes of rights. Framing the same argument in terms of a concept that has become crucial for development work, de Greiff argues that perhaps the most significant contribution transitional justice can make to development is to strengthen the norms that underlie participatory citizenship. Transitional justice, then, can contribute to development if seen as an instrument of social integration.

In conclusion, it must be stressed that transitional justice processes are not all, or always, motivated by the laudable objectives outlined above. In practice, calls for justice in the aftermath of conflict are not always based on only the noble goals outlined above. Post-conflict justice is inherently political. A new regime's call for justice is sometimes self-serving. A successor regime may want a show of justice to enhance its own legitimacy. It may also seek to put former leaders on trial to undermine or de-legitimize political opposition.

1.4 Range of Potential Transitional Justice Mechanisms

Transitional justice, at its core, involves a range of tools and processes, and choices among them (Sriram *et al.* 2009). The range of mechanisms which are adopted by societies seeking to overcome the challenges arising from legacies of past human rights abuses include the following processes.

1.4.1 Criminal prosecutions

States have the duty to investigate and, if there is sufficient evidence, the duty to submit to prosecution persons alleged to be responsible for human rights violations and, if found guilty, the duty to punish them. Conversely, victims have both moral and legal rights to receive remedies for human rights abuses that, in cases of gross violations of international human rights law and serious violations of international humanitarian law, include prosecutions. The failure of states to investigate and prosecute human rights violations is the clearest indication of impunity. Impunity has negative consequences not only upon the victims of human rights abuses, but upon the quality of government, the legitimacy of the state and the capacity of its institutions to deliver basic services that they are mandated to provide, especially providing security and guaranteeing peace. Societies seeking to overcome the social and political problems linked to past human rights abuses often have to grapple with the question as to how to end impunity.

During transitions to democracy that many states across the world experienced during the 1970s and 1980s, successor regimes routinely opted to grant amnesties and pardons for the crimes committed in the course of armed conflicts or by repressive governments. The last two decades have seen the development of international norms rejecting blanket amnesties for serious violations of human rights in general and international crimes in particular. Criminal prosecutions have now attained the status as the uniform and most preferred of transitional justice processes, at least as far as serious violations of international crimes are concerned (Drumbl 2000b). In helping societies deal with a legacy of past mass abuses, the process of criminal accountability can serve several functions. Criminal prosecutions address the desire of victims for justice and help best to heal their wounds and to restore self-confidence through public acknowledgement of suffering and determination of responsibility for that suffering. Promoters of criminal prosecutions as a mechanism of transitional justice also argue that prosecutions can serve to reduce victims' sense of marginalization and grievance, to re-establish trust between victims and the state, to promote and reflect a new set of social norms, and to promote the process of reforming institutions of the new government (van Zyl (u.d.)). Kritz argues that prosecutions can provide victims with a sense of justice and catharsis – a sense that their grievances have been addressed and can more easily be put to rest, rather than smouldering in anticipation of the next round of conflict. They provide a public forum for the judicial confirmation of historical facts. They can also establish a new dynamic in society, an understanding that aggressors and those who attempt to abuse the rights of others will henceforth be held accountable (Kritz 1997).

In addition, prosecutions are promoted as being useful for avoiding unbridled private revenge and other acts of 'self-help justice' that can trigger social and political disturbance. Prosecution may promote peace by removing perpetrators of gross human rights abuses from the political system and depriving them of the capacity to wage war against or otherwise destabilize the new regime. Prosecution serves to establish individual accountability, eradicating attribution of collective guilt to a community, which is a source of negative stereotyping that may provoke more violence. Prosecutions are seen as the most potent deterrent against future abuses of human rights and the most effective insurance against sustained violence and atrocities. They can successfully break the vicious circle of impunity that causes injustice in many parts of the world. Finally, the pursuit of criminal sanctions against perpetrators of war crimes, genocide and crimes against humanity is a duty under international law. Human rights trials are said to have induced a 'justice cascade' whereby norms and practices that focus on accountability have spread between those countries pursuing transitional justice (Sikkink 2011).

There are at least four possibilities for prosecutions of persons responsible for gross violations of international human rights law and violations of international humanitarian law constituting crimes under international law.

1.4.1.1 Prosecutions before national courts

As states have the primary responsibility for preventing human rights violations that take place on their respective territories and ensuring accountability on the part of perpetrators of such crimes, national prosecutions are the primary forum for investigation, prosecution and punishment of human rights violations. The ideal forum for prosecutions of human rights violations are the national courts of the states in which the crimes were committed. Transitional justice scholars have outlined a long list of advantages that prosecution of war crimes before domestic courts have. It is argued that prosecution before domestic courts serves some important purposes, distinct from those that underlie international trials. Domestic trials can enhance the legitimacy and credibility of a fragile new government, demonstrating its determination to hold individuals accountable for their crimes. Because domestic trials tend to be high-profile proceedings that receive significant attention from the local population and foreign observers, they can provide an important focus for rebuilding the domestic judiciary and criminal justice system, establishing the courts as a credible forum for the redress of grievances in a non-violent manner. Finally, domestic courts can be more sensitive to the nuances of local culture, and resulting decisions 'could be of greater and more immediate symbolic force because verdicts would be rendered by courts familiar to the local community' (Kritz 1997: p. 6).

National institutions are able to handle larger numbers of suspects relative to international tribunals or foreign courts exercising universal jurisdiction, which have very restricted capacity and have to be selective in the choice of cases that they take on. In-country prosecutions provide a sense of ownership of the accountability mechanisms to which the society that was a victim of the human rights abuses resorts. They provide a sense of empowerment to the people of a post-conflict society, and to victims of past human rights abuses in particular. Being closer to the victims, national prosecutions are more likely to have an impact in changing values and human rights practices than trials conducted by remote tribunals based abroad. National prosecutions are likely to contribute more effectively to the processes of building sustainable national capacity to organize and conduct national prosecutions of human violations. Thus, legitimate national prosecutions are more likely to have a greater impact on long-term prospects for the rule of law and respect for human rights than prosecutions undertaken by distant and foreign judicial entities. National prosecutions are less costly than trials by international and foreign tribunals and are thus more sustainable as a more efficient way of utilizing the immense resources that the international community provides for promoting the rule of law to transitional states through the prosecution of perpetrators of atrocity.

Unfortunately, national prosecutions often have significant shortcomings with their capacity constrained by lack of adequate domestic human, material and financial resources. Judiciaries of transitional societies often not only lack the necessary professional skills, but may be subject to government control or interference, which compromises their independence and the legitimacy of their proceedings. National prosecutions may not be effective in advancing the goals of transitional justice in the absence of a commitment on the part of the new regime to genuine political reform that guarantees democracy and the rule of law. Where conflict has come to an end through the outright victory of one side, national prosecutions are invariably selective, targeting only the losers in the conflict.

1.4.1.2 Trials by international criminal tribunals

Whereas national institutions have the primary responsibility and should have priority to prosecute international crimes and other gross human rights abuses, there are situations where international criminal justice is more appropriate. The last two decades have been a time of phenomenal development of international criminal justice. Public outrage about the atrocities that were committed during the conflicts of the former Yugoslavia and Rwanda compelled the major powers to support the establishment of the International Criminal Tribunal for the Former Yugoslavia and the International Criminal Tribunal for Rwanda. The establishment of the ad hoc United Nations tribunals generated significant expectations about the contribution of international criminal justice to transitional justice. The two tribunals raised hopes that they would help to discredit delinquent leaders, render vengeance less tempting, give victim groups valuable moral power, contribute to national reconciliation and help to establish the rule of law in post-conflict societies, as well as to help prevent future conflicts through the threat of prosecution (Akhavan 1997, 2001).

The two tribunals served as a source of inspiration and prototypes for the establishment of a permanent international criminal court, an aspiration that was realized with the adoption of the Rome Statute of the International Criminal Court (ICC) in 1998. The treaty establishing the ICC entered into force on 1 July 2002 and represents the climax of a long campaign to constitute a critical and permanent component of the machinery for bringing perpetrators of gross human rights violations to justice. The ad hoc United Nations tribunals are in the process of implementing their respective completion strategies. The ICC, on the other hand, is still in its early stages of development. The Office of the Prosecutor of the ICC is investigating situations in Uganda, the Democratic Republic of Congo, Central African Republic, Sudan (Darfur), Kenya, Libya and Côte d'Ivoire. The Prosecutor is carrying out preliminary examinations of situations in Afghanistan, Colombia, Georgia, Honduras, Nigeria, the Republic of Korea, Guinea and Palestine.[4]

International criminal tribunals have certain advantages over other domestic alternatives. Kritz argues that:

> An international tribunal is better positioned to convey a clear message that the international community will not tolerate such atrocities, deterring, one hopes, future carnage … in the country in question and worldwide. It is more likely to be staffed by experts able to apply and interpret evolving international standards in a sometimes murky field of the law. It can more readily function – and be perceived as functioning – on the basis of independence and impartiality rather than retribution. Relative to the

> often shattered judicial system of a country emerging from genocide or other mass atrocities, an international tribunal is more likely to have the necessary human and material resources at its disposal. An international tribunal can also do more than local prosecutions to advance the development and enforcement of international criminal norms. Finally, where the majority of senior planners and perpetrators of these atrocities have left the territory where the crimes were committed or are otherwise inaccessible for apprehension and prosecution by national authorities (as is the case in both Rwanda and Bosnia), an international tribunal stands a greater chance than local courts of obtaining their physical custody and extradition. (Kritz 1997: p. 4)

While the institutions of international criminal justice that the international community has developed to deal with the challenge of violent conflict are a significant development in the fight against impunity, they have also been the subject of criticism over a wide range of issues, including the lack of a legal framework for engagement with victims in capacities other than witnesses, mismanagement and failure to provide the societies that they were established to help with a measure of ownership of their work. The impact of these institutions in changing values and establishing norms in the societies that they were established to help is certainly contested, but this is an issue for which an assessment can only be made in the long term.

1.4.1.3 Hybrid courts

By the end of the 1990s, the high expectations that the establishment of the ad hoc United Nations tribunals had initially raised were beginning to be tempered by reality, as the limitations of truly international tribunals became apparent. The limitations and shortcomings of the United Nations ad hoc tribunals (including lack of domestic ownership, failure to establish strong legitimacy in the societies they had been established to help, instances of mismanagement, exorbitant costs and long duration of trials) combined to erode support for ad hoc international tribunals among major constituencies, particularly members of the Security Council and (western) donor countries. At the same time, international human rights norms on serious international crimes had developed to a point where it was no longer an option for policy makers to revert to the old policies of turning a blind eye to instances of massive human rights abuses. As a result, support for the establishment of a permanent international criminal court to deal with the most serious violations of international crimes remained strong in the international community, as it was recognized that there were and would continue to be compelling situations of massive human rights abuses that the states involved could not or would not prosecute fairly and effectively, either due to a lack of capacity or political will. The concept of hybrid courts (also known as mixed tribunals) primarily evolved as an alternative to the establishment of more ad hoc tribunals to address human rights abuses in such situations pending the establishment of a permanent international criminal court.

The hybrid courts that have been established to deal with such situations include the Serious Crimes Panels in East Timor, the Regulation 64 Panels in the courts of Kosovo, the War Crimes Chamber of the State Court of Bosnia Herzegovina, the Special Court for Sierra Leone, the Cambodian Extraordinary Chambers and the Special Tribunal for Lebanon. Hybrid tribunals are usually based in the countries whose situations they are established to address. The courts apply domestic law that has, where necessary, been reformed to accord with international standards (Dickinson 2003). They are staffed by a mixture of national and international legal personnel. Learning from the experiences of the United Nations tribunals, hybrid courts have usually undertaken stronger outreach and media efforts, to enhance legitimacy within the societies they have been established to help.

Hybrid tribunals address situations where there is no opportunity for international criminal justice and the domestic judicial system lacks capacity to investigate and prosecute the relevant crimes effectively and in good faith. Supporters argue that hybrid tribunals combine the best of international justice, in that they may be more impartial, because of the participation of foreign legal professionals, and of domestic justice, in that they may be more legitimate and locally accessible, as they primarily conduct their trials in the territories of the affected states (Dickinson 2003).[5] The inclusion of national legal and other professionals helps to bring a measure of 'national ownership' to the tribunals' work while still addressing the international community's concerns about impartiality, competence and the 'international' nature of the crimes addressed.[6] Involvement by the national judiciary and domestic personnel imparts a sense of local ownership to the tribunal's work, which usually increases accessibility, accountability and perceived legitimacy for the local, affected community. Local legal personnel are familiar with local laws, language and customs, enabling them to take into account factors that might escape international personnel. Local personnel can serve as a valuable resource for elucidating the national legal system to international personnel. Additionally, the inclusion of local staff and judges is seen as a way to enhance the capacity of national judicial systems once internationalized trials are over (Dickinson 2003). Hybrid tribunals can strengthen the capacity and legitimacy of local institutions by promoting the legal training of local personnel. It is argued that hybrid tribunals also have the advantage of being located close to where the crimes took place. Through public stigmatization and just retribution, local trials are able to expose those responsible for atrocities to the local population, leading to gradual reconciliation and a cathartic process for the victims. Proximity to the events in question also gives these tribunals immediate access to potential evidence and witnesses (Raub 2009). However, in practice hybrid tribunals have not always demonstrated the advantages that that their supporters claim they enjoy over truly international and domestic tribunals. Hybrid tribunals have generally been under-resourced by the international community and though they attract legal professionals with high levels of expertise, their impact on building the capacity of the national justice institutions has been minimal (Cohen 2002).

1.4.1.4 Trials based on universal jurisdiction

The least commonly applied basis for prosecution of violations of human rights law and international humanitarian law is universal jurisdiction. Universal jurisdiction means the *ability* of the court of any state to try persons for crimes committed outside its territory which are not linked to the forum state by the nationality of the suspect or of the victims at the time of the crimes or by harm to that state's own special national interests (Hall 2010).

The framework of criminal justice processes comprising national prosecutions, trials by hybrid tribunals and international criminal justice still leaves gaps in enforcement of domestic laws and international law obligating states to investigate, prosecute and punish serious violations of human rights law and international humanitarian law. Some repressive regimes have in the past attempted to shield their officials from responsibility for human rights abuses by conditioning transition to democracy on amnesties enshrined in domestic law. Some armed conflicts (such as Rwanda's) involving grave human rights abuses come to an end through the outright military victory of one party. In situations where members of the victorious side have been responsible for human rights abuses, the transitional justice processes that the new regime undertakes are more likely to focus solely on the crimes of the vanquished. In other situations (such as Mozambique's), armed conflicts are often brought to an end by negotiated settlements that may grant amnesties or pardons to officials of the state or armed groups that are parties to the peace agreements. In still other situations, such as in Liberia, a newly installed democratic government led by persons who may not have played any role in past violence may be too weak and fragile to bring perpetrators of atrocities to justice. Perpetrators of human rights abuses who lose in armed conflicts often flee to foreign countries, where they may seek asylum and are out of reach of the jurisdiction of the states in which they committed crimes. There are many scenarios under which persons responsible for grave human rights abuses may be beyond the reach of the law, either because they control the machinery of the state, wield strong influence in it, have negotiated amnesties or immunities, or the state is too weak to apprehend and punish them, or they flee to a foreign land to avoid the reach of the state in which they committed crimes.

The concept of universal jurisdiction provides opportunity for the investigation and prosecution of international crimes that on account of a lack of capacity or will are not being investigated and prosecuted genuinely by national courts of the state where the crimes occurred or in the state of nationality of the suspect or the victim. The principle of universal jurisdiction helps to advance accountability and to combat impunity making it possible to prosecute the crimes of such perpetrators in foreign courts, in the event that such perpetrators should be found within the territorial boundaries of foreign states.

Until the 1990s, most states were very reluctant to exercise universal jurisdiction for human rights violations, even where domestic laws permitted or even obligated them to do so. The turning point for the principles of universal jurisdiction was the attempt by Spanish judges to secure the arrest of former Chilean dictator Augusto Pinochet for crimes committed during his rule in Chile. Since then, a large number of states have enacted domestic laws to prosecute extraterritorial conduct, even if international treaties do not contain specific obligations to do so. States have also been more willing to undertake trials based on universal jurisdiction. Because of the exceptional circumstances in which universal jurisdiction applies and the jurisdictional, political and financial limitations involved in undertaking investigations and prosecutions in these circumstances, universal jurisdiction is the least significant of possibilities for holding perpetrators of human rights abuses accountable through prosecutions. Nevertheless, universal jurisdiction is still a significant component of the global framework of legal mechanisms for combating impunity for human rights abuses. Universal jurisdiction has in practice demonstrated that it can be an effective complement to other transitional justice processes.

1.4.2 Truth commissions and other truth-seeking mechanisms

Truth commissions have their origins in the transitions from authoritarian regimes to democratic states in Latin America in the early 1980s where efforts at prosecution of perpetrators were stymied by the power that members of the former military regimes still wielded and the threat they posed to nascent democracies. Truth commissions were then used to achieve some measure of accountability for the crimes of the past and to issue reports, which made their findings publicly known. The focus on 'truth' was a response to the clandestine nature of the crimes of the former regimes and the particular and pervasive use of 'forced disappearances', a crime whose impact is aggravated by denial and secrecy. These initial commissions were limited in nature. They took testimony behind closed doors and moved little beyond the facts related to specific incidents, often saying little about the historic context, causes or consequences of the violence they had documented. The limited nature of these commissions was a result of both a lack of experience with truth commissions as well as the bargains that had been struck with the outgoing regimes.

Since those early days, truth commissions have been transformed in terms of their legal status, objectives, mandates, powers and methods of work. Since these initial or 'first-generation' truth commissions, there has been a significant evolution (Valji 2009). Contemporary truth commissions now generally employ public hearings for victims as well as institutional and thematic hearings which explore the role and impact of the conflict on key groupings and institutions in society. They are also increasingly being adapted to meet the needs of their local contexts. Some recent commissions have moved beyond the traditional focus on political and civil rights and are increasingly addressing the linkages of these rights to socio-economic crimes which are equally (or more) relevant for individual countries and are often inextricably linked to the nature of the conflict itself. Equally, truth commissions are adapting and incorporating local justice and reconciliation processes to deepen their impact and relevance amongst the local populations. As the idea of mandatory prosecution for certain violations of human rights law has gained currency within the United Nations and among other international actors, to the point that today international law forbids amnesty for certain international crimes, truth commissions have gradually moved towards a model that is intended to complement justice mechanisms, instead of replacing them. Truth commissions and prosecutions are no longer mutually exclusive; the two processes should ideally complement each other (Kritz 1997). Truth commissions should only be part of a society's strategy for dealing with past abuses.

Truth commissions are officially sanctioned, temporary, non-judicial or quasi-judicial fact-finding bodies (UNOHCHR 2006a: p. 1). These bodies are usually granted a relatively short period for carrying out their investigations before completing their work with a final public report. The core activities of each commission usually include collecting statements from victims and witnesses, conducting thematic research, including analysis of gender and child violations and their causes and consequences, organizing public hearings and other awareness programmes, and publishing a final report outlining findings and recommendations. Their primary purpose is to investigate past abuses in an attempt to understand the extent and patterns of past violations, as well as their causes and consequences. Each truth commission is a unique institution with variation in overall powers, design and focus. Some have the powers of search and seizure, and the right to gain access to official offices and official documents without warning. Others have had to rely on voluntary cooperation. Some can recommend prosecution or amnesty, or name individual perpetrators. Others cannot. Truth commissions can also differ vastly in their mandates, principle objectives, size and composition. However, they have certain common institutional characteristics that include official law or decree that confers wide powers of investigation; a focus on the past rather than ongoing human rights abuses; a temporary mandate for a designated period of time; and a specific mandate identifying the acts and time period to be investigated. This includes the production of a final report at its conclusion; a focus on investigating patterns of rights abuse over a set period rather than single incidents; a victim-centred nature; and an official status or relationship to the state (Hayner 2001; United States Institute of Peace 2008).

Truth commissions are generically assumed to promote a very wide range of objectives, including the establishment of the truth about the past; accountability, including punishment of perpetrators; acknowledgement of responsibility for crimes of the past and for victims' experiences of these crimes; amnesty; apology for the suffering of the victims; promoting coexistence; facilitating confession, repentance, mercy, forgiveness and healing; restoring the dignity of the victims and responding to some of their needs, such as their need to clarify the legal status of disappeared relatives in order to gain access to social benefits; establishing an inclusive narrative of the country's past and thus ensuring a common set of premises from which to build for the future; making a moral/symbolic break with the past (*nunca mas* or 'never again'); punishment; contributing to the development of a culture of respect for human rights and the establishment of democracy and the rule of law; promoting reconciliation and national unity; facilitating reconstruction; facilitating restoration, including reparations to victims; responsibility; preventing future abuses by recommending reparations or institutional reforms and by reaffirming social norms; promoting peace and serving as a platform for nation-building and reconciliation (Soota 2006; United States Institute of Peace 2008; Skaar 2011: p. 8).

Popkin and Roht-Arriaza define the four main goals of truth commissions as contributing to transitional peace by 'creating an authoritative record of what happened; providing a platform for the victims to tell their stories and obtain some form of redress; recommending legislative, structural or other changes to avoid a repetition of past abuses; and establishing who was responsible and providing a measure of accountability for the perpetrators'.[7] In a holistic approach to transitional justice, the recovery of truth serves as both a cornerstone of justice and a triggering device for legal justice, reparations and institutional reforms aimed at preventing massive abuses from happening again (Rotberg 2000; Cobián and Reátegui 2009: p. 148). Some of their objectives, such as the compilation of an objective historical record, social science research into the ultimate causes of atrocities and a listing of recommendations for reparations, may be within reach. Other goals, such as national reconciliation and healing, and accountability for criminal perpetrators, may be more ambitious and aspirational. The ultimate objective of a truth commission is to help a society understand and acknowledge a contested or denied history, and to bring the voices and stories of victims to the public at large, to the end that victims and the perpetrators may begin to mend their relations on the basis of the public acknowledgement of the former's suffering.

Truth commissions enjoy a very favourable standing in policy, human rights advocacy and international development circles. However, truth commissions can and often have limitations. The focus on the past can miss the way in which violence, rooted in the legacy of the past, takes new forms through the transition period which equally undermine the goals of the rule of law, human security, peace and non-repetition. Truth commissions may be established by a new regime for selfish or self-serving reasons, including a desire to discredit prior regimes and political opposition in general, to legitimize the new political dispensation or to shield their own members from prosecutions. Truth commissions that lack a mandate to 'name names' may be perceived as a cover-up for past wrongdoing. The non-binding nature of the recommendations of truth commissions may perpetuate perceptions of victimization rather than bring closure and healing to victims. There is no means of determining the extent to which truth commissions, as other transitional justice processes, are able to achieve their intended objectives.

Whether a truth commission succeeds in its objectives and has the desired impact may depend on a multiplicity of factors including: timing; political will and strength of mandate; integrity, impartiality and independence of commissioners; availability of resources; organization of the commission's functioning, including its transparency and ability to afford all stakeholders (especially victims) opportunity to participate in its proceedings; and the broader political context of change, particularly the nature of political transition in the country in question.

1.4.3 Reparation

Reparation is an umbrella designation for a set of measures that provide redress for victims of gross violations of international human rights law, serious violations of international humanitarian law and violations of international criminal law. The term 'reparation' encompasses restitution, compensation, rehabilitation, measures of satisfaction (such as public apologies, public memorials) guarantees of non-repetition and changes in relevant laws and practices, as well as bringing to justice the perpetrators of human rights violations (United Nations Human Rights Committee 2004; Orentlicher 2005). With the exception of restitution and compensation, measures of reparation are usually cumulative. The guiding principles of a proper reparations programme are meant to acknowledge the wrongdoing done to victims, to improve the quality of their lives, to afford recognition through affirmation and acknowledgement of the harm suffered, and to build civic trust and solidarity (Soota 2006: p. 319).

There have been efforts by various human rights courts and treaty bodies to clarify the nature and scope of the right to reparation. One such effort, undertaken by the Sub-Commission on Prevention of Discrimination and Protection of Minorities towards the end of the 1980s, resulted in the adoption by the United Nations General Assembly of the Basic Principles and Guidelines on the Right to a Remedy and Reparation for Victims of Gross Violations of International Human Rights Law and Serious Violations of International Humanitarian Law (herein after referred to as the Basic Principles and Guidelines on the Right to a Remedy and Reparation). Principle 15 provides:

> Adequate, effective and prompt reparation is intended to promote justice by redressing gross violations of international human rights law or serious violations of international humanitarian law. Reparation should be proportional to the gravity of the violations and the harm suffered. In accordance with its domestic laws and international legal obligations, a

> State shall provide reparation to victims for acts or omissions which can be attributed to the State and constitute gross violations of international human rights law or serious violations of international humanitarian law. In cases where a person, a legal person, or other entity is found liable for reparation to a victim, such party should provide reparation to the victim or compensate the State if the State has already provided reparation to the victim.

The essence of restitution is to restore the victim of a breach of an obligation under domestic or international law to the position that he or she would have been in but for the breach. Reparation must, as far as possible, wipe all of the consequences of the illegal act and re-establish the situation that existed before the breach (Basic Principles and Guidelines on Right to a Remedy and Reparation, principle 19). Restitution is the primary form of reparation. The primacy of restitution was confirmed by the Permanent Court of Arbitration in the Chorzow Factory Case when it said that the responsible state was under 'the obligation to restore the undertaking and, if this is not possible, to pay its value at the time of the indemnification, which value is designated to take the place of restitution which has become impossible'. When restitution is not materially possible or if restitution entails efforts or costs out of proportion, then instead of restitution, the state in breach can pay compensation (Buyse 2008: p.131).[8] Restitution may include, as appropriate, restoration of liberty (as, for example, in cases of detention in violation of international human rights law or of prison sentences resulting from unfair trials),[9] restoration of enjoyment of human rights, restoration of identity, restoration of family life and restoration of citizenship,[10] return to one's place of residence (where the government has illegally expelled the victim from the country,[11] or the victim has been compelled to leave his or her country of nationality because of persecution or the government's failure or refusal to protect him or her),[12] restoration of employment (or, if reinstatement is not possible, provision of similar employment)[13] and return of property.[14]

Compensation for immaterial damage is a form of monetary reparation for physical or mental suffering, distress, harm to reputation or dignity or other moral damage. Compensation is a secondary form of reparation in the sense that a state has the obligation of compensation for damage 'not made good by restitution', covering 'any financially assessable damage including loss of profits insofar as it is established' (Buyse 2008: p. 131).[15] The role of compensation is to fill in any gaps so as to ensure full reparation for the damage suffered (as long as the damage is financially assessable).[16] Compensation is for any damage caused by the act of the state in breach, whether material or moral. The Inter-American Court of Human Rights has held that international law does not recognize the concept of punitive or exemplary damages.[17]

The right of victims to compensation is established in a wide range of treaties,[18] as well as the jurisprudence of courts[19] and human rights bodies. The treaty bodies of the United Nations have recognized a right to compensation even where it is not explicitly mentioned in the particular treaty.

The Human Rights Committee recommends, as a matter of practice, that states should award compensation.[20] The right to compensation has also been recognized in numerous resolutions of the UN Commission on Human Rights[21] and its special procedures.[22]

The UN Basic Principles and Guidelines on the Right to a Remedy and Reparation[23] provide that *compensation* should be provided for any economically assessable damage, as appropriate and proportional to the gravity of the violation and the circumstances of each case, resulting from gross violations of international human rights law and serious violations of international humanitarian law, such as a) physical or mental harm; b) lost opportunities, including employment, education and social benefits; c) material damages and loss of earnings, including loss of earning potential; d) moral damage; e) costs required for legal or expert assistance, medicine and medical services, and psychological and social services. These categories of damages or compensation have been recognized by human rights courts and treaty bodies: loss of earnings;[24] other material damage;[25] lost opportunities, including employment and education;[26] immaterial/moral damage; physical and mental harm.[27]

The amount of compensation is equivalent to what restitution in kind would have offered, i.e. on the value lost as compared to the situation if the illegal act had not occurred.[28] In some situations, the appropriate remedy may be collective compensation for a community, in addition to individual remedies (Lutz 1995).[29]

The right to rehabilitation is guaranteed in several human rights treaties and declarations.[30] UN Basic Principles and Guidelines on the Right to a Remedy and Reparation[31] provide that *rehabilitation* should include medical and psychological care as well as legal and social services. The Working Group on Enforced or Involuntary Disappearances understands rehabilitation as, amongst others, 'medical care and rehabilitation for any form of physical or mental damage' (UNCHR 1999: para. 75). The concept of rehabilitation is not only relevant for physical or psychological damages; rehabilitation can also be of a social nature (Droege 2006: p. 145). Victims are entitled to rehabilitation of their dignity, their social situation and their legal situation (UNCHR 1999: para. 75). Some of these measures, such as legal rehabilitation through rectification of criminal records or invalidation of unlawful convictions may also fall under the category of the remedy of 'restitution'.

Satisfaction is a different, non-financial form of reparation for moral damage or damage to the dignity or reputation. Satisfaction becomes relevant when the other remedies of restitution and compensation cannot result in full reparation. The UN Basic Principles and Guidelines on Remedy and Reparation[32] provide that:

> *Satisfaction* should include, where applicable, any or all of the following:
> Effective measures aimed at the cessation of continuing violations;
> Verification of the facts and full and public disclosure of the truth to the extent that such disclosure does not cause further harm or

threaten the safety and interests of the victim, the victim's relatives, witnesses, or persons who have intervened to assist the victim or prevent the occurrence of further violations;

The search for the whereabouts of the disappeared, for the identities of the children abducted, and for the bodies of those killed, and assistance in the recovery, identification and reburial of the bodies in accordance with the expressed or presumed wish of the victims, or the cultural practices of the families and communities;

An official declaration or a judicial decision restoring the dignity, the reputation and the rights of the victim and of persons closely connected with the victim;

Public apology, including acknowledgement of the facts and acceptance of responsibility;

Judicial and administrative sanctions against persons liable for the violations;

Commemorations and tributes to the victims;

Inclusion of an accurate account of the violations that occurred in international human rights law and international humanitarian law training and in educational material at all levels.

International tribunals have decided that a condemnatory judgment constitutes satisfaction in itself, since an independent and impartial tribunal states with legal authority that the victim has suffered a violation of his or her human rights.[33] International courts and human rights bodies, such as the Human Rights Committee[34] and the Inter-American Court of Human Rights,[35] have asked states to make their judgments public. The Inter-American Court, however, considers that in cases of gross human rights violations, a judgment alone does not suffice to constitute adequate reparation; such violations call for compensation.[36] In cases of gross human rights violations, a mere declaration by a court will usually fail to do justice to the victim.[37]

The UN Basic Principles and Guidelines on Remedy and Reparation[38] provide that reparation includes guarantees of non-repetition and that guarantees of non-repetition should include, where applicable, any or all of the following measures, which will also contribute to prevention:

Ensuring effective civilian control of military and security forces;

Ensuring that all civilian and military proceedings abide by international standards of due process, fairness and impartiality;

Strengthening the independence of the judiciary;

Protecting persons in the legal, medical and health-care professions, the media and other related professions, and human rights defenders;

Providing, on a priority and continued basis, human rights and international humanitarian law education to all sectors of society and training for law enforcement officials as well as military and security forces;

Promoting the observance of codes of conduct and ethical norms, in particular international standards, by public servants, including law enforcement, correctional, media, medical, psychological, social service and military personnel, as well as by economic enterprises;

Promoting mechanisms for preventing and monitoring social conflicts and their resolution;

Reviewing and reforming laws contributing to or allowing gross violations of international human rights law and serious violations of international humanitarian law.

1.4.4 Institutional reform

Institutional reform refers to processes that change public institutions, including those that may have perpetuated conflict or served a repressive regime, and transforming them into institutions that are more effective and accountable and thus better able to support the transition, sustain peace and preserve the rule of law. Reforming public institutions is a core task in countries in transition from authoritarianism or conflict to democracy and peace (United Nations 2004). Institutional reform is grounded in the right of victims of human rights violations to cessation and guarantee of non-repetition, which are considered forms of reparation. Institutional reform aims at transforming institutions that are ineffective and lacking in legitimacy into public bodies that enjoy civic trust and have capacity to protect human rights and to deter future human rights abuses.

Institutional reform contributes to achievement of transitional justice policies in two principal ways. First, fair and efficient public institutions play a critical role in preventing future abuses. Second, institutional reform contributes to transitional justice in that it enables public institutions, in particular in the security and justice sectors, to provide criminal accountability for past abuses (UNOHCHR 2006: p. 3). A reformed police service, for example, can professionally investigate the abuses committed during the period of conflict and a reformed justice system is able to conduct independent and impartial and therefore credible trials of crimes. However, institutional reform processes have other benefits as well. Institutional reforms make institutions accountable to the people and become protectors and defenders rather than a threat to the safety and security of citizens.

Institutional reform, to be credible and effective in promoting respect for human rights and to prevent recurrence, must address the very institutions that were responsible for human rights abuses or that failed to stop or prevent them in the past. In particular, but not exclusively, the process of institutional reform aims to transform the security sector and the justice sector. The security sector refers to 'the structures, institutions and personnel responsible for the management, provision and oversight of security in a country' (United Nations 2008a).

Institutional reform measures may include, for example, the creation of oversight, complaint and disciplinary institutions and procedures including a National Human Rights Commission to ensure respect for human rights and justice; the reform or establishment of legal frameworks (including Constitutions) governing the organization and operation of public institutions; the development or revision of ethical guidelines and codes of conduct; providing human rights and professional training to personnel to address individual as well as organizational shortcomings; changing symbols that are associated with abusive practices; and the provision of adequate salaries, equipment and infrastructure. Effective reform efforts might also have to review the functioning of an entire public sector and consider merging, disbanding or creating public institutions. The precise content and scope of those measures will depend on the country's circumstances (UNOHCHR 2006: p. 4).

1.4.4.1 Vetting

Institutions commit, or fail to prevent or stop, human rights violations through the agency of individual officials. Strategies for reforming institutions with a view to making them more effective in ensuring respect for human rights and preventing recurrence of violence must necessarily address the problem of the integrity and capacity of the personnel of the relevant institutions to support institutional goals of promoting respect for human rights, accountability and the rule of law in general. The principal method of reforming the personnel of institutions critical to achievement of these goals is vetting. Vetting refers to the process of assessing the integrity of members of institutions that have previously been responsible for human rights abuses to determine their suitability for continued public service (United Nations 2004: p. 17). Vetting procedures evaluate, in particular, a person's adherence to relevant standards of human rights and professional conduct, including financial propriety (UNOHCHR 2006c: p. 4). Vetting processes seek to determine if the prior conduct (including, most importantly from a transitional justice perspective, their respect for human rights standards) of government officials warrants their exclusion from public institutions. 'Exclusion' here includes both terminating employment and restricting access to employment.

The public, and particularly victims of rights abuses, is unlikely to rely on institutions that retain or hire individuals with serious integrity deficits. Vetting processes aim at excluding such persons from public service in order to re-establish civic trust and restore legitimacy to public institutions. Vetting public employees, in particular in the security and justice sectors, is now widely recognized as an important measure of institutional reform in countries emerging from conflict or authoritarian rule (Mayer-Rieckh 2006). Vetting generally needs to be part of a much broader reform of the institution concerned. Institutional reform, in turn, needs to be part of a broader comprehensive transitional justice policy if it is to contribute to the goal of creating institutions that ensure respect for human rights and promote reconciliation and peace. Vetting and institutional reform should not be considered as an alternative to other transitional justice processes.

1.4.5 Traditional justice/informal/local justice systems

The development of transitional justice has been driven by the western-oriented human rights activism and international human rights organizations, including the United Nations and regional human rights mechanisms. These forces have situated the basis for transitional justice in international law. The approaches to fighting impunity that the transitional justice project has adopted in the course of its development has privileged criminal prosecutions through the formal justice system as the primary mechanism of accountability for very serious human rights abuses.

The end of the Cold War led to a proliferation of civil wars in a diverse range of developing countries whose societies have pluralistic legal systems. In many of these societies, the majority of citizens have little engagement with formal justice and look to local or traditional mechanisms for resolving disputes in society. Policy makers deliberating approaches to transitional justice in these societies encountered the challenge of integrating traditional justice mechanisms into the policy, legal and practical frameworks for state building and peacebuilding.

In the United Nations 2004 report on the rule of law, the UN Secretary General acknowledged that 'due regard must be given to indigenous and informal traditions for administering justice or settling disputes, to help them to continue their often vital role and to do so in conformity with both international standards and local tradition' (United Nations 2004: p. 12). The application of conventional transitional justice approaches to such societies raises questions of relevancy, legitimacy and efficacy.

With its community Reconciliation Programmes, East Timor was the first state to turn to traditional justice mechanisms to address a legacy of gross human rights abuses. Rwanda's adoption of Gacaca tribunals as the principal mechanisms of accountability for crimes relating to the genocide has attracted intense international attention and scholarly focus about the potential role of traditional mechanisms in transitional justice. The ICC's investigation into the crimes of the leadership of the Lord's Resistance Army in northern Uganda has prompted a debate not just about the role of traditional justice mechanisms in general, but about their engagement with international human rights mechanisms, including the complementary provisions of the Rome Treaty of the ICC. Other examples of instances where traditional conflict resolution mechanisms have been used to address legacies of violent conflict include the reconciliation processes in Sierra Leone, the Palaver Huts process in Liberia, the Conseil National des Bashingantahe in Burundi, and the healing rituals of the Curandeiros in Mozambique and the Mato Oput in Uganda (Huyse and Salter 2008). The role of traditional conflict resolution mechanisms in peace-building processes of countries in or emerging from violent conflict remains a hotly debated and controversial subject, in Africa especially.

Traditional justice systems have over the past two decades emerged as a significant addition to the range of mechanisms that societies in or emerging from periods of gross human rights abuses choose to address legacies of violence (Mutisi 2009; Shaw and Waldorf 2010). Traditional justice systems are a component of informal systems of mechanisms of dispute resolution, falling outside the scope of the formal justice system. Traditional justice systems are culture and community specific. They can take many different forms, and vary extensively from community to community. These systems often rely on negotiation and mediation, leading to consensus and compromise. Their primary aim is to mend or maintain relations between members of the community. These systems are not static as their role in society evolves with changing social norms and rules governing a particular society.

Promoters of traditional justice mechanisms argue that these have advantages over transitional justice processes. Unlike prosecutions, which focus on individual responsibility, traditional justice can contribute to determining patterns and causes of previous violence. While prosecutions are necessarily processes of confrontation between two opposing sides to determine which side is right, the starting point of traditional justice processes is that they aim at restoring the relationship between the parties. Traditional justice mechanisms are often premised on restorative justice principles. Benefits of local justice lie in the fact that problems can be resolved quickly, in close proximity to where the conflict took place, at low cost, in the local language, and in a way that is familiar to participants. Traditional justice mechanisms are accessible, home-grown, locally owned, culturally embedded. They are accessible to local and rural people in that their proceedings are carried out in the local language, within walking distance, with simple procedures that do not require the services of a lawyer, and without the delays associated with the formal system. In most cases, the type of justice they offer – based on reconciliation, reparation, restoration and rehabilitation – is more appropriate to people living in close-knit communities who must rely on continuous social and economic cooperation with their neighbours. They help in educating all members of the community as to the rules to be followed, the circumstances which may lead to them being broken, and how ensuing conflict may be peacefully resolved. The fact that they employ non-custodial sentences effectively reduces prison overcrowding, may allow prison budget allocations to be diverted towards social development purposes, permits the offender to continue to contribute to the economy and to pay reparation to the victim, and prevents the economic and social dislocation of the family (Penal Reform International 2000). Rwanda's Gacaca courts have demonstrated some of these positive aspects of traditional justice.

Traditional justice mechanisms have limitations, however. They are often dominated by men and often insensitive to gender. Their decisions are often not legally binding and may therefore be unenforceable, a factor that undermines their legitimacy. Their functioning may violate international human rights norms and standards of due process and the right to a fair trial. In societies which have experienced inter-ethnic or inter-communal strife or violence, traditional mechanisms may no longer enjoy legitimacy to adjudicate disputes in ways that promote social healing.

In its report on the role of traditional justice and reconciliation after violent conflict (Huyse and Salter 2008), based on a series of case studies of Uganda, Sierra Leone, Burundi, Rwanda, Mozambique and Liberia, the International Institute for Democracy and Electoral Assistance (IDEA) concludes that traditional justice mechanisms and processes constitute an important aspect of home-grown governance resources and as such deserve to be given greater recognition and support in both nationally directed and internationally supported efforts to promote peace with justice. The study concludes that appropriately understood, used and applied traditional justice mechanisms are potentially important tools of and for, peace building and social healing in the aftermath of violent conflict within a society, not as contradictory to or competing with but as complementing other approaches. In this sense they stand to contribute to the establishment of the political and social platform required for the construction [and in some cases reconstruction] of sustainable democratic institutions, processes and structures.

2 A Decade of Atrocities

2.1 Introduction

Rwanda experienced horrendous violence, including genocide, during the 1990s. This book discusses the processes of accountability with which Rwanda has attempted to address the legacy of that violence. This chapter aims to provide the context for the discussion of the mechanisms of accountability for atrocity that are the subject matter of the book. The chapter discusses the broader historical background to the genocide and provides a brief history of the genocide itself. It also discusses a unique and defining character of the genocide of the Tutsi of Rwanda, namely the participation of a very large number of private citizens in committing atrocities. The large-scale participation of private citizens in committing atrocities has influenced the nature and scope of the peace-building processes (including processes of accountability for past human rights violations) that Rwanda has undertaken to address the legacy of the genocide.

2.2 Historical Background to the Genocide

Rwanda has a history of conflict going back centuries. Over the past half a century, conflict within Rwandan society has periodically turned violent. This violence reached its peak during the 1990s, when the country experienced human rights violations on a massive scale, including genocide.

Understanding and explaining the causes of conflict in Rwandan society is not an easy task, particularly given that it is believed that misconceptions, flawed interpretations and deliberate distortions of the country's history have played a role in shaping and driving conflict (Des Forges 1999: pp. 31–64; Prunier 1995: pp. 1–40). The history of Rwanda, much like the history of many other deeply divided societies, is subject to a great deal of controversy. The absence of documentary records, lack of scientific research and reliance on oral accounts of the past have led to the creation of a body of history which is a mixture of myth and fact. Opinions about Rwanda's past vary greatly, depending on the origins, political ideology and experiences of a proponent of any particular point of view.

It is widely acknowledged that by the mid-eighteenth century, Rwanda was already a centralized state, inhabited by the Twa, Tutsi and Hutu communities. The state was organized as an absolute monarchy, ruled by an all-powerful king, whose being was considered sacred. The king ruled through a hierarchy of competing chiefs, the majority of whom were Tutsi. Access to public office and control of resources went hand in hand. Not all Tutsi were members of the ruling class. Some of the chiefs responsible for land were Hutu. While the terms 'Hutu' and 'Tutsi' existed in pre-colonial times, their meaning and political significance varied over time and differed from one region of the country to another. Newbury (1988) states that social stratification between the two groups was not static or unchanging. Generally, however, it is accurate to say that whereas the exploitation, exclusion and marginalization inherent in the social, economic and political organization of pre-colonial Rwanda affected Tutsi of lower social status, they exacted a higher toll on the Hutu as they were the majority of the population and were less likely to rise socially, economically or politically.

Racial prejudice rooted in questionable anthropological theories shaped colonial policy in Rwanda. Colonial officials and missionaries believed that the Tutsi were members of an exotic race superior to the other indigenous peoples and adopted policies that discriminated against other groups. Administrative reforms that the colonial government carried out in the 1920s and 1930s removed the few Hutus who were then still in power from office and increased the power of the Tutsi aristocracy. Sons of Tutsi notables had exclusive access to education and employment in the formal sector. The politicies of the colonial government not only consolidated inequalities between Hutu and Tutsi, they also hardened the stratification of Rwandan society and helped to intensify bi-polar differentiation between Hutu and Tutsi (Newbury 1995a: p. 12). The colonial government exacerbated the hardships of the common people by a variety of other unpopular policies, including a system of forced labour, payment of burdensome taxes and compulsory cultivation of certain crops, especially coffee. Responsibility for the enforcement of the harsh and unpopular policies fell upon the Tutsi chiefs, who often resorted to abuse of their subjects to appease colonial masters. The policies of the colonial administration and the Catholic Church have played a role in fuelling resentment, hatred, divisions and violence in Rwanda society (Longman 2010).

Partly as a result of colonial state building, transformations in clientship relations and unpopular labour policies, a movement agitating for the emancipation of the Hutu from the double yoke of colonialism and Tutsi domination begun to take hold after World War II (Newbury 1988: p. 181). The leaders of the movement were opposed to independence before resolution of the problem of inequalities between ethnic groups. Rather than acknowledge the need for political reform and seek a negotiated settlement, Tutsi elites instead pushed for acceleration of the process of decolonization in order to preserve the existing order and to safeguard their control of power. The colonial government (due to a number of factors, including the stance of the Tutsi elites on the issue of decolonization, pressure on Belgium from the United Nations to undertake some democratic reforms before granting Rwanda independence, and the influence of much younger and more progressive missionaries) switched allegiances and threw its weight behind the Hutu emancipation movement, and was joined by the Church. Together, the colonial government and the Church used their influence to effect a transfer of power (called the '1959 Revolution') from the Tutsi aristocracy to Hutu elites through a series of policies and actions (Lemarchand 1970; Harroy 1984; Destexhe 1994; Kakwenzire and Kamukama 1999; Melvern 2000a: pp. 14–15; IRDP 2003).

The abolition of the monarchy and overthrow of the Tutsi aristocracy did not, however, lead to the establishment of democracy or greater social equality. Within a few years, the government had become intolerant of all opposition. Political dissent was not tolerated. Opposition legislators were murdered. Opposition parties were banned. Rwanda became a one-party state in 1965. Power became concentrated within a narrow circle of politicians from the President's home district in southern Rwanda. The concentration of power in the hands of politicians from southern Rwanda gave rise to grievances among politicians and military officers from the north over political and economic exclusion. These grievances led to a *coup d'état* by army officers hailing from the north, led by General Juvenal Habyarimana, in July 1973 (Desrosiers and Thomson 2011: p. 433). The 1973 military *coup d'etat* resulted in the decimation of the top leadership of the ruling party of the day and the ascension of new elites hailing from the north of the country to power. General Habyarimana proceeded to establish another monolithic, authoritarian regime dominated by elites from his own home region.

From 1959, the Tutsi community were victims of officially sanctioned persecution. Tens of thousands of Tutsi perished in anti-Tutsi violence that followed the overthrow of the monarchy (Lemarchand 1970: p. 224). Successive attempts by Tutsi insurgents to regain power during the 1960s failed to dislodge the new regime from power and only served as a catalyst for further atrocities against the Tutsi who remained in Rwanda (Reed 1995; Melvern 2000a: pp. 16–20; Stromseth 2003: pp. 90–1). Racism and discrimination against the Tutsi who survived these attacks became institutionalized. Government institutions (including educational institutions) carried out virulent propaganda inciting hatred against the Tutsi. Violence and other human rights abuses against the Tutsi were glorified as acts of heroism. Government placed discriminatory limitations on Tutsi access to education, employment or service in the military and security services (Desrosiers and Thomson 2011: p. 432). Impunity for atrocities against members of the Tutsi community became the norm (Ngoga 2009). Government policy, driven by anti-Tutsi racism, condemned Tutsi refugees to perpetual exile.

The policy of the government of Rwanda on the question of refugees was to encourage the refugees to integrate in the societies of the countries in which they had received asylum (Reed 1996: p. 483). Unfortunately, the states in which the refugees had settled were no more welcoming. Three decades after they had left Rwanda, Rwandan refugees still faced systematic discrimination in most of the countries in which they lived. The policy denying refugees the right to return set the country on a course of inevitable violent conflict. Deprived of the right to return to Rwanda and condemned to eternal statelessness, the refugees came to the conclusion that they had no option but to return to Rwanda by force of arms if necessary. The 1980s National Resistance Movement (NRM) rebellion against the Uganda government provided Rwanda's refugees with the opportunity to acquire military skills that could be useful in the event that they launched their own armed struggle to overthrow the Rwanda regime (Watson 1991; Melvern 2000a: p. 27). By the time the NRM came to power in Uganda in 1986, it counted thousands of Rwandese refugees among its ranks, including its officer corps. Rwandan refugees were now strategically positioned to recruit more troops, to organize a grassroots movement of supporters among refugee communities in Central Africa and to make preparations for an invasion of Rwanda (Reed 1995: p. 49, 1996: p. 485; Otunnu 1999). The combination of the Rwanda government's uncompromising policy on the question of the return of Tutsi refugees and the existence of a restive exile community with a cohesive armed organization led by experienced and ideologically committed military commanders at its disposal set the stage for armed military confrontation unlike any other that Rwanda had experienced since independence. The refugees launched their invasion of Rwanda under the banner of an organization called the Rwandese Patriotic Front (RPF), whose military wing was called the Rwandese Patriotic Army (RPA) on 1 October 1990 (Watson 1991).

At the time of the RPA invasion, the regime was also facing political pressure from within. By the end of the 1980s, Rwanda was experiencing economic hardship arising from a fall in world coffee prices and bad weather affecting crop harvests. Worsening economic conditions led to increased discontent with the regime. A home-grown, unarmed opposition movement heavily influenced by similar movements which were challenging authoritarian regimes across much of French-speaking Africa was growing. The call for democratic change in Francophone Africa was boosted by an ultimatum that French President Mitterrand issued to governments of client states at the June 1990 France-Africa summit in Le Baule. President François Mitterrand indicated that it was time for these states to embark on democratization, and that French aid to African countries would henceforth be given out on a scale commensurate with their efforts at democratization. Rwanda's President Habyarimana had returned from the conference to announce proposals for the introduction of multi-party politics in Rwanda. The RPF invasion came at a time when Rwanda's government had begun taking some tentative steps towards political reform which had produced some degree of political liberalization, including the emergence of an independent press and opposition groups (Newbury 1995b; Vandegiste 1999b; Mamdani 2001).

The war that started in October 1990 hastened this reform process (Newbury 1998). The RPA invasion weakened the regime and emboldened the unarmed internal opposition. The opposition exploited the military pressure exerted by the RPA to extract concessions from the regime to accept the sharing of power and to undertake democratic reform. In 1991, the ruling party reluctantly agreed to share power with the unarmed political opposition. The opposition parties also lent their support to the peace process between the government and the RPF. The peace talks, mediated by Tanzania, were supported by the international community. These talks were carried out from 1991 to 1993.

The human rights situation in Rwanda progressively worsened while the government and the RPF negotiated a peace settlement. The government responded to the RPA invasion and to demands for political reform by seeking to consolidate the Hutu community behind the ruling party through persecuting the Tutsi (UNCHR 1993: para. 21; Bradley 1998; Ingelaere 2006: p. 391). The ruling elite attempted to rally the populace behind the regime with anti-Tutsi political rhetoric and policies. The government used its control of government-owned media outlets (especially the radio) to incite hatred and violence against the Tutsi by labelling them as accomplices of the invaders (Africa Watch 1992; UNCHR 1993: paras 56–8). During this time, the military command issued a document, later widely distributed across the country, which equated all Tutsi with 'the enemy' (Africa Watch 1992; Des Forges 1999: pp. 56–8). As the civil war settled into something of a stalemate, the regime escalated its killings of the Tutsi and political opponents (Destexhe 1994: pp. 46–7). During this period, the government was responsible for widespread human rights abuses, including at least 16 major episodes of massacres against the Tutsi community (Africa Watch 1992; Des Forges 1999). The human rights abuses that the Tutsi were subjected to during this period included killings of innocent civilians, summary executions of non-combatants suspected of being sympathizers of the RPF, kidnappings, involuntary disappearances, arbitrary imprisonment, death threats, rape, torture, burning of homes and destruction of crops and verbal abuse (Africa Watch 1992; UNCHR 1993). The attacks against members of the Tutsi community appeared to be organized and coordinated by state officials (UNCHR 1993: para. 42). These killings and other human rights violations were carried out by private citizens (generally members of militia groups associated or allied with extremist political parties loyal to the regime who were led to believe in a very real RPF 'threat') (Prunier 1995: pp. 109–10), members of the military and police, local government officials, clandestine organizations (death squads) and private individuals. The military provided training to the militia groups that were involved in committing killings against the Tutsi. The military also set up a 'self-defence' programme under which it provided guns, ammunition and grenades to local administration organs for use in committing killings (Africa Watch 1992). The army's involvement in massacres and other killings of Tutsi during the period before the genocide was confirmed by a commission set up by the government under pressure from human rights organizations and the international community (UNCHR 1993: para. 36).

The gravity of the human rights situation in Rwanda during this period prompted Rwandan civil society groups to form a coalition that in 1992 appealed to the international community for assistance with the investigation of the alarming human rights situation in the country. Four international human rights organizations responded to the appeal and formed a non-official international Commission of Inquiry to investigate the human rights situation in Rwanda.[1] The Commission visited Rwanda between 7 and 21 January 1993 and issued a report on its findings in March 1993 (Fédération Internationale des Ligues des Droits de l'Homme *et al.* 1993). The Commission's report established, *inter alia*, that massacres and other extrajudicial killings had been committed in Rwanda since the beginning of the war. It documented more than 2,000 killings and an unspecified number of other attacks against civilians, kidnappings and other violations, including persecution of the independent media. The report revealed that state officials at the highest levels, including the President, were directly or indirectly responsible for most of those violations, indicated that there were death squads operating in the country, and stated that the President and the government tolerated and encouraged the activities of armed militia groups attached to political parties in violation of Rwandan law. The report further indicated that these groups were now taking the lead in violence against the Tutsi and members of the opposition on behalf of the state and that the RPF was also responsible for some human rights abuses. According to the Commission, some of the abuses that had been committed by state officials amounted to acts of genocide, as the majority of the victims were Tutsi and the victims were targeted for the sole reason that they were Tutsi. The Commission also found that more recently, an increasing number of Hutu had also been targeted because they belonged to political parties opposed to the President and the ruling party; that the Rwandan army had killed soldiers of the RPA after they surrendered; and that the judicial system had failed to provide justice to victims of the above-mentioned human rights abuses. The Commission recommended that the President commit to peace, respect for human rights and protection of all Rwandans by the state. In addition, the Commission called for the disbanding of militia groups, the continuation of investigations and prosecution of all infractions against human rights and the continuation of investigation of mass graves.

The government generally accepted the findings of the Commission. However, according to a report of the United Nations Commission on Human Rights' Special Rapporteur on Extra-judicial, summary or arbitrary executions (UNCHR 1993), government officials and groups associated with the ruling party failed to heed the report's recommendations but instead continued committing human rights abuses. A day after the Commission left Rwanda, government forces resumed the killings and murdered an estimated 300 to 500 people, some of whom had testified to the Commission. These crimes were never investigated or punished by the government. State-inspired violence against the Tutsi continued unabated until the outbreak of the genocide in April 1994 (Melvern 2000a).

Even as the violence in Rwanda mounted, the peace talks between the coalition government and the RPF evolved into a comprehensive negotiation of a process to establish democracy and the rule of law in Rwanda. A successful outcome of the talks threatened to undermine the ruling party's control of power. The President's inner circle, his party, and the military and security services were determined to hold on to power at all costs. Despite this opposition, the talks culminated in the signing of a comprehensive final accord in August 1993. By the end of the talks, the RPA had grown to a formidable military force. The RPF was able to obtain very favourable terms for settlement of the conflict. The agreement covered the areas of the rule of law,[2] power sharing in a transitional government,[3] repatriation of refugees and resettlement of displaced persons,[4] integration of the forces of the two parties,[5] and other miscellaneous issues.[6] The agreement provided for the establishment of a broad-based transitional government in which the government, the unarmed opposition parties and the RPF would share power. It guaranteed the RPF participation in the military and security services on terms virtually equal to the government's. The agreement called for the removal of public officials responsible for human rights abuses, permitted the return of refugees, and envisaged the holding of free and fair elections within 22 months. President Habyarimana would remain Head of State, but the office of President would be almost ceremonial. Executive power would be vested in a council of ministers in which the RPF and the unarmed opposition parties would be the majority. The former ruling party, the Mouvement Révolutionnaire National pour le Développement (MRND), would be only a minority partner in the transition government. Its members faced the prospect of being brought to justice for human rights abuses and other crimes that they had committed and continued to commit while in office.

The peace agreement that the parties concluded in August 1993 failed to end the war. The regime had negotiated the peace accords under pressure from the international community (Organisation of African Unity 2000: chap. 8), but lacked the political will to implement the proposed settlement. The elements from Northern Rwanda that controlled power in Rwanda had been marginalized during the peace talks and were determined not to concede control of power. These elements tried to frustrate the implementation of the peace agreement by all means at their disposal (Jones 2000; Mamdani 2001: pp. 185–233). The tactics used included violent murders of members of the opposition and orchestrating splits within the political parties which were supposed to take part in the transition government in order to make it impossible to form the institutions (especially the parliament and government) envisaged by the accords. The regime sustained the stalemate for more than six months after the signing of the peace agreement. By the beginning of April 1994, the patience of the international community had run out and pressure on the regime to implement the peace treaty reached its peak. Regional and other powers insisted that the regime implement the peace agreement. On 6 April 1994, when President Habyarimana was murdered, the peace agreement had yet to be implemented. The killing of the President set in motion violence that led to the genocide of the Tutsi and the massacres of possibly thousands of Hutu opponents of the regime. President Habyarimana's death provided extremists within government, the military and security services, and the ruling party with the pretext they needed to derail implementation of the peace agreement and the democratization process in order to hold onto power (Destexhe 1994: p. 28; Ball 1999: p. 162; Mamdani 2001: p. 217; Prunier 2001).

The regime hardliners sought to retain power by orchestrating a campaign of genocide targeting the Tutsi community and massacres of Hutu opponents of the regime (Jones 1999), beginning with the core of what would have been the leadership of opposition parties in the transitional government. The violence unleashed by the genocide spilled into the Democratic Republic of Congo (DRC), which Rwanda has invaded twice and sent its forces into several more times in attempts to destroy forces responsible for the genocide and other armed groups. Hundreds of thousands of Rwandan refugees may have perished at the hands of the Rwanda military during these operations (UNOHCHR 2010).

2.3 The Genocide

2.3.1 Planning of the genocide

The exact details of the planning for the genocide of the Tutsi (its origins, the membership of the leadership that conceived the plan and its ultimate direction) remain and will probably always be a matter of controversy and speculation. Some researchers, including Des Forges and Melvern, have suggested that the plan to carry out genocide against the Tutsi may have been hatched as far back as 1991 or 1992. They have also argued that the final adoption and execution of the plan was the work of military officers and members of President Habyarimana's inner circle led by Colonel Théoneste Bagosora (Des Forges 1999: p. 185; Melvern 2004; Human Rights Watch 2006b).

Colonel Bagosora was a retired military officer and Directeur de Cabinet, or Chief of Staff, and effectively deputy to the Minister of Defence at the time of the outbreak of the genocide. During the 1990s, the Office of the Prosecutor of the ICTR pursued a strategy to prove the existence of a master plan of genocide against the Tutsi through a very large trial involving dozens of former government and military officials. The Chambers refused to approve the consolidation of the cases in question. The Prosecutor then sought to prove the master plan of the genocide against the Tutsi through a trial of Bagosora, who was believed to be the real power behind the scenes during the genocide, and a smaller number of senior military officers. Bagosora was charged with conspiracy to commit genocide; genocide; complicity in genocide; and murder, rape, persecution, extermination and 'inhumane acts' as crimes against humanity (including the murder of ten Belgian peacekeepers who were serving with the United Nations Assistance Mission in Rwanda (UNAMIR) on 7 April 1994). Bagosora was also charged with the killing of civilians, outrages on personal dignity and 'violence to life' as serious violations of Common Article 3 (Geneva Conventions). The Amended Indictment of 12 August 1999 charged that Colonel Bagosora developed a plan whose intent was to 'exterminate' the Tutsi civilian population. In executing this plan, Bagosora allegedly organized, ordered and participated in massacres perpetrated against the Tutsis and moderate Hutus in Rwanda.

The Prosecutor failed to prove the allegation that Colonel Bagosora masterminded the genocide, and he was acquitted of the charge of conspiracy of genocide. While the Trial Chamber did not rule out the possibility that there was a plan to carry out the genocide, it ruled that there was not sufficient evidence to prove beyond reasonable doubt that Bagosora or his co-accused had committed the alleged conspiracy.[7] The verdict in the Bagosora case thus ended the ICTR's attempt to establish the existence of a national-level conspiracy to commit genocide against the Tutsi. On the other hand, there is more than ample proof (including the findings in many judgments of the ICTR and the admissions in the guilty plea of Jean Kambanda) that the genocide was planned.[8]

Certain policies and actions of the government and ruling party during the years leading up to the genocide may be an indication that preparations for the genocide began well before the final Arusha Peace Accords were signed on 4 August 1993 (Jones 1999: p. 145). Those who believe that preparations for the genocide started well before 6 April 1994 point to certain activities – such as the creation and operation of a military commission chaired by Bagosora in 1991 that determined the 'enemy' of the state as all Tutsi; the promotion of extremism in Rwandan politics (through the establishment of new anti-Tutsi political parties and extremist factions within established political parties which were hostile to the Tutsi community); the creation, arming and training of civil militia groups (accessible only to members of the ruling party and groups associated with extremist anti-Tutsi policies) by the military;[9] the purchase and distribution of large quantities of conventional and unconventional weapons to citizens and members of militia groups even after the signing of the peace agreement; and the establishment of death squads – as proof that planning for the genocide started well before 6 April 1994 (Human Rights Watch 1994a; Des Forges 1999).[10] Another activity that points to early preparations for mass violence and possibly genocide was the establishment of infrastructure for the dissemination of propaganda against the Tutsi community and opposition politicians. Preparations in this regard involved the establishment of anti-Tutsi media outlets (the most famous ones were the *Kangura* newspaper[11] and Radio RTLM) to complement the state-owned media in disseminating anti-Tutsi propaganda. It has also been established that some lists of individuals targeted for massacre were drawn up well in advance of the outbreak of the violence on 6 April 1994 (African Rights 2000). Although the Tutsi were identified as the principal targets in these lists, members and particularly leaders of opposition parties were also listed as potential targets. All indications are that the drawing up of lists was mainly done in the capital, Kigali. No evidence of the systematic compilation of lists of potential victims across the country prior to the genocide has come to light.

Knowledge about the details of the planning of the genocide remains scant in the public domain. The subject of responsibility for the conception and direction of the Rwanda genocide at the national level is the last frontier of scholarship on the genocide; it is the single aspect of the genocide about which so little is known. There are, nevertheless, useful indications as to where the search for the individuals who bear ultimate responsibility for the genocide can begin. Circumstantial evidence surrounding the genocide suggests that its principal organizers were individuals or groups determined to preserve the political status quo. The ease with which these individuals or groups were able to seize control of the machinery of the state, especially the military apparatus, suggests that they were already part of the inner circle of the elites who were already in control of the levers of power in Rwanda. The capacity that these individuals or groups demonstrated in eliminating or marginalizing military or political leaders (especially those from the centre and south of the country) who were not in support of the genocide, building and sustaining a broad and unified coalition of Hutu leaders willing to join hands with them in exterminating the Tutsi, setting up a new government outside the constitutional framework, and mobilizing and manipulating all machinery of the state to orchestrate a very effective nationwide campaign of genocide and massacres of the opposition provides some guidance about the identity of the individuals and groups who constituted the leadership who bear ultimate responsibility for the genocide. The core group probably came from the northern part of Rwanda. They must have included holders of key commands of the military establishment. They were also able, at critical times, to co-opt other people from outside this inner circle to help them carry out their plans.

2.3.2 Implementation of the genocide

The precise time when the definitive decision to carry out a genocide against the Tutsi was made remains a mystery. There is ample evidence that plans to carry out attacks not necessarily with genocidal intent against the Tutsi community and political opposition started as early as 1991.[12] The unofficial International Commission of Inquiry that investigated the human rights situation in Rwanda in early 1993 indicated that past and then ongoing attacks against the Tutsi community may have constituted genocide. There has been no conclusive independent finding, however, that the preparations for and perpetration of violent attacks against the Tutsi community between October 1990 and April 1994 (including the creation and work of a military commission chaired by Colonel Bagosora in 1991; the creation, arming and training of civil militia groups by the military; the purchase of conventional and unconventional weapons and their distribution to militia groups and private citizens; the establishment of death squads and the drawing up of lists of Tutsis living in certain parts of the country) had a genocidal intent, an intent to destroy the Tutsi community 'in whole or in part' in terms of the Genocide Convention. What can be inferred from the events that followed the death of President Habyarimana is that around 6–7 April 1994, or soon thereafter, some individuals or groups who wielded power or influence within the regime of the assassinated President either made a decision to execute a prearranged plan of genocide or decided to escalate existing plans to carry out attacks against members of the Tutsi community to an all-out campaign of genocide of the Tutsi community.

The leadership of the extremists opposed to the peace agreement and the political reforms envisaged in the agreement sprang into action within hours of the President's death. The number one priority of these individuals or forces was to seize control of the country's military and use it to advance their goals of preserving their control of political power, through exterminating the Tutsi and eliminating all opposition. Some members of the Rwanda military (the Forces Armées Rwandaises, FAR) initially fought against the Presidential Guard, trying to stop the slaughter (Prunier 1995: p. 229). Some military officers who were opposed to the genocide appealed for help from the international community to stop the atrocities. However, the effective command of the military was firmly in the hands of officers who were opposed to the peace process and political reform. The most influential members of the military command and the members of the critical units of the military machinery were from the President's home region and were equally opposed to the peace process and political reform. The minority of the military officers who were opposed to the genocide were easily outmanoeuvred and marginalized. The leadership of extremists who were opposed to the peace process and political reform and were planning attacks against the Tutsi and members of opposition parties were able to co-opt the majority of the military into their plans with ease (Des Forges 1999: pp. 182–5, 192).

The death of the President had left opposition leaders, especially the then Prime Minister and the Prime Minister nominated under the peace accords, as the most senior political leaders under the Constitution. The extremists opposed to the peace process and the political reforms envisaged in the agreement moved to prevent a constitutional succession by hunting down and killing opposition leaders and leaders of government institutions (including the Prime Minister and the President of the Constitutional Court) who could have obstructed their plans by setting up a government committed to pursuing a peaceful settlement (Reed 1996: p. 496; Ball 1999: p. 165). Along with the political leaders, the extremists behind the violence also started eliminating other dissident voices, such as journalists and human rights activists who had been critical of the regime (Des Forges 1999: p. 205).

The group's next step in the process of consolidating their control of the machinery of the state was to take control of public administration organs. In the hours after the President's death, Colonel Bagosora and several other military officers who were allied to the late President and the ruling establishment had established a military crisis committee that they wanted to assume power from the civilian government. Officers who were not close to the ruling establishment opposed the proposal. Bagosora and fellow extremist military officers were compelled to cede power to a civilian government, albeit one that they would have control over.

In order to facilitate their plans for the destruction of the Tutsi community, the principal organizers of the genocide devised strategies to build or enhance intra-Hutu solidarity in general and solidarity within the extremist Hutu political movement in particular. These forces sought to enhance Hutu solidarity by co-opting politicians from the south of the country, whom the regime had previously marginalized, through appointment to prominent positions in a new government. The organizers of the genocide appointed Hutu from the south to important positions, including the Presidency of the Republic, the Office of the Prime Minister, head of the military and key cabinet positions (Des Forges 1999: p. 166). Only members of the extremist factions of established political parties opposed to the peace process were appointed to the government. Jean Kambanda's plea of guilt (since recanted) researched by both Des Forges (1999) and Prunier (2001) has indicated that opposition and local government leaders who were opposed to the regime, committed to democracy and opposed to the genocide were eliminated while military and civilian officials who were not enthusiastic about the genocide were sidelined or removed from office.[13]

Having secured control of the central government and the military and security services at national level, the organizers of genocide then set out to use these structures and their resources to ensure the success of their plans to exterminate the Tutsi at the grassroots level.[14] The forces behind the genocide directed, supervised and supported local government institutions from provincial level down to village level to ensure that all Tutsi in their respective areas were killed. By using the army, police and leaders of local government to organize the killings, the organizers of the genocide were able to expand the genocide to almost all parts within days. The military and police provided weapons, ammunition, supervision and, if necessary, reinforcements to ensure the success of massacres of the Tutsi in their respective areas of operations (Des Forges 1999: pp. 223–7). According to Des Forges and Prunier (Des Forges 1999: pp. 179–80; Prunier 1995: p. 244), local government officials in turn relied heavily on the militia of extremist factions of political parties to spearhead the massacres in their respective provinces, districts, sectors and villages.

The principal organizers of the genocide also adopted a series of other strategies to ensure that no Tutsi survived the campaign of genocide in any part of the country. These strategies included: intimidating the international community through acts such as the killings of Belgian peacekeepers, to ensure that there would be no humanitarian intervention to assist persons targeted by the massacres; using state-owned and private media outlets, particularly the radio, to incite and direct atrocities (Thompson 2006; Destexhe 1994: p. 31); imposing an around-the-clock curfew across the country to prevent potential victims of massacres from organizing to protect themselves and to make it difficult for potential victims from going into hiding or attempting to escape (Des Forges 1999: p. 166); imposing and strictly enforcing restrictions on movement through the establishment of a requirement for travel permits and the setting up of roadblocks (manned by soldiers, police, militia and individual citizens) across the country's highways, roads and even paths to identify and apprehend Tutsi who were fleeing;[15] using national identity cards (that specified a citizen's identity) to identify the Tutsi to be killed (Des Forges 1999: p. 212–14); establishing a so-called civil defence system whose declared mission was self-defence, but whose real mission was to carry out massacres of members of the Tutsi community; organizing, as part of the civil defence system, night patrols ostensibly for the purpose of preventing infiltration by the RPA, to ensure that Tutsi did not escape from the killers under cover of darkness (Des Forges 1999: p. 212–14); encouraging potential victims to congregate in large numbers at public places (such as churches, schools, stadiums and hospitals) with false promises of security and protection to make it easier and faster to massacre them; intimidating, threatening, coercing and punishing individuals and communities opposed to the genocide or willing to protect potential victims; deploying militia from other areas to areas whose communities were unenthusiastic or unable to carry out or complete massacres of the targeted victims and distributing money, alcohol and food, making promises of opportunities to rape Tutsi women and to loot the property of victims to encourage participation in committing atrocities. When there were no longer any Tutsi left in homes or public places, the killers undertook searches for survivors in forests, swamps, fields and the homes of Hutu who were suspected of hiding Tutsi (Hatzfeld 2008).

The Rwanda genocide was marked not just by the speed at which it was carried out and the popular participation that it attracted, but also by the brutality of extreme proportions that it manifested (African Rights 2000; Gourevitch 1998; Hatzfeld 2000, 2008). Victims were subjected to depraved, painful and humiliating treatment of every imaginable description. Victims were tortured, both physically and psychologically, before being killed. Crude weapons that caused slow and very painful death killed most of the victims. The most widely used weapon was the machete, which was used to cut off the limbs of victims. Wooden clubs with a bulging end from which protruded iron nails were very potent in smashing the skulls of victims. Occasionally guns, bows and arrows were also used. The perpetrators of the genocide did not always kill their victims straight away. Perpetrators often tried to inflict pain and mental anguish by cutting off water or food supplies before the final onslaught. Victims were sometimes subjected to slow painful deaths; some of their limbs such as legs or arms would be cut off and they would be left to bleed to death for periods that sometimes extended to days. Other victims were buried alive or had their hands and legs tied up and were drowned in rivers and lakes. Some victims were forced to kill their children, spouses, relatives or friends before being killed themselves.

One of the most horrific aspects of the genocide was the treatment of Tutsi women (Human Rights Watch 1996; Green 2002; African Rights 2004). Tens of thousands of women were subjected to rape (often gang rape) and other sexual abuse (Hubbard 2007). Neither the children nor the very old were spared. Rape was fuelled by hate propaganda before and during the genocide. The sexual violence aimed to humiliate and dehumanize the victims, to inflict maximum pain and ultimately to physically destroy the victims personally as well as to destroy the reproductive capacity of the Tutsi. Rape was often committed in public places such as roadblocks. Women were humiliated by being raped in the presence of their children, siblings, spouses or parents. The victims were subjected to insults. Victims of sexual violence were often paraded or made to walk long distances naked, and made objects of scorn and humiliation in the communities in which they had lived. Women's genital organs were pierced with pointed foreign objects such as spears, arrows and broken bottles, sprayed with pepper or cut off completely (Nowrojee 2005). Some had parts of their bodies that symbolise feminine beauty such as breasts, legs, noses and fingers cut off. After all the humiliation and infliction of pain, many of the victims of rape were killed. The dead bodies of victims were often left naked in public places. Some rape victims were not killed but kept as sexual slaves to some of the criminals (Green 2002). Many of the women who were victims of rape were infected with HIV and have either died or are dying of HIV/AIDS (African Rights 2004). Many survivors of the genocide became pregnant as a result of the genocide rape and gave birth to and have had to raise children born of those traumatic experiences (African Rights 2004).

The genocide had devastating consequences on Rwandan society in general and on the Tutsi community in particular. It is estimated that more than a million people had lost their lives by the time the genocide came to an end (Ministère de l'Administration Local, de l'Information et des Affaires Sociales 2002). The genocide, it is generally believed, claimed at least three-quarters of the Tutsi population (Des Forges 1999: p. 1). It has also been estimated that the massacres of Hutus who were targeted because of their presumed sympathy for the Tutsi may have claimed an additional 100–200,000 lives (Uvin 2000). The violence that Rwanda experienced occasioned immense suffering to literally millions of its citizens. More than two million Rwandans were internally displaced at the end of the genocide. Several million more had followed the interim government to exile as it fled (Bradley 1998: p. 132; Halvorsen 1999: p. 307; Prunier 1995: pp. 312–55). The genocide led to the virtual collapse of state institutions, to widespread destruction of private property and public infrastructure and to loss of social capital of inestimable value. The war and genocide left the country's economy in ruins. The genocide left Rwandan society more polarized along ethnic lines than ever before.

2.4 The Problem and Significance of Popular Participation in Genocide

The plan to exterminate the Tutsi was an enterprise of mammoth proportions; it brought together a very large number of people with one common goal: the destruction of the Tutsi community. While the genocide may have been the brainchild of a small group of individuals with personal and collective motives, its execution was the handiwork of multitudes. Over the course of the period during which it was carried out, the Rwanda genocide was transformed from being a project of political elites to a truly popular enterprise. Many individuals and groups accommodated, embraced, owned and advanced the genocide, with varying degrees of passion or commitment. A very large number of people bear personal responsibility for the crimes that were committed in the context of the genocide (Destexhe 1994: pp. 65–7; Straus 2007: p. 31). Participants in the genocide came from diverse social, professional, political and regional backgrounds. No segment of Rwandan society was unrepresented in the enterprise of implementing the genocide. On the contrary, the enterprise of genocide attracted a significant if not substantial following in every segment of Rwandan society. Perpetrators of the genocide came from the following groups.

2.4.1 The leadership of the political establishment

The organization of the genocide had a pyramid structure. At the top of the pyramid were the principal organizers. The identity of the membership of the core leadership responsible for the conception and direction of the genocide remains a matter of speculation. What is certain is that the leadership that conceived and directed the genocide comprised elements of the elites who controlled power in Rwanda prior to the genocide. This core leadership group comprised, in all likelihood, Colonel Bagosora and other members of the late President's inner circle, leaders of the ruling party and leaders of the military (Des Forges 1999: pp. 185–6; Human Rights Watch 2006b). This core leadership played the most decisive role in driving the genocide. It organized the swift elimination of opposition politicians whose alternative voices might have tempered the violence that was engulfing the country. It successfully organized the co-option of the leadership and broad membership of extremist factions of political parties behind their mission of exterminating the Tutsi. It marginalized military officers who were not committed to the plan of genocide against the Tutsi and massacres of political opposition. It put in place a puppet civilian government that helped popularize the genocide across the country. It was able to ensure that all organs of the state adopted the conduct of the genocide as their primary priority. Together with the puppet government that they established, the principal organizers of the genocide directed the campaign of genocide across the country.

2.4.2 Military, police and security services

The political establishment's plan for the extermination of the Tutsi was made possible by its control of the military, police and security services. From 1990, the leadership of the military took a leading role in the development of the concept of the Tutsi as the 'enemy'. It indoctrinated its members with anti-Tutsi propaganda, incited or allowed soldiers to commit atrocities against the Tutsi and trained and armed the militia that were instrumental in making the campaign of genocide successful. After the start of the genocide, the military adopted the campaign of genocide as part of its mandate. Rwanda had an army in excess of 40,000 men at the time of the genocide. It had police forces (the Gendarmerie and Police Communale) of several thousand. Not all elements of the military or police embraced the plan to exterminate the Tutsi or participated in the massacres of members of opposition parties. There were elements of these institutions that initially resisted joining the campaign of genocide. The majority of the military may not have had an opportunity to participate in committing atrocities against the Tutsi and political opposition because they were at the front fighting the RPA. However, the military, police and security services eventually all ended up being under the control of the organizers of the genocide. The military leadership incited, encouraged or ordered soldiers and policemen to commit or participate in atrocities against the Tutsi, who were all officially considered as the 'enemy'. The army distributed some of the weapons (through local government organs) that were used to commit the genocide. It provided organizational and logistical support to local leaders and militia and other groups which were leading the killings. Where civilians appeared reluctant to attack or were unable to subdue large groups of Tutsi, the army and police forces usually led the way, until civilians overcame their fear or reluctance (Des Forges 1999: p. 224). The army also manned roadblocks across the country to prevent the Tutsi from escaping. During the period of the genocide, the primary function of the two police forces (the Gendarmerie and Police Communale) was to support and facilitate the success of the genocide in the areas they were responsible for. The genocide might never have been possible and would certainly never have been as deadly as it turned out without the support that these institutions provided to the genocide campaign in terms of indoctrination, training, arming, logistical support, operations and coordination and supervision. While the precise number of soldiers and policemen who participated in the genocide is difficult to determine, it may be in the thousands or even tens of thousands.

2.4.3 Central government

The principal organizers of the genocide were able to extend the genocide from the capital to others parts of the country through the co-option of a wide cross-section of extremist Hutu politicians whom they constituted into the 'interim government', every single member of whom was allied with the extremist factions of their respective parties (Des Forges 1999: pp. 196–8). The members of the coalition of extremists represented in the interim government worked together or separately to incite, coerce, organize, support and lead the general population in the conduct of the genocide. The interim government mobilized popular support for the genocide through collective as well as individual declarations inciting violence against the Tutsi. Its members promoted violence against the Tutsi by exhorting the Hutu population to 'be vigilant in detecting the enemy and its accomplices', meaning the Tutsi (Des Forges 1999: pp. 190, 191, 345, 400, 415). Members of the government convened public meetings, especially in communities that were initially reluctant to participate in the killings, to warn the population to look out for the 'enemy' (meaning the Tutsi).[16] The members of the government also supported the campaign of genocide through other activities such as issuing directives to local government organs to organize massacres, encouraging militia groups of their respective political parties and other groups to get involved in committing atrocities, distributing arms and ammunition (to local government leaders, members of the militia, community 'self-defence' forces and members of the public) and supervising the progress of the genocide.[17] The members of the interim government made extensive and deadly use of the media, especially the radio, to incite hatred and violence against the Tutsi (Thompson 2006). Additionally, the interim government removed from office local government leaders who did not embrace, or were opposed to or reluctant to participate in, the genocide and replaced them with officials who were willing to lead the campaign of genocide in areas under their control.[18] Officials of departments of government at the national level also supported the genocide by diverting public funds to support operations to commit atrocities and putting government resources and assets, especially motor vehicles, at the disposal of military, police, militia and other groups that were involved in committing atrocities.

2.4.4 Political parties

Political parties played a very critical role in advancing the campaign of genocide. The leadership and membership of the factions of political parties that were opposed to the peace process and the reforms envisaged in the peace accords made a very critical contribution to the success of the campaign of genocide. Among political parties, the party that bears the greatest responsibility for the genocide is the then ruling party, the MRND. From the outbreak of the war in 1990, the leadership of the party was instrumental in inciting hatred and violence against the Tutsi community and political opposition as a strategy to unite the Hutu population behind the regime (Kakwenzire and Kamukama 1999). However, the MRND is not the only political party whose leadership and members participated in the genocide. At the time of the genocide, almost every major registered political party had split into moderate and extremist factions. Moderate factions supported the peace process and transition to democracy. Extremist factions were united by their anti-Tutsi ideology. When the genocide broke out, extremist factions of the political parties allied themselves with the organizers of the genocide and supported the campaign of genocide in many ways. They bestowed legitimacy, nationally and internationally, upon the organizers of the genocide by allowing them to claim that they had set up a broad-based government that represented and served the interests of all the people of the country. The leadership of the extremist political factions took an active role in promoting massacres at the provincial, district, sectoral and even village level. These factions of political parties had membership across the country. The factions put their militia at the disposal of the organizers of the genocide for use in the campaign of genocide. The factions encouraged their members to actively participate in the atrocities. The number of members of these militia has been estimated to have been around 50,000 (Prunier 1995: p. 243). Leaders and members of the militia associated with the various political parties (the two most prominent of which were the Interahamwe and Impuzamugambi) were the vanguard of the mobs that roamed the country committing atrocities.

The militias were the backbone of the civilian participation in the genocide. Members of the militias were often the most ideologically extreme, the most brutal, the most enduring of perpetrators of atrocities targeting the Tutsi community. The majority of the members of the militia were young men. The militia operated as one group in most areas. In most cases, these groups were mobile, moving from locality to locality depending on the need for their services. In each area, the militia were under direction or at the very least at the disposal of the local administration officials such as the mayor (*bourgmestre*) or the governor (the *prefet*) or the local military commander. These militia led roadblocks, night patrols, house-to-house searches and hunting for Tutsi in swamps, forests, fields and other places where Tutsi were reported or suspected to be hiding. The members of the extremist factions of political parties, and especially the members of their militia, took a leading role in implementing the genocide. The Rwanda genocide would probably not have succeeded to the extent that it did without the use of civilian militia of extremist political parties.

2.4.5 *Local government*

The main instrument of the principal organizers of the genocide and the central government for the effective prosecution of the genocide were local government organs. Rwanda has always had effective local government structures. The principal organizers of the genocide and the central government used these structures, ordinarily meant for facilitating effective delivery of public services, to facilitate the genocide. Rwanda was, at the time, divided into prefectures (provinces), communes (districts), sectors and cells. The interim government organized meetings of prefects (provincial governors) and issued instructions to them to organize and supervise killings in areas under their authority and to instruct bourgmestres (mayors of districts) to do likewise. Provincial and district authorities were responsible for the implementation of the civil defence system. They organized provincial and district security council meetings (*inama z' umutekano* in Kinyarwanda), ostensibly to discuss the security situation in their respective areas. The real objective of these security council meetings was to give directions to the lower level organs to organize massacres of the Tutsi in areas under their control. The meetings in each area were attended by local government leaders such as counsellors, civil servants, representatives of the army, police and security services as well as prominent private citizens. Local government organs distributed arms supplied by the central government and the military for use in committing atrocities. Local government organs were also responsible for organizing night patrols to ensure that potential victims did not escape.

2.4.6 Civil society

In development and democratic governance discourse, civil society is often portrayed as an agent of positive, transformative change. One would therefore have expected civil society in Rwanda to have taken a stand against the genocide. On the contrary, much of civil society in Rwanda either stood by or fell in line behind the plans of the organizers of the genocide. Civil society organizations, including the media and human rights NGOs were either totally silenced or co-opted. Not even the church, which occupied a very influential position in Rwanda's social and political system and would perhaps have been the only institution that could have been immune from reprisals, spoke out against the genocide. Elements of civil society, in fact, actively participated in the genocide. Of the constituent elements of civil society, the media played the most decisive role in advancing the genocide. The organizers of the genocide owe their success, in part, to the control they were able to exercise over both private and public media outlets (IRPD 2003). State-owned and private media outlets were very instrumental in both inciting hatred and violence against the Tutsi and in directing attacks against the community. Print and radio journalists used the media to spread anti-Tutsi hatred, to incite violence and genocide against the Tutsi and to direct and coordinate attacks against the community. This propaganda either exaggerated dangers posed to the Hutu community by the RPA or incited hatred and violence against Tutsi and their sympathizers (Reed 1996: p. 496).

2.4.7 *Private citizens*

A very large number of ordinary citizens share responsibility for the genocide. The factor that by far accounts for the extraordinary success of the campaign of genocide against the Tutsi community was the effectiveness of the organizers' strategy to involve as much of the population as possible in committing atrocities (African Rights 2000; Des Forges 1999). The principal organizers of the genocide were able to convince prominent personalities, especially politicians from the ruling party and extremist factions of political parties, to join the campaign of genocide against the Tutsi. These prominent personalities, working with local government organs, were able to incite hatred against the Tutsi community and to convince a significant part of the population that the Tutsi were a mortal enemy that had to be destroyed. Genocide became, in the eyes of a large number of citizens, a form of service to the community. Hundreds of thousands of ordinary civilians responded to persuasion, incitement and coercion by political, military and civil society to participate in genocide. In almost every village across the country, many if not most of the men (and sometimes women and children) volunteered or were coerced to serve in searches of homes, on night patrols, at roadblocks or in hunting expeditions in which Tutsi were found and murdered. A very large number of private citizens participated directly in killings, torture, rape and other sexual violence, pillage and destruction of property. Citizens who were well to do provided money, alcohol and food to motivate other citizens to participate actively in committing atrocities. Others provided logistical support, by availing their motor vehicles to transport the gangs that spearheaded the attacks. Individuals reported the hiding places of potential victims who had survived earlier attacks. A very large number of private citizens, numbering at least hundreds of thousands, participated in the genocide in some way. The widespread participation of the masses in committing atrocities is one of the distinguishing features of the Rwandan genocide (African Rights 2000; Des Forges 1999; Ball 1999: p. 168; Daly 2002a: p. 362; Straus 2007). The genocide was largely executed using ordinary citizens, motivated by a wide range of factors including ideology, coercion, prospects of pillage, plunder, sexual gratification, desire for vengeance and other diverse reasons.

2.5 Conclusion

Rwanda has a history of social conflict going back centuries. The principal driver of the conflict is grievances over perceptions of social, economic and political marginalization and exclusion. From the middle of the twentieth century, the nature of the conflict and relations between the country's two major communities became radicalized, as elites incited and promoted inter-ethnic hatred and violence in the process of competition for political power. Since then, conflict in Rwanda has periodically turned violent. The most significant outbreak of such violence occurred in 1990, when Tutsi refugees invaded Rwanda from Uganda. Facing internal and external pressures for political reform, the government of the day sought to stave off demands for political change by inciting violence against and persecuting the Tutsi community. Pressure from regional and internal powers compelled the government to sign a peace agreement to end the war and to pave the way for democratic reform. The political establishment vigorously opposed both the peace process and the proposed political reforms, and used the assassination of the President in April 1994 as a pretext to thwart both processes. The ruling establishment decided to carry out genocide of the Tutsi community as a strategy to preserve its control of political power. The principal organizers of the genocide were able to co-opt a broad section of elites behind their plan to exterminate the Tutsi community. These elites helped to popularize the genocide among ordinary citizens across the country. A small minority of Rwandese courageously opposed the genocide. The majority of the population were powerless bystanders. Nevertheless, the campaign of genocide became a popular enterprise. A distinguishing feature of the Rwanda genocide is the scale of popular participation in the atrocities. The processes of accountability for atrocity with which Rwanda and the international community have responded to the legacy of the genocide are discussed in the next four chapters. These processes have been shaped, more than any other factor, by the element of the widespread social participation in atrocities.

3 Accountability for Mass Atrocity

Challenges, Choices and Goals of Transitional Justice in Post-Genocide Rwanda

3.1 Introduction

The previous chapter discussed the historical background to the Rwandan conflict, and provided the reader with basic knowledge of the violence, particularly genocide, that this conflict spawned during the 1990s. Knowledge of the conflict, and of the violence associated with it, is critical to understanding the choices of transitional justice processes that Rwanda has made. Chapter 3 discusses the context in which the transitional justice that Rwanda has pursued was adopted and implemented. It discusses the challenges that the reconstruction of Rwanda from the consequences of war and genocide posed, and provides insights as to how the development of policies relating to the country's reconstruction in general, and to the challenges associated with the management of the legacy of the genocide in particular, were carried out. It discusses the factors that shaped the choices of transitional justice mechanisms that Rwanda chose to pursue, the role that processes of accountability for atrocity have occupied in the framework of policies on the country's reconstruction, and the objectives that the transitional justice processes that Rwanda adopted were intended to achieve.

3.2 Challenges of National Reconstruction in the Aftermath of War and Genocide

The war and genocide of the 1990s had catastrophic consequences for Rwanda. The violence that the country experienced during the period had a devastating impact on its social fabric, economy and the state's capacity to deliver essential public services. The country's reconstruction faced a host of challenges related to the violence experienced. The choices that Rwanda made as to how it should deal with the legacy of that violence, and of the genocide in particular, were shaped by the country's socio-political situation. These choices were part of the new government's strategies for the stabilization and reconstruction of the country. In order to understand the rationale behind the choices of the transitional justice mechanisms that Rwanda chose to pursue, one needs to appreciate the challenges that the recovery, reconstruction and development of the country posed after the war and genocide. These challenges included the following.

3.2.1 Lack of safety and security

Between April and July 1994, Rwanda's political, military and law enforcement institutions and much of civil society worked together to further one common mission: the extermination of the Tutsi through a campaign of genocide (African Rights 2000; Des Forges 1999; Prunier 1995). Institutions of the state, instead of enforcing and upholding the law, became part of a nationwide criminal enterprise to exterminate a section of the population. The government of the day distributed weapons to members of militia groups, trained them in the use of the weapons and provided incentives to citizens to encourage them to participate in committing atrocities (Des Forges 1999: pp. 65–137). Committing atrocity was portrayed in government propaganda as a patriotic act, a fulfilment of civic duties (Thompson 2006). Large numbers of citizens responded positively to this incitement and participated in committing atrocities (Des Forges 1999: pp. 260–2). By the end of the genocide, the public had lost all confidence in the state and its institutions as guarantors of public security and the protection of citizens against human rights violations. Rwanda's post-genocide government faced the challenge of restoring public confidence in the country's legal system and in the institutions of the state to ensure safety and security to citizens.

3.2.2 Social polarization

Cleavages between the Hutu and Tutsi communities have historical origins stretching back decades, and perhaps centuries (Organisation of African Unity 2000). Divisions between the Hutu and the Tutsi deteriorated during the colonial period as a result of policies of the colonial government that discriminated against the Hutu community (Mamdani 2001: p. 40). Post-independence governments exacerbated the state of bad relations between the country's two major communities even further through persecution and institutionalized discrimination against the Tutsi community (Prunier 1995; IRPD 2003). Government propaganda and the education system of post-independence Rwanda systematically dehumanized the Tutsi community (Rudasingwa 1994; Organisation of African Unity 2000: Chapter 3). Official policy treated the Tutsi as little more than aliens, a people with limited rights, whose lives were in certain situations entirely dispensable and at the mercy of the government and its officials (Ngoga 2009: pp. 312–24). Between 1973 and 1994, competition for power and resources gave rise to new cleavages between Hutu from the North and those from the South of the country (Kakwenzire and Kamukama 1999: p. 64; Straus 2007: p. 23). However, the genocide eclipsed these cleavages between North and South and re-established the schism between the Hutu and Tutsi communities as the dominant dividing line in Rwandan society. The Tutsi generally came out of the experience of the genocide with the perception that the majority of the Hutu community were either perpetrators of, or accomplices to, the genocide (Gourevitch 1998). The genocide ruptured relations between the Hutu and Tutsi communities at the individual, community and national level (Haile 2008: p. 11). The war and the genocide ended with the victory of the Tutsi-dominated RPF rebel movement, a development that caused dismay in the Hutu population (Mamdani 2001; Prunier 1995). Could the new regime avoid seeking revenge? Would the regime seek to dominate the Hutu majority and re-impose Tutsi hegemony as the propaganda of the previous government had warned? Rwanda was a bitterly divided country after the war and genocide (Cannon 2005: pp. 10–11; Habimana 2009). The prevailing social polarization had strong implications for efforts to restore law and order, to promote peace and stability and to rebuild the country (Organisation of African Unity 2000: Chapter 23).

3.2.3 Managing social tensions inherent in the pursuit of justice in the context of large-scale popular participation in mass atrocity

The Rwandan genocide is unique among modern genocides and other situations of mass atrocity in the extent to which ordinary people participated in committing atrocities (Straus 2004). While state institutions planned and directed the Rwanda genocide from the top, it was largely carried out using a grassroots army of private citizens (Des Forges 1999; Straus 2004). The large-scale participation of private citizens in committing atrocities presented the new government with complex dilemmas. The country did not have the capacity to deal with violence on the scale of the genocide in accordance with existing legislation (Meyerstein 2007). The justice system had collapsed as a result of the war and genocide (Kirby 2006). The country had no functioning courts, prosecution service or police. Policing functions were being performed by soldiers who had no police training (ACCT 1994; Vandegiste 1997: p. 13). The country's prisons did not have the capacity to accommodate the large and growing prison population of genocide suspects. Managing problems arising from mass social participation in atrocity raised a number of very difficult issues that the post-genocide government had to confront (Meyerstein 2007: p. 472). How should a state whose justice system has been destroyed deal with the perpetrators of mass atrocity? How does a society that has experienced mass atrocity balance due process considerations with the need to ensure public order and promote the rule of law? Is it acceptable for the government to apprehend and detain persons suspected of atrocity even though it does not have the capacity to ensure a fair trial without undue delay? What strategies are necessary to build capacity to handle crimes involving large-scale popular participation? Would the process of trying and punishing so many members of one ethnic group worsen relations between the two ethnic groups? How could accountability for genocide be reconciled with strategies to promote reconciliation in a situation where the perpetrators were predominantly of one ethnic group? How does a society divided by past violence balance the objectives of eradicating impunity and promoting peaceful coexistence between survivors and the rest of society? The post-genocide government was under pressure to devise policies and approaches to mediate the tensions between the parties to the conflict over the question of justice.

3.2.4 Addressing the needs and concerns of survivors of the genocide

The genocide had a catastrophic impact on the Tutsi community and Rwandan society. More than a million people may have lost their lives in the course of the genocide (Ministère de l'Administration Locale, de l'Information et des Affaires Sociales, Rwanda 2002)[1] and more than three-quarters of the entire Tutsi population may have perished (Des Forges 1999: p. 16). Tens of thousands of victims who survived the genocide had experienced horrendous physical abuse of every description, including rape and/or gruesome torture (Human Rights Watch 1996; African Rights 2004; Hubbard 2007). It has been reported that between 250–500,000 women and girls may have been victims of rape and other forms of sexual violence during the period of the genocide (Organisation of African Unity 2000: para. 16.170). Rape was often preceded or followed by acts of humiliation and other forms of violence often leading to death. A very large proportion of the women who were raped during the genocide were infected with HIV/AIDS (Human Rights Watch 1996; Africa Rights 2004). Many Tutsi women and girls also became victims of enslavement during the genocide (Human Rights Watch 1996; Nowrojee 2005). Hutu women married to Tutsi lost husbands and children. The genocide had a very devastating impact on children who were targeted for slaughter in an attempt to ensure that there were no remnants of the Tutsi left for posterity (Human Rights Watch 2003). Large numbers of children who survived the slaughter were orphaned or separated from their families by the war and genocide. It has been reported that this number could be as high as 300,000 (Organisation of African Unity: para. 16.56).

Survivors were traumatized by the suffering they had experienced. They were often socially marginalized and most were economically destitute. They lived with the risk that those responsible for the deaths of their relatives and their own suffering might be tempted to silence them by killing them. Survivors of the genocide needed reassurance that their persecution was over, that the days of impunity for human rights violations had ended, and that they would be safe and secure in the future. They also needed to have their trust in the humanity of the Hutu community restored. The post-genocide government had the difficult challenge of meeting the basic humanitarian and security needs of survivors; defusing survivors' anger, mistrust and temptation to take the law into their own hands in reprisal or revenge killings; restoring their confidence in the power of the state to protect all; reassuring survivors that those who had victimized them would be brought to justice; and creating conditions necessary to enable them and the rest of Rwandan society to overcome the legacy of past divisions, conflict and violence and to build a secure shared future.

3.2.5 The crisis of internally displaced persons and refugees

Almost every person who was living in Rwanda in 1994 was at one time or another displaced during the conflict (Algard 2005: p. 34). Government propaganda led the Hutu community to believe that the RPA was responsible for massive indiscriminate killings of civilians. This propaganda reached its peak during the three months of the genocide (Chrétien 1995). As a result of this propaganda, the Hutu population often fled as the RPA advanced into their areas. Most communities in Rwanda were displaced at least once during the course of the genocide (IRDP 2003: p. 101). Communities from central and southern Rwanda established large camps of internally displaced persons in south-western Rwanda after the arrival of Operation Turquoise, the UN-sanctioned French military mission in June 1994.[2] There were more than 1,800,000 Rwandans living in these internally displaced persons (IDP) camps at the end of the genocide (Prunier 1995: p. 312). The defeat of the government responsible for the genocide in July 1994 led to an unprecedented new exodus of refugees (Adelman and Suhrke 1999; Organisation of African Unity 2000; Prunier 1995: p. 312). A large part of the population followed the deposed government and its forces as they fled to exile. There were more than 3,000,000 Rwandan refugees living in camps in neighbouring countries (Adelman and Suhrke 1999: pp. 307–20; Prunier 1995: pp. 312–55; IRDP 2003: p. 101). The civilian, military and militia leadership that had led the genocide in Rwanda was able to impose itself on the refugee population and to recreate the power structures they had once led in Rwanda in refugee camps in Congo (Halvorsen 1999: pp. 310–11; Strain and Keyes 2003: p. 94). These camps were militarized (Halvorsen 1999) and the groups in control of the camps continued to carry on very hostile propaganda against the new government (Berry and Berry 1999: pp. 87–122). Through propaganda and physical coercion, they were able to effectively obstruct the return of those refugees who wished to go back to Rwanda. Refugees who attempted to return were killed, as a sign to the rest of the refugee population that they should not consider the option of returning until the leadership of the camps allowed them to do so (Halvorsen 1999: p. 310). Fear of victimization by justice processes intended to deal with genocide was cited as one of the reasons hindering refugees from returning to Rwanda (Scharf 1999: p. 629). A fair and effective justice system was considered to be critical to the resolution of the problem of internally displaced persons and refugees. Credible processes of dealing with atrocities associated with the genocide, it was hoped, would encourage and facilitate the return and reintegration of refugees in their communities.

3.2.6 Threats of resurgence of armed conflict

Once established in the Congo, the leaders of the deposed government and military began preparing for a return to power in Rwanda (Amnesty International 1995a; Human Rights Watch 1995). Their aim was to return to power by force of arms (Human Rights Watch 1995; Prunier 1995: pp. 315–16; Tully 2003: p. 390). According to Human Rights Watch (1995), they recruited and trained additional troops from the youth in the refugee camps and re-armed, often using proceeds from the sale of supplies provided by the international community for humanitarian assistance to the refugees. The insurgents soon started launching attacks against Rwanda from refugee camps across the border. The attacks mainly targeted genocide survivors and government officials (Amnesty International 1996b). The presence of a very large, hostile and militarized population close to Rwanda's borders was a formidable threat to the country's fragile security and its long-term stability (Haile 2008: p. 15). The existence of an armed, externally based opposition propagating sectarian violence undermined the Rwandan government's policies to improve safety and security inside the country, promote national reconciliation, encourage the return and reintegration of refugees, and facilitate social and economic reconstruction.

3.2.7 Challenges relating to economic recovery, reconstruction and development

Rwanda's economy was already in dire straits prior to the genocide. It is widely believed that economic factors played a part in precipitating or encouraging the genocide (Uvin 1998: pp. 82–102; Organisation of African Unity 2000: Chapter 5). The war and genocide brought the country's economy to the brink of total collapse (World Bank 1998; Ministry of Finance and Economic Planning, Rwanda 1999; Daly 2002a: p. 366; Cannon 2005: pp. 5–7). There was widespread destruction of public infrastructure and private property. International trade came to a halt, and government revenues dried up completely as the machinery of the state collapsed. Development assistance, which Rwanda had greatly depended upon prior to the genocide, also came to a halt (Prunier 1995: pp. 312–15). Even humanitarian assistance that the country so badly needed was withheld for some time after the genocide. The collapse of the country's economy had a huge impact on the welfare of the population in the aftermath of the genocide. Social services previously provided by the government ceased to be available. Poverty levels worsened since sources of livelihood had been destroyed (Organisation of African Unity 2000: Chapter 17). The country's recovery would depend on the capacity of the government to organize urgent humanitarian support for victims of the war and genocide, to provide essential services to the population in general and to address the problem of poverty that many believed was one of the root causes of the Rwanda conflict (Organisation of African Unity 2000: Chapter 17;

Cannon 2005: pp. 5–7). Peace and stability were a prerequisite for economic recovery and justice was expected to contribute to both goals.

3.3 Choices of Policies and Processes for Accounting for Genocide

3.3.1 The RPF's approach to governing Rwanda in the aftermath of the genocide

The RPF interpreted its military victory over the organizers of the genocide as a mandate to reconstruct Rwanda on its own terms. The analogy that the party adopted to characterize its role in the post-genocide political dispensation was that it was the 'engine' of the government. In practice, this policy meant that although other political parties could take part in the day-to-day management of the country, the RPF had almost absolute discretion in determining what the policies of the government on major issues would be. Policy proposals would originate from the party. The party would formulate the policies through its internal debates. The party's policy proposals would be presented to its partners in government for formal approval. The RPF's overwhelming dominance of the political system ensured that the other parties represented in the transitional government did not have the clout to reject or substantially alter policy proposals advanced by the RPF.

Rwanda's initial responses to the challenge of accountability for the genocide were developed through the same process. The RPF took the view that justice for the genocide was not just a legal matter of concern only to lawyers; it was a political issue that was central to the organisation's mission of rebuilding Rwanda. Shortly after the end of the genocide, the RPF commenced an internal debate on how the country would deal with the question of accountability for the genocide. The consultations, hosted and led by the then President, Pasteur Bizimungu, brought together a very wide cross-section of the leadership of the party, including the Vice President and other party leaders, cabinet ministers, Members of Parliament, judges and prosecutors, the entire leadership of the military, senior civil servants and senior party workers. As a result of historical factors that could be traced to the external origins of the RPF (the organization was established by exiles, the vast majority of whom were Tutsi), the majority of the participants in the consultations were Tutsi. While consultations included a very significant number of officials whose families had perished in the genocide, the majority of the participants were Tutsi who returned to Rwanda from the diaspora. Only a minority of the participants were Hutu.

As a member of the RPF and a senior representative of the organization in the transitional government, I was involved in most of the organization's high-level debates about the government's reconstruction policies after my return to Rwanda in August 1994. I was also one of the few people in the senior leadership of the organization with legal training. As a result, I played a very active role in internal organizational debates about the restoration of the country's justice system and the establishment of mechanisms of accounting for the genocide even before I was appointed to a formal office in the justice sector. At the beginning of 1996, I was transferred to the Ministry of Justice. As Deputy to the Minister, I was not only responsible for the day-to-day management of the department, but I also led the formulation and implementation of policies on law and justice issues, including the critical issue of reckoning with the legacy of the genocide. It is in this capacity that I participated in the internal RPF debates about policy responses to the genocide. When the RPF reached a consensus on the approach to accountability for genocide and had it adopted by the government at large, it was my responsibility to lead the implementation of the adopted policies.

3.3.2 Policy issues

In the genocide's aftermath, the necessity of a legal response to the genocide was not seriously contested (Graybill and Lanegran 2004: p. 8). The leadership that had responsibility for planning and directing the genocide were on the run. A government dominated by the Tutsi had taken over. The Hutu who remained inside the country were keen to distance themselves from any role in the atrocities that had been committed. Everyone in Rwanda, official and private citizen alike, proclaimed their support for justice for the genocide. The necessity for justice for crimes that had been committed during the course of the genocide was one of the exceptional situations in Rwandan society where there was a broad cross-ethnic consensus on a major policy issue.

Given the existing consensus on the need for accountability for genocide, the debate on accountability centred on the modalities of ensuring that justice for the genocide was rendered in a way that supported the country's reconstruction agenda.

In spite of unanimous agreement among all stakeholders on the need for accountability, there were still many concerns, within and outside of Rwanda, regarding the process of bringing perpetrators of the genocide to justice (Sarkin 2001: p. 144). The issues that confronted us as we (as policy makers) considered our options in terms of providing justice for the genocide included the following: What objectives should justice for the genocide aim to achieve? What mechanisms or processes were ideal for achieving the intended objectives? Should the state pursue universal accountability through the criminal justice system, by seeking to investigate, prosecute and punish all of the perpetrators according to existing laws? Was universal accountability through the criminal justice system feasible, given the state of the justice administration system (which had almost completely been destroyed as a result of war and genocide) and the high level of popular participation in atrocity? Was it possible to hold fair trials for mass atrocity in an environment of such intense social polarization? If genocide-related litigation was to be dealt with through criminal prosecutions, should the ordinary courts conduct the trials, or should special courts be established for the purpose of trying the genocide cases? Was it realistic to seek to apply the strict letter of the law in a context where a very large number of citizens had participated in committing atrocities? Was it advisable, for example, to retain capital punishment, given that the large number of citizens who had participated in genocide came exclusively from one community? Or should the state, for the sake of promoting national stability, explore ways of dealing with the 'small fish' more leniently than current law allowed while still upholding the principle of individual criminal responsibility? How would the country find the human and financial resources to undertake investigations and trials on such a large scale, given the state of the justice system and the economy? Should the country deal with the trials on its own or should it seek international assistance (financial as well as human resources) in dealing with accountability for the genocide? What role should international criminal justice play in accountability for the genocide? If it were not possible or appropriate to deal with genocide-related crimes through the criminal justice system, should the country consider alternatives to criminal prosecutions? If alternatives to criminal prosecutions were acceptable or indeed inevitable, what would such alternatives be? Was a truth and reconciliation commission an appropriate response to the Rwanda genocide? How could the process of ensuring justice for the genocide be harmonized with other strategies to stabilize the country? Considering that a very large number of members of the Hutu community had participated in committing atrocities, was it possible to have universal accountability and national reconciliation and stability at the same time?

The process of determining appropriate mechanisms of accountability for the genocide called for a careful balancing of the interests and concerns of a large number of stakeholders. The stakeholders in the process included the government, survivors of the genocide and other human rights abuses, persons suspected or accused of having taken part in the genocide and their relatives and sympathizers, the Tutsi community who had not been victims of the genocide, Hutus who had not participated in the atrocities (including the leadership of the political parties that were junior partners in the Transitional Government) and the international community. All of these groups had interests and concerns that they wished to see addressed by and during the process of accountability for the genocide. The government's primary objective was to restore public order, to stabilize the country and to create an environment conducive to national recovery, reconstruction and development (Ministère de Finance, Rwanda 1996). The Tutsi community in general, and survivors of the genocide in particular, hoped that accountability processes would end impunity once and for all by conveying an unequivocal message that those who commit atrocities against fellow citizens would henceforth be held accountable (Office of the President, Rwanda 1995). The Hutu community equally needed reassurance that their human rights would be respected under the new political dispensation and that any measures to seek justice for the genocide would be fair (MDR 1994). Persons suspected or accused of participation in the genocide and their families needed assurances that there would be no victimization and that any charges against them would be investigated and tried fairly and without undue delay.[3] The Hutu community had a compelling interest in ensuring that guilt was individualized, so that the whole community would not be tainted by attribution of collective guilt. The interest of the international community was mainly to have a response to the genocide that would contribute to the establishment and maintenance of peace and stability in Rwanda and the Great Lakes region as a whole.[4] Rwanda's recovery and stabilization was not of exclusive concern to policy makers and citizens of Rwanda. The situation in Rwanda, and in particular its stability, was truly a matter of international concern in the aftermath of the genocide. The genocide had demonstrated that mismanaging a conflict could have grave consequences for international peace and security.

In the mid-1990s when we were grappling with the question as to what could be the appropriate policy responses to the legacy of the genocide, the field of transitional justice was not as well researched, published and developed as it is today. Indeed, the term 'transitional justice' itself had only recently been coined (Teitel 2010). We were, of course, familiar with general knowledge about the Nuremberg trials, truth commissions including South Africa's and the recent establishment of the ICTY. We did not, however, consult and were not influenced by any literature or expertise on transitional justice as part of our search for an appropriate response to the legacy of the genocide. More than anything else, our deliberations on how to respond to the genocide were driven by analysis of the challenges that the reconstruction of the country posed and of the strategies that were in our opinion necessary to address those challenges. Our engagement with transitional justice only really began with the convening of the conference that the government organized at the end of 1995 for the purpose of facilitating dialogue with the international community on the issue of accountability for the genocide. Our familiarity with transitional justice theory and transitional justice processes of other post-conflict societies grew from then onwards. However, Rwanda's policy makers have never looked to transitional justice literature and the experiences of other societies for guidance on the design of Rwanda's own accountability mechanisms. We were always of the view that Rwanda's situation was unique and were focused on designing responses to address Rwanda's exceptional circumstances.

3.3.3 ***Processes***

3.3.3.1 International Criminal Tribunal for Rwanda

Before the above-mentioned internal RPF consultations had made any headway in fashioning a national legal framework for accountability for the genocide, the Rwanda government was compelled to take a stand on the establishment and organization of an international tribunal to try crimes relating to the genocide. Some of the major powers in the international community set in motion the process for establishment of a tribunal to try crimes relating to the Rwanda genocide even before the genocide had come to an end. The US government is said to have been considering a proposal to establish a mechanism for the trial and punishment of crimes relating to the Rwanda genocide as early as June 1994 (Schabas 2006: p. 27). On 1 July 1994, the Security Council passed a resolution to establish a commission of experts with a structure and mandate to the commission that had earlier recommended the establishment of the ICTY (United Nations 1994g). In September 1994, the commission presented its initial report, recommending the expansion of the ICTY's jurisdiction to cover human rights violations that had been committed in Rwanda. By then, the United Nations and especially the members of the Security Council were already holding informal consultations on the establishment of a tribunal for Rwanda. The Rwanda government was consulted on a draft of the statute for the proposed court, but given only a very short time in which to respond to the proposal. The RPF had initially supported the establishment of an international criminal court to try crimes relating to the genocide on account of several reasons, which are discussed in detail in Chapter 4. The RPF organized internal consultation on the draft statute. The consultative meetings expressed reservations about certain aspects of the draft statute of the tribunal that are also detailed in Chapter 4. The Rwanda government dispatched a delegation to the United Nations headquarters to articulate its views during the final round of the negotiations that preceded the establishment of the ICTR. Rwanda's views on the statute of the proposed tribunal failed to sway the tribunal's supporters, and the resolution establishing the ICTR was adopted on 8 November 1995 (United Nations 1994m).

3.3.3.2 Domestic prosecutions

The internal RPF consultations on a domestic response to the legacy of the genocide resumed after the United Nation's decision to establish the ICTR. All the key principles, which were subsequently adopted by the government and parliament as the core elements of the legal framework for bringing perpetrators of genocide to justice, were initially discussed and agreed upon in advance by the RPF consultations forum. Our discussions led to the conclusion that the issue of accountability could not be dealt with in isolation from the wider process of national reconstruction. The genocide could not be dealt with as an ordinary crime. The objective of our policies on accountability for the genocide we agreed would be to complement other government initiatives designed to build a peaceful and stable society able to deal with the social, political and economic challenges that the country faced, some of which have been described in the previous section of this chapter.

The discussions on accountability were influenced, above all else, by the urgency of the need to heal divisions in Rwandan society that were a legacy of the genocide. The consultations also decided that the primary response to the legacy of the genocide should be criminal prosecutions. The trials would be conducted in accordance with pre-1994 criminal law. Specialized courts would be established to handle the trial genocide cases. The trials would aim at universal accountability by all persons who had participated in committing atrocities. Perpetrators would be categorized into groups according to the degree of the seriousness of the crimes they were accused of. Only suspects who bore the greatest responsibility would bear the full rigour of the law, including capital punishment. Attempts would be made to treat leniently suspects who were not among planners, leaders or perpetrators of particularly heinous crime including sexual violence. Incentives would be offered to encourage perpetrators to cooperate in telling the truth about how the genocide had been organized and carried out.

The choice of criminal prosecutions as the preferred mechanism of accountability for the genocide was influenced by a number of factors. The approach of prosecutions had the support of genocide survivors. Criminal prosecutions were considered by survivors to be the ideal response to the country's entrenched culture of impunity for human rights violations. Victims, understandably, wanted the sternest punishment possible. Survivors argued that it was not only fair but necessary to 'just apply the law'. Criminal prosecutions offered, at least in theory, persons accused of genocide the best opportunity to be tried through a process that applied well-known rules with guarantees of being treated fairly. Prosecutions offered the best opportunity for trials seeking to conform with international human rights standards. Prosecutions were also attractive to the government, in that they would help to emphasize Rwanda's new aspiration to be a state governed by the rule of law.

The choice of pre-1994 criminal law as the applicable law to govern genocide was aimed at avoiding violation of the principle against retroactive legislation. The establishment of specialized chambers in the courts and specialized sections in the prosecution service dedicated exclusively to the handling of the genocide cases was intended to ensure that the genocide caseload was dealt with as expeditiously as possible. Categorization of suspects aimed to balance the need for accountability with the necessity to stabilize the country, by making it possible to deal with the 'small fish' more leniently than the existing law allowed while applying the full force of the law against perpetrators who bore the most responsibility, in order to send a clear message about impunity for human rights violations.[5] Sexual violence was included in the category of crimes that would attract the most severe punishment in acknowledgement of the horrendous nature of the sexual violence that Tutsi women, girls and sometimes men had been subjected to during the genocide. The exclusion of capital punishment for all but a small minority of perpetrators who bore the greatest responsibility was necessary to avoid aggravating the already polarized relations between the country's two major communities.

The 'guilty plea and confession' programme aimed to expedite the processing of the genocide caseload and to make it easier to establish the truth about how the genocide had been organized and carried out.

The consultations considered the option of using what has subsequently come to be known as the 'hybrid courts' system to deal with the genocide caseload. The proposal to use hybrid courts arose out of recognition of the country's lack of domestic capacity to investigate and prosecute the very large number of crimes that had been committed during the genocide. The proposal to use foreign legal professionals in processing the genocide caseload was ultimately rejected on account of several reasons, including the prevalence of strong feelings on the part of many of the participants that the deployment of foreign legal professionals in the country's justice system would be an unacceptable infringement of national sovereignty; lingering resentment against the international community on account of its failure to prevent or stop the genocide; suspicion that foreign legal professionals could be vulnerable to manipulation by foreign powers sympathetic to the ousted regime and perpetrators of the genocide; and a determination on the part of the new government to establish sustainable capacity to deal with the challenge of responding to the genocide and administration of justice in general.

Some outsiders at the time counselled the government to consider a role for a truth and reconciliation commission, with or without amnesty for the perpetrators (Graybill and Lanegran 2004: p. 8). We never seriously considered the option of using a truth and reconciliation commission. Feelings about the genocide were still raw. A truth commission was considered by both policy makers and victims of the genocide to be a grossly inadequate response to the horror of the genocide. A truth commission was also considered to be inadequate for addressing the country's deeply entrenched culture of impunity (Fierens 2005).

Once the RPF leadership had agreed upon the framework of an accountability regime that it wished to establish, details of the proposals were communicated to junior partners in government through the cabinet. The government approved the proposals. The government did not, however, organize any extensive public consultation on the proposals. The only forum at which the proposals were discussed in detail was an international conference that the Office of the President organized for the purposes of presenting the proposals to national and international stakeholders and experts (Ministère de Finance, Rwanda 1996). The conference's agenda covered a wide range of issues relating to the genocide, but its primary goal was to seek the input of international experts on the legal framework for the conduct of genocide trials that the RPF and government had formulated. The task of working out details of the draft legislation to govern the conduct of genocide cases was entrusted to one of the working groups of the conference. The working group produced a draft of a bill that it presented to the plenary of the conference. A number of international experts stayed in Rwanda for some days after the conference to complete the proposed legislation. The draft of the law was then presented to the Ministry of Justice. The Ministry of Justice made some structural modifications to the draft of the legislation that the conference experts had prepared before submitting it to the Cabinet, which approved the draft and forwarded it to Parliament for debate. Parliament eventually passed the law on genocide trials in August 1996, after often emotional and sometimes acrimonious debates.[6] A number of foreign experts continued to provide some legal advice to the government during and after the law on organization of genocide trials was adopted.

3.3.3.3 Gacaca

Within two years after prosecutions before domestic courts and the International Criminal Tribunal for Rwanda got underway, it was already apparent that conventional domestic prosecutions could not effectively address human rights violations on the scale of the atrocities that had been committed in Rwanda.

By the middle of 1998, Rwanda had well over 135,000 genocide suspects in detention (Office of the President, Rwanda 1999: para. 74; Amnesty International 2002b: p. 8). Hardly any Hutu family was without a family member or relative in detention on genocide-related charges (Organisation of African Unity 2000; paras 18.5–18.6). Most of the genocide suspects had been in pre-trial detention for several years. The arrest and detention of most of the suspects violated the applicable provisions of the Criminal Procedure Code. Most of the suspects did not have any files (dossiers) indicating the nature of the charges against them or the evidence substantiating those charges (UNCHR Rights 1998b: para. 14). Conditions of detention in Rwanda's prisons were at the time considered by human rights organizations to constitute cruel, inhuman or degrading treatment or punishment (Moussali 1998; Amnesty International 2000: para. 21). Several thousand suspects died in prison each year because of the cramped conditions, malnutrition, poor hygiene and lack of adequate medical care (UNOHCHR 1994a: paras 43 and 46; Human Rights First 1997). Over 11,000 genocide detainees are reported to have died in detention between 1994 and 2002 (Megwalu 2006: p. 27).

While it was generally acknowledged that the performance of the criminal justice system had improved and continued to improve (Amnesty International 1997b; Vandegiste 1997: p. 19; Moussalli 1998), the number of trials completed each year was still insignificant compared to the number of suspects awaiting trial (Pitsch 2003; Uvin 2003a; Tiemessen 2004). The justice system was so overwhelmed by the genocide caseload that even very serious crimes such as rape were not being investigated and prosecuted (Office of the President, Rwanda 1999: para. 73).

The slow pace of the genocide trials was a result of many factors, including cumbersome and time-consuming legal procedures (Office of the President, Rwanda 1999: para. 79), inadequate personnel, lack of adequate skills, lack of basic resources (especially logistics for investigations) and lack of motivation on the part of staff (due to poor remuneration and other unsatisfactory working conditions). As a result of its failure to deal effectively with the genocide caseload, the criminal justice system did not enjoy a high level of public confidence (Sarkin 2001: p. 150; Vandegiste 2001a: p. 267; Habimana 2009). Some in government, and particularly the President, were critical of the criminal justice system because it did not provide opportunity for popular participation in the accountability process.[7]

The slow pace of the genocide trials was a source of strong frustration for all of the major stakeholders in the justice for genocide process, especially genocide suspects (Sarkin 2001: p. 149) and victims (Vandegiste 2001a: pp. 267–8). The prolonged and indefinite detention of such a large number of members of one ethnic community in harsh conditions posed major political, social and economic problems for the government (Uvin 2003a: p. 116). Many women and sometimes children spent much of their time commuting to detention centres to take provisions to detained relatives instead of working on farms or attending school. The withdrawal of so much labour from production increased poverty and hardship in communities. The detention of a significant proportion of the Hutu men not only occasioned social and economic hardships to their families, but also led to strained relations between Hutu and Tutsi (especially genocide survivors) in every community (Sarkin 2000). The problem of a large prison population had many strategic implications. The arbitrary detention of so many members of the Hutu community undermined initiatives to promote reconciliation and to ensure national stability. It exposed the government to constant international criticism (Amnesty International 2004). It deprived justice sector institutions of resources that could be used for development purposes. The government relied on assistance from the international community for the greater part of the budget for the upkeep of its prisons. The government's dependence on foreign assistance for running the prison system made it vulnerable to external pressure (Pitsch 2003: p. 12). The government needed to take urgent measures to address the adverse social, political and economic problems that the prolonged detention of such a large number of genocide suspects had given rise to (Graybill 2004). Previous attempts by the government to reduce the prison population had been unsuccessful.

The inability of the criminal justice system to process the genocide caseload effectively had an adverse impact on the government's performance in terms of addressing the social and political challenges of post-war reconstruction, already discussed at the beginning of this chapter. Upon taking power in 1994, the RPF had given itself a mandate to govern for a transitional period of five years. In 1998, the end of that mandate was drawing to a close. The RPF was preoccupied with the problem of how to manage the transition from the governance arrangements that had been adopted in 1994. As part of the process of mapping out a strategy for exit from transitional governance arrangements, the RPF organized a series of consultations (which came to be known as the Urugwiro Reflection Meetings) to discuss the major challenges that the country still faced in the process of reconstruction after war and genocide and the strategies that were necessary for addressing those challenges.

The RPF has been the dominant political force in post-genocide Rwanda. The choices of accountability mechanisms that Rwanda has made have reflected the party's policy preferences, which in turn are shaped by its own political interests. During the years immediately after the genocide, the RPF primarily developed policy on the country's reconstruction programme, including policy on accountability for the genocide, through its internal organs. The RPF engaged its junior partners in government on the accountability question after the party had decided on the approach of its choice. By the late 1990s, the RPF had consolidated its control over the machinery of government. The organization still dictated policy on accountability (as well as policies on other national issues), but it formulated the policies through the agency of the formal organs of government that it still dominated. The Urugwiro Reflection consultations were again hosted by the then President, Pasteur Bizimungu, but now in his official capacity as President and not a member of the RPF. The meetings took place on most Saturdays during the latter part of 1998 and the early part of 1999. The items on the agenda of the meetings included a review of the challenges that the government had inherited upon taking office in 1994, an assessment of the progress that had been made in addressing those challenges, taking stock of the problems and challenges that the country still faced, and making recommendations on how those continuing problems and challenges should be addressed. Participants in the meetings included the entire cabinet, the leadership of the legislature, the judiciary, the armed forces, provincial governors, advisors to the President and the Prime Minister, representatives of the political parties, and other opinion leaders who were invited on the basis of individual merit.[8]

During the discussions of the Urugwiro Reflection Meetings, justice again emerged as one of the major areas of concern. The problems relating to justice were discussed over the course of 11 meetings, which took place between 1 August 1998 and 13 February 1999. I participated in the forum's discussions on the subject of justice in my capacity as Prosecutor General.[9] The meetings reviewed the performance of the justice sector, particularly the management of the genocide caseload. The majority of the participants in the meetings (with the exception of legal professions leading justice sector institutions) came to the overwhelming view that the performance of the justice system in general was unsatisfactory (Office of the President, Rwanda 1999: p. 47). The justice system was, the participants believed, characterised by slow procedures, lack of appropriate skills on the part of the personnel, and instances of corruption in the handling of litigation, including cases relating to the genocide (Office of the President, Rwanda 1999: para. 73).

The Urugwiro Reflection Meetings took note of the enormous burden that the genocide had placed on the country's system of justice administration (Office of the President, Rwanda 1999: para. 74). The forum came to the conclusion that the formal justice system was not an appropriate mechanism for dealing with the crimes that had been committed during the genocide (Office of the President, Rwanda 1999: para. 80). The participants stressed that slow progress of the formal justice system in processing genocide-related cases was a source of discontent across Rwandan society and a hindrance to national and individual reconciliation (Office of the President, Rwanda 1999: para. 79). There was strong public discontent over the detention of genocide suspects in the inhumane conditions of pre-trial detention without any prospect of trial in the foreseeable future (Office of the President, Rwanda 1999: para. 89; Sarkin 2001: pp. 148–50). Survivors of the genocide were unhappy that the justice system was unable to bring to justice the persons that they held responsible for their victimization. The impact of the justice system's failure to deal with the genocide caseload, the majority of the participants believed, could have far-reaching, undesirable consequences for the reconstruction, stabilization and development of the country. After much debate, the Urugwiro Reflection forum resolved that it was necessary to adopt an alternative approach to the process of accountability for genocide embodied in Organic Law 8/96 on genocide trials (Office of the President, Rwanda 1999: para. 80).

After long deliberations on what the alternative to criminal prosecutions could be, the President proposed the adoption of a modified version of a traditional justice process known as *Gacaca* as the mechanism by which most of the cases of genocide and related crimes should be adjudicated (Office of the President, Rwanda 1999: paras 81, 86). Some of the participants in the Urigwiro meetings, including me, found the proposal unappealing. Genocide survivors generally viewed the proposal unfavourably, considering it to be merely a step toward granting amnesty to persons accused of crimes associated with the genocide. Legal professionals had reservations about entrusting the adjudication of such serious cases to lay, and sometimes illiterate, citizens. Gacaca was premised on the assumption that individuals in communities would willingly and freely tell the truth about how the atrocities in their respective communities had been planned and carried out. On the basis of what I already knew about how strained relations between victims and members of their respective communities were, I personally had strong doubts that citizens would volunteer to tell the truth about the genocide at the expense of implicating relatives, friends and neighbours who had participated in committing atrocities.

However, Gacaca had at least one unquestioned advantage over the ordinary criminal justice system. Part of the appeal of Gacaca was that it would be more legitimate in the perception of the public. Many in the Hutu community felt that the Tutsi dominated the formal justice system. Participants in the Urugwiro Reflection Meetings were more diverse than the participants in the RPF consultations. Many more Hutu participated in the debate on the establishment of Gacaca than had taken part in the earlier RPF consultations. The idea of taking genocide cases to community courts that would naturally be dominated by Hutu citizens made Gacaca a very attractive proposition to the Hutu community, and to Hutu members of government in particular. The President's passionate advocacy for Gacaca and the strong representation of the Hutu community in the Urugwiro Reflection Meetings helped ensure the adoption of the proposal to create Gacaca courts.

The task of preparing detailed proposals on the establishment of Gacaca courts was entrusted to a commission that was established on 17 October 1998, of which I was part (Office of the President, Rwanda 1999: para. 89). The Commission's mandate was to make proposals on the modalities of implementing the proposal to establish Gacaca courts; to study the political and social consequences of implementing the proposal; to make recommendations in general as to how genocide trials could be expedited and properly conducted with the objective of eradicating impunity and promoting social harmony; to make proposals for amendments to the law which regulated the conduct of genocide trials at the time; to propose a new sentencing regime which reduced penalties and/or offered alternatives to imprisonment (particularly community service) with respect to genocide offences alleged to have been committed by the rank and file among perpetrators; to propose a draft message to be addressed to the population both to explain why it was necessary to transfer trials of genocide cases to Gacaca courts and to encourage the population to participate in the processs; and lastly, to prepare a budget proposal and timelines for the implementation of the decision to establish the proposed court system.

We submitted a draft report outlining proposals for a legal framework for the establishment of Gacaca tribunals (Office of the President, Rwanda 1999: paras 89–91). The Urugwiro forum discussed the Commission's proposals, to which it made substantial modifications. The forum also made recommendations on new laws as well as amendments to existing laws that would be necessary to pave the way for the establishment of Gacaca. The Urugwiro forum assigned specific tasks to various government agencies to ensure the successful implementation of the Gacaca project (Office of the President, Rwanda 1999: paras 92–107). The Ministry of Justice was given the task of following up the legislative process for the establishment of Gacaca. The Ministry of Local Government was tasked with responsibility for preparing the citizenry for the introduction of Gacaca. The Ministry of Justice made additional changes to the above-mentioned Commission's proposals and submitted a draft bill to the cabinet. The draft bill was introduced in the Transitional National Assembly subsequent to its adoption by cabinet. The law establishing the Gacaca tribunals came into force in January 2001.[10]

3.4 Objectives of Rwanda's Accountability Mechanisms

The objectives of the accountability processes discussed above that Rwanda has undertaken in response to the consequences of the war and genocide of the 1990s have been diverse. Some of the objectives are common to transitional justice in general, as outlined in Chapter 1. Others are specific to the Rwanda situation. Some of the objectives are common to all the accountability processes. Other objectives are unique to a specific mechanism.

The objectives that are common to all three of the accountability mechanisms that Rwanda has pursued include the following.

The most immediate objective of Rwanda's accountability processes has been simply to 'stabilize the country' (Scharf 1999: p. 630). The violence that Rwanda experienced during the 1990s left the country's economy, infrastructure and machinery for delivery of public services completely destroyed. The conflict also destabilized social equilibrium and left Rwandan society deeply traumatized and bitterly divided. The state was very fragile and relations between its people were marked by deep mistrust and resentment, if not outright hatred. The odds against the restoration of the country to a functioning, effective and stable state were very daunting. The difficult challenges of restoring order, delivering basic social services and leading the country's reconstruction and development faced by the government could not be addressed effectively unless the country was pacified, relations between citizens were improved and the trust of citizens in the state was restored to a certain degree. While we as policy makers recognized that the long-term solution to the challenges that the country faced was establishing democracy and the rule of law and promoting national unity and reconciliation, these could only be long-term ambitions. The government needed short- and medium-term strategies to facilitate the processes of recovery, reconstruction and development. As a government, we had to find answers to questions such as: How could we guarantee the safety and security of all citizens? What could we do to limit or eliminate the risk of revenge or reprisals for the genocide? What did we need to do to ensure peaceful coexistence between survivors of the genocide and the families and communities of the perpetrators? What could the government do to restore some trust between citizens on both sides of the conflict to get them to work together to rebuild the country and a shared future? What strategies could we adopt to attract urgently needed humanitarian and development assistance or to facilitate economic recovery?

During the various internal debates that the RPF had about the process of reconstruction in the aftermath of the genocide, the then President coined the term 'stabilization of the country' as an objective of the government. Looking back, I would describe what the President meant by that term as the creation of the minimum conditions necessary for all segments of Rwandan society to start collaborating effectively in rebuilding the country and sustaining the operation of its social, economic and political systems. The minimum conditions envisaged in the concept of 'stabilization of the country' included at least a guarantee of an end to violence, a commitment on the part of all parties to seek a peaceful path out of the conflict and the establishment of some trust between citizens and the government.

In the course of the above-mentioned debates on Rwanda's reconstruction strategies, all stakeholders agreed that justice was necessary for the country's stabilization. Justice for genocide would give confidence to the general population and to the Hutu community in particular, that they would be treated fairly under the new government and that there would no collective attribution of responsibility for the genocide. Justice for the genocide could convince victims not to seek revenge, and to let the law take its course. It was hoped that justice would, by facilitating establishment of the truth and acknowledgement of the suffering of the victims, help to rebuild relations between victims and perpetrators and their families and communities and to improve relations between the Hutu and Tutsi communities in general. By helping to improve relations between citizens on both sides of the ethnic divide, justice would make the country less likely to explode into sectarian violence again. Justice could help restore public confidence in the state's ability and its commitment to protect the rights of all citizens. These conditions, it was hoped, would help the people of Rwanda to begin collaborating in the process of repairing the damage that the genocide had caused to the country's infrastructure, human capital and social fabric. The policies on accountability that Rwanda adopted in the aftermath of the genocide were essentially aimed first and foremost at stabilizing the country.

'Stabilization' was one of the objectives of Gacaca. At the time of the 1998–99 Urugwiro Reflection Meetings at which the proposal to substitute the jurisdiction of ordinary courts in relation to the genocide with trials by Gacaca was discussed, Rwanda still remained fragile. While law and order had been restored across the country, relations between Rwanda's constituent communities were still characterized by mistrust at best. An insurgency led by the forces responsible for the genocide remained active in the DRC. The ordinary criminal justice system had failed to make a dent in the large and growing genocide caseload. The government could not afford to release the genocide suspects out of fear of the message that the releases would send (that it was condoning impunity and encouraging future violence) and it could not try them due to lack of capacity. The justice system's inability to try or release genocide suspects was deeply resented in the Hutu community. The problem of how to deal with the genocide cases had become a heavy political burden for the government. While the adoption of Gacaca had other long-term objectives, it also had the short-term goals of defusing the political and social crisis that the large genocide caseload posed and averting the ominous consequences that the continued detention of such a large number of members of the Hutu community in appalling conditions could have on the country's stability and the feasibility of its reconstruction programmes.

A very important objective of the processes of accountability that Rwanda has undertaken is to establish the truth about how the genocide was organized and carried out (Uvin 2003a; Wolters 2005a: p. 1; Kirby 2006: p. 100; Molenaar 2006: p. 26; Le Mon 2007; Meyerstein 2007: p. 472; Sosnov 2008: p. 25; Penal Reform International 2010b: p. 14). The organizers of the genocide portrayed the atrocities that were directed against the Tutsi community as legitimate self-defence against security threats posed by the

Tutsi (Des Forges 1999: pp. 278–83). The forces responsible for the planning and direction of the genocide continued to justify the genocide even after they were defeated and driven to exile (Berry and Berry 1999: pp. 87–122). Inside Rwanda, most of the people who had lived through the genocide (bystanders and perpetrators alike) equally feigned ignorance about atrocities that had taken place in their own communities. The majority of the tens of thousands of genocide suspects that the government was holding in detention all claimed to be innocent (Drumbl 1998). The reluctance of individuals and communities to acknowledge the truth about the genocide undermined efforts to promote reconciliation, peace and long-term stability.

The benefits that were expected from processes to establish the truth about the genocide included individualization of guilt (to prevent collective stigmatization of the Hutu community as a whole); acknowledging the wrong that had been done to the victims, recognising their suffering and honouring the memory of those victims who had perished; helping victims come to terms with the past and to build a future shared with the rest of Rwandan society; and mending relations between victims and perpetrators to facilitate reconciliation. It was hoped that the acknowledgment of victims' suffering would facilitate the mending of broken relations, the rebuilding of trust and the promotion of reconciliation between victims and perpetrators and their families and communities. By facilitating reconciliation, establishment of the truth would contribute to promoting peace and long-term stability. The truth, it was hoped, would also serve to deter future atrocities. Exposure of the nature and consequences of the atrocities would educate the population on the need to avoid similar atrocities in the future. Establishing the truth about how the genocide was organized and carried out was necessary in order to create an uncontested historical record of the circumstances of the genocide, so that revisionists would not in the future seek to alter the history of the events. Establishing the truth about the genocide would pre-empt possible (or more likely, inevitable) attempts by revisionists to rewrite the history of the genocide and to deny that the genocide ever occurred, and to facilitate the formulation of policies to prevent the recurrence of genocide or other similar violence. The Rwanda government wanted the truth about the genocide established in order to consolidate its credibility and to undermine the legitimacy of the forces responsible for the genocide, which continued their attempts to return to power through the use of force. By detailing the role of the various perpetrators (especially the leaders) in the atrocities, truth-telling mechanisms would serve to delegitimize perpetrators as players in national politics. The public exposure and stigmatization of the perpetrators was particularly necessary to ward off pressure (by some Western governments) to negotiate a political settlement with the perpetrators of the genocide and to share power with them (Prunier 1995: pp. 312–55).

Another important objective of the accountability processes that Rwanda has undertaken is to ensure accountability for the crimes that were committed during the genocide (Wolters 2005a; Le Mon 2007: p. 16). Victims of human rights abuses have a right to a remedy, which includes the investigation, prosecution and punishment of the crimes that have been committed (United Nations 2006).[11] Victims of the Rwanda genocide articulated this demand intensely and incessantly. In seeking ways to bring the perpetrators of the genocide to justice, the post-genocide government was responding, in part, to this demand.

The accountability processes Rwanda has implemented have also aimed to promote national unity and reconciliation (Penal Reform International 2010b: p. 14). The genocide left Rwandan society polarized along ethnic lines. The prevailing social polarization stood in the way of national reconstruction and sustainable peace. The broad spectrum of the political groups that were represented in the first post-genocide government generally agreed that national recovery and durable peace and stability would not be possible without reconciliation at individual, community and national level and that accountability for the genocide was a prerequisite for such reconciliation to take hold. Justice for both the victims and persons accused of genocide and related crimes, it was hoped, would help repair relations between individuals, between them and their communities and between communities. Some scholars have claimed (quite erroneously) that unity and reconciliation were never part of the discourse on justice during the period immediately after the genocide (Sarkin 2001: p. 154). These are far-fetched misconceptions. From the very beginning, promoting reconciliation was always one of the principal objectives of Rwanda's accountability programme (Bradley 2004; Wolters 2005b: p. 2; Kirby 2006: p. 100). I know from personal experience of participation in internal Rwanda policy debates of the time that reconciliation was always at the top of our priorities. Whether the policies we pursued were appropriate for reaching that goal is a different matter. The goal of healing individual and social wounds, promoting reconciliation and rebuilding community was also behind the decision to set up the Gacaca system (Bradley 2004; Longman 2006a; Clark 2007).

The transitional justice processes Rwanda has carried out have also aimed at eradicating impunity, promoting a culture of respect for human rights and preventing future atrocities, especially against the minority (Vandegiste 2001a: p. 261; Ironside 2002; Uvin 2003a; Wolters 2005a: p. 1; Kirby 2006: p. 261; Longman 2006a; Oomen 2006; Sosnov 2008; Penal Reform International 2010b: p. 14; Takeuchi 2011). The Tutsi community and opponents of the successive Rwanda regimes were victims of gross human rights abuses from 1959 (Lemarchand 1970; Ngoga 2009: pp. 321–4). The governments of the day and their officials (and during times of political tensions, even private citizens) had an unfettered licence to kill and commit other gross human rights violations against the Tutsi and opponents of the regime. These abuses were portrayed as acts of patriotism. Only a very small proportion of these crimes were ever investigated and prosecuted (Riddell 2005).[12] The majority of the crimes were never followed up by judicial or law enforcement agencies (Ngoga 2009: pp. 321–4). The narrative of the Rwanda conflict espoused by the post-genocide government and the Tutsi community always stresses the very decisive role that impunity is believed to have played in making the 1994 genocide possible (Office of the President, Rwanda 1995; Strain and Keyes 2003: p. 87). The goal of eradication of impunity and the aspiration to establish a culture of respect for fundamental human rights (especially of the rights to life and the integrity of the person) to ensure that gross human rights violations would never happen again in Rwanda were key objectives of Gacaca (Vandegiste 2001a: p. 261; Ironside 2002; Uvin 2003a; Wolters 2005a: p. 1; Kirby 2006: p. 261; Longman 2006a; Sosnov 2008).

Advancing the rule of law was not always expressly articulated as one of the goals of Rwanda's transitional justice agenda, but was nevertheless always a key objective of the country's accountability processes. Post-independence Rwanda had a history of gross human rights abuses against the Tutsi and opponents of the government dating back to 1959 (Lemarchand 1970: pp. 197–227; Des Forges 1999: p. 40; Mamdani 2001: pp. 129–31). Rwanda was one of the first countries in post-independence Africa to become a one-party state. Government was generally very repressive throughout this period and practised institutionalized discrimination (on a regional as well as ethnic basis) against certain sections of the population (Des Forges 1999: p. 400). The executive dominated other branches of government, including the judiciary (Bouvier *et al.* 1992). The judiciary was politicized and subservient to the executive branch of government, was not independent or impartial and was not effective in safeguarding the rights of citizens (Fierens 2005; Ngoga 2009). The security services, the military establishment and the members of the ruling elite were above the law. While the genocide was partly a result of entrenched impunity, that impunity was a manifestation of the absence of the rule of law. The absence of the rule of law is one of the root causes of the Rwanda conflict. The genocide served to make a very strong case for political reforms to promote human rights, democracy and the rule of law if Rwanda was to have any prospect of durable peace, stability and sustainable development (Office of the President, Rwanda 1995). The ultimate goal of the transitional justice processes that Rwanda has undertaken has always been envisaged to build a peaceful and stable society of citizens who no longer live in perpetual fear of violence and other human rights abuses. The processes of accountability for atrocity that Rwanda has undertaken were considered to be an integral part of the government's strategies for promoting peace and stability anchored in the rule of law. The government hoped that these processes would help promote the rule of law by stressing basic principles and values of the rule of law such as the supremacy of the law, individual personal responsibility for human rights violations, equality of all citizens, non-discrimination and accountability of public officials and institutions for human rights violations (Gahima 2002).

3.4.1 Objectives specific to Gacaca

As indicated in section 2 of this chapter, there were over 130,000 genocide suspects in custody in Rwanda by the late 1990s. The criminal justice system could not cope with the genocide caseload. It was estimated that the investigation and prosecution of the existing genocide caseload alone could take decades to conclude (Vandegiste 2001a; Fierens 2005; Schabas 2005a). Yet, it was widely believed that the genocide suspects who were in custody were only a fraction of the citizens who had participated in committing atrocities. The slow pace of the genocide trials was a source of legal as well as political problems for the government. Indefinite pre-trial detention of tens of thousands of suspects in harsh conditions violated many aspects of the right to fair trial, created tensions between Tutsi and Hutu inside and outside government and generated hostility towards the government among members of the Hutu community. The government could not afford to be indifferent to the negative public perceptions of the justice system's handling of investigations and prosecutions of genocide. It needed to devise a system of accountability for genocide that was both credible in the perception of the majority of the population and able to deal with genocide cases fairly and effectively. Gacaca was adopted as the principal mechanism for accounting for genocide because it addressed both of these considerations (Ironside 2002; Uvin 2003a; Mibenge 2004: p. 412; Tiemessen 2004; Molenaar 2005: p. 46; Kirby 2006; Meyerstein 2007: p. 472; Penal Reform International 2010b: p. 14). In addition, Gacaca aimed to reduce the number of genocide suspects in detention (Clark 2010; Takeuchi 2011).

Gacaca has also aimed at facilitating the return and re-integration of persons accused of genocide into their respective communities (Penal Reform International 2010b: p. 14). The large-scale participation of citizens in committing atrocities meant that, potentially, large numbers of perpetrators from virtually every village in Rwanda were liable to serve very long terms of imprisonment. The prolonged imprisonment of such very large numbers of perpetrators from one ethnic community was neither politically expedient nor sustainable. It would undermine efforts to improve relations between survivors and the rest of their communities. It would continue to alienate much of the Hutu population from the government. By undermining the processes of building social cohesion and promoting reconciliation, the imprisonment of a large number of members of the Hutu community would ultimately prove detrimental to the country's long-term stability. At the same time, however, the release of persons responsible for genocide back into their respective communities without any form of accounting was bound to offend survivors and equally to undermine prospects for reconciliation. Rwanda had to find a way to deal with perpetrators of genocide in a manner that ensured accountability and facilitated the smooth reintegration of perpetrators into their communities, while at the same time maintaining or promoting social cohesion. Gacaca aimed to facilitate such reintegration of persons responsible for genocide by giving the power to judge genocide cases to the very communities from which the perpetrators came and to which they would return after completing their sentences (Tiemessen 2004: p. 61).

Some of the factors that influenced the adoption of Gacaca as the principal mechanism of accountability for the genocide have not been officially acknowledged. For example, one of the objectives of Gacaca was to help

Rwandan society reach a form of 'closure' on the issue of the genocide. Five years after the genocide, the issue of accountability for the genocide still divided Rwandan society and its management remained a major preoccupation of the government and Rwandan society at large. The country needed, at some point in the foreseeable future, to reach closure with regard to the genocide to be able to focus more on pressing development challenges. The country could not, however, reach closure until a process of reckoning with the legacy of the genocide was over. The intense preoccupation of Rwandan society with genocide litigation was a hindrance to the stabilization of the country and to processes of national reconstruction and development (Office of the President, Rwanda 1999). One of the key objectives for the establishment of Gacaca was to help hasten the country's progress towards closure with regard to accountability for the genocide. By expediting the accountability process, Gacaca would enable Rwandan society to begin the slow but necessary process of putting the tragedy of genocide behind it and to devote more attention and resources to the challenges of social, economic and political development. This fundamental objective of Gacaca has not been prominently highlighted or openly acknowledged (to avoid causing offence to survivors), but it was nevertheless a factor that critically influenced the establishment of Gacaca courts.

Literature on Gacaca to date has not recognized how establishment of the institution was also strongly driven by the political calculations of the ruling party, the RPF. In 1994, the RPF gave itself a mandate to govern the country for five years pending the holding of elections. By 1998, the party had come to the conclusion that it was not ready to organize elections and that it could not be certain of winning if elections were to be held. The government had spent the period since the genocide addressing many critical challenges, including the pacification of the country, the repatriation of internally displaced persons and refugees, the restoration of social services, the re-launching of economic activities and fighting off the Congo-based insurgency. Rwanda was still deeply divided along ethnic lines and fragile socially and politically. The government had not developed a legal framework for regulating political activities beyond the transition. Not only was the RPF not ready to organize elections, it was apprehensive that their chances of winning if elections were to be held immediately were compromised. The RPF was intent on staying in power, as its leadership believed (and still believes) that its role in stopping the genocide has earned it the moral right to lead Rwanda. One of the issues that was certain to put the RPF at a severe political disadvantage if elections were to be held was justice for genocide. The Hutu community, who constitute the majority of the population, had bitter grievances over the government's handling of the cases of the more than 130,000 members of the Hutu community who were in prison at the time. One of the compelling motivations behind the decision of the RPF to adopt Gacaca as the principal mechanism of accountability for the genocide was to make progress in addressing the grievances of the Hutu community in relation to justice for genocide well before the RPF had to submit itself to the electorate.

3.5 Conclusion

The development of policies and processes on accountability for atrocity that Rwanda has pursued have been influenced by many factors, including the nature of the violence that Rwanda experienced during the 1990s, the degree of popular participation in that violence, the manner in which the armed conflict of the period ended, the political governance arrangements that post-genocide Rwanda adopted and, above all, the challenges that the post-genocide government faced in the process of leading the recovery, reconstruction and development of the country in the aftermath of the war and genocide. The post-genocide government considered accountability for the genocide to be a prerequisite for national recovery, reconstruction and development and for sustainable peace. The transitional justice processes with which the country attempted to address the legacy of the violence of the 1990s were an integral part of the new government's reconstruction agenda. The next three chapters discuss the three mechanisms of accountability for atrocity (international criminal justice, domestic prosecutions and Gacaca) with which Rwanda has endeavoured to reckon with the genocide's legacy. A fourth chapter will discuss the trials of crimes relating to the Rwanda genocide that have been undertaken by other states on the basis of the principle of universal jurisdiction. The four chapters will explore the legal frameworks for the trials that have been carried out under each process, the challenges that these trials have faced, and the extent to which they have met the objectives that they were intended to achieve, if at all.

4 Accountability, Justice and the Role of the International Criminal Tribunal for Rwanda

4.1 Introduction

In November 1994, the United Nations Security Council set up the International Criminal Tribunal for Rwanda (ICTR) to bring to justice the persons responsible for the atrocities that had been committed during the Rwanda genocide (United Nations 1994m). The establishment of the ICTR followed the establishment a year before of a similar tribunal, the International Criminal Tribunal for the Former Yugoslavia (ICTY) in response to atrocities that were committed in the course of the wars that were precipitated by the break-up of the Federal Republic of Yugoslavia (United Nations 1993b). The two ad hoc United Nations tribunals were a bold attempt at giving effect to the principles of international human rights law and international humanitarian law. The ICTR's early years were tumultuous and the tribunal attracted widespread criticism about its performance. The tribunal survived the challenges and setbacks of those early years to continue its work, and is set to close its operations in 2014 (United Nations 2010).

The legacy of the tribunal's shortcomings in those formative years has haunted the institution to its final days. The imminent closure of the tribunal makes its legacy a subject of vigorous debate in Rwandan society and strong scholarly interest, and it raises a number of issues. To what extent has the ICTR fulfilled its mandate? Which of its objectives has the tribunal achieved and which remain elusive? What factors influenced its development and performance, and are responsible for its successes and failures? What impact has the tribunal had on the development of international criminal law and transitional justice? What is the legacy of the tribunal in Rwanda? What lessons does the tribunal's work have for the field of international criminal justice and transitional justice in general?

This chapter seeks to address these and other related issues. Building on the theoretical framework of transitional justice outlined in Chapter 1, the chapter discusses the legal basis of the duty of states under international law to prosecute violations of international human rights law and international humanitarian law. It examines the factors that led to the establishment of the tribunal in particular, the debates that the government of Rwanda had with the international community about the tribunal's organization and functioning and the objectives that the framers of the tribunal's statute aspired to accomplish. The chapter next reviews the performance of the tribunal through the years, exploring the factors that had an impact on its capacity to perform its mandate, and the strategies that it adopted to address the various challenges that initially threatened to lead it to failure. The tribunal was primarily established to serve the people of Rwanda. This chapter explores the complicated relationship between the tribunal and its various stakeholders in Rwandan society. It then discusses the tribunal's completion strategy, examines the extent to which the tribunal has succeeded, if at all, in delivering on its mandate, and deliberates on the legacy of the institution and its implications for international criminal justice and transitional justice in general.

4.2 The Duty of States under International Law to Prosecute Violations of Human Rights

The role of criminal prosecutions in transitional justice is briefly discussed in Chapter 1. States have the primary responsibility to ensure compliance with international human rights law and international humanitarian law within their respective territories. As such, states have obligations to ensure accountability for violations of human rights. Accountability for violations of human rights law and international humanitarian law is broader than the investigation, prosecution and punishment of perpetrators. In addition to criminal sanctions, perpetrators of human rights violations may also be held accountable through other measures such as disciplinary administrative sanctions and reparation. Nevertheless, prosecution is considered to be the primary means of holding perpetrators of serious violations of human rights and humanitarian law accountable. This is the view that has been expressed by the Human Rights Committee.[1] States have an obligation to investigate, prosecute and punish perpetrators of gross human rights violations and to combat impunity. A large number of treaties specifically obligate state parties to investigate, prosecute and bring to justice the perpetrators of specific offences.[2] The duty to prosecute and punish perpetrators of human rights violations can also be found in a large number of declaratory instruments.[3] The European Court of Human Rights has held that the obligation to investigate, prosecute and punish abuses of human rights law flows from the substantive guarantees of the European Convention on Human Rights (such as the prohibitions of torture, and cruel, inhuman and degrading treatment, the protection of the right to life or private life), but that it is part of the right to a remedy, guaranteed in Article 13 of the Convention.[4] Other alternative measures are complementary to, and not a substitute for, prosecution and punishment in cases involving very grave violations of human rights law and international humanitarian law.

The duty of states to provide a remedy for violations of human rights law and international humanitarian law is not synonymous with an individual victim's right to have a perpetrator prosecuted. The duty to prosecute or otherwise hold a perpetrator accountable is related to the general obligation of a state to prevent future violations, rather than the individual's right to a remedy. Prosecution is not a compulsory remedy for violations of human rights law and international humanitarian law. The duty to hold perpetrators accountable and to ensure remedies for victims may be satisfied by mechanisms other than prosecution (United Nations Human Rights Committee 1992: para. 20). States may discharge their obligation under international law to prosecute persons responsible for violations of human rights law and international humanitarian law through selective trials or exemplary trials and need not necessarily prosecute each and every person suspected of crimes committed before or during the transition (Vandegiste 2009: p. 470). However, international law, human rights law and humanitarian law obligate states to prosecute and punish persons responsible for certain gross human rights violations. It is an established principle of international law that crimes against humanity impose an obligation on states to prosecute and punish perpetrators.[5] States also have a mandatory obligation to prosecute and punish the crime of genocide.[6] States are obliged to prosecute or extradite persons responsible for crimes against peace, war crimes and crimes against humanity (ILC 1950: Article 6). Other gross violations of human rights that entail the duty of states to prosecute and punish include slavery, trafficking in human beings,[7] child pornography,[8] or violent acts of racial discrimination,[9] extra-judicial executions, torture and ill-treatment, and enforced disappearances. Amnesties that foreclose prosecution of those responsible for genocide, crimes against humanity, war crimes or gross violations of human rights are inconsistent with states' obligations under international law (Orentlicher 2005: principle 24). 'United Nations-endorsed peace agreements may never promise amnesties for genocide, war crimes, crimes against humanity or gross violations of human rights' (United Nations 2004).

4.3 Establishment and Objectives of the ICTR

4.3.1 Background to the establishment of the ICTR

As the genocide raged in Rwanda in 1994, the major world powers, particularly the United States, downplayed the severity and genocidal character of the atrocities (Melvern 2000a; Power 2001). However, the pretence that the atrocities that were then going on in Rwanda were just another of the usual tribal conflicts so common in Africa had become untenable by the middle of May 1994. Following a May mission to Rwanda, the United Nations High Commissioner for Human Rights issued a report that confirmed that atrocities on a horrendous scale had been committed and were continuing in Rwanda (UNOHCHR 1994).[10] The Security Council, in the preamble of its resolution of 17 May 1994 on the situation in Rwanda, requested the Secretary General 'to present a report as soon as possible on the investigation of serious violations of international humanitarian law committed during the conflict' (United Nations 1994d). On 8 June 1994, Security Council resolution S/RES/925 finally used the word 'genocide', noting that 'reports indicating that acts of genocide have occurred in Rwanda' and stating that 'genocide constitutes a crime punishable under international law'. A special session of the United Nations Commission on Human Rights on the situation in Rwanda that was convened in Geneva on 24 and 25 May 1994 recognised that breaches of international humanitarian law and human rights law had been and were still being committed in Rwanda, and decided to appoint a Special Rapporteur on the situation in Rwanda without delay (UNCHR 1994b). The Special Rapporteur's reports confirmed that grave, massive and systematic violations had taken place in Rwanda; that the media had incited these violations; that the violations had largely targeted the Tutsi population; that the atrocities may constitute genocide; and that the vast majority of the violations were the responsibility of the government and militia groups allied with it (Magnarella 2000: p. 37). The reports recommended the establishment of an international ad hoc tribunal or the enlargement of the jurisdiction of the Yugoslav Tribunal to bring those responsible for the Rwanda genocide to justice (UNCHR 1994e).

Once the scale and nature of the atrocities that had been committed became publicly acknowledged, the establishment of some mechanism to bring its perpetrators to justice became inevitable. The Security Council had established the ICTY a year earlier to address atrocities that were committed during the conflicts in the Former Yugoslavia. In setting up the ICTY, the Security Council had set a precedent that had to be followed for Rwanda as well, given the gravity of the situation in that country. Most observers suggest that it is most unlikely that the Security Council would have set up the ICTR had a precedent not been set by its earlier decision to establish the ICTY (Mutua 2000).

Much is often made of the fact that the ICTR was set up at the request of the government of Rwanda. A more accurate way to explain the situation would be to say that Rwanda acquiesced with the determination of the international community to establish the tribunal. Nothing better illustrates the real driving force and motives behind the push for the establishment of the Rwanda tribunal than the manner in which Rwanda's purported request to the Security Council to establish the tribunal was made. At end of June 1994, the United States Secretary of State, Warren Christopher, had indicated his government's support for an international war crimes tribunal for Rwanda (Greenhouse 1994). In early August, the US Assistant Secretary of State for Human Rights, John Shattuck, visited Kigali to convince the government to support the proposal to establish an international criminal tribunal to deal with the aftermath of the genocide (Lewis 1994; Rawson 2001).[11] Ambassador Shattuck's meetings led to what has often been described as Rwanda's 28 September 1994 formal request to the United Nations to establish a tribunal (United Nations 1994i). David Rawson, the United States Ambassador to

Rwanda prior to, during and immediately after the genocide, has written that the actual request was drafted at the US embassy in Kigali, taken to the Rwandan Minister of Justice to sign, and swiftly brought to the United States by John Shattuck (Rawson 2001).

The government of Rwanda admittedly had its own interests in having a tribunal to bring perpetrators of the genocide to justice established. President Bizimungu reiterated Rwanda's support for the establishment of the proposed court in his October 1994 address to the United Nations General Assembly, declaring that 'it is absolutely urgent that this international tribunal be established' (United Nations 1994j: p. 14). The fact remains, however, that the tribunal was established partly, if not mainly, to serve the interests of its international community.

The Security Council set in motion the process that led to the establishment of the Rwanda tribunal on 1 July 1994, when it passed Resolution S/RES/935(1994) requesting the Secretary General to establish a commission of experts to review the evidence of grave violations of international law committed in Rwanda, including possible acts of genocide. The commission of experts would be similar in structure and mandate to the Commission whose work paved the way for the establishment of the ICTY (United Nations 1994g: Article 1). The preamble of the Resolution expressed its 'grave concern at the continuing reports indicating that systematic, widespread and flagrant violations of international humanitarian law, including acts of genocide, have been committed in Rwanda', and recalled that 'all persons who commit or authorise the commission of serious violations of international humanitarian law are individually responsible for those violations and should be brought to justice' (United Nations 1994g: paras 7 and 8). The Secretary General appointed the Commission on 26 July 1994. On 1 October 1994, the Commission of Experts issued an interim report, which concluded that massive violations of international humanitarian law (including the Convention on the Prevention and Punishment of the Crime of Genocide) resulting in massive loss of life had been committed as part of a systematic plan to exterminate the Tutsi population (United Nations 1994j). The report recommended that the persons responsible for the crimes should be brought to justice by an independent tribunal (United Nations 1994j: para. 150) through the expansion of the jurisdiction of the Yugoslav tribunal to cover the Rwanda situation (United Nations 1994j: para. 149).

4.3.2 Rwanda and contentious negotiations on the establishment of the ICTR

Consultations on a draft statute to establish a tribunal to deal with the Rwanda situation began even before the Commission of Experts issued its interim report. A major issue of contention during these consultations was whether the Rwanda situation should be referred to the ICTY or a separate tribunal should be established to deal exclusively with the Rwanda situation.

The Commission of Experts had apparently initially preferred the second option, but reportedly recommended the first under pressure from the US government (Schabas 2006: p. 29). Concern then arose that a decision to deal with the Rwanda situation through the expansion of the jurisdiction of the ICTY might create a perception that the Rwanda genocide was not being given due recognition. A draft resolution, co-sponsored by the United States and New Zealand, proposing the establishment of an independent court with its own trial chambers, but sharing an Appeals Chamber and a Prosecutor with the Yugoslav tribunal, was eventually adopted as the baseline for negotiations. This draft of the statute of the proposed tribunal became the subject of controversial debate between the government of Rwanda and representatives of the governments that were taking a lead in preparations to establish a court to try and punish crimes that had been committed in the course of the genocide.

As the initial informal consultations gave way to formal negotiations, differences of opinion arose between the government of Rwanda and the principal promoters of the proposal to establish a tribunal to deal with the Rwanda situation (Akhavan 1996: pp. 505–8; Mutua 1997: p. 178; Kamatali 2003).

The government and the promoters of the proposed tribunal disagreed on its temporal jurisdiction. The proposed tribunal's promoters wanted its jurisdiction to be limited in time. The draft statute proposed to limit the temporal jurisdiction of the tribunal to the period from 1 January to 31 December 1994. The government preferred the jurisdiction of the proposed tribunal to cover a longer span of time, ideally from October 1990 (Goldstone 2000: p. 11). The rationale for the government's position was that the tribunal's jurisdiction should include the serious and widespread violations of human rights that had been committed by and under the previous government from the beginning of the war in 1990 to the end of the genocide (United Nations 1994j: Statement of the Permanent Representative of Rwanda; Schabas 2006: p. 11). The government was also concerned that limitation of the temporal jurisdiction to the calendar year of 1994 might exclude crimes that may have been committed as part of the preparations for the genocide prior to 1994 (United Nations 1994j: Statement of the Permanent Representative of Rwanda; Magnarella 2000: p. 42).

The Rwanda government and the representatives of the states that were pushing for the fast establishment of the tribunal were also divided on its structure. The Commission of Experts had recommended the extension of the mandate of the Yugoslav tribunal to deal with the Rwanda genocide (United Nations 1994j: para. 149; Schabas 2006: p. 29). The government took strong exception to the proposal to deal with the Rwanda genocide by extending the mandate of the ICTY. It considered the proposal to deal with the Rwanda situation by extending the jurisdiction of the Yugoslav tribunal as an unacceptable failure to recognize the gravity and significance of the Rwanda genocide. The government of Rwanda instead advocated the establishment of a completely separate tribunal, with its own Prosecutor and Appeals Chamber, as a better option both because this alternative arrangement (in its view) recognized the significance of the genocide and would lead to a more effective tribunal (United Nations 1994j: Statement of the Permanent Representative of Rwanda). Negotiations led to a compromise to establish a separate tribunal for Rwanda. However, the draft still provided that the Rwanda and Yugoslav tribunals would have a common Prosecutor and that the Appeals Chamber of the ICTY tribunal would also serve as the Appeals Chamber for the Rwanda tribunal. Rwanda opposed the arrangement of having a common Prosecutor and Appeals Chamber for both tribunals to the very end (United Nations 1994j: Statement of the Permanent Representative of Rwanda).

The parties also had differences on the crimes that the jurisdiction of the proposed tribunal would cover. The draft statute included genocide, war crimes and crimes against humanity in the subject matter jurisdiction of the proposed court. The government of Rwanda was of the opinion that its jurisdiction ought to be limited exclusively to genocide (United Nations 1994j: Statement of the Permanent Representative of Rwanda). In taking this stand, the government was primarily motivated by concerns that the proposed court should not be bogged down in investigating anything other than the most serious offences (United Nations 1994j: Statement of the Permanent Representative of Rwanda). The majority of the members of the Security Council, on the other hand, remained of the opinion that the jurisdiction of the court should include war crimes and crimes against humanity, not least because there was a need to address crimes alleged to have been committed by the RPA as well as some Tutsi civilians.

The government and sponsors of the draft resolution on the establishment of the proposed tribunal could not reach a consensus on its location. The government was of the view that trials of genocide suspects on Rwandan territory, even when conducted by an international court, were preferable to trials by a court based in a foreign country to which the Rwandan public would not have access. The government's view, in particular, was that the trial of the leadership that had planned and directed the genocide would have a far greater impact on fighting impunity, promoting respect for human rights and promoting peace in Rwanda than trials held in a foreign country (United Nations 1994j: Statement of the Permanent Representative of Rwanda, p. 16). The government therefore strongly argued that the proposed court should be based in Kigali, its capital (Goldstone 2000: pp. 111–12; Magnarella 2000: p. 42). The sponsors of the draft resolution and other like-minded states were of the firm view that it was necessary to base the court outside Rwanda in order to safeguard its independence as a judicial institution (Møse 2005).

The draft statute provided that the penalty imposed by the tribunal would be limited to imprisonment and that in determining the terms of imprisonment the trial chamber would have recourse to the general practice regarding prison sentences in the courts of Rwanda. In effect, the statute by implication excluded capital punishment as a possible sentence for persons who would be tried by the tribunal. Rwanda still had the death penalty on its statute books in 1994. The government was of the strong view that the leadership responsible for the genocide should bear the full brunt of the law, including the death penalty, as an expression of Rwandan society's revulsion and repudiation of the atrocities for which these leaders were responsible. Since the proposed international court was possibly the only venue where this leadership would ever be brought to justice, the government argued that the court should have the capacity to impose capital punishment. The exclusion of the option of capital punishment from the penalties that the statute of the tribunal could impose for offences within its jurisdiction would lead to the absurd situation where persons who bore the greatest responsibility for the genocide would be treated more leniently than some of the followers they had incited and led in committing atrocities, who were going to be tried in domestic courts and would be liable to capital punishment (United Nations 1994j: Statement of the Permanent Representative of Rwanda, p. 16).

The Rwanda government not only wanted the court to be based in Rwanda; it also wanted the state of Rwanda to play a role in the functioning of the court. The draft statute provided that the organs of the tribunal would be the Chambers (comprising two Trial Chambers and an Appeals Chamber, with judges to be appointed by the United Nations General Assembly from a list submitted by the Security Council[12]), the Prosecutor (appointed by the Security Council upon nomination by the Secretary General[13]) and the Registry (headed by the Registrar, to be appointed by the Secretary General after consultation with the President of the Tribunal).[14] The Registry and Office of the Prosecutor would have such additional staff as would be necessary for their work, and all such staff would be appointed by the Secretary General on the recommendations of the Registrar and the Prosecutor respectively. The government of Rwanda fought for a right to participate in the process of selection and appointment of the tribunal's officials in order, it argued, to ensure that states that had supported the regime responsible for the genocide would not gain control of the tribunal's organs and be in positions to protect their allies who were responsible for genocide (United Nations 1994j: Statement of the Permanent Representative of Rwanda, p. 16). The government also wanted to have Rwandans participate in all organs of the tribunal (United Nations 1994j: Statement of the Permanent Representative of Rwanda, p. 16). The sponsors of the draft resolution and other members of the Council, on the other hand, wanted to keep Rwanda's influence on the tribunal to a minimum in order to preserve the institution's integrity and independence (Schabas 2006: p. 11). They were determined not to allow the government to have any control over the functioning of the proposed tribunal.

Lastly, the government and the promoters of the proposed tribunal disagreed on the powers of other states in relation to the commutation of sentences of persons convicted by the tribunal. The draft also had a provision that permitted states (in which persons sentenced to imprisonment by the tribunal would be imprisoned) to offer pardons or commutation of sentence to such prisoners, in accordance with their laws, subject to notification to the tribunal and approval by the President of the Tribunal, acting in consultation with the judges, on the basis of the interests of justice and general principles of law.[15] The government of Rwanda was concerned that this provision was open to abuse (United Nations 1994j: Statement of the Permanent Representative of Rwanda, p. 15). The government was particularly concerned that some foreign governments that it considered to be sympathetic to the former regime could use the statute's provision relating to commutation of sentences to reduce the prison sentences imposed by the tribunal on former allies serving time in their countries (United Nations 1994j: Speech of the Permanent Representative of Rwanda, p. 15; Schabas 2006: p. 11).

The government of Rwanda's stance during the negotiations over the draft of the statute of the tribunal was influenced by several factors, including mistrust of the international community (attributable to the failure of the international community to prevent, stop or mitigate the genocide); genuine concern that the tribunal might end up being manipulated or controlled by hostile governments sympathetic to the forces responsible for the genocide; a desire on the part of the new government to assert national ownership over the international aspect of mechanisms for accountability for the genocide; and determination on the part of the new government to assert sovereignty in dealings with the international community during the country's reconstruction process. The government's stand on the proposed state was also influenced by considerations relating to the necessity to protect its military from exposure to prosecutions by the proposed court.

However, the government's negotiating capacity was also constrained by lack of expertise, particularly expertise on the international human rights system and transitional justice issues. The officials who were in charge of the negotiations on the draft statute on behalf of the government were new to government and had no expertise on international human rights, international humanitarian law and international criminal law. The government did not have the opportunity to seek outside expert help either, due to the speed with which the promoters of the proposed tribunal were rushing to set it up. Had the government had ample time to consider the issues and the opportunity to seek expert assistance, it may well have taken a more balanced approach to some of the issues over which it maintained a hard-line stand to the very end. The negotiations between the government and the sponsors of the resolution to establish the tribunal ended in deadlock. The Security Council eventually decided to go ahead and set up the tribunal, in spite of Rwanda's continuing objections (United Nations 1994k).

Some of the demands that the government of Rwanda made during the negotiations over the content of the draft statute were entirely legitimate or at least defensible. The Rwanda government's proposals for a separate prosecutor and a large number of judges have been vindicated. The international community has tacitly acknowledged the shortcomings of the original structure of the tribunal by instituting certain changes to the tribunal's organizational structure, including the creation of additional trial chambers, the appointment of ad hoc judges and the appointment of separate prosecutors for the Rwanda and the Yugoslav tribunals (United Nations 2003a, 2003b). These changes have brought the organization of the tribunal in line with the arrangements that the government of Rwanda advocated during negotiations over the establishment of the tribunal.

Rwanda's attempt to assert a degree of national ownership over the tribunal was understandable. Absence of ownership by the societies that United Nations ad hoc international criminal tribunals have been established to help remains one of the biggest weaknesses of such tribunals. Rwanda's desire for a role in the functioning of the tribunal, including the participation of Rwandan legal professionals in all aspects of the tribunal's work, has been vindicated by the international community's embrace of hybrid courts systems for the situations in East Timor, Kosovo, Sierra Leone and Cambodia. The concerns about national ownership of transitional justice processes and accountability of international criminal tribunals to the societies which such tribunals are established to help, which the government of Rwanda first raised in 1994 during the negotiations over the establishment of the tribunal, were far-sighted. These issues went on to become major themes in the debate on the role and relevance of international criminal justice in post-conflict countries during the next decade (Schabas 2006: p. 11).

With the benefit of hindsight, it is also now evident that some of the concerns that the government expressed seem to have been unwarranted; some of its demands were out of the bounds of reason. The government would have been better advised not to take the hard-line stand that it took on the issue of the death penalty. It was not reasonable to expect the international community to reach some compromise that would have allowed the Rwanda tribunal to administer the death penalty. Given Rwanda's intense social polarization, it was only right that the government's demands for a role for the government in the selection and appointment of officials to the tribunal, including judges, were rejected. The Rwanda tribunal has been accused by its critics of providing one-sided justice. The tribunal's integrity would have been subjected to even stronger criticism had its statute permitted the government to play a role in the tribunal's affairs. The location of the court outside Rwanda was equally a far-sighted decision. The tribunal and the Rwanda government have often had a tense relationship; the location of the tribunal outside of Rwanda served to protect the tribunal's integrity and independence to some degree.

4.4 Objectives of the ICTR

The ICTR is a creation of the Security Council, a political institution whose decisions are primarily influenced by political considerations. In making decisions on matters before them, the Council's members are understandably motivated first and foremost by their own national interests. At the same time, the members of the Council, and its permanent members in particular, share certain interests and values with many other states that are not members of the body. Members of the Council consult with, and take into account, policies and representations of other (and especially like-minded) states in dealing with issues with which the Council is seized. The decisions of Council members are also influenced by non-political bodies, including civil society. As a result, decisions of the Council are often compromises reflecting accommodation of the varied interests of a wide range of stakeholders. Like other decisions of the Security Council, the decision to establish the ICTR was a result of broad agreement between groups of stakeholders sharing some common interests but also having their own interests to take into account. The stakeholders in the process of establishing the tribunal included the members of the Council, other states, regional groupings of states, the government of Rwanda and civil society, especially human rights organizations that had campaigned for the establishment of a court to ensure justice for the victims of the genocide.

The motives behind the decisions of the Council are not always clear-cut. The declared or apparent objectives of the Council's decisions are not necessarily the only or even the principal rationales for the body's decisions. The objectives of the international community in setting up the Rwanda tribunal can be categorized into two groups, namely primary objectives and secondary objectives. The overriding objective of at least some of the major promoters of the project to establish the Rwanda tribunal (particularly the US and indeed the other major world powers) was to deflect blame for having failed to prevent, stop or mitigate the genocide. The major powers of the Western world ceaselessly preach about their societies' commitment to universal human rights, democracy and the rule of law. The Rwanda genocide had, thanks to the ease of communications in the modern era, taken place before the very eyes of policy makers in these countries. The leaders of these democracies deliberately chose to do nothing to stop or mitigate the extent of the genocide. Some in fact worked to obstruct efforts to help the victims (Melvern 2000a, 2000b: pp. 9–11). The deliberate decisions of leaders of the major world powers to do nothing to protect or otherwise help the victims of the genocide, not only represented a failure of institutions, they also represented moral failings on the part of the institutions' leaders.[16] Many commentators argue that the rush to set up a criminal court to try perpetrators of the genocide was motivated, perhaps more than anything else, by a desire to erase the memory of these moral failings, to assuage the guilt of Western leaders for not having intervened to stop or mitigate the genocide (Ironside 2002; Kamatali 2003: p. 119). The United Nations ad hoc tribunals 'were established more as acts of political contrition, because of the egregious failures to swiftly confront the situations in the former Yugoslavia and Rwanda, than as part of a deliberate policy, promoting international justice' (Zacklin 2004: pp. 541–5; Moghalu 2005: p. 49).

Another factor, which heavily influenced the decision to establish the Rwanda tribunal, was the need to avoid the appearance of racism and discrimination. Having decided to set up a tribunal to deal with the situation in the Former Yugoslavia, the international community had little choice but to support the establishment of an international criminal tribunal to deal with the Rwanda situation as well (Zacklin 2004: pp. 541–5; Moghalu 2005: p. 49). A decision not to set up a tribunal to deal with the Rwanda situation would have been perceived as racist. Most observers agree that it is highly unlikely that enough support would have been mobilized to establish the Rwanda tribunal had the establishment of the Yugoslav tribunal not set a precedent (Akhavan 1996: p. 501).

There were, without doubt, many in the international community who genuinely believed in the necessity of, and advocated for, the establishment of the proposed court in the hope that such a tribunal could aid Rwanda's recovery and transition to a normal, peaceful and stable society. The secondary objectives for the establishment of the ICTR included the following (Akhavan 1996: pp. 504–5; Carroll 2000).

4.4.1 Holding perpetrators accountable

The core mission of the Rwanda tribunal was to try and punish persons responsible for genocide and other serious violations of international humanitarian law (Scharf 1999: p. 628).[17] Rwanda had just experienced a genocide involving massive loss of life. Many of the perpetrators had fled to other countries. There was a consensus, in and outside Rwanda, that the perpetrators should be brought to justice but Rwanda was unlikely to ever get custody over these fugitives. The genocide had left Rwanda very deeply divided along ethnic lines. Most observers had serious concerns as to whether it would be possible to have genocide trials that were perceived as fair to all parties, particularly for those most responsible for the genocide, in Rwanda's domestic courts (Scharf 1999: p. 628). An independent and impartial international tribunal was considered necessary to ensure that justice was not only done, but also seen to be done in the trials of persons accused of responsibility for the genocide. The ICTR was established to provide a venue where persons responsible for the genocide could be brought to justice by an independent and impartial court (United Nations 1994j: Statements of the Permanent Representatives of France, p. 3, New Zealand, p. 5, the United Kingdom, p. 6, Spain, p. 12, Oman, p. 16). At the meeting of the Security Council at which the resolution establishing the tribunal was adopted, the Permanent Representative of the Russian Federation expressed the opinion that accountability was the principal objective of the tribunal with the statement: 'those responsible must receive the punishment they deserve – and this is the major, but not the sole task of the international tribunal to be created' (United Nations 1994j: p. 2). The Representative of Nigeria expressed the same sentiment with the words: 'The issue at stake is the need to punish collectively criminal acts against humanity' (United Nations 1994j: p. 3). The Permanent Representative of Brazil put it another way, saying that the urgent need to bring to justice those responsible for the series of heinous massacres was the overriding purpose of the international tribunal (United Nations 1994j: p. 10).

4.4.2 Fighting impunity and promoting respect for human rights in Rwanda and other countries

A related objective for the establishment of the Rwanda tribunal was to fight impunity for human rights abuses, not only in Rwanda but globally as well (United Nations 1994j: Statement of the Permanent Representatives of Argentina, p. 8 and Oman, p. 16). The tribunal was being established partly to promote compliance with international law, especially the law of armed conflict, and to eradicate or reduce impunity for gross human rights abuses (United Nations 1994j: Statement of the Permanent Representatives of the Russian Federation and Czech Republic, p. 2 and p. 7). The tribunal's establishment was part of an ongoing process to develop international mechanisms for promoting respect for human rights and promoting peace through combating impunity for gross human rights abuses (Carroll 2000: p. 173). Several of the representatives of members of the Security Council who took part in the meeting to consider the adoption of the resolution establishing the tribunal drew attention to the implications of the decisions to set up the two adhoc United Nations tribunals for the international human rights protection regime. The French, Russian and Spanish representatives on the Council expressed the hope that the Rwanda tribunal would provide lessons for the establishment of a future permanent international criminal court (United Nations 1994j: pp. 2–4). This rationale for the establishment of the tribunal has often been reiterated by members of the Security Council during the course of meetings to consider the annual reports and reports on the completion strategies of the two tribunals (United Nations 2000: Statement of the Permanent Representative of Canada, p. 113).

4.4.3 Deterrence of future human rights violations

At the end of the genocide, the forces responsible for the genocide relocated to Zaire[18] and began preparations to return to power in Rwanda by force of arms (Austin 1994; United Nations 1994j: Statements of the Representatives of the Czech Republic, p. 7 and Spain, p. 13; Human Rights Watch 1995). There were also reports of continuing human rights abuses inside Rwanda (Amnesty International 1994, 1995c). The tribunal was established not only to punish the persons responsible for the genocide, but also to act as a deterrent against the continuation or resumption of human rights abuses within

Rwanda and the neighbouring countries in which Rwandans had sought refuge (United Nations 1994j: p. 170). The 'deterrence' aspect of the tribunal's mandate is alluded to by references in the preamble to Resolution 955 to the Security Council being 'determined to put an end to such crimes' (United Nations 1994m, para. 6) and 'ensuring that such violations are halted and effectively redressed' (United Nations 1994m, para. 8).

4.4.4 *Facilitating the return of Rwandan refugees*

Another objective of the tribunal's establishment appears to have been to facilitate the return of the millions of Rwandan refugees who had fled the country at the end of the genocide (United Nations 1994j: Statements of the Representatives of the Russian Federation, p. 2, New Zealand, p. 5; Scharf 1999: p. 628). The numbers of Rwandan refugees living in neighbouring countries was around 3 million at the time (Prunier 1995: p. 205). The refugee crisis was a political, economic and environmental disaster for Zaire and a serious security threat for Rwanda. This refugee crisis could not be resolved unless the stranglehold that the leadership of those most responsible for the genocide had over the refugee camps and their residents was broken. Many in the international community believed that the establishment of the tribunal would break the control of these leaders and their political and military organizations within the refugee camps, if not by apprehending and bringing the leaders to justice, by at least driving them underground as fugitives from justice (Akhavan 1996: p. 505). It was also hoped that the tribunal would contribute to the resolution of the Rwanda refugee crisis by encouraging refugees to return home, guaranteeing fair and impartial justice (United Nations 1994j: p. 2).

4.4.5 *Restoration and maintenance of peace*

Yet another objective of the tribunal was to contribute to the restoration and maintenance of peace in Rwanda and the Great Lakes region of Central Africa as a whole (United Nations 1994j: Statements of the Representatives of the Russian Federation, p. 2, Argentina, p. 8, Pakistan, p. 10, Spain, p. 12 and Oman, p. 16; United Nations 1994m; Scharf 1999: p. 629). A recurring theme in the speeches that were made on the occasion of the adoption of the resolution establishing the Rwanda tribunal was that its establishment was an exercise of the inherent power of the Security Council to ensure international peace and security. The establishment of the tribunal would, it was hoped, contribute to the restoration and maintenance of peace by reducing or destroying the capacity of the forces responsible for the genocide to wage war against the state of Rwanda or to destabilize neighbouring countries. The indictment, apprehension, trial and punishment of persons who bore the greatest responsibility for the genocide would deprive them of their constituencies, access to resources and freedom to organize and wage war.

4.4.6 Promoting reconciliation in Rwanda

The tribunal was also expected to contribute to national reconciliation in Rwanda (United Nations 1994j: Statements of the Representatives of the Russian Federation, p. 2, Argentina, p. 8; Pakistan, p. 10, Spain, p. 12, Nigeria, p. 13 and the United States, p. 18; United Nations 1994m; Kamatali 2003; Møse 2005; Morrison *et al.* 2008). The genocide affected every community in Rwanda. At least three-quarters of the Tutsi community perished during the events. Most of the survivors of the genocide lost generations of family and friends. The genocide had attracted widespread citizen participation and, as a result, ruptured relationships between the Tutsi and Hutu in every community across the country. Rwanda was deeply divided along ethnic lines at the end of the genocide. Many, if not most, of the Tutsi survivors were of the view that the Hutu population as a whole bore some responsibility, in varying degrees, for the genocide. Many in the Hutu community, on the other hand, were still in denial, often not only disavowing any personal role in the conduct of the genocide, but even refusing to acknowledge that any atrocities had taken place in their communities at all. Many in the Hutu community were more concerned with the suffering of members of their own community at the hands of the victors.

The high level of mistrust between the country's two major communities was detrimental to the country's prospects for peace and long-term stability. Rwanda's transition to a peaceful and stable state would depend on the ability of its people to overcome a history of mistrust, hatred and gross human rights violations, and to work together to build a shared future. It was generally agreed there could be no durable peace or stability in Rwanda until the communities whose relations had been ruptured by the war and genocide were reconciled. Reconciliation was, on the other hand, not possible until the legacy of the war and genocide was addressed. Many in the international community shared the view that justice (through the proposed court as well as through national courts) for the genocide had an important role to play in facilitating the process of national reconciliation. The tribunal would contribute to the process of reconciliation by facilitating acknowledgement of the suffering of all the victims, holding perpetrators of genocide and other human rights abuses accountable, and promoting a culture of respect for fundamental human rights.

4.4.7 Supporting the rebuilding of Rwanda's justice system

There also appears to have been an expectation that the tribunal would contribute to the process of rebuilding Rwanda's judicial system. The preamble to the Security Council Resolution establishing the tribunal refers to the need for 'international cooperation to strengthen the courts and judicial system of Rwanda, having regard, in particular, to the necessity for those courts to deal with large numbers of suspects' (United Nations 1994m).

4.5 A Review of the Performance of the Tribunal through the Years

Building a consensus for the establishment of the tribunal was the easy part of the process of ensuring that those responsible for the genocide were brought to justice. Developing the tribunal into an effective, credible institution able to carry out its mandate and to achieve its objectives was a more difficult task. The tribunal had to be set up from the ground. Its development was a slow process. The Security Council designated Arusha, Tanzania as the seat of the tribunal on 22 February 1995 (United Nations 1994m). The first judges of the tribunal were only elected in May 1995. The judges held their first plenary session in The Hague in June 1995, because the tribunal's own premises in Arusha were not yet ready (ICTR 1996a: para. 20). At this session, the judges adopted the tribunal's Rules of Procedure and Evidence (ICTR 1996a). The Agreement between the United Nations and the host country, Tanzania, concerning the tribunal's headquarters was signed on 31 August 1995. The first Registrar of the Tribunal was not appointed until September 1995. The tribunal only moved into its premises in Arusha a year after its establishment, in November 1995. The tribunal's first indictment, concerning eight individuals suspected of crimes alleged to have been committed in Kibuye prefecture, in Western Rwanda, was confirmed on 28 November 1995 (ICTR 1996a: paras 31, 44).[19] The first suspect was transferred to the seat of the tribunal in May 1996.[20] The first accused persons to appear before the tribunal made their initial appearance in accordance with the procedure laid down in rule 62 of the Rules of Procedure and Evidence on 30 and 31 May (Pillay *et al.* 1998). The tribunal's first trial commenced in January 1997 (ICTR 1997).

The tribunal had a very slow start. Its slow progress during those formative years caused near universal disappointment. The tribunal soon drew intense criticism from both within Rwanda and the wider international community. Critics of the tribunal included not only the government and other stakeholders in Rwanda (Peter 1997), but also human rights organizations, academics and representatives of states that financed the tribunal's operations (Amnesty International 1998; International Crisis Group 2001a, 2002a; Zacklin 2004). The issues over which the tribunal was often criticized during its early years include the following.

The tribunal got off to a very slow start in identifying, and seeking the apprehension and transfer of persons suspected of crimes within its jurisdiction. During the first several years of its existence, the tribunal often issued only opportunistic indictments, seeking custody of suspects who had been located and apprehended on the initiatives of third parties, including the Rwanda government. The tribunal's slow progress in identifying and pursuing suspects, especially those who bore very great responsibility for the genocide, caused frustration not only on the part of victims but also on the part of many in the international community, including some governments upon whom the tribunal depended for political, financial and other assistance. Perceptions that the tribunal was not effective in identifying and pursuing significant numbers of suspected perpetrators of genocide during its early years adversely affected perceptions about the tribunal within and outside Rwanda (Bonner 1994).

Even when the tribunal was able to secure custody of suspects, it could not organize trials of the cases of suspects who were already in its custody within a reasonable time. Suspects often spent very long periods in pre-trial detention.[21] When the tribunal was able to put on trials, the trials were extraordinarily long, partly as a result of the complexity of cases, the volumes of documents subject to disclosure, the large number of witnesses, the necessity for interpretation of testimony from Kinyarwanda into French and English (the tribunal did not at the time have facilities for simultaneous interpretation), ongoing investigations by the Office of the Prosecutor and defence, and non-availability of witnesses and defence counsel, most of whom lived outside Africa. Delays of trials also arose from frequent changes in prosecution strategy, frivolous defence motions, successive amendments of indictments initiated by the Prosecutor, large numbers of interlocutory motions and appeals, delays in translation of documents and repeated adjournments of cases. Many defence counsels were often not available when needed for trials. The staff of the Office of the Prosecutor were often unprepared to proceed with trials. Lack of judicial control of proceedings also contributed to the inefficiency of the tribunal in its early years (United Nations 1999b: paras 35–82; ICTR 2001: paras 40–5; United Nations 2001b: Statement of ICTR President, pp. 7–8; ICTR 2002: para. 17; Moghalu 2002: pp. 32–4; ICTR 2003b, 2004b). During its early years, the tribunal's chambers completed very few trials each year.[22] The tribunal's failure to deliver tangible results in the form of trials completed within a reasonable time had an adverse impact on perceptions of the institution (United Nations 2000: Statements of the Permanent Representative of the Russian Federation and the Representative of Jamaica).

The tribunal also attracted criticism concerning alleged violations of fair trial rights of accused persons, including failure to bring suspects before judges for their initial appearance within the prescribed time; delays in obtaining indictments of suspects already in custody; unreasonable delays in hearing defence motions; detention of suspects in unauthorized detention centres; making illegal arrests and failure to provide suspects with access to counsel (Amnesty International 1998). In a number of cases, prosecutors failed to apply for indictments within the deadlines set by the Rules of Procedure and Evidence (Amnesty International 1998: pp. 24–7). The tribunal also generally failed to comply with the requirements of the right of accused persons to trial without undue delay. Suspects spent many years waiting for the opportunity to have their cases heard. Trials that did begin proceeded at a very slow speed, and most defendants spent many years in pre-trial detention. The Appeals Chamber was so frustrated by some of the irregularities in the arrest and detention of suspects that in one case it granted the motion of an important defendant for the squashing of the indictment against him and permanently stayed all proceedings in the case.[23] The government of Rwanda reacted to the decision of the Appeals Chamber by announcing an intention to suspend cooperation with the tribunal, a move that would have seriously hurt the tribunal's ability to operate. The crisis was only averted because a differently constituted Appeals Chamber reversed the earlier decision.[24]

Some defence counsel abused the tribunal's legal aid scheme. Some defence personnel ingeniously prolonged proceedings for financial gain by filing an immense number of motions, many of which were frivolous. Some of the defence counsel did not have adequate professional skills (United Nations 1999b). Others solicited and/or accepted requests for fee-splitting arrangements with clients. Other members of defence teams gave valuable gifts and other forms of indirect support and maintenance to their clients and their clients' relatives. Some defence teams also hired friends or relatives of their clients as defence investigators (United Nations 2001a, 2002). A significant number of the investigators hired by defence teams were themselves suspected of being responsible for atrocities (REDRESS/African Rights 2008a). The tribunal failed to exercise appropriate oversight of the legal aid system and to prevent these unethical malpractices (United Nations 2001a, 2002). The above abuses of the legal aid scheme by some members of defence teams led to some embarrassing situations, including instances where the tribunal had to indict persons who were being paid through its funds.[25]

The Rwanda tribunal was also strongly criticized, particularly by the government of Rwanda, for unsatisfactory treatment of victims of the genocide. During the tribunal's early years, its management, and the registry in particular, took the court's obligation of impartiality to extremes. The tribunal initially tried to distance itself from victims in the belief that this was necessary in order to protect the tribunal's independence and impartiality. The tribunal failed to reach out to victims, to understand their views and concerns in relation to its work, to explain its work to them and to provide them with the opportunity to meaningfully participate in its work. Victims only participated in the court's work as witnesses for the prosecution. The Office of the Prosecutor did not adequately brief witnesses for the prosecution on how the adversarial system of trials works. Consequently, many witnesses were unprepared for the aggressive cross-examination to which they were subjected by defence counsel, and the experience of testifying at the tribunal was traumatic for some of them. It was also often claimed that the tribunal failed to make adequate measures for the protection of prosecution witnesses.

Lastly, the tribunal was also criticized for inefficient use of the financial resources that the international community provided to finance its operations. The tribunal's judicial outputs were meagre relative to the substantial resources at its disposal. At the height of their operations, the combined budgets of the two United Nations tribunals represented 15 per cent of the entire budget of the United Nations. The high cost of the two tribunals and their perceived failure to provide value for money was one of the factors that undermined support for the two institutions, particularly among donors (Drumbl 2002a: p. 8). This lack of support in time led to demands by the major donors for completion strategies to ensure that there would be a cut-off date for the mandate of the two tribunals. Issues relating to the efficiency of the tribunal were also a constant source of friction between the Rwanda government and the tribunal. The government of Rwanda saw the tribunal as a competitor for resources and was of the view that the resources that the international community provided to finance the tribunal's operations could have been put to better use through investment in enhancing the capacity of national rule of law institutions, such as the courts, prosecutions service, prisons and police.

The above shortcomings of the tribunal can be attributed to a number of factors. The most critical of these factors was probably the lack of an appropriate prosecution strategy (United Nations 1997). The tribunal's early years were marked by a haphazard approach to investigations and prosecutions. In view of large-scale citizen participation in committing atrocities, the tribunal should have focused on suspects who bore the greatest responsibility. Unfortunately, the Office of the Prosecutor did not, as it should have, decide in advance the profile of the suspects that it would pursue. Its initial approach was simply to divide its investigators into separate teams and to assign these teams to investigate genocide in general, in certain parts of the country, without identifying the suspects whose activities the investigations would focus upon (Scharf 1999: p. 634). The investigation teams set their own strategies and did not for the most part benefit from supervision by their superiors or the guidance of the Prosecutor (Scharf 1999: p. 634). In addition to investigations based on a geographical approach, the tribunal also usually sought arrest and indictment of whatever suspects were arrested by states, regardless of their role or status in the institutions that were responsible for the planning or execution of the genocide (Waldorf 2004). The critical role that the lack of an appropriate prosecution strategy played in hampering the tribunal's capacity to fulfil its mandate was stressed by the Office of Internal Oversight Services in its 1997 Audit and Investigation Report on the tribunal (United Nations 1997).[26]

The other major factor, which hampered the tribunal's performance in its early years was the mismanagement of its affairs, particularly by the Registry (Mutua 1997: p. 178). The Registry frustrated the efforts of other organs of the tribunal by failing to hire the required personnel, and delaying or failing to provide necessary support such as transport and office equipment. The extent of the problem of mismanagement within the tribunal was later exposed by reports of the Office of Internal Oversight Services. The reports indicated that the tribunal's management suffered from poor financial and administrative management, favouritism, irresponsive bureaucracy and lack of coordination, lack of effective planning and lack of flexibility (Vandegiste 1997; Carroll 2000: p. 182; Moghalu 2005: p. 232). The Office of Internal Oversight Services' 1997 report concluded that not a single administrative area of the tribunal functioned effectively (United Nations 1997: para. 9).

Mismanagement within the tribunal was not, however, limited to the Registry; it extended to the Chambers and Office of the Prosecutor as well. Judges were in recess for very long periods and were often absent from Arusha due to poor planning, often leaving the tribunal's courtrooms unused while the number of suspects waiting in pre-trial detention increased year after year (International Crisis Group 2001a: pp. 10–13; United Nations 2001b: Statement of ICTR President, p. 6).

Most of the tribunal's shortcomings in the early years of its mandate were ultimately a result of internal weaknesses, especially lack of effective leadership. Weak management affected all the constituent organs of the court. As a result of poor management, staff lacked basic resources and facilities, including vehicles, communications facilities, and office equipment and supplies to enable it to function well (ICTR 1997: para. 48, 1998: paras 4–6). The management of the tribunal, and the Registry in particular, failed to provide the resources that the organs of the tribunal needed in order to perform their functions properly (United Nations 2001a, 2002). The organs of the tribunal responsible for staff recruitment often failed to hire vital staff for which the tribunal had funding (ICTR 1998: paras 4–5; United Nations 1999c). Many critical posts for which the General Assembly appropriated funding went unfilled for a long time (Human Rights First 1997: p. 17; ICTR 1998: para. 15). The personnel whom the tribunal hired did not always have the qualifications that their jobs required (ICTR 2001: paras 94–7; International Crisis Group 2001a: pp. 11–12, 2002a). Trial attorneys without trial experience were recruited to undertake and supervise investigations and prosecutions (United Nations 1997: para. 52). The tribunal hired investigators with little or no experience in criminal investigations (United Nations 1997: para. 53). A significant proportion of the tribunal's personnel were short-term staff seconded by their governments, the use of which undermined continuity and institutional effectiveness (Vandegiste 1997: p. 36). Lack of sound management systems frustrated many of the competent people within the institution and many of them left the tribunal (United Nations 1997: para. 38).

Most critics of the tribunal have often attributed its early failings to the Registry and the Office of the Prosecutor. Not many observers have focused on the contribution that the Chambers made to the problems that the tribunal experienced. The Chambers, especially the Presidency, failed to coordinate the different organs of the tribunal. The Chambers failed to exert adequate control over the proceedings (International Crisis Group 2001a). In the early years, the court was more often than not in recess and went for long periods without hearing any cases. The Chambers frequently ordered or granted adjournments of cases for what many considered inordinately long periods. The long duration of trials increased the cost of trials and caused frustration to both the victims and suspects.

The inherent difficulties of establishing an international criminal tribunal from the ground up were further compounded by other internal problems, in addition to weak management. In particular, the friction that existed between the Registry, on the one hand, and the Chambers and the Office of the Prosecutor on the other (in connection with issues such as the hiring of staff and procurement of equipment), often hampered effective functioning of the institution as a whole (ICTR 1997: para. 57; United Nations 1999b: para. 21; International Crisis Group 2001a: p. 12). The Statute of the Tribunal states that the Registry shall be responsible for the administration and servicing of the tribunal.[27] The Rules of Procedure and Evidence provide that the President shall supervise the activities of the Registry and that the Registrar shall consult with the President before recommending the hiring of staff, and that the Registrar, under the authority of the President, shall be responsible for the administration and servicing of the tribunal (Rules 19 and 33). In practice, the Registry has for much of the tribunal's existence operated as an autonomous entity free from supervision of, and accountability to, the other organs of the tribunal. Meanwhile, other organs of the tribunal (the Chambers and the Office of the Prosecutor) remained of the view that the Registry was exceeding its authority and that it was an obstacle to their ability to perform their respective functions (United Nations 1997: paras 49–52, 60–3). The different organsof the tribunal often failed to adequately coordinate their activities (United Nations 1999b: Statement of the Permanent Representative of Argentina, p. 5), impacting the effective functioning of the organization as a whole.

However, the tribunal's performance was also affected by factors over which its organs had no control, including the location of the tribunal, the tribunal's organizational structure, lack of cooperation from some states (including Rwanda, on occasions), weak support from the United Nations secretariat and problems in locating suspects. The location of the tribunal in Arusha, Tanzania contributed to the slow start and unsatisfactory performance of the tribunal during the early years after its establishment. Arusha lacked adequate infrastructure and communication facilities (Møse 2005: p. 2). Many observers have been of the view that the relatively remote location of the tribunal made it difficult to attract and to keep qualified personnel (United Nations 2000: Statement of the Prosecutor, p. 21). The tribunal's isolation hampered its ability to attract top-level judges, prosecution staff and defence counsel (Schabas 2006: p. 11). The structure of the tribunal involved the dispersion of key components of the organization's machinery to three different countries separated by long distances, which was not conducive to its efficient operation. The organizational structure placed impossible demands on the Prosecutor, whose contribution to the work of the tribunal in the early part of its work was critical to the institution's success. The Prosecutor could not provide the Office of the Prosecutor with the leadership, guidance and supervision that was required for the effective functioning of such a new and complex institution.

International tribunals depend on state cooperation to function, particularly as regards vital matters such as gathering evidence and arrest of suspects (United Nations 1999b: para. 25). Whereas many states from the very beginning willingly cooperated with the tribunal in apprehending suspects on their territories, some states were less cooperative and their reluctance to provide assistance to the tribunal impeded its work in the early years (Barria and Roper 2005: p. 360; Human Rights First 1997: p. 12). Even states willing to cooperate with the tribunal sometimes took inordinately long periods to enact legislation to provide a legal framework for such cooperation. The Belgian Parliament did not pass a law on cooperation with the tribunal until 22 March 1996. France adopted a law for the same purpose on 22 May 1996, but did not issue the ministerial directive on implementation of the law until 30 August 1996. The cooperation of states which were initially unwilling to provide assistance to the tribunal (states such as Kenya, the Democratic Republic of Congo and Cameroon) was often secured only after the application of diplomatic pressure, principally by the United States government. With a few exceptions, even those countries that were initially reluctant or unwilling to help the tribunal generally cooperated with it in subsequent years. However, a few countries, including Kenya (United Nations 2008b, Statement of ICTR Prosecutor, pp. 9–11) and the Democratic Republic of Congo (International Crisis Group 2001a: pp. 14–15; (United Nations 2004b, 2008b: Statement of ICTR Prosecutor, pp. 9–11) continue to fail to apprehend and surrender some suspects on their territories.

The functioning of the tribunal was also adversely affected by the absence of the disciplining influence of an authority exercising oversight over it. In the usual national setting, such authority would be provided by the sovereign government of the state. The executive may not interfere with the judicial functions of courts, but it is entitled to demand accountable management from the judiciary. In the case of the UN tribunals, oversight responsibilities in theory devolved to the UN Security Council, General Assembly and Secretariat. However, none of these organs appears to have provided effective oversight for the tribunal. The United Nations Secretariat, acting in the belief (mistaken in the view of some, including the Office of Internal Oversight Services) that it was necessary to avoid involvement in the tribunal's management problems in order to safeguard the tribunal's independence, generally maintained a hands-off approach to the operations of the UN tribunals (United Nations 1997: paras 64–9). The evidence suggests that, once a few key administrators were selected, the UN Secretariat failed to take responsibility for providing essential support to the tribunal.

The Office of Internal Oversight Services has, in its reports, identified lack of adequate support from the UN Secretariat as one of the causes of the deficiencies and failures that permeated key facets of the tribunal's administrative operations during the 1990s (Scharf 1999: p. 634). The result of the hands-off approach of the Secretariat, Security Council and General Assembly to the management of the tribunal's administrative functions was that the tribunal was not accountable to any outside institution in any meaningful sense. Lack of effective oversight and supervision affected the performance of the tribunal. The Office of Internal Oversight Services recommended that the UN Secretariat should take greater responsibility for assisting the Secretary General in the implementation of Security Council resolution 955 (1994) by, in particular, making practical arrangements for the tribunal's effective functioning (United Nations 1997: para. 73).

The tribunal's performance was also affected by understandable difficulties in locating fugitives. Virtually all persons who took a significant role in planning, organizing and leading the genocide left Rwanda in 1994. Most of these leaders initially sought refuge in the Democratic Republic of Congo (formerly Zaire) and subsequently relocated to countries around the world. Over the years, many of these suspects have kept low profiles. Some have even changed their identities. Tracking these suspects has not been an easy task for the tribunal.

4.5.1 Reforming the ICTR

The problems that the tribunal faced, and the criticism that was directed towards it, during its initial years have had a lasting impact on the institution's development. The 1997 Office of Internal Oversight Services' report on the functioning of the tribunal was a wake-up call for the United Nations. The United Nations responded to the report by carrying out some far-reaching management personnel changes. The Registrar, Deputy Prosecutor and several other senior officials of the tribunal were replaced. These personnel changes were meant to send an unmistakable signal that the Secretariat and the Security Council expected the tribunal to improve its performance. Following that shake up, and due to continuing pressure from within and outside the United Nations, the tribunal began implementing reforms to improve both its performance and public perceptions of the institution (Carroll 2000: pp. 194–5). The management sought to improve performance, first and foremost, by improving coordination ofthe activities of the various organs. Coordination between the organs was enhanced through a number of mechanisms, including the establishment of the Coordination Council (ICTR 1996b: Rule 23ter). Comprising the President, Prosecutor and Registrar, the Coordination Council was established to harmonize planning of the activities of the tribunal's three principal organs (Rule 23bis). The tribunal streamlined the planning and conduct of trials through the New Trials Committee, comprising representatives of Chambers, various sections of the Registry, and the Prosecution, which aimed to improve the trial readiness of new cases (United Nations 2001b: Statement of ICTR President; United Nations 2003c: p. 9). The tribunal also tried to improve its performance by introducing wide-ranging reforms of its procedures. The Rules of Procedure and Evidence of the Court were amended time and time again (as indicated below) to facilitate more efficient conduct of the court's proceedings (Møse 2005: pp. 10–11; ICTR 1998, 2000a: p. 15, 2001: para. 36, 2002: para. 17; United Nations 2001b: Statement of ICTR President, pp. 7–8).

a) Institution of pre-trial and pre-defence status conferences, through which the Chambers could order parties to disclose information (including evidence and other information such as lists of witnesses that the parties intend to call, with a summary of the facts and the specific allegations in the indictment on which the witnesses will testify), identify contested matters, and order parties to file briefs addressing factual or legal issues (Rule 73bis).
b) Introduction of new rules to enable the tribunal to make rulings on motions expeditiously by requiring motions to be in writing, and allowing decisions on motions to be decided orally or in writing (Rule 73).
c) Allowing motions to be decided by a single judge (Rule 54bis).
d) Introducing deadlines for the filing of some categories of motions and a general time limit for responding to motions (Rules 72 and 73).
e) Introducing a provision which allowed the Chambers to impose sanctions against counsel who brought motions that, in the opinion of the court, were frivolous or an abuse of the process of the court (Rule 73).
f) Ensuring greater control of proceedings by judges through control of the number of witnesses a party is allowed to call; reducing the length of examination in chief of both parties and reducing cross-examination time.
g) Introduction of the rule allowing a Chamber to continue cases in the event of the sickness or absence of one of the judges, to allow judges who are no longer on the court to complete partly heard cases in which they had participated, and to allow new judges to join panels of partly heard cases when some former members of the panels are unable to proceed with the cases that they had started hearing (Rule 15bis).
h) Imposing a requirement that each accused person have two counsel and insisting that one counsel continues to act in the case in the event of the other being absent (Rule 44).
i) Introducing regulations which allowed as evidence written depositions by expert witnesses, without the need for the appearance of such experts in person before the tribunal, subject to the other side's acceptance of the testimony.
j) Establishing a procedure to facilitate plea agreements where an accused expressed a willingness to plead guilty (United Nations 2001b: Statement of ICTR President, pp. 7–8; United Nations 2003c).
k) Introducing measures to improve translation services.

l) Introduction of simultaneous interpretation of cases (though the Annual Reports suggest that simultaneous interpretation was not introduced in practice until 2004).

Rationalization of the tribunal's procedures was also key to reform. The Chambers tried to improve the conduct of trials by streamlining the tribunal's operations and rationalizing the use of its resources. The Chambers increased the number of trials by increasing the number of days spent on hearings, conducting trials on a 'twin-track' basis (hearing two cases in consecutive slots) and using a 'shift system' (using one courtroom for two cases, with one case being heard during the morning and early part of the afternoon and the second case being heard during the afternoon and early evening). The Security Council has also sought to improve the tribunal's performance by reforming the organizational structure of the tribunal. A long-standing criticism of the tribunal (dating back to the time when the court was established) was the institution of a common Prosecutor for both the Rwanda and Yugoslav tribunals. Some critics of the arrangement (including the government of Rwanda) always cited the arrangement as one of the causes of the tribunal's unsatisfactory performance (United Nations 1994j: Statements of the Permanent Representatives of Rwanda: p. 15). In 2003, the Security Council finally acknowledged the validity of these concerns by amending the statute of the tribunal to include a provision for the appointment of a prosecutor dedicated exclusively to the Rwanda tribunal (United Nations 1997). The Security Council also amended the statute of the tribunal to create a third chamber and to permit the appointment of *ad litem* judges, increasing the number of *ad litem* judges who could serve at any one particular time and permitting *ad litem* judges to handle pre-trial matters (United Nations 2003e).[28]

4.6 Relations between ICTR and Rwandan constituencies

Although the core mission of the tribunal was to bring persons responsible for the genocide and other grave human rights abuses to justice, the objectives for its establishment also included the achievement of certain socio-political goals, including eradication of impunity, deterring further human rights abuses, restoring and maintaining peace, promoting the rule of law and facilitating national reconciliation. The success of the tribunal in promoting these socio-political objectives depended, to a large extent, on the perceptions of Rwandan stakeholders about the tribunal's effectiveness in addressing issues of concern to the respective groups. Perceptions about the tribunal had an important bearing on its effectiveness in carrying out its mandate, on its ability to achieve the objectives for which it was established and on its legacy (Carroll 2000: pp. 184–5).

The relationship between Rwanda and the tribunal has been the subject of a great deal of commentary (Straus 2007). Unfortunately, most of the writing on the subject only focuses on the interaction between the tribunal and the government and rarely addresses the issue of the perceptions and attitudes of other segments of Rwandan society towards the tribunal. While the relationship between the tribunal and government is obviously very important, narrowing the inquiry about the tribunal's relationship with Rwandan society to its interaction with the government misses the point that Rwandan society is not monolithic. The government's views and policies towards the tribunal do not necessarily represent all shades of opinion and varieties of interests among all Rwandan stakeholders. On the contrary, Rwandan society is deeply divided on many political issues, and few subjects divide Rwandan society as strongly as justice for the violence experienced during the 1990s. The work of the tribunal is a process on which many segments of Rwandan society with diverging interests have different perspectives. The following sub-sections describe the relationship of the tribunal with various stakeholders in Rwandan society.

4.6.1 The Rwandan government

Most commentators have generally portrayed the state of relations between the government of Rwanda and the tribunal as having been consistently poor throughout the period of the tribunal's existence (Peskin 2005; Reyntjens 2011; Waldorf 2011a). The real situation of this relationship is more complex.

There is substance to the claim that relations between the tribunal and the government were always fraught with tensions, particularly during the tribunal's early years. The government generally had an unfavourable perception of the tribunal as a result of several factors and the relationship started off on the wrong footing from the very beginning. The sense of betrayal which many in Rwanda felt towards the international community for its failure to prevent, stop or mitigate the extent of the genocide generated very strong resentment towards international institutions in general, and United Nations institutions in particular (Aptel 1997; International Crisis Group 2001a, 2002a). The Security Council's decision to establish the tribunal over the fervent objections of the Rwanda government served to further undermine domestic support for the tribunal even before it came into being.

In the very first years of the tribunal's existence, the relationship between the tribunal and the government was affected by the tribunal's management problems and other shortcomings (United Nations 2000: Statement of the Permanent Representative of Rwanda: p. 19), which were widely publicised. The tribunal's unsatisfactory performance in carrying out its mandate during this period was a matter of great concern to the government (Drumbl 2002a: p. 8) and it affected the government's perception of the court (Ministry of Justice u.d.).

In addition, the government's attitude towards the tribunal was at various times adversely affected by several others factors, including competition between the tribunal and the government over custody of suspects, the Appeals Chamber's decision in the Barayagwiza case[29], the tribunal's plans to investigate and prosecute human rights violations alleged to have been committed by the RPA, employment of Rwandan exiles opposed to the government (including genocide suspects) within the services of the tribunal (United Nations 2001b: Statement of Rwandan Minister of Justice, p. 19), and issues relating to the treatment of prosecution witnesses, most of whom were genocide survivors (United Nations 2001b: Statement of Rwandan Minister of Justice, p. 14).

The leadership of the government, military and militia groups responsible for the genocide sought refuge in countries across the world after fleeing from Rwanda (Aptel 1997: p. 679). Rwanda often made requests for the extradition of fugitives whom the tribunal was interested in. The tribunal invoked the right of primacy under its statute to override the extradition requests of the government and the competing requests for transfer of genocide suspects were usually resolved in the tribunal's favour.[30] Competition between the tribunal and the government for custody of suspects caused friction between the two in the late 1990s. In time, however, the government recognized that the pursuit of suspects that the tribunal was also interested in was a lost cause and did not pursue such suspects (Carroll 2000: pp. 194–5). The government actually became a strong advocate of transfers of genocide suspects to the tribunal. Claims by some scholars that ICTR prosecutors consistently clashed with the government of Rwanda over custody of suspects (Peskin 2011: p. 174) are completely unfounded.

As a government, we recognized from the very beginning that in spite of its weaknesses and shortcomings, the tribunal was an invaluable instrument for ensuring justice for the genocide, particularly as concerned the persons who bore the greatest responsibility for its conception and direction. We shared with the tribunal the same common interest of seeking to bring persons responsible for the genocide to justice. The success of the tribunal presented a unique opportunity to advance our own goals and objectives. We were very keen to help the tribunal to succeed in this regard in any way we could, the tribunal's weaknesses and shortcomings notwithstanding. The claim by some scholars that the government of Rwanda had a policy to deliberately sabotage the tribunal (Peskin 2005) has no basis. We were critical of the tribunal (as many non-Rwandans were), but we also genuinely wanted the tribunal to succeed in bringing those responsible for the genocide to justice. The government's poor perception of the effectiveness of the tribunal did not in any way hinder it from helping the tribunal as our common interests were at stake.

In line with our policy of facilitating the tribunal's pursuit of its mandate, we generally provided all the support that the institutions of the tribunal requested most of the time. The day-to-day working relationship between both senior officials and other employees of government and the tribunal was quite harmonious and beneficial to the tribunal most of the time (United Nations 2000: Statements of the Prosecutor and the Permanent Representative of Rwanda, p. 4; ICTR 2001: para. 16, 2005a: paras 48–49; Moghalu 2002: p. 29). The Prosecution Service, police and local government authorities across the country provided invaluable assistance to investigators and other personnel of the tribunal as they went about their work. The tribunal's success in bringing to justice a very large number of the leadership that bears responsibility for the genocide is owed in part to the strong support that institutions and officials of the Rwanda government have provided over the years.

There were admittedly a few times when cooperation between the tribunal and the government of Rwanda was seriously threatened by issues over which agreement could not be reached. One such issue was the Barayagwiza case, the event that perhaps tested the relationship between the government and the tribunal the most. At stake was a decision of the Appeals Chamber to dismiss the indictment against Jean-Bosco Barayagwiza with prejudice and to order his release.[31] Barayagwiza had previously been a prominent scholar and extremist Hutu politician. He was also a key founder of Radio RTLM (which was very instrumental in inciting and directing the genocide). Barayagwiza was arrested in Cameroon on 27 March 1996 and detained from that date pending a decision by the Cameroonian authorities on Rwanda's extradition. The Cameroon Court of Appeal eventually rejected Rwanda's extradition request and ordered Barayagwiza's release on 21 February 1997.

On the day that the Cameroon Court of Appeal ordered Barayagwiza's release, the Prosecutor made a request for his provisional detention. The Prosecutor followed up with a request for orders for his arrest and transfer to the tribunal on 24 February 1997. The order for Barayagwiza's arrest and transfer to the tribunal was granted by a Cameroonian judge on 3 March 1997. Barayagwiza remained in the custody of the Cameroonian authorities pending a decision of the President of Cameroon on the tribunal's request for Barayagwiza's transfer. On 29 September 1997, Barayagwiza filed a writ of habeas corpus, but the application was overtaken by a 21 October 1997 decision of the President of Cameroon authorizing Barayagwiza's transfer to the tribunal. Barayagwiza was transferred to the tribunal's Detention Unit on 19 November 1997 but did not make his initial appearance before the tribunal until 23 February 1998, contrary to the provision (Rule 40bis) of the Rules of Procedure which required that an initial appearance take place within30 days. On 24 February 1998, Barayagwiza filed a motion seeking to nullify his arrest and detention, but the Trial Chambers did not rule on the motion until 17 November 1998, when his motion was dismissed. Barayagwiza filed an appeal against the dismissal of the motion to quash the order for his arrest and detention. The Appeals Chamber, in November 1999, allowed Baragyagwiza's appeal, dismissed the indictment against him with prejudice, and ordered Barayagwiza returned to Cameroon, on the grounds that Barayagwiza's due process rights (including the right to be informed promptly of the charges against him, the right to appear before a judge without undue delay for his initial appearance, and the right to have the motion challenging the legality of his arrest and detention heard within 30 days as provided by the Rules of Procedure) had been violated.

The decision to dismiss the indictment against Barayagwiza with prejudice was received by the government of Rwanda and genocide survivors with outrage. Our view was that Barayagwiza was accused of very grave crimes relating to the genocide in Rwanda; that the tribunal had a legal obligation either to try such crimes or to surrender persons accused of them to jurisdictions that are able and willing to try them; that the delays on the basis of which the indictment against Barayagwiza was dismissed were of the tribunal's own making; that if the tribunal could not try the accused, it should surrender him to Rwanda or another state for trial; that the dismissal of the indictment against the accused with prejudice was both unjustified and an error which occasioned a gross miscarriage of justice.[32] We were very concerned that as a result of the tribunal's mishandling of the cases of many of the suspects who were in its custody, the Appeals Chamber's decision in the Barayagwiza case would set a precedent that would lead to the release of many of the suspects who were in the tribunal's custody, as many of them had to varying degrees been affected by delays in the processing of their cases similar to Barayagwiza's experience. We responded to the Barayagwiza decision by announcing plans to suspend cooperation with the tribunal. What critics of the government failed to notice was that the government's statement indicated that it would suspend all cooperation 'excepting what the government was legally required to do'. I personally drafted that statement. We were sensitive to the fact that the jurisdiction of the tribunal was founded in a resolution of the Security Council under Chapter VII of the UN Charter, which was binding on all states, including Rwanda. In the event, we were well aware that the tribunal represented the only prospect of bringing the perpetrators of the genocide to justice. It was never the government's intention to suspend all cooperation with the tribunal as such. Our statement was merely designed to press our case that the tribunal should either try Barayagwiza on the merits or transfer him to Rwanda or any state willing to try him. The Appeals Chamber allowed me to appear before it to argue the case for review of the order dismissing the charges against Barayagwiza with prejudice. The Prosecutor and most states and prominent international human rights organizations interested in the work of the tribunal shared our view that neither Barayagwiza nor other genocide suspects in the custody of the tribunal should escape justice on the basis of technicalities attributable to the tribunal's unsatisfactory performance.

The international community (including governments and human rights organizations) largely supported Rwanda's stand that Barayagwiza should not escape justice. The Prosecutor shared Rwanda's concerns regarding the potential implications of the decision in the Barayagwiza case for a large number of cases in the tribunal's docket. A differently constituted Appeals Chamber found that the remedy issued in the November 1999 order was disproportionate to the circumstances, revoked Barayagwiza's release and determined that violations of his rights should be remedied at trial.[33] The review of the Barayagwiza decision resolved a crisis that could have had far-reaching implications for the tribunal's future. As a matter of fact, with the exception of a decision to withhold the issue of a visa to the new Prosecutor for two weeks, Rwanda's cooperation with the tribunal went on very smoothly even during this period (Cruvellier 2010: p. 108).

The government's support for the tribunal's work in Rwanda was consistent even during times of tension with the ICTR. Whereas there were always issues over which the government and the tribunal did not share a common view and occasions when disagreements over these issues led to tensions in the relationship (ICTR 2002: para. 87), quite often, collaboration at a technical level was maintained even as the official rhetoric seemed to signal a breakdown of relations. This was the situation even during the Barayagwiza case. Claims by Peskin (2011: p. 177) and other scholars that the government actually stopped cooperating with the tribunal until the Appeals Chamber reversed the Barayagwiza decision are untrue. The perception that the tribunal and the government had a consistently acrimonious or confrontational relationship and that it was always the policy of the Rwandan government to undermine the tribunal's work does not accurately reflect the true state of affairs. The government may have had misgivings about the tribunal's performance but equally it always wanted the tribunal to succeed in its mandate to investigate and prosecute genocide (United Nations 2001b: Statement of Rwandan Minister of Justice, p. 14). With the exception of the issue of investigations of crimes attributed to the RPA, the government not only cooperated with but also actively went out of its way to assist the tribunal to perform its mandate. Criticism of the tribunal was used as a means to pressure the tribunal over issues that the government felt strongly about, but withdrawing support for the work of the tribunal was never considered an option (United Nations 2001b: Statement of Rwandan Minister of Justice, p. 14).

Some scholars have written that the Rwandan government's and my own criticism of the tribunal was connected to the tribunal's plans to investigate and prosecute crimes alleged to have been committed by the RPA. Our criticism of the tribunal (see, for example, Ministry of Justice, u.d.) was a genuine reflection of our views on its performance. The nature of the engagement between the government of Rwanda and the tribunal on the issue of crimes attributed to the RPA is often misrepresented. Equally, the impact of the government's policy in respect of investigations pertaining to those crimes has been exaggerated by scholars (e.g. Peskin 2005; Waldorf 2011a).

The tribunal has had four prosecutors during the course of its existence: Richard Goldstone (1994–96), Louise Arbour (1996–99), Carla Del Ponte (1999–2003) and Hassan Bubacar Jallow (2003–to date). It has been reported that the tribunal started investigations of cases against members of the RPA during the 1990s under the tenure of Louise Arbour (Peskin 2005: p. 223). Goldstone and Arbour did not at any time seek the government's support towards investigation of the crimes allegedly committed by the RPA.

Carla Del Ponte, the third Prosecutor, was the first Prosecutor of the tribunal to openly declare (in 2000) that she was pursuing investigations of the alleged crimes and to seek government support for those investigations (United Nations 1994j: Statement of the Prosecutor, p. 11; ICTR 2001: para. 117). Del Ponte reportedly entrusted these investigations to a unit called the Special Investigations Team. In meetings with the President, the Head of the Military Prosecution Service and me, during the early 2000s, Prosecutor Del Ponte indicated that she planned to investigate some cases involving allegations against members of the RPA, as required by her mandate. The President initially responded to the Prosecutor's request for assistance with assurances that the government would indeed cooperate with the proposed investigations. Relying on the President's assurances, Del Ponte forwarded a number of dossiers in respect of which her office needed additional investigatory support to the Rwanda Military Prosecutor's Office.

Many scholars of the tribunal and Rwanda's transitional justice processes misrepresent the scope of the investigations that Del Ponte proposed to carry out. The Prosecutor did not seek to investigate a large number of cases. She was at pains to point out that she wanted to investigate only a few cases. The Prosecutor wanted, she indicated, to pursue these few cases to respond to criticism that the tribunal was only trying and punishing members of one side to the conflict. The Office of the Prosecutor has never demonstrated any intention to undertake a comprehensive investigation and prosecution of crimes attributed to the RPA.

However, even the minimal demands of the ICTR were not acceptable to the military. After some procrastination, President Kagame instructed the Chief Military Prosecutor to inform Del Ponte in categorical terms that the military justice system (and, in effect, the Rwanda government) would not cooperate with her offices' investigations of crimes attributed to the RPA. In deciding to confront the Prosecutor directly and to declare that the government would not cooperate with or support the tribunal's investigation or prosecution of allegations against members of the RPA, the Rwanda military establishment was influenced by several factors. One of these factors was the determination of this leadership to do anything in its power to avoid trials that would undermine the legitimacy that the RPA claimed from its role in stopping the genocide. Another of these factors was that the military establishment essentially believed that the Prosecutor would not get the support of the international community in undertaking such trials. The Rwanda military establishment's decision not to cooperate with the tribunal's plans to investigate and prosecute crimes attributed to its members was, I believe, heavily influenced by signs coming from London and Washington that the Prosecutor could not count on the backing of the governments of the United Kingdom and the United States were she to seek indictments against members of the RPA. In my discussions of the issue with President Kagame, he was always of the view that the international community did not have the moral right or the political will to seek indictments and to undertake trials of RPA members who may be implicated by the investigations of the Prosecutor.

Another factor that may have led the military leadership to decide not to cooperate with the Prosecutor's proposed investigations was the possible conviction that the tribunal could not investigate the cases effectively without the government's assistance. The military and security services were able to use the coercive powers of the state to disrupt the tribunal's work should the Prosecutor insist on pursuing the proposed investigations. At certain critical junctures in the history of the relationship of the tribunal with Rwanda, the security services had demonstrated their almost unfettered capacity to undermine the tribunal's effectiveness by a number of strategies, including the manipulation of civil society organizations (especially organizations representing genocide survivors and the local media) and control of access to witnesses. The government's security services often used survivors of the genocide to attack the credibility of the tribunal. On other occasions, the security services used administrative measures, such as imposing new requirements for the issue of travel documents to witnesses going to testify at the tribunal, to halt the court's operations.

Faced with a strongly recalcitrant attitude on the part of the government to the issue of investigations of allegations of human rights abuses attributable to the victors, Del Ponte reckoned that she could still get the government to cooperate through the application of diplomatic pressure by Western countries. The Prosecutor embarked on a mission to lobby some Western governments, with special emphasis on the governments of the United Kingdom and the United States, to exert pressure on the Rwanda government to cooperate with the investigations of allegations against members of the RPA.

The Prosecutor's efforts to mobilize diplomatic pressure to bear on the government were unsuccessful. None of the major powers offered to help the Prosecutor in applying pressure upon the government to cooperate with the proposed investigations. On the contrary, the governments of the United Kingdom and the United States in particular may have, knowingly or otherwise, encouraged Rwanda's military leadership to defy the Prosecutor. In 2002, President Kagame met Jack Straw, the then United Kingdom Foreign Secretary, to discuss bilateral and regional issues. According to sources in the Foreign Office at the time, the Foreign Secretary departed from the briefing that civil servants had prepared and launched an unprompted scathing attack on the tribunal. Although it may not have been the Foreign Secretary's intention, the meeting marked a turning point in the dialogue between the Rwanda government and the tribunal on the question of accountability for the crimes alleged to have been committed by members of the RPA. President Kagame returned from the meetings in the United Kingdom firmly resolved to defy the tribunal's attempt to pursue the allegations against his men. The Foreign Secretary's conduct had the effect of giving President Kagame confidence that major powers would not support the tribunal in the event of a showdown with the Rwanda government over the issue of indictments of members of the RPA.

In 2003, the United States government, through its Ambassador-at-Large for War Crimes Issues, offered to mediate the dispute between the government and the Prosecutor over the matter of the investigations of human rights abuses alleged to have been committed by the RPA. Rwanda did not request the mediation. The US government suggested the negotiations on its own initiative. At the May 2003 meetings that we and Del Ponte held in Washington a tentative agreement was reached, under which the tribunal would give Rwanda the first opportunity to investigate and prosecute some of the cases that the Prosecutor wanted to be investigated and tried. The tribunal would monitor the investigations and trials to verify whether they were conducted in good faith. In the event that the tribunal determined that the investigations and trials had not been conducted in good faith, the tribunal would have the right to retry the cases. My delegation was happy with the arrangement.

As Prosecutor General, it fell to me to convince the Rwanda military to cooperate with the limited number of investigations of crimes attributed to the RPA that Del Ponte wished to pursue. On my delegation's return to Rwanda, President Kagame decided not to take leadership on the issue, and said he would leave it to us to convince the rest of the leadership of the military and security services to decide whether to accept or reject the terms of the agreement that we had reached with the Prosecutor during our meetings in Washington. Not surprisingly, the military leadership emphatically rejected our advice to cooperate with the Prosecutor. Opposition to the proposed investigations remained strong within the Rwandan military establishment. The President and rest of the leadership of the Rwanda military had ultimately come to the conclusion that they did not have to cooperate with the tribunal in its investigations and prosecutions of crimes attributed to the RPA.

The Prosecutor herself had a change of mind and subsequently withdrew from the agreement. Nevertheless, the meetings in Washington were very significant for both Rwanda and the tribunal. The significance of the meetings was that the US government had conveyed the message that the exercise of the powers of the Prosecutor was negotiable. Having repudiated an agreement that the US had brokered, the Prosecutor knew she could not count on the US government to support her in any future confrontation with the government of Rwanda over issues relating to abuses alleged to have been committed by the RPA.

Del Ponte's mandate in respect of Rwanda was terminated by the Security Council in September 2003. Contrary to claims (Peskin 2011: p. 178) that Rwanda may have had secret understandings with the governments of the United Kingdom and the United States to remove Del Ponte, we were taken by complete surprise by the decision to terminate her mandate in respect of the Rwanda tribunal. With Del Ponte's departure, the issue of the crimes alleged to have been committed by members of the RPA immediately ceased to be a sticking point between the Rwanda government and the tribunal. After assuming office in 2003, Prosecutor Jallow avoided making any decision on the allegations against members of the RPA by reiterating, year after year, that he was reviewing the cases and carrying on further investigations. The Prosecutor ultimately decided not to seek any indictments against members of the RPA. Rwanda's military establishment had judged (rightly, as it turned out) that the international community did indeed not have the political will to enforce the arrest and trial of members of the RPA for any human rights abuses that they may have committed during the 1994 events.

Save for a brief period between 2002 and 2003, the government of Rwanda and the tribunal have enjoyed a degree of harmonious cooperation that is not often appreciated. There have been difficult moments in that relationship. However, few of the conflicts that have arisen between the government and the tribunal were significant enough to affect ongoing collaboration. The issues that were of such strong significance as to have potential to disrupt the otherwise smooth collaboration between government institutions and the tribunal were few and far from frequent. On the single issue that had the potential to lead to a total breakdown of relations, namely the pursuit of justice for crimes attributed to members of the RPA, the Prosecutors of the court decided to defer to the wishes of the government. Successive prosecutors of the Rwanda tribunal made strategic decisions to deal with the crimes attributed to the RPA in ways that sought to avoid precipitating a backlash from the Rwandan government that might jeopardise the entire work of the tribunal. The declarations of the successive prosecutors expressing intentions to investigate crimes allegedly committed by the RPA would appear to have been merely intended to appease or pacify those in the international community who still advocated for holding members of the RPA accountable. The influence of the issue of human rights abuses allegedly committed by the RPA on the policies of the government towards the tribunal has been exaggerated. The tribunal has never seriously pressured the Rwandan government to cooperate with or support investigations of abuses attributable to its military. No foreign government or organization (including the Security Council) has ever sought to exert pressure on the government to provide support to the tribunal to enable it to pursue the cases against the RPA. Whereas there were occasions when the relationship between the tribunal and the Rwanda government became very contentious, in general, the government and the tribunal have enjoyed a productive, mutually appreciated and fairly harmonious relationship over most of the tribunal's life.

4.6.2 Survivors of the genocide

Survivors of the genocide are a very important interest group in matters relating to both national and international mechanisms of accountability for the genocide and as such are a very important constituency of the tribunal.

Genocide survivors have had an ambivalent relationship with the tribunal throughout the duration of its existence. On one hand, survivors have valued the institution for its unique capacity to bring perpetrators of the genocide to justice. Survivors recognized that the tribunal provided the best, if not the only, realistic opportunity for bringing the perpetrators of the genocide who were living outside Rwanda to justice. Survivors have strongly supported the tribunal, particularly through providing evidence as witnesses before the tribunal.

At the same time, survivors of the genocide have over the years had concerns that have affected their support for and trust in the tribunal (Drumbl 2002a: p. 16). Many survivors harboured suspicions about a United Nations court from the very beginning, given that the United Nations had abandoned them in their most urgent time of need by failing to act to prevent or stop the genocide. They saw it then as an institution set up, in the wake of the genocide, by an international community that was more interested in symbolic responses rather than in meaningful justice (REDRESS/African Rights 2008b: p. 55).

The slow pace of the tribunal's work has always been a source of great frustration for survivors (Strain and Keyes 2003: p. 107; Burnet 2009: p. 175). Survivors' perceptions of the tribunal were also adversely affected by widely disseminated reports of mismanagement and corruption within the tribunal as well as by occasional scandals such as the hiring of genocide suspects and the discovery of fee-splitting arrangements between defence counsel and persons on trial before the tribunal. Other factors, events and circumstances that have over the years contributed to undermining the image of the tribunal among genocide survivors include misgivings over the propriety of some of the tribunal's judicial decisions (including the widely criticized decision to quash the indictment of Jean-Bosco Barayagwiza and the acquittal of several of the most notorious defendants (REDRESS/African Rights 2008b: p. 56; Habimana 2009)),[34] the imposition of sentences that are, in the opinion of survivors, disproportionately lenient relative to the crimes for which accused persons have been convicted (Hirondelle News Agency 2009), lack of an effective witness protection system,[35] failure to prepare witnesses for the rigours of cross-examination in an adversarial setting (Drumbl 2002a: p. 16; Moghalu 2002: p. 29), the failure, discussed in a later chapter, to adequately take into account the prevalence of rape and other crimes affecting women (REDRESS/African Rights 2008b: p. 56) and the humiliating treatment of some prosecution witnesses by the officials responsible for witness protection and even by Chambers on some occasions.[36] Although not necessarily significant when viewed individually, the above events and circumstances have collectively served to enhance negative perceptions of the tribunal within the community of genocide survivors.

Genocide survivors' perceptions about the tribunal have also been adversely affected by the treatment accorded accused persons by the tribunal. The tribunal has endeavoured to treat persons in its custody in accordance with international standards relating to the treatment of prisoners.[37] The statute of the tribunal excluded capital punishment, even while capital punishment still applied to Category 1 suspects in Rwanda's justice system.[38] The tribunal's detention facility in Arusha offers better accommodation than what the majority of Rwandans live in. Whereas victims of the genocide (including women and girls who were infected with HIV/Aids as a result of rape during the genocide) have generally had problems in getting access to necessary healthcare, detainees in the custody of the tribunal have access to very good medical care (Drumbl 2002a: p. 10). Victims of the genocide, on the other hand, did not receive comparable or indeed any medical assistance even when they were witnesses in cases before the tribunal (United Nations 2001b: Statement of Rwandan Minister of Justice, p. 15). Some of the persons who have been tried by the tribunal have benefited financially from their trials by being able to provide employment to friends and relatives on defence teams, financed through the tribunal's budget and through fee-splitting arrangements with defence counsel (United Nations 1997). The image that most Rwandans have of persons on trial before the tribunal is one of well groomed men wearing designer suits living in luxury that is unimaginable to most of their compatriots. Survivors' support for the tribunal has been tempered by strong misgivings arising from the perception that the tribunal places a disproportionate emphasis on the rights of the accused (Tiemessen 2004: p. 29).

The tribunal's lack of powers to provide reparations for victims of the crimes that it tries has hurt its standing in the perception of survivors. Under Rwanda's legal system, victims of crime have a right to seek damages during the course of the criminal trials of the perpetrators.[39] The statute of the tribunal does not, however, make any provision for the award of damages or provision of other modes of reparation. Issues relating to reparations are only addressed in the Rules of Procedure and Evidence. Rule 106 of the Rules of Procedure and Evidence provides:

> Rule 106: Compensation to Victims
>
> A The Registrar shall transmit to the competent authorities of the States concerned the judgement finding the accused guilty of a crime which has caused injury to a victim.
>
> B Pursuant to the relevant national legislation, a victim or persons claiming through him may bring an action in a national court or other competent body to obtain compensation.
>
> C For the purposes of a claim made under Sub-Rule (B) the judgement of the Tribunal shall be final and binding as to the criminal responsibility of the convicted person for such injury.

The tribunal's lack of authority to order payment of compensation to victims was displeasing to survivors, particularly those who agreed to testify in the tribunal's proceedings. The government shared survivors' views on the issue of reparations (United Nations 2001b: Speech of Jean de Dieu Mucyo,

Rwandan Minister of Justice, p. 15). The tribunal's lack of authority to provide monetary or material compensation to victims adversely affected its appeal to survivors of the genocide (Moghalu 2002: p. 29).

4.6.3 *Political opposition in Rwanda*

The Rwanda opposition movement has generally been very critical of the tribunal. The views of opponents of the current government of Rwanda on the tribunal reflect their policies on the situation in Rwanda. The opposition to the current government is largely made up of political elites who went into exile in the aftermath of the RPF's military victory in 1994. The opposition includes people who were involved in planning and carrying out the genocide as well as people who did not play any part in committing atrocities. The opposition is predominantly Hutu, and is largely based outside Rwanda. The political philosophy, which unites this opposition movement, is that the current government is a dictatorship and that it is controlled by a minority ethnic group, some of whose members committed grave violations of human rights abuses themselves during and after the 1990–94 war. The Rwanda opposition movement has long advocated that the tribunal should take measures to bring members of the RPA to justice for crimes that they are alleged to have committed during and after the genocide. The opposition movement has always expressed regret over the limitation of the tribunal's temporal jurisdiction to the calendar year 1994. The opposition would instead have preferred to have the tribunal's jurisdiction extended to include the period after the end of the war, as they argue that the RPA continued to commit atrocities against members of the Hutu community after it came to power (RDR 2000).

Various opposition groups and individuals have over the years lobbied and pressured successive prosecutors to follow up the allegations of human rights violations attributed to the RPA. The prosecutors have all failed to heed calls to address these crimes. The failure of the tribunal to investigate and try any allegations of human rights abuses by the RPA has led the largely Hutu opposition to the conclusion that the tribunal is not independent and impartial, and that the tribunal is biased against the Hutu community – a tool of victor's justice (Barayagwiza 2000: para. 177). Some Rwandese associated with the previous government go further and argue that the tribunal's exclusive focus on the genocide and its failure to prosecute any of the crimes attributed to the RPA is a result of a deliberate conspiracy against the Hutu community by the entire international community (Barayagwiza 2000: para. 215).

4.6.4 *Perceptions and attitudes of the general public towards the tribunal in Rwanda*

There is little published research documenting public attitudes in general towards the tribunal. The general population in Rwanda has not been adequately informed about the tribunal's work (Moghalu 2002: p. 22). The tribunal has been based in another country and its proceedings are accessible to only a very small minority in Rwandese society. Reporting on the tribunal has not been adequately informative. The media in Rwanda has rarely published any detailed analysis of issues relating to the tribunal and has only reported major events happening at the tribunal. Media coverage of issues relating to the tribunal has generally reflected government policy towards the tribunal. Media coverage of the tribunal inside Rwanda has been heavily influenced by the government and organizations representing survivors, and has tended to focus more on the tribunal's failings.

The government dominates the media in Rwanda and has used its clout in the media market to influence public opinion on issues of major concern, including the work of the Rwanda tribunal. The Rwandan public has been exposed to one-sided, negative reporting on the Rwanda tribunal and this reporting has in all probability affected public attitudes towards it. However, in the absence of any systematic surveys, it is difficult to make an accurate assessment of public attitudes towards, and perceptions of, the tribunal. Lack of a free press and the limitations on freedom of expression that prevail in Rwanda make it difficult to gain even accurate anecdotal evidence about what the general population thinks of the tribunal's effectiveness in carrying out its mandate.

A human rights activist who was one of the leaders of LIPRODHOR (the most prominent domestic human rights organization prior to a government crackdown on independent civil society organizations during the mid-2000s), has described public attitudes towards the tribunal in a short article entitled 'What Does International Justice Look Like in Post-Genocide Rwanda?' (Habimana 2009). According to Habimana, public perceptions of the tribunal in Rwanda are overwhelmingly negative: most Rwandans believe the tribunal was designed by the United Nations to save face for doing too little to save Rwanda.

Apart from government influence, negative perceptions of the tribunal among the general population have also resulted from a number of other factors, including what most Rwandans perceive as the tribunal's incompetence and ineffectiveness, particularly in the light of the huge financial resources at its disposal. It is also claimed that most Rwandans, like the government, object to the location of the seat in a foreign country and the exclusion of capital punishment from the penalties the tribunal is able to impose. However, most Rwandans also trust the tribunal to be more impartial than national courts and have high regard for its witness protection programme. Harsh criticism of the tribunal by the government has widespread influence among the public, particularly because survivors and the Tutsi generally dominate both state-controlled and privately owned media. The negative image of the tribunal, the article asserts, undermines Rwandans' hope for justice in general and international justice, in particular. The belief that public attitudes towards the tribunal are negative is shared by some external observers (Thomson 1999; International Crisis Group 2001a, 2002a; Waldorf 2011a; Ironside 2002).

It may reasonably be concluded that there are at least some significant segments of Rwandan society that hold negative views on the tribunal. The human rights abuses of which members of the RPA are accused caused substantial suffering and loss of human life. The memory of those abuses lives on amongst those who survived them. The tribunal's failure to investigate, try and punish these crimes cannot but be a source of grave disappointment on the part of the victims. The tribunal's failure to render justice in an even-handed and neutral manner affects its legitimacy amongst at least part of the population (Carroll 2000: pp. 184–5; Cruvellier 2010). Some would go so far as to argue that the tribunal is perceived by the majority of the Hutu population as international punishment by the victors with the blessing and support of the international community (Mutua 1997: pp. 186–7).

4.7 The Completion Strategy of the ICTR: Endgame

The ICTR, like its sister tribunal for the former Yugoslavia, is currently implementing the final stages of its completion strategy. Completion strategies for the two tribunals became necessary as a result of several developments. Although the former leadership of the Yugoslav tribunal has claimed credit for initiating the completion strategies process (Morrison *et al.* 2008: p. 695), the truth about the origins of the completion strategies of the two tribunals is more complex. During the 1990s and early 2000s, the two United Nations tribunals were often criticized for a variety of shortcomings, including the slow pace of their trials,[40] violations of accused persons' fair trial rights, including prolonged pre-trial detention, inefficient use of resources, lack of effective management systems and their failure to undertake effective outreach programmes with a view to making the tribunals relevant to and credible in the perception of the societies they were set up to help (United Nations 1999b: Statement of the Permanent Representatives of Argentina, p. 5; Morrison *et al.* 2008: p. 695). Some of the criticism of the two tribunals may have been objective and constructive. Some was probably uninformed, lacking in objectivity and on occasions self-serving, as in the case of criticism by states that were not cooperating well with the tribunals. Criticism of the two tribunals by the governments of Rwanda and some states of the Former Yugoslavia, for example, may on occasions have been intended to undermine the tribunals in reprisal for their attempts to investigate and prosecute allegations against members of the respective government's political leadership or military (Erlanger and Gall 2000; Peskin 2005).

Criticism of the two tribunals had a strong impact on shaping attitudes about their work, about the quality of their leadership, and above all about their effectiveness in carrying out their respective mandates. By around 2000, many in the international community were openly questioning the effectiveness of these institutions and their suitability as responses to legacies of atrocity.

Deep-rooted concerns about their efficiency and effectiveness undermined their credibility and siphoned off much-needed political support. As Judge Erik Møse has written, this was a time when 'tribunal fatigue' had already set in (Morrison *et al.* 2008: pp. 698–9). Some influential states which provided the bulk of the funding for the United Nations came to see the imposition of limits to the duration of the tribunals' mandates as a necessary cost-containing measure. The states which formed the core constituency of the tribunals were already focusing on the establishment and strengthening of the permanent international criminal court as the new priority with regard to the future of international criminal justice (Schabas 2006: p. 31). These states had no compelling reason to perpetuate recourse to the 'ad hoc tribunal' mechanisms. This core constituency may also have come to the conclusion that the two tribunals had served their primary objectives. The tribunals had originally been set up primarily to assuage the guilt of the West over its failure to stop, prevent or mitigate the atrocities that had been committed in the former Yugoslavia and Rwanda. The need for atonement (through the two tribunals) became less necessary as memories of the atrocities the tribunals had been established to punish faded. The completion strategies were responses to unavoidable external pressures, political and economic, to wind up the two tribunals as soon as practically possible.

The behind-the-scenes debates about the future of the two tribunals took place in an environment in which the two tribunals were in a politically weakened position. The compromise that came out of the discussions was a decision to put the two institutions on a tight leash, to push them to improve their performance, and to impose a cut-off date for the completion of their work. Each tribunal was to be required to commit to a plan ('completion strategy') outlining how it proposed to complete or otherwise dispose of its caseload (United Nations 2003a). The 'completion strategies' had to ensure the completion of all investigations by the end of 2004, completion of all first instance trials by 2008, and completion of all appeals and closing down of the two tribunals in 2010 (United Nations 2003a: Article 6). The completion strategies committed the tribunals to concentrating on the prosecution and trial of the most senior leaders responsible for the crimes within the tribunals' jurisdiction and to transfer cases involving intermediate or lower-rank accused persons to national jurisdictions. In order to ensure strict compliance with the goals set forth in the completion strategies, the Security Council mandated the tribunals' Presidents and Prosecutors to report their progress on implementation of the completion strategies every six months (United Nations 2003a: Article 6).

4.7.1 Completion of the tribunal's judicial duties

The ICTR presented the first version of its Completion Strategy in 2003. At the time of its presentation, the tribunal had completed first instance trials of 21 persons. Four trials involving 12 persons were then in progress. Thirty accused persons were in detention awaiting trial. Sixteen indicted persons were still at large. In presenting the strategy, the Prosecutor indicated that he expected to seek indictments against an additional 26 more suspects (ICTR 2003a). The Completion Strategy sought to meet the requirements of the Security Council to prepare for the end of the tribunal's mandate through two approaches. The first approach was to enhance the capacity of the tribunal to use available resources to increase its judicial output. The second was to transfer some of the tribunal's caseload to national jurisdictions (United Nations 2003e: Statement of ICTR Prosecutor, pp. 13–16; ICTR 2006d). The tribunal proposed to increase its judicial output by improving overall coordination of planning through the Coordination Council; twin-tracking cases (each Chamber trying two cases simultaneously), adopting a shift system for the use of courtrooms (each courtroom to be used for one case in the morning and early afternoon and for a different case in the afternoon and evening); establishing more trial chambers or sections of chambers (particularly through the use of *ad litem* judges); enhancing judicial control of proceedings; increasing the number of trial teams in the Office of the Prosecutor; allowing *ad litem* judges to participate in pre-trial proceedings; improving the capacity for the translation of documents; and enhancing coordination of pre-trial proceedings through a newly established New Trials Committee comprising representatives of the three organs of the tribunal (ICTR 2003a: pp. 11–12).

The Completion Strategy envisaged that the court would complete its workload between 2007 and 2011 depending on a number of factors, including the possibility of a reduction in the number of pending investigations, the response of the Security Council to the tribunal's request for an increase in the number of *ad litem* judges, the creation of additional chambers or sections of chambers, the number of guilty pleas that would be made, success in the transfer of cases to national jurisdictions, as well as the progress of the Office of the Prosecutor in tracking fugitives. The completion strategy of the tribunal has been modified and updated periodically, in conformity with the provisions of Resolution 1534 (United Nations 2004b).

In line with the Completion Strategy, the tribunal officially ended the investigation stage of its mandate, the first formal milestone in its completion strategy, on 1 January 2005. However, the tribunal was not able to meet the Security Council's deadlines for the completion of trials and the Council had to extend the deadline for the completion of trials on several occasions. In December 2010, the Security Council set a final deadline of no later than 31 December 2014 for the closure of the tribunal (United Nations 2003a: Article 3).

At the time of writing, the tribunal is currently involved in diverse activities related to preparations for closure, in addition to completing trials of the few remaining cases. The tribunal is preparing the records to be transferred to a successor institution that will deal with residual issues relating to the tribunal's work. It has undertaken evidence preservation hearings in respect of some of the cases that it proposes to pass on to the successor mechanism.

The tribunal is also reviewing witness protection orders that it has passed, and withdrawing or reviewing those that are no longer necessary, to ensure that the successor mechanism, with its limited resources, will not be unnecessarily tasked with continuing to monitor protected witnesses who no longer need protection. The tribunal has continued to improve awareness of its work through its outreach programme in Rwanda and Tanzania and it continues its capacity-building support for legal institutions in Rwanda. The tribunal's Prosecutor (who is also the Prosecutor of the Mechanism) continues to be actively engaged with matters relating to cooperation between states and the tribunal, ensuring the arrest of the remaining fugitives, the possible referral of cases to national jurisdictions, the transfer of convicts for the enforcement of their sentence, assistance to national jurisdictions interested in investigating and trying crimes within the competence of the tribunal, either as a result of Rule 11bis transfers or in exercise of universal jurisdiction, and the relocation of acquitted persons and persons who have served their sentence (ICTR 2011b). The tribunal has also been actively involved in litigation relating to its applications to transfer some of the tribunal cases to national jurisdictions. The subject of transfers of cases to national jurisdictions under the provisions of Rule 11bis of the Rules of Procedure and Evidence is discussed exhaustively in Chapter 5.

4.7.2 Residual mechanism

The proposal to close the ad hoc United Nations tribunals raised many issues, including the following: What institutions would supervise the execution of the decisions that the tribunals have made? What institutions would review those decisions, if the interest of justice so required? What would the tribunals do with cases of suspects that they had arrested but were unable to apprehend by the time of closure? What would the institutions do with evidence that they had gathered in the course of investigations that had not led to the issue of indictments and trials? How would the witnesses who had been provided with protection assistance by the tribunals continue to be protected after the tribunals closed? How should the records of the tribunals be managed following their closure? (Oosthuize and Schaeffer 2008; REDRESS/FIDH, 2009).

Following a long process of study and consultations, the United Nations Security Council decided to address these and related issues through the establishment of the International Residual Mechanism for Criminal Tribunals (the IRMCT) in 2010 through a resolution taken under Chapter VII of the UN Charter.[41] The Mechanism came into existence on 1 July 2012 as concerns the ICTR, and a year later with regard to the ICTY. The Mechanism is common to the two tribunals, but will have two separate branches, one for each tribunal.[42] The Mechanism will comprise one Trial Chamber for each branch and a common Appeals Chamber. A single prosecutor, with a deputy in charge of each of the two branches, will serve the Mechanism. The President of the Mechanism will be the only permanent judge. The President will appoint judges to deal with the business of the Mechanism from a list approved by the General Assembly. Judges will be paid only when they are in service.

The Mechanism will essentially have the same structure and jurisdiction as the ICTR and ICTY.[43] The task of the Mechanism is expressed as to:

> continue the jurisdiction, rights and obligations and essential functions of the ICTY and the ICTR, respectively, subject to the provisions of this resolution and the Statute of the Mechanism, and all contracts and international agreements concluded by the United Nations in relation to the ICTY and the ICTR, and still in force as of the relevant commencement date, shall continue in force *mutatis mutandis* in relation to the Mechanism.[44]

The functions of the Mechanism will include trials of fugitives,[45] review of judgments and other decisions of the tribunals, management of tribunal archives,[46] management of Witness Protections Programmes of the tribunals, supervision of execution of sentences imposed by the tribunal, and handling issues relating to the repatriation or relocation issues that arise with respect to individuals who are acquitted or who have served their sentences.

The Mechanism will not be able to issue new indictments for international crimes.[47] It will only have powers to issue new indictments and to try offences involving alleged interference with the administration of justice (such as intimidation of witnesses), contempt and perjury that arise during the remaining cases. The prohibition of new indictments has come as a disappointment to those, in relation to Rwanda, who had hoped that the United Nations would use the residual mechanism to redeem the tribunal of the burden of the legacy of its failure to address atrocities that were committed against members of the Hutu community during Rwanda's armed conflict of the 1990s.

The Mechanism has concurrent jurisdiction with national courts over persons whom it is competent to try, but has primacy over national courts.[48] At any stage of the procedure involving a person covered by Article 1, paragraph 2 of the Statute, the Mechanism may formally request national courts to defer to its competence in accordance with the present Statute and the Rules of Procedure and Evidence of the Mechanism. The resolution establishing the Mechanism urges and the Statute of the Mechanism requires the Mechanism to actively undertake every effort to refer those cases which do not involve the most senior leaders suspected of being most responsible for crimes to competent national jurisdictions in accordance with their respective Statutes and Rules of Procedure and Evidence.[49] The Trial Chamber may order such referral *proprio motu* or at the request of the Prosecutor, after having given to the Prosecutor and, where applicable, the accused, the opportunity to be heard and after being satisfied that the accused will receive a fair trial and that the death penalty will not be imposed or carried out. The Mechanism shall monitor cases referred to national courts by the ICTY, the ICTR and the Mechanism itself, with the assistance of international and regional organizations and bodies. After an order referring a case has been issued by the ICTY, the ICTR or the Mechanism and before the accused is found guilty or acquitted by a national court, where it is clear that the conditions for referral of the case are no longer met and it is in the interests of justice, the Trial Chamber may, at the request of the Prosecutor or *proprio motu* and upon having given to the State authorities concerned the opportunity to be heard, revoke the order and make a formal request for deferral.[50]

The President, Prosecutor and Registrar of the Mechanism were appointed and took office on 1 March 2012 for four-year terms. The judges were sworn in May 2012. The Mechanism commenced operations in July 2012 as planned.

4.8 Assessing the Impact and Legacy of the Tribunal

As the ICTR winds up its work, it is timely to begin contemplating its impact and legacy. Has the tribunal adequately performed its mandate? To what extent has its work advanced the goals and objectives for which it was established? Has the tribunal had any impact in terms of the objectives that the Security Council had in mind when it established the institution, and if so, to what extent? What will the lasting legacy of the institution be?

The impact and legacy of the ICTR cannot be discussed in isolation from that of the ICTY. The two ad hoc United Nations tribunals were twin institutions, set up by the same institution with more or less the same objectives. They faced similar challenges. In carrying out their mandates, they have been the subject of strong criticism since their establishment during the 1990s. This criticism has often centred around a number of issues, including the slow pace of proceedings (leading to frustration on the part of both suspects and victims and to human rights violations); the high cost of the tribunals (the tribunals consumed a disproportionate share of the resources that the international community makes available to promote the rule of law in the respective post-conflict states); and efficiency (the judicial output of the tribunals did not reflect the immense resources at their disposal).

The tribunals were also criticized for their failure to engage victims adequately, to address their concerns and to provide them with the opportunity to participate in their work. The general opinion among commentators is that, at least initially, the tribunals were too removed – physically as well as psychologically – from the societies in question to have any significant relevance to them (Drumbl 2002a: p. 8). The tribunals' pursuit of neutrality tended, deliberately or inadvertently, to sideline the victims of the conflicts they were dealing with from their processes (Drumbl 2002a: p. 42). The geographic remoteness of the two tribunals from the states whose conflicts they were dealing with, which was intended to insulate them from local influence, had the adverse effect of alienating them from the very people they were meant to serve. The tribunals did not initially recognize the critical need to interact with, and justify their relevance to, the societies they were established to help, who should have been their primary constituencies. They were rather more preoccupied with meeting the expectations of their international constituencies at the expense of being accountable to the societies they were formed to assist (Drumbl 2002a: p. 9). The ad hoc tribunals have not afforded the victims' societies a share of the ownership of their work, and thus many in those societies have felt deeply estranged from the institutions.

In spite of the above criticism, the ad hoc tribunals have played a very useful role in advancing the goals of transitional justice in the societies they were established to help. They have been important developments in the field of transitional justice. What remains uncertain is the extent to which the institutions have achieved the intended long-term goals.

The Rwanda tribunal was built from the ground. Its principal targets were dispersed across the world and many suspects tried to change their identities to evade justice. Initially, some states were not cooperative in apprehending suspects wanted by the tribunal. In spite of these hurdles, the tribunal has been able to apprehend and bring to justice a sizeable number: it has approved indictments against 92 suspects during its lifetime. As at 4 November 2011, the tribunal had completed work at the trial level with respect to 76 of the 92 accused, which included two referrals to national jurisdictions, two withdrawn indictments, and two indictees who died prior to or in the course of trials. It had delivered 50 first-instance judgments involving 70 accused, 9 of whom had pleaded guilty. Appellate proceedings have been concluded in respect of 37 persons. The persons whom the tribunal has brought to justice for crimes that were committed during the context of the genocide include the most senior civilian and military leaders of the government on whose watch the genocide was planned and carried out, together with leaders of civil society who also played a leading role in the genocide. Nine fugitives remain at large (ICTR 2011b). The tribunal has substantially performed its core mandate to prosecute persons responsible for genocide and other serious violations of international humanitarian law that were committed during the Rwanda conflict in 1994.

At the time of the tribunal's establishment, representatives of some of the members of the Security Council suggested that one of the objectives for its establishment was to facilitate the return of the millions of refugees who had fled from Rwanda at the end of the genocide. The refugees returned to Rwanda, but their return had nothing to do with the tribunal. Most were returned from the Congo by force of arms, and from other states in the Great Lakes region of Central Africa through peaceful bilateral agreements between the governments of those states and Rwanda.

The forces that had planned and directed the genocide were still a very strong political force as the tribunal began its work. These groups controlled millions of Rwandan refugees living in neighbouring states, and were training and recruiting combatants and waging war against the state of Rwanda with a view to recapturing power. The tribunal's work drove much of the leadership of these groups underground. A large number of the former leaders of political and military institutions that had planned and directed the genocide were eventually arrested and transferred to the tribunal. The arrest and detentions of these political, military and civil society leaders deprived them of capacity to continue to wage war against the new government. In apprehending and bringing to justice some of the leaders of the insurgent groups that were waging war against Rwanda, the tribunal delegitimized and weakened these groups politically and militarily and may thus have contributed to ensuring peace and stability in Rwanda in the short term (Van den Herik 2005: p. 263; Kamatali 2003: p. 127).

The lasting impact of the tribunal in advancing its long-term goals, namely fighting impunity, promoting respect for human rights, promoting reconciliation and ensuring sustainable peace, is strongly contested. The capacity of the tribunal to contribute to the attainment of these objectives has been undermined by a number of factors, the most significant of which is its failure to address the question of human rights violations alleged to have been committed by the RPA against members of the Hutu community. Hassan Jallow, the fourth and last of the tribunal's prosecutors, has essentially abdicated the ICTR's responsibility of ensuring that individuals from both sides of the conflict are brought to justice for their crimes (Peskin 2011: p. 174). Many commentators share the opinion that the tribunal's failure to investigate and prosecute violations of human rights by the victors has undermined both its credibility and its ability to contribute to the advancement of the objectives for which it was established (Van den Herik 2005: p. 264; Silva-Leander 2008: p. 1612; Peskin 2011).

Due to the tribunal's lack of even handedness, its work is perceived as victor's justice by a significant part of the Rwandan society, especially in the Hutu community. There is a broad consensus, at least amongst the Hutu who live in the diaspora, not only that the tribunal has been indifferent to the suffering of their community, but that its actions have victimized them.[51] The perception of the work of the tribunal as victor's justice by the majority of the Hutu community has undermined the tribunal's capacity to promote reconciliation in Rwanda.

In the absence of genuine reconciliation, it may be unrealistic to argue that the tribunal has made any significant contribution to prospects for sustainable peace in Rwanda. In spite of its contribution in facilitating the arrest and trial of a very large number of some of the people who bear the greatest responsibility for the genocide, the tribunal is unlikely to have any long-term impact in fighting impunity, deterring human rights abuses, promoting reconciliation and advancing sustainable peace.

The tribunal's failure to address the human rights abuses attributed to the RPA may have repercussions that will reverberate beyond Rwanda. One of the objectives for the tribunal's establishment was to fight impunity and to promote respect for human rights, not just in Rwanda but across the world. Its failure to provide impartial justice may encourage impunity by encouraging the perception that international criminal justice mechanisms only target the losers in conflicts and are powerless or not interested in dealing with crimes by perpetrators of atrocity who remain in power. The message conveyed by the ICTR is that there will only be consequences for egregious human rights abuses if a party to a conflict loses political power; those who retain or come to power after violent conflict are still guaranteed impunity for their crimes.

The tribunal's handling of the issue of crimes attributed to the RPA has exposed a fundamental weakness of the ad hoc United Nations tribunals. The rationale for international criminal justice is that independent and impartial international institutions are necessary to ensure that there is justice for crimes, especially crimes by leaders who bear the greatest responsibility for atrocity, which domestic courts are not able or willing to judge fairly and in good faith. There is abundant evidence that the RPA may have committed very extensive human rights violations during and immediately after the genocide. Rwanda's military establishment has always made it very clear, both by its actions and its categorical pronouncements, that it is not willing to try or allow the trial of its members by an outside jurisdiction for crimes that they are alleged to have committed during and immediately after the genocide. The ICTR was the only court that had both the legal authority and the power (backed by a resolution of the Security Council under Chapter 7 of the UN Charter) to investigate and try these crimes in good faith. The tribunal has failed in its mandate to investigate the alleged crimes. Knowing that the Rwanda government had no intention whatsoever to investigate and try the crimes in good faith, the management of the Office of the Prosecutor still made a political decision not to investigate and seek indictments for the crimes. In a national setting, a prosecutor who makes a politically motivated decision not to investigate and prosecute crimes that he or she is required by law to pursue would be liable to professional discipline by the relevant professional responsibility bodies or censure by appropriate national authorities according to law. Prosecutors of the ad hoc tribunals are, on the other hand, not accountable to anybody. There is no mechanism for seeking redress for arbitrary, politically motivated decisions that prosecutors of the ad hoc tribunals have made.

4.9 Conclusion

The ICTR is in the final stretch of its winding-up process and is expected to finally close its doors in 2014. The tribunal had a difficult beginning. Even organs and officials of the United Nations itself were critical of its weaknesses and shortcomings (ICTR 1999: p. 23; Møse 2005: p. 6). Some of these shortcomings were a result of internal weaknesses; others were attributable to external factors over which the tribunal had no control. The criticism that the tribunal faced on account of its shortcomings in its early years had a very profound impact in shaping attitudes towards the institution in Rwanda and beyond (Moghalu 2002). The tribunal would spend the rest of its existence trying to overcome the legacy and shortcomings of its early period.

Under the pressure of both the United Nations and the tribunal's various constituencies, including donors and the government of Rwanda, the tribunal undertook reforms to improve its capacity to carry out its mandate. These reforms, particularly during the presidency of Judge Erik Møse, went a long way towards addressing concerns about its performance. As a result, the tribunal has substantially been able to carry out its core mandate of bringing persons who bear the greatest responsibility for the genocide to justice. The tribunal has managed to bring to justice a very large number of the political, military and civil society leadership who would otherwise have escaped justice for responsibility for horrendous atrocities.

The ICTR has also played a very important role beyond providing justice for the victims of the Rwanda genocide. The work of the Rwanda tribunal, as well as its Yugoslav counterpart, has helped to consolidate the principle of individual criminal responsibility for egregious human rights abuses (Møse 2005: p. 15). The two ad hoc tribunals have advanced the development of international human rights law, international humanitarian law and international criminal law. The two tribunals helped to generate momentum for the establishment of the permanent International Criminal Court and their work has constituted a very significant development in the fight against impunity and in the development of the field of transitional justice. The experience of the ad hoc United Nations tribunals has demonstrated that the architecture of international criminal justice crafted by the international community to deal with the challenge of accountability for atrocity is capable of giving effect to principles enshrined in human rights instruments that had for decades been little more than wishful aspirations.

However, the diverse experiences of the ICTR and ICTY have also shown that the existing system of international criminal justice still has serious flaws and shortcomings. International criminal justice mechanisms do not as yet provide a sense of ownership over their processes to the societies that they are established to help. They depend unduly on state cooperation, and are impotent in the face of recalcitrant governments. These mechanisms are eager to take action against weak parties or losers of armed conflicts, but are unlikely to pursue perpetrators of atrocity who come to or remain in power after conflict in the absence of strong diplomatic support or pressure from the major powers of the West. These judicial institutions are vulnerable to external manipulation, and are often driven to make selective and partisan decisions and choices, depending on how the major Western powers that fund and control them choose to use their power and influence to shape their agendas. Their management is not accountable to any outside body or subject to any independent oversight, with the result that there is no mechanism for seeking redress when they make politically motivated choices and decisions.

The ICTR's legacy within Rwanda is mixed. The tribunal deserves credit for its success in bringing persons who bear the greatest responsibility for the genocide to justice. However, the trials were not intended to be an end in themselves. The tribunal was established, at least in part, to help Rwanda in its reconstruction and development process by promoting certain socio-political goals (Morrison *et al.* 2008: p. 682). The extent to which the tribunal's work has contributed to the achievement of these goals is a matter of vigorous debate both amongst Rwandans and scholars of Rwanda. The long-term impact of the tribunal's work in terms of the achievement of the socio-political objectives that underpinned the establishment of the tribunal (as well as Rwanda's other peace-building processes) is highly questionable.

5 National Prosecutions

5.1 Introduction

The Rwanda genocide was an experience that shook the very foundations of Rwandan society. The brutality and scope of the violence experienced in 1994 defied and still defies imagination or rationalization. Even finding words that can adequately describe the suffering of its victims is difficult. In the aftermath of violence of this nature, the necessity for justice was not a subject of contentious debate. Justice, all stakeholders agreed, was the very minimum that our society owed the victims. The question was, what form would justice take?

In the genocide's immediate aftermath, the wounds of the violence that Rwandan society had recently gone through were still raw. It was not politically feasible to respond to the victims' demand for justice by advocating any alternative short of dealing with the legacy of the violence according to the letter of the law. In 1996, the Rwanda government adopted a policy that aimed to pursue universal accountability for crimes that were committed in the context of the genocide through indiscriminate prosecution of all suspected perpetrators by the ordinary criminal justice system.[1] While the letter of the law was clear as to how the transgressions that the genocide involved should be dealt with, the complicating factor was that the genocide had attracted large-scale popular participation. The policy that the post-genocide government adopted of seeking to try and punish all suspected perpetrators still raised a number of questions. Was the genocide practically possible to achieve universal accountability for mass atrocity, especially where it involved large-scale popular participation? Could the country mobilize the necessary financial and material resources required to carry out investigations and trials on such a mammoth scale? Would the justice system have sufficient human resources to handle the genocide caseload? Did the available justice sector professionals have the expertise to deal with cases of such complexity effectively? Would they be able to investigate and prosecute the genocide and related crimes in accordance with basic human rights standards? Would the courts try the genocide cases fairly and in an impartial manner, or would the trials turn out to be instruments of the victor's justice? In short, did the criminal justice system have the capacity to investigate and try the genocide caseload fairly and effectively?

More importantly, the decision to reckon with the legacy of the genocide with a policy aiming at universal accountability raised the question of whether criminal prosecutions are an appropriate response to a situation of mass atrocity involving large-scale popular participation. Do indiscriminate criminal prosecutions in such situations necessarily advance the goals of transitional justice? Are criminal prosecutions alone adequate to address the needs of a society that has experienced mass atrocity, or do they need to be complemented with other non-legal alternatives?

This chapter discusses the process of trials of crimes relating to the genocide that have been undertaken by Rwanda's formal criminal justice system. The theoretical framework of the field of transitional justice in which these prosecutions are situated has been discussed in Chapter 1. The legal basis of the duty of states to prosecute violations of international human rights law and international humanitarian law were discussed at the beginning of the preceding chapter. The starting point of this chapter is an exploration of the challenges and constraints that Rwanda's initial attempts to address the legacy of the genocide through domestic criminal prosecutions faced and the various strategies that the post-genocide government adopted to promote its transitional justice goals through domestic prosecutions. The chapter evaluates the impact of these domestic prosecutions in advancing the government's transitional justice goals, the factors that account for the failure of these trials to achieve their original objectives, and the implications of the domestic prosecutions that Rwanda's courts have undertaken for the field of transitional justice. The chapter concludes with a discussion of the proceedings of the ICTR and courts of other states that have considered applications to transfer cases or requests to extradite genocide suspects for trial in Rwanda.

5.2 Challenges and Constraints to Achieving Fairness and Due Process in Prosecutions of the Rwanda Genocide

Rwanda's attempt to investigate and prosecute the genocide caseload through the ordinary criminal justice system was constrained by a multitude of challenges. The country had never had an independent and impartial system of administration of justice prior to the genocide (Van Lierop 1997; Human Rights First 1997). Commentators have variously described Rwanda's pre-genocide justice system as having been 'no more than a corrupt caricature of justice' (Schabas 1997), 'decrepit' (Human Rights Watch 2008: p. 1), and 'weak and flawed' (Amnesty International 2004: p. 5). A study that was commissioned by Rwanda's Ministry of Justice in 1992 concluded that the country's system of administration of justice was in an appalling state (Bouvier *et al.* 1992). The judiciary was understaffed, its personnel lacked the skills to perform their functions and the justice system lacked resources to function effectively. The judiciary was neither independent nor impartial: it was subject to the complete control of the Executive (Fierens 2005). The judiciary and law enforcement institutions lacked competence to perform their respective functions effectively (ACCT 1994; Fierens 2005). The genocide resulted in the virtual collapse of an already weak and discredited system of administration of justice (Schabas 1994; Strain and Keyes 2003: p. 110).

As a result of the war and genocide the courts, prosecution service and judicial police ceased operations. The prisons system had collapsed. Rwanda had never had a professional bar association. The country had no legal aid system (Drumbl 1998). There were no institutions or systems to provide professional education and training for the personnel of the justice sector institutions. The government needed to devise strategies to ensure that institutions such as the courts, prosecution service, judicial police and the prisons system resumed operations and to establish new institutions and systems such as the police, bar, legal education and training institutions and legal aid mechanisms that did not exist prior to the genocide.

Development of human resources was by far the most challenging of the many things that had to be done for investigations and prosecutions of the crimes that had been committed in the context of the genocide to proceed. Many staff of justice sector institutions were killed during the genocide (Amnesty International 2004: p. 6). Most of the staff that had survived the atrocities went into exile (Morris 1997). Justice sector institutions were all greatly understaffed with estimates that no more than 20 per cent of staff remained in Rwanda after the genocide (Schabas 1994). As of May 1996, only about 50 of the judges who sat in courts with criminal jurisdiction had returned to work (Human Rights Watch 2008: p. 12). By October 1994, only 14 of the more than 87 prosecutors who comprised the prosecution service prior to the genocide had returned to work (Vandegiste 1997: p. 9). An estimated 39 of the more than 193 members of the judicial police returned to work after the genocide (Vandegiste 1997). The functioning of the courts and the prosecution service was further handicapped by a lack of adequate support staff including clerks and administrative staff (UNOHCHR 1996). The prisons service had very few members of staff with the training and know-how to process the inflow of inmates (Neher *et al.* 1995: p. 30). The management of the country's prisons had been taken over by the military, whose personnel had no knowledge of the prison service's systems and procedures (ACCT 1994: p. 14).

Not only were justice sector institutions understaffed, the available personnel lacked the skills required to undertake the complex process of investigating and prosecuting the genocide caseload. Shortages of qualified and experienced personnel raised concerns about the fairness of the criminal justice system in general and the credibility of the process of judging genocide cases in particular (Amnesty International 2004: p. 7). Most of the personnel of the justice sector had minimal or no legal education or experience in their respective field (Bouvier *et al.* 1992). The number of qualified lawyers working in the courts and prosecution service during the period immediately after the genocide was about 20. A good proportion of these lawyers had no previous experience in the justice system (ACCT 1994: p. 7). A significant proportion of the lawyers who were recruited into the justice system had been trained in common law countries and were handicapped by a lack of knowledge of the French language (the language in which most of Rwanda's legislation and most legal commentary was written) (Schabas 1994) and lack of familiarity with Rwanda's civil law system.

The problems arising from the lack of necessary knowledge and technical capacity was compounded by poor infrastructure across the justice sector. The courts, prosecution service, police and the prisons service lacked basic infrastructure (Morris 1997). Buildings of the justice sector institutions had been damaged or destroyed during the war and genocide (UNOHCHR 1996: p. 6). Judges and other justice sector personnel had no courtrooms or offices to work from or to secure their records. The personnel of the justice sector institutions lacked accommodation and, as a result, many of them were unable to work in the areas to which they were posted (Neher *et al.* 1995: p. 18; UNOHCHR 1996: p. 6). The prisons system (comprising about 17 establishments across the country), in particular, had acute problems with a lack of appropriate infrastructure. The capacity of the prisons system prior to the genocide was estimated to have been between 12,000 and 15,000 (Human Rights First 1997; Vandegiste 1997: p. 15). The prisons system now had to accomodate a population many times that capacity, with prisons severely overcrowded. The number of persons being detained was increasing with every passing month. This number stood at around 40,000 in May 1995 (Neher *et al.* 1995: p. 15), 80,000 in September 1996 (Human Rights First 1997), 108,000 in May 1997 (Vandegiste 1997: p. 15) and 115,000 in August 1997 (Vandegiste 1997: p. 15). The combination of overcrowding and poor living conditions (including lack of proper sanitation, lack of adequate nutrition and lack of adequate medical care) led to very high mortality rates in the prisons system (UNOHCHR 1996: paras 43 and 46; Human Rights First 1997).[2]

The capacity of the justice system to deal with the genocide caseload was also hampered by an acute lack of essential financial and material resources. Not only had the infrastructure of justice institutions been damaged or destroyed during the conflict, vehicles, furniture and other equipment belonging to justice sector institutions had been looted during the last stages of the conflict. Members of the ousted government emptied the treasury before leaving the country. The country's economy had collapsed and the state was receiving little revenue from taxes. Institutions of the criminal justice system now lacked even the most basic requirements including office equipment and stationery (Neher *et al.* 1995: p. 17). The prosecution service and police lacked logistical support to enable them to send their staff to the field to carry out investigations (ACCT 1994: p. 14). The personnel of justice sector institutions lacked copies of the laws that they were supposed to consult and apply (Neher *et al.* 1995). Lack of financial and material resources made it difficult to recruit and retain personnel in the sector. Many of the members of staff whom justice sector institutions recruited and trained during the years after the genocide left for better paying jobs after completing their training (Human Rights First 1997).

The re-building of an effective and credible criminal justice system also called for a necessary but delicate process of disengaging the military of the victors from the machinery of justice. With the defeat of the government responsible for the genocide, all of its institutions (including central government and local government and the military, security and police services) ceased operations as their members fled to exile. The only cohesive and effective institution that exercised authority throughout the country after the departure of the old regime was the RPA. Its members assumed the powers and functions of local and central government institutions, including policing, pending the appointment of civilian officials. The army soon began making arrests and detaining genocide suspects.

When the new government finally began appointing new local government officials, these officials joined military personnel in undertaking arrests and detaining genocide suspects. Officials of military and local government organs continued to make arrests and to detain genocide suspects even after justice sector institutions resumed operations. The military often flouted the authority of judicial and law enforcement institutions. Decisions of the judiciary and prosecution service to release genocide suspects were often overruled or ignored by the military, which was in charge of detention facilities (UNOHCHR 1996: para. 108). The military often rearrested suspects that judicial officials released for lack of evidence or non-compliance with arrest procedures. Some of the suspects that the military rearrested became victims of enforced disappearances (ACCT 1994: pp. 11–12). Prosecutors, judges and civilian police were frequently subjected to interference and intimidation by the military (UNOHCHR 1996; Amnesty International 2004: p. 2). This interference contributed to the explosive growth of the prison population during the years after the genocide and was, to a large extent, responsible for the eventual failure of the criminal justice system in processing the genocide caseload.

Lack of security and fears for personal safety adversely affected the capacity of judicial and law institutions to investigate and prosecute genocide cases fairly and effectively. Judges, prosecutors and judicial police officers who made the decisions to release suspects on account of lack of evidence or non-compliance with the procedures set out in the Criminal Procedure Code were sometimes arrested and imprisoned by the military themselves (ACCT 1994: pp. 12–13; UNOHCHR 1996: para. 109). On occasions, some of the judges, prosecutors and members of the judicial police who overruled decisions of the military were killed (Human Rights First 1997). At least one defence lawyer, one of only a handful who were willing to represent genocide suspects at the time, is known to have disappeared during this time. Justice sector professionals, who made decisions that the military did not agree with, faced very grave personal risks, including death or disappearance. Witnesses in genocide cases were also exposed to security risks. As a result of the scale of the genocide, the government lacked the capacity to provide security for witnesses. Genocide survivors were often blamed by their communities for arrests of genocide suspects. Many witnesses were killed in efforts to suppress evidence implicating some perpetrators (African Rights 1996). The killing of genocide survivors with a view to suppressing evidence on the genocide continued to be a major problem for many years after the genocide (African Rights 1996; Parliament, Rwanda 2004).

One of the most difficult challenges that the justice system of Rwanda faced as it began the process of dealing with the genocide caseload was weak public confidence. A country's justice system cannot function properly and meet the legitimate expectations of citizens when it does not enjoy public confidence. At least a significant part of the Hutu population perceived the justice system as a tool of the new government, delivering victor's justice (Vandegiste 1997: p. 40). This lack of public confidence in the justice system was due to a number of factors, including residual prejudice resulting from anti-Tutsi propaganda by post-independence governments, incitement of anti-Tutsi violence and hatred during the genocide, guilt and group solidarity on the part of the perpetrators of genocide and their relatives and communities, human rights abuses that were committed by the RPA against Hutu civilians during the conflict, the arbitrariness of the mass arrests and detentions of genocide suspects that were carried out by the military in the wake of the genocide, the dehumanizing conditions in which the ever increasing number of genocide suspects were detained, the domination of the new system of administration of justice by members of the Tutsi minority, and the inability of the justice system to deal with the cases of persons accused of genocide within a reasonable time. All these factors contributed to enhancing the alienation of an already hostile and prejudiced population to the new government and its institutions (including judicial and law enforcement agencies) and policies. Lack of public confidence in the justice system had very important implications for the process of dealing with the genocide caseload. The population was not supportive of the work of investigative organs and judicial authorities. Much of the public refused to cooperate in identifying the persons who had committed atrocities (Vandegiste, 1997: p. 22). The task of identifying perpetrators was often left to genocide survivors, who knew least about what had happened during the genocide as they would have been in hiding or on the run.

5.3 Building Capacity to Conduct Domestic Prosecutions

5.3.1 Institutional development

A prerequisite for the implementation of the policy on accountability for atrocity that the post-genocide government adopted was to re-establish judicial and law enforcement institutions to develop their capacity to perform their functions. It was also necessary to set up additional new institutions, such as defence services, that were required for the effective functioning of the criminal justice system in general, and for the investigation and prosecution of the genocide caseload in particular. With a view to enhancing the capacity of the justice sector to process the genocide caseload, the government mobilized financial resources from donors such as Belgium, the United States, Germany, Canada and the Netherlands, the latter, by far the most generous in providing funding for human resource and infrastructure development and for acquisition of materials and equipment (Vandegiste 1997: p. 8). The support that donors provided was critical to enabling justice sector institutions to resume operations and to start processing the genocide caseload.

Lack of capacity to carry out criminal investigations was the most critical bottleneck in the justice system's handling of the genocide caseload. Under the Criminal Procedure Code, investigative functions were shared by the civilian judicial police and the gendarmerie. Both of these institutions operated under the supervision and direction of the prosecution service. The prosecution service had authority to undertake investigations on its own initiative and to take over investigations from the other investigative agencies at its discretion. In the aftermath of the genocide, neither the judicial police nor the gendarmerie was in a position to conduct a significant level of investigations of the genocide caseload (UNOHCHR 1996: para. 13). The government had to re-establish the two institutions and to build their capacity to investigate crime, particularly on the genocide caseload. A new gendarmerie, recruited from the RPA, was established (UNOHCHR 1996: para. 35). The judicial police was reinvigorated, with the recruitment and training of hundreds of new employees (UNOHCHR 1996: para. 13).

Access to legal representation is a critical element of the right to fair trial and access to justice in general.[3] The establishment of a bar to support the operations of the justice system and the conduct of genocide trials was a priority during this period. Legislation establishing the bar and regulating legal practice was enacted in 1997.[4] The legislation also provided for the establishment of a corps of paralegal judicial defenders who were entitled to practise before the courts of first instance, including the specialized chambers trying genocide cases (Vandegiste 1997: p. 8). The Rwanda bar was launched, with an initial membership of 44 members. Rwanda's bar was too small to provide legal services effectively to all persons accused of genocide. In any event, the majority of genocide suspects were too poor to afford the services of lawyers. Lack of legal representation for suspects and defendants put the credibility of genocide trials into question.

To address the need for legal representation for the defence in genocide cases, the government accepted an offer from Avocats Sans Frontières, a Belgian non-governmental organization, to provide legal aid in genocide trials using teams of lawyers from Francophone countries. However, Avocats Sans Frontières could at any one time only deploy around a dozen lawyers to assist defendants in genocide trials. This level of support was not adequate to meet the demands for legal services in relation to genocide trials. In order to enhance access to legal aid, the government reached an agreement with the Danish Centre for Human Rights to train and finance paralegals to provide legal advice and representation in genocide cases (Danish Centre for Human Rights 2000). An American organization called Legal Aid Rwanda provided pre-trial legal advice to genocide suspects. The services that the above and other non-governmental organizations provided helped to improve the quality and enhance the credibility of the genocide trials (Danish Centre for Human Rights 2004).

Rwanda lacked capacity to provide the education and professionals necessary to its immense human resource needs. Prior to the genocide the only avenue for professional training open to the personnel of Rwanda's justice sector was France's École Nationale de la Magistrature. Only 18 Rwandans had been admitted to the academy between 1966 and 1993 (ACCT 1994: p. 9).

Some donors and other international partners urged the government to seek the assistance of foreign lawyers to help the justice sector deal with the genocide caseload (Vandegiste 1997: p. 10). The government did not consider the use of foreign lawyers appropriate (Neher *et al.* 1995: p. 53) and instead opted to rely exclusively on national staff. An intensive programme was undertaken to recruit, train and equip nationals to handle the genocide caseload. Steps were taken to train large numbers of lawyers through the National University. Pending the availability of university-trained lawyers, the government embarked on a large-scale exercise to recruit, train and deploy new para-legal personnel for the justice sector. The number of students admitted to the law degree programme at the National University was dramatically increased, initially to over 400 students per year. Arrangements were made to recruit professors from bilingual, civil law countries to provide instruction to Anglophone students. As commencement of investigations and trials of genocide cases could not wait for the graduation of lawyers from the university, the government recruited high-school graduates or people with some years of university education, provided them with training and appointed them as judicial police, prosecutors and judges. Training of judicial investigators (organized and financed by the Belgian organization Reseau de Citoyens, RCN) began in early 1995 and programmes to train judges and prosecutors soon followed (ACCT 1994: p. 15). These training programmes were initially carried out by non-governmental organizations, particularly the RCN. In due course, the government established its own judicial training centre to provide continuing professional development to justice sector personnel.

The human resources development strategies that justice sector institutions adopted to deal with the challenge of investigating and prosecuting the genocide caseload have been criticized for a number of shortcomings, including the use of non-lawyers to prosecute and judge cases as complex as genocide (Cousineau 1996); the inadequacy of the training that was provided to the new recruits to the sector (the training, which lasted 3–6 months, is said to have been too short, considering the candidates' lack of prior legal education and experience in the justice sector and the complexity of the cases that they were expected to handle) (Cousineau 1996: pp. 176–8); lack of attention to building capacity for providing legal representation to genocide suspects; disproportionate representation of the Tutsi minority among the new recruits to the justice sector (labelled by some critics as a deliberate process of 'Tutsification' of the judiciary) (Cousineau 1997: pp. 176–8; Sarkin 1999); and lack of government policies to ensure retention of personnel (a very substantial proportion of the newly trained members of the staff of justice sector institutions would leave for better paying jobs after very short durations of service) (UNOHCHR 1996: para. 39).

These criticisms are not without justification. In retrospect, it is evident that the training that was provided to recruits to the various justice sector institutions may not have been adequate, given the complexity of the cases that judicial and law enforcement institutions were handling. The duration of the various training programmes should perhaps have been made longer. Some use should have been made of foreign lawyers during the process of rebuilding domestic capacities. Experienced foreign lawyers could have provided critical mentoring skills to new entrants to the justice sector. Strategies for capacity development for the justice sector should from the very beginning have included support for the development of capacity for legal representation of genocide suspects, to ensure equality of arms. Although the charges of deliberate 'Tutsification' of the judiciary are unjustified, as recruitment was genuinely based on merit,[5] greater attention should still have been paid to diversity issues. Some affirmative action steps should have been implemented to ensure that the justice system was adequately inclusive of all communities.

In spite of the above shortcomings, the approach to the development of human resources adopted by the justice system still appears defensible, even in retrospect. The approach offered the only prospect of commencing genocide trials with a minimum of delay. The use of non-lawyers for the investigation and prosecution of the genocide caseload was the only viable option for the government, given that tens of thousands of suspects were already in pre-trial custody. The reliance on Rwandan nationals to process the genocide caseload ensured national ownership, affordability and sustainability of the process of accountability for genocide.

5.3.2 Other strategies to promote respect for human rights in the prosecution of genocide

In addition to investing in institution building, the Rwandan government also undertook a wide range of other initiatives to enhance compliance by the institutions of the criminal justice system with basic human rights in the investigation and prosecution of genocide crimes.

5.3.2.1 Training police and military

One of the factors that contributed to large-scale arbitrary arrests of genocide suspects in the years immediately after the genocide was lack of knowledge of the laws and procedures governing arrest and detention on the part of military personnel. The members of the army and the new police (the gendarmerie), who were responsible for law enforcement in Rwanda after the genocide, had no police training or experience and were unfamiliar with laws governing the functioning of the criminal justice system and procedures governing arrest and detention of criminal suspects. With a view to reducing or eliminating arbitrary arrests and detention, the government organized programmes to provide training to the police and other members of the military on arrest and detention procedures (UNOHCHR 1996: para. 21). The programmes were fairly successful. By mid-1997, most arrests and detentions of genocide suspects complied with the provisions of the Criminal Procedure Code and were supervised by the prosecution service (Vandegiste 1997: p. 13).

5.3.2.2 Commissions de Triage

The large-scale arrests and detentions that the army and local government officials carried out after the genocide were extremely unpopular, especially within the Hutu community. The arrests and detentions were also very unpopular with the personnel of the judiciary and the prosecution service. On their own initiative or upon applications by some of the genocide suspects, judges, prosecutors and judicial police officials began to make orders for the release of some of the genocide suspects whose continued detention was considered unlawful. Decisions by the courts, the prosecution service or the judicial police to release some of the genocide suspects for lack of evidence or non-compliance with prescribed procedures invariably provoked a backlash from the military, who claimed that the releases of genocide suspects were motivated by bias, and driven by ethnic partisanship. The mutual distrust, that existed between the judiciary and prosecution service on one hand and the military on the other, reached such a crisis point that the Cabinet had to intervene and impose a solution as to how the problem of detentions that did not comply with the prescribed procedures should be dealt with. In October 1994, the Cabinet tried to resolve the impasse by establishing ad hoc screening commissions (*Commissions de Triage*).

The commissions, established at the level of each province, were composed of the local prosecutor and representatives of the military, the police and the civilian intelligence services. The objective of the commissions was to conduct a rapid screening of the prison population and to release those suspects against whom there were no cases with merit (UNOHCHR 1996; Vandegiste 1997: pp. 13–14). The establishment of the screening commissions was controversial and widely criticized by human rights organizations as unwarranted interference by the executive in judicial matters. The authority of the commissions was also strongly contested by members of the legal profession, especially in the judiciary and prosecution service. The commissions had no basis in law. They had no standard guidelines to guide their operations, no dedicated personnel and no fixed times for meetings. Most of the members of the commissions did not give the commissions priority, as the commissions were not their primary responsibility. The commissions lacked effective supervision. They also lacked cohesion and their members were often unable to reach consensus on the cases that they were considering (Amnesty International 2004: p. 4). The commissions proved to be ineffective in carrying out their mandate (UNOHCHR 1996: para. 74). The government tried to make the commissions more effective by decentralizing their functions to lower levels of territorial administration (by establishing the commissions at commune/district rather than prefecture/province level) and by setting up technical committees to support the commissions by carrying out investigations on their behalf. Not even these changes were enough to improve the performance of the triage commissions (UNOHCHR 1996: para. 74). The government finally abandoned use of the triage commissions in 1996.

5.3.2.3 Mobile Investigation Units ('Groupes Mobiles')

Following the failure of the screening commissions, the government next tried to address the problems of arbitrary detentions and the large backlog of pending genocide cases through the establishment of mobile investigation units that were known as *Groupes Mobiles*. The groups were established in 1997. The mission of the Groupes Mobiles was to carry out intensive investigations to help identify detainees against whom there was no adequate evidence and to release such detainees. The goal of the units was to contribute to reducing prison overcrowding and to expedite investigations of the genocide caseload in general. The Groupes Mobiles process was a great improvement on screening commissions. The groups were composed of members of the judicial police and gendarmerie, both of which had legal authority to carry out investigations, to order arrests and to release suspects in appropriate cases. The Groupes Mobiles operated under the coordination and supervision of the prosecution service as the law mandated (Vandegiste 1997: p. 14). The members of the groups were provided with appropriate short-term training. The groups were provided with adequate personnel and resources (including vehicles, fuel and allowances for investigators) to enable them to perform their functions. Decisions of the groups (with regard to choice of upholding or terminating the detention of genocide suspects) were based on evidence gathered from field investigations, as opposed to the arbitrary administrative decisions of the *commissions de triage*. However, even the Groupes Mobiles were ultimately unsuccessful in achieving the goal of significantly reducing the large number of genocide suspects in arbitrary pre-trial detention, mainly due to the very large size of the genocide caseload. The groups nevertheless made a very useful contribution to improving investigations of genocide cases.

5.3.2.4 *Guilty Plea and Confession Programme*

The government's next (and by far the most ambitious) strategy for improving the processing of the genocide caseload was a Guilty Plea and Confession Programme that was introduced by Organic Law 8/96 on the organization of prosecutions of genocide (Morris 1997: p. 689). The aim of the Guilty Plea and Confession Programme was to expedite the processing of genocide cases through confessions. The government hoped that the programme would expedite genocide trials by offering incentives (in the form of reduced sentences) to perpetrators to plead guilty. The reduction of sentence would depend on the category in which the offences a suspect was accused of were placed.[6] The programme was open to all suspects. However, category 1 suspects were not eligible for reduction of sentences in exchange for confession.[7] Admissibility of a plea of guilt and confession was conditional on full disclosure of all offences that a suspect had committed and details of the facts about the crimes and an offer of apology.[8]

Thousands of suspects responded to the invitation to join the Guilty Plea and Confession. However, the programme was not successful in expediting the investigation of genocide cases, nor in reducing the size of the prison population or reducing the backlog of pending genocide cases. The relative failure of the Guilty Plea and Confession Programme was due to a number of factors (Vandegiste 1997: pp. 23–5) including the lack of an effective strategy to educate prisoners about the programme; exclusion of category 1 suspects from the benefits of the programme (influential elites who were not eligible to join the programme discouraged other detainees from participation); the government's failure to separate detainees willing to confess from those opposed to the programme; lack of access to legal advice to clarify the advantages of joining the programme (Amnesty International 1997b); lack of trust in the good faith of the government to release prisoners who would plead guilty; fear that confessing to genocide would trigger civil liability and demands for reparations; lack of a witness protection programme; collective solidarity and group adhesion among prisoners; and concerns over the potential for retribution (Drumbl 1998). Drumbl (1998, 2004) and others have also argued that the Guilty Plea and Confession Programme's lack of appeal to the majority of the prison population was also attributable to political factors, including continuing adherence to the ideology of genocide (many who had participated in committing atrocities were not yet convinced that they had done anything wrong) and political calculations that the insurgents who were fighting to overthrow the new government during the late 1990s would regain power and release suspected perpetrators of genocide who were already in custody.

5.3.2.5 Group trials and 'itinerant' courts

Two other strategies that were adopted in an attempt to improve capacity for processing genocide cases were the adoption of a policy to try genocide cases in groups involving large numbers of suspects, and the conduct of trials in rural areas using mobile courts (Moussalli 1998). Although the genocide was centrally organized at the national level, the modalities of carrying it out were worked out at the local level in every area. Crimes of genocide that were committed in every locality were in effect almost always a joint criminal enterprise in which large numbers of people from the same area (assisted, in some cases, by persons from outside their communities) cooperated. Group trials saved time and resources by ensuring that evidence to prove crimes that were committed by a group in a given locality was adduced once in proceedings to which as many members of the group as possible were parties, instead of presenting the same evidence over and over again in separate individual criminal trials. However, the organization of group trials presented logistical challenges. Group trials involved many witnesses and travel to courts located far from the area where the majority of the witnesses lived. These trials lasted many days. Organizing, transporting and looking after witnesses for such trials was a difficult exercise. Justice sector institutions resolved the logistical challenges of conducting group trials by setting up mobile courts to hold trials in the communities where the crimes had taken place and where the majority of the witnesses lived. Group trials and mobile courts significantly improved the pace of genocide trials during the period just before the introduction of the Gacaca system.

A problem that was to pose continuing political, practical and legal challenges for the government in its pursuit of accountability was the lack of capacity within the prison system to handle the large prison population in accordance with accepted human rights standards. Reform of the prisons system was a very important part of enhancing respect for human rights in the process of investigation and prosecution of genocide. The government took a number of steps to improve the functioning of the prisons system. These measures included ending military management of the prisons system; re-establishment of a civilian, justice sector-supervised prisons system; recruitment of civilian prison guards; improvement of the skills of the newly recruited prisons personnel; increasing the operational capacity of the prisons system (through refurbishment and extension of existing facilities and construction of new detention facilities) (UNOHCHR 1996: pp. 15–16); establishment of separate and improved detention facilities for women and for juveniles; release of minors who were not criminally liable and the elderly and the very sick from custody;[9] improvement of conditions of detention, particularly medical care and nutrition, largely through the assistance of the

International Committee of the Red Cross; progressive transfer of genocide suspects from unofficial detention centres to regular prisons; and the establishment of systems and procedures in the judicial police and prosecution service to ensure that all new arrests and detentions complied fully with the relevant provisions of the Criminal Procedure Code. By and large, the changes that were carried out in the prisons system improved detention conditions in official prisons (Vandegiste 1997: p. 16). However, conditions in provisional detention centres located at district headquarters (that were referred to as 'cachots') remained very poor until they were closed.

Justice sector institutions faced very difficult challenges in organizing the investigation and prosecution of the genocide caseload from the very beginning. As a result of the above challenges which institutions of the justice sector in post-genocide Rwanda were faced with, implementation of the policy to pursue, try and punish all perpetrators of genocide was an uphill task. The government adopted a range of strategies to address these challenges. There was, however, no single blueprint for the rebuilding and reforming of the justice system that was followed consistently. The process of trying to enhance the capacity of the criminal justice system, to enable institutions of the sector to conduct genocide investigations and trials effectively and in compliance with basic human rights standards and norms was a continuous one. The processes of change and reform of the justice sector that were undertaken during the years immediately after the genocide were largely driven by the need to address social and political problems that were a direct result of the implementation of the policies on accountability for atrocity that the country had decided to pursue.

5. 4 Taking Stock of Rwanda's Domestic Prosecutions Process

Rwanda's initial choice of domestic prosecutions as the principal mechanism for addressing the legacy of the genocide was an unprecedented undertaking. No other society had ever attempted to enforce universal accountability for crimes committed in a context of mass atrocity involving popular participation. The policy on accountability for the genocide that the post-genocide government adopted led to the arrest and detention of an extremely large number of citizen suspects (Vandegiste 1997: p. 12; Amnesty International 2004). The policy of seeking universal accountability for the genocide was adopted at a time when Rwanda still lacked functioning justice sector institutions. As a result, tens of thousands of Rwandans were arrested and detained in arbitrary circumstances by unauthorized officials on the basis of unverified allegations made by victims or other citizens. In many cases, the suspects were detained without even any documentation indicating their identities and the nature of the charges against them (Moussalli 1998; UNCHR 1999). The majority of the suspects who were arrested and detained during the years immediately after the genocide had to wait for several years before they were informed of the specific charges against them and of the facts to support the charges (ACCT 1994: pp. 11–12; Cousineau 1996: pp. 183–5).

The challenges of organizing the investigation and prosecution of the crimes that were committed in the context of the genocide were daunting. Rwanda's judiciary and law enforcement institutions adopted various strategies, discussed in section 3 of this chapter, to enhance their capacity to investigate and try the genocide caseload. The government, with the support of donors, invested immense resources and political capital in the rebuilding of the institutions of the justice sector to enable them to perform their respective functions, with the handling of cases relating to the genocide at the very top of priorities. The strategies and programmes that the government pursued to build the capacity of judicial and law enforcement institutions to investigate genocide and related crimes were not in vain. Arbitrary arrests became the exception rather than the norm. New detentions increasingly complied with the applicable criminal procedure law. The trials that the domestic courts conducted progressively improved in quality (Vandegiste 1997: p. 19; Amnesty International 2000: pp. 3–5; Strain and Keyes 2003: p. 115). Defendants had greater access to legal representation and to their dossiers prior to trial. Defendants also had more time to prepare their defence. Judges more regularly granted applications for adjournments to enable accused persons to prepare their defence. Civil parties increasingly appeared in court to pursue claims to act as witnesses and to seek compensation. The genocide trials that the formal justice system conducted gradually became widely regarded as being generally fair (Vandegiste 1997: pp. 39–40).

In spite of the immense resources and efforts that the post-genocide government and donors devoted to enhancing the capacity to investigate and try the crimes that had been committed in the context of the genocide, Rwanda's justice system was still unable to cope with the huge genocide caseload. While it was generally acknowledged that the performance of the criminal justice system had improved and continued to improve (Amnesty International 1997b; Vandegiste 1997: p. 19, Moussalli 1998), the number of trials completed each year was still insignificant compared to the number of suspects awaiting trial (Pitsch 2003; Uvin 2003a; Tiemessen 2004). By the middle of 1998, Rwanda had well over 135,000 genocide suspects in detention (Office of the President, Rwanda 1999: para. 74; Amnesty International 2002b: p. 8). The scale of the genocide's violence and the high level of citizen participation in committing atrocities made it virtually impossible to investigate and prosecute all offences relating to the genocide through the formal criminal justice system. The genocide caseload was simply too big for Rwanda's fledgling criminal justice system to handle, regardless of the effort and resources that were invested. The justice system was so overwhelmed by the genocide caseload that even very serious crimes such as rape were not being investigated and prosecuted (Office of the President, Rwanda 1999: para. 73).

Not only were our attempts to bring alleged perpetrators of genocide to justice through the formal criminal system doomed to fail, they compounded the fragile situation in the country by occasioning grave violations of human rights on an extensive scale. Initially, there were several thousand children among the persons who were arrested and detained for crimes associated with the genocide. Many of the children were detained with adults (UNCHR 1999: paras 117–22). Some genocide suspects were detained in military facilities, to which neither the general public nor the Red Cross had access (Vandegiste 1997: p. 17; Amnesty International 2000: pp. 114–18). Detainees who were held in military-run detention centres and irregular detention facilities at district administration headquarters (cachots) were often subjected to maltreatment, including torture (Vandegiste 1997; Amnesty International 2004).

Detention conditions were appalling even in facilities controlled by civilian authorities. Detention facilities housed detainees far in excess of their intended capacity. The arrest and detention of tens of thousands of persons suspected of involvement in the genocide left Rwanda's prisons so overcrowded that many of the suspects did not even have room for standing, sitting or sleeping (Human Rights Watch 1995). Ventilation, lighting and sanitation conditions were appalling in most detention centres (Moussalli 1998: paras 50–55), food supplies were inadequate and medical care was unsatisfactory (Moussalli 1998). The cramped detention conditions encouraged the spread of deadly contagious diseases, including tuberculosis (Moussalli 1998). Most human rights organizations and observers (domestic as well as international) who monitored the conditions of Rwanda's detention facilities, particularly during the first five years after the genocide, were of the view that detention in these conditions constituted cruel, inhuman or degrading treatment or punishment (Amnesty International 1997a: p. 24; Moussalli 1998; Amnesty International 2000: para. 21). Neither the efforts of the government nor the support of its international partners were able to resolve effectively the problem of inhumane detention conditions. Several thousand suspects died in prison each year because of the cramped conditions, malnutrition, poor hygiene and lack of adequate medical care (UNOHCHR 1994a: paras 43 and 46; Human Rights First 1997). Preventable diseases, malnutrition and the debilitating effects of overcrowding reportedly resulted in the death of around 11,000 detainees during the period 1994–2001 (Amnesty International 2004: p. 4; Megwalu 2006: p. 27). More detainees died of preventable causes, including disease, malnutrition, poor sanitation and lack of adequate medical care than the criminal justice system was able to try each year (Amnesty International 1997a).

The failings of the criminal justice system in relation to the investigation and trial of cases relating to the genocide had many adverse, unintended consequences. The slow pace of the genocide trials was a source of deep frustration for all of the major stakeholders in the justice for genocide process, especially genocide suspects (Sarkin 2001: p. 149) and victims (Vandegiste 2001a: pp. 267–8).

The arbitrary, prolonged, indefinite detention of a very significant proportion of the members of one ethnic community in harsh conditions posed major political, social and economic problems for the government (Uvin 2003a). Hardly any Hutu family was without a family member or relative in detention on genocide-related charges (Organisation of African Unity 2000: paras 18.5–18.60). Many women and sometimes children spent much of their time commuting to detention centres to take provisions to detained relatives instead of working on farms or attending school. The withdrawal of so much labour from production increased poverty and hardship in many communities. The detention of a significant proportion of the Hutu men not only occasioned social and economic hardships for their families, but also led to strained relations between Hutu and Tutsi (especially genocide survivors) in every community (Sarkin 2000).

The failure to deal effectively with the genocide caseload undermined public confidence in the justice system (Sarkin 2001: p. 150; Vandegiste 2001a: p. 267; Habimana 2009). The arbitrary detention of so many members of the Hutu community also undermined initiatives to promote reconciliation between survivors and alleged perpetrators, between survivors and their communities and between the Tutsi and Hutu communities. The human rights abuses that the arrest and detention of tens of thousands of members of the Hutu community occasioned were largely perceived as persecution. The grievances of the Hutu community against the criminal justice system and the government in general were exacerbated by the government's unwillingness to address the question of human rights abuses that had been committed against members of the Hutu community during and after the events of 1994. The detention of so many members of the Hutu community and the government's failure to address the violence that the Hutu community experienced undermined the government's legitimacy in the perception of the majority of the population (Amnesty International 2004) and was detrimental to the success of efforts to stabilize the country.

The process of domestic prosecutions with which the post-genocide government responded to the genocide did not bring satisfaction to survivors either. In my experience of dealing with issues relating to accountability for the genocide, I found that survivors had their own concerns and grievances about the government's efforts to investigate and punish the genocide that included the failure to consult them adequately and to take their views into account as it developed policies on accountability for the genocide; the slow speed of genocide investigations and prosecutions; the failure of criminal prosecutions to disclose the truth about how the genocide was committed in their communities and who bore responsibility for it; the failure of the justice system to devote adequate resources to the investigation and prosecution of sexual violence (Human Rights Watch 1996); lack of effective witness protection mechanisms (African Rights 1996); lack of compensation and other means of reparation; and suspicions that the genocide was being exploited for political purposes by the government.

Rwanda's initial reliance on domestic prosecutions to address the legacy of the genocide failed to satisfy the yearnings of any of the stakeholders (the survivors and persons accused of genocide) for justice. The policy of seeking accountability for the genocide through indiscriminate criminal prosecutions was not effective in helping to promote the primary goals of transitional justice, namely establishing the truth, ensuring accountability, promoting reconciliation and providing effective reparation to victims and survivors. Instead of helping to advance the rebuilding of trust between victims and those they held responsible for their suffering, domestic prosecutions were instead having the effect of consolidating mistrust and entrenching grievances between victims and genocide suspects and their families and between survivors and their communities. The process of domestic prosecutions also undermined public confidence in the justice system and in the state as a whole and as such was detrimental to the long-term prospects for peace and stability.

By the end of the 1990s, the problem of how to manage the issue of accountability for genocide had reached a crisis point. While impunity for the crimes that had been committed during the course of the genocide was not an option, it was also evident to both the legal professionals who were involved in the day-to-day management of the crisis and the rest of the government that maintaining the status quo was equally untenable. A consensus developed across government that the approach of dealing with the aftermath of the genocide by investigating and prosecuting the crimes of all perpetrators through the formal criminal justice system was not workable. In view of the very large number of suspects who were already in detention, an alternative approach was imperative. The government needed to take urgent measures to address the adverse social, political and economic problems that the prolonged detention of such a large number of genocide suspects had given rise to (Graybill 2004). It was in acknowledgement of the fact that the formal justice system could not conceivably ever investigate and try the full genocide caseload in a timely, effective and fair manner that the government initiated the debates that ultimately led to the adoption of Gacaca as the principal mechanism of accountability for the genocide.

I have personally never been enthusiastic about Gacaca. I always had reservations about the process that I discuss in the next chapter. However, like many of my counterparts in government, I had by the end of the 1990s come to the conclusion that the policy that we had initially adopted (involving the indiscriminate pursuit, prosecution and punishment of all perpetrators) could not be implemented. After several years of intimate involvement in virtually all aspects of the process of pushing the process of domestic prosecutions forward (including policy development, legal reform, institutional development, management of prisons, capacity building and oversight of prosecutions of genocide), I had come to the realization that our judicial system could not handle the volume of cases that the genocide had occasioned. In the words of Schabas (1997), the whole endeavour was an attempt at 'Searching for Solutions to Impossible Problems'. Perhaps no judicial system has ever been designed to deal with crime involving such a high level of popular participation. Moreover, the adverse consequences that our uncompromising attempts to investigate and prosecute cases relating to the genocide had given rise to had led me to question whether, even assuming that it was possible to try all the crimes, such a course of action would lead to the realization of the transitional justice goals that we had in mind. At the time, my preference in terms of an alternative approach to accountability for the genocide was a combination of criminal prosecutions and a South African-style Truth and Reconciliation Commission. However, the idea of such a Truth and Reconciliation Commission was a non-starter, as amnesty still remained an anathema to the majority of the Tutsi community.

As a result of the progressive extension of the Gacaca courts' jurisdiction, Rwanda's formal criminal justice system has come to play only a relatively minor role in the country's framework for ensuring accountability for genocide. Nonetheless, the process of domestic prosecutions has had a profound impact on Rwanda's post-genocide reconstruction process. The process of domestic prosecutions affected tens of thousands of individuals directly (as they were arrested in arbitrary circumstances and detained in often appalling conditions for many years). The formal justice system also indirectly affected even more citizens, as the people who were victims of the above arrests and detention had families who cared about them and who were often affected materially, socially and pschycologically by the arrests and detentions. The process of domestic prosecutions shaped public perceptions about the government's commitment to human rights, democracy and the rule of law. It had an immense impact on relations between Rwanda's constituent communities. The experience of domestic prosecutions is a critical part of the legacy of Rwanda's transitional mechanisms.

In 2008, Rwanda enacted new legislation that transferred virtually all genocide cases that hitherto had remained in the formal justice system to Gacaca courts.[10] In future, the formal criminal justice system will only have jurisdiction to try genocide cases transferred from the ICTR and foreign jurisdictions and new cases of genocide which may come to light after the completion of the Gacaca process. The issue that arises with regard to genocide cases that will remain within the jurisdiction of the formal justice system is whether the system is now able to meet basic minimum requirements of a fair trial that it was not able to guarantee in the past.

5.5 Rule 11 bis Transfers and Extradition of Genocide Suspects from Third-Party National Jurisdictions to Rwanda[11]

Most if not all of the public officials and civil society leaders who were involved at the highest levels in the planning and direction of the genocide left Rwanda in 1994, along with many of the other perpetrators (REDRESS 2008a). In the years immediately after the genocide, we (as in the government of Rwanda) shared the popular perception of the ICTR as a mismanaged and ineffective institution. We believed that the ICTR was not making sufficient efforts to track and apprehend persons responsible for the genocide. As a result, the Rwanda government actively sought the extradition of genocide suspects from other states, in spite of indications that many states were reluctant to return genocide suspects to Rwanda at the time. As the ICTR became more effective at tracking and apprehending genocide suspects, the pursuit of suspects living in other countries ceased to be a pressing priority for the government. As Prosecutor General, I did not include the pursuit of genocide suspects living abroad as one of the priorities of my office. We were under immense pressure to get to grips with the huge internal caseload of genocide cases and comfortable to leave the pursuit of genocide suspects living abroad to the ICTR, with its superior resources, powers and diplomatic support.

As a result of several factors that are discussed in Chapter 4 (section 7, 'The Completion Strategy of the ICTR'), the ad hoc United Nations tribunals were compelled by the Security Council to draw up blueprints (Completion Strategies) for the winding up of their activities. In August 2003, the Security Council passed a resolution (United Nations 2003a) calling upon the ICTY and ICTR to take all possible measures to complete all trial activities at first instance by the end of 2008. The completion strategies had to ensure the completion of all investigations by the end of 2004, completion of all first instance trials by 2008, and completion of all appeals and closing down of the two tribunals in 2010. The completion strategies committed the tribunals to concentrating on the prosecution and trial of the most senior leaders responsible for the crimes within the tribunals' jurisdiction and to transfer cases involving intermediate or lower-rank accused persons to national jurisdictions. In order to ensure strict compliance with the goals set forth in the completion strategies, the Security Council mandated the presidents and the prosecutors of the tribunals to report their progress on implementation of the completion strategies every six months.

The ICTR presented the first version of its completion strategy in July 2003. The strategy sought to meet the requirements of the Security Council to prepare for the conclusion of the tribunal's mandate through two approaches. The first approach was to enhance the capacity of the tribunal to use available resources to increase its judicial output. The second approach was to transfer some of the tribunal's caseload to national jurisdictions (United Nations 2003e: Statement of ICTR Prosecutor, pp. 13–16; ICTR 2006d). The ICTR completion strategy envisaged that the court would complete its workload between 2007 and 2011 depending on a number of factors, including the possibility of a reduction in the number of pending investigations, the response of the Security Council to the tribunal's request for an increase in the number of *ad litem* judges, the creation of additional chambers or sections of chambers, the number of guilty pleas that would be made, success in the transfer of cases to national jurisdictions, as well as the progress of the Office of the Prosecutor in tracking fugitives.

The ICTR Completion Strategy proposed to transfer or transmit the cases of at least 49 genocide suspects to national jurisdictions. 'Transfer' refers to the sending of cases for which an indictment has already been issued by the tribunal to national jurisdictions. Transfer is subject to approval by chambers, following a motion filed by the Prosecutor. 'Transmission' refers to the handing over of case files relating to suspects who have not yet been indicted by the tribunal, and does not require approval by chambers. The 49 cases that the Prosecutor proposed to transfer or transmit to national jurisdictions included five cases of suspects who had already been indicted by the tribunal and were in the tribunal's custody, 12 indictees who were fugitives and 32 suspects against whom no indictments had been issued (ICTR 2010a). The Prosecutor outlined the criteria for determining the cases that the tribunal would retain and try and those that it would transfer to national jurisdictions. These criteria included the alleged status and extent of participation of the suspect in the genocide; the connection an accused individual's case may be alleged to have with other cases; the need to cover the major geographical areas of Rwanda in which atrocities were allegedly committed; the availability of evidence with regard to the individual concerned; the concrete possibility of arresting the individual concerned; and the availability of investigative material for transmission to a state for national prosecution (ICTR 2003b: p. 6).

When the Security Council compelled the ICTR to commit to a completion strategy that set 2004 as the cut-off date for investigations and the ICTR drastically scaled down the number of cases that it would investigate and try, it became evident that the majority of genocide suspects who had fled Rwanda in 1994 were now likely to escape attempts to hold them accountable. The Rwanda government was compelled to reconsider its strategies for ensuring that genocide suspects living in other countries could be brought to justice. Over the past decade, Rwanda has stepped up efforts to ensure that the cases that the ICTR would not try as a result of the limitations imposed by the ICTR's completion strategy would be transferred to Rwanda. Rwanda also stepped up efforts to secure the extraditions of persons suspected of involvement in the genocide from other countries. The government set up a Fugitives Tracking Unit, used the services of INTERPOL to locate genocide fugitives and started submitting extradition requests to various states. In 2007, INTERPOL established the Rwandan Genocide Fugitives Project, designed to facilitate arrests through coordination of the activities of Rwandan authorities and the national investigative authorities of countries where alleged genocide suspects are living.[12]

The related issues of extradition of genocide suspects from other countries and the transfer of cases from the ICTR to Rwanda have been extremely sensitive in and outside Rwanda. Rwanda shares jurisdiction to try the crimes that were committed during the course of the genocide with the ICTR. The government of Rwanda is of the view that it should have priority to try genocide suspects that the ICTR cannot bring to justice on account of the limitations imposed by its completion strategy. Similarly, the Rwanda government has until recently maintained that Rwanda should have the opportunity to prosecute and punish genocide suspects found in other states that are unwilling to prosecute and punish them. On the other hand, some commentators and critics of the government of Rwanda argue that neither the ICTR nor any of the states from which Rwanda seeks to extradite genocide suspects should send the suspects to Rwanda because the country's justice system cannot guarantee the suspects fair trial (RNC 2012). The views of commentators and government critics who oppose transfers of genocide cases to Rwanda are shared by many if not most of the Hutu community elites. The ICTR has focused exclusively on crimes that were committed by Hutu extremists against the Tutsi. As a result of the ICTR's failure to investigate and prosecute crimes attributed to the RPA, many if not most of the Hutu regard the ICTR as a one-sided and partisan institution that colludes with the government of Rwanda to deny the Hutu justice (FDU-Inkingi 2009; PDR Ihumure 2012).

The issues of transfer of ICTR cases to Rwanda and extradition of genocide suspects from states in which genocide suspects have settled or are found, remains controversial and raises several critical questions. Does Rwanda's system of administration of justice have the capacity to conduct the trials of such complex cases in a competent manner? Is Rwanda's justice system able to provide adequate fair trial guarantees for genocide suspects whose cases may be transferred from the ICTR or other states? Are Rwanda's courts going to provide an independent and impartial forum for the trial of the suspects? What legal or policy reforms should Rwanda undertake to satisfy the ICTR or states considering extraditing genocide suspects to Rwanda to ensure that their trials will be conducted in conformity with international human rights standards? What guarantees should the ICTR or national authorities of the states from which Rwanda is seeking extradition of suspects request from the government of Rwanda to ensure that the cases are tried fairly? What mechanisms can the ICTR or states considering transferring cases or suspects to Rwanda put in place to ensure that the guarantees of fair trial contained in Rwanda's laws or bilateral agreements between Rwanda and states that extradite genocide suspects to Rwanda are respected in practice?

When the first version of the completion strategy was initially presented to the Security Council, the major stumbling block to the transfer of cases to Rwanda was that Rwanda still had capital punishment on its statute books. The likelihood of transfer of genocide suspects to a jurisdiction which still retained the death penalty was a matter of concern to many, including the suspects (ICTR 2003b: p. 10). There were also concerns that the judiciary, the prosecution service and the bar of Rwanda may not have adequate skills to try the cases in accordance with international standards of fair trial (United Nations 2001b: Statement of the Prosecutor, p. 12; ICTR 2003b: p. 10) and that the judiciary in Rwanda was not independent (ILAC 2007: p. 20; Morrison *et al.* 2008: p. 699; Roth 2009b).

With regard to fair trial rights, there was concern that persons whose cases would be transferred to Rwanda would not have adequate opportunity for effectively defending themselves (ILAC 2007: pp. 19–20; Morrison *et al.* 2008: pp. 683–90). It would be difficult for accused persons to get local lawyers they could trust to represent them effectively. It was also thought that witnesses living in Rwanda would be too afraid to testify for the defence, and that defence witnesses living abroad would not be able to get the immunity and security guarantees necessary to enable them to testify in person in proceedings before Rwandan courts.

Rwanda carried out many legislative reforms that sought to address concerns over the capacity of its court system to try cases that may be transferred from the ICTR or other foreign jurisdictions, impartially and in full respect of the rights of the accused (Morrison *et al.* 2008: p. 707). It abolished the death penalty.[13] The government has carried out a restructuring of its entire justice system, creating new justice sector institutions that are better organized, staffed by better qualified personnel and better resourced (Human Rights Watch 2008). The government has also introduced new laws that seek to make legal processes more efficient and expeditious.[14] New laws have been introduced to regulate the conduct of trials of cases that may be transferred from the tribunal and other national jurisdictions.[15] A new prison that complies with international standards of detention was constructed to house detainees to be transferred from the tribunal. In order to demonstrate that this particular detention facility met international standards, Rwanda even offered to host persons who have been tried and convicted by the Special Court for Sierra Leone.

In response to the reforms of the justice system undertaken by Rwanda, the ICTR prosecutor exercised his discretion to transmit over 30 case files to Rwanda and one case to Belgium (United Nations 2005: Statement of the Prosecutor, p. 15). The transfer of cases of persons who had already been indicted proved more difficult. With the exception of Rwanda, most states that the prosecutor approached were unwilling to volunteer to accept the referral of cases from the ICTR (United Nations 2005a: Statement of the Prosecutor). The cost involved in investigations and prosecutions of cases referred by the ICTR was one of the factors that made states reluctant to agree to referral of ICTR cases to their own jurisdictions (Møse 2005: p. 3). Apart from Rwanda, only a few other states (France, Norway and Belgium) agreed to accept referrals from the ICTR. Two cases were transferred to France in 2007.[16] An attempt to transfer the case of Michel Bagaragaza to Norway and the Netherlands failed because of legal reasons.[17] Transfers to African countries were not possible either because of a lack of capacity or necessary legislation (REDRESS 2008a). Rwanda remained the only country which has unconditionally sought to receive cases from the tribunal (United Nations 2005a, 2009a) and the prosecutor made applications to transfer five cases to Rwanda.

The reforms that Rwanda had undertaken were not, however, adequate to allay concerns about the capacity of the country's justice system to guarantee the fair trial of the cases that might be transferred to it. The trial chambers turned down all five applications.[18] The chambers did not give consistent reasons for rejecting the Prosecutor's applications to transfer cases to Rwanda. However, the grounds for refusal of the applications that were cited in the decisions included lack of an appropriate legal framework for the prosecution of certain offences created by the tribunal's statute, risk of punishment that violated the right of the accused not to be subjected to 'cruel, inhuman or degrading punishment', concerns about the risk of abuse of certain aspects of the right to fair trial and concerns regarding the independence of the judiciary in Rwanda.

In the Hategekimana case,[19] the trial chamber indicated that one of the factors that led it to deny the application for referral was that it was not clear that Rwanda law criminalizes command responsibility, one of the modes of criminal participation with which the accused had been indicted. All the decisions held that the penalty of imprisonment with 'special conditions, including solitary confinement' that the accused were liable to if they were to be transferred to Rwanda constituted 'cruel, inhuman or degrading punishment', which is prohibited under the Convention against Torture. With regard to fair trial rights, the chambers were not satisfied that the accused would enjoy 'equality of arms' in preparing and presenting their defence. In particular, the chambers indicated that they were not satisfied that the accused would be in a position to call witnesses residing in and outside Rwanda to the same extent and in the same manner as the prosecution. The chambers acknowledged that the defence may encounter problems in obtaining witnesses inside Rwanda because they might be too afraid to testify and witnesses living outside Rwanda would not have adequate guarantees to enable them to travel to testify in Rwanda. The trial chamber in the Munyakazi decision[20] also denied the transfer on the ground that, in its view, Rwanda does not respect the independence of the judiciary judges. A judge sitting alone on a transferred case would be particularly susceptible to external pressure, the chamber in the Munyakazi case said.

The appeals chamber confirmed the five decisions, but narrowed down the grounds upon which the applications were rejected. The appeals chamber upheld the refusal to transfer the cases only on the grounds that persons transferred to Rwanda risked being sentenced to life imprisonment in solitary confinement and that there were problems in securing the testimony of defence witnesses. Other grounds that had been advanced by the defence and human rights NGOs that appeared *amicus curiae* in the proceedings (including claims that Rwanda's law did not recognize the concept of criminal enterprise, that Rwanda's judiciary lacked independence and that there was risk of torture) were rejected by the appeals chamber.

The decisions of the trial and appellate chambers to turn down applications to transfer cases to Rwanda initially threw the tribunal's completion strategy into disarray. Rwanda responded to the denial of the prosecutor's applications for referral of the five above mentioned cases by carrying out additional legislative reforms. In May 2009, Rwanda amended its law on the transfer of cases from the ICTR and other jurisdictions with a view to addressing the concerns that the five decisions had raised.[21] The amendments abolished the practice of solitary confinement, limiting the maximum penalty to life imprisonment. The law provided that no person would be criminally liable for anything said or done in the course of a trial, subject to relevant laws on contempt of court and perjury. The amendments also authorized delivery of testimony outside Rwanda by video-link or in person before a foreign judge or a commissioner designated by Rwandan courts, to address the concerns of defence witnesses who did not feel secure to travel to Rwanda to testify in person. The government also reinforced its witness protection programmes, by creating separate programmes for the prosecution and for the defence witnesses.

On the basis of the additional reforms that Rwanda had undertaken, the ICTR prosecutor filed new requests for the transfer of the cases of Fulgence Kayishema and Charles Sikubwabo in October 2010. The first of the second round of Rule 11 bis applications for referral of cases to Rwanda to be confirmed was Uwinkindi. The appeals chamber approved the transfer of Uwinkindi to Rwanda on 28 June 2011.[22] The court based its decision to approve the referral of the Uwinkindi case on the changes that Rwanda had made to its laws in respect of the issue of solitary confinement, evidence that Rwanda had adopted measures bringing conditions of detention in line with the guidelines set by UN General Assembly Resolution 43/173 (United Nations 1988), adoption of new laws regarding witness immunity as well as the creation of a new witness protection programme. The court ordered that the trial of the case and conditions of detention should be monitored by the African Commission on Human and Peoples' Rights. The ICTR has since approved the transfer of an additional seven cases to Rwanda.[23] Thus the battles over the transfer of ICTR cases to Rwanda finally and decisively resolved in the Rwanda government's favour.

5.5.1 Extradition of genocide suspects from other states

The Rwanda government's efforts to secure extradition of genocide suspects from other states have until recently been largely unsuccessful. French courts have blocked extradition of genocide suspects to Rwanda in a large number of cases.[24] Courts in Switzerland, the United Kingdom, Germany and Finland have similarly blocked the extradition of genocide suspects to Rwanda. The decisions of the courts of various over rejecting Rwanda's extradition requests have generally been based on concerns countries lack of judicial impartiality and independence and the risk of violation of fair trial rights.

However, the Rwanda government's push to secure extradition of genocide suspects from other countries is now gathering momentum. In 2009, the Supreme Court in Norway upheld a decision of a lower court authorizing the extradition of genocide suspect Charles Bandora[25] to Rwanda to face charges in connection with the 1994 genocide. Canada and the United States have used immigration proceedings to deport genocide suspects to Rwanda. The United States has already transferred two genocide suspects to Rwanda.[26]

In January 2012, Canada finally gave effect to a decision of the Supreme Court paving the way for the deportation of Leon Mugesera[27] to Rwanda.

An extradition request to Sweden in connection with the case of Sylvere Ahorugeze has led to a significant breakthrough in Rwanda's efforts to secure extradition of genocide suspects from European countries.[28] Ahorugeze, a former head of the Rwandan Civil Aviation Authority, arrived in Denmark in 2001 and was granted refugee status. Some time after September 2007, the Rwandan authorities requested his extradition from Denmark to answer charges of involvement in genocide and crimes against humanity. The Rwanda government failed to provide Denmark with satisfactory evidence in support of the extradition request, and the Danish authorities did not respond to that request. In July 2008, Ahorugeze travelled to Sweden, where Swedish police arrested him in compliance with the international alert and warrant of arrest that had led to his earlier arrest in Denmark.

In August 2008, the Rwandan prosecution service formally requested Ahorugeze's extradition from Sweden so that he could be prosecuted for genocide, murder, extermination and involvement with a criminal gang. A Swedish court authorized Ahorugeze's detention on suspicion of genocide. Following the prosecutor's opinion favouring extradition, the Supreme Court concluded that there was no general legal obstacle to sending Ahorugeze to Rwanda to stand trial on charges of genocide and crimes against humanity. The Supreme Court added that it assumed the Swedish government would consider further information before it took its final decision whether to extradite. Ahorugeze challenged Sweden's decision to extradite him to Rwanda before the European Court of Human Rights, claiming that if extradited to Rwanda he would risk being tortured or otherwise ill-treated or would be at risk of persecution because he was a Hutu, in violation of Articles 3 and 6 of the European Convention on Human Rights which prohibit inhuman or degrading punishment and protect the right to a fair trial, respectively. On 27 October 2011, the European Court of Human Rights (ECHR) decided the *Ahorugeze* v. *Sweden* case, in which it was held that the extradition of Ahurogeze to Rwanda would not violate Articles 3 or 6 of the European Convention on Human Rights. In this case, the ECHR set a high standard for finding that an extradition violates Article 6 of the European Convention on Human Rights. The court set the 'flagrant denial of justice standard' for prohibiting extradition under Article 6, and determined that, given Rwanda's recent legislative reforms, the suspect would not face the risk of an unfair trial.

The *Ahorugeze* v. *Sweden* case was influenced by the Uwinkindi and Bandora cases, in which a trial chamber of the ICTR and the Supreme Court of Norway had approved the transfer or extradition of genocide suspects for trial in Rwanda. The *Ahorugeze* v. *Sweden* decision was confirmed on appeal.[29] The impact of the ECHR's decisions on Ahorugeze personally is uncertain. The Swedish Supreme Court released Ahorugeze from detention on 27 July 2011 and he returned to Denmark. It is unclear whether Denmark will now respond favourably to Rwanda's request for Ahorugeze's extradition. It is expected, however, that the ECHR's final decision in the *Ahorugeze* v. *Sweden* case will have a far reaching impact on Rwanda's large number of extradition requests that are now pending before various states, particularly in Western Europe. Governments of states that are hosts to genocide suspects are likely to prefer extraditing suspects to Rwanda instead of undertaking trials by their own courts based on the principle of universal jurisdiction. The ECHR judgment may also help to speed up the conclusion of extradition treaties with Rwanda where treaties are a precondition for extradition.

Many of those who bear great responsibility for the Rwanda genocide remain at large (REDRESS 2008a). In order to fight impunity in Rwanda, it is necessary to bring these perpetrators to justice, either in Rwanda or in the countries where they have settled. Most of the states that are hosts to persons suspected of involvement in the genocide have demonstrated little political will to prosecute. It is appropriate that persons accused of involvement in the genocide should be transferred or extradited to Rwanda where host countries are unable or unwilling to try the crimes for which they stand accused. However, effective mechanisms need to be put in place to ensure that genocide suspects transferred or extradited to Rwanda can receive a fair trial.

Commenting on the subject of Rule 11 bis transfers of ICTR cases to Rwanda, Schabas (2009c: p. 58) writes:

> The transfer proceedings demonstrate the potential for synergy that exists between international and national criminal justice systems. There can be no doubt that in terms of justice in Rwanda, the whole process has been extremely salutary. The death penalty has been abolished, and not only for the transfer cases but for the country as whole. The applications for transfer have provided an important stimulus to Rwanda to make improvements in a range of areas, including prison conditions and the training of judicial personnel. They have heightened the awareness within the country of the importance of a truly independent and impartial judiciary. This may have further benefits along the line, because courageous and activist judges will stimulate other reforms, and provide a foundation for greater democracy, as they have done in many developing countries.

There is no doubt that Rwanda's justice system has benefited from the reforms that the country has undertaken in an attempt to meet the requirements for Rule 11 bis transfers. The judiciary now benefits from the legal framework, technical skills, and infrastructure and material resources that have been put in place to build domestic capacity to conduct trials of genocide suspects who may be transferred from the ICTR or extradited from other states. However, the critical issue at stake in the process of determining whether extraditions of Rule 11 bis transfers to Rwanda are appropriate is not whether there are the laws on Rwanda's statute books that guarantee that the right to fair trial, criminalization of torture and the independence of the judiciary, but whether these guarantees are respected in practice. The decisions of the ICTR and ECHR that have paved the way for Rule 11 bis transfers and extraditions to Rwanda have dealt with this issue only superficially, if at all.

The degree to which a country's judiciary is autonomous and free from external influence cannot be determined independently of the country's general human rights situation. The human rights situation in Rwanda does not protect the judiciary from external interference or pressure. The country's political system is completely dominated by the ruling party, the RPF (Straus and Waldorf 2011a). The party itself is controlled by the military and security services and it exercises absolute control over all branches of government, including the judiciary. All mid and senior level appointments to public office, including appointments to the judiciary, are made by organs of the ruling party, after unauthorized vetting by the security services. The military and security services are able to control appointments to all significant public offices, including appointments to the judiciary, through the above-mentioned vetting processes. State organs such as the Senate and the Superior Council of the Judiciary that appoint judges only ratify decisions that have already been made internally by the party leadership. The vast majority of Rwanda's judges are active members of the party. Judges are compelled to pay financial contributions to the party and to participate in senior level party meetings and other activities. Judges, like other party members, are subject to the disciplinary mechanisms of the party. The party ensures that the primary obligation of the members, including judges, is to the party, rather than to the state or the people. The party removes public officers, including judges, from offices at will.[30]

In Rwanda, the president and the security services sometimes overrule decisions of judicial institutions.[31] Judges who do not toe the line are removed from office.[32] Not only are the courts powerless to protect citizens from abuse of power, they are used to persecute opposition leaders and government critics.[33] The government of Rwanda has enacted laws (Example: Law No. 18/2008 Relating to the Punishment of the Crime of Genocide Ideology) that stifle the exercise of the rights of freedom of expression and political participation under the guise of fighting the crimes of genocide ideology, divisionism, sectarianism and endangerment of state security (Amnesty International 2011). These anti-democratic laws are strictly enforced through a compromised judiciary. The military and intelligence services of the Rwanda government often arbitrarily arrest persons perceived as opponents or critics of the government and detain them incommunicado in secret detention facilities where they are denied access to legal representation, medical treatment and visits by family members.[34] The military and intelligence services are also responsible for torture,[35] enforced disappearances[36] and extra-judicial executions (Amnesty International 2011). State officials even organize extra-judicial killings of government opponents in foreign countries.[37] Members of the military and officers of security agencies who commit human rights violations against civilians or fellow officers enjoy absolute impunity.[38]

The ICTR, the ECHR and government authorities in countries such as the United States, Canada, the United Kingdom, Sweden and Norway are willing to sanction the transfer of genocide suspects for trial in Rwanda merely on the basis of the reforms of laws that Rwanda has carried out and diplomatic assurances. Respect of the right to fair trial does not depend on the mere existence of laws guaranteeing respect of the right to fair trial, but rather on the actual respect of these rights in practice. The Rwanda state places very severe limitations on the free exercise of civil and political rights, including the right to fair trial in other cases. The persons whose cases the ICTR seeks to transfer to Rwanda or those whose extradition from other countries Rwanda requests are often regarded in Rwanda as being among the leadership that organized and directed the genocide in various capacities. These suspects have been the objects of very extensive adverse publicity in Rwanda. Rwanda's judiciary is legally independent but vulnerable to manipulation in cases in which the executive has an interest. While it is possible to have a fair trial in criminal cases that are not politically sensitive, fair trial cannot be guaranteed in cases involving defendants considered opponents or critics of the current government. There is a very great risk that genocide suspects transferred to Rwanda could be victims of unfair trials. There are legitimate grounds for concern that the Rwanda judiciary may not be able to conduct independent and impartial trials of persons whose cases are transferred from the ICTR or of those who may be extradited from other states. The failure of ICTR decisions relating to applications for Rules 11 bis transfers to Rwanda to recognise that the domination of the judicial system by one group in a society which is deeply divided, particularly along ethnic lines is a material factor in determining the risk of miscarriage of justice is a very grave shortcoming.

Ongoing efforts to secure extradition of genocide suspects to Rwanda third-party states are not willing to prosecute the crimes attributed to the suspects are laudable. Mechanisms should be put in place, however, to prevent the miscarriage of justice in the trials of cases of suspects transferred from the ICTR or extradited from other states. The most effective mechanism for ensuring a fair trial in these cases would be to set up a hybrid tribunal similar in structure to the War Crimes Chamber of the State Court of Bosnia and Herzegovina.[39] The ICTR and states considering transfer or extradition of genocide suspects to Rwanda should consider conditioning such transfer or extradition on the inclusion of foreign judges on panels of the Rwanda High Court that will try the cases in question. This would give Rwanda the opportunity to bring the suspects to justice while at the same time assuring the suspects, the ICTR or the states extraditing the suspects that the cases in question are tried fairly and impartially. I believe the government of Rwanda would agree to this condition if it were the only option for ensuring that genocide suspects are returned to stand trial in Rwanda. The inclusion of foreign judges on Rwanda's war crimes court would not now be as politically objectionable as it was immediately after the genocide; Rwanda has already set a precedent of using foreign judges by hiring expatriate judges to sit on its commercial courts.

5. 6 Conclusion

Rwanda initially attempted to reckon with the legacy of the genocide principally through domestic prosecutions. The country's transitional justice policy aimed at universal accountability through the prosecution of each and every alleged perpetrator by the ordinary criminal justice system. The ambitious attempt to ensure accountability for genocide through a policy of indiscriminate investigations and prosecutions of crimes associated with the genocide was undertaken in the face of many daunting challenges, including weak institutions, destroyed infrastructure, lack of human resources with appropriate skills and financial constraints. Rwanda adopted a variety of strategies and programmes to address these challenges. The strategies that Rwanda implemented to build capacity to prosecute genocide and related crimes helped to improve the quality of trials, but were unsuccessful in dealing effectively with the large volume of cases of genocide suspects who were in custody. As a result, the handling of the cases of the vast majority of persons accused of genocide occasioned grave violations of fundamental human rights norms. The formal criminal justice system was neither able to deliver justice for the victims of genocide in a timely manner nor to guarantee respect of the right to fair trial for persons suspected of genocide. The country's attempt to address the legacy of the genocide by mass prosecution of alleged perpetrators not only proved unworkable, but also had unintended consequences with significant adverse social and political implications.

Rwanda's ambitious but ultimately unsuccessful attempt to achieve universal accountability for genocide through criminal prosecutions in the ordinary criminal justice system has at the very least raised very strong doubts about the propriety of indiscriminate prosecutions as a tool for promoting the goals of transitional justice in situations of mass atrocity, especially mass atrocity involving large-scale popular participation. The experience of the process of domestic prosecutions undertaken by Rwanda to address the legacy of the genocide suggests that universal accountability may not be feasible or even desirable in situations of atrocity involving large-scale popular participation, and that in such circumstances, domestic prosecutions may need to be complemented by non-prosecutorial mechanisms to serve better the goals of transitional justice. At the end of the 1990s, Rwanda adopted one such mechanism: Gacaca became the primary process by which Rwanda would reckon with the legacy of the genocide. The next chapter discusses the Gacaca process and the extent to which it has addressed the shortcomings of criminal prosecutions in the framework of Rwanda's transitional justice architecture, if at all.

6 Seeking Alternative Accountability Mechanisms

The Gacaca Courts

6.1 Introduction

The post-genocide government of Rwanda adopted the Gacaca courts as the principal mechanism of accountability for the genocide after coming to the conclusion that domestic prosecutions in the formal criminal justice system were not an appropriate approach to the realization of its transitional justice goals. The Gacaca courts were formally closed in June 2012. The government has staked its authority and legitimacy on Gacaca as the cornerstone of its peace-building programme. Since its adoption, Gacaca has caught the imagination of scholars and policy makers across the world, many of whom have embraced it as an innovative and practical blend of retributive and restorative justice that could legitimately complement the formal criminal justice system in promoting the goals of transitional justice (Ironside 2002; Wierzynska 2004; Megwalu 2006). Gacaca has also been widely criticized for a wide range of shortcomings (Sarkin 2001; Amnesty International 2002a, 2002c; Waldorf 2006b). Despite this strong criticism, the Gacaca system maintains a devoted following of supporters among scholars, development practitioners and policy makers (Daly 2002a: p. 362; Borocan 2004: p. 399; Wierzynska 2004; Clark 2007, 2010). Some of Gacaca's supporters have gone so far as to suggest that it represents a possible model for other transitional societies that have to deal with legacies of past human rights abuses (Harrell 2003; Lahiri 2009). The adoption of Gacaca as Rwanda's primary mechanism of accountability for atrocity raised a number of issues: Does it have any advantages over criminal prosecutions as an instrument of reckoning with the legacy of the violence that Rwanda experienced during the 1990s? Does it have the capacity to deliver the objectives that it was designed to promote? Does it offer any lessons as to how societies that have previously suffered grave human rights abuses can reckon with such abuses? What implications does the experience of Gacaca have for the role of traditional justice mechanisms in the framework of transitional justice?

The role of justice mechanisms based on custom, tradition and social norms in transitional justice in general has been discussed in Chapter 1. This chapter discusses Gacaca, the modified version of the neo-traditional Rwandan justice mechanism adopted by Rwanda as its primary mechanism of accountability for genocide and other crimes that were committed between 1990 and 1994. It explains the structure, functions, powers and procedures of the remodelled Gacaca as the principal mechanism for reckoning with the genocide's legacy. The chapter then discusses the implementation of Gacaca, and assesses both its positive outcomes as well as its weaknesses, and examines the extent, if any, to which Gacaca has succeeded in helping Rwanda achieve its transitional goals. The chapter concludes with a review of Phil Clark's work on Gacaca, especially the book *The Gacaca Courts, Post-Genocide Justice and Reconciliation in Rwanda – Justice without Lawyers* (2010), which challenged all previous scholarship on Gacaca as deeply flawed and reflects on Gacaca's lessons for transitional justice.

6.2 The Gacaca Courts in Rwanda: Origins, Organization, Functions and Competences

6.2.1 Origins

The inspiration for the establishment of Rwanda's Gacaca was a traditional conflict resolution mechanism of the same name. Rwanda's pre-colonial history is unwritten and much of it is contested. Information relating to traditional Gacaca is not an exception to this reality (Molenaar 2005: p. 13). However, existing literature suggests that there are some characteristics of traditional Gacaca that most writers on the subject agree upon, characteristics that Gacaca shares with the traditional mechanisms of justice of many other African societies.

Traditional Gacaca dealt with disputes in accordance with customary law and practice, instead of written laws. Gacaca were non-permanent and ad hoc arrangements (Amnesty International 2002b: p. 20). Their procedures were flexible and informal. Disputes were usually adjudicated by elders who usually enjoyed respect within the community (Tully 2003: p. 395). The members of these panels were men; women were excluded unless they happened to be claimants or defendants (Borocan 2004: p. 376). The composition of the Gacaca varied from case to case, depending on the choice of the parties (Haile 2008: p. 33). Submission of disputes to Gacaca mediation or arbitration was voluntary. Gacaca did not have powers to dispense justice in cases of serious crime (Molenaar 2005: p. 16).

The chiefs or the king exercising judicial power tried serious matters such as murder, stock theft or conflicts involving senior public officials (Tully 2003: p. 395). Traditional Gacaca mainly dealt with civil matters such as succession, land disputes, claims for compensation for loss of crops destroyed by livestock, and general family relations between members of a particular community (Mibenge 2004; Tiemessen 2004). The elders who presided over traditional Gacaca were, within certain boundaries, free to determine the sanctions that best served the interests of the community. Decisions were consensual and represented a compromise between the collective and individual interests (Corey and Joireman 2000: p. 89; Amnesty International 2002b: p. 11). The community considered guilt for the transgressions to extend to the accused person's family. Sanctions resulting from the disputes typically involved payment of compensation. The elders who acted as judges or arbiters had no power to impose prison sentences or other forms of punishment (Meyerstein 2007: p. 472; Haile 2008: p. 33). Disputes that Gacaca could not resolve were referred to chiefs. Problems that chiefs could not resolve could be referred or appealed to superior chiefs and ultimately the king. Gacaca could also be called upon to assist criminal courts in investigating or ascertaining evidence. Social pressure was the principal motivation for compliance with the decisions of Gacaca. The objective of the process was to repair or sustain social peace, cohesion and order, after sanctioning the violation of shared values, and to re-integrate the offender into the community (Tully 2003: p. 395; Borocan 2004: p. 376; Graybill 2004: p. 1123; Karekezi *et al.* 2004: p. 73; Mibenge 2004: p. 413; Tiemessen 2004: p. 61; Molenaar 2005: p. 13).

Gacaca was never static. It is an organic, dynamic system that has undergone changes throughout the centuries of its existence (Clark 2007). Gacaca survived the advent of colonialism and continued to function side by side with Western-style courts applying written, non-customary law (Graybill 2004: p. 23; Clark 2007: pp. 775–80; Meyerstein 2007: p. 472). However, the role of Gacaca in Rwandan society was weakened during the colonial period, with the introduction of Western laws and a Western judicial system and an enhanced role for chiefs appointed by the government (Molenaar 2005: pp. 11–18; Longman 2006a). During the post-independence period, Gacaca became more formal, as most of its traditional functions were taken over by local government officials who in certain instances replaced community elders as the arbiters of disputes between members of the community (Megwalu 2006). Forms of Gacaca continued to be practised after the genocide, as local administrators brought community members together to resolve disputes over property as refugees returned to the country (Longman 2006a: p. 13).

The form of Gacaca that Rwanda has adopted to judge genocide cases differs greatly from the traditional Gacaca (Sarkin 2000: p. 119). Unlike traditional Gacaca, the new Gacaca was created by written laws and is an integrated part of the formal state system of administration of justice. It has applied state law instead of custom and relies on the coercive powers of the state instead of social control to function. It has dealt with very serious crimes. It has had formal rules of procedure and was not as flexible as the traditional counterpart. The new Gacaca has had powers to impose penal sanctions, whereas the traditional form merely awarded compensation as a remedy. The old Gacaca was purely restorative; the new has combined restorative and retributive justice functions. Under the new Gacaca, the consent of the parties to the process has been irrelevant, as appearance is compulsory not only for the accused but for the public at large (Molenaar 2005: p. 13; Haile 2008: p. 33).

6.2.2 Organization, functions and competences

Gacaca courts were initially established by Organic Law 40/2000 that came into force on 15 March 2001.[1] Like Organic Law 8/96, Organic Law 40/2000 still grouped suspected perpetrators of genocide and related offences into four categories.[2] Organic Law 40/2000 provided that all genocide-related cases, with the exception of cases involving the new Category 1 offences, would henceforth be tried by Gacaca courts.[3] The prosecution service would still have the power to investigate genocide and related crimes, but it would be required to verify whether the cases it was investigating had not been heard or determined by any Gacaca tribunal.[4] The prosecution service would have to submit all dossiers that it investigated to the competent Gacaca court.

Gacaca courts have been recognized as fully-fledged judicial institutions under Rwandan law.[5] The courts were organized in a hierarchy based on the territorial organization of the country.[6] Organic Law 40/2000 established a four-tier hierarchy of Gacaca courts, with 12 Gacaca courts at the province level at the apex of the system, 100 district courts, 1,545 sector courts and 9,011 cell courts.[7] In 2004, the government introduced new legislation, Organic Law 16/2004,[8] that reorganized the Gacaca system by, among other changes, abolishing Gacaca courts at the district and provincial levels, leaving one Gacaca court at each cell and establishing two courts at sector level,[9] a court of first instance and an appellate court.[10] Each Gacaca court had three organs, namely a general assembly, a bench or panel of judges and a coordinating committee.[11] The basic qualification for election as a Gacaca court judge is being a person of integrity and being recognized as such by peers in the community. Other qualifications include being at least 18 years old and a resident of one of the cells of the relevant cell or sector;[12] not having a record of having participated in genocide; not having been tried and convicted definitively of a crime in respect of which a penalty of more than six months imprisonment was imposed; not having sectarian tendencies; being of high morals and good conduct; being truthful and honest; not having a temperament that makes one inclined to deny other people the opportunity to express their views; not being an adherent or believer in the ideology of genocide, which was defined as '[consisting] of behaviour, a way of speaking, written documents and any other actions meant to wipe out human beings on the basis of their ethnic group, origin, nationality, region, colour of skin, physical traits, sex, language, religion or political opinions.'[13] Persons holding public office, including officials of central or local government, serving members of the military or police forces, career judicial officials, and leaders of political organizations were barred from serving as Gacaca judges.[14] Persons whose names appeared on the official list of genocide suspects were not eligible for election as Gacaca judges.[15]

Gacaca judges could cease to hold or be removed from office on a number of grounds, including failing to attend three successive meetings of the court without convincing justification, promoting sectarianism, disclosing details of in-camera court proceedings, showing indications of being an adherent of the ideology of genocide, or doing any act inconsistent with the attribute of being a person of integrity.[16] A president and two vice presidents as well as two secretaries elected from among the judges of the court constituted the coordination committee of each Gacaca court. The members of the committee had to be able to read and write Kinyarwanda.[17]

6.2.3 Procedures of Gacaca

The procedures of Gacaca courts were regulated by legislation as well as administrative directives issued by the National Service for Gacaca Jurisdictions. Proceedings of Gacaca courts could be commenced either by a Gacaca court taking over dossiers that had previously been investigated by the prosecution service or by Gacaca courts starting investigations of their own. Proceedings of Gacaca were conducted in three phases.

The first stage of Gacaca proceedings was the information-gathering phase (Rettig 2008: p. 32). This stage involved the drawing up of six lists:

1. List of residents of the cell in April 1994 and their current status (whether alive and in the *cellule*, moved away, in prison, deceased or unknown);
2. List of residents who died in the cell during the genocide;
3. List of residents who died outside the cell during the genocide;
4. List of persons from outside the cell who died within its borders;
5. Inventory of physical and property damage or stolen goods;
6. List of persons accused of being perpetrators.

The information-gathering phase was by law the responsibility of the Assembly of the Cell Gacaca Court. In practice, however, the process was conducted by local government leaders known as *Nyumbakumi* (heads of groupings of ten households) completing forms of the above lists with the required information. Once the forms were completed, a meeting of the General Assembly of the Cell Gacaca Court was convened. These lists were then read to the meeting of the General Assembly for validation. The General Assembly could add new accusations or delete unfounded allegations (Megwalu 2006: p. 22).

The second stage of Gacaca, which was also conducted by the cell Gacaca court, is the categorization of the suspects identified during the information-gathering phase (Algard 2005: p. 18; Molenaar: 2005 p. 31; Rettig 2008: p. 31). The General Assembly undertook the categorization of suspects at the conclusion of the information-gathering phase. Upon completion of the categorization process, the cases were transmitted to the Gacaca courts that had jurisdiction to try them. Cases that fell within the competence of the formal courts were transmitted to the prosecution service.[18]

The final stage of the proceedings of Gacaca courts, the trial phase, was conducted by the panel of judges of the competent Gacaca court.[19]

All Gacaca courts had power to conduct follow-up investigations with respect to evidence received; to receive confessions, guilty pleas and communications of repentance and apology from persons who participated in genocide and related crimes; to decide upon applications for removal of one or more of their number from the panel; to hear and determine cases falling within their jurisdiction; and to hear appeals against decisions of subordinate Gacaca courts.

Gacaca courts enjoyed the normal powers and privileges ordinarily accorded to other courts.[20] Gacaca court proceedings were open to the general public, subject to certain restrictions on observers, researchers and journalists, who had to have an official permit to observe the proceedings and were required to present themselves to local government officials prior to the proceedings of the Gacaca courts.[21] Gacaca hearings could be held in camera, if necessary on account of reasons of public order or good morals.[22] Proceedings before Gacaca courts were informal. The conduct of Gacaca proceedings was not subject to the normal criminal procedure law of Rwanda. Some procedural guidelines for the conduct of trial of Gacaca courts are set out in the legislation establishing Gacaca courts.[23] Additional guidelines were developed and issued by the National Service for Gacaca Jurisdictions. It is doubtful, however, whether non-compliance with any of these guidelines would in any situation be a ground for invalidating a decision of a Gacaca court.

Every citizen was required to participate in the proceedings of the Gacaca within whose territorial jurisdiction she or he resided. It was an offence to refuse to testify in Gacaca proceedings when required to do so.[24] Any member of the General Assembly had a right to provide evidence. Suspects and defendants in the Gacaca system were not allowed to be represented by counsel.[25] Deliberations of the panels of judges were conducted in secrecy. Judgments of Gacaca courts were issued in open court and in writing.[26] Gacaca courts were authorized to try suspects *in absentia* where the defendants could not be traced.[27] Gacaca courts had powers to impose any of the penalties available under the Penal Code, including life imprisonment. However, Gacaca did not have much discretion in terms of the sentences they could impose. Sentences in Gacaca proceedings were strictly regulated by legislation; a Gacaca court could only impose a sentence within a specified range set for each category of offences.[28] The range of sanctions applicable to each category of offence in turn depended on a variety of factors, including the nature of the offence a suspect was accused of, the category in which the accused had been placed, the role of the accused in the planning and execution of the offence, whether the accused had joined the Guilty Plea and Confession Programme and, if so, at what stage the offer to join the Confession and Guilty Plea Programme was made, as well as whether the accused person was an adult or a juvenile person at the time of committing the offence in question.

The penalties that Gacaca courts were empowered to impose for offences under legislation governing genocide trials have varied over the years. The trend since the passage of Organic Law No. 40/2000 has generally been to reduce penalties for offences that Gacaca have jurisdiction to try. The considerations which have influenced the development and evolution of this sentencing policy have included the following: ensuring more expeditious disposal of the genocide caseload; ensuring a substantial reduction in the size of the prison population in order to reduce the financial and political costs associated with maintaining such a large detainee population; encouraging establishment of the truth about the conduct of the genocide; encouraging perpetrators to acknowledge their wrong doing and to apologize to victims for their crimes with a view to facilitating reconciliation; facilitation of the smooth re-integration of the large number of detained genocide suspects into their respective communities; combating impunity for gross human rights abuses in general and sexual violence in particular; and ensuring the treatment of juveniles in a manner that more closely conforms to relevant international human rights standards.

The above-mentioned policy goals of the sentencing system of Gacaca courts were promoted through a range of strategies. To fight impunity, stiff penalties were provided for perpetrators who bore the greatest responsibility (Category 1).[29] Penalties designed to publicize the atrocities that were committed, with a view to shaming perpetrators and to deter recurrence of violence, were introduced.[30] The Guilty Plea and Confession Programme played a key role in the management of the Gacaca process by providing incentives to genocide suspects to cooperate with investigations and judicial institutions.[31] These incentives were not originally available to but were later extended to perpetrators of Category 1 offenders.[32] An acknowledgement of the need to address the concerns of victims is evident in the requirement for apology as a prerequisite for acceptance of guilty pleas and confessions of persons accused of genocide.[33] Community service was also introduced as a substitute for part of a prison term.[34] Sentences of juveniles were also significantly reduced,[35] and perpetrators of crimes relating to property (Category 3 suspects) were exempted from custodial sentences.[36] The penalty of community service was introduced to address social and political problems arising from prison overcrowding and to facilitate the re-integration of perpetrators back into their respective communities. Legislation introduced in 2008 provided that the custodial part of Category 2 genocide perpetrators' sentence would be commuted to community service if it was proved that the community service part of an offender's sentence was executed in an exemplary manner.[37] This provision provides the government with a legal basis for commuting custodial sentences of all perpetrators who have participated in the Guilty Plea and Confession Programme. It is now very unlikely that any of the Category 2 suspects who have joined the Guilty Plea and Confession Programme will ever be required to serve time in prison at all. The legal provisions and administrative decisions that make it possible for perpetrators of genocide to perform only community service and to avoid service of substantial time in prison are viewed unfavourably by survivors (Wolters 2005b: p. 16).

6.3 Implementation of Gacaca

Gacaca was implemented in three stages: the preparations stage, the pilot project phase and the nationwide implementation stage.

The government launched the preparations stage with a process of raising public awareness about the proposed system and putting in place government-wide systems and processes to implement and support the operation of Gacaca. The public education campaign started well before legislation establishing Gacaca was enacted (Borland 2003). The campaign continued for most of the duration of the Gacaca process and has included activities such as producing and disseminating messages about Gacaca through radio, film, print and other media; conducting training programmes for leaders who would be involved in the process of implementing Gacaca; convening community meetings to explain the Gacaca system to the population and undertaking various other activities, including theatre performances (Bababola *et al.* 2003; Algard 2005). The objectives of the awareness campaign included: a) explaining the objectives and advantages of Gacaca to the public; b) addressing the concerns of stakeholders, especially genocide survivors, about the proposed system; c) informing the public on how the Gacaca system would operate and explaining the role that citizens were expected to play in it; d) encouraging citizens to participate in the process; and e) encouraging the population, especially persons who had participated in committing atrocities, to cooperate in facilitating the Gacaca process by coming forward to tell the truth.

The preparation stage of Gacaca also involved the establishment of organs, structures and systems to facilitate the functioning of the proposed courts. The implementation of Gacaca called for reorganization of the functioning and priorities of existing justice institutions – especially the judiciary, prosecution service, police and local government bodies – to position them to support the operations of Gacaca. Activities that were undertaken during this stage as part of the process of establishing the machinery for the implementation of Gacaca included the elections of Gacaca judges; the design and delivery of training to the elected judges; the establishment of structures to supervise the operation of Gacaca and the setting up of a database for cases to be transmitted to Gacaca courts once they commenced operations.

The second stage of the process of implementing Gacaca was the pilot project phase (Meyerstein 2007: p. 474). The government initially planned to roll out Gacaca across the country at the same time. However, some non-governmental organizations, donors and members of the legal profession responsible for the setting up of Gacaca urged the government to consider beginning its implementation with an experimental phase to help identify the key problems that nationwide implementation was likely to raise. The experience gained during the experimental phase would be used to adjust the Gacaca system to ensure optimal results once it was introduced in all parts of the country. The government accepted the proposal to launch Gacaca with a pilot phase and it was undertaken in two parts over a three-year period (2002–5). The areas in which it was conducted were chosen because they had a high proportion of genocide suspects that had volunteered to participate in the Guilty Plea and Confession Programme (Amnesty International 2002a,

2002c; Molenaar 2005: p. 52). The decision to start Gacaca in areas with a high concentration of confessions was intended both to reward the detainees who had joined the Guilty Plea and Confession Programme (by having their cases heard first) and to encourage additional confessions. Other factors which affected the choice of pilot areas were whether the respective areas had the necessary infrastructure and equipment to support the implementation of the Gacaca process, the level of community enthusiasm for Gacaca, and the availability of relatively competent residents to serve as judges in the area's Gacaca courts (Molenaar 2005: p. 52; Penal Reform International 2010b: p. 21).

The pilot phase brought to light many potential problems for the nationwide implementation of Gacaca courts. The large number of judges on each Gacaca court made it difficult to convene and conduct meetings of the court organs. Public confidence in the Gacaca system was found to be weak. A significant part of the population in many areas was reluctant to participate in Gacaca at all (Haile 2008: p. 39–41). According to many researchers (Wolters 2005b), elites within different communities in particular avoided participating in Gacaca; their attendance was particularly low at the stage where the courts were supposed to name the perpetrators. Absenteeism and late arrival of participants for Gacaca meetings (due to domestic commitments including farming, attendance of social functions including church, and lack of confidence in the Gacaca process) led to low productivity (Honeyman *et al.* 2004). Proceedings of many courts also suffered from weak management and organizational skills on the part of judges and local government officials responsible for Gacaca. Judges often failed to prepare adequately for the meetings and they (as well as members of the public) were not adequately informed about Gacaca's functioning. Intimidation and coercion of witnesses was widespread (Le Mon 2007).[38] Physical attacks against survivors, though not widespread, were common (Human Rights Watch 2007: p. 6). Some of the Gacaca judges were themselves implicated in atrocities. The inability of Gacaca to deal with complaints of crimes alleged to have been committed by members of the military of the current government discouraged significant numbers of citizens in some areas from participating in Gacaca courts. Gacaca judges generally lacked motivation. Judicial corruption was identified as a problem of significant concern (Wolters 2005b: p. 17; Kirby 2006: p. 111; Le Mon 2007: p. 116).

The government used the feedback from the pilot phase to restructure Gacaca with a view to improving its capacity to deal with the genocide caseload more effectively (Clark 2007: p. 13; Meyerstein 2007: p. 475; Lahiri 2009: pp. 325–6). The government undertook a number of reforms as a result of lessons learnt from the pilot phase: Gacaca courts at the provincial and district levels were abolished. Jurisdiction over the cases that fell within the competence of district and provincial Gacaca courts was transferred to the more numerous sector Gacaca courts.[39] The categorization of suspects was revised further: Categories 2 and 3 under Organic Law No. 40/2000 were combined into a new Category 2, and the old Category 4 became Category 3.[40] The structure of Gacaca was changed. The number of judges on each Gacaca court was reduced from 19 to 9 (with 5 alternates) to make it possible to have more competent judges. This new arrangement also aimed to make it easier for the members of each court to meet and to conduct the business of the court more efficiently.[41] Public awareness activities were intensified. Additional training programmes for Gacaca judges and the officials of the National Service for Gacaca Jurisdictions were developed and carried out (Umugwaneza 2005). A manual was developed and disseminated to judges to help them carry out their tasks.[42] Template forms to help Gacaca judges at every stage of proceedings of Gacaca were designed, refined and distributed to officials of Gacaca courts. A system of providing some minimal compensation to judges of Gacaca courts was established. Modalities were established for examining cases of Gacaca judges accused of complicity in genocide.[43]

Nationwide implementation of the Gacaca project began with the launch of the information-gathering phase in 2005. The government initially wanted to have all Gacaca trials completed before the end of 2006. However, the judgment phase of the process was put on hold in 2006 pending the enactment of new legislation to harmonize the organization of Gacaca with the new organization of the local government system (Waldorf 2006b: p. 19). The judgment phase began nationwide in July 2006 (Human Rights Watch 2011, p. 23). A new deadline (end of 2008) for the completion of Gacaca trials was set. In response to government pressure, Gacaca courts across the country disposed of the cases in their jurisdictions with extraordinary speed, completing almost all trials in a period of less than two years (Takeuchi 2011). Gacaca finally closed down in June 2012.

6.4 Looking Back at a Decade of Gacaca: Promise Unfulfilled?

The Gacaca process was an unprecedented response to mass atrocity both in terms of its scope and its ambitions. It is still too early to make an accurate assessment of its lasting impact. It is possible, however, to make some tentative observations about the quality of the trials that Gacaca has undertaken and the extent to which Gacaca will be able to meet its goals. Gacaca has undoubtedly had some positive attributes. It has compelled Rwandan society to confront the genocide more systematically than the process of criminal prosecutions that preceded it. It has served to individualize guilt, making it easier to promote peaceful coexistence (if not reconciliation) by dispelling misconceptions about the collective guilt of the Hutu community for the genocide (Daly 2002a: p. 375). Gacaca has enhanced opportunities for establishing the truth about the genocide (Algard 2005; Sosnov 2008). Gacaca courts have gone further in comprehensively establishing the truth about the genocide than the formal justice system could ever have done. Gacaca has localized justice, making it accessible to people who might never have received any justice at all had the genocide caseload remained in the formal justice system (Daly 2002a: p. 377; Borocan 2004: p. 381). Gacaca has expanded access to justice for both victims as well as persons suspected of being perpetrators of genocide (Mibenge 2004: p. 422). Prior to Gacaca, most of those who were in detention awaiting trial for crimes linked to the genocide had little or no prospect of being brought to trial within their lifetimes. Gacaca has helped Rwanda achieve the once seemingly unattainable goal of disposing of the huge genocide caseload (Penal Reform International 2010a, 2010b). Gacaca has proved more able to guarantee respect of the right to trial without undue delay than the formal justice system.[44] Gacaca has helped Rwanda to dispose of the large backlog of pending genocide cases and to drastically reduce the number of persons accused of or responsible for genocide who are in detention. Approximately 66,000 genocide suspects were released from detention between 2002 and 2006, for example (Megwalu 2006: p. 18). In reducing the prison population and bringing to an end the process for trials of genocide cases, Gacaca may have moved Rwanda closer to closure of the litigation concerning the genocide, providing an opportunity for greater attention to be focused on building a stable and secure future. As such, Gacaca may have contributed to progress towards the realization of some of the key objectives of the transitional justice processes undertaken by Rwanda. The government and outsiders who are favourably disposed towards Gacaca praise the system as an innovative and useful path in the search for truth, justice and reconciliation in the aftermath of genocide (Uvin and Mironko 2003; Borocan 2004; Wierzynska 2004; Mutisi 2009; Clark 2010).

Gacaca is not without its failings. Despite its positive aspects, the Gacaca process remains deeply controversial, particularly in Rwandan society. Gacaca experienced challenges and had inherent limitations that have had a negative impact on its potential and early promise. These challenges and limitations which, according to critics, have had a negative impact on Gacaca's capacity to achieve its fundamental objectives include the following.

6.4.1 *Absence of community*

Gacaca's capacity to achieve its intended objectives has been severely constrained by the absence of community (Daly 2002a: pp. 378–81; Bradley 2004). Underlying a neo-traditional conflict resolution mechanism such as Gacaca is a notion of community, defined as the existence of closely-knit groups of people sharing the same values and expectations (Uvin 2003b: p. 120). As a result of war, genocide and the massive population movements that Rwanda has experienced since the early 1990s (including massive internal displacement, the exile of millions of citizens, the repatriation and resettlement of hundreds of thousands of Tutsi refugees who had fled Rwanda since 1959, and the forced relocation of many communities to grouped settlements under the government's villagization programme), many communities comprise people who did not live together before the genocide (Borocan 2004: p. 391; Human Rights Watch 2006c: p. 126). Residents of many communities in post-genocide Rwanda have no historical connections to one another, do not constitute cohesive communities and do not necessarily share a desire to work together to create a cohesive community (Daly 2002a: p. 391). The factors (including common values, shared interests, cohesion and trust in existing social institutions and systems) that made traditional Gacaca acceptable and effective in resolving conflict and maintaining harmony are lacking in most Rwandan communities today. Local justice that relies on the participation of the population depends on the existence of a strong community to succeed. If community trust is weak, then local justice (particularly punitive justice) will fray the social fabric (Rettig 2008: p. 46). The radical changes that have altered the makeup of many communities in Rwanda since 1994 have weakened the capacity of such communities to work together in resolving common problems, including the challenge of accountability for the genocide and other human rights violations experienced during the 1990s (Borocan 2004: p 356). Survivors and the majority of the members of the Hutu community have different perceptions about the past. The two groups have participated in Gacaca for different and divergent goals, linked to the defence or promotion of personal, family, group or sectarian interests rather than to promote community-wide goals and concerns (such as establishing the truth, mending relations with the victims and perpetrators and their families, and working to build a shared secure future).

6.4.2 Retributive justice

Gacaca was adopted both to try and punish the crimes that were committed in the context of the genocide as well as to promote the restoration of constructive relationships between both sides of the violence experienced during the 1990s. In practice, the two goals have proved contradictory and incompatible. Many in the Hutu community had relatives, friends and neighbours who were accused of genocide. Their primary objective in participating in Gacaca has been to secure the release of these relatives, friends and neighbours, not necessarily to advance the goals of truth or justice. The potential consequences of conviction for genocide (including detention for very long periods, being stripped of civil rights, social ostracization, and risk of revenge attacks) left many in the Hutu community little choice but to defend relatives, friends and neighbours accused of genocide at all costs, regardless of their role in the genocide. In many communities, the retributive aspect of Gacaca had the impact of transforming Gacaca into a bitter, partisan contest between survivors and relatives and sympathizers of people accused of genocide. It is conceivable that it might have been easier for survivors and communities, some of whose members were accused of participation in genocide, to reach common ground about the events of the genocide if Gacaca had not had powers to impose heavy criminal sanctions. The endowment of Gacaca with jurisdiction to punish (as severely as ordinary courts are able to) crimes that were committed during the context of the war and genocide has imperilled the realization of Gacaca's restorative justice goals.

6.4.3 Lack of even-handedness

Gacaca has been further undermined by its lack of even-handedness in addressing the suffering of all victims (Mutisi, 2009: p. 23). Gacaca has focused exclusively upon the crimes that targeted the Tutsi community and those whom perpetrators of the genocide presumed to be sympathizers of accomplices of the Tutsi, and failed to address crimes against members of the Hutu community attributed to the RPA (Oomen 2006: p. 19). Organic Law 40/2000 originally included crimes attributed to the RPA within the scope of Gacaca's jurisdiction. However, at the launching of Gacaca, the President orally directed (in a nationwide radio broadcast the night before the first election of Gacaca judges) that Gacaca courts should not deal with these crimes. The law governing Gacaca was subsequently amended to exclude jurisdiction for human rights violations alleged to have been committed by the RPA from the mandate of Gacaca courts. The government of Rwanda insists that human rights abuses that may have been committed by members of the RPA were neither systematic nor widespread; that the crimes were acts of individuals and that they have been and will continue to be investigated and punished by the competent military authorities whenever they are reported (Ngoga 2009). Gacaca's one-sided focus on the genocide and its failure to address the issue of war crimes and crimes against humanity that were committed against victims in the Hutu community resulted in frustration on the part of many in the Hutu community and has discouraged active and constructive Hutu participation in Gacaca (Longman 2006a: p. 36; Waldorf 2006b). The government's adamant refusal to countenance the investigation and prosecution of crimes attributable to its military has undermined the credibility of popular support for and participation in Gacaca (Borocan 2004: p. 390; Tiemessen 2004; Algard 2005: p. 73; Waldorf 2006b: p. 21). Many scholars shared the view that the exclusion of crimes that were committed against members of the Hutu community by elements of the victors has undermined community ownership of Gacaca, and that this risks transforming Gacaca into a kind of victor's justice (Molenaar 2005: p. 62; Haile 2008: p. 16; Takeuchi 2011: p. 17). Many in the Hutu community and political opposition have deep grievances over Gacaca's lack of even-handedness (Burnet 2009: p.179; FDU-Inkingi 2012).

6.4.4 Human rights abuses

Gacaca's credibility and effectiveness have also been affected by the legacy of human rights abuses to which persons accused of involvement in the genocide have been exposed. Tens of thousands of citizens were arrested and detained on genocide charges in the years after the genocide. These arrests and detentions were for the most part arbitrary and detainees were kept in conditions that human rights observers and other commentators agree constituted 'cruel, inhuman and degrading treatment or punishment' (Amnesty International

1997a: p. 24). The pre-trial detention of these suspects extended, in many cases, to periods of as long as ten years or more. Gacaca was established, in part, to address the problems of the large backlog of genocide cases and the huge population of genocide suspects who were being held in pre-trial detention. While Gacaca has contributed to addressing problems of prison overcrowding and a huge caseload of pending genocide cases, it has led to further abuses against genocide suspects as well. The regime of lenient penalties that Gacaca offered was only available to genocide suspects who joined the Guilty Plea and Confession Programme. Genocide suspects who refused to join the programme continued to be held in pre-trial detention many years after their arrest. Gacaca cases have been affected by corruption (Algard 2005: p. 38). Gacaca proccedings have in some areas been compromised by external interference, with officials using their positions to protect themselves, family members, friends and others by preventing negative testimony from being heard and recorded (Meyerstein 2007: p. 489; FDU-Inkingi 2012).

During Gacaca trials, genocide suspects did not enjoy equality of arms (Borocan 2004: p. 388; Longman 2006a: p. 29). The resources of the state were overwhelmingly used to support the investigation, prosecution and trial of the charges against the suspects. Accused persons did not have comparable opportunity or resources to seek evidence exonerating them. Genocide suspects tried by Gacaca were not permitted to have legal representation, even when they had their own resources to pay for such services (Sarkin 2001: p. 166; Werchick 2001: p. 17; Borocan 2004: p. 388; Mibenge 2004: p. 422; Haile 2008: p. 27; Rettig 2008: p. 26). Suspects implicated during the data collection, validation and categorization stages of Gacaca were denied the opportunity to respond to evidence incriminating them (Meyerstein 2007: p. 489; Penal Reform International 2010b: p. 29). Suspects were only allowed to respond to evidence that incriminated them belatedly during the judgment phase (Penal Reform International 2006). Defendants in Gacaca cases had minimal information about the charges against them and the supporting evidence prior to commencement of trials (Amnesty International 2002b: p. 19). They did not have adequate time to prepare for their defence (Ironside 2002; Haile 2008: p. 28) and were required to answer any new allegations that were levelled against them during the proceedings spontaneously, without adequate time to study the charges and evidence and to frame appropriate defences. The Gacaca system has not provided adequate guarantees for impartiality, defence and equality before the law (Uvin 2003a: p. 118).

Some commentators have argued that the violations of human rights inherent in Gacaca should be tolerated because even the formal justice system was not able to guarantee respect of such rights (Uvin 2003b: p. 119; Megwalu 2006: p. 18). It is also argued that fair trial standards should not apply to Gacaca because these human rights standards were not developed with the realities of poor, post-conflict societies such as Rwanda in mind (Tully 2003: p. 414; Borocan 2004: p. 393; Meyerstein 2007: pp. 500–2). The argument that fair trial guarantees are Western impositions that ought to be optional in poor post-conflict societies needs to be challenged (Haile 2008: pp. 33, 36). International human rights standards are neither a luxury nor a cultural phenomenon. Fair trial rights are a critical part of the infrastructure for promoting the rule of law, protecting fundamental human rights and defending important values (Haile 2008). No legal system should try a person for a crime, particularly a very serious crime such as genocide, if it cannot guarantee a fair trial. A tribunal that has power to try very serious offences and to impose very stiff penalties needs to conform to local laws and international human rights norms regarding fair trial (Daly 2002a: p. 396). The failure of Gacaca courts to guarantee respect of fair trial rights undermined the potential of Rwanda's transitional justice processes to contribute to national reconstruction (Mutisi 2009). Unfair trials also undermine confidence in the justice system and efforts to promote a culture of respect for human rights, establish the rule of law and promote peace (Amnesty International 2002b: p. 2; Organisation of African Unity 2000).

By the time Gacaca was established, the trust of the people in the ability of Rwanda's judicial institutions to deal with the genocide caseload had sunk very low (Office of the President, Rwanda 1999). The introduction of Gacaca initially raised expectations that the population would embrace the process (Bababola *et al.* 2003), yet it has not succeeded in undoing the damage caused by the failings of the formal justice system. The long history of abuses of the human rights of persons suspected of involvement in the genocide may have irreparably damaged public confidence in the mechanisms with which Rwanda has attempted to address the legacy of the genocide, including Gacaca. In many communities, most citizens have resisted participation in Gacaca, partly as a form of protest against the abuses that the justice system inflicted against members of those communities accused of genocide.

6.4.5 Constraining socio-political environment

Gacaca has also been adversely impacted by the socio-political context in which it has been implemented (Mutisi 2009: p. 23). The large-scale arrests and prolonged pre-trial detention of genocide suspects in harsh conditions from 1994 onwards generated very intense grievances on the part of many in the Hutu community towards the government and genocide survivors (Organisation of African Unity 2000: paras 18.59, 18.60). The government's failure to hold its military accountable for human rights violations, and to democratize, has hardened anti-government and anti-Tutsi feelings in Rwanda even further (Zorbas 2004). Rwandan society remains deeply divided along ethnic lines (Sarkin 1999b: p. 800; Waldorf 2004: p. 138; Burnet 2007: p. 2). Accountability for genocide and Gacaca in particular is one of the many issues that deeply divide Rwandan society (Rettig 2008). Some reports have indicated that as implementation of Gacaca at national level got underway, an atmosphere of pervasive fear spread across the country, to the extent that tens of thousands of citizens fled the country. This pervasive fear was present throughout the duration of the implementation of Gacaca (Richters *et al.* 2005: p. 213; Thomson 2011b: p. 378). Intense polarization within Rwandan society has made the likelihood of biased Gacaca judgments very high (Borocan 2004: p. 387; Mibenge 2004: p. 422). There have been political as well as personal incentives and motivations for Gacaca judges to be biased in the exercise of their judicial functions (Sosnov 2008). Gacaca judges are likely to be influenced by, among other factors, their personal experiences, political allegiances and inclinations, relations with the defendants and their families or security concerns in deciding the cases before them. According to some scholars, the impartiality of Gacaca judges cannot be assured because of the socio-political environment, which is characterized by intense politicization of personal disputes, strong disaffection towards government and polarization of society along lines of ethnicity that prevailed in Rwanda during the implementation of Gacaca (Rettig 2008; Reyntjens 2011). The risk of exposure to miscarriage of justice affected both persons accused of genocide as well as victims of genocide (Borocan 2004: p. 387). Gacaca has also been implemented in a repressive political environment, and the oppressive and unequal political climate has cast a shadow upon the process (Oomen 2006: pp. 18, 20; Purdekova 2011). These factors have affected Gacaca's legitimacy in the perception of many citizens and, as a result, many have not been willing to participate in the process freely and have rather found ways of passive resistance to it (Thomson 2011a).

6.4.6 State capture

The Rwanda government made Gacaca the showpiece of its peace-building agenda. The government wanted Gacaca to be completed smoothly and expeditiously, in line with its objectives that are outlined in Chapter 2. Due to a number of factors (discussed in the preceding paragraphs), Gacaca became unpopular with large segments of Rwandan society and citizens opposed to Gacaca demonstrated their passive resistance by refusing to turn up for Gacaca meetings. The government resorted to coercion and threats of punishment to compel citizens to participate (Penal Reform International 2006: p. 17; Thomson 2011b). Forced to attend meetings against their will, citizens often adopted a new strategy of resistance by refusing to contribute to the deliberations of the meetings. The government still insisted that Gacaca cases be completed under strict timelines. Most of the Gacaca judges did not have the technical and management skills to move Gacaca at the speed at which the government wanted. In an attempt to expedite the processing of cases, the government increasingly relied on government institutions to drive Gacaca forward. The investigation phase of the Gacaca process was turned over to local government officials, although under the law this task was a function of judges (Penal Reform International 2006; Meyerstein 2007). As a result, Gacaca judges were marginalized during the investigation phase. The use of administration officials instead of Gacaca judges for data collection transformed the investigative stages of Gacaca from being a judicial process to an administrative procedure. Some commentators argue that the local administration officials who compiled the necessary forms during the information-gathering phase had disproportionate power to influence the nature and amount of information that would form the basis of the case files setting out the accusations against suspects (Human Rights Watch 2007: p. 20). Lack of openness, transparency and opportunity for public participation in the information-gathering process undermined the credibility of Gacaca.

In 2007, agents of the National Service for Gacaca Jurisdictions assumed extensive powers over the categorization of genocide suspects (Human Rights Watch 2008: p. 20). The organs of central and local government increasingly exercised dominant control of the investigation functions of Gacaca courts during their existence (Lahiri 2009: p. 331). Some scholars of Gacaca contend that local government officials, rather than Gacaca judges, directed and dominated the proceedings of Gacaca in many communities (Algard 2005: p. 68; Waldorf 2006b: p. 28). Government essentially captured Gacaca to enable its work to be completed at all costs. Some commentators argue that the interference of government officials in the operation of the Gacaca system adversely affected public participation in Gacaca and adversely compromised its integrity and legitimacy (Penal Reform International 2006: p. 17; Meyerstein 2007: p. 489). Gacaca has not been a truly independent system of courts and it has not lived up to the promise of being a popularly owned process in many communities (Human Rights Watch 2011). The capture of Gacaca by the state and state functionaries has had a negative impact on its capacity to contribute to the attainment of the goals of Rwanda's transitional justice agenda (Waldorf 2006b; Takeuchi 2011; Thomson 2011b).

6.4.7 *Lack of reparation*

Another factor that undermined the popular ownership and legitimacy of Gacaca and its capacity to contribute to the attainment of the objectives of Rwanda's transitional justice programme was the absence of a government policy on reparations for victims of both the genocide and human rights abuses attributable to the RPA (Mibenge 2004: p. 422; Waldorf 2006b: pp. 56–9; Meyerstein 2007: p. 486). Survivors of the genocide have, individually or collectively through the organizations that represent them, always demanded reparations, especially compensation. Survivors regard reparations as an integral part of the quest for justice for genocide. Many of the survivors of the genocide are destitute and they need the compensation to meet pressing economic and social needs (Hirondelle, 13 January 2009). Survivors' demand for compensation has grown as government has moved away from the strict application of the law and adopted policies that seek to treat perpetrators of the genocide ever more leniently. The government has, largely as a result of concerns over affordability, been unwilling to commit to payment of compensation to survivors. Some victims (intervening as *parties civiles* in genocide proceedings) have sought and received damages from the formal courts.[45] Unfortunately, none of the awards of damages that the ordinary courts have made have been enforced (Algard 2005: p. 42). The failure of the government to adopt a reparations programme has discouraged some survivors from participating in Gacaca (Waldorf 2006b). Lack of prospects for justice and for reparation for victims of human rights abuses attributable to the RPA has similarly discouraged many Hutus from participating in Gacaca in good faith.

6.4.8 Security considerations

The participation of genocide survivors in Gacaca was also discouraged by security concerns (Mutisi 2009: p. 23). Lack of effective mechanisms for the protection of survivors and witnesses has also been a concern, and was so from the very beginning of the Gacaca process (REDRESS/African Rights 2008b). The Gacaca process posed security risks to victims, witnesses, including survivors, and even judges (Algard 2005; Thomson 2011b: p. 385). Gacaca trials in many areas have taken place in an environment of intense division and mistrust between members of the different communities. The majority of Hutu in many communities either kept silent during Gacaca proceedings or only intervened to defend accused persons (Rettig 2008: p. 40). The task of confronting persons suspected of genocide and providing evidence against them was, in many communities, left to survivors (Penal Reform International 2006; Rettig 2008). Genocide survivors are few in each community and most are very poor and marginalized. Undertaking the task of exposing crimes that were committed by people who have bigger families, stronger ties with the rest of the community and more resources often exposes survivors and witnesses to mortal danger (Corey and Joireman 2000). The government's policy was that security for victims and witnesses will be ensured through enhancing the security of their respective communities in general. This approach to the protection of witnesses in genocide cases (particularly survivors) was not adequate and many witnesses have been subjected to harassment and intimidation (Algard 2005: p. 28; Sosnov 2008). Some witnesses were killed (Mibenge 2004: p. 18). Ibuka, the umbrella organization representing genocide survivors, has documented killings of at least 167 survivors during the period 1995–2008 (Hirondelle, 15 July 2008). Attacks against witnesses were aimed at discouraging or punishing testimony before Gacaca courts (Wolters 2005b: p. 18; Le Mon 2007: p. 16). Harassment, intimidation and violent attacks against witnesses and judges succeeded in discouraging some witnesses from participation in Gacaca (Algard 2005: p. 29; Le Mon 2007; Meyerstein 2007). The overall inability of the state to provide adequate security for witnesses in genocide cases and survivors severely constrained the functioning of Gacaca (Borocan 2004: p. 391; Meyerstein 2007: p. 490).

The factors discussed above have undermined the appeal and legitimacy of Gacaca. Gacaca's compromised legitimacy made citizens unwilling to participate voluntarily in the process (Waldorf 2006b; Human Rights Watch

2011; Takeuchi 2011; Thomson 2011b) and lack of legitimacy has in turn undermined Gacaca's effectiveness in promoting its goals. Chapter 9 evaluates the extent to which the transitional justice processes undertaken by Rwanda, especially Gacaca, have achieved the transitional justice objectives they were intended to achieve. The conclusion of this evaluation is that whereas the transitional justice processes in question, including Gacaca, have achieved some of their short-term objectives, long-term objectives such as reparation for victims, reconciliation, establishment of democracy and the rule of law, ending impunity and ensuring sustainable peace largely remain elusive.

6.5 Interpreting Phil Clark: A General Critique of *The Gacaca Courts, Post-Genocide Justice and Reconciliation in Rwanda – Justice without Lawyers*

Phil Clark's *The Gacaca Courts, Post-Genocide Justice and Reconciliation in Rwanda – Justice without Lawyers* (2010) is the first book-length academic analysis of Rwanda's Gacaca courts. The book is undoubtedly a work of significant importance to scholarship of Gacaca. Its purpose is expressed to be 'to explore the nature of Gacaca, to identify its objectives, and judge its effectiveness in responding to the legacies of the genocide' (Clark 2010: p. 4). One reviewer has expressed the view that it may turn out to be the definitive work on Gacaca (Caplan 2011). Clark has also written several review articles and book chapters on Gacaca (2007, 2009a, 2009b, 2009c). His scholarship departs from other established scholarship on Gacaca and he goes to great lengths to distinguish his work from other scholarship on the subject. To facilitate this distinction, Clark identifies three categories of scholarship on Gacaca: 'the dominant view', comprising scholars who, according to the author, view Gacaca as a primarily judicial institution whose sole objective is retributive justice aimed at punishment and deterrence; a second group that perceives Gacaca as the Rwandan state's coercion of popular involvement, and the state's interference in Gacaca in order to collectivize the guilt of all Hutu; and a third group, that Clark considers himself to be part of, which argues that Gacaca aims both to punish perpetrators as well as to achieve other post-genocide objectives, particularly reconciliation (Clark 2010: pp. 4–5). Clark argues that apart from his own groundbreaking work, all other existing scholarship (by scholars in all of the three above-mentioned groups) on Gacaca is deeply flawed (2010: p. 91). Gacaca, the book argues, represents a radical, comprehensive approach to transitional justice (p. 343) and is a holistic response to the legacies of the genocide (p. 27). The book concludes that Gacaca has been successful in facilitating truth telling and truth hearing and in providing for positive peace by creating a dialogical space for the resolution of people's past conflicts (p. 342). It also asserts that Gacaca has proven effective in many communities at initiating restorative justice, forgiveness and reconciliation, even though these objectives stretch beyond the timeframe of Gacaca (p. 342).

The author's repeated, emphatic and unapologetic assertions that all other scholarship on Gacaca is flawed leave readers of his work in a quandary. How can so many scholars on a subject go so wrong? On what basis does the author reach the conclusion that this vast body of scholarship is flawed? Is Clark's criticism of other scholarship grounded in a sound theoretical framework of the fields of transitional justice, peace building and human rights as we know them? Are his conclusions supported by facts, both from his own research and from other scholarship? Does Clark's scholarship correctly interpret the situation on the ground? Is its interpretation an accurate and objective assessment of Gacaca or not? These are issues that every student of Gacaca who reads the book and the author's other writings on Gacaca confronted with from the start. Clark's findings and conclusions on Gacaca compel every serious reader of the work to seek answers to the above questions. This section proposes to explore answers to some of the questions.

Clark's conclusions (as set out in this book and other writings) on the success of Gacaca in achieving its objectives are at variance with the vast body of other independent scholarship on the subject. For scholars of Gacaca and other professionals interested in the subject, the book's unconventional and controversial findings and conclusions call for interpretation or explanation. I am of the view of that the conclusions of *Gacaca Courts, Post-Genocide Justice and Reconciliation in Rwanda – Justice without Lawyers* on the effectiveness of Gacaca in achieving its objectives are unwarranted. This section sets out the basis of my views on this subject.

6.5.1 Lack of grounding in mainstream transitional justice theory

The book argues that Gacaca is unique among transitional justice processes, and attributes its purported uniqueness and attraction to its hybridity, demonstrated by its combination of 'pragmatic' and 'profound' objectives. It claims to be the first and only work of scholarship on Gacaca to interpret correctly that 'Gacaca is designed to pursue a combination of pragmatic and profound objectives' (2010: p. 82). The book does not offer any definition of what constitutes a 'pragmatic objective' and a 'profound objective'. I understand 'pragmatic objective' to refer to initiatives intended to address a social or political problem of pressing concern, that is not linked to a particular policy objective of transformative societal change. I understand a 'profound objective' to refer to an objective associated with addressing one or more aspects of the fundamental causes of the underlying conflict and linked to aspirations to build a peaceful and stable society able to manage and resolve its conflict in constructive ways. Clark asserts that scholars and other commentators whose work comprises what he refers to as the 'dominant narrative' consider punishment and deterrence to be the sole objective of processes of accountability in general, and Gacaca in particular (pp. 27, 82, 96). The 'dominant narrative', he suggests, considers punishment alone to be the only adequate response to crimes such as genocide (2010: p. 220). According to the book, proponents of the 'dominant narrative' do not recognize the social political objectives of Gacaca, especially reconciliation, as an objective of transitional justice processes in general and Gacaca in particular (pp. 92, 97).

Clark's interpretation of Gacaca is based on a significant misunderstanding of transitional justice theory. Gacaca is a hybrid in the sense that it is a new institution that applies statutory criminal law (whose application is normally exclusively reserved to the formal justice system) in the context of popular justice administered by lay people. That apart, there is nothing new or unique about Gacaca's pursuit of a multiplicity of goals of short- and long-term implications. Transitional justice processes aim to help a society emerging from violent conflict or authoritarian rule to build peace and stability. The choices that each society in transition makes as to which transitional justice processes it should pursue are determined by its context. Necessarily, therefore, all transitional justice processes combine both pragmatic and profound objectives that mirror the particular challenges that the society in question has to deal with. As is amply demonstrated in Chapter 1's exploration of the theoretical framework of transitional justice, all of Gacaca's goals that Clark labels as its 'profound' goals (namely truth, justice, peace, healing and forgiveness and reconciliation) are already recognized as objectives of transitional justice in general (Crocker 1999; Vandegiste 2009). Transitional justice theory also holds that the objectives of transitional justice processes are necessarily intimately linked (United Nations 2004: paras 24–7). The multiple goals that each transitional justice process pursues may be complementary (United Nations 2004), but they may also be in conflict (Crocker 1999). The author's claim that his book is the first and only work of scholarship to interpret correctly that 'Gacaca is designed to pursue a combination of pragmatic and profound objectives' has no basis. A large number of scholars have long explored the social and political objectives of Gacaca (Borocan 2004; Daly 2002a; Drumbl 2000a, 2000b, 2001, 2002b, 2004; du Toit 2011; Gahima 2002; Haile 2008; Ingelaere 2006, 2008, 2009a, 2009b, 2010; Karekezi *et al.* 2004; Lambourne 2005; Longman 2004a, 2006a, 2009, 2010, 2011; Thomson 2009, 2011a, 2011b, 2011c; Waldorf 2006a, 2006b). This vast body of scholarship has long recognized and explored the full range of the objectives of Gacaca that Clark's work discusses.

6.5.2 Failure to appreciate the role of human rights in establishing legitimate transitional justice processes

The book dismisses criticism of Gacaca's failure to comply with human rights standards relating to justice as unwarranted. Most other scholars, the book argues, have a 'mistaken assumption that Gacaca fails to provide impartial decision-making and to guarantee legal safeguards; virtues which they claim result solely from a strict due process approach to justice' (Clark 2010: p. 348). Clark argues that the principle that 'justice should be a neutrally determined, universal virtue and free from all value-laden claims by specific individuals or groups' should not be applied to Gacaca (p. 92). In any event, the author continues, 'most observers have grossly overstated the predicted or observed problems with Gacaca ... the hybridity of Gacaca's methods has facilitated both legal protection of individual suspects and a high degree of popular participation' (p. 343). According to the book, proponents of the dominant narrative 'mischaracterize Gacaca as a form of mob justice, which fails to protect innocent suspects ... these critics ignore Gacaca's formal boundaries, which limit the negotiated aspects of hearings, and protect the rights of suspects' (p. 352). Gacaca, Clark argues, represents a radical, comprehensive approach to transitional justice (p. 343) to which the provisions of international human rights instruments are not relevant or applicable. The concept of the right to fair trial that is the basis for much of the human rights-related criticism of Gacaca ought not to be applied to Gacaca.

The book's argument that the concept of 'fair trial' protected by international law should have no application to Gacaca or other traditional justice mechanisms has no basis in Rwandan or international law and is certainly not supported by established scholarship in the fields of transitional justice. The right to fair trial applies to all proceedings of a judicial nature, including traditional justice mechanisms. The Human Rights Committee has found that the right to trial by an independent and impartial tribunal 'is an absolute right that may suffer no exception' (UNOHCHR 1987: para. 5.2). Commenting on Article 14 of the International Covenant on Civil and Political Rights (ICCPR), the Human Rights Committee, in General Comment 13, has said: '[t]he provisions of Article 14 apply to all courts and tribunals within the scope of that article whether ordinary or specialized' (UNOHCHR 1984: para. 4). The right to fair trial applies to even traditional or customary mechanisms of justice (African Commission on Human and Peoples' Right 1999a). Paragraph 4 of the African Commission on Human and Peoples' Rights Dakar Declaration on the right to fair trial in Africa (African Commission on Human and Peoples' Rights 1999b) has stated:

> It is recognized that traditional courts are capable of playing a role in the achievement of peaceful societies and exercise authority over a significant proportion of the population in African countries. However, these courts also have serious shortcomings, which result in many instances in a denial of a fair trial. Traditional courts are not exempt from the provisions of the African Charter relating to fair trial.

The Principles and Guidelines on the Right to a Fair Trial and Legal Assistance in Africa provide (African Commission on Human and Peoples Rights 2001: Article R) that traditional courts, where they exist, are required to respect international standards on the right to a fair trial. No circumstances whatsoever, whether a threat of war, a state of international or internal armed conflict, internal political instability or any other public emergency, may be invoked to justify derogations from the right to a fair trial.

However, the rationale for respect of the right to fair trial in Gacaca is not limited to legal reasons. Human rights practices have tremendous implications for the effectiveness of transitional justice processes, and criminal trials in particular. Unfair trials create or perpetuate grievances that may give rise to a desire for revenge and to fresh outbreaks of violence. Unfair trials hinder the restoration or building of constructive relationships between victims and perpetrators. They undermine the legitimacy of the state and the commitment of the government to the rule of law. Violations of human rights principles in the implementation of transitional justice processes have the potential to affect adversely prospects for reconciliation, peace and stability, and political transition.

There are social and political reasons that make respect for human rights in transitional justice processes critical. Respect of the right to fair trial has implications for the effectiveness of prosecutions, or trials by traditional conflict resolution mechanisms such as Gacaca, in achieving the goals of transitional justice. Unfair trials render judicial processes illegitimate in popular perception. They enhance, instead of dissipating, grievances between the parties who have been in conflict. Unfair trials undermine efforts to rebuild relations of trust between parties in the proceedings. They are an obstacle to reconciliation and sustainable peace. Gacaca are courts with all the power of ordinary criminal justice courts, but lacking the safeguards that the law avails to defendants in ordinary criminal cases. Gacaca's limitations in achieving its objectives are partly a result of deep grievances of many in the Hutu community that Rwanda's transitional justice processes (including Gacaca) have violated their human rights and the human rights of relatives, friends and members of their community. The principal problem with Gacaca is not that it violates human rights norms (which it does) that Rwanda is obligated to uphold; the major problem is that it has an adverse impact on relations between victims and the majority of the people in their communities. It has also become a new source of grievance by the Hutu community against the government and the minority Tutsi community. The book's argument that human rights standards should have no application to Gacaca has no legal, social or political justification.

I recognize that Gacaca could never have been able to comply fully with all the legal requirements covered by the right to fair trial. I also acknowledge that Gacaca had the potential to play a useful role in advancing the goals of transitional justice in the aftermath of the violence that Rwanda experienced. In hindsight, I now believe that it was not appropriate to give Gacaca the full range of the powers that criminal justice courts have. Gacaca should, in my opinion, have served as a decentralized truth commission without the powers of criminal courts to sentence suspects to imprisonment. The powers of prosecution and punishment would be left to the ordinary courts, that would try only as many cases (mainly of persons who bore great responsibility for the crimes that were committed) as they could try fairly. Gacaca would only have jurisdiction for crimes that were committed by the rank and file and its powers would extend to power to award compensation or to order community service. The decisions of Gacaca courts should have been open to review by the ordinary courts.

6.5.3 Misrepresentation of other scholarship on Gacaca

The book makes many unfounded claims and outright misrepresentations about other serious scholarship on Gacaca. It argues that previous scholarship on Gacaca which it labels as the 'dominant narrative' is all deeply flawed (Clark 2010: p. 83). According to Clark, the dominant narrative comprises mainly 'observers … [who] lack the experience of first hand observations of Gacaca hearings' (pp. 6–7); interprets Gacaca 'solely on the basis of its legal instruments' (pp. 96, 347); neglects 'the importance of popular ownership over, and evolving interpretations of, Gacaca' (pp. 28, 91, 347); considers punishment and deterrence to be the sole objective of criminal prosecutions of gross human rights violations in general, and Gacaca in particular (pp. 27–8, 82, 93, 95–6, 348); shares 'the unconvincing view that justice, which is determined formally to facilitate exclusively deterrent outcomes, is an adequate response to crimes such as genocide' (p. 347); does not recognize the social and political objectives of Gacaca, especially reconciliation (pp. 82, 92, 97); 'holds that non-legal pursuits are inappropriate at Gacaca' (p. 351); seeks 'to dissolve any possible link between retributive or deterrent justice and notions of restoration and reconciliation (p. 245); or has failed to analyse Gacaca 'as a dynamic, lived, social legal institution' (p. 347) or to explain why it is important to analyse Gacaca on the basis of the population's views and participation in Gacaca (p. 5). All these claims about previous scholarship on Gacaca are entirely unfounded. Clark argues that the dominant narrative 'provides an extremely narrow view of Gacaca, and in the main, criticizes it for failing to achieve ends for which it was never, or at least only particularly, intended' (p. 28). The book contends that the dominant narrative ignores 'the importance of concepts of public collaboration, negotiation and engagement through the daily running of Gacaca … By not only ignoring the effects of popular involvement in Gacaca … but by also viewing popular involvement in Gacaca as an anathema to impartial justice, proponents of the dominant discourse on Gacaca fail to recognize the kinetic nature of Gacaca' (p. 348). Clark also claims that the dominant view neglects 'the virtual impact of external social and political developments elsewhere in Rwandan culture on the ways in which the community interprets, and participates in Gacaca' (p. 347).

The book's claim to be the groundbreaking work in terms of identifying the objectives of Gacaca has no basis. The objectives of Gacaca have long been extensively documented in legislation, policy documents and academic scholarship (Borocan 2004; Daly 2002a; Drumbl 2000a, 2000b, 2000b, 2001, 2002b, 2004; du Toit 2011; Gahima 2002; Haile 2008; Ingelaere 2006, 2008, 2009a, 2009b, 2010; Karekezi *et al.* 2004; Lambourne 2005; Longman 2004a, 2006a, 2009, 2010, 2011; Thomson 2009, 2011a, 2011b, 2011c; Waldorf 2006a, 2006b). The claims that the dominant narrative considers deterrent justice to be the sole objective of Gacaca, regards criminal justice as the only appropriate response to crimes such as genocide and does not recognize that Gacaca has non-legal objectives such as reconciliation are untrue. Much of the scholarship criticized (Ingelaere 2006, 2008, 2009a, 2009b;

Oomen 2005, 2006, 2009; Rettig 2008, 2011; Thomson 2009; Waldorf 2004, 2006a, 2006b; Zorbas 2004) is grounded in transitional justice theory, which recognizes that punishment in criminal prosecutions is only part of a wide range of complementary processes that post-conflict societies need to undertake to build peaceful and stable societies. Transitional justice theory recognizes that justice is a means to an end (promoting the building of peaceful, stable societies governed in accordance with the rule of law) and not an end in itself. Neither the scholars nor the human rights organizations such as Amnesty International and Human Rights Watch whose work is critiqued in the book have argued or advocated that retributive justice is, or should be, the sole objective and end goal of transitional justice processes, in Rwanda or in other parts of the world. Much of the scholarship criticized by the book analyses Gacaca on the basis of extensive field research exploring how Gacaca operates in practice and not on the exclusive basis of Gacaca's legal instruments. All the scholarship recognizes the social and political objectives of Gacaca and much is the result of extensive research at grassroots level, for extended periods in many cases. (See, for example: Ingalaere 2003, 2006, 2008, 2009a, 2009b, 2010; Rettig 2008, 2011; Strauss…., Thomson 2009, 2011a, 2011b, 2010; Waldorf 2006a, 2006b, 2009, 2011a, 2011b). The book's claim, that all scholarship of the dominant narrative is not based on first knowledge of the operation of Gacaca, are unfounded.

6.5.4 Failure to take into account the prevailing social and political context

Transitional justice processes are a major aspect of peace building, an umbrella term for many different activities that non-violently seek to prevent, reduce, resolve, transform and help people recover from violence in all forms, including structural violence that has not yet led to massive civil unrest (Schirch 2008: p. 7). The impact of transitional justice is hard to measure (Van der Merwe *et al.* 2009). There is a consensus, however, that transitional justice processes (and all other processes aimed at peace building in the aftermath of violent conflict) cannot achieve their intended objectives if they are not part of a comprehensive process of reform that addresses the root causes of the conflicts that the particular society has experienced in the past. The Carnegie Endowment's Commission on the Prevention of Deadly Conflict (1997) defined peace building as 'structural prevention' which consists of strategies to address the root causes of deadly conflict. Necessarily, therefore, the success of transitional justice processes is intimately connected with, and very dependent upon, the social and political environment prevailing in a particular society, which is in turn shaped by conflict in a particular society.

By contrast, *The Gacaca Courts, Post-Genocide Justice and Reconciliation in Rwanda* discusses the extent to which Gacaca has achieved its intended objectives in total isolation from the root causes of conflict and the social and political context prevailing in Rwanda. The author's failure to connect the process of

Gacaca to the crucial social and political environment in which Gacaca has been implemented and the limits that this political environment has had on Gacaca's ability to achieve its objectives may well be the book's greatest weakness.

The war, genocide and other violence that the people of Rwanda experienced during the 1990s left them bitterly divided. The RPF exploited its military victory to monopolize political power and has used its absolute control of the state to engineer what is considered by many to be a successful experiment of post-conflict reconstruction (Straus and Waldorf 2011). The post-genocide government is credited with success in the restoration of order, rebuilding the machinery of government, providing social services and promoting economic growth (McDoom 2011). The ruling party claims that economic development can only be assured and sustained by continued restrictions of civil and political rights. Post-genocide Rwanda transitioned to one-party dictatorship with a false façade of a democracy. The government has imposed strict control on the exercise of the rights of freedom of expression and political participation and does not allow open debate about the human rights practices of its military and security services, ethnicity, or the distribution of power between the different social or ethnic groups or political participation in general. The government is controlled by a small group of elites from the Tutsi minority. The majority Hutu are excluded from a meaningful share of power. The government relies on repression (including arbitrary arrests, malicious prosecutions, enforced disappearances, extra-judicial killings and other forms of persecution) to stay in power. There is no system of checks and balances in Rwanda's government. The judiciary and legislature are not independent. Civil society, including the media, is stifled by government control and cannot operate freely. Agents of the state continue to enjoy impunity for grave human rights abuses. The accountability processes that Rwanda and the international community have undertaken have focused exclusively on the genocide and have overlooked the suffering of the Hutu community.

While Clark writes that he recognizes 'the crucial national social-political context within which Gacaca operates' (2010: p. 25), there is no indication in the text that these factors have in any way influenced his analysis of Gacaca. The book discusses Gacaca in total isolation from essential elements of this context. This shortcoming calls into question the credibility of its positive analysis of Gacaca's impact.

6.5.5 Narrow scope of analysis

Lastly, Clark's analysis of the impact of Gacaca is very narrow in scope. There are certain important objectives of Gacaca that the research for this book did not succeed in identifying. These objectives include eradication of impunity, promoting a culture of respect for human rights, advancing the rule of law, empowerment of the citizenry, helping Rwandan society to reach closure in relation to accountability for genocide and preparing the ground for the RPF to participate competitively in the elections that were to mark the end of the transition period. The objectives of Gacaca that the book does not discuss are precisely the objectives in respect of which Gacaca has demonstrated its greatest weaknesses. The book's failure to address some of the fundamental objectives of Gacaca makes its discussion of Gacaca superficial.

Clark's work is an important contribution to knowledge about Gacaca. However, the book has very significant shortcomings. It does not identify the full range of Gacaca's objectives. Its analysis downplays the significance of many of Gacaca's obvious weaknesses, including its failure to address grievances of the Hutu victims, lack of even-handedness in providing justice for victims, non-compliance with human rights standards, constraints to the establishment of the truth and Gacaca's tendency to enhance tensions between victims and their communities and between the Hutu and Tutsi in general. The book's analysis steers away from discussing aspects of Gacaca's transitional justice objectives, such as the eradication of impunity, the promotion of a culture of respect for human rights, advancing democracy and facilitating 'national closure' on the issue of accountability for the genocide, that the Rwanda government considers sensitive or objectionable. Its analysis is not grounded in a sound understanding of the theories, principles and best practices of the fields of transitional justice, human rights and peace building on which Gacaca, like other transitional justice mechanisms, should be grounded. The book misrepresents the thrust of a vast body of scholarship that it labels as the 'dominant narrative' on Gacaca. Most significantly, it fails to analyse the impact of the constraining socio-political environment prevailing in Rwanda on Gacaca's capacity to achieve its intended objectives.

The book's factual findings and conclusions about the effectiveness of Gacaca are in many instances inconsistent. Consider, for example, the following declarations made in the book in the light of its overall conclusions that Gacaca has achieved its objectives: 'Feelings of fear and uncertainty which [the] … social, legal and political environment instills in the population greatly affect popular involvement in Gacaca and justice and reconciliation more broadly' (2010 p. 19); the RPF committed atrocities after the genocide (p. 20) and 'the atmosphere of violent retribution created by the massacres lingers in the current context, causing many genocide suspects to fear the prospect of return to their communities where they will face Gacaca and creating unease among the Hutu population in general' (p. 20); the RPF has since 1994 worked to consolidate monopoly of political power and to impose its political dominance (p. 21); there has been 'limited national discussion … since 1994 … on key issues of Rwandan ethnicity and the root causes of the genocide (p. 219); Gacaca is perceived by members of the Hutu as one-sided (p. 210); government rarely discusses the extensive participation of state actors in Gacaca, which undermines the notion of Gacaca as an entirely popular enterprise driven by local agents (p. 146); '[t]here is little doubt many detainees confess to crimes significantly less severe than those they actually committed during the genocide' (p. 101). The book's selective use of data on Gacaca raises questions about the work's scholarly value.

6.6 Conclusion

In 2003, Uvin wrote:

> Finally, the way in which the Gacaca process unfolds will be profoundly affected by broader social and political trends, both nationally and locally. The extent to which people distrust or dislike the government (perhaps because they suffered heavily from the counter-offensives against rebel infiltration, or because they judge the central government to be increasingly unrepresentative and exclusive), the memories they carry about the behaviour of government soldiers immediately after the genocide, and even general economic trends (e.g. the impact of localized famines) – all these factors are bound to influence people's willingness to engage in the risky process of Gacaca. While these factors fall outside the design of the law, they may well be the key factors that determine its success or failure. (2003b: p. 121)

Uvin's writing has been profoundly prophetic. At its inception, Gacaca was generally favourably perceived as a bold, if overly ambitious, undertaking with largely noble ideals. Harshly criticized by political opponents of the Rwanda regime, human rights commentators and most academic scholars of the Rwanda genocide, Gacaca has nevertheless had some positive outcomes. It offered Rwanda the only viable opportunity of providing justice for the victims of the genocide and it has done so more effectively than prosecutions in the ordinary criminal justice system could ever have done. Gacaca has also helped to address some of the social and political problems (including the large backlog of pending genocide cases and harsh overcrowding of prisons) arising from the pursuit of criminal cases against hundreds of thousands of members of the Hutu community for crimes connected with the genocide. Gacaca has not, however, been successful in achieving its long-term objectives such as promoting reconciliation, advancing the rule of law, ending impunity and ensuring sustainable peace and stability.

Gacaca's potential to achieve its long-term objectives was adversely affected by several factors, including its pursuit of retributive justice, its lack of even-handedness and constraints associated with the socio-political environment in which it has been implemented. Gacaca's appeal and legacy have also been adversely affected by widespread human rights abuses that its implementation occasioned to those who were affected by it and by the capture of the process by state institutions and functionaries. Gacaca's lack of even-handedness undermined its legitimacy with many in the Hutu community (Zorbas 2004; Wolters 2005b; Waldorf 2006b; Haile 2008; FDU-Inkingi 2012). Gacaca's retributive aspect motivated many in the Hutu community to obstruct the pursuit of truth, in the interest of shielding relatives, friends and neighbours from responsibility for their crimes. Some commentators believe the active participation of the Hutu community in Gacaca was also discouraged by grievances that the ruling party has excluded the community from a meaningful share of political power (Thomson 2009, 2011a, 2011b; Takeuchi 2011; Thomson and Nagy 2011). As a result of the resistance of many in the Hutu community to the Gacaca process, the government was in many instances compelled to rely on coercion to move the Gacaca process forward. Expediency has been prioritized at the expense of due process and fairness (Sarkin 2001: p. 164). Gacaca involved violations of fair trial guarantees that are likely to have led to widespread miscarriages of justice (Longman 2006a; Rettig 2008). It has proved vulnerable to abuse by key stakeholders, including the perpetrators and victims of mass atrocity, the population at large, as well as officials of the government (Penal Reform International 2010a: pp. 43–5). Some research suggests that Gacaca exposed and may even have deepened conflict, resentment and ethnic disunity in some communities (Rettig 2011; Thomson 2011b).

The record of Gacaca at grassroots level is at best mixed. As one scholar has noted:

> Some trials end with the community largely satisfied; others leave survivors, prisoners, and their families frustrated. While some judgments are clear-cut, others seem arbitrary. And while Gacaca's successes (achieved against great odds) should be celebrated, its problems (some inevitable, some not) also should be taken seriously. (Rettig 2008: p. 33)

At national level, Gacaca's legacy is on balance negative. Like Rwanda's other peace-building initiatives, it has not addressed some of the root causes of conflict in Rwandan society. Gacaca may have played a useful and perhaps invaluable role in the short term. Its longer-term benefits are less obvious and will be debated for a long time to come.

Rwanda's experience with Gacaca has lessons for other societies that may have to deal with legacies of mass atrocity. The implementation of Gacaca has demonstrated that justice mechanisms based on custom or tradition can play a very useful role in the framework of transitional justice processes in societies with pluralistic legal systems. Traditional justice mechanisms can be more effective than criminal prosecutions in the formal court system in reckoning with legacies of massive violations of human rights, especially in situations where the violence has involved large-scale popular participation. Rwanda's experience with Gacaca suggests, however, that traditional justice systems work best when they aim to promote restoration, and have inherent limitations as tools for the investigation, trial and punishment of grave human rights abuses. When endowed with jurisdiction to try and punish international crimes, traditional justice mechanisms are likely to lead to extensive human rights abuses that undermine the capacity to advance the goals of transitional justice.

7 Trials Based on the Principle of Universal Jurisdiction

7.1 Introduction

A large number of states have undertaken investigations and, sometimes, prosecutions of crimes alleged to have been committed as part of the Rwanda genocide on the basis of the principle of universal jurisdiction. This chapter discusses the background to the problem of the presence of persons suspected of involvement in the Rwanda genocide in various states, the rationale and legal basis for the exercise of the principle of universal jurisdiction for international crimes and other gross human rights violations in general, and the strategies that various states have put in place to make it possible for their courts to exercise universal jurisdiction for international crimes in general, and crimes relating to the Rwanda genocide in particular. An overview of the experiences of prosecutions, based on the principle of universal jurisdiction, by various states of crimes alleged to have been committed during the Rwanda genocide follows. The chapter concludes with a discussion of the lessons that have been learned from attempts to ensure justice for the Rwanda genocide through the instrumentality of the principle of universal jurisdiction.

7.2 Background to Prosecutions of Crimes Associated with the Rwanda Genocide through Universal Jurisdiction

In July 1994, the RPA took control of Rwanda and brought the genocide to an end. With the military defeat of the government that had planned and directed the genocide, millions of Rwandans fled en masse out of the country. Among the Rwandans who left the country were persons who bore responsibility to varying degrees for genocide, war crimes, crimes against humanity and other gross violations of human rights. These perpetrators included the leaders of the military and security institutions, government agencies, militia groups and civil society organizations who played a leading role in ensuring the success of the genocide. Most of the perpetrators who fled Rwanda in 1994 initially sought refuge in countries in Eastern and Central Africa. In time, those who could afford it moved on to countries beyond. The spread of Rwandan refugees across the world particularly intensified after the Rwandan military launched attacks against the camps of Rwandan refugees in the Congo during 1996–97. Rwandan refugees, including perpetrators of genocide, can now be found in every part of the world, and have settled in large numbers in Europe, North America and a large number of countries in Africa, with the exception of North Africa (SALC/REDRESS 2012).

It can be safely assumed that in every large community of Rwandans now settled in any foreign country, there are likely to be persons who are responsible for genocide and other gross human rights violations. Bringing these perpetrators of atrocity to justice has presented challenges both to the state of Rwanda and to the international community. In the aftermath of the genocide, the government of Rwanda did not have the human and material resources to investigate and prosecute the cases of tens of thousands of genocide-accused persons who were in its custody, let alone pursue the perpetrators who had settled in foreign countries. Rwanda had extradition treaties with only a few states. Many governments had strong misgivings about the state of the country's justice system and many states were unwilling to return persons accused of involvement in the genocide for trial in Rwanda. Rwanda's justice system lay in shambles, and many states had legitimate concerns about the country's capacity to provide fair trial of any suspects who might be returned. It was, as a result, virtually impossible for Rwanda to obtain custody of suspects living in foreign countries. Until recently, Rwanda has been unable able to secure the extradition or transfer of persons suspected of genocide-related crimes from foreign countries for trial in its courts.

The ICTR was tasked to bring persons responsible for the genocide to justice. However, the tribunal could only try a relatively small number of the perpetrators who had escaped from Rwanda. By the early 2000s, the ICTR was already under pressure to scale down indictments and to implement a completion strategy. The stage seemed set to enable a very large number of the people who bore significant responsibility for crimes that were committed during the genocide to escape justice.

The principle of universal jurisdiction has been exploited by victims, civil society advocacy groups and interested governments to narrow the impunity gap that domestic prosecutions, proceedings before Gacaca tribunals and international criminal justice have left in relation to the crimes that were committed during the Rwanda genocide. The principle of universal jurisdiction has provided the opportunity to provide justice to victims of crimes whose perpetrators fled to Rwanda in or after 1994 that might otherwise have gone unaccounted for.

7.3 Rational and Legal Basis for Universal Jurisdiction for International Crimes in General

7.3.1 Rationale for universal jurisdiction

'Universal jurisdiction' refers to the competence of a national court to try a person suspected of a serious international crime – such as genocide, war crimes, crimes against humanity or torture – even if neither the suspect nor the victim are nationals of the country where the court is located ('the forum state'), and the crime took place outside that country (Reydams 2003; Hall 2010).

When violent conflict involving human rights abuses has occurred, trials by the state in which the crimes were committed (the 'territorial state') are preferable to trials abroad. The territorial state is preferable because it enjoys the advantage of being where most of the evidence is located and where the majority of victims are present. Domestic trials of those responsible for committing human rights violations are likely to have a greater impact on victims and society as a whole than trials conducted by courts of foreign countries that have no link to the conflict in the context of which the crimes being tried were committed.

However, fair and effective investigation and prosecution of human rights abuses by the territorial state are not always possible. Persons responsible for grave human rights abuses may be able to escape justice in the territorial state for a variety of reasons. Perpetrators may control the machinery of the territorial state or wield strong influence in the society in question. The territorial state may be unwilling to investigate or prosecute the crimes due to state involvement or acquiescence in the crimes. Some conflicts (such as Mozambique's) are often brought to an end by negotiated settlements that may grant amnesties or pardons to officials of the state or insurgent groups that are parties to the peace agreements. In other situations, repressive regimes may seek to shield their officials from responsibility for human rights abuses by conditioning the transition to democracy on amnesties enshrined in domestic laws. The state may simply be too weak to apprehend and punish perpetrators. The legal system of the state in which the abuses have been committed may not be in a position to provide justice to victims. The domestic judiciary may have been destroyed as a result of the conflict. A newly installed democratic government may be too weak and fragile to bring perpetrators of atrocities to justice. Such is the case in Liberia, for example. Some armed conflicts (such as Rwanda's) involving grave human rights abuses come to an end through the outright military victory of one party. In such situations, the transitional justice processes (including criminal prosecutions) that the new regime undertakes are more likely to focus solely on the crimes of the vanquished. Perpetrators of grave human rights violations may also seek to avoid justice by fleeing from the territorial state and seeking asylum in other countries, either in their rightful names or under newly assumed identities. There may be legal or political reasons that make the extradition of such perpetrators to the territorial state impossible. These are just some of the circumstances in which persons responsible for grave human rights abuses may be able to escape justice in the states in which they committed crimes.

A system of international criminal justice (comprising the ad hoc tribunals as well as the permanent ICC) has been developed to close the impunity gap that results when the states in which international crimes are committed are unable or unwilling to investigate, prosecute and, if the evidence so warrants, punish perpetrators of serious human rights violations. However, international criminal tribunals can only reduce but not eliminate this gap in mechanisms to fight impunity. International criminal tribunals have limited capacity to try significant numbers of suspects. Their mandates are generally limited to crimes committed in specific conflicts. Their jurisdiction is limited in geographical scope and temporal mandate. With regard to the ICC, the powers of the prosecutor are also subject to strong limitations. As a result of these circumstances, international criminal justice does not always provide effective access to justice to victims of human rights abuses that the forum state is unable or unwilling to investigate, prosecute and punish in good faith.

The rationale for the exercise of universal jurisdiction is that when crimes of concern to the international community have been committed, and the states that enjoy traditional jurisdiction are unable or unwilling to act, there is an interest in the international community to take action in order to preserve peace. The concept permits an interested state to exercise jurisdiction over crimes that the forum state is unable or unwilling to investigate and try. The state undertaking the investigation and prosecution is acting on behalf of the international community, which has an interest in the preservation of the world order (Bassiouni 2002b: pp. 950–6). The principle of universal jurisdiction not only serves to fight impunity, it also helps to advance accountability by making it possible to investigate, prosecute and punish international crimes that domestic courts and international criminal tribunals are not addressing.

7.3.2 *Legal basis for universal jurisdiction*

The principle of universal jurisdiction for international crimes is based on the recognition that certain crimes are of a particularly egregious nature that they are a matter of international concern, due to their 'heinous nature and disruptive impact on peace and security' (Bassiouni 2001: p. 153). It is argued that the horrific nature of such crimes requires the extension of the jurisdiction of domestic courts to ensure that perpetrators are brought to justice, wherever they may be. Proponents of the strict application of the principle of universal jurisdiction argue that all states have a duty and an obligation to hold perpetrators of international crimes (especially genocide, war crimes, crimes against humanity and torture) accountable and that victims of serious international crimes have a right to justice everywhere in the world. The right of states to exercise universal jurisdiction to investigate and prosecute serious international crimes may be based on treaties as well as customary international law. The principle of universal jurisdiction is permissive: states are permitted but not obliged to investigate and prosecute unless a mandatory, treaty-based obligation to investigate and prosecute exists.

There is a consensus that the courts of most states have universal jurisdiction for war crimes, including torture and grave breaches of the Geneva Conventions. Such jurisdiction is based on accession to the Geneva Conventions and the Convention against Torture. Each of the Geneva Conventions of 1949 contains a provision to the effect that:

> Each High Contracting Party shall be under the obligation to search for persons alleged to have committed, or to have ordered to be committed, such grave breaches, and shall bring such persons, regardless of their nationality, before its own courts.[1]

The Convention against Torture and Other Cruel, Inhuman or Degrading Treatment or Punishment provides:

> **Article 4**
>
> 1. Each State Party shall ensure that all acts of torture are offences under its criminal law. The same shall apply to an attempt to commit torture and to an act by any person which constitutes complicity or participation in torture.
> 2. Each State Party shall make these offences punishable by appropriate penalties which take into account their grave nature.
>
> **Article 5**
>
> 1. Each State Party shall take such measures as may be necessary to establish its jurisdiction over the offences referred to in article 4 in the following cases:
>   (a) When the offences are committed in any territory under its jurisdiction or on board a ship or aircraft registered in that State;
>   (b) When the alleged offender is a national of that State;
>   (c) When the victim is a national of that State if that State considers it appropriate.
> 2. Each State Party shall likewise take such measures as may be necessary to establish its jurisdiction over such offences in cases where the alleged offender is present in any territory under its jurisdiction and it does not extradite him pursuant to article 8 to any of the States mentioned in paragraph I of this article.
> 3. This Convention does not exclude any criminal jurisdiction exercised in accordance with internal law.

The International Convention for the Protection of All Persons from Enforced Disappearances provides:

> Each State Party shall likewise take such measures as may be necessary to establish its competence to exercise jurisdiction over the offence of enforced disappearance when the alleged offender is present in any territory under its

> jurisdiction, unless it extradites or surrenders him or her to another State in accordance with its international obligations or surrenders him or her to an international criminal tribunal whose jurisdiction it has recognized.[2]

Claims of universal jurisdiction for genocide and crimes against humanity are based on customary international law. There is no consensus, but it is widely accepted that international law permits all states to exercise universal jurisdiction in respect of genocide and crimes against humanity as well[3] and, possibly, serious violations of the laws of war in internal armed conflicts.[4]

7.4 Strategies for Enhancing the Role of the Principle of Universal Jurisdiction in Accountability for International Crimes

Over the past two decades, national authorities in many states, including Austria, Belgium, Canada, Denmark, Finland, France, Germany, Sweden, the Netherlands, Senegal, Spain, the UK and the US have initiated criminal proceedings against suspected perpetrators of war crimes, torture, crimes against humanity and genocide committed in Rwanda as well as other countries, including Afghanistan, Argentina, Chad, Chechnya, DRC, the Former Yugoslavia, Iraq, Mauritania, Sierra Leone, Tunisia and Uganda. At the same time, victims have invoked the principle of universal jurisdiction to file complaints against human rights violations alleged to have been committed in Algeria, Chad, China, France, Israel, Rwanda, Tunisia and the US. The developments in the domains of international human rights law, international humanitarian law, international criminal law and transitional justice emphasizing the need for accountability for gross human rights abuses that have occurred over the past two decades have led to, amongst other things, the development of state practice relating to the application of the principle of universal jurisdiction. States, especially in Western Europe and North America, have developed strategies to enhance, facilitate and streamline the application of the principle of universal jurisdiction to the investigation and prosecution of international crime. These strategies have included the following measures.

7.4.1 Legal reforms

Traditionally, one of the main obstacles to the application of the principle of universal jurisdiction to the investigation and prosecution of international crimes has been the absence of relevant implementing legislation. While most states acknowledge in principle their obligation under treaties as well as customary international law to investigate and prosecute international crimes, this obligation may not be reflected in domestic laws. The laws of some states do not explicitly confer jurisdiction to try extraterritorial crimes to their courts. States may not have legislation defining the crimes that may be tried on the basis of the principle of universal jurisdiction (Human Rights

Watch 2006c). Many states have undertaken reforms of their laws and their courts' jurisdiction to try international crimes or to stream mechanisms for the applications of the principle of universal jurisdiction to the investigation and prosecution of such crimes (Amnesty International 2011). The legal reforms undertaken by various states that have had a bearing on the prosecution of crimes relating to the Rwanda genocide are discussed below in the section that discusses national experiences of prosecutions of crimes relating to the Rwanda conflict.

7.4.2 Setting up of specialized units to track war criminals and to investigate and prosecute international crimes

States have attempted to enhance their capacity for effective investigation and prosecution of international crimes on the basis of the principle of universal jurisdiction by establishing specialized war crimes units. The first specialized units to work on the investigation of international crimes were established to investigate and prosecute Nazi-era crimes.[5] These earlier specialized units were not successful, and most were eventually disbanded. The challenge of dealing with the problem of the presence of war criminals from the many conflicts that broke out in many parts of the world in the aftermath of the end of the Cold War gave impetus to renewed efforts to devise mechanisms to enhance the effectiveness of investigations and the prosecution of international crimes. In recognition of the fact that investigations and prosecutions of international crimes are complex and challenging activities that require specialized knowledge, skills and approaches, a number of countries, particularly in Western Europe (Belgium, Denmark, Germany, the Netherlands, Norway, Sweden and the UK), but also the US and Canada, have established new specialized units in their immigration, police and prosecution services to detect, investigate and prosecute persons suspected of serious international crimes (REDRESS/FIDH 2010). The Council of the European Union has encouraged member states 'to consider the need to set up or designate specialist units within the competent law enforcement authorities with particular responsibility for investigating and, as appropriate, prosecuting [international] crimes' (European Union 2003: Article 4). Denmark established the Special International Crimes Office in 2002. In 2009, Germany restructured and reinforced the Central Unit for the Fight Against War Crimes and Further Offences pursuant to the Code of Crimes Against International Law (ZBKV). In 2010, France established a specialized unit to investigate international crimes within the gendarmerie. The Netherlands has appointed an investigative judge to work exclusively on international crimes (REDRESS/FIDH 2010). The establishment of specialized units to investigate and prosecute brings the advantage of a consistent and coherent approach to accountability for international crimes, rendering investigations and prosecutions more effective, and allowing for the accumulation of expertise and the sharing of experiences (REDRESS/FIDH 2010: p. 21). These specialized units have played a crucial role in the prosecution of international crimes (including crimes relating to the Rwanda genocide) that have been undertaken in Europe and Canada since the 1990s.

7.4.3 *Establishing mechanisms for promoting cooperation between states in the investigation and prosecution of international crimes*

In addition to establishing specialized units, states have also sought to enhance their capacity to investigate and prosecute international crimes through inter-state cooperation, including through the exchange of information. The Council of the European Union has adopted a decision whose aim is to 'increase cooperation between national units in order to maximize the ability of law enforcement authorities in different Member States to cooperate effectively in the field of investigation and prosecution of persons who have committed or participated in the commission of genocide, crimes against humanity or war crimes … as defined in Articles 6, 7 and 8 of the Rome Statute of the International Criminal Court of 17 July 1998' (European Union 2003: Article 1). The decision provides that member states shall assist one another in investigating and prosecuting the said crimes in accordance with relevant international agreements and national law, and shall to that end coordinate ongoing efforts to investigate and prosecute persons suspected of having committed or participated in the commission of genocide, crimes against humanity or war crimes and take the necessary measures to ensure that the relevant national law enforcement and immigration authorities are able to exchange the information which they require in order to carry out their tasks effectively. Member states of the European Union have established a network to implement this Council decision.

7.5 Overview of National Experiences of Investigations and Prosecutions of Crimes Arising from the Rwanda Conflict on the Basis of the Principle of Universal Jurisdiction

As indicated in section 2 above, many of the people who participated in the Rwanda genocide, including some who took a leading role in planning and directing it managed to escape to other countries and many of these suspects have settled in countries in Europe, North America and Africa (REDRESS 2008). The investigation and prosecution of crimes alleged to have been committed during the Rwanda genocide by Rwandans now living in foreign countries has played a crucial role in the development of institutional mechanisms and state practices pertaining to the application of the principle of universal jurisdiction for violations of international human rights law and international humanitarian law. The states whose courts have been seized with cases relating to the Rwanda genocide include the following.

7.5.1 *Switzerland*

Switzerland was the first country to prosecute a person suspected of crimes relating to participation in the Rwanda genocide on the basis of the principle of universal jurisdiction. Fulgenze Niyonteze,[6] a former district mayor, fled Rwanda after the genocide and was granted asylum in Switzerland in 1995. He was arrested by Swiss authorities in August 1996 and charged with murder, attempted murder and incitement to murder, war crimes, genocide and crimes against humanity. Niyonteze was tried by a military court, as it was the only court that had jurisdiction to try the crimes of which Niyonteze was accused of under Swiss law. The counts of genocide and crimes against humanity were dropped at the beginning of the proceedings, as Swiss criminal law did not legally recognize those crimes at the time. On 30 April 1999, the military tribunal found Niyonteze guilty of assassination, instigation of assassination and violations of the laws of war, and sentenced him to life imprisonment and to 15 years of exclusion from Swiss territory.[7] On appeal, the Military Appeals Tribunal confirmed the conviction for violations of the laws of war, but acquitted Niyonteze of the charges of murder, and reduced the sentence to 14 years' imprisonment and to 15 years' exclusion from Switzerland.[8] In April 2001, the Tribunal Militaire de Cassation, the highest Swiss military court in times of peace, upheld the decision of the Appeals Tribunal.[9] Niyonteze's conviction for war crimes in an internal armed conflict was the first conviction by a municipal court exercising universal jurisdiction under the 1949 Geneva Conventions and Additional Protocol II. Swiss authorities have opened a criminal investigation against former Rwanda Minister of Environment, Gaspard Ruhumuriza, regarding allegations that he was responsible for conduct amounting to genocide in 1994.

7.5.2 *Belgium*

Belgium has led the world in putting the principle of universal jurisdiction into practice. Its law on the prosecution of international crimes[10] has been widely praised by the human rights movement and vilified by governments for its expansive scope.

Many Rwandan genocide suspects and victims of the genocide have settled in Belgium, and have in many cases become naturalized citizens of Belgium. Belgium has demonstrated the strongest commitment of any state to the application of the principle of universal jurisdiction to cases relating to the Rwanda genocide. Its leading role in the application of the concept of universal jurisdiction to the Rwanda genocide may be explained by several factors. These factors include Belgium's commitment to the concept of universal jurisdiction in general; the murder of Belgium members of the United Nations peacekeeping mission that was deployed in Rwanda at the beginning of the genocide; the fact that large numbers of Rwandan refugees, including persons responsible for crimes connected with the Rwanda genocide, have sought and continue to seek asylum in Belgium; colonial links with Rwanda (including responsibility for some policies that exacerbated ethnic conflict in Rwanda); and Belgium's widely criticized decision to withdraw its peacekeepers from Rwanda as the genocide got underway. Many commentators argue that Belgium's withdrawal of its peacekeepers doomed the UN peacekeeping, and may unwittingly have given the rump government that was then in power the signal that the international community would not intervene to stop the genocide of the Tutsi.

Belgium has investigated and prosecuted a significant number of cases relating to crimes alleged to have been committed in the course of the genocide. The first of these cases was the landmark Butare Four case.[11] This case was Belgium's first attempt to apply its 1993 law against war crimes,[12] which gave Belgian courts universal jurisdiction for international crimes. The case was also the first jury trial of alleged violations of international humanitarian law by a municipal court. The trial of the case opened in 2001. The four accused included a university administrator (Vincent Ntezimana), a businessman (Alphonse Higaniro) and two Catholic Church nuns (Consolata Mukangango and Julienne Mukabutera). The jury trial resulted in the conviction of all four, and they were sentenced to prison terms ranging between 12 and 20 years on 8 June 2001.

In response to criticism and diplomatic pressure by several states, particularly the US, relating to the expansive scope of its universal jurisdiction laws, Belgium changed the provisions of its law on universal jurisdiction in August 2003: Law of 17 April 1878 Containing the First Title of the Criminal Procedure Code. The new provisions were effected by amendments to the Belgian Criminal Code and Criminal Procedure Code. With the amendments, Belgium retains universal jurisdiction but in a restricted form. These amendments provide that Belgian courts have jurisdiction over genocide, crimes against humanity and war crimes, as well as ancillary offences, only if the accused is Belgian or has primary residence in Belgian territory, if the victim is Belgian or had lived in Belgium for at least three years at the time the crimes were committed, or if Belgium is required by treaty to exercise jurisdiction over the case. The amendments also provide for jurisdiction over summary and indictable offences under Belgian law that are also offences under the law of the place of commission, as long as the alleged perpetrator has primary residence in Belgian territory, the public prosecutor orders the prosecution, and either the victim or his/her family has filed a complaint, or the state where the offence took place has advised Belgian authorities to prosecute.[13]

Belgian courts have continued to investigate and prosecute cases of crimes alleged to have been committed during the Rwanda genocide under the terms of the revised law on prosecution of international crimes. The Kibungo case[14] was the first case relating to the Rwanda genocide that courts in Belgium tried after the adoption of the 2003 amendments to the law on prosecution of international crimes. It involved charges against two businessmen (Etienne Nzabonimana and Samuel Ndashyikirwa) who were accused of participation in the massacres alleged to have been committed in the Kibungo area of Rwanda. Nzabonimana was accused of helping to organize the killings of civilians by the Interahamwe militias. On 29 June 2005, Nzabonimana and Ndashyikirwa were found guilty of war crimes and sentenced to 12 and 10 years' imprisonment respectively. The decision of the Cour d'Assises in this case involved several interesting facts, including the fact that the accused could be convicted for crimes committed against persons who had not been identified. Furthermore, the court considered as extenuating circumstances the tense situation in Rwanda at the time of the killings, as well as the incitement of racial hatred by the RTLM radio station.

While the majority of the cases relating to the Rwanda genocide that Belgium has investigated and tried involved Rwandan victims, Belgium has also used its law on universal jurisdiction to provide justice to Belgian victims of the Rwanda conflict. Belgium has tried a former officer of the former army of Rwanda, Major Bernard Ntuyahaga,[15] for the brutal murder of the 11 Belgian peacekeepers who were killed in Rwanda at the beginning of the genocide. The charges against Ntuyahaga also included the murder of Prime Minister Agathe Uwilingiyimana and other persons, some of whom were not identified. This case was significant, as it was the only one in which the victims included Belgian citizens. The case had a convoluted history. Belgium initially issued an international arrest warrant for Major Ntuyahaga on 29 May 1995. Ntuyahaga surrendered to the ICTR but the ICTR subsequently decided not to proceed with the case against and set him free, and a struggle between Rwanda and Belgium for his custody ensued. The ICTR ruled that it that it had no mandate to deliver him to any national authority. The Republic of Tanzania eventually decided to extradite Ntuyahaga to Belgium, where his trial before the Cour d'Assises of Brussels began on 19 April 2007. Major Ntuyahaga was convicted and sentenced to 20 years' imprisonment by the Belgian Cour d'Assises for the murder of ten Belgian peacekeepers and an unknown number of other victims, who were killed between 7 April and 6 June 1994.

Another important case relating to crimes that were committed during the Rwanda genocide that has been tried by Belgian courts is the Nkezabera case.[16] Ephrem Nkezabera was a former President of the Commission of Economic Affairs and Finance within the national committee of the Interahamwe militia and Director of the Commercial Bank of Rwanda. He had assisted the Office of the Prosecutor of the ICTR in its cases against other genocide suspects and received immunity from the office. In the early 2000s, the Office of the Prosecutor decided to use him as a prosecution witness in some of its cases. The ICTR could not use him as a witness before he was tried of crimes for which he was personally responsible. For the purposes of establishing Nkezabera's credibility, the prosecutor requested Belgium to 'arrest' and to try him. Belgium cooperated and arrested Nkezabera in June 2004 (Cruvellier 2010: p. 54). Before the Brussels Cour d'Assises, Nkezabera was accused of violations of international humanitarian law, including murder, attempted murder and rape. Nkezabera had originally been charged with crimes of genocide as well, but these charges were dismissed by the court, as the crime had been introduced into Belgian law in 1999, five years after the

Rwanda genocide. Nkezabera admitted the majority of the alleged offences that he was charged with, including financing and arming the Interahamwe militia in order to exterminate the Tutsi and Hutu opponents of the regime, the incitement of massacres and the financing of the Radio Libre des Mille Collines, which was instrumental in inciting massacres. However, Nkezabera disputed the charges of sexual violence. The charges against Nkezabera included allegations of 'murder or rape of an unspecified number of people in unspecified places on unspecified dates between 6 April and 2 July 1994'. Nkezabera, who was suffering from cancer at the time of his trial, did not attend any of the proceedings in the case. He was convicted of the charges against him, including an 'indeterminate' number of murders and rapes committed by him or under his orders. Nkezabera was sentenced to 30 years imprisonment, instead of life imprisonment, due to his cooperation with the prosecution. The trial of Nkezabera was significant because of its contribution to knowledge of the organization and financing of the genocide. The case was also significant because its judgment was the first instance in Belgian judicial history when rape was held to be a war crime. On 1 March 2010, the court granted Nkezabera's application for the setting aside of his conviction and sentence *in absentia* and ordered a retrial. Nkezabera succumbed to liver cancer on 24 May 2010 before the case against him could be retried.

Belgium continues to carry out investigations against Rwandans suspected of involvement in the genocide. Persons who are now in custody awaiting trial in Belgium for crimes alleged to have been committed include Mathias Bushishi (a former prosecutor in the southern Rwandan town of Butare), Ernest Gakwaya, known as 'Camarade', Emmanuel Nkunzuwimye, aka 'Bombok' and Col. Jean Marie Vianney Ndahimana, alias 'Rumende', a former officer in the former Rwanda government army. Ndahimana was Commandant of Camp Kigali military base during the genocide and he is accused of having participated in killings both in Kigali and in the former Kibuye Prefecture, his home area.

7.5.3 Netherlands

Prior to 2003, Dutch legislation already provided for universal jurisdiction over war crimes (and torture).[17] In 2003, the Netherlands enacted the International Crimes Act to incorporate crimes listed in the ICC Statute (genocide, crimes against humanity and war crimes) into domestic Dutch criminal law. Since the adoption of the International Crimes Act, the Netherlands has been able to prosecute violations of international humanitarian law under the universality principle. The International Crimes Act does not, however, have retroactive effect (Ryngaert 2007). Under the Act, Dutch courts may only seize cases without a traditional link to the Netherlands (that is, when the crime was not committed in Dutch territory, by or against Dutch nationals) when the offence involves genocide, war crimes, crimes against humanity or torture and the suspect is present in the country.

The Netherlands has conducted one trial, against Joseph Mpambara, relating to the Rwanda conflict.[18] Mpambara is a brother of Obed Ruzindana, one of the genocide suspects who has been tried and convicted by the ICTR and sentenced to 25 years' imprisonment. Mpambara arrived in the Netherlands on a fake Ugandan passport in 1998. He sought asylum in the Netherlands, claiming that he faced persecution in Rwanda as result of having testified in the defence of his brother at the ICTR. Mpambara's asylum application was unsuccessful, and he was arrested by Dutch authorities in 2006 on the basis of a referral of his case to the Netherlands by the ICTR Prosecutor in the framework of the tribunal's completion strategy. Mpambara was charged with genocide, war crimes and torture. He was originally also charged with genocide. An issue arose as to whether the Dutch courts had jurisdiction to try the crime of genocide under the principle of universal jurisdiction when neither the alleged perpetrator nor the victims had any connection with the Netherlands at the relevant time. On 24 July 2007, the Hague District Court held that Dutch courts did not have universal jurisdiction over the crime of genocide under the provisions of Dutch criminal law that was then in force. In addition, the court ruled that Dutch courts had no jurisdiction over cases of genocide derived from the referral of cases to the Netherlands by the ICTR, in the absence of a treaty from which the Netherlands could derive competence to take over the prosecution from the ICTR.[19] An appeals court confirmed this decision. On 21 October 2008, the Supreme Court of the Netherlands, affirming the rulings from the two lower courts, held that although Dutch courts clearly had universal jurisdiction over the crime of genocide for acts committed after new legislation was passed in 2003, they did not have such jurisdiction over acts constituting genocide before that time. The ruling did not, however, affect the prosecution of war crimes and torture. Mpambara's trial in respect of the charges of war crimes and torture began on 13 October 2008. On 23 March 2009, he was found guilty of torture and sentenced to 20 years' imprisonment. He was acquitted of war crimes, on the grounds that there was not a sufficient nexus between the crimes that he had committed and the armed conflict. The main basis for the acquittal in respect of the war crimes charges was the fact that Mpambara was not a public officer or part of the military. The prosecutor and civil claimants appealed against the trial court's judgment. The Hague Court of Appeal confirmed Mpambara's conviction, and he was also convicted for additional war crimes for which he had previously been acquitted (on the basis that his actions were not linked to the genocide) and was sentenced to imprisonment for 30 years. Mpambara was acquitted of two charges of rape.[20]

The problem of Dutch courts' lack of jurisdiction over genocide based on events that took place prior to 2003 has been an impediment to the referral of cases to the Netherlands by the ICTR. Michel Bagaragaza, a former Director General of a parastatal organization in charge of the tea industry in Rwanda, reportedly cooperated with the Office of the Prosecutor for many years in its investigations of other suspects.[21] The Office of the Prosecutor wanted to use Bagaragaza as a prosecution witness in some of its cases. To establish his credibility as a prosecution witness, the Office of the Prosecutor wanted Bagaragaza to be tried before taking the stand against other suspects. As part of an understanding with Bagaragaza, the Office of the Prosecutor promised to refer his case to a European country, presumably because he would receive a shorter sentence and be detained in better conditions. The Office of the Prosecutor applied for referral of Bagaragaza's case to Norway. However, the trial chamber denied the Prosecutor's request for referral of Bagaragaza's case to Norway on the ground that Norway did not have laws criminalizing genocide on its statute books.[22] On 30 August 2006, the Appeals Chamber of the International Criminal Tribunal for Rwanda dismissed an appeal by the ICTR Prosecutor, agreeing with the reasoning and conclusion of the trial chamber that it would be inappropriate to transfer Bagaragaza's case to Norway because that country lacked jurisdiction to try the accused for the serious violations of international law of genocide. The Office of the Prosecutor next attempted to transfer Bagaragaza's case to the Netherlands. In light of the decisions in the Mpambara case, the Netherlands could not try Bagaragaza for genocide either. Dutch prosecutors informed the tribunal that their courts did not have any jurisdiction to try the case. The referral of Bagaragaza's case to the Netherlands was revoked in 2008.

A new case relating to the Rwanda genocide is currently underway in the Netherlands. Yvonne Ntacyobatara Basebya became a Dutch citizen in 2004. The Dutch International Crimes Unit originally launched an investigation against Basebya's husband. These investigations did not provide any compelling evidence against the husband, but allegedly implicated the wife, instead, in atrocities. Yvonne Basebya was arrested in June 2010 and as she is a Dutch citizen, she can, unlike Mpambara, be tried of genocide in the Dutch courts. Nyacyobatara's case will be the first genocide trial in the Netherlands. The District Court in The Hague suspended the pre-trial detention of Ntacyobatabara Basebya, on account of delays in bringing the case to trial. The trial is scheduled to start in October 2012.[23]

7.5.4 *France*

French law does not recognize absolute universal jurisdiction based on customary international law. At the time of the Rwanda genocide, French law provided for a limited form of universal jurisdiction. The law governing universal jurisdiction of French courts is set out in Article 689-1 of the Code of Criminal Procedure:

> In accordance with the international agreements referred to in the following articles, any person who has committed one of the crimes listed in these articles outside the territory of the French Republic may be prosecuted and convicted by the French courts if she/he is in France.

The provisions of the present article apply also to any attempt to commit these crimes, whenever such is punishable by law.

French law has incorporated universal jurisdiction based on treaty obligations in respect of the crimes of torture and crimes relating to the physical protection of nuclear material, the protection of the European Union's financial interests and the fight against corruption involving Officials of the European Communities or officials of Member States of the European Union, and crimes defined as terrorism.[24] French criminal procedure law did not implement the provisions of the Geneva Conventions relating to universal jurisdiction, despite the fact that the Conventions require the state to exercise universal jurisdiction over crimes defined by the Conventions. French courts have held that they do not have universal jurisdiction for crimes against humanity and genocide. In March 1996, in the case of Wenceslas Munyeshyaka, a Rwandan refugee in France investigated for genocide, torture and inhuman and degrading treatment, the Indictment Division of the Court of Appeal in Nîmes found that it did not have jurisdiction to try offences committed abroad by a foreigner against foreigners since the Code of Criminal Procedure did not at the time provide for the jurisdiction of French courts in such a case.[25]

In January 1995, France enacted legislation permitting the exercise of absolute universal jurisdiction in the limited context of offences within the jurisdiction of the ad hoc United Nations international criminal tribunals for Rwanda and the Former Yugoslavia.[26] The universal jurisdiction of the French courts under the two laws was limited *ratione materiae*, *temporis* and *loci* by the provisions of the relevant resolutions of the Security Council. Since 1995, French courts have exercised jurisdiction over crimes within the competence of the ICTR so long as they were committed between 1 January 1994 and 31 December 1994 on the territory of Rwanda and, in respect of Rwandan citizens, on the territory of neighbouring states. On 9 August 2010, France enacted Law No. 2010-930 adapting criminal law to the Statute of the International Criminal Court. Law No. 2010-930 amends the Article 689-1 of the Code of Criminal Procedure, and gives French courts jurisdiction to try cases of international crimes against a person who resides in the territory of France and who has committed abroad a crime within the jurisdiction of the ICC, if the conduct is punishable under the laws of the state where the crime is committed or where such state is party to the Rome Statute, or where such person is a national of a state party to the convention, and when no international or national jurisdiction requires the surrender and extradition of the person concerned.

France has by far the largest number of on going investigations of crimes relating to the Rwanda genocide. As of January 2012, French investigative authorities had opened investigations against at least 25 Rwandan genocide suspects, including Agathe Habyarimana (the widow of assassinated President Juvenal Habyarinama), Laurent Bucyibaruta, Laurent Serubuga, Cyprian

Kayumba, Fabien Neretse, Fabien Nsabimana, Rwamucyo Eugene, Dominique Ntawukuriryayo, Stanislas Mbonampeka, Kamali Isaac, Kamana Claver, Col. Bivugabagabo Marcel, Simbikangwa Pascal, Tegera Pierre, Twagira Charles, Ngenzi Octavien, Habyarimana Joseph, Camy (Kanyamihigo) Paul, Barahira Tito, Bwigenzare Manasse, Nyombayire Venuste, Nsengiyumva Hyacinthe Rafiki, Wenceslas Munyeshyaka, Dr Sosthene Munyamana and Venuste Nyombayire. Most of the cases against these suspects were, as in Belgium, initiated by victims or civil society organizations, not the state investigative authorities.

Unlike Belgium, France has failed to complete any of the investigations of Rwanda genocide cases that it has commenced and is yet to bring a Rwanda genocide case to trial. Most of the cases have been in the investigation phase for close to two decades. The government of France has not provided the human and financial resources required for the investigations to be completed. Two investigative judges handling the Rwanda genocide cases requested to be relieved of their other judicial duties to dedicate themselves to the large number of outstanding investigations relating to the Rwanda genocide, but their requests were turned down (REDRESS 2010).

Rwanda has filed extradition requests for some of these suspects. Most of the extradition requests to date have been turned down by French courts. France appears to be neither willing to extradite the genocide suspects whose cases its justice system is investigating to Rwanda, nor to try the suspects of the alleged offences in French courts. While the judicial decisions declining to extradite suspects for trial in Rwanda due to concerns about the risk of unfair trial are consistent with the decisions of courts in other European countries, France's failure to investigate diligently the cases of genocide suspects living in France and to try their cases in French courts where the evidence warrants is difficult to understand or defend. It is widely suspected that France's failure to make any progress in investigating and prosecuting the Rwanda genocide cases that its judicial authorities have opened investigations into may be due to a lack of political will. The pre-genocide government of Rwanda enjoyed extremely good relations with France. On the other hand, the current government of Rwanda has, until recently, had extremely poor relations with successive French governments. The government of Rwanda has accused French institutions and political leaders, including some who remain politically active, of responsibility for or complicity in the genocide against the Tutsi (Mucyo 2008). France's failure to investigate and prosecute the cases relating to the Rwanda genocide that have been brought against suspects now living in France serves neither the victims nor the suspects. While victims await justice with no end in sight, the genocide suspects who are the subjects of ongoing French investigation remain in limbo, unable to prove their innocence and to move on with their personal lives and professional aspirations.[27]

France has instituted a judicial investigation of the attack against the plane in which President Habyarimana was travelling at the time of his assassination.

The indictment in the case, issued by anti-terrorist Judge Bruguière in November 2006, charged members of the Rwanda military, including its most senior commanders, with crimes of premeditated murder and terrorism. Rwanda responded to the indictment by suspending diplomatic relations with France. As a result of bilateral efforts to mend relations between the two countries, France agreed to reopen investigations into the case that continue.

7.5.5 *Finland*

One trial relating to the Rwanda conflict, involving former church pastor François Bazaramba, has been held in Finland.[28] Bazaramba sought asylum in Finland in 2003. Rwanda sought extradition of the pastor and he was arrested and detained on genocide charges in 2007. Bazaramba was alleged to be responsible for organizing the killing of civilians in the town of Nyakizu during the genocide. In February 2009 the Finnish Ministry of Justice refused to authorize the extradition of Bazaramba to Rwanda to face prosecution, citing decisions of the ICTR as well as German and French courts relating to the risk of violation of the right to a fair trial under Rwanda's justice system. The Finnish Ministry of Justice indicated that it had 'neither any reason to question the conclusions of the ICTR nor any grounds to assess the prevailing circumstances in Rwanda any differently to the ICTR' (Ministry of Justice, Helsinki, 2009). Bazaramba was tried and convicted of genocide and five counts of murder, and acquitted of ten other counts of murder. The Bazaramba case was the first genocide case to be prosecuted in Finland.

7.5.6 *Denmark*

Denmark first attempted to investigate and try crimes relating to the Rwanda genocide with the arrest of Sylvere Ahorugeze. Ahorugeze, a former Director of Rwanda's Civil Aviation Authority, had been tried and convicted of genocide and crimes against humanity by a Rwanda Gacaca court. Rwanda sought Ahorugeze's extradition from Demark. Rwanda and Denmark did not have an extradition treaty at the time. Danish authorities decided to arrest Ahorugeze and try him in Denmark on the basis of the principle of universal jurisdiction. Danish investigators conducted an investigation in Rwanda that failed to produce enough to justify the prosecution of the suspect in Denmark. Danish prosecutors dropped the case against Ahorugeze for lack of evidence, and Ahorugeze was thereafter released and awarded damages. Ahorugeze was subsequently arrested in Sweden on the basis of the INTERPOL arrest warrant that had led to his arrest in Denmark.

Demark has proceeded with the trial of one Rwandan, Emmanuel Mbarushimana, for crimes alleged to have been committed during the Rwanda genocide. Mbarushimana was arrested in December 2010 after living in Denmark under a false name since 2001. Mbarushimana had been tried *in absentia* and sentenced to life imprisonment in Rwanda in 2008. The Danish court of first instance held that there was no legal basis in Denmark to prosecute foreigners charged with genocide in another country.[29] An appellate court upheld the lower court's decision,[30] holding that the 1955 Danish Act Concerning the Punishment of Genocide[31] could not be used to prosecute genocide extra-territorially because the wording of the law does not manifest an intention to give the law extraterritorial jurisdiction. The court also ruled that the Genocide Convention does not obligate a state party to prosecute crimes of genocide committed outside the jurisdiction of the state country. The court's jurisdictional ruling resulted in the dismissal of the genocide charges. The Mbarushimana case is significant not only because it was Denmark's first attempt to prosecute genocide on the basis of universal jurisdiction, but also because of its interpretation of the obligations of state parties to the Genocide Convention. Danish authorities have indicated that they intend to proceed with the trial of Mbarushimana for killings classified as murder, instead of genocide.

7.5.7 *Germany*

German law on international crimes is codified in its Code of Crimes Against International Law of 26 June 2002. Germany has exercised universal jurisdiction under the International Crimes Act to investigate several cases relating to the Rwanda conflict. In January 2011, the Frankfurt High Regional Court commenced the trial of Onesphore Rwabukombe, who was mayor of Muvumba Commune in northern eastern Rwanda at the time of the genocide. Rwanda had initially requested Rwabukombe's extradition, and he was arrested and detained pending extradition proceedings in 2008. German courts turned down Rwanda's request for Rwabukombe's extradition to Rwanda due to concerns about the risk of unfair trial. German authorities decided to prosecute Rwabukombe in Germany instead. The Rwabukombe case is Germany's first trial relating to the Rwanda genocide. At the time of writing, the trial of Rwabukombe was still in progress before the Frankfurt Regional High Court.

Trials of Rwanda genocide cases in foreign courts are usually expensive and logistically challenging because of the need to transport and accommodate large numbers of witnesses to provide evidence in person. Their transportation sometimes leads to diplomatic incidents, as some witnesses often decide not to return to Rwanda and opt to seek political asylum instead. The Rwabukombe trial has set a precedent by making extensive use of video conferencing technology to take the testimony of some of the witnesses living in Rwanda. Increased use of video conferencing technology will reduce the costs of trials relating to the Rwanda genocide conducted by other states on the basis of the principle of universal jurisdiction. It is hoped that a reduction in the costs of these trials will encourage states that have refrained from conducting trials of Rwanda genocide cases due to financial considerations to do so in the future.

7.5.8 *Spain*

Spanish courts have exercised universal jurisdiction since passage of the Organic Law on Judicial Power in 1985.[32] The law provided that Spanish courts have jurisdiction over acts perpetrated by Spanish nationals and acts perpetrated by foreigners outside of Spain if such acts are alleged to constitute genocide, terrorism, war crimes, piracy or unlawful seizure of aircraft, counterfeiting of foreign currency, crimes related to prostitution, trafficking in psychotropic, toxic or narcotic drugs and any other crime which should be prosecuted by Spain in accordance with international treaties, especially international humanitarian law and human rights treaties.[33] Article 23.4 of Act No. 6/1985 has been amended on several occasions. In 2003, Spain enacted an amendment to regulate jurisdiction of Spanish courts in respect of crimes that may fall within the competence of the ICC.[34] This amendment gave the ICC primacy in the case of complaints that may be filed with Spanish courts. In 2005, an amendment of Article 23.4 of Act No. 6/1985 introduced provisions regulating prosecution of the crime of female genital mutilation, in respect of which universal jurisdiction may be exercised by Spanish courts only where the perpetrators are present in Spain.[35] A 2007 amendment to Article 23.4 of Act No. 6/1985 extended universal jurisdiction of Spanish courts to the crimes of human trafficking or smuggling of persons.[36]

Spanish courts have been as proactive in applying the principle of universal jurisdiction to international crimes as their counterparts in Belgium. Spanish courts have made a very significant contribution to the development of international criminal law and the fight against impunity, particularly through their handling of cases relating to past human rights abuses in Latin America. Spanish courts have also initiated proceedings relating to alleged human rights abuses in other parts of the world, including China/Tibet, Israel and the United States. The expansive scope of Spanish law on universal jurisdiction has been widely criticized, in much the same way as the Belgian law on the subject has been the subject of criticism. This criticism, and pressure from states such as Israel and China as well as the African Union, eventually compelled Spain to curtail the scope of universal jurisdiction. In 2009, Spain adopted a new law, Organization Act No. 1/2009,[37] governing universal jurisdiction for international crime. Article 1 of Act 2009 provides:

> Without prejudice to the provisions of international treaties and agreements signed by Spain, in order for Spanish courts to have jurisdiction over the [...] offences [listed in Art. 23.4 of Act No. 6/1985], it must be established that the alleged perpetrators are present in Spain, that there are victims of Spanish nationality or that there is some relevant link with Spain and, in any event, that no other competent country or international court has initiated proceedings, including an effective investigation and, where appropriate, prosecution, of such crimes.

> The criminal proceedings initiated in a Spanish court shall be temporarily stayed where it has been established that proceedings based on the alleged acts have been initiated in the country or by a Court referred to in the previous paragraph.

Under the new provisions, the application of the principle of universal jurisdiction is restricted to cases where there is a link to Spain, which may include the Spanish nationality of the victim, the presence of the alleged perpetrator on Spanish territory or any other relevant link with Spain. Under the new provisions, Spanish courts defer to the primacy of international criminal courts or of other international tribunals or tribunals of other states, so long as those states are able and willing to investigate, prosecute and if necessary punish the alleged crimes effectively.

The Audiencia Nacional has invoked the principle of universal jurisdiction to investigate one significant case relating to violations of international human rights law and violations of international humanitarian law that were committed in both Rwanda and the Democratic Republic of Congo by soldiers and officers of the army of the current government of Rwanda. On 6 February 2008, Spanish Investigative Judge Andreu Merelles issued an indictment charging 40 current or former high-ranking Rwandan military officers with serious crimes including genocide, crimes against humanity, war crimes and terrorism, perpetrated over a period of 12 years from 1990 to 2002.[38] The case was initiated by complaints from families of nine Spaniards who were killed, harmed or disappeared during the relevant period, but the indictment was subsequently expanded to include crimes committed against Rwandan and Congolese victims, primarily against members of the Hutu community. The persons under investigation in this case originally included President Kagame, the current President of Rwanda, as one of the suspects. The Audiencia Nacional ruled that it did not have competence in respect of Paul Kagame, on account of the protection accorded to him by the immunity of an incumbent Head of State under international law.[39] The court ruled, however, that lack of competence was restricted to President Kagame, and that it was competent to prosecute the other military officers named in the indictment. The case against the remaining suspects is a very sensitive subject in Rwanda, as it targets virtually all the top leadership of the command of Rwanda's military. The Rwanda government has not only refused to cooperate with the Spanish investigation, but has successfully convinced the African Union to pass a resolution committing African states not to cooperate in the prosecution of the case and another one underway in France that similarly targets very significant figures in Rwanda's military leadership.

Spain's application of the principle of universal jurisdiction raises moral, legal and philosophical issues. While Spanish law permits the exercise of universal jurisdiction to prosecute non-Spanish citizens for crimes, including genocide, crimes against humanity, war crimes and torture committed outside Spain, and refuses to recognize amnesties for such crimes in other countries, Spanish courts continue to uphold amnesty for Franco-era crimes and deny Spanish victims the rights and remedies that victims of foreign conflicts have in Spanish courts. The case against Judge Baltasar Garzón illustrates the incomprehensible and indefensible double standards of the Spanish legal system in dealing with past human rights abuses.

Between 2006 and 2008, family members and associations representing victims of the Franco-era human rights abuses filed petitions alleging that members of the 'Junta de Defensa Nacional', or National Defence Movement, established in 25 July 1936 by dissident generals in support of Franco, had systematically and illegally detained, tortured and killed their relatives during and after the Spanish civil war.[40] The victims' families and associations representing families of victims requested fact-finding missions to ascertain the fate of family members, the exhumation and identification of victims' remains and criminal investigations of those crimes with a view to obtaining effective remedies for the violation of their rights to truth, justice and reparation.[41] The petitions were submitted to the Audiencia Nacional, and allocated automatically to the Juzgado Central de Instrucción No. 5 of the Audiencia Nacional directed by Judge Baltasar Garzón Real.

Judge Baltasar Garzón opened an investigation into some 114,000 cases of forced disappearance allegedly committed during the Franco regime. Judge Garzón considered the disappearances as crimes against humanity committed as part of a systematic attempt to eliminate political opponents. He considered the crimes as ongoing unlawful detentions – and therefore not subject to the prohibition of retroactive application of criminal law or expiry of the period of limitation. Although Judge Garzón subsequently ceded jurisdiction over the petitions to lower courts and sought the direction of the Supreme Court when the lower returned the dossiers to the Audiencia Nacional, far right-wing political groups lodged criminal complaints of abuse of power against Judge Garzón,[42] arguing that the judge had consciously overstepped his judicial power and breached the 1977 Amnesty Law.[43] Judge Garzón was suspended from office as a result of these petitions. The Supreme Court admitted the criminal complaint against Judge Garzón and put him on trial.[44] Judge Garzón and the Spanish Prosecution Service asked the Supreme Court to exercise its power to dismiss the case, in vain. They then challenged the legality of the proceedings and the challenges were similarly dismissed.

The Supreme Court subsequently dismissed the charges of abuse of power against Judge Garzón, but upheld the validity of the 1977 Amnesty Law on the basis of a restrictive interpretation of the principle of legality.[45] The court rejected the continuing 'crime argument' and held that notwithstanding Spain's ratification of treaties declaring that the statute of limitations does not apply for serious international crimes, these treaties could not be retroactively applied to the crimes in question.

7.5.9 Norway

Norway did not introduce the crimes of genocide, crimes against humanity and war crimes into its domestic law until the passage of Act No. 28 of 20 May 2005 amending the General Civil Penal Code. Act No. 28 was brought into force by Amendment to the General Civil Penal Code, LOV-2005-05-20-28, on 7 March 2008. The amendment permitted limited extraterritorial jurisdiction to Norwegian courts over non-Norwegian nationals for offences alleged to have been committed, subject to several cumulative requirements, such as the presence of the accused in Norwegian territory, prohibition of double incrimination, a requirement that the offence is considered a crime under international law, and that prosecution should be in the public interest. Prior to the adoption of the Act of Amendment to the General Civil Penal Code, LOV-2005-05-20-28, genocide and crimes against humanity committed abroad could only be prosecuted under cover of charges of offences such as murder, assault and other crimes that were defined under the country's penal code. Article 12.4 of the General Civil Penal Code provided that Norwegian criminal law shall be applicable to acts committed abroad by a foreigner when the act either constitutes murder, assault and certain other crimes under Norwegian law, or is a felony also punishable according to the law of the country in which it is committed, and the offender is resident in the realm or is staying therein.

Norway's justice system had the opportunity to consider whether Amendment to the General Civil Penal Code, LOV-2005-05-20-28 could be applied retroactively in the case of Mirsad Repak.[46] Repak, a Bosnian former member of a Croatian paramilitary organization called the Croatian Defense Forces (HOS), was accused of committing war crimes against 18 Serb civilians in the Dretelj detention camp in southern Bosnia during the 1992–95 Bosnia war. Repak arrived in Norway in 1993 as an asylum seeker and obtained Norwegian citizenship in 2001. Repak was charged with alleged crimes against humanity, war crimes, torture and rape. Repak pleaded not guilty to the charges, insisting that he was only following orders. Repak's trial was the first war crimes trial in Norway since the end of World War II. Like the consitutions and laws of many other states, the Constitution of Norway prohibits legislation from having retroactive effect. The trial court convicted Repak of war crimes and handed him a five-year prison sentence in December 2008, but acquitted him of the charges of crimes against humanity on the grounds that the Amendment to the General Civil Penal Code, LOV-2005-05-20-28 could not apply retrospectively. Both the defendant and the prosecutor appealed. The case went all the way to the Norwegian Supreme Court. The Norwegian Supreme Court[47] held that Amendment to the General Civil Penal Code, LOV-2005-05-20-28 could not be applied retrospectively, because that would infringe Section 97 of the Norwegian Constitution. Repak could, however, still be tried for other crimes under the Norwegian penal code not affected by the retroactivity principles.

The decision of the Norwegian Supreme Court in the Repak case has implications for cases of Rwandan genocide suspects now living in Norway.

In the light of the Repak decision, Norway has two options on how to deal with the cases of Rwandan genocide suspects residing in Norway: either to extradite them to Rwanda or to try them of ordinary crimes and war, including breaches of the Geneva Conventions and the Convention Against Torture, that were already crimes under Norwegian law at the time of the Rwanda genocide. Norway appears to have decided to take the approach of extradition.

In 2007, the Norwegian National Authority for Prosecution of Organized and Other Serious Crimes started investigation against 19 Rwandese staying in Norway accused of having participated in the genocide in Rwanda. So far, 17 of the cases have been closed due to lack of evidence. The agency is investigating one of the two cases that was not closed; the investigation of the case is expected to be completed during 2013.

The other investigation that was not closed related to Sadi Bugingo. Bugingo, who has lived in Norway since 2002, was arrested on genocide charges in May 2011. He was indicted by Norwegian authorities on 17 September 2012 and is accused of having participated in the killings in the Kibungo area, of at least 2000 persons, under especially aggravating circumstances offences as part of genocide.[48]

The indictment and prosecution of a foreigner staying in Norway for offences committed abroad has to be approved by the King in Council, which took place on Friday 7 September 2012. The trial of Bugingo, in the first instance before the Oslo District Court, commenced on 24 September 2012. About 20 witnesses were expected to be brought from Rwanda to Norway to testify in the Bugingo case. About 80 other witnesses were expected to give their evidence and to be cross-examined by video link. Norway is also carrying out investigations against Eugene Nkuranyabahizi.[49]

Norway is also processing a request for the extradition of a third genocide suspect, Charles Bandora, to Rwanda. Charles Bandora, a businessman, fled Rwanda after the genocide and eventually settled in Malawi. Rwanda issued an INTERPOL Red Alert notice in respect of Bandora, and he was held briefly by Malawian authorities. Released by Malawian authorities, Bandora fled to Belgium, where he made an unsuccessful request for asylum and was again arrested (SALC/REDRESS 2012: p. 19). Due to the fact that he arrived in Belgium with a forged passport containing a Norwegian Schengen visa, Bandora was expelled from Belgium and transported to Norway, and was arrested on arrival at Oslo Airport on 8 June 2010. Bandora was charged by the Norwegian authorities of using a passport that does not belong to him. Rwandan authorities had gotten wind of Bandora's presence in Europe and they submitted a request for his extradition to Norway, which was received in July 2010 while Bandora was still in Norwegian custody. In July 2011, the Oslo District court granted Rwanda's request for his extradition. Bandora appealed. The Court of Appeal affirmed the decision of the District Court.

In November 2011, Norway's Supreme Court rejected Bandora's appeal against an order for his extradition to Rwanda. At the time of writing, Bandora was still in custody in Norway, pending a final decision on Rwanda's extradition request by the Ministry of Justice. Should the Ministry of Justice decide to extradite, the subject of the extradition request has 3 weeks to challenge that decision. The final decision on extradition is dealt with by the King in Council. Bandora may also challenge the order for his extradition to Rwanda before the European Court of Human Rights.

The Norwegian courts' lack of jurisdiction to prosecute genocide and crimes against humanity committed prior to 7 March 2008 has prevented the referral of cases to Norway by the ICTR.[50]

7.5.10 United Kingdom

The United Kingdom considers that under international law, universal jurisdiction in its true sense is only clearly established for a small number of specific offences: piracy and war crimes, including grave breaches of the Geneva Conventions of 1949 (Permanent Mission of the UK to the United Nations 2011). Courts in the UK also have universal jurisdiction over 'grave breaches' of the Geneva Conventions committed after 1957.[51] The Geneva Conventions Act 1957 implements the Geneva Conventions of 1949, which require states to establish universal jurisdiction over grave breaches in international armed conflicts (not internal armed conflicts) (Permanent Mission of the UK to the United Nations 2011). Courts in the UK have had universal jurisdiction in respect of torture since the adoption of the Criminal Justice Act 1988. This Act implemented Articles 4 and 5 of the 1984 Convention Against Torture, which required states to establish extraterritorial jurisdiction over the crime of torture. The Criminal Justice Act 1988 permits prosecution of torture committed after 1988, regardless of where the crime was committed, and regardless of whether or not the alleged crime has any connection to the UK.[52]

The first successful prosecution under universal jurisdiction laws in the UK occurred in July 2005, when Afghan militia leader Faryadi Zardad was tried and convicted of acts of torture and hostage-taking that had taken place in Afghanistan in the 1990s. Zardad was sentenced to 20 years of imprisonment.[53] In practice, the UK courts only exercised 'extraterritorial jurisdiction' in relation to these crimes; that is, jurisdiction could only be exercised when the accused had been present in the UK to be arrested (Joint Committee on Human Rights 2009: p. 8). The UK does not recognize absolute universal jurisdiction based on customary international law for genocide, crimes against humanity and war crimes in internal armed conflicts. As a result of accession to the Rome Treaty of the ICC, the UK enacted the International Criminal Court Act 2001, which established jurisdiction over British citizens and residents for war crimes in internal armed conflicts ('civil wars'), as well as international armed conflicts, genocide and crimes against humanity committed after the date the Act came into force in 2001. The limited scope of universal jurisdiction under this law (restricting jurisdiction to British citizens or residents and to crimes that were committed after 2001) was widely criticized, as it would exclude cases of war criminals suspected of responsibility for crimes committed in conflicts that took place prior to 2001, including the Rwanda genocide.

The unsatisfactory state of UK law relating to the accountability of suspected war criminals present on UK territory was demonstrated in the case of four Rwandans (Vincent Bajinya aka Brown, Celestin Ugirashebuja, Charles Munyaneza and Emmanuel Nteziryayo), accused of genocide by the Rwanda government.[54] The government of Rwanda requested extradition of the four from the UK. United Kingdom law enforcement authorities arrested and detained the four in December 2006 pending extradition proceedings over the genocide charges. Munyaneza was also subject to additional proceedings for falsifying his name in order to obtain refugee status in the UK. In June 2008, a District Judge ruled that the cases should be sent to the Secretary of State for consideration that extradition be ordered. In August 2008, the Secretary of State informed all four men that she was ordering their extradition to Rwanda. Rwanda and the UK did not have a bilateral extradition treaty at the time. The UK government proposed to extradite the four to Rwanda on the basis of a bilateral Memorandum of Understanding. The four men lodged appeals against the decision of the District Judge and the Secretary of State to order extradition. Two High Court Judges agreed with the four, ruling that there was a 'real risk' that the men would suffer a 'flagrant denial of justice by reason of their likely inability to adduce the evidence of supporting witnesses' if they were extradited to Rwanda. The court also said that a real risk existed of interference in the judiciary by the government of Rwanda. The four men were ordered to be released from custody after the judges refused to grant the request of the Crown Prosecution Service (representing the Government of Rwanda) for leave to appeal the ruling. The decision of the High Court in respect of the four Rwandans marked the first time that a UK court has blocked an extradition request on the basis that it would violate Article 6 of the European Convention on Human Rights. The High Court ordered the release of the four genocide suspects from custody, despite upholding the lower court's conclusion that the evidence presented by the Rwandan government showed that the men had a case to answer for their role in the genocide. At the time, the UK could not try the four men of genocide or crimes against humanity, as universal jurisdiction for genocide, crimes against humanity and war crimes in internal conflicts under the International Criminal Court Act only existed in respect of crimes committed after 2001.

The decision of the High Court reversing the order for the extradition of Bajinjya, Ugirashebuja, Munyaneza and Nteziryayo gave an impetus to efforts to convince the UK government to close the impunity gap that the International Criminal Court 2001 left in respect of the crimes of genocide, crimes against humanity and war crimes in internal armed conflicts committed prior to 2001. In 2009, the UK passed new legislation, the Coroners and Justice Act 2009, under which the jurisdiction of British courts for crimes which fall within the jurisdiction of the ICC was pushed back to 1991.[55] As a result of this amendment to the International Criminal Court Act 2001, British courts now have jurisdiction over crimes relating to the Rwanda genocide. There is no indication, however, that the UK government is making any attempts to hold trials of cases in relation to the Rwanda genocide. Bajinya and the other Rwandans accused of involvement in the genocide who successfully fought attempts to extradite them to Rwanda have appealed to the UK government to try them in British courts.[56] The UK government has not responded to these requests.

7.5.11 Canada

Canada attempted its first prosecution of war crimes that were committed abroad in the landmark *R.* v. *Finta* case. Finta had served as a Hungarian police commander during World War II. He immigrated to Canada in 1948 and became a Canadian citizen in 1956. Canadian authorities received information that as Commander of the Gendarmerie in the city of Szeged, Finta had participated in the deportation of Jews to their deaths. In 1988, Finta was charged with manslaughter, kidnapping, unlawful confinement and the war crimes provisions of the Criminal Code in relation to his alleged activities as a police officer assisting the Nazis in the forced deportation of 8,617 Jews from Szeged. Finta's defence was based on the argument that he had only been following orders and was only responsible for transporting Jews. Finta was acquitted after a six-month jury trial. The acquittal was upheld by the Ontario Court of Appeal in 1992.[57] In 1994, the Supreme Court of Canada confirmed the decision of the Ontario Court of Appeal, upholding a jury acquittal.[58] The Supreme Court recognized the constitutionality of the impugned war crimes provisions of the Criminal Code while establishing a high standard of proof for the prosecution of war crimes and crimes against humanity. The Finta decision brought to an end Canada's short-lived attempt to prosecute foreign war criminals in Canadian courts.

Following the unsuccessful attempt to prosecute Finta, Canada focused on citizenship immigration proceedings (through which war criminals are stripped of citizenship and deported to the countries where they committed crimes) rather than criminal prosecutions in dealing with alleged war criminals living in Canada.

Canada's most famous attempt to use immigration proceedings to deport an alleged war criminal from its territory in the aftermath of the failed attempt to prosecute Finta was the immigration case against Leon Mugesera. Mugesera is a Rwandan university professor who was also active in politics in Rwanda during the 1990s Rwanda war. The professor was a strong activist of the ruling party. In 1992, Mugesera made a speech in which he called for genocide, crimes against humanity and murder to be committed against Tutsis. The speech was widely criticized, and the government of the day came under pressure to arrest and punish Mugesera. To escape possible arrest, Mugesera fled to Canada, where he sought political asylum. Mugesera's asylum application was rejected, and the Minister of Citizenship and Immigration ordered his deportation to Rwanda. Mugesera appealed the decision to the Immigration Tribunal. The tribunal ordered that the Minister of Citizenship and Immigration could deport Mugesera, on the basis that the above mentioned speech rendered him inadmissible to Canada before he entered in 1993. The speech was said to constitute incitement to genocide; instigation of extermination, murder and persecution, as crimes against humanity; and persecution. Mugesera applied for a judicial review of the decision of the Immigration Tribunal. The Trial Division of the Federal Court partly upheld the tribunal's decision, specifically agreeing that the speech made him answerable for crimes against humanity.[59] However, the Appeal Division completely reversed the deportation order, holding that the speech, although awful in its message, did not amount to a crime against humanity.[60] The government appealed to the Canadian Supreme Court. In a unanimous judgment, the Supreme Court overturned the decision of the Appeal Division in June 2005 and upheld the deportation order against Mugesera.[61] Canadian authorities did not attempt to deport Mugesera to Rwanda for many years after the Supreme Court decision. On 6 December 2011, the Minister of Citizenship and Immigration served Leon Mugesera with notification that he would be deported from Canada in accordance with a previous order of the Canadian Supreme Court. Mugesera's last-minute attempts to have another judicial stay of the order for his deportation were unsuccessful. Mugesera was finally deported to Rwanda in January 2012.

While Canada, like many other countries, continues to invoke immigration laws to keep war criminals from entering or staying within its territory, it has also resumed prosecution of war criminals in its courts. In 2000, Canada passed the Crimes Against Humanity and War Crimes Act. The Act was adopted mainly to implement Canada's obligations with respect to the International Criminal Court. However, it also aimed to provide for the prosecution of international crimes before Canadian courts. With the passage of the Act, Canadian courts now have jurisdiction to prosecute war criminals for extraterritorial crimes. Canada has also established a specialized war crimes investigation unit.

R. v. *Munyaneza*[62] was the first case to be tried under Canada's Crimes Against Humanity and War Crimes Act. Munyaneza arrived in Canada in 1997 on a false Cameroon passport. He immediately applied for asylum, claiming that because he was a Hutu, he would be killed if he were sent back to Rwanda. Munyaneza's claim of political asylum was denied, largely on the basis of evidence provided by the Royal Canadian Mounted Police that linked him to massacres during the Rwandan genocide. Munyaneza was arrested in October 2005, and charged with seven counts related to the genocide (murder, causing physical and mental harm), crimes against humanity (murder, sexual violence) and war crimes (murder, sexual violence and pillage). The Munyaneza trial lasted two years and included evidence from multiple nations. At the end of the trial, Munyaneza was convicted and sentenced to 25 years without parole. The Munyaneza case was a landmark case in Canada's attempts to use the law to contribute to the promotion of respect for international human rights law and international humanitarian law. As well as being the first successful trial under the principle of universal jurisdiction in Canada, it was the first time that a case involving the Rwandan genocide had been heard before a single judge.

In *R.* v. *Mungwarere*, another Rwandan has been charged with crimes relating to the Rwanda genocide. This is the second prosecution under the Crimes Against Humanity and War Crimes Act 2000 and the trial commenced 28 May 2012.

7.5.12 United States

At the time of the Rwanda genocide, jurisdiction over the crime of genocide in the United States was governed by the Genocide Convention Implementation Act (the Proxmire Act).[63] The Proxmire Act only allowed for prosecution of genocide in the US where 'the offense is committed within the United States'[64] or where 'the alleged offender is a national of the United States'.[65] At the time, US courts did not have jurisdiction over extraterritorial crimes against humanity, war crimes or torture. US President Ronald Reagan signed the Torture Convention on 18 April 1988 and on 27 October 1990 the US Senate gave its advice and consent to ratify the treaty with several reservations, understandings and declarations. Thereafter, there were several unsuccessful attempts to implement the Torture Convention in domestic legislation. It was not until 30 April 1994 that the House and the Senate were able to pass legislation, called the Extraterritorial Torture Statute Act,[66] to implement the Torture Convention. The Extraterritorial Torture Statute constitutes section 506 of the Foreign Relations Authorization Act, Fiscal Years 1994 and 1995. Pursuant to the legislation and Article 27 of the Convention Against Torture, the Extraterritorial Torture Statute went into effect on 20 November 1994, 30 days after the US had ratified the Convention Against Torture. The Extraterritorial Torture Statute provides that US courts have jurisdiction in torture cases if 1) the alleged offender is a national of the US; or 2) the alleged offender is present in the US, irrespective of the nationality of the victim or alleged offender.[67] In 2007, the US enacted the Genocide Accountability Act of 2007.[68] This Act expands the jurisdictional bases of the US law criminalizing genocide, the Proxmire Act, to allow prosecution of any perpetrator of genocide found in the US. Courts in the US now have jurisdiction over genocide where:

> 3. the alleged offender is an alien lawfully admitted for permanent residence in the United States (as that term is defined in section 101 of the Immigration and Nationality Act (8 U.S.C. 1101));

4. the alleged offender is a stateless person whose habitual residence is in the United States; or
5. after the conduct required for the offense occurs, the alleged offender is brought into, or found in, the United States, even if that conduct occurred outside the United States.[69]

Passage of the Genocide Accountability Act has not led to any policy change with regard to the prosecution in the US of persons suspected of involvement in the Rwanda genocide. Not a single prosecution under the Act has been initiated before US courts. Twelve years elapsed before the US brought the first ever prosecution under the Extraterritorial Torture Statute.[70] Although US courts have jurisdiction to try international crimes, the US government still prefers to deal with war criminals, including persons suspected of involvement in the Rwanda genocide, through deportation proceedings (Rosenbaum 2007).

The first known case of a Rwandan charged in the US with criminal charges linked to the Rwanda genocide was the case of Jean-Marie Vianney Mudahinyuka. Mudahinyuka illegally entered the US in 2000. US government authorities subsequently received information that Mudahinyuka had participated in the genocide and was responsible for crimes including murder and rape. Mudahinyuka was arrested in 2004 and indicted on immigration fraud offences and assault. During the arrest, Mudahinyuka had assaulted an Immigration and Customs Enforcement (ICE) agent and grabbed the agent's weapon. In June 2005, Mudahinyuka was convicted of immigration fraud (lying on his US immigration forms to gain entry to the US as a refugee) and assault against a federal officer by a federal court. He was sentenced to 51 months in a federal prison for the offences.[71] Because Mudahinyuka had been convicted of an 'aggravated felony', the US Department of Homeland Security (DHS) thereafter commenced expedited removal proceedings against Mudahinyuka and ultimately ordered Mudahinyuka removed to Rwanda. Mudahinyuka then applied for withholding of removal and protection under the Convention Against Torture (CAT), arguing that he would be subject to persecution and torture if returned to Rwanda, where he has been accused of participating in the 1994 Rwandan genocide.

The immigration judge presiding over Mudahinyuka's case held that Mudahinyuka was ineligible for withholding of removal under either the Immigration and Nationality Act or the CAT, because his conviction for assaulting federal officers was a 'particularly serious crime'. In the alternative, the immigration judge found Mudahinyuka to be barred from relief under the Immigration and Nationality Act because he participated in the persecution of Tutsis in the 1994 Rwandan genocide. Finally, the judge also determined that Mudahinyuka did not qualify for deferral of removal under the CAT because he failed to demonstrate that it is more likely than not he will be tortured if removed to Rwanda. The immigration judge's decision was upheld in all material respects by the Board of Immigration Appeals (BIA), which adopted and supplemented the judge's decision. Mudahinyuka then appealed the BIA's decision to the United States Court of Appeals for the Seventh Circuit. Noting its lack of jurisdiction, the Seventh Circuit declined to disturb the immigration judge's decision regarding Mudahinyuka's commission of a 'particularly serious crime' and the resultant statutory bar, and declined to address the judges' alternative holding that Mudahinyuka was ineligible for withholding of removal because he participated in the 1994 genocide. The Seventh Circuit denied Mudahinyuka's petition for review as it pertained to his request for deferral of removal under the CAT, finding that Mudahinyuka had a reasonable opportunity before the immigration judge to present evidence in his favour and that the judge had applied the correct standard for the admission of expert testimony.[72] Upon Mudahinyuka's release from prison he was deported to Rwanda, where he was wanted on charges of genocide and crimes against humanity.

In April 2005, Enos Kagaba,[73] a Rwandan businessman who arrived in the US from Zambia on forged documents, was arrested at the Minneapolis-St. Paul International Airport as he attempted to gain entry into the US, and charged with trying to enter the country without valid documents and misrepresenting his identity. Subsequently, the ICE's Human Rights Violators and Public Safety Unit became aware that Rwanda had issued an international warrant of arrest against him for crimes relating to the Rwanda genocide. Pursuant to a provision of the Immigration and Nationality Act, added by Congress in 1990, that renders any alien who engaged in conduct that is defined as genocide removable from the country, the US government ordered Kagaba's deportation to Rwanda.[74] Kagaba filed a petition with the 8th Circuit Court of Appeals to prevent his deportation. The Federal Immigration Appeals Court rejected the appeal and ordered Kagaba deported to Rwanda, instead of returning him to Zambia. Kagaba's case was the first incidence in the United States of a removal order based on allegations of genocide. The government invoked the Extraterritorial Torture Statute to establish jurisdiction over Kagaba. Upon his return to Rwanda, Kagaba was imprisoned without trial for a period of six years. In November 2011, he was tried and convicted of genocide and sentenced to imprisonment for life in a very brief trial by a Gacaca court.

In 2008, another Rwandan, Prudence Kantengwa, was arrested due to a 15-count indictment alleging visa fraud (18 U.S.C. § 1546), perjury (18 U.S.C. § 1621) and obstruction (18 U.S.C. § 1505).[75] The indictment alleged that Kantengwa had participated in the genocide and lied in her visa application and in her application to stay in the US. On 7 May 2012 Kantengwa was convicted of fraud in immigration documents, visa fraud, perjury during testimony before an immigration judge and obstruction of administrative proceedings.

A similar case has been brought against another Rwandan, Beatrice Munyenyezi.[76] In the case, the US authorities issued an indictment against Beatrice Munyenyezi who arrived in the US in 1995 and became a US citizen in 2003. Munyenyezi comes from a family that was prominent under the previous regime. Her husband and mother-in-law (Arsene Ntahobari and Pauline Nyiramasuhuko, respectively) had been tried and convicted by the ICTR of crimes relating to the genocide. The indictment in the case charges Munyenyezi with two counts of procuring citizenship unlawfully by making material misrepresentations on a number of occasions before and after she came to the US. In particular, the indictment alleges that Munyenyezi participated, committed, ordered, oversaw, conspired to, aided and abetted, assisted in and directed persecution, kidnapping, rape and murder during the Rwandan genocide of 1994 and that she misrepresented these facts in order to obtain immigration and naturalization benefits. The jury in the Munyenyezi was deadlocked on the issue of the defendant's participation in the genocide and the presiding judge declared a mistrial in the case on 15 March 2012. The accused has been granted bail pending a retrial.

A Burundian national, Lazare Kobagaya, has been tried in the US on immigration offences that would have required proof of his participation in the Rwanda genocide.[77] Kobagaya was charged with unlawful procurement of citizenship or naturalization (naturalization fraud), in violation of 18 U.S.C. § 1425(a) (Count One), and fraud and misuse of visas, permits and other documents (visa fraud), in violation of 18 U.S.C. § 1546(a) (Count Two). The US government claimed that Kobagaya had lied about his participation in the Rwanda genocide in his application for naturalization as a US citizen. The case was the first in the US to require proof of commission of the crime of genocide. The jury was not able to reach a unanimous verdict on Count One (18 U.S.C. § 1425(a)) and returned a guilty verdict on Count Two (18 U.S.C. § 1546(a)). The court declared a mistrial as to involvement in the genocide. The prosecution informed the defence that they planned to retry that aspect of the case. The defence filed a motion for acquittal. In its response to the defence motion for acquittal, the prosecution revealed that it had failed to disclose statements that had been made by a former consular officer in Nairobi in relation to the case. The officer stated that even if she had known that Kobagaya was in Rwanda in 1994, she would not have questioned him about the genocide for his visa and alien registration application because he was not Rwandan, but rather a Burundian national. A key argument in the defence's case was that Kobagaya's presence in Rwanda during the genocide was not a material fact that would have caused further investigation by US immigration officials if Kobagaya had disclosed it in his immigration papers. Kobagaya had not made that disclosure regarding his presence in Rwanda in his application. The defence wrote a letter to the presiding judge stating that it would seek sanctions for the government's failure to disclose information from the consular officer. Prosecutors were compelled to request the judge not only to dismiss the charge against Kobagaya of lying on his citizenship application, but also to set aside his visa fraud conviction.

Current trends indicate that the US investigation and prosecutorial bodies are experiencing difficulties in establishing solid cases against the genocide suspects upon whom they have focused their investigations.

7.6 Challenges and Obstacles to the Exercise of Universal Jurisdiction in Respect of Crimes Relating to the Rwanda Genocide

Attempts to seek justice for victims of the crimes that were committed during the Rwanda conflict of the 1990s through judicial proceedings in third-party states on the basis of the principle of universal jurisdiction are constrained and hampered by a number of challenges and obstacles.

The pre-genocide regime in Rwanda enjoyed excellent relations with a large number of other governments. In the aftermath of the genocide and the defeat of the government that planned and directed the genocide, officials of the ousted government and other Rwandans who had participated in committing atrocities sought asylum in states (such as Kenya, Zaire, now the Democratic Republic of Congo, Gabon and Cameroon) whose governments were sympathetic to their cause. Instead of helping the Rwanda government to bring persons who bore responsibility for genocide to justice or investigating and prosecuting the crimes in their own courts, governments of such states often provided suspected genocide suspects with protection.

Genocide suspects who did not enjoy high-level political protection in the countries of initial refuge soon moved away from the vicinity of Rwanda to distant countries. Many of them changed their identities. Some even changed their nationality by registering as Congolese or Burundians with the United Nations Office of the High Commissioner for Refugees (UNHCR), or with national refugee commissions. Many genocide suspects have become naturalized citizens of other states, either through legitimate channels or through bribery and the use of fake documents (SALC/REDRESS 2012: p. 18). It is not a coincidence that a significant number of the Rwandan genocide suspects who have been apprehended and brought to justice in Europe and North America have often been found to have arrived with false identities, assisted by real or forged passports of third-party states.[78] The pursuit of justice for the victims of crimes relating to the Rwanda genocide is hampered by systematic efforts on the part of the criminals to hide their real identities and their whereabouts.

Africa has generally lagged behind the rest of the world in ensuring accountability for crimes associated with the Rwanda conflict. While most of the refugees who fled Rwanda in the aftermath of the genocide remain in Africa and it is reasonable to assume that the majority of perpetrators remain in Africa, not a single African country has undertaken the prosecution of crimes alleged to have been committed in the course of the genocide. Even African governments that have not been sympathetic to genocide suspects have demonstrated little political will to investigate and prosecute crimes relating to the 1990s Rwanda conflict. In addition to lack of political will, the failure of African states to ensure accountability on the part of persons who bear responsibility for crimes relating to the Rwanda conflict may also be attributed to lack of appropriate legal frameworks and technical capacity.

Most states in Africa do not have laws incorporating international crimes into domestic legislation. In most of the states in the region, legal frameworks that would make it possible for domestic courts to exercise extraterritorial or universal jurisdiction over international crimes, including crimes committed during the 1990s conflict, are either absent or inadequate. Problems relating to lack of appropriate laws are exacerbated by technical constraints such as lack of expertise and insufficient resources (SALC/REDRESS 2012).

Legal, technical, financial and political obstacles to justice for the victims of the atrocities that were committed during the Rwanda conflict of the 1990s are not peculiar to Africa. Justice for the victims of Rwanda's violent past is elusive even in the affluent states in Europe and North America, which have significant populations of Rwandan refugees who may include persons responsible for genocide. Personal and collective narratives of Rwanda's past and its current situation divide Rwandan society along ethnic lines and political affiliation. Immigration, police and judicial officials of foreign states do not always have adequate knowledge of Rwandan society in general or the politics of its conflict in particular. In every investigation relating to the Rwanda conflict that investigative and prosecutorial bodies of states that are host to genocide suspects undertake, these agencies are certain to be confronted by narratives that are deeply influenced by ethnic affinity and political bias. That even states (such as the United Kingdom and France) whose laws permit the exercise of universal jurisdiction for international crimes and whose judicial systems have the necessary technical and financial resources to investigate and prosecute crimes alleged to have been committed by the Rwandan immigrants that they have welcomed as refugees have chosen not to carry out any prosecutions is an indication of the difficulties that officials of foreign governments face in making sense of allegations and counter-allegations of human rights abuses by the parties to the Rwanda conflict. It is possible that faced with these difficulties of determing the truth, most foreign officials often choose to do nothing about crimes attributed to genocide suspects living on their territories. It is not a coincidence that Belgium, with its historical links with Rwanda and deep knowledge of Rwandan society, has made more progress in carrying out investigations and prosecutions based on exercising universal jurisdiction in respect of crimes relating to the Rwanda genocide than any other state.

The pursuit of justice in respect of the crimes that were committed during the 1990s Rwanda conflict is impeded by technical constraints even in states with advanced and well resourced justice and law enforcement systems. Investigations and prosecutions of international crimes are complex. They require expert skills that many states may not initially have. Building the capacity required to carry out such investigations and prosecutions effectively is, even in the most favourable of circumstances, a challenging and long-term undertaking. Few if any states have invested adequately in building such capacity. The absence of such capacity is demonstrated not just by the fact that few states have undertaken such investigations and trials, but by the outcomes of the few cases that are prosecuted. In the United States, for example, investigations and prosecutorial agencies have only been able to convince a jury to return a verdict of guilty in a case involving alleged participation in the Rwanda genocide in just one instance, this in spite of the enormous resources that the US government spends on investigating and prosecuting cases of crimes linked to the Rwanda genocide.[79]

State practices and policies on whether and when to support investigations and prosecutions of extraterritorial international crimes are also influenced by financial considerations. Investigations and prosecutions of crimes alleged to have been committed in conflicts in distant lands whose languages, culture, history and society officials of foreign investigations and prosecutorial agencies may not be familiar with are very costly.[80] During these times when governments in every part of the world are struggling to keep vital national programmes funded, spending on investigations and trials of crimes that were committed two decades ago in a small state of little strategic interest such as Rwanda is not a priority. Governments have generally underfunded units in charge of investigations and prosecutions of war crimes, including crimes relating to the Rwanda genocide. In France and Belgium, for example, investigations of crimes relating to the Rwanda genocide are supervised by only one or two investigative judges who are not exclusively dedicated to cases connected with the Rwanda genocide.

Even outside Africa, the pursuit of justice in respect of the crimes that were committed in the course of the 1990s Rwanda conflict is hampered by lack of political will. Many of the governments of states in Europe that are host to genocide suspects have generally been reluctant to extradite such suspects to Rwanda due to concerns about the risk of unfair trials. While these governments often proclaim that their states shall not be safe havens for war criminals and pay lip service to the need for accountability for crimes linked to the Rwanda genocide, they fail to take any steps to make such accountability possible. Nothing illustrates this lack of political will more than the fact that the vast majority of the cases that have been commenced in France and Belgium (the states that have opened the most investigations in respect of crimes stemming from the Rwanda genocide) were initiated by non-governmental organizations or victims rather than the state institutions tasked with investigating and prosecuting these crimes. Lack of political will can be the only explanation for why rich states with developed legal systems and advanced economies such as the United Kingdom and France are yet to organize any trials for the genocide suspects whom their own courts have refused to extradite to Rwanda due to fair trial concerns. Problems due to lack of political will to pursue prosecutions (especially of officials of sitting governments or former officials of influential states) remains pervasive (Human Rights Watch 2006c: p. 4).

Even in the relatively advanced legal systems of Western Europe and North America, accountability for crimes relating to the Rwanda genocide has in some instances been impeded by lack of appropriate legal frameworks. Many states lack laws authorizing trials of international crimes, especially genocide, on the basis of the principle of universal jurisdiction based on customary law. Trials of genocide suspects have been aborted in the Netherlands,[81] Norway,[82] France[83] and Denmark[84] because the courts in those countries have ruled that they did not have jurisdiction to try extraterritorial crimes, even in situations where the suspects were living in those countries. Lack of jurisdiction in such cases may be rectified by amending existing laws, as France, the United Kingdom, Norway and other states have done. However, the concerns of the victims of the Rwanda conflict are not a priority in many of the countries where genocide suspects have settled. Amendment of domestic laws to allow the exercise of universal jurisdiction may take a long time or may never happen at all. Even where new legislation permitting the exercise of universal legislation is brought onto the statute books, it may not be helpful in ensuring justice for the victims of the Rwanda conflict of the 1990s. The Norwegian Supreme Court has held such legislation is not applicable to crimes that were committed before the legislation came into force.[85]

Charges of international crimes are particularly prone to manipulation for political reasons. A new government may seek to use charges of human rights abuses to silence foreign-based political opposition. Losers of armed conflicts may use allegations of human rights abuses to undermine the legitimacy of the new political order. The history of Rwanda has been prone to manipulation by both sides of the Rwanda conflict. There is a widespread perception among Rwandan refugees that charges of involvement in the genocide that the Rwanda government levels against many refugees are politically motivated. Some Rwandan refugees admit that they too have used the opportunity of lodging complaints, particularly in Spain and France, against members of the current government of Rwanda as a strategy to fight the government.[86] The principle of universal jurisdiction for crimes relating to Rwanda is delicate because it has proved to be very prone to abuse.

Success in carrying out investigations and prosecutions of international crimes based on the principle of universal jurisdiction depends on the cooperation of the states where the crimes took place. Governments will rarely, if ever, cooperate with investigations of crimes alleged to have been committed by their officials. The Rwanda government's policy on universal jurisdiction demonstrates this point. The government has always welcomed and actively assisted the investigation and prosecution of genocide and other grave violations of human rights that were committed against the Tutsi and political opposition by the previous government. On the one hand, the government has resisted and opposed, in the strongest terms possible, any attempts by foreign investigative and prosecutorial bodies to investigate and prosecute allegations of human rights violations attributed to members of military and security services. In 2008, the Rwanda government severed diplomatic relations with France after a French investigative judge issued international warrants for the arrest of officers alleged to have been involved in the missile attack on the aircraft in which the Presidents of Rwanda and Burundi, along with their entourages, perished in 1994. The government of Rwanda has similarly reacted violently to the issue of international warrants for the arrest of members of its military leadership by Spanish authorities. As a result of the Rwanda government's refusal to cooperate with investigations of foreign investigative and prosecutorial bodies of crimes alleged to have been committed by members of its military, the investigation and prosecution of crimes relating to the Rwanda conflict that foreign jurisdictions have carried out on the basis of the principle of universal jurisdiction have dealt exclusively with the crimes of the vanquished, the Hutu political, military and civil society leaders of the previous regime. The implication of the reality that states do not usually cooperate with investigations of crimes alleged to have been committed by their own officials is that the exercise of the principle of universal jurisdiction for international crime is likely to further the agenda of the victors, rather than address the past violence of the relevant society in an even-handed manner. It is not surprising, therefore, that in the view of many in the Hutu community, trials of genocide suspects based on universal jurisdiction are as much victor's justice as national trials in Rwanda and trials by the ICTR have been.[87]

7.7 Conclusion

The manner in which Rwanda's armed conflict of the 1990s ended, with the military defeat of the forces that planned and led the implementation of the 1994 genocide, resulted in an unprecedented dispersal of large numbers of perpetrators of very grave human rights abuses, including genocide, crimes against humanity and war crimes, across the world. Rwanda's ordinary courts and the Gacaca tribunals have mostly tried only the rank and file participants in the genocide. While the ICTR has played a crucial role in bringing perpetrators who bear the greatest responsibility to justice, it has tried only a small proportion of this group of perpetrators. The majority of the political, military and civil society leaders who led the campaign of the Rwanda genocide remain at large. The genocide's aftermath created an opportunity to test both the promise and the limitations of the exercise of the principle of universal jurisdiction for the most egregious human rights abuses. Experience of the application of the principle of universal jurisdiction to accountability for crimes relating to the Rwanda conflict has to date demonstrated that while it is in theory a critical component of global strategies to fight impunity for gross human rights abuses, it has strong limitations in practice. Its potential for contributing effectively to the fight against impunity for international crimes is frequently constrained by the absence of appropriate legal frameworks, resource constraints and lack of political will on the part of the governments of the various states in which perpetrators have settled. The last two chapters will discuss the impact, if any, that the processes that have been undertaken to ensure accountability for crimes that were committed during the course of Rwanda's 1990s conflict, including trials based on the principle of universal jurisdiction, have had in achieving the objectives of transitional justice in Rwanda.

8 Untold Story, Unfinished Business

Confronting the Crimes of the Victors

8.1 Introduction

The genocide against the Tutsi and massacres of Hutus who were considered opponents of the government of the day were without doubt the most extreme of the violence that Rwanda experienced during the 1990s. This book does not in any way seek to downplay, let alone deny, the extent, significance or very grave consequences of the genocide against the Tutsi and massacres of Hutu opponents of the government that planned and directed the genocide. Neither does this work seek to put the genocide on a par with any other violations of human rights that took place during this period. The genocide was a unique catastrophe that will always occupy a singular place in the history of Rwanda. The genocide and massacres against Hutu Rwandans whom the regime in power in Rwanda in 1994 considered its opponents were not, however, the only human rights violations that took place in Rwanda during the 1990s. There have long been allegations, strongly contested by Rwanda's current government (Kagame 2009), that the victors may themselves have committed war crimes and crimes against humanity during and after the genocide (Des Forges 1999; Organisation of African Unity 2000; Prunier 1995). Almost two decades after the genocide, the topic of the allegations of human rights abuses by the victors remains one of the major issues that still deeply divide Rwandan society.

No aspect of the Rwandan conflict generates as much controversy as the issue of the extent to which the RPA was responsible for human rights abuses during and after 1994. Some Hutu, particularly the leaders of the forces that planned and directed the genocide and other opponents of the current government, to this day deny that there was any genocide of the Tutsi. These groups assert, instead, that the violence that Rwanda experienced in 1994 was nothing more than reciprocal killings by two groups that were then at war. Some even claim that the Hutu were the real victims of the violence that Rwanda experienced in 1994 (Ntamabyariro 1999). The current government of Rwanda on the other hand denies that its army was responsible for widespread and systematic abuses against unarmed civilians. The government generally portrays the purveyors of the 'double genocide' theory and advocates for justice for Hutu victims of atrocity as revisionists who seek to deny the genocide against the Tutsi or are sympathetic to those responsible for it.

The accountability processes that Rwanda has undertaken have done little to shed light on the issue of allegations of human rights abuses on the part of the victors. Many questions relating to this aspect of the violence that Rwanda experienced during the 1990s remain unresolved. Was the RPA responsible for gross human rights violations against innocent Hutu non-combatants? What was the extent of the atrocities, if any, that were committed against Hutu non-combatants by victors? Were the human rights violations attributed to the RPA merely isolated criminal acts of individuals or systematic attacks organized and led by military commanders at various levels? Were the attacks, if any, extensive enough to constitute a 'reverse genocide', as members of the ousted regime and some other opponents of Rwanda's current government assert? This chapter aims to shed some light on the above questions. It discusses the human rights practices of the army and security services of the RPA before, during and immediately after the genocide, and examines the extent to which Rwanda's accountability processes have addressed the violations of human rights attributed to the victors. The chapter also explores the possible implications of the failure of Rwanda's transitional justice process to address the crimes of the victors and discusses the question whether lack of impartiality negates the value of the transitional justice processes that Rwanda has undertaken.

8.2 The Human Rights Record of the RPA

There are long-standing allegations that the RPA may have committed gross human rights abuses before, during and after the genocide (Silva-Leander 2008: p. 1608). Reports of allegations of widespread human rights abuses on the part of the RPA were emerging even before the genocide ended. A report on the situation in Rwanda published by Human Rights Watch at the beginning of May 1994 concluded that there was no evidence that the RPA had engaged in any widespread slaughter of the population, but it indicated that there were reports of less systematic abuses (Human Rights Watch 1994b). Reports of RPA abuses persisted following the genocide. A report on the situation in Rwanda presented by the UN Secretary General to the Security Council on 25 July 1994 noted that several hundred thousand people had already been killed, largely by government forces. The report indicated, however, that the RPA was responsible for summary or arbitrary executions carried out as acts of revenge (United Nations 1994g).

The preliminary report of the Commission of Experts, which was established by the Secretary General at the request of the UN Security Council to investigate the violations of international humanitarian law that had been committed in Rwanda, concluded that government forces and allied militia groups largely bore responsibility for the atrocities that had been committed in Rwanda, but indicated that, although massacres perpetrated by the RPA were less systematic than those of the armed forces and Hutu militia, the RPA was nevertheless responsible for certain crimes against humanity (United Nations 1994h: para. 83). The Commission's report stated that there existed substantial grounds to conclude that mass assassinations, summary executions, breaches of international humanitarian law and crimes against humanity had been perpetrated by Tutsi elements against Hutu individuals. The Commission noted, however, that it had not uncovered any evidence to indicate that Tutsi elements had committed any criminal acts with intent to destroy the Hutu ethnic group in terms of the definition of genocide under the 1948 Genocide Convention (United Nations 1994h: para. 83).

In its second and final report, the Commission of Experts reaffirmed its earlier finding that mass murders, summary executions, breaches of international humanitarian law and crimes against humanity had been perpetrated by Tutsi elements against Hutu individuals (United Nations 1994h: para. 8). The Commission again indicated that it was unable to establish any genocidal intent in the atrocities that members of the RPA were reported to have committed. Neither did the Commission find any evidence to indicate that the killings of Hutus by individual RPA soldiers were systematic, or were sponsored, or even approved of, by government officials or army commanders (United Nations 1994i). However, the Commission expressed grave concern over continuing violence against innocent non-combatants by RPA soldiers. The Commission recommended that investigations of violations of international humanitarian law and human rights law attributed to the RPA be continued by the prosecutor of the ICTR. The Commission undertook to turn over files relevant to this aspect of the violence to the Prosecutor (United Nations 1994i: para. 100).

The situation of human rights in Rwanda during and after the genocide was also the subject of a series of reports of the Special Rapporteur of the UN Commission on Human Rights, Rene Degni Segui. The first of the reports, submitted following a visit that the Special Rapporteur made to Rwanda in mid-May 1994, indicated that in the areas controlled by the RPA, cases of massacres reported were rather rare, perhaps because little was known about them (UNCHR 1994c: para. 22). The report claimed, however, that members of the RPA were carrying out summary executions and were responsible for disappearances in areas under the organization's control (1994c: paras 22, 49). The Special Rapporteur's follow-up reports concluded that gross human rights abuses, including summary executions, abductions and enforced disappearances, arbitrary arrests and detentions, and other human rights abuses, had been committed by the RPA and were continuing. The Special Rapporteur did not make any estimates of the number of victims of the human rights violations attributable to the RPA. However, the Special Rapporteur's reports progressively became more critical of the post-genocide government's human rights practices, drawing attention to the prevailing insecurity and continuing human rights violations by the military against civilians. The reports of the Special Rapporteur did not suggest that the government was directly responsible.

Rather the reports indicated that human rights violations occurring after the genocide were committed 'either by the civilian population itself, by soldiers at the civilian population's request or on their own initiative' (UNCHR 1994e: para. 40).

In October 1994, Amnesty International published a report on the situation of human rights in Rwanda that alleged that deliberate and arbitrary killings, abductions and disappearances had been committed by the RPA during the genocide and were continuing. According to the report, many of the killings had taken place in reprisal attacks against civilians (Amnesty International 1994). The report also indicated that there were deliberate executions carried out in the course of screening the population for members of the Interahamwe militia and other persons suspected of being responsible for genocide. The report attributed responsibility for most of the killings to the RPA, but also revealed that civilian supporters of the RPA were being allowed to kill opponents or persons suspected of being perpetrators of the genocide. The Amnesty International report did not attempt to estimate the number of victims of the attacks, but it indicated that the executions could possibly have claimed thousands of lives in the northern part of Rwanda alone. Amnesty International considered the human rights violations attributable to the RPA to be so very grave that it recommended the establishment of an independent commission of inquiry with the specific responsibility to investigate reports of human rights violations both in areas under the RPA's control before July 1994 and in the country as a whole since that date (Amnesty International 1994).

The most authoritative account of the crimes alleged to have been committed by the RPA during this period is generally considered to be the seminal report on the Rwandan genocide that was published by Human Rights Watch and the International Federation for Human Rights (Des Forges 1999). The report concluded that:

> In their drive for military victory and a halt to the genocide, the Rwandese Patriotic Front killed thousands, including non-combatants as well as government troops and members of militia. As RPF soldiers sought to establish their control over the local population, they also killed civilians in numerous summary executions and in massacres. They may have slaughtered tens of thousands during the four months of combat from April to July. The killings diminished in August and were markedly reduced after mid-September … (Des Forges 1999: p. 692)

Further light has also been shed on the human rights practices of the RPA during and after the genocide by Rwanda's own genocide investigations. Evidence of human rights abuses on the part of the RPA has come to light in all parts of the country. In the course of investigating genocide crimes, the police and prosecution service in Rwanda have often been told of two waves of killings: the genocide and reprisal attacks which took place after the genocide had come to an end.

During my time of service as Prosecutor General, I personally conducted investigations of genocide cases in the Kibuye, Butare and Kibungo provinces of Rwanda. I had access to the contents of hundreds of dossiers that I reviewed as part of my oversight of domestic prosecutions of the crimes that were committed in the context of the genocide. I visited every prison across the country and interacted with a large number of genocide suspects. I did not, in the course of these activities, come across evidence indicating that the RPA was responsible for acts constituting genocide as it is legally defined. However, my experience left no doubt that members of the RPA had committed widespread human rights violations across the country.

Since the establishment of the Gacaca courts, citizens participating in Gacaca in various parts of the country have tried to raise the issue of human rights abuses alleged to have been committed by the RPA (Penal Reform International 2001, 2002a, 2002b, 2003a, 2003b, 2003c, 2006, 2010a).

The crimes that were committed by members of the RPA during and after the genocide fall into five categories: ordinary crimes of violence unrelated to the genocide that were committed by individuals (Prunier 1995: pp. 332–3; United Nations 1994f; UNCHR 1994c, 1994d, 1994e); revenge or reprisal killings by individuals or groups that were not acting in an official capacity (Prunier 1995: p. 332); killings of civilians by soldiers in the course of combat operations (Des Forges 1999: pp. 702–5); indiscriminate massacres of civilians (Des Forges 1999: p. 705); and targeted killings of political and other figures who were suspected either of being responsible for genocide or of belonging to the extremist political organizations responsible for the genocide (Des Forges 1999: p. 709).

The RPA has also been accused of committing gross human rights violations against Rwandan refugees during the 1996–97 war in the Democratic Republic of Congo, formerly known as Zaire (Bradol and Guibert 1997; Dialogue 1997; Organisation of African Unity 2000). In 1996, Rwanda sponsored and led a rebellion against the government of Zaire, and its then President, Marshal Mobutu (Pomfret 1997). The Rwanda government used a rebel group known as the Alliance of Democratic Forces for the Liberation of Congo-Zaire (AFDL) as a cover for an operation to dismantle camps of Rwandan refugees inside Zaire and to attack and destroy insurgent groups (comprising former members of the Forces Armées Rwandaises (FAR) and militia groups that had participated in the genocide) that were waging war and threatening the security of Rwanda (Amnesty International 1996b; Pomfret 1997). In the course of dismantling the refugee camps and the pursuit of these insurgents, the RPA and/or its Congolese allies are reported to have committed widespread human rights abuses against Rwandan civilians (United Nations 1996a, 1998a; Amnesty International 1997d; Human Rights Watch 1997; International Centre for Human Rights and Democratic

Development 1998; Adelman 2003). The AFDL and its allies or benefactors, including the RPA, successfully obstructed investigations of the above mentioned allegations by the United Nations (1996a). Later attempts by the United Nations to investigate atrocities that were committed against both Rwandans and Congolese during the war that led to the ousting of President Mobutu from power in Congo were equally frustrated by the new government of the Democratic Republic of Congo.

The atrocities that were committed against Rwandan refugees in the Democratic Republic of Congo during 1996–97 returned to the limelight in 2010, when the Office of the United Nations High Commissioner for Human Rights published the Report of the Mapping Exercise documenting the most serious violations of human rights and international humanitarian law committed within the territory of the Democratic Republic of the Congo between March 1993 and June 2003 (UNOHCHR 2010). The mapping exercise has its origins in the United Nations' earlier investigations of human rights violations that were committed in Congo from 1993 to 1997. In September 2005, the UN peacekeeping mission in Congo, MONUC, discovered three mass graves in Rutshuru, in North Kivu province of eastern Congo, relating to crimes committed in 1996 and 1997. The discovery of the mass graves prompted a re-opening of investigations of human rights violations that were committed dring the 1996–97 DRC war. The Office of the High Commissioner for Human Rights, with the support of the UN Secretary General, initiated the mapping exercise and broadened its mandate to include crimes committed during Congo's conflict from 1993 to 2003 as well. The report included a section narrating the horrendous attacks that Rwandan Hutu refugees in the DRC suffered at the hands of the Rwanda military and its allies. The report stated that the attacks against Rwandan refugees by members of the RPA and/or their allies may have constituted crimes that can be classified as genocide. The report further made recommendations, involving a combination of Congolese, foreign and international jurisdictions, on how the crimes that all the armed groups implicated by the report committed could be brought to justice. The Rwanda government's vitriolic response to the mapping report focused not on denying the alleged atrocities per se, but on attacking the report's categorization of the crimes as possible acts of genocide.

It may never be possible to establish an accurate account of the human rights violations that members of the RPA were responsible for during and after the genocide. The Rwanda military successfully established systems to control access to information relating to its conduct of the wars that it fought in Rwanda and in the Congo during the 1990s (Gowing 1998; Des Forges 1999: p. 522). Restriction of access to areas of combat limited the opportunity for human rights organizations and the media to monitor and report upon the human rights practices of the organization during this critical period (Des Forges 1999: p. 522). There are reports that the RPA has systematically worked to destroy incriminating evidence during the intervening period.

The RPF has, since taking power, restricted the opportunity to publicly discuss allegations of human rights abuses attributed to its military wing. Nevertheless, there is now a consensus among scholars of Rwanda and other commentators that the RPA was indeed responsible for atrocities against unarmed civilians during and after the genocide, in both Rwanda and in the Congo (Des Forges 1999: pp. 701–35; Organisation of African Unity 2000: Chapter 22; Prunier 1995). Not all the killings committed by the RPA were isolated incidents of revenge as the military establishment in Rwanda seeks to portray them. The seminal Human Rights Watch report quoted above on the Rwanda genocide has indicated that the killings by members of the RPA were widespread, systematic and involved large numbers of participants and victims (Des Forges 1999: p. 734). This conclusion was endorsed by the panel of very eminent personalities, which was established by the Organisation of African Unity (2000: Chapter 22). There is also empirical research available, which suggests that the RPA may indeed have been responsible for widespread killings of innocent civilians (Verwimp 2003).

8.3 Selective Accountability: Human Rights Violations and the RPA

The military in Rwanda effectively control the government from behind the scenes (Ghai 2009: p. 9; Beswick 2012). The policies of the government, including the policies on accountability for past human rights violations, are in effect the policies of the military and the ruling party that formal government institutions implement on their behalf. Due to the control that the military exercises over the Rwanda state, the policies on accountability for atrocity that the government has pursued have reflected the interests, preferences and expectations of the military and security services.

Officially, the government of Rwanda does not deny that members of its military committed human rights abuses against civilians during and after the genocide. General Kagame, who has been at the helm of the RPA since 1990, along with other commanders as well as the political leaders of the RPF, have long acknowledged that some members of the RPA were indeed responsible for human rights abuses during and after 1994 (United Nations 1994h). The government only disputes the claim that the crimes in question were widespread, organized and systematic, or sanctioned by military commanders (Kagame 2009). The government claims that killings and other crimes by members of the RPA were not organized, supervised or condoned by military superiors, and that they were merely 'isolated incidents', committed by individual servicemen (Tiemessen 2004: pp. 69–70). Rwanda's military establishment claims that violent acts against innocent civilians by members of the RPA were a rare occurrence and that they were a result of poor discipline and a desire for revenge by young soldiers who had lost their relatives during the genocide, rather than a result of an organized, centrally directed strategy (Longman 2004b: p. 167). According to scholars of the genocide, 'any hint that the RPF might be guilty of massive human rights violations [has always been] immediately countered by the regime with an indignant reminder of the genocide' (Prunier 1995: p. 362).

It has not been possible for victims of the crimes alleged to have been committed by members of the RPA to put the government's claims about the nature and scope of these crimes to the test. Through legislation as well as administrative measures, the government of Rwanda has made it impossible to ascertain the truth regarding the allegations of human rights abuses that have been levelled against the RPA. The government does not tolerate any public debate about the human rights violations that the RPA is alleged to have committed (Zorbas 2004). Persons who criticise the RPA for its human rights practices or for its perceived record of exclusion are accused of sowing division and brutally silenced (Longman 2004b: p. 167). The government has historically dealt with demands for justice for crimes that were committed by members of its military during and after the genocide by simply reiterating standard denials of widespread massacres and promises that the military justice system will investigate and prosecute any isolated cases of human rights abuses that may be brought to its attention. The mechanisms of accountability for atrocity that Rwanda has undertaken in response to the aftermath of the genocide have in practice miserably failed to investigate, prosecute and punish the crimes of the victors.

8.3.1 Gacaca

Gacaca courts were officially adopted as Rwanda's principal mechanism of accountability for genocide in 2001. The law that initially established the Gacaca courts included war crimes, crimes against humanity and breaches of Additional Protocol II to the Geneva Conventions in the subject matter jurisdiction of Gacaca courts.[1] However, on the eve of the elections of the first Gacaca judges, the President of Rwanda publicly announced that Gacaca courts would not have jurisdiction to investigate and try allegations of human rights abuses by the members of the RPA.[2] The 2004 amendment of the law governing the operations of Gacaca courts formally removed war crimes and breaches of Additional Protocol II to the Geneva Conventions from the subject matter jurisdiction of Gacaca courts.[3] Organic Law 10/2004 still contains a reference to crimes against humanity.[4] Conceivably, this provision brings some of the crimes that members of the RPA may have committed within the jurisdiction of Gacaca courts (Fierens 2005: pp. 908–9). In practice, however, Gacaca courts have been expressly forbidden by administrative directives from dealing with cases involving human rights violations that were allegedly committed by members of the RPA (Longman 2004b: p. 167). Gacaca judges have been instructed that Gacaca courts do not have jurisdiction to deal with any offences attributable to the RPA. Some individuals in communities across Rwanda have still courageously made demands for justice for the victims of these crimes (Penal Reform International 2002a; Molenaar 2005:

pp. 58–9). Gacaca courts have responded to these demands by reiterating the policy of the government in respect of these crimes, namely that the allegations of human rights violations against members of the RPA were not part of the mandate of Gacaca and that any complaints regarding the crimes should be reported to military authorities which would investigate the allegations and take appropriate action, including bringing perpetrators to justice where the evidence warranted (Tiemessen 2004: pp. 69–70). The Gacaca system has thus been unable to address the human rights violations alleged to have been committed by the victors of Rwanda's armed conflict (Waldorf 2006b; Meyerstein 2007: pp. 485–6). The government's refusal to allow Gacaca courts to receive and adjudicate complaints of violations of human rights abuses attributed to the RPA has adversely affected the credibility of the Gacaca process within Rwandan society (Honeyman *et al.* 2004: p. 11).

8.3.2 National prosecutions

The exclusion of human rights violations attributed to the RPA from the subject matter jurisdiction of Gacaca courts would not by itself have been a major problem had the government intended to address allegations of the abuses in good faith by other means. The Rwanda military maintains its own separate justice system that exercises exclusive jurisdiction for crimes committed by members of the military and civilian accomplices. Under Rwanda's legal system, offences committed by members of the military are tried by the military court system. Even civilian accomplices of military offenders are subject to the jurisdiction of military courts.[5] Victims of the human rights abuses that were committed by the RPA have found it difficult to report and pursue complaints with military authorities (Richters *et al.* 2005: p. 209). In some cases, citizens have reported killings that were committed by members of the RPA to the police and prosecution service, but these institutions can only refer the cases to the military. During my time as Prosecutor General, my office referred some cases to the prosecution service of the military justice system. None of the cases that the civilian justice system forwarded to the military prosecution department during my tenure resulted in prosecutions.

Citizens in many communities raised issues relating to human rights violations alleged to have been committed by members of the RPA during the course of Gacaca. Very few, if any, of these complaints have been followed up by the investigative, prosecutorial and judicial organs of the Rwandan military system; only an insignificant number of complaints of human rights abuses attributable to the RPA have been investigated (Tiemessen 2004; Human Rights Watch 2008: pp. 89–109). As of July 2008, the military justice system had prosecuted crimes involving approximately 115 members of the RPA that were committed against civilians during and immediately after the genocide. The majority of the defendants in these cases were low-ranking soldiers (Human Rights Watch 2008: p. 90). Only a small number of RPA officers have been prosecuted for offences relating to the violence of 1990s and only a minority of the defendants in the cases that were prosecuted were convicted. Very light sentences have been imposed in the minority of cases that have resulted in convictions (Human Rights Watch 2008: p. 90; Rettig 2008: p. 32) and even these light sentences were sometimes not executed (Algard 2005: pp. 19–21). The general consensus among scholars of Rwanda is that Rwanda's military justice system has failed to investigate and prosecute in good faith crimes alleged to have been committed by its members during and after the genocide. Rather, the prosecutions that have been undertaken appear to have been intended to shield members of the RPA from rendering an account for crimes for which they are accused of being responsible.

8.3.3 Trials by the ICTR

The subject matter jurisdiction of the International Criminal Tribunal for Rwanda (ICTR) includes crimes against humanity and war crimes.[6] The expectation of the members of the Security Council and other states who were involved in the process of establishing the Rwanda tribunal was that it would bring to justice persons who were responsible for crimes that fell within its jurisdiction, regardless of the parties to the Rwanda conflict to which they belonged (United Nations 1994l). The UN Security Council reiterated on many occasions, particularly during the first ten years of the ICTR's mandate, the need for the tribunal to investigate and prosecute human rights violations that may have been committed by members of the RPA. Yet, the tribunal has not issued even a single indictment in respect of crimes that members of the RPA are alleged to have committed. The choices that successive prosecutors of the tribunal have made to refrain from seeking any indictments against members of the RPA appear, at least in part, to have been a result of strategic decisions to avoid confrontation with the government of Rwanda that could have paralysed the operations of the Rwanda tribunal (Peskin 2008). All the prosecutors who have served the tribunal consciously decided not to pursue any investigation of the attack against the plane of President Habyarimana that sparked the genocide. The last and longest serving of the tribunal's prosecutors inexplicably decided to deal with the question of the crimes alleged to have been committed by members of the RPA by transferring cases relating to the crimes that his office had investigated to Rwanda's military justice system (ICTR 2009b), even though Rwanda evidently lacked the will to investigate and try these cases in good faith. Most surprisingly, the Prosecutor even transferred to Rwanda's military justice system the most prominent and sensitive of these cases, the Kabgayi case.[7] The case involved the killing of more than a dozen people in Gitarama, including three bishops, nine priests and another senior clergyman of the Catholic Church, most of whom were Tutsi. Human rights organizations and other critics of the ICTR argue that this particular case was not prosecuted in good faith by Rwanda (Roth 2009b).

The tribunal, like Rwanda's domestic accountability processes, has failed to address the crimes of the victors.

The accountability processes that Rwanda has undertaken have been selective and partisan. Rwanda's domestic justice institutions (formal as well as traditional) have failed to investigate and prosecute in good faith and to punish the human rights violations that members of the RPA committed against non-combatant Hutu civilians, or to otherwise establish the truth about the allegations in an objective and impartial manner (Tiemessen 2004: pp. 69–71; Waldorf 2006b; Human Rights Watch 2008: pp. 89–91; Rettig 2008: p. 26). The accountability processes that Rwanda has undertaken have, to date, almost exclusively targeted perpetrators of genocide against the Tutsi and massacres of Hutu opponents of the pre-1994 regime that were committed by individuals and groups on the losing side. A similar one-sidedness has been evident in the work of the tribunal. The national and international processes of transitional justice mechanisms that Rwanda has implemented have failed to address the allegations of gross human rights abuses on the part of the victors seriously and in good faith.

8.4 Potential Implications of the Failure to Address Human Rights Violations Allegedly Committed by the Victors

Rwanda's failure to address the question of the gross human rights violations that are alleged to have been committed by the victors has serious implications for both the country and the international community.

Post-genocide Rwanda has presented the international community with many complex challenges (Uvin 2001: p. 177), but few aspects of Rwanda's post-genocide reconstruction have posed such challenging dilemmas to the international community as the human rights practices of the victors, and the issue of accountability for human rights violations allegedly committed by members of the RPA during and in the aftermath of the genocide in particular. The international community welcomed the RPA's success in ending the genocide and restoring order to Rwanda. The international community has largely been supportive of the government's handling of the post-war and genocide reconstruction process. This supportive attitude of most governments and international organizations towards the post-genocide Rwanda government and its policies and programmes is understandable, particularly in light of the widely acknowledged challenges that the government faced on assuming office. However, the human rights record of the government's army and security services has also confronted the international community with serious practical and moral questions and choices. Do individuals, leaders and institutions who or which stand by while atrocity rages have a moral right to seek to hold accountable those who courageously stand up to evil? Is it justifiable to undermine the credibility and effectiveness of a new regime that appears to offer the only hope of restoring security and stability to a war-torn country by insisting on arrests and prosecutions of its members, and particularly its leaders, for wartime human rights violations? How can the international community reconcile the important values, which the law of human rights seeks to promote, with the necessity to nurture a fragile peace? If even the victors must be held to account, what leverage does the international community have to ensure that crimes attributable to the perpetrators who come to or remain in power after war can be investigated and prosecuted fairly and effectively? How can the international community ensure that efforts to bring members of a new regime to justice for wartime human rights violations do not lead to the undesirable consequence of politically strengthening perpetrators of worse atrocities? These are questions that have arisen in many post-conflict contexts, and continue to trouble those working in the field of transitional justice. In the Rwandan context, these issues raise particularly intractable questions, given that those yet to be held to account are also those that brought an end to genocide, against a background of inaction and failure to protect by the international community.

During the years immediately following the genocide, some in the international community (including members of the UN Security Council), made occasional demands for accountability for the crimes that members of the RPA are reported to have committed (United Nations 2003a; United Nations 2003e: Statement of the Permanent Representative of Mexico). However, external demands for accountability for these crimes have gradually died away. The international community has, by default, chosen to deal with the issue of the responsibility of members of the RPA for the crimes by abandoning the search for truth and justice and sanctioning impunity.

Several factors have influenced the responses of international actors to human rights practices of the RPA during and after the genocide. The Rwanda government tries to silence criticism of the human rights practices of its military and security services by harping at the failure of the international community to stop or mitigate the genocide (Roth 2009a; Reyntjens 2011; Zorbas 2011). Policy makers in foreign governments and international institutions seek to avoid criticism for that failure. These policy makers also seek to avoid the risk of destabilizing Rwanda and precipitating a fresh outbreak of sectarian violence that they believe could arise as a result of weakening the RPA. There have in the past been concerns that any weakening of the RPA could lead to the strengthening of the forces that were responsible for the genocide as political players. There is also concern that destabilization of Rwanda could aggravate the already fragile situation in the Great Lakes region of Central Africa, especially in the neighbouring Democratic Republic of Congo, where the Rwanda military retains enormous capacity to wreak havoc. Policy makers in foreign governments and international organizations fear that initiatives to seek to hold to account Rwanda's military for past and ongoing abuses could provoke Rwanda's military to destabilize the DRC further. More recently, Rwanda's role as a provider of competent United

Nations peace-keeping forces has made it even more unlikely that foreign governments and international institutions will engage the Rwanda government on its governance deficits, including the human rights malpractices of its military.

The policies of both the Rwanda government and the major world powers and international institutions on the question of human rights violations attributable to the victors of the Rwanda conflict have raised an important question: Does the truth about human rights practices of the victors of armed conflicts matter? Or is justice for victims of the human rights violations abuses by victors negotiable or dispensable? If justice for the crimes of the victors is important, what are the implications of the failure to address seriously the crimes of the victors?

The truth about the crimes of the victors matters. Conservative estimates suggest that tens of thousands of people may have lost their lives at the hands of the RPA (Des Forges 1999: p. 734; Organisation of African Unity 2000, Chapter 22). These are, by any standards, atrocities that neither Rwandan society nor the international community should ignore or should ever have ignored. Rwanda can only ignore the crimes in question at its peril. The problem of accountability for these crimes has profound implications for Rwanda's efforts to fight impunity for gross human rights abuses and to promote a culture of respect for human rights, its transition to democracy, the chances of success in reconciling its divided people, and prospects for ensuring sustainable peace and stability in the long term.

The failure of Rwanda's accountability processes to address the issue of the human rights violations that may have been committed by the victors raises the possibility that the genocide trials that Rwanda has undertaken will be etched in the collective memory of the Hutu community as nothing more than victor's justice (Silva-Leander 2008: p. 1612). There is a general consensus among scholars of the Rwanda genocide that the failure of the accountability processes that Rwanda has undertaken to address the allegations of human rights violations attributable to the victors undermines the country's efforts to fight an entrenched culture of impunity (Strain and Keyes 2003: p. 116). Accountability processes that target only one side of the conflict are unlikely to be credible tools to combat impunity; they may encourage further violence and human rights abuses (Sarkin 2001: p. 171; Algard 2005: p. 21).

By failing to investigate and punish war crimes and crimes against humanity that were committed against members of the Hutu community effectively and in good faith, the government of Rwanda has missed an opportunity to deal with the past in a manner that promotes national reconciliation and healing (Megwalu and Loizides 2010). A society with a history of intractable violent conflict can only overcome the social polarization that past violence has spawned by recognizing, acknowledging and making amends for the suffering of victims on all sides. The uneven-handedness of the accountability processes that Rwanda has undertaken may undermine initiatives to promote national unity and reconciliation (Tiemessen 2004: p. 71; Algard 2005: p. 21).

Rwanda's failure to address issues relating to violence against members of the Hutu community has undermined public trust in government and its policies, including policies pertaining to national reconciliation (Organisation of African Unity 2000: para. 22.41). It has also fostered political tensions and further divided the country (Longman 2004b). The failure of Rwanda's domestic justice institutions and international criminal justice to address the human rights practices of the victors enhances the appeal of politicians and political groupings that espouse extremist anti-Tutsi policies, including genocide negationism (Zorbas 2004: p. 41). Rwanda's failure to provide justice for the victims of the violence that the Hutu community suffered during the 1990s is a source of bitter grievances against the government and hostility towards the Tutsi community in contemporary Rwanda.

The failure of domestic accountability mechanisms and international criminal justice to address allegations of human rights abuses against members of the Hutu community during and after the genocide is also a hindrance to progress towards democratization and establishment of the rule of law in Rwanda. The Rwanda government's adamant refusal to agree to any credible process of accountability for crimes that were committed against members of the Hutu community is driven, at least in part, by considerations relating to the need to protect the credibility and legitimacy of the RPF organization, the reputations of its military leaders and its hold on power (Tiemessen 2004: p. 65). The RPF claims to be entitled to a dominant role in Rwanda's politics since 1994 (RPF 1994). This claim is premised on the moral authority that the organization claims to derive from its role in stopping the genocide (Longman 2004b: p. 162). The moral authority, legitimacy and possibly the very survival of the RPF as a political player in Rwanda would be adversely affected by any process irrefutably establishing the responsibility of its members for widespread and systematic atrocities. To avoid being condemned to political marginalization or oblivion, the RPF is prepared to do everything in its power to ensure that its reputation (and hence the rationale for its monopoly of political and economic power) is not called into question. Perpetrators of atrocity are unlikely to allow competition for power, as their conduct would become a legitimate campaign issue in free and fair elections. Success in the transition to democracy in Rwanda will remain elusive as long as perpetrators of atrocity among the victors remain in power and are not brought to account.

Rwanda's failure to ensure even handed accountability also undermines prospects for sustainable peace and stability in Rwanda and the Great Lakes region of Central Africa. Victor's justice encourages perceptions within the Hutu community that they are victims of double standards, that the international community is indifferent to the violence and discrimination to which they have been subjected, and that the only way to resolve such discrimination is to resort to armed violence. The long-term peace and stability of Rwanda requires that the truth about the nature and scope of the human rights abuses that were committed against the Hutu community be established, that the suffering of the victims of the crimes be formally and openly acknowledged, that responsibility for the crimes be determined, and that the perpetrators of the crimes (especially those most responsible) be brought to account in some way. The failure of Rwanda's government and of the international community to address the grievances of the Hutu community may serve to inspire renewed violence rather than promote peace and stability. Unless the truth about violence against the Hutu community is confronted, acknowledged and satisfactorily redressed, its legacy could well haunt future generations of Rwandans and lead to new outbreaks of violence (Le Mon 2007: p. 20). New violence in Rwanda could in turn lead to catastrophic consequences for some of Rwanda's neighbours, as the aftermath of the 1994 genocide has demonstrated. Both Rwanda and the international community have a vested interested in seeing to it that the grievances of the victims of the victor's crimes are addressed in a constructive, fair and effective way.

The Rwanda government's resolute opposition to demands for credible and impartial mechanisms to establish the truth about the allegations of human rights violations attributed to the RPA undermines efforts to achieve the objectives of the country's transitional justice and peace-building processes. The victims of the human rights violations attributable to the victors are entitled to justice, just like the victims of the genocide. The issue of anti-Hutu violence is too critical to Rwanda's present and future to be simply ignored indefinitely. Confronting the issue of atrocities that may have been committed against innocent Hutu civilians by the victors is a challenge that Rwanda cannot delay forever. It is absolutely necessary that Rwandan society at some point addresses the issue of crimes against humanity, war crimes and other violations of human rights attributable to the victorious parties in the Rwanda conflict.

8.5 'Victor's justice': Negating the Importance of Transitional Justice in Rwanda?

The accountability mechanisms with which Rwanda has sought to address the legacy of the violence that the country experienced during the 1990s have been tainted by accusations that they represent yet another example of 'victor's justice' (Corey and Joireman 2000; Tiemessen 2004: p. 69; Wolters 2005b: p. 14). Rwanda's failure to address gross human rights violations attributed to the victor raises the question of what impact this lack of impartiality has on the country's transitional justice processes. Is 'victor's justice' of no value? Or can transitional justice that is not even-handed still serve a useful purpose?

Some argue that the credibility and ultimate effectiveness of any transitional justice mechanism is determined by its perceived legitimacy and impartiality (Borocan 2004). However, although impartiality in the dispensing of justice may be the ideal, it remains the exception rather than the norm in most post-conflict situations. Most armed conflicts come to an end through the outright military victory of one of the parties. Victors rarely ever concede to demands to hold their members, and especially their leaders, accountable for human rights violations that they may have committed during and after conflict. Rwanda is neither the first, nor likely the last, situation where there will be resort to uneven-handed justice after violent conflict involving gross human rights abuses. In practice, the responses of most societies emerging from violent conflict involving gross human rights abuses are often limited to either collective amnesia or 'victor's justice'. In so far as the term 'victor's justice' suggests that the extent of a group's political power determines whether one is the dispenser of justice or subject to it, the complaint still holds true in most cases.

The Charter and proceedings of the Nuremberg trials offer lessons as to how 'victor's justice' can, in spite of its obvious shortcomings, still have a positive impact on setting norms and establishing important values. The Nuremberg trials have been criticized for a number of shortcomings, including application of *ex post facto* laws (prosecuting and punishing defendants for crimes expressly defined for the first time in an instrument adopted at the conclusion of the war), functioning on the basis of limited procedural rules that did not adequately protect the rights of the accused, lack of opportunity for defendants to submit their cases for consideration by an appellate court and, most significantly, being trials conducted by a victor's tribunal before which only the vanquished were called to account for violations of international humanitarian law (Scharf 1995). In spite of the above shortcomings, the Nuremberg Charter and proceedings are widely recognized to be among the most significant developments in international law and international human rights law in particular during the twentieth century.

The Nuremberg experiment did not live up to the promise of a new era in which atrocity would be unfailingly punished in all circumstances. However, Nuremberg laid the foundations of the regime for accountability for atrocity that the international community has since built upon to create a framework for dealing with situations of grave human rights abuses. Nuremberg established several principles of international human rights law that became critical building blocks of the architecture of the regime for accountability for gross human rights abuses that the international community continues to develop (ILC 1957: para. 97; Kritz 1996b: p. 22; Ratner *et al.* 2009). Nuremberg firmly established the principle that 'No state or power may commit crimes against its citizens and go unpunished' (Bosch 1970). The proceedings of the Nuremberg trials inspired the adoption of the Universal Declaration of Human Rights as well as the 1948 Convention on the Prevention and Punishment of the Crime of Genocide (Shattuck 2006). Contemporary mechanisms of accountability for atrocity owe their existence in large measure to Nuremberg (Shattuck 2006).

Processes of accountability for atrocity that are not entirely even-handed may still be worth pursuing, for a number of reasons. Justice for atrocities committed by the defeated parties in conflicts is often both a legal imperative as well as a political necessity. States have a legal duty to provide remedies, including prosecutions, punishment of offenders and reparations, to victims of such crimes.[8] The crimes for which the defeated parties are responsible may be so horrendous that they cry out for a response. There usually is very strong public demand for justice in the aftermath of atrocity or other gross human rights abuses. The successor regime must necessarily respond to this yearning for justice because of legal, moral and political reasons. The prosecution and punishment of perpetrators of atrocities who are defeated in armed conflicts are both legitimate and desirable. The necessity for justice for the atrocities that the vanquished may have committed does not become any less compelling just because the victors may themselves be responsible for crimes of lesser (or equal) gravity.

Accountability processes that do not deal with the human rights violations committed by all the parties to a conflict in an even-handed manner may still serve a useful purpose by documenting, for posterity, a historical record of the atrocities for which members of the losing side were responsible. Establishing the truth about the nature, extent and responsibility for the worst atrocities committed is necessary in order to deny persons who bear responsibility for such atrocity the opportunity to revise and distort history in the future. Establishing an incontestable record of the human rights violations attributable to the vanquished is still important, notwithstanding that the conduct of the victors remains unaccounted for. Few would seriously argue that the processes that have served to shed light on the Holocaust or the genocide of the Tutsi have been worthless, just because they were not even-handed.

Justice for human rights violations, however limited in scope, also serves to dissipate victims' thirst for revenge. Failure to bring perpetrators of atrocity who lose a war to justice may encourage individual acts of vengeance by the victors as an alternative response. Victims, perpetrators and successor regimes are all better served by retributive justice, however uneven-handed, than by the alternative of unbridled revenge. Societies (including non-democratic ones like Rwanda) which have experienced gross human rights abuses promote more peaceful coexistence better by treating the vanquished in accordance with established laws and due process than by giving free reign to desire for unbridled revenge.

Accountability processes that are not even-handed may also still have an important role in standard setting and in reaffirming the fundamental values of international human rights law. Though incomplete or inadequate, accountability processes such as those pursued by Rwanda may nonetheless have an important normative value, as the legacy of Nuremberg and the experience of both the United Nations ad hoc tribunals clearly shows.

Finally, accountability processes may also serve a role in deterring human rights abuses, even where they lack impartiality or are otherwise incomplete. The current international regime for investigating, trying and punishing atrocity is still in its infancy, having begun to take shape only in the closing decades of the twentieth century. There is yet no evidence to prove conclusively the theory that accountability deters impunity for human rights violations in practice. It is possible, however, that the processes of investigation, prosecution and punishment of atrocity that Rwanda has undertaken, for the first time in its history, may have pedagogical value, serving to educate citizens on the illegality and severe potential consequences of participation in committing atrocity. These lessons may well have some impact in discouraging large-scale social participation in atrocity in the future. At an international level, the mechanisms of accountability for atrocity that the international community has established and continues to expand may (over a longer period of time) prove useful in deterring gross human rights abuses. It would be preferable to err on the side of seeking to prevent or reduce the commission of atrocities than to do nothing.

The Rwanda genocide was only the third unambiguous case of genocide during the twentieth century. The genocide decimated the Tutsi community, led to massive destruction that had a devastating impact on Rwandan society as a whole, and set in motion events that eventually resulted in a regional conflict which has claimed millions of innocent lives in the Great Lakes region of Central Africa. The genocide caused outrage among survivors and was condemned, in the strongest terms, by the international community when it was over. Accountability for the genocide was an absolute necessity for both Rwandan society and humanity at large.

The mechanisms of accountability for genocide that Rwanda has undertaken have admittedly not been even-handed. However, these mechanisms have still played a useful role in the process of Rwanda's reconstruction and have responded to the strong domestic as well as international demand for accountability. The genocide trials that Rwanda has undertaken have compelled Rwandan society to confront the genocide, to determine issues of responsibility for it and to start dealing with its consequences. These processes have brought to justice a very large number of the persons who bear the greatest responsibility for the violence experienced during the 1990s. The promise of justice was instrumental in helping to avert a very real danger of large-scale revenge attacks or a resumption of fully-fledged conflict between the country's two major communities in the aftermath of the genocide. The accountability processes implemented by Rwanda have contributed to the process of stabilizing the country. Although this stability may not be long term or sustainable, it has enabled the post-genocide government to devote the necessary attention and resources to responding to the humanitarian, reconstruction and development challenges that the country faced in the aftermath of the genocide. Rwanda's progress in socio-economic reconstruction and development since the genocide is widely praised (McDoom 2011; Ndaruhutse 2011; World Bank 2011; Zorbas 2011: p. 105). The progress in socio-economic development achieved by Rwanda would not have been possible without the stability that has come with its accountability processes, despite their limited scope and taint of partiality. These processes have helped to promote peaceful coexistence, if not reconciliation. They have served to individualize guilt. By helping to dispel the misconceptions (widespread among survivors and the Tutsi community at large) about the collective guilt of the Hutu community for the genocide, accountability for the genocide has made it possible to begin the tenuous process of rebuilding trust between members of communities that have been deeply divided by the experience of genocide (Daly 2002a: p. 375).

8.6 Conclusion

The violent conflict that Rwanda experienced during the 1990s occasioned immense suffering to all communities in all parts of the country. Despite strong evidence to the contrary, the Rwanda government contests claims that the members of the Hutu community suffered widespread and systematic human rights violations at the hands of the military wing of the party that won the conflict's armed aspect. Rwanda has undertaken an unprecedented exercise to investigate, prosecute and punish crimes that were committed in the course of the war and genocide, using domestic mechanisms as well as international criminal justice. Both these domestic and international processes have focused exclusively on the suffering of the Tutsi community, and have failed to address the violence that was directed at the Hutu community by elements of the victors. The lack of even-handedness in these accountability processes raises the question of whether they have still served a useful purpose. In spite of their lack of even-handedness, the accountability processes have indeed served some useful purpose but what remains uncertain is the extent to which the full range of objectives that Rwanda's transitional justice processes were intended to promote have been achieved, if at all. The overall impact of these transitional justice processes is the subject of the next chapter.

9 Assessing the Impact and Legacy of Rwanda's Mechanisms of Accountability for Atrocity

9.1 Introduction

The 1994 genocide was a catastrophic experience for Rwandan society, and its consequences were far reaching and enduring. The genocide has implications for virtually every aspect of Rwanda's recovery, reconstruction and development. The post-genocide government has made accountability for atrocity one of the pillars in the country's recovery, reconstruction and development efforts and peace-building initiatives. Post-genocide Rwanda has undertaken vigorous attempts to secure accountability through criminal prosecutions, using both national and international mechanisms. National mechanisms of accountability comprise the ordinary courts and Gacaca tribunals, and the United Nations' International Criminal Tribunal for Rwanda has rendered international criminal justice.

Rwanda's attempt to bring perpetrators of atrocity to justice is without precedent (Drumbl 2002a: p. 5; Strain and Keyes 2003: p. 122). No other society has ever attempted to investigate, try and punish crimes of mass atrocity, on the scale of what Rwanda has attempted to do. Yet, processes of accountability are not an end in themselves. Transitional justice processes aim to achieve certain objectives leading to positive social change. The question of the extent to which the processes of accountability that Rwanda has undertaken have achieved their intended purposes and objectives is very pertinent. Evaluation of the effectiveness of transitional justice mechanisms is a complex and often controversial exercise (Van der Merwe *et al.* 2009). However, there is a substantial body of empirical research and other evidence on Rwanda's legal responses to the genocide, on the basis of which it is possible to at least make a preliminary assessment of the country's transitional justice processes in achieving the intended objectives.

The ultimate test of the success of transitional justice processes is their lasting impact on the society that they are adopted to help, on whether they have contributed to consolidating the rule of law and respect for human rights, building social cohesion and enhancing prospects for long-term peace. As Gacaca and the ICTR wind up, the long-term impact of the transitional justice processes implemented by Rwanda is very topical. The people of Rwanda, scholars, policy makers and others interested in post-genocide Rwanda's reconstruction cannot but ask some crucial questions. To what extent have the accountability processes succeeded in achieving their intended objectives? Which of the intended objectives have been realized and which remain elusive? What factors have helped or constrained the realization of the intended goals and objectives? What are the implications of the country's success or failure to achieve the goals and objectives of Rwanda's transitional justice agenda? The answers to these questions may well be crucial for Rwanda's future.

Rwanda's transitional justice processes were intended to facilitate the attainment of a range of objectives which have been discussed in other parts of this book, especially Chapter 3. The country has expended a tremendous amount of resources (both domestic and foreign) and invested so much hope in processes to ensure accountability for the genocide. The government considers the accountability processes that it has undertaken to be a crucial component of its vision and programme for building a prosperous, peaceful and stable society. This chapter aims to explore the extent to which Rwanda's transitional justice processes have achieved the objectives that they were designed to promote. It includes a discussion of the ICTR's role and impact on Rwanda's reconstruction and political transition.

9.2 Assessing the Impact of Rwanda's Accountability Mechanisms

Opinions as to the effectiveness of Rwanda's mechanisms of accountability for atrocity vary widely, depending on one's perceptions of Rwanda's political transition since the genocide. The Rwanda government and supporters of its policies (domestic as well as foreign) assert that the country's accountability processes have been just and fair, that justice is making an effective contribution to national reconciliation and reconstruction, and that the country is now a peaceful, stable, democratizing state, partly as a result of the transitional justice processes that have been undertaken (Clark 2010; Ngoga 2009). Some scholars have lauded Gacaca, in particular, as a better alternative to punitive, procedural, Western-style justice for purposes of accountability for the genocide (for example, Longman 2006b; Meyerstein 2007; Venter 2007; Clark 2010). On the other hand, some critics of the policies of the government argue that Rwanda's accountability processes have been nothing more than victor's justice. They contest Rwanda's claim to being a democracy governed by the rule of law, and assert that it remains unstable and prone to violent conflict, its large-scale accountability processes notwithstanding (Waldorf 2006b: p. 3; Thomson 2011b). There are other observers whose views are somewhere in between, depending on the issues. Where does the truth lie? What impact have Rwanda's efforts to address the legacy of the genocide through criminal justice mechanisms (contemporary as well as traditional) had? Have Rwanda's attempts to ensure accountability for atrocity helped the country to achieve, wholly or even partially, the objectives that they were intended to achieve?

9.2.1 Accountability

States have a duty to provide a legal remedy for victims of gross human rights violations (Bassiouni 2002: p. 43; United Nations 2006: Principles 2(c) and 12). The right to a remedy has been characterized as one of the most fundamental and essential rights for the effective protection of all other human rights (United Nations 2001c: para 9). This obligation of states to provide a legal remedy for victims of violations of gross human rights violations is well grounded in international law (Vandegiste 2009: p. 431). The duty of a state to provide a domestic legal remedy for victims of violations of human rights is established in many international human rights treaties[1] and regional human rights instruments.[2] The right to a remedy has been refined by the jurisprudence of a large number of international and regional courts, as well as other treaty bodies and complaints mechanisms. It is further supported by various declarations considered as having the status of soft law.[3] A remedy is only considered adequate if it is prompt and effective, through providing meaningful access to justice.[4] International human rights bodies have considered that the right to an effective remedy encompasses the right to a prompt, thorough, independent, impartial and effective investigation.[5] The nature of the remedy varies depending on the right that is at stake. The provisions of relevant treaties and the jurisprudence of courts and human rights mechanisms indicate that in the case of gross human rights violations, states have an obligation to guarantee a remedy of a judicial nature (Droege 2006: p. 53). The African Charter on Human and Peoples' Rights, for example, provides that all remedies should be judicial.[6]

The core of Rwanda's transitional justice processes are the trials that have been conducted to hold perpetrators of the genocide accountable. Rwanda's attempts to bring perpetrators of mass atrocity to justice are unprecedented. No other society has ever attempted to investigate, try and punish perpetrators of atrocity in which such very large numbers of ordinary citizens have participated.

Gacaca courts have tried as many as 1,951,388 genocide suspects over the last decade (Musoni 2012; Ndori 2012). Upwards of 1,270,336 were tried in the third category, which was composed of people who either looted or destroyed property. The rest were convicted of more serious crimes including war crimes and crimes against humanity. A total of 1,678,672 genocide suspects were found guilty, while 272,716 were acquitted. Approximately 75,000 of the suspects who were convicted by Gacaca courts are fugitives (Musoni 2012). Rwanda's formal court system has tried between 10,000 and 11,000 genocide suspects (Ingelaere 2008: p. 45; Drumbl 2009: p. 41). The ICTR has undertaken trials of a large number of senior political, military and civil society leaders who are suspected of bearing responsibility for the genocide. As at 11 May 2012, the ICTR had completed the work at the trial level with respect to 83 of the 93 accused that it has indicted. This included 52 first-instance judgments involving 72 accused, 9 of whom had pleaded guilty. Appellate proceedings had been concluded in respect of 43 persons. Nine of the suspects who have been indicted remain fugitives. No other society has ever undertaken trials for human rights violations on the scale of what Rwanda has attempted to do.

The accountability processes undertaken by Rwanda have not been without serious shortcomings. Gacaca, in particular, has had problems that even its supporters, such as Clark (2010), acknowledge. Gacaca has not addressed the crimes that were committed by some members of the RPA against innocent non-combatants. Many members of the Hutu community view Gacaca as one-sided justice, which does not provide justice for crimes committed by the RPF (FDU-Inkingi 2012; Ingabire 2012; Mahoro 2012). Many Hutu have been unwilling to disclose the truth about the events of the genocide in their communities. Most of the participants in Gacaca, including those who claimed that they had confessed their crimes, lacked remorse and tended to explain their crimes in terms of elite coercion or being caught in the general mayhem of 1994, instead of accepting personal responsibility. Gacaca has involved extensive abuses of fair trial rights that may have led to miscarriage of justice in many cases. Genocide survivors resent Gacaca, perpetrators and the government, as they do not consider that the penalties that Gacaca provides for perpetrators who join the confession programme to be commensurate with crimes of the gravity of genocide and other crimes that were committed in the context of the genocide (Clark 2010: pp. 252–3). None of the mechanisms of accountability with which Rwanda has tried to reckon with the legacy of the genocide have met all the expectations of all the various stakeholders.

The accountability processes undertaken by Rwanda have largely succeeded in facilitating accountability and providing justice for the victims of the genocide. Gacaca in particular has made it possible for more victims of genocide to have access to justice than would have been possible through the domestic formal justice system or international criminal justice. However imperfect, Rwanda's accountability processes can be credited with the historic achievement of having translated human rights norms into enforceable remedies for victims of the genocide. The mechanisms have demonstrated that perpetrators of atrocity can be held accountable for their crimes.

Like Clark, I disagree with the opinion advanced by scholars such as Waldorf and Thomson that the Rwanda government has used Gacaca to impose collective guilt on the Hutu community (Straus and Waldorf 2011b: p. 12; Thomson 2011b: pp. 377–8; Waldorf 2011b: p. 50). On the contrary, Gacaca has tried to individualize guilt in the face of concerted popular resistance to efforts to establish the truth about how the genocide was organized and carried out and to ascertain responsibility for the crimes that were committed during the genocide. I am of the view that in the light of the relatively light sentences that Gacaca offers for perpetrators who join the confession programme, it has if anything erred on the side of leniency towards perpetrators. The downside of the accountability processes that Rwanda has undertaken is that they have not been even handed. These processes have failed to provide justice for victims of the human rights violations that were committed by the victors.

9.2.2 Contributing to the restoration of law and order and the maintenance of public security

Rwanda's post-genocide government inherited a state in which public order had broken down completely. State institutions had become criminalized. Lawlessness was the order of the day. Public confidence in the state's capacity to provide security to citizens was very low. The new government resorted to draconian measures to restore law and order, arresting and detaining tens of thousands of genocide suspects without due process (Borocan 2004: p. 374). These measures helped to restore public order. There were admittedly revenge and reprisal attacks after the genocide, but the large-scale attacks against the Hutu community that many, in Rwanda and abroad, had feared, were avoided. The government has been largely effective in maintaining public order ever since the genocide. Rwanda has little serious crime and is reputed to be the safest country in its region (Burnet 2007). Sectarian violence (in the form of attacks against genocide survivors) occasionally takes place, but is not widespread (Mutara 2009).

Some may question whether, given the violations of fair trial rights that domestic accountability processes have occasioned, it can be claimed that there has been a positive aspect to the process of arresting, detaining and trying genocide suspects. Arrests of genocide suspects were inevitable, perhaps even necessary, in the aftermath of the genocide. The scale and brutality of the genocide was such that the government simply could not have avoided taking suspects into custody. The country had just experienced a genocide that had claimed up to a tenth of the population. The institutions of the justice system had stopped functioning. It would have been untenable for the government to refrain from taking action against persons accused of being responsible for the atrocities until the justice system was re-established and effective. Indeed, the formal justice system would not be effective in dealing with the genocide caseload even today. It is possible that had the government not sanctioned the arrests of genocide suspects, many of the suspects might have been targeted for revenge. The large-scale arrests and detentions may have helped the country to avoid widespread revenge and reprisal killings, enhanced the security of genocide survivors and may also have defused the serious risk of a resumption of sectarian violence.

Rwanda is today by and large safe and effectively governed, relative to many other African states (Jordaan 2006: p. 333; Takeuchi 2011). It can be argued that by convincing victims of genocide not to take the law into their own hands, but to trust the state to deal with their grievances through legal channels, domestic accountability processes are at least partly responsible for the Rwanda government's success in restoring and maintaining public order. However deeply flawed the mechanisms of accountability for genocide have been in terms of guaranteeing respect of fair trial rights, they have still had some positive influence. They helped to defuse the temptation for victims to seek revenge and to take the law into their own hands, they have contributed to restoring a degree of citizens' confidence in the capacity of state institutions to maintain law and order and they have contributed to the enhancement of public security.

9.2.3 Expediting trials of the genocide caseload

Rwanda initially attempted to reckon with the legacy of the genocide with prosecutions through the ordinary courts. In 1999, the Rwanda government decided to shift primary responsibility for adjudication of the genocide caseload to Gacaca courts, in the hope that a Gacaca system would be able to process the genocide caseload more expeditiously than the formal justice system had so far been able to do. The Gacaca system has had some serious shortcomings.[7] It should be beyond dispute, however, that Gacaca has been phenomenally successful in expediting the investigation and trial of genocide-related cases (Ingelaere 2008; Clark 2010). The process of establishing Gacaca courts and preparing them to conduct trials took a long time. However, once the system started operating nationally, it was able to dispose of pending genocide litigation very swiftly. The investigation phase of Gacaca was carried out over the second half of 2005. The trial phase, which commenced in 2006, was carried out and virtually completed over a period of less than two years. Gacaca closed operations in June 2012 (Musoni 2012; Ndori 2012). Gacaca courts have been successful in achieving the government's objective of expediting the processing of genocide cases. Resolution of the huge backlog of pending cases has effectively addressed certain social and political problems that the existence of the backlog had created, helping to bring forward a time when the government and citizens of Rwanda can put the challenges of organizing and conducting genocide trials behind them and devote more attention to issues of development.

9.2.4 Reducing the prison population

The problem of the huge backlog of pending genocide cases went hand in hand with a related problem of a very burdensome prison population. Prior to the adoption of Gacaca as the principal mechanism of accountability for genocide, the government was not only concerned about the evident incapacity of the formal justice system to process the genocide caseload in a timely manner, it was equally strongly concerned about the very large size of the prison population. Prisons were overcrowded, and the detentions of most of the suspects in custody were considered to be arbitrary (Amnesty International 1995a, 1996a, 2000, 2002b) and inhumane by international human rights organizations (Amnesty International 1995a, 1996a, 2000, 2002b).

The conditions of detention facilities attracted harsh criticism, domestically and externally. The detention of very large numbers of members of the Hutu community in these harsh conditions adversely affected public perceptions and attitudes towards the government across the country. The maintenance of a large prison population put the government in the vulnerable position of having to depend on the international community for the food, sanitation and medical care requirements of the prisoners. The government needed to reduce the prison population to levels that it could afford to finance on its own. It also needed to reduce spending on prisons, and to use the savings to fund development activities in the justice sector or other development priorities. Lastly, the government needed to address the social, economic and political problems to which the incarceration of a large number of male members of the Hutu community had given rise.

The government has over the years adopted various strategies to reduce the prison population. These strategies have included enhancing compliance with the provisions of the Criminal Procedure Code on matters relating to arrest and detention; releasing elderly, sickly and juvenile detainees from custody; establishing a Guilty Plea and Confession Programme that enabled genocide suspects to benefit from a more lenient sentencing regime and to move out of the prison system quickly; adopting a policy to allow suspects to stay out of prison before and during trial; and introducing community service as an alternative to serving time in prison. These measures resulted in the release of more than 60,000 suspects between 2003 and 2007 alone.[8] Gacaca has been particularly instrumental in resolving the problem of the huge prison population that Rwanda was grappling with when it was first introduced (Clark 2010). The success of Gacaca in reducing the number of genocide suspects or perpetrators in detention should be of help to the government as it seeks to address the social, economic and political problems that the detention of a very large number of members of the Hutu community had previously given rise to.

9.2.5 Truth telling

The role of truth telling in transitional justice has already been discussed in Chapter 1. Victims of serious human rights violations have a right to the truth.[9] This right has its origins in international humanitarian law, where it was developed to address issues relating to missing persons. As international law has evolved to apply in all situations of serious human rights violations, the scope of the right to the truth has expanded. In the field of human rights, the right to the truth first evolved in relation to cases of enforced disappearances and it has gradually been extended to other serious human rights violations, including extra-judicial killings and torture. The Human Rights Committee has made it clear that the right to the truth applies to human rights violations in general (United Nations 1996b).[10]

The legal right of victims of human rights violations to the truth has been recognized by both international and regional human rights instruments.

The United Nations' Updated Principles for the Protection and Promotion of Human Rights through Action to Combat Impunity establish as fundamental rights the 'inalienable right to the truth', 'the duty to remember', the 'victim's right to know' and 'guarantees to give effect to the right to know' (Principles 2–5). A society's history is part of its heritage, and this includes the history of its oppression. Preserving this history is thus important, in particular to guard 'against the development of revisionist and negationist arguments' (Principle 3). The Inter-American Commission on Human Rights has stated that 'Every society has the inalienable right to know the truth about past events, as well as the motives and circumstances in which aberrant crimes came to be committed, in order to prevent repetition of such acts in the future' (Inter-American Commission on Human Rights 1986).

The right to the truth implies knowing the entire truth as to events that occurred, their specific circumstances and who participated in them. Its scope now includes the entitlement to seek and obtain information on the causes leading to the person's victimization; the causes and conditions pertaining to serious violations of international human rights and humanitarian law; the progress and results of investigations of the violations; the circumstances and reasons for the perpetration of crimes under international law and gross human rights violations; the circumstances in which the violation took place; in the event of death, missing or enforced disappearance of victims, the fate and whereabouts of the victims or their remains; and the identities of the perpetrators (UNOHCHR 2006b). This knowledge must be disclosed and made public. In the interpretation of the Inter-American Commission of Human Rights, the right to the truth means a judicial search for the truth and investigation, and to judicial sanctions of the perpetrators. A non-judicial body such as a truth commission cannot substitute this right.[11] The inalienable character of the right to the truth means it that it should not be subject to any limitations. Furthermore, its close relationship to other non-derogable rights, such as the right not to be tortured, means that the right to the truth should also be considered non-derogable (UNOHCHR 2006b: para. 60).

The right to the truth is both an individual right enjoyed by victims in their personal capacity, as well as a collective right. While each individual victim has the right to know the truth about violations affecting him or her, the truth also has to be told at the level of a society to safeguard against the recurrence of such violations (Principle 2 of the Updated Set of Principles).[12] The Inter-American Court of Human Rights has held that truth plays both a preventive and reparatory role for family members of victims and for society at large.[13] The state has responsibility for giving effect to the right to the truth. The Updated Principles emphasize that states must take appropriate measures to give effect to the right to know the truth.

Establishment of the truth was always one of the objectives of Rwanda's accountability processes.[14] The government of Rwanda and supporters of Gacaca claim that Gacaca has been effective in establishing the truth about the violence of the past. The most prominent of scholars who credit Gacaca with success in achieving its objectives, including establishing the truth, is Phil Clark (2006, 2007, 2009a, 2009b, 2009c, 2010).

I share Clark's rejection of the claim by some scholars, such as Waldorf (2006b, 2011b) and Ingelaere (2009a), that Gacaca is designed to be a top-down process by which the state imposes legal and historical truths on the population, that the state has used Gacaca to impose collective guilt and that it encourages punitiveness against the Hutu community. That the Rwanda genocide happened is a historical fact. The ordinary criminal justice system did not have capacity to try all genocide cases. Gacaca is an imperfect process, but it still is a useful mechanism (a definitely more effective process than other processes that Rwanda has tried to use) for establishing a historical record of what happened during the genocide and for holding perpetrators of genocide accountable. I also agree with Clark's view that 'Gacaca provides a vital dialogical space in which Rwandans tell and hear narratives about the events and effects of the genocide ... [and] has provided a forum for collective discussions that have not occurred elsewhere in Rwandan society' (Clark 2010: p. 218).

Rwanda's transitional justice processes have made a significant contribution towards the establishment of the truth about the genocide. Trials by both the ordinary courts and Gacaca tribunals have helped to establish a degree of truth about the genocide. Gacaca has, by compelling each community to recall and recount its experiences during the genocide, vastly enhanced opportunities to establish the truth about the genocide at a micro level (Mibenge 2004: p. 422; Sosnov 2008: pp. 136–40). The ICTR has also helped to establish a historical record of the genocide and has even taken judicial notice of the genocide.[15]

However, I do not share Clark's unqualified conclusion that Gacaca has been successful in establishing the truth about the violence that Rwanda experienced during the 1990s. There have been very significant obstacles to the establishment of the truth about the genocide and other violence experienced before, during and after 1994. Ethnicity has had a strong influence on shaping citizens' attitudes about the genocide and accountability for it (Tiemessen 2004: pp. 70–1). Very few of the people responsible for the genocide acknowledge their wrongdoing, let alone express remorse for their actions (Drumbl 1998: p. 26). Much of Rwandan society remains in a state of denial about the genocide. Although the atrocities were often committed in broad daylight and in full public view (Hatzfeld 2003), most citizens deny personal knowledge of (let alone involvement in) the atrocities that took place in their communities (Penal Reform International 2003b, 2003c; Longman 2004b: p. 170). Many in the Hutu community are reluctant to disclose the truth about the genocide and to name those responsible for the atrocities that took place in their communities (Penal Reform International 2003b, 2003c; Fierens 2005). There has been a profound reluctance in many communities to participate in Gacaca (Penal Reform International 2002a: pp. 16, 41, 2003c: p. 64; Borocan 2004: p. 392; Rettig 2008: p. 26). Many in the Hutu community often opted not to attend or participate actively in Gacaca proceedings in order to avoid having to discuss the events that took place during the genocide. Some researchers have reported that there are indications of a widespread conspiracy of silence about the genocide in many communities (Rettig 2008: pp. 35–42; Burnet 2009: p. 179; Purdekova 2011: p. 494).

The government has only been able to get the population to participate in Gacaca through coercion (Penal Reform International 2002b: pp. 8–9, 2003c: p. 65; Waldorf 2006b: p. 23; Rettig 2008: p. 32; Thomson 2011b). Even when they have participated in Gacaca meetings, most citizens have chosen not to contribute to the discussions (Sosnov 2008). Participants who have relatives and friends on trial have generally been more interested in defending accused relatives than revealing or seeking the truth (Waldorf 2006b: p. 25; Ingelaere 2008: p. 12). Some in the Hutu community even deny that the genocide ever occurred at all and classify the violence of 1994 as merely a civil war in which human rights violations were committed by both sides (Drumbl 1998; Sosnov 2008). Lack of meaningful voluntary participation in Gacaca on the part of the majority of the population has hindered efforts to establish the truth (Le Mon 2007: p. 18).

The only segment of Rwandan society that has been forthcoming in disclosing the truth is genocide suspects who have joined the Guilty Plea and Confession Programme (Penal Reform International 2002b: p. 25). However, even these perpetrators often fail to make complete and unqualified confessions of serious crimes. The general consensus is that even the 'confessions' of genocide suspects who have joined the Guilty Plea and Confession Programme are not complete; participants only admit to relatively minor crimes and withhold evidence relating to more serious offences (Penal Reform International 2002b: p. 25). Many among them remain unwilling to accept personal responsibility for their crimes, or to express remorse (Wolters 2005b: pp. 9–12; Ingalaere 2008). Even Clark acknowledges that 'there is little doubt many detainees confess to crimes significantly less severe than those they actually committed during the genocide' (Clark 2010: p. 101) and that only a very small proportion of confessed perpetrators expressed genuine remorse for their crimes, with most claiming that they were either merely present when the crimes were committed or they were coerced by political elites to commit these crimes (Clark 2010: p. 225).

Not only have many Hutu refused to tell the truth about the genocide in their communities (Clark 2010: pp. 209–12), they have often lied about the events for a number of reasons. I do not share the opinion that has been expressed by some scholars and adopted by Clark (2010) that the reluctance of individuals and communities to tell the truth about what happened during the genocide is necessarily linked to the Rwandan cultural preference for silence and secrecy. There are other factors that account for this 'silence', including the need to protect and defend relatives and friends implicated in the genocide, reaction against Gacaca's discriminatory character (as demonstrated by its failure to address the suffering of Hutu community members), and individual and collective non-violent resistance against the programmes (especially Gacaca) of a regime that many do not consider legitimate.

The majority of those who have been accused of genocide do not display any remorse; they proclaim their innocence of the crimes they have been accused of and see themselves as prisoners of war who have simply ended up on the losing side (Drumbl 1998; Sosnov 2008).

Gacaca has not lived up to expectations of becoming a forum where victims and perpetrators could discuss the events about the genocide in an environment of mutual respect, empathy and honesty. The same dynamics that hinder acknowledgement of the truth in criminal proceedings in the formal criminal courts have been at play in Gacaca. In many communities, Gacaca became a contest between survivors on one hand and the accused and their families on the other. The task of laying charges and searching for the truth is left to genocide survivors, as the rest of the people in their communities either keep silent or defend their accused kith and kin (Oomen 2005: p. 905; Meyerstein 2007: p. 489). Yet, survivors know the least about what happened during the events because they were either in hiding or on the run at the time (Molenaar 2005: p. 37; Longman 2006a). In some communities, genocide survivors and others have organized themselves to fabricate testimony and evidence against certain people (Burnet 2009: p. 179). The role of survivors and other witnesses in shouldering the burden of pushing efforts to establish the truth has often exposed them to hostility, marginalization and, occasionally, violence (Ingelaere 2008; Le Mon 2007: p. 17). Attempts have also been made to silence – through corruption (Le Mon 2007: pp. 16–20), coercion (Sosnov 2008), killings and other attacks (Mibenge 2004: p. 418; Wolters 2005b: p. 16) – people willing to discuss honestly what happened.

Rwanda's accountability processes have been far from successful as truth-telling mechanisms. The truth that has been established is not the complete truth, nor is it comprehensive (Sosnov 2008: pp. 136–40). These processes have not helped to establish a historical narrative that all Rwandans agree with or relate to (Richters *et al.* 2005: p. 211; Haile 2008: p. 50). The accountability mechanisms have focused exclusively on the genocide and the massacres that were committed against Hutu moderates (Waldorf 2006b). Gacaca has not addressed the grave human rights violations that were committed against members of the Hutu community at all (Clark 2010: pp. 210–11; FDU-Inkingi 2012). The trials have produced a limited sense of individual responsibility or blameworthiness in only a small minority of genocide perpetrators (Drumbl 1998, 2002b: p. 16). The Hutu community has by and large been reluctant to acknowledge the full truth about the genocide and these massacres (Sarkin 1999b: p. 799; Oomen 2005: p. 904). The government has limited opportunity to discuss violence that is alleged to have been committed by the RPA. None of the accountability mechanisms undertaken by Rwanda addressed the violence that was committed against the Hutu community in Rwanda during and after the genocide and against

Hutu refugees in the Democratic Republic of Congo.[16] The decision to exclude completely allegations of human rights violations by the members of the RPA from the scope of the accountability processes means that only a partial accounting can be achieved (Longman 2006a: p. 39; FDU-Inkingi 2012).

As the IDEA study, *Traditional Justice and Reconciliation After Violent Conflict*, has noted:

> One overarching and omnipresent opinion accompanies the Gacaca process: the truth is absent. This has serious consequences for the system in its essence and hampers its ultimate objectives. The surfacing of the truth functions as the cornerstone of the entire transitional justice architecture in post-genocide Rwanda, as we have argued. The reasons why there is no truth are multiple and complex (Ingelaere 2007). The 'truth' is, in the first place, curtailed by the *a priori* defining parameters of what the 'truth' can be, methodologically and ideologically, but also by the features of Rwandan culture. The 'truth' is mostly 'forensic' because it is derived from a criminal procedure. It varies according to locality since it surfaces through the dynamic of local constellations idiosyncratically subverting and interpreting the truth-generating procedures. The 'truth', furthermore, has a high degree of instrumentality as it is sought through confrontation along group based (mostly ethnic) lines, not deliberation or dialogue. It has a certain degree of arbitrariness resulting from the principle of 'confession and denunciation without verification.' As a result the 'truth' is 'partial' in the sense of 'incomplete' and 'deformed', but also 'one-sided' and 'one-dimensional,' lacking a broadly based contextual anchoring. (Ingelaere 2008: p. 56)

The same observations apply to the other accountability processes that Rwanda has undertaken. These mechanisms have not provided a narrative of the Rwanda conflict (and of the genocide in particular) that all victims are ready to accept as fairly reflecting their experiences and addressing their grievances.

9.2.6 Reparation

Reparation is a core objective of all transitional justice processes. Its role in transitional justice in general has similarly been discussed as part of the theoretical framework of transitional justice in Chapter 1.

The human rights violations that were committed during the war and genocide that Rwanda experienced during the 1990s caused the death of at least hundreds of thousands of people and occasioned suffering to millions more. As a result of those massive violations of human rights law and international humanitarian law, including genocide, millions of survivors are entitled to reparation for the suffering that they were subject to and for the loss of family members who perished. Providing reparation for victims of the violence that the country experienced during the 1990s has been a very challenging exercise for Rwanda.

The government has adopted some policies and undertaken some programmes to address victims' demands for reparation. The most significant of these policies and activities are the trials of genocide-related cases that the country has undertaken. Rwanda observes an annual, week-long commemoration of the genocide in April each year. During this period of annual mourning and remembrance, victims and survivors of the genocide are publicly honoured across the country and in government-sponsored events abroad. The government has also established and maintains hundreds of memorial sites throughout Rwanda.[17] The government has established a fund, the Fonds National pour l'Assistance aux Rescapés du Génocide (known as FARG) to help needy genocide survivors, to which it contributes 6% of its annual budget.[18] Other funding for FARG comes from a tax on every public servant's earnings, individual donations, grants from foreign countries and damages payable by persons convicted of participating in genocide.[19] FARG supports survivors of the genocide by providing funding for education, housing and medical treatment.

The above efforts to provide some form of reparation for the human rights violations that were committed during the war and genocide have not, however, been satisfactory to the victims. Most significantly, the government's reparation initiatives do not address the demands, grievances and legitimate rights of members of the Hutu community who were victims of human rights violations attributed to the military of the current government (Thomson 2011b). Without official acknowledgement of these crimes, it has not been possible to establish the truth about them. The victims have not received justice and reparation has not been possible (Waldorf 2009). Neither do victims of the human rights violations attributed to the RPA receive support from FARG.[20] The government says that it has other programmes, run by local government authorities, which provide comparable assistance to needy citizens who are not genocide survivors. Nevertheless, victims of the crimes attributed to the RPA, and the Hutu community in general, are bitter about FARG's discrimination against victims of war crimes and crimes against humanity alleged to have been committed by the RPA. Victims of these crimes also harbour deep grievances over the fact that they are denied the right to remember and honour relatives and members of their community who died as a result of the crimes in question (Thomson 2011b: pp. 379–80). Some scholars of the Rwanda genocide argue that the Rwandan government's genocide commemorations and national mourning practices generate a polarizing discourse that defines all Tutsi as genocide victims and all Hutu as genocide perpetrators (Burnet 2009: p. 184).

Even Tutsi victims of the genocide are discontented with the government's record on reparation. The genocide survivors' discontent revolves around their inability to date to receive compensation. Prior to the introduction of Gacaca courts, survivors, like victims of other crimes prosecuted under Rwandan law, could join criminal proceedings as civil parties and claim compensation for moral and pecuniary damages and for restitution. In Rwanda's civil law system, victims of crime did not have to wait for the conclusion of criminal trials to be able to file civil proceedings claiming damages. Genocide survivors lodged claims for compensation against both alleged perpetrators and the state in trials before specialized chambers starting in 1996. The adjudication of genocide cases by specialized chambers was very slow: only a few thousand trials were completed between 1996 and the introduction of Gacaca in the early 2000s. Between 2000 and 2006, Rwanda's justice system was preoccupied with rolling out Gacaca, and few genocide cases were tried by the ordinary courts. In over the 10,000 cases (REDRESS/African Rights 2011) that were concluded by the ordinary courts before and after the adoption of Gacaca, damages were routinely awarded, often against both individual defendants as well as against the state. However, the judgments in these cases were not enforced (Vandegiste 2001b: p. 10) because the defendants were either fugitives or unwilling or unable to settle the claims against them and the government was yet to adopt a policy on compensation for genocide victims. The slow pace of genocide trials and the government's failure to develop a policy on compensation has always been frustrating for survivors of the genocide (REDRESS/African Rights 2011).

The country-wide implementation of Gacaca between 2005 and 2007 finally provided the majority of genocide victims with the opportunity to press their claims for compensation. The Organic Law 40/2000 that introduced Gacaca jurisdictions declared civil actions against the state inadmissible 'on account of it [the government] having acknowledged its role in the genocide and that in compensation it pays each year a percentage of its annual budget to the Compensation Fund. This percentage is set by the financial law.'[21] Under Organic Law 40/2000, survivors could still make civil claims for compensation before Gacaca,[22] but the compensation was limited to material losses and 'body damages'. Gacaca jurisdictions could not decide upon claims for moral damage.[23] Gacaca jurisdictions were to draw up a list of victims who had suffered material losses or bodily harm and make an inventory of those losses, as well as allocate damages. All judgments by ordinary and Gacaca courts awarding compensation for material 'and body damages' were to be forwarded to the Compensation Fund for Victims of the Genocide and Crimes against Humanity, with the Fund to 'fix the modalities for granting compensation'.[24] The establishment of the Compensation Fund would have enabled survivors to enforce their reparation awards against the Compensation Fund, rather than against the individual perpetrator. Since 2009, only FARG can undertake civil action against persons accused of crimes classifying them in the first category.[25]

Gacaca courts have tried 1,951,388 defendants, of whom 1,678,672 have been found guilty and 272,716 have been acquitted of crimes relating to the genocide. The almost one and three-quarters of a million defendants who have been convicted by Gacaca represent a very significant fraction of Rwandans who were adults in 1994 (Musoni 2012). While Gacaca has judged a huge number of cases in which damages have been awarded or are due, it has not enabled victims of genocide to actually receive compensation. The government has still not adopted any policy on compensation for the rights violations that were committed during the 1990s conflict. It has also failed to set up the Compensation Fund that legislation establishing the Gacaca courts anticipated. Consequently, victims have no avenue for seeking enforcement of awards that have been made by Gacaca courts. Some victims have attempted to enforce their claims against individual perpetrators, but such enforcement is difficult. Aside from the inability of perpetrators to pay awards, survivors have reportedly been threatened when seeking to enforce awards and local government officials who are supposed to facilitate enforcement are not helpful to victims, probably because of having been bribed (REDRESS/African Rights 2011: p. 5).

The government's failure to develop a policy on compensation for victims of the genocide was largely a result of financial constraints. Given the scale of the genocide, the country's economy could not generate the resources to meet the claims of all the victims to whom compensation was due. Moreover, the government has pressing social problems to address. The country depended disproportionately on humanitarian and development assistance to finance its social and development programmes and the devotion of a substantial part of the national budget to satisfy claims of genocide survivors for compensation would have had an adverse impact on the implementation of such programmes.

Gacaca's compensation awards have given rise to additional tensions and grievances between survivors and perpetrators and their families, and between the Hutu community and the government. In a country like Rwanda where most people are poor, defendants in genocide cases do not have the financial resources to settle the claims victims. The only assets that perpetrators have are their homes and pieces of land on which their families live and farm for survival. Gacaca's awards of compensation to victims of the genocide have become politicized. Hutu opponents of the government claim that the awards are a strategy by the Tutsi-dominated government to dispossess the entire Hutu community and to render the community destitute.[26]

9.2.7 Advancing national unity and reconciliation

One of the objectives of transitional justice processes is to promote reconciliation after divisions that arise in society as a result of human rights violations. The promotion of national unity and reconciliation has been a key objective of Rwanda's accountability processes and an overarching priority of the post-genocide government (Zorbas 2004: p. 37; Richters *et al.* 2005: p. 205; Melvin 2012: p. 2). Indeed, the policy of national unity and reconciliation has been the backbone of the Rwandan government's reconstruction strategy following the 1994 genocide (Thomson 2011a). Post-genocide Rwanda has adopted a wide range of policies and undertaken many initiatives (in the domain of justice as well as other areas) to promote national unity and reconciliation (National Unity and Reconciliation Commission 2001). The non-legal initiatives, that have been undertaken by the government with a view to promoting reconciliation, include the restoration and maintenance of public security; the abolition of identity cards classifying citizens by ethnicity and the prohibition of references to ethnicity in official documents; the repatriation and resettlement of more than two million refugees and about a million internally displaced persons (National Unity and Reconciliation Commission 2001); the re-integration of thousands of members of the former government army into the military; the enactment of legislation to punish the propagation of discrimination and sectarianism;[27] the introduction of public service recruitment and management policies based more on merit rather than patronage; the introduction of merit-based admission to educational institutions; the establishment of the National Unity and Reconciliation Commission,[28] the National Human Rights Commission[29] and the Demobilisation and Re-integration Commission; the undertaking of many anti-corruption programmes; and the adoption of a national poverty reduction programme (see also Richters *et al.* 2005: p. 206; Melvin 2012: pp. 3–4).

The government and supporters of its policies positively assert that the above-mentioned policies and activities have made reconciliation a reality (Gourevitch 2009; Thomson 2011a, 2011b). It is undeniable that the policies and programmes undertaken by the government have had some positive impact on Rwandan society. The peace-building policies and strategies that the post-genocide government has pursued, including its transitional justice programmes, have made a positive contribution towards reducing social tensions and establishing negative peace. (Negative peace is defined as the absence of violence and as structural violence, where the absence of violence is combined with closure of avenues for challenging the status quo and expressing grievances in a peaceful way (Department for International Development 2010: p. 9).) The stabilization of Rwanda and the creation of conditions that have made coexistence between the parties to the Rwanda conflict possible is a very significant achievement, given the violence (including genocide) that Rwandan society experienced during the 1990s.

Nevertheless, the impact of the peace-building policies and programmes on achieving positive reconciliation remains a much contested subject. Many scholars and commentators question the reality and depth of reconciliation in Rwanda and the impact of processes of accountability for atrocity, in particular, in facilitating the realization of national reconciliation (Zorbas 2004; Waldorf 2006b; Haile 2008). Even Clark, arguably the most prominent of the minority of scholars who praise Gacaca for its achievements, concedes that Rwanda's transitional justice processes, including Gacaca, have not been successful in achieving positive reconciliation (Clark 2010).

I do not share the views of scholars such as Waldorf who claim that the main factor that has made Rwanda's accountability processes, especially Gacaca, ineffective in fostering reconciliation is the state's politicization of Gacaca in order to collectivize the guilt of the Hutu population (Waldorf 2011b). Nevertheless, I share the view that the accountability processes that Rwanda has carried out have very strong shortcomings as instruments of promoting reconciliation. Several factors have constrained the capacity of Rwanda's transitional justice processes to advance national reconciliation. One of these factors is the reluctance of the majority of Rwandans to acknowledge the truth about how genocide was carried out in their respective communities. Another is the unwillingness of many of the perpetrators to express remorse for their crimes and the suffering that such crimes occasioned to victims (Drumbl 1998; Ingelaere 2008; Rettig 2008).

The potential of Rwanda's accountability processes to advance reconciliation has also been undermined by other policies and practices of the post-genocide government, including its top-down imposition of a narrative of the Rwanda conflict that does not reflect the experiences and grievances of members of the Hutu community; the unwillingness of the victors of Rwanda's armed conflict to engage in dialogue with the opposition on ways to address the root causes of the conflict; the ruling party's manipulation of the process of transition during the early 2000s to entrench itself in power instead of facilitating a transition to democracy; the monopolization of political power by elites from the Tutsi minority; and the current government's intolerance and persecution of political opposition.

Prospects for reconciliation in Rwanda have been particularly undermined by the RPF's manoeuvres to monopolize political power. The Rwanda conflict, including the genocide, was largely a result of a struggle for political power and access to resources (Haile 2008: p. 42). Conflict over these issues continues. The RPF used the transition period (1994–2003) to consolidate its hold on power. From 1995, the organization gradually marginalized and eventually excluded the other political parties from meaningful political participation. Many of the leaders of opposition parties who were part of the broad-based government that was set up after the genocide were removed from office, and some were subjected to persecution after leaving office and compelled to go into exile (Reyntjens 2004; Wolters 2005b: p. 15). While the RPF built a formidable grassroots organization across the country, other political parties were banned from recruiting members, holding meetings or carrying out any other activities whatsoever during the transition period (Reyntjens 2004; Wolters 2005b: p. 15). The only party that was considered as being realistically capable of offering significant opposition to the RPF was banned prior to the 2003 elections (Reyntjens 2004; Wolters 2005b: p. 15). The so-called transition to democracy failed to establish a more inclusive political order, and has instead consolidated authoritarian rule (Rafti 2008). Space for political participation narrowed instead of expanding as a result of the 2003 elections (ICCO *et al.* 2003; p. 26). The transition led to the consolidation of what many scholars of Rwanda consider to be, a one-party minority regime (Nifosi 2005; Rafti 2008), dominated by a small group of military officials from the minority Tutsi group (Burnet 2007: p. 2). It is widely acknowledged that the Hutu community is marginalized from a meaningful share of power and access to resources and they question the government's legitimacy (Drumbl 2002b: pp. 31–2; Vandegiste 2001a: pp. 266–7).

The majority of the Hutu political elite class that was ousted from power in 1994 remains in exile, unreconciled to the new political order, biding time and hoping for a regime change. Almost 20 years after the genocide, Hutu armed insurgents continue to wage war against the Rwandan state from their sanctuaries in the Congo. The externally based opposition calls for dialogue about the country's conflict, but the government says that the country's conflict has been resolved: Rwanda is now one reconciled and united nation and there is no need for negotiation of a political settlement. As some commentators have noted, the government of Rwanda has engaged in political rhetoric and various initiatives targeted at reconciliation; however, the reconciliation that the government envisions is politically constructed on Tutsi terms, which are insufficient for ensuring the long-term stability of Rwanda (Corey and Joireman 2000: p. 88). The politics of ethnicity remain intractable (Takeuchi 2011: p. 31).

The capacity of Rwanda's transitional justice processes to advance reconciliation has also been undermined by the legacy of widespread human rights abuses that were committed against members of the Hutu community during and after the genocide (including the atrocities that were committed against Rwandan refugees in the Congo and the arbitrary arrests and detentions, extending to many years in most cases, of tens of thousands of genocide suspects) and the failure of the accountability mechanisms that Rwanda has undertaken to address the human rights violations in question (Drumbl 2002a: p. 31, 2002b: p. 17). These human rights abuses have given rise to bitterness and resentment on the part of many in the Hutu community (Sarkin 1999b: p. 787, 2000: p. 113; Richters *et al.* 2005: p. 209; Le Mon 2007: pp. 18–19; Haile 2008: p. 16). The government's failure to investigate and punish RPA abuses is widely believed to be a strong hinderance to reconciliation (Le Mon 2007: pp. 18–19; du Toit 2011: p. 21). Some scholars and organizations working on peace and conflict issues in the Great Lakes region of Central Africa, such as the International Crisis Group, argue that the failure of Rwanda's transitional justice processes to address the human rights abuses that were committed against members of the Hutu community, especially the massacres of refugees in the Congo, has become one of the main justifications for latent and explicit denial of the genocide against the Tutsi (Eltringham 2004: p. 145). The greviances of members of the Hutu community over human rights violations attributed to the RPA and the political exclusion of the Hutu community from a meaningful share of power in post-genocide Rwanda's political system are perhaps the most significant hindrances to reconciliation in post-genocide Rwanda. From the perspective of genoicde victims, the capacity of Rwanda's accountability processes to advance reconciliation has been limited by the government's failure to formulate and implement a coherent policy on reparation (Wolters 2005b: pp. 16–17).

Not only have Rwanda's transitional justice processes failed to foster positive reconciliation, they may have contributed to exacerbating conflict in Rwandan society (Rettig 2008; Burnet 2009: p. 186; Mutisi 2009; Thomson 2011b). Many in the Hutu community argue that Rwanda's accountability processes (and Gacaca in particular) are a form of persecution of their community (Mahoro 2012; Call 2004: p. 105). The negative attitudes of many in the Hutu community against Rwanda's accountability processes (including Gacaca) have been shaped by a wide range of events, policies and practices of the Rwanda government including the mass arrests and detentions of genocide suspects during the early 1990s; the detention of the genocide suspects in inhumane and quite often life-threatening conditions; the failure of Rwanda's justice system to organize trials for genocide suspects who were held in pre-trial detention for periods which exceeded ten years for some suspects; the one-sided nature and discriminatory character of Rwanda's accountability processes (including the ICTR), demonstrated by their failure to address human rights violations that were committed against members of the Hutu community during and after the genocide; the failure of Rwanda's political and legal systems (including Gacaca) to publicly acknowledge the atrocities that were committed against members of the Hutu community (in Rwanda and the DRC, during and after the genocide), to investigate and punish the crimes in good faith and to allow survivors of these crimes to memorialize loved ones who perished in those atrocities; the use of coercion to compel citizen participation in Gacaca; perceptions (however mistaken) that awards of reparations to victims of genocide are a strategy to dispossess and impoverish the Hutu population; and continuing impunity for human rights abuses committed by agents of the state against citizens. The processes of justice for genocide have, instead of facilitating reconciliation, become a source of new and deep-rooted grievances in the Hutu population that add a new dimension to the Rwanda conflict.

Gacaca, in particular, has aggravated cleavages in Rwanda society. One of the major objectives of Gacaca was to promote social harmony and reconciliation.[30] From the very beginning, it was recognized that Gacaca was very vulnerable to political, social, psychological and even economic dynamics (Uvin 2003a: p. 121). Research indicates that it has indeed fuelled – or at least aggravated – conflict, resentment and ethnic disunity (Molenaar 2005: p. 98). Gacaca has undisputedly been divisive (Amnesty International 2002b). The government itself acknowledges the existence of these divisions as it continues to wage war against what it says is a worrying resurgence of genocide ideology (Human Rights Watch 2008: pp. 34, 41; Ngoga 2009). As a result of Gacaca, survivors have become more marginalized and face increased hostility and ridicule in their communities (Molenaar 2005: p. 98).

Mistrust between survivors and the rest of the population has given way to open hostility in some places. Attacks against survivors and other witnesses have become a major national problem (Commission Nationale des Droits de L'Homme, Rwanda 2003; Parliament, Rwanda 2004). Gacaca has led to increased tensions within the Hutu community, between perpetrators who have confessed to their crimes and families of accused persons who are implicated by such testimony (Algard 2005: p. 29). Gacaca may have led to a worsening rather than healing of divisions within Rwandan society (Sosnov 2008: p. 142–5; Burnet 2009: p. 187).

The impact of Rwanda's accountability processes in promoting reconciliation is at best mixed (Drumbl 2002b: p. 31; Longman and Rutagengwa 2006: p. 176; Buckley-Zistel 2009; Thomson 2011a, 2011b, 2011c). The social conditions of post-genocide Rwanda remain constructed in terms of ethnic identity (Tiemessen 2004: p. 69). The marginalization and exclusion of the Hutu population and the suppression of legitimate political opposition in general have very profound implications for the security and long-term stability of Rwanda. In the absence of a concurrent political settlement that ends authoritarian rule, and political exclusion of the majority of the population in particular, the processes of accountability that Rwanda has carried out have limitations as instruments for advancing the process of reconciliation and other transitional justice objectives that Rwanda expected from its accountability processes. There cannot be genuine reconciliation while grievances about political participation, accountability for human rights abuses, access to resources and other issues continue to fester, particularly in the Hutu community (Waldorf 2004: p. 139; Naftalin 2011: p. 24). As one scholar has observed:

> Broadly speaking, the proposition that the Gacaca process or retrospective justice in general can bring about reconciliation presumes that the single most important source of societal division is the legacy of human rights atrocities. Yet, the atrocities in Rwanda, like most other atrocities are consequences of the means used to resolve conflicts rooted elsewhere, mainly in the struggle for political power and resources. Therefore, reconciliation presupposes a political process and institutional design that addresses the underlying causes of the conflict which are still in place in Rwanda. The politicisation of Hutu and Tutsi identities and perceptions that one group is dominating the other are still prevalent features of Rwandan society, although the dominant and subordinate groups have changed positions. To the extent that the problem is not addressed through an appropriate political design, mechanisms focusing on the injustices of the past can be sources of renewed injustice, suspicion and conflict rather than reconciliation, particularly when the mechanisms themselves are perceived to be unjust. (Haile 2008: p. 43)

Rwanda's failure to democratize and the persecution of political opposition that the government finds necessary to safeguard its control over power hinder reconciliation. Justice can only facilitate reconciliation if it is part of a wider, comprehensive settlement of a nation's conflicts that addresses the major issues that cause conflict. Vandegiste's comments on this issue point to the challenge that Rwanda needs to address:

> Genuine reconciliation at the community level and national levels may be the end result of a lengthy process of acceptance of both justice and democracy (or, to avoid a taboo word, 'power sharing'). For justice to be accepted as an instrument of reconciliation, it must meet certain conditions that go beyond criteria of impartiality of the judiciary. These conditions include its embeddedness in an overall process towards transparency, political participation and inclusiveness. At the same time, history has shown that in the context of Rwanda's plural society, political participation can by no means equal majority democracy, but requires a balanced system of power sharing, including the protection of minority rights and security guarantees. (2001a: p. 278)

Rwanda's reconciliation process is a work in progress, and it still has a long way to go. The initiatives that the government has undertaken in an attempt to promote reconciliation may have achieved a substantial measure of peaceful coexistence, but ethnic divisions remain a matter of grave concern (Burnet 2007: p. 2; FDU-Inkingi 2012). The accountability mechanisms that Rwanda has relied upon for its transitional justice agenda have profound limitations as tools for bridging the divide between the country's two major communities and are unlikely to have a very significant impact in promoting reconciliation. Far from helping to heal and reconcile Rwandan society, Rwanda's accountability processes may in fact enhance rather than diminish inter-ethnic division (Le Mon 2007: p. 17).

9.2.8 Eradicating impunity and fostering a culture of respect for human rights

The deterrence effect of criminal justice in general remains a contested matter, in Rwanda as elsewhere. Nonetheless, advocates of transitional justice argue that accountability for past human rights abuses has the potential to change human rights practices and to deter future human rights abuses. Some scholars argue that human rights trials can increase the likelihood of future atrocities, exacerbate conflict, and undermine efforts to create democracy (Snyder and Vinjamuri 2003). However, a review of data on domestic and international human rights prosecutions in 100 transitional has suggested that human rights prosecutions after transition may lead to improvements in human rights protection, and that human rights prosecutions have a deterrence impact beyond the confines of the single country (Kim and Sikkink 2010). One of the principal objectives of Rwanda's accountability processes was to eradicate impunity.[31] The long-term impact of Rwanda's accountability mechanisms on human rights practices is difficult to determine. It may on the one hand be argued that Rwanda's unprecedented attempt to hold each and every person who participated in the genocide accountable cannot but have an impact on human rights practices. Being accused of genocide in post-genocide Rwanda had extremely grave consequences for suspects, including prolonged detention without trial, detention in harsh conditions, risk of revenge attacks and, for social and political elites, exclusion and marginalization from mainstream society. It is possible that some in Rwandan society may indeed have drawn the lesson from the country's accountability processes that it is not acceptable to commit human rights abuses against fellow citizens and that such abuses will always be punished and should not be repeated. There have been attacks against genocide survivors, but sectarian violence is no longer a problem. The human rights practices of state institutions and officials have improved greatly since the 1990s. Perceptions of security have improved within the country as incidents of human rights abuses went down in numbers (Ingelaere 2008: pp. 31–2).

On the other hand, it is difficult to see how Rwanda's accountability processes can effectively and permanently change the attitudes and values that have fuelled impunity in the past when they have only singled out the losers and have not addressed the crimes of the victors. Rwanda's accountability processes have exclusively focused on the genocide. The genocide is only one aspect of the violence that Rwanda experienced during the 1990s. The vast majority of members of the RPA responsible for human rights violations have never been brought to justice. Not only do they remain in service, they have prospered professionally, and still occupy positions of immense power. Some scholars of transitional justice argue that the credibility and effectiveness of any transitional justice mechanism is predicated upon its perceived legitimacy and, ultimately, even-handedness and ability to deliver genuine justice to all segments of society – victims and perpetrators alike (Borocan 2004: p. 400; Call 2004: p. 109). Rwanda's accountability processes have not offered such even-handedness and are, as a result, perceived as victor's justice by the majority of the population (Ingelaere 2008: p. 56; Corey and Joireman 2000: p. 89; Sosnov 2008: pp. 136–40).

The accountability processes that Rwanda has undertaken can at best be said to have a mixed record as far as the goal of eradicating impunity is concerned. While mass atrocity has ceased agents of the state are to this day still able to commit human rights abuses (killings, torture and disappearances) without fear of being held accountable (Reyntjens 2004: pp. 194–7). Although the human rights practices of the army and security services have improved as violent armed conflict has abated, impunity on the part of state officials remains a problem (Ingelaere 2008: pp. 43–4). Even Clark, whose overly positive assessment of Gacaca is considered by most other scholars of Rwanda to be questionable, acknowledges that Gacaca, the principal mechanism with which Rwanda has sought to address the legacy of the genocide, has not had the deterrent impact that its designers had hoped for (2010: p. 255).

The failure of Rwanda's accountability processes to investigate in good faith and to punish allegations of human rights abuses attributable to the RPA perpetuates the very culture of impunity that the country's transitional justice mechanisms intended to eradicate (Zorbas 2004: p. 41). Many scholars of Rwanda are of the view that the goal of eradicating impunity will be elusive as long as crimes attributed to the RPA remain unaccounted for (Vandegiste 2001: p. 251; Borocan 2004: p. 390; Tiemessen 2004: p. 69; Algard 2005; Kirby 2006: p. 116).

9.2.9 Promoting democracy and the rule of law

The impunity that victims of human rights violations and scholars of and commentators on Rwanda believe partly accounts for the 1994 genocide was directly linked to the absence of the rule of law. Consequently, the promotion of the rule of law emerged as one of the key objectives of Rwanda's accountability processes. The post-genocide government took power at a time when state institutions had become criminalized and lawlessness was the norm rather than the exception across the country. Rwanda has since made some progress in establishing the systems and institutions of governance of a normal state. Large-scale killings of unarmed civilians have stopped. The level of violence in Rwandan society has been drastically reduced as armed conflict has ebbed. Law and order have been effectively restored, and public security is generally adequate. The country has enacted a Constitution and other laws that, in theory, guarantee respect for most fundamental human rights. The country has also adopted very progressive policies in relation to gender equality, including affirmative action in public service. Rwanda has undertaken reforms of the justice system that are making the system more efficient and effective (Human Rights Watch 2008: p. 44).[32] Many aspects of the human rights situation in Rwanda have experienced remarkable progress since the genocide (Department of State 2009).

In spite of the above positive developments, the state of the rule of law in Rwanda remains very unsatisfactory. The ruling party, the RPF, enjoys unchallenged power. The party exercises absolute control over all organs of the state (Reyntjens 2004: p. 190). The RPF itself, like the government, is under the control of the President, in whom the Constitution vests virtually absolute powers.[33] The executive effectively controls all of the other organs of the state (Burnet 2007: p. 2; Ghai 2009: p. 27). The political system lacks checks and balances. Branches of government other than the executive are deprived of their autonomy and legitimacy (Nifosi 2005: p. 85). The legislature is a rubber stamp for the executive (Burnet 2007: p. 4). The independence of the judiciary is compromised (Jordaan 2006: p. 344; Burnet 2007: p. 4).[34] The government's own human rights watchdog, the National Commission for Human Rights (NCHR), has 'acted more as a public relations organ of the government' (Department of State 2005). The executive is itself controlled by a small group of military and security services officials from behind the scenes

(Prunier 1995: p. 67; Zorbas 2004: p. 45; Ghai 2009: p. 9). The army and security service are above the law and not accountable to the civilian authorities (Stroh 2009: p. 20). The military, especially the officer corps, is made up almost exclusively of Tutsi officers (Vandegiste 2001a: p. 257). The Hutu who serve in government are only surrogates of the RPF, kept in office, often for very brief periods, for the sole purpose of giving the government an appearance of embracing political pluralism (Reyntjens 2004). The majority of the population does not consider the government as legitimate (Vandegiste 2001a: pp. 266–7; Kayumba *et al.* 2010).

The unrivalled political supremacy that the RPF now enjoys in Rwanda has not been achieved through an open and free process of competition for power with other political forces, but through repressive laws, administrative practices and the use of the security services to frustrate the exercise of the civil and political rights of opponents of the regime and citizens in general (Longman 2004b: pp. 162, 166–7; Oomen 2005: p. 906; Naftalin 2011: p. 23).

Rwanda is a very tightly controlled society (Wolters 2005b: p. 15). The government relies on repression to enforce its control of the population (Richters *et al.* 2005: p. 218). Legal, administrative and physical obstacles have been put in place to make it all but impossible to contemplate peaceful political opposition or freedom of expression (Naftalin 2011: p. 23). The government exercises zero tolerance of political opposition or criticism. The security services regard dissent and criticism of the government as treason (*The East African*, 4 December 2006). The law places very severe restrictions on the ability of opponents of the government to organize and advocate their policies to the population.[35] The government has in the past used smear campaigns and insults to intimidate opponents, whether they are international non-governmental organizations, civil society groups, newspapers or political parties (Christian Aid 2004; Burnet 2007: p. 7). Intimidation against government opponents has gone to the extent of making threats of physical violence, including death. In one speech that preceded the 2003 elections, the President threatened that those opposed to the government would be 'wounded' and 'ground to dust'.[36] People who are perceived as posing a potential challenge to the RPF are subjected to persecution that makes their political activities impossible (ICCO *et al.* 2003; Longman 2004b: pp. 162, 166–7). Persecution of opponents of the government has included constant police surveillance, assaults, arrests, illegal detention and politically motivated prosecutions.[37] Politically motivated violence continues to stifle freedom of expression (Longman 2004b). Opponents of the regime have become victims of extra-judicial killings and involuntary disappearances (Burnet 2007: pp. 8–9; Amnesty International 2011).[38] Even some opponents of the regime who flee to exile still meet death in mysterious circumstances.[39] Opponents and critics of the regime who are victims of human rights violations do not have the opportunity to seek redress from the courts. Impunity on the part of the military and the security services has long been a major problem (Vandegiste 2001: p. 267). And it remains so.

The government has enacted legislation to punish sectarianism and discrimination.[40] The government has since 2003 used accusations of 'sectarianism', 'divisionism' and 'spreading of genocide ideology' to curtail political opposition and civil society work, most specifically human rights work (Zorbas 2004: p. 44; Article 19 2009; Ghai 2009: pp. 30–2; Thomson 2011a: p. 4; Melvin 2012: p. 4). These crimes are not properly defined in the relevant legislation. The government has exploited the ambiguity of the anti-sectarian legislation to limit freedom of expression and to persecute individual opponents and critical members of civil society, especially human rights organizations and the media (Burnet 2007: p. 2). Charges of sectarianism have been levelled against political parties across the spectrum, including the Liberal Party for its advocacy on behalf of survivors of the genocide (Christian Aid 2004: p. 13).

Rwanda's transition to democracy has floundered. Rwanda's new Constitution, rather than enhancing opportunity for competition and diversity, has imposed drastic limitations on the exercise of the right of political participation. The Constitution and the laws that govern the operation of political parties make it not just difficult, but impossible for the opposition to form political parties and to compete for political power,[41] creating what one scholar has termed a situation of electoral authoritarianism (Stroh 2009: p. 19). A plethora of state security and military apparatuses make it all but impossible for any political opposition to exist, let alone work freely. There is no meaningful competition for political power between political parties and thus no real opportunity to change the government through elections (NEPAD 2006; Burnet 2007: p. 3; Longman 2011: p. 27). The legal and administrative restrictions on space for political participation have been so draconian that the opposition has stopped participating in elections. No genuine opposition parties participated in the 2008 parliamentary and 2010 Presidential elections. Rwanda holds regular elections, but their outcome is predetermined because there is effectively no opportunity for the opposition to function legally (National Democratic Institute 2003; Stroh 2009). Opportunities for political participation are severely restricted (Burnet 2003). Elections are systematically manipulated and heavily conditioned by the RPF in order to ensure its electoral victory (Nifosi 2005: p. 85; Ghai 2009: p. 27; Longman 2011: pp. 38–41).

The Rwanda government does not tolerate criticism of its policies, including policies on justice, let alone opposition (Le Mon 2007: p. 19; Lahiri 2009: p. 331; Longman 2011: pp. 27–34; Straus and Waldorf 2011b: p. 10; Thomson 2011a: p. 4). Freedom of expression is severely limited (Ghai 2009: p. 27; Pall 2010; Melvin 2012: p. 4). The law guarantees freedom of the press but the media remains tightly controlled by the government (Burnet 2007: p. 5). The government has justified the restrictions on the media by referring to the genocide: it argues that the restrictions on freedom of speech and expression are necessary to prevent ethnic strife and to ensure national stability (Straus and Waldorf 2011b: p. 4). Media outlets are either state-controlled, co-opted or constantly under siege. The government has used the curbs on the media to suppress criticism or dissent (Department of State 2005: Section 2; Nifosi 2005: p. 89). The government has regularly arrested journalists, seized issues of journals and closed publishing houses (Longman 2011: p. 35). The security services sometimes co-opt independent journalists by paying them money. Journalists who refuse to toe the line or be co-opted have often been subjected to threats and intimidation; some have either been killed or have become victims of involuntary disappearance (Reyntjens 2004: pp. 196–7). Others have had to flee into exile to escape persecution. Threats, intimidations and other forms of persecution at the hands of the security services have created a climate whereby journalists exercise self-censorship in order to avoid the wrath of the security services (Reyntjens 2004: pp. 196–7). Freedom House has reported that the 'Rwandan media are officially censored and constrained by fear of reprisals. Journalists interviewed admitted that they censor their own writing and that the authorities have made it clear that certain topics cannot be discussed' (Freedom House 2003).

Civil society as it exists in other countries, in the sense of a counterbalance to government, does not really exist in Rwanda. Civil society as a whole operates under very tight restrictions in post-genocide Rwanda (Straus and Waldorf 2011b: p. 10). Civil society groups, which do not toe the government line, are not allowed to operate freely (International Crisis Group 2002b; Nifosi 2005: p. 89). Civil society organizations speak publicly and influence decision making only when their views are in line with those of the RPF and the government (Burnet 2007: p. 4; Reyntjens 2004: p. 185). The government exercises intense control over the non-governmental sector by both overt and covert methods (Christian Aid 2004: p. 15). The regime has so systematically intimidated, co-opted and suppressed civil society that Rwanda lacks independent social organization capable of articulating most public interests (Longman 2011: pp. 26–31). Independent human rights organizations, in particular, have been a target of the security services. Human rights groups and their members have been subjected to harassment, intimidation and all kinds of restrictions and persecution (Amnesty International 2005; Department of State 2005; Nifosi 2005: p. 89), including freezing of assets, threats of dissolution of the organizations, restrictions on the ability to have meetings, engineering the replacement of organizational leadership, and forcing organizations to align their views with government policy (Department of State 2005: Section 4). Critical voices in civil society and the media have been silenced (Burnet 2007: p. 2) and the regime has become even more repressive since the end of the transition in 2003 (Burnet 2007: p. 2).

Although large-scale violence has dramatically reduced in Rwanda over the years, and the majority of the population now enjoys relative security (Nifosi 2005: p. 85), repression has become consolidated and institutionalized since the 2003 elections (Nifosi 2005: p. 85; Reyntjens 2006). The security services have so intimidated the population that they no longer find it necessary to resort frequently to killings or enforced disappearances to deter opposition.

Rwanda is today a country in which people live in permanent fear of the security services (Christian Aid 2004: pp. 6–7; Richters *et al.* 2005: p. 213).

The explicitly violent and repressive way in which the RPF deals with the opposition and civil society has turned Rwanda back into a de facto one-party regime with a democratic façade (Reyntjens 2004: p. 43; Nifosi 2005: p. 93). Gacaca was a product of the Urugwiro Reflection Meetings, a process that originally aimed to draw a roadmap for transition to a democratic political order. The transition to democracy that the Urugwiro Reflections Meetings envisioned for the country never took place. Rwanda emerged from the 1994–2003 transitional period with the ruling party consolidating its monopoly of political power (Nifosi 2005: p. 93; Rafti 2008). Gacaca has been implemented in a repressive political environment (Sarkin 2001; Le Mon 2007; Haile 2008; Oomen 2009: pp. 192–5; Thomson 2011b). Repression has eroded public confidence in government in general and the justice system (including Gacaca) in particular (Borocan 2004: pp. 390–2; Tiemessen 2004: p. 331). Lack of progress towards democracy and the rule of law have reduced the popular appeal of Gacaca, its potential to function effectively and its ability to achieve intended objectives (Borocan 2004: pp. 390–2; Wolters 2005a). The impact of Rwanda's accountability processes on promoting the rule of law has, at best, been very limited (Takeuchi 2011). Most scholars of transitional justice are of the view that processes of accountability for past human rights abuses are unlikely to achieve their objectives in the absence of democracy (Sarkin 2000: pp. 116, 120; Richters *et al.* 2005: p. 218).

9.2.10 Promoting sustainable peace and stability

Peace building has been defined as the full range of approaches, processes and stages needed for the transformation of conflict toward more sustainable, peaceful relationships and governance modes and structures (Boutros-Ghali 1992, 1995). A common definition of conflict is 'a struggle over values and claims to scarce status, power and resources' a struggle in which the aims of opponents are to neutralize, injure or eliminate rivals (Coser 1956: p. 8). Conflict may be inter-personal, intra-group and inter-group. Peace building assumes that conflict is a natural part of human existence and that the goal of peace building is to transform the destructive ways in which society deals with conflict to lead to more constructive outcomes (Caritas 2002: p. 58). The field of peace research differentiates between negative peace, defined as the absence of violence and as structural violence, where the absence of violence is combined with the closure of avenues for challenging the status quo and expressing grievances in a peaceful way (Department for International Development 2010: p. 9), and positive peace, defined as 'social peace, respect for the rule of law and human rights, and social and economic development, supported by dynamic and representative political institutions capable of managing change and resolving disputes without resorting to violent conflict' (2010: p. 9).

> Structural violence refers to the disabilities, disparities, and even deaths that result when systems, institutions, or policies meet some people's needs and rights at the expense of others'. Societies that permit or encourage economic and social disparity, exclude some groups from full participation in decision-making and public life, or direct harm toward some people, suffer more from all forms of violence, both public and private. (Schirch 2008: p. 7)

Peace building centres on relationship-building and repairing processes, but is not limited by them (Schirch 2008: p. 8).

Transitional justice processes are a major aspect of peace-building processes in societies with legacies of violent conflict. Transitional justice can assist a society that has experienced conflict to confront and address the root causes of past conflict. Processes such as accountability, truth telling and reparation can help individuals and communities move towards reconciliation, understood as a multi-faceted and long-term process of building civic trust between citizens and the state, and among citizens themselves after a conflict. Justice in particular is a very critical component of strategies for reconciliation (Pankhurst 1999: p. 254). Justice for atrocity can facilitate the development of relations of trust between individuals, between individuals and groups, between groups that have had antagonistic relationships and between citizens in ways that make a society progressively more conflict-resilient.

The promotion of sustainable peace and stability was the ultimate objective of Rwanda's accountability processes as well as its other peace-building strategies. In evaluating whether these accountability processes are contributing effectively to promoting peace and stability, it is necessary to explore the core causes of the Rwanda conflict. The instability and violence experienced by Rwanda has largely resulted from conflict over unresolved issues relating to governance. Disputes over political representation, political participation, access to resources and respect for fundamental human rights lie at the heart of the conflict in Rwanda over the last 50 years (Sarkin 1999b).

Rwanda has initiated and implemented a very wide range of policies, processes and programmes (including Gacaca) as part of its peace-building agenda. The Rwanda government claims credit for restoring law and order and for bringing about sustainable peace and stability to the country (Kagame 2009, 2010). This assessment is shared by a minority of scholars and commentators. Clark (2010) argues that Gacaca has been effective in promoting peace in Rwanda through providing a forum for in-depth dialogue and debate on issues of communal importance to Rwandan society, through facilitating truth telling and truth hearing and in promoting positive peace by creating a dialogical space for the resolution of peoples' past conflicts (Clark 2010: pp. 231–342). Clark further argues that the dialogue of Gacaca hearings is a training ground for non-violent conflict resolution outside of Gacaca (Clark 2010: pp. 232, 234) and that it has the potential to embody civic virtues of communal engagement, dialogue and debate that are important for building trust and long-term peace.

While I recognize that the many initiatives (including Gacaca) that Rwanda has undertaken as part of its peace-building agenda may have contributed to a degree of 'negative peace' (Clark 2010: p. 237), I believe Clark's claim that 'Gacaca has also proven vital in the construction of positive peace ... [and] currently constitutes a rare forum in which the engagement between previously antagonistic parties necessary for maintaining long-term peace can occur' (2010: p. 237) has no factual basis. Clark's arguments on the effectiveness of Gacaca in promoting peace in Rwanda are not grounded in a sound understanding of the theoretical underpinnings of the process of peace building. According to scholarship on peace building, effective peace-building processes are built on certain key principles that include engagement between parties in conflict on the root causes of conflict, participatory processes and the restoration and rebuilding of relations between parties previously in conflict, leading to reconciliation, policies and practices that address the root causes of conflict in the society in question (OECD 2001).

The main causes of conflict in Rwandan society include grievances held by both the Hutu and Tutsi communities over perceptions of social, economic and political humiliation, discrimination, marginalization and exclusion at one time or another in the country's history; the legacy of colonialism; policies of dictatorial regimes that have promoted racism and prejudice hatred; competition between elites for power and opportunity of access to resources; manipulation of the population by elites to advance their political goals, leading to ethnic prejudice and hatred; grievances rooted in experiences of violence and impunity; failure on the part of successive governments to create the conditions for refugees to return peacefully rather than by force; structural violence rooted in socio-economic inequalities; and lack of democratic institutions to provide protection to citizens as well as facilitate the resolution of conflict in constructive ways (Cannon 2005: pp. 7–10; Silva-Leander 2008: pp. 1606–7; McDoom 2011).

In *The Gacaca Courts, Post-Genocide Justice and Reconciliation in Rwanda: Justice without Lawyers*, Clark discusses the concept of engagement in relation to Gacaca, quoting Porter, who defines engagement as 'practices involving honest committed encounters with others, not least those with whom we disagree the most' (2010: p. 166). Clark stresses his conviction that 'there can be no reconciliation (nor several of Gacaca's other aims) without genuine engagement between parties previously in conflict' (p. 166). He goes on to write:

> Engagement entails antagonistic parties debating the root causes of their conflicts ... it recognizes that there will be deep-rooted animosity between individuals and between groups after an event as destructive as genocide ... Implicit in Gacaca is the view that reconciliation after genocide will require difficult dialogue, a genuine confrontation with the sources of conflict, and parties' mutual dedication to rebuilding fractured

> relations … For engagement to be productive, it requires immense dedication of the parties involved, a genuine sense of trust between them and effective forms of mediation to ensure that this sense of trust is maintained. (pp. 166–7)

The Rwanda government has not allowed, let alone facilitated, such engagement. Clark's claim that Gacaca promoted positive peace by facilitating dialogue on the root causes of conflict in Rwandan society is absolutely without basis. Clark's assertion that Gacaca courts have provided Rwandans with an opportunity to engage in open dialogue on the root causes of conflict in Rwandan society (2010: p. 231) is unfounded. Neither Gacaca, nor indeed any of the other peace-building processes that Rwanda has undertaken, are yet to address the fundamental root causes of conflict in Rwandan society (Richters *et al.* 2005: p. 210). Participants in Gacaca are not expected to discuss and have not discussed the root causes of the genocide, let alone the causes of the wider and continuing Rwandan conflict (Thomson 2011a: p. 7). The very same factors that have driven conflict in Rwanda in the past remain potent.

On assuming power in 1994, the RPF promised not only to restore security and to maintain peace, but also to establish democracy, the rule of law and respect for human rights, and to address the major causes of conflict that had until then devoured the country (RPF 1994). The RPF initially set up a broad-based, multi-party government in the spirit of the power-sharing arrangements set out in the Arusha Peace Agreement, subject to exclusion of the political groups and individuals that had participated in the genocide (RPF 1994; Vandegiste 2001a: p. 256). The experiment with genuinely broad-based, multi-party government was, however, very short-lived.

Relations between the RPF and its partners in government got off to a very bad start, largely as a result of allegations of widespread human rights abuses by the RPA, which the military leadership appeared unable or unwilling to control or punish (MDR 1994), and disputes over apportionment of power between the RPF and other political parties in government. The leadership of the RPA not only failed to hold the military accountable, it also defiantly defended the army's actions in cabinet (Twagiramungu 1995). Disagreements over the handling of allegations of rights abuses by the military and the apportionment of power (between the RPF and other political parties) within the government led to the ousting of the Prime Minister and other opposition politicians (Amnesty International 1995c; Sendashonga 1995; Twagiramungu 1995).

From the third quarter of 1995 forward, Rwanda's government remained a multi-party government only in name (Vandegiste 2001a: p. 256). The 1995 ousting of opposition politicians from government started a trend towards progressive consolidation of the RPF's control of the machinery of the state and set a pattern of intolerance for political opposition that has only grown more strident with the passage of time (Reyntjens 2004: p. 180; Longman 2011: p. 32). Not only did the RPF seek to stifle criticism within the government, it also made it progressively difficult for alternative voices to hold the government accountable from outside the machinery of government. Throughout the period of the transition, the RPF continually devised strategies to weaken, disable and destroy political opposition. The RPF strictly enforced a ban on all political activities against other political parties, but did not make any effort to observe the ban itself.

The period before the 2003 elections that were supposed to mark the end of the transition, in particular, witnessed intensified activity on the part of the RPF to destroy the last of the remaining opposition before the elections and to put in place mechanisms to ensure a smooth path to its electoral victory. As the 2003 elections approached, the police, security services and military increased persecution of potential opponents of the regime. The RPF orchestrated the banning of the Mouvement Démocratique Républicain (MDR), the only one among existing political parties that was considered capable of mounting a credible challenge to the RPF during the elections that were due shortly (Reyntjens 2004: p. 184; Oomen 2005: p. 900; Clark 2007; Longman 2011: p. 33). An attempt by former President Pasteur Bizimungu, perhaps the only remaining political leader who could have challenged the RPF after the banning of the MDR Party during the elections, to set up a new party, was stopped (ICCO *et al.* 2003: p. 24; Reyntjens 2004: p. 193). The former President and other promoters of the proposed party were arrested and imprisoned on what are trumped up charges (Human Rights Watch 2008: pp. 53–8). Genuine opposition parties were denied registration, and security agencies made it difficult for independent candidates to register as candidates in the elections.

The fact that the 2003 presidential and parliamentary elections would not be free and fair was only too apparent even before the elections were held (Oomen 2005: p. 901). The elections were indeed marred by widespread malpractices (Jordaan 2006: p. 333). Writing on the eve of the elections, Uvin noted:

> What Rwanda is currently going through is not a process of democratisation as much as a formal election painted on top of an increasingly totalitarian state. The closing off of all political space, the maintenance of a climate of fear, the intimidations and disappearances of potentially critical voices, the banning of the sole opposition party with some possible popular grounding, the attacks on key civil society organisations and the further muzzling of the press – all point to the undeniable fact that there is, in 2003, no free choice in Rwanda. As a matter of fact, this year of so-called democratisation has seen an actual reduction in political space. (Uvin 2003b: p. 1)

The harassment of opposition political parties was even more severe in the run-up to the 2010 elections (Longman 2011: p. 34). The political transition Rwanda began after the genocide has, instead of leading to democracy, resulted in the legitimization and consolidation of authoritarian minority rule (Nifosi 2005: p. 93). The majority of the population have no opportunity for meaningful political participation. Political power is vested in a narrow leadership that does not necessarily represent its own ethnic minority group, let alone the whole population. Not only does the system of government exclude the majority ethnic group from meaningful political participation (Sarkin 2000: p. 120; Reyntjens 2011), it tolerates no political opposition of any kind, regardless of the ethnicity of the opponents (Silva-Leander 2008: p. 1614). Political opposition, Hutu and Tutsi alike, has been systematically repressed and most if its leadership has been compelled to go into exile (Reyntjens 2006).

Critics of the government that remain inside Rwanda, as well as organizations and individuals who may be perceived as threats by the government, are accused of 'divisionism' at the slightest indication of dissent, where 'divisionism' is loosely defined as an attempt to separate the two main ethnic groups (Reyntjens 2006). Rwanda is in fact far less free than it was prior to the 1994 genocide. The military officers who dominate the political system are afraid to embrace democracy, in the belief that they can only protect their privileged position and safeguard the security of the Tutsi community by clinging to absolute power. The issues of representation, opportunity for political participation, access to resources and respect for human rights (especially civil and political rights) that have previously driven conflict in Rwanda remain unresolved (Sarkin 1999b: p. 799; Vandegiste 2001a: p. 252). The RPF has unwittingly fulfilled the worst predictions of its early critics. Hutu extremists warned before the genocide that the armed struggle of the RPF was an attempt to return the country to minority Tutsi domination, and that prophecy has come to pass (Sarkin 2000; Drumbl 2002b: pp. 32–3; Kayumba *et al.* 2010).

The Rwanda conflict has in effect really never ended. Rwanda may be at peace internally, but it is a peace maintained by force of arms. A progressive closing down of political space has accompanied the peace that the country currently enjoys (Jordaan 2006: p. 336). The RPF justifies the stifling political context that it has imposed on the country on the grounds that the policies and practices it has adopted are necessary measures to maintain stability and to prevent a recurrence of genocide (Tiemessen 2004: p. 67; Oomen 2005: p. 900). Yet, the government's policies are likely to lead to the very dangers that it seeks to avoid. The suppression of all political opposition in general and the exclusion of the Hutu from a meaningful share of power in particular, perpetuates perceptions of victimization (Drumbl 2002a: pp. 32–3), which in turn fuels violence. Some scholars of Rwanda argue that Rwanda's authoritarian rule may prove disastrous for the country's long-term stability, as it prevents the public from expressing its interests through productive, peaceful, political means and also prevents the regime from benefitting from the contribution of much of the population (Longman 2011: p. 26). Deprived of the opportunity for political participation on an equal footing, the Hutu community and other opponents of the regime may yet again, in years to come, fall prey to incitement to liberate themselves from oppression and minority domination by resorting to violence (Waldorf 2004: p. 138). More particularly, by refusing to make compromises, to open up the political space and to agree to at least share power, the ruling party once again risks not only losing power by force, but also exposes all Tutsi to the risk of violence, even violence of genocidal proportions, at some indeterminate future time (Waldorf 2004: p. 138; Haile 2008: p. 50). Rwanda can only begin to hope for lasting peace when it has devised a political system grounded in the rule of law that allows majority rule while providing adequate guarantees for the minority (Sarkin 1999a: p. 832, 2001: p. 171; Vandegiste 2001: pp. 257–8; Tiemessen 2004: p. 67). As long as Rwanda is unable to resolve its governance problems, the risk of violent sectarian conflict will remain (Silva-Leander 2008: p. 1616). Former President Bizimungu once stated:

> We are persuaded that if things continue, the Hutus will prepare for war and in fifteen or twenty years, they will have driven out the Tutsis, with the conceivable consequences that would entail. Mechanisms need to be set up so that each community can have a hand in government, until we have forged a national identity that transcends Hutu/Tutsi divisions ... Rwanda is not a constitutional state and it has enormous problems. The inequalities in the promotions system stir so much discontent. If the situation does not change, the only possible outcome is violence. The war of 1990 is not over ...[42]

As a result of the draconian restrictions on the exercise of the rights of freedom of expression and political participation in force in Rwanda, Rwandans have not had any opportunity to discuss freely the root causes of conflict in Rwandan society. Many in the Hutu harbour strong if not bitter grievances that have been shaped by the experience of violence, political exclusion and lack of justice for their suffering. Reconciliation between Rwanda's two major communities remains elusive for the time being (Takeuchi 2011). Due to the country's lack of significant progress towards reconciliation and democratization, Rwandan society remains deeply divided by ethnicity and politics. Longman asks a very relevant question: 'The willingness to forgive authoritarianism during the Habyarimana regime made the genocide possible. Will the world allow the same mistake to be repeated under Kagame?' (2011: p. 43).

Rwanda's post-genocide government has failed to address the major root causes of the country's conflict, especially the tensions that exist around the nexus between ethnicity and access to power and resources (Vandegiste 2001: p. 278; Drumbl 2002a: p. 18; Christian Aid 2004; Naftalin 2011: p. 24). Neither Gacaca nor any of the other policies, processes and programmes that constitute Rwanda's peace-building agenda has, as yet, advanced Rwandan society to 'positive peace.' The accountability processes that the country has undertaken are unlikely to have any significant impact in ensuring sustainable peace and stability in the absence of progress towards more democratic, inclusive and accountable government. Accountability processes cannot be prospects for peace and stability in the absence of genuine, inclusive efforts to address the fundamental causes of conflict.

9.3 Assessing the Legacy of the International Criminal Tribunal for Rwanda

The ad hoc United Nations tribunals for Rwanda and the former Yugoslavia are now in the stages of winding up. The experiences of the two tribunals have important implications for the future of legal mechanisms of accountability for atrocity worldwide. It is timely to begin contemplating their legacies and the legacy of the ICTR cannot be considered in total isolation from that of the ICTY. The questions that need to be posed include the following: Have the tribunals achieved the objectives for which they were established? Has the Rwanda tribunal, in particular, had any impact in terms of the objectives that the various members of the Security Council had in mind when they voted for its establishment (Waldorf 2004)? Has the tribunal made any significant contribution to advance the goals and objectives of Rwanda's transitional justice agenda? What will the lasting legacy of these tribunals be?

The Rwanda Tribunal, and indeed its Yugoslav counterpart, has been the subject of strong criticism over the years.[43] This criticism has often centred around a number of issues, including the slow pace of proceedings (leading to frustration on the part of both suspects and victims, and to human rights violations); the high cost (with the tribunals consuming a disproportionate share of the resources that the international community makes available to promote the rule of law in the respective post-conflict states); efficiency (considered unsatisfactory, given their low output, particularly during their early years); and failure to adequately engage victims, to address their concerns and to provide them with opportunity to participate in their proceedings. The overwhelming opinion among scholars of the United Nations tribunals is that, at least initially, the tribunals were too removed – physically as well as psychologically – from the societies they were established to help to have any significant relevance for them (Drumbl 2002b: p. 8). The tribunals' pursuit of neutrality tended, deliberately or inadvertently, to sideline the victims of the conflicts they were dealing with from their processes (Drumbl 2002b: p. 42). The geographic remoteness of the two tribunals from the states whose conflicts they were dealing with, which was intended to insulate them from local influence, had the adverse effect of alienating them from the very people they were meant to serve. The tribunals did not initially recognize the critical need to interact with, and justify their relevance to, the societies they were established to help, who should have been their primary constituencies. Instead they were rather more preoccupied with meeting the expectations of their international constituencies at the expense of being accountable to the societies they were formed to assist (Drumbl 2002b: p. 9). The ad hoc tribunals did not afford the victims' societies a share of the ownership of their work, and thus many in those societies felt deeply estranged from the institutions.

Nevertheless the ad hoc United Nations tribunals have been a positive development in the fight against impunity for gross human rights abuses.

They have raised international awareness of what happened in the countries where the conflicts they are dealing with took place. They have helped to establish objective historical records about the respective conflicts (Drumbl 2002b: p. 9). The tribunals have demonstrated that international humanitarian law and international human rights law, fields of law that had for a long time been merely a collection of legal principles without practical application, are capable of enforcement. The tribunals have made accountability for atrocity a reality by apprehending, trying and punishing some of those who bear the greatest responsibility for the atrocities that were committed during the conflicts of Rwanda and the Balkans (Drumbl 2002b: p. 40). The Rwanda tribunal, in particular, has indicted, apprehended and tried a substantial number of the most senior leaders of the government, military and civil society who were instrumental in planning and directing the genocide. The ad hoc tribunals have laid a foundation for the permanent International Criminal Court, which will hopefully in time evolve into an effective tool against impunity for egregious human rights abuses.

The ICTR has substantially performed its core mandate to prosecute persons responsible for genocide and other serious violations of international humanitarian law that were committed during the Rwanda conflict in 1994 (Van den Herik 2005: p. 263). In apprehending and bringing some of the perpetrators who bear great responsibility for the genocide to justice, the tribunal may have contributed to maintaining peace and stability in Rwanda in the short term (Kamatali 2003: p. 127; Van den Herik 2005: p. 263). The tribunal has contributed substantially to the development of international law (Drumbl 2002b: p. 9; Jallow 2009). Through its groundbreaking judgments, it has provided clarity and definition to the concept of genocide, acknowledged the importance of sexual violence as a form of war, prosecuted the wrongful use of the media as a weapon of hatred, clarified the application of the Geneva Conventions to civilian perpetrators and shown that sovereign immunity has no place in the modern world (Jallow 2009: p. 270).

The Rwanda tribunal was the first international tribunal to issue a judgment in a trial involving charges of genocide. This was done in the Akayesu case.[44] Genocide had never been defined by a court of law prior to this decision. The case raised a very important issue as to whether a group (the Tutsi in this case) which, although stable and membership is by birth, does not meet the definition of any one of the four categories of groups (national, ethnic, racial or religious groups) expressly protected by the Convention on the Prevention and Punishment of the Crime of Genocide, could still be protected under the convention. The Akayesu case provided a groundbreaking definition of ethnicity. The court took the approach that too narrow an interpretation of the Genocide Convention went against its purpose, which was to ensure the protection of any 'stable and permanent group'. The court also defined the elements of the crime of genocide, holding that what was required was to prove the crime was not the actual destruction of the protected group, but the 'special intent' of the accused, to destroy, in whole or in part, the protected group.

The Akayesu case also advanced a progressive understanding of sexual violence.[45] The case resulted in the first conviction of rape as a crime against humanity and genocide and the judgment gave the first ever definition of rape in international law, finding that rape is an act of aggression that 'cannot be captured in a mechanical description of objects and body parts'.[46] It defined rape as 'physical invasion of a sexual nature, committed on a person under circumstances which are coercive',[47] which went far beyond the usual definition framed in terms of consent and penetration. The case also provided an equally broad definition of sexual violence, finding that sexual violence need not even be physical.[48]

In the media case[49] the ICTR issued a judgment that has contributed immensely to defining the boundaries between freedom of expression and incitement of hatred, discrimination and criminal violence. This was the first ever decision by an international criminal tribunal to result in a conviction of media leaders for inciting genocide and it differentiated statements of ethnic pride (protected by virtue of freedom of expression) from incitement to hate. The court held that the application of a democratic principle such as freedom of expression must vary from state to state. The judgment also defined the meaning of 'direct incitement' of genocide, finding that it need not draw an immediate response.

The Rwanda tribunal has issued judgments, which have clarified the application of the Geneva conventions to civilians. Historically, the conventions were thought to apply only to members of the military and governments. The principles, which were established in the Akayesu, Rutaganda,[50] Semanza[51] and Musema[52] cases, extended command responsibility outside the military and government context and into the private corporate environment. The ICTR has also advanced the definition of conspiracy in international law.[53]

Last but not least, the tribunal has given judgments, which have laid to rest the question as to whether sovereign immunity can be a defence against charges of international crimes. The ICTR was the first international tribunal to convict a head of government of genocide and crimes against humanity.[54] The tribunal has made it clear that sovereign immunity no longer applies, that even heads of state and government can be held responsible, as subjects bound by international legal obligations, for breaches of international law.

The ad hoc tribunals have generated substantive law, thereby serving an important expressive and jurisprudential function (Drumbl 2009: p. 41). They will leave a highly developed and sophisticated body of law in which the definition and scope of war crimes, crimes against humanity and genocide have been explored, along with the various forms of participation and liability, the available justifications and defences, procedural matters, issues concerning the rights of the accused and sentencing (Schabas 2006: p. 44). The decisions of the ICTR in the above cases have served to expand the protection of victims of human rights abuses by clarifying various legal concepts. The body of law that the two United Nations tribunals have developed is now widely consulted and relied upon by jurisdictions across the world (Schabas 2006: pp. 44–6). It will be useful for the permanent International Criminal Court.

However, international criminal tribunals still have certain shortcomings as well. There is no indication that the ICTR and ICTY are as yet having any significant impact on promoting reconciliation within the societies that were affected by the conflicts that they have been dealing with (Rodman 2008). The tribunals may have made groundbreaking contributions to the development of international law, but there is no evidence that they are effective in deterring atrocity or ensuring greater respect for human rights, at least not in the Great Lakes region of Central Africa (Rodman 2008). Judging by the violent conflicts that have ravaged Central Africa and surrounding regions (including Darfur) over the past decade, it is clear that the ICTR has not had any significant impact on deterring conflict or ending impunity for atrocities.

International criminal tribunals depend on the cooperation of states to be able to carry out their mandates effectively, and are at times impotent when the major powers lack the political will to support some aspects of their work. International criminal tribunals are particularly weak in addressing atrocities attributable to individuals or groups that remain in power (Peskin 2005). They may, in some cases, help sitting governments to consolidate their power and to stigmatize political opponents, while shielding their own illiberal practices from scrutiny, as has been the case in Rwanda (Drumbl 2009: p. 42). The Rwanda tribunal's handling of allegations of human rights abuses attributable to the RPA best illustrates this aspect of the weaknesses of existing mechanisms of international criminal justice. One of the major differences between the Rwanda and the Yugoslav tribunals is that whereas the Yugoslav tribunal has targeted persons who bear the greatest responsibility for atrocity in all groups that were parties to the conflict, the Rwanda tribunal has only brought indictments against members of the losing side.

The question of human rights violations attributable to the RPA is the factor that will have the greatest impact on the legacy of the Rwanda tribunal. The ICTR's failure to investigate and prosecute violations of human rights by the victors has undermined both its credibility and its ability to contribute to the advancement of the objectives for which it was established, especially the objective of eliminating impunity (Van den Herik 2005: p. 264). The tribunal's work is perceived as victor's justice by a significant part of Rwandan society and its failure to address RPA abuses could have repercussions that may reverberate beyond Rwanda's borders. The ICTR's failure to provide impartial justice may encourage impunity, by leaving the perception that international criminal justice mechanisms only target the losers in conflicts and are powerless or not interested in dealing with crimes by perpetrators of atrocity who remain in power.

9.4 Conclusion

In the aftermath of the genocide, the government of Rwanda considered it absolutely imperative to ensure accountability for the atrocities that were committed during the course of the war and genocide. Rwanda responded to the legacy of the violence of war and genocide with a very ambitious programme of accountability mechanisms that aimed to seek out and bring to justice every perpetrator. These accountability processes have undeniably had some positive impact on Rwanda's recovery and reconstruction, and they have arguably had important short-term benefits. Impunity for gross human rights has been challenged in Rwanda for the first time in its history. Rwandan society has been compelled to confront some aspects of its past violence. The truth about the genocide, if not all previous violence, has been substantially established and documented. A very large number of perpetrators of atrocity have been made to account for their crimes, and victims of the crimes have received some justice. The processes of accountability for atrocity that Rwanda has applied have made a positive contribution to national reconstruction. Law and order have been re-established, and some degree of peaceful coexistence between Rwanda's divided communities has been achieved, partly as a result of these mechanisms.

The long-term impact of the accountability processes undertaken by Rwanda is less certain. Reconciliation and the promotion of peace in post-conflict situations are not the exclusive responsibility of the justice system. If other government policies foster injustice and divisiveness, the best court system in the world will not lead to reconciliation (Organisation of African Unity 2000). Rwanda's socio-political situation still manifests a wide range of obstacles to reconciliation and peace (Cooke 2011). Impunity remains entrenched. The state of the rule of law remains a matter of grave concern. Instead of progressing towards being a more open, democratic and inclusive society, the country has instead drifted towards more stringent authoritarianism. Rwandan society has not had any open debate about the violence of the past that addresses the grievances of all victims. The government has unilaterally imposed its own version of the history of the conflict. This version focuses exclusively on anti-Tutsi violence in general and the genocide in particular and does not reflect the experiences of a very significant part, if not the majority, of Rwandan society, particularly from the Hutu community. The country's accountability processes have been one-sided. They have been selective and partisan, investigating and prosecuting only the genocide and overlooking human rights violations that were committed by the victors. Rwandan society remains deeply divided along ethnic lines. As a result of the situation that prevails in the country, Rwanda's ambitious accountability processes have had some fundamental shortcomings (Drumbl 2002b: p. 11). These processes have not been able to achieve their long-term, transformational objectives because the country has not yet satisfactorily addressed the root causes of its conflict. Rwanda cannot have effective transitional justice processes without making progress towards democracy (Sarkin 2000: p. 121, 2001: p. 169–70; Oomen 2006: p. 20). The contribution of Rwanda's accountability processes promoting the long-term utilitarian goal of mitigating the risk of future violence and bloodshed remains doubtful (Drumbl 2002b: p. 11).

10 Tentative Lessons from Rwanda's Mechanisms of Accountability for Atrocity

10.1 Introduction

This chapter discusses the implications of Rwanda's accountability processes for the field of transitional justice. It argues that Rwanda's transitional justice processes are of significant importance for the field of transitional justice in general, and for societies that are dealing or may have to deal with legacies of mass violence involving large-scale popular participation in atrocity in particular. The chapter discusses the critical question as to whether the conventional orthodoxy of the fields of transitional justice and human rights that assumes or indeed advocates that all serious human rights violations have to be prosecuted applies to situations of mass violence involving large-scale popular participation. The chapter simultaneously seeks to identify the lessons that Rwanda's transitional justice experiences offer about the role and limitations of alternative mechanisms of accountability, especially conflict resolution mechanisms based on customary law and tradition, and reparation programmes in addressing legacies of mass atrocity. Lastly, it discusses the lessons that the experience of Rwanda's transitional justice mechanisms offer on the links between transitional justice and political transition, the impact of international relations on the effectiveness of transitional justice processes, and the connection between the concept of the responsibility to protect and the legitimacy of transitional justice mechanisms, especially international criminal justice.

10.2 Relevance of Rwanda's Accountability Processes to the Field of Transitional Justice

Each conflict or post-conflict society's choices as to how it should deal with a history of past human rights violations are shaped by its own particular circumstances. Transitional justice processes are part and parcel of processes of state building and peace building after violent conflict. The challenges facing societies emerging from violent conflict differ from country to country. Consequently, strategies for national reconstruction and development in the aftermath of violent conflict must necessarily vary from country to country.

There cannot be standard responses to legacies of past human rights abuses: legal responses to mass atrocity must be contextual (Sarkin 2001: p. 148; Borocan 2004; United Nations 2004: para. 19). Judicial responses to legacies of mass atrocity depend on events of the past, the obstacles of the present and the future needs of society (Sarkin 2000: p. 116). The modalities of securing accountability for past human rights violations, encouraging reconciliation and healing, and ensuring sustainable peace and development should vary depending on the circumstances of each situation (Drumbl 2002b: p. 7). Nevertheless, the state-building and peace-building experiences of one society may have important lessons for other conflict and post-conflict situations.

Rwanda's accountability processes, like transitional justice processes in other conflict situations, have been shaped by events of the past, and the social and political conditions that have prevailed in the country in the aftermath of the violence of the 1990s. The factors that have shaped the policies and processes with which Rwanda has responded to the legacy of that violence include the country's long history of impunity for gross human rights abuses, the brutality, scale and consequences of the genocide, the high level of popular participation in atrocities and the manner in which the armed conflict of the 1990s came to an end. Above all, the government's policy responses to the legacy of violence of the 1990s were influenced by the overarching objective of creating an enabling environment for national recovery, reconstruction and development. The military defeat of the forces responsible for the genocide and the rise to power of a government dominated by the victims ensured that justice for the genocide would not only be possible but was inevitable (Graybill and Lanegran 2004: p. 8). The military victory of the RPF also enabled the post-genocide government to have almost total discretion in determining its policies relating to the reconstruction of the country, including accountability for atrocity (Sarkin 2001).

Accountability for genocide was a key pillar of the government's reconstruction programme, seen as a prerequisite for the restoration of order, for reconciliation and for the future stability of the country and its successful reconstruction and development. From the beginning, criminal prosecutions emerged as the preferred mechanism of accountability. In light of the violence of the genocide, it was not politically feasible at the time to advocate, let alone adopt, exclusively restorative approaches to justice for the violence that genocide victims had suffered. Survivors were demanding justice according to the laws of the land. The government's ability to provide justice for the violence of the genocide had strong implications for its own legitimacy. The post-genocide government was compelled by circumstances to pursue an approach that would aim for universal accountability for all crimes that were committed in the context of the genocide through the ordinary criminal justice system.

At the same time, the same circumstances (especially the high level of popular participation in atrocity) dictated that the government explore ways of tempering the rigour of the law and of dealing with the vast majority of the perpetrators more leniently than the strict letter of the law required. If the government's main concern in the immediate aftermath of the genocide was to reassure survivors, the priority, as the country stabilized, became to enhance its legitimacy in the perception of the wider (majority Hutu) population. The government's initial approach to accountability, premised on universal individual accountability in a strictly criminal justice setting, had alienated much of the country's population. The government adopted Gacaca as the principal mechanism of accountability for genocide, in part to address this alienation. The adoption of Gacaca signified the beginning of a progressively more restorative approach to justice for the genocide. Gacaca has sought to achieve objectives of both individual criminal accountability and restoration.

Rwanda's transitional justice processes have drawn the field of transitional justice into uncharted waters. As a result of the policy of pursuing universal accountability for atrocities that involved large-scale popular participation, Rwanda has carried out what is arguably the most ambitious effort any society has ever undertaken to ensure accountability for atrocity (Drumbl 2002a). The country's efforts to ensure effective individual accountability for all crimes that were committed in the context of mass atrocity are unprecedented. Rwanda could not achieve the goal of universal accountability through prosecutions by the ordinary criminal justice system, and so introduced Gacaca, a mechanism premised on popular participation in dispensing justice that blends retributive and restorative justice objectives, to the field of transitional justice. Rwanda's experiment of transforming a conflict resolution mechanism, based on customary law and traditional practices and designed as an instrument of restorative justice, into a criminal court with jurisdiction to try and punish serious violations of human rights law and international humanitarian law, has been a groundbreaking development in transitional justice.

Rwanda's attempts to reckon with the legacy of the genocide have thus pushed the limits of the existing theoretical framework on how societies should reckon with legacies of past violence. The country's innovations in the field of transitional justice have been applauded and criticized in equal measure (Waldorf 2006b; Clark 2010). The vigorous debates about the merits and legacies of Rwanda's accountability processes raise important questions for transitional justice scholarship. How should a society that has experienced mass atrocity involving large-scale popular participation reckon with the legacy of such violence? Is it desirable or appropriate to try and punish all perpetrators who participated in mass atrocity involving large-scale popular participation? Are prosecutions alone an adequate legal response to a legacy of mass atrocity? Does universal accountability for mass atrocity involving large-scale popular participation help or hinder the advancement of the objectives of transitional justice? Is it necessary, in dealing with a legacy of mass atrocity, to consider alternatives to criminal prosecutions? What are the options of such alternatives? Are traditional justice processes of conflict resolution viable forms of transitional justice? To what extent should such alternative mechanisms of accountability be bound by international human rights norms? All these are issues that Rwanda has grappled with and they are of critical relevance to the field of transitional justice.

10.3 Lessons from Rwanda's Accountability Processes

It is too early yet to tell what the long-term impact of the accountability processes with which Rwanda has attempted to deal with the legacy of the war and genocide of the 1990s on Rwandan society will be. It is possible nonetheless to discern some tentative lessons to date from the experience of implementing these processes. With the caveat that responses to each conflict situation must necessarily be contextual, the following remarks explore the tentative lessons or insights that other societies dealing with legacies of mass atrocity may draw from Rwanda's experience.

10.3.1 Criminal prosecutions in the context of mass atrocity

The Rwanda genocide was unique in the extent to which large numbers of ordinary citizens participated in committing atrocity (Waldorf 2006b: p. 12; Straus 2007). Rwanda initially responded to the genocide with a policy that relied exclusively on criminal prosecutions that aimed to identify, prosecute and punish each and every perpetrator through the ordinary criminal justice system (Schabas 2005a: pp. 880–6; Burnet 2009: p. 174). This attempt to attain universal accountability through indiscriminate criminal prosecutions of all perpetrators in the ordinary criminal justice system ultimately proved unworkable. The country resorted to Gacaca, a system of courts manned by lay people, to achieve its goal of universal accountability. Rwanda's processes of accountability have provided the first opportunity to test the relevance of the theoretical framework of transitional justice to situations of mass atrocity involving large-scale popular participation.

Rwanda's Gacaca courts have tried cases of almost two million genocide suspects. The accountability processes that the country has implemented have helped Rwandan society to achieve some important short-term objectives (such as restoring order, establishing some truth about the genocide, identifying and holding many perpetrators accountable, and stabilizing the country). These processes have, however, been less effective in achieving some fundamental objectives of transitional justice, such as ending impunity, reconciliation, consolidating peace and advancing democracy and the rule of law. The mechanisms have failed to provide justice for victims of crimes that were committed by the victors. The historical record of the Rwanda conflict that the processes have established is highly contested in Rwandan society. The Hutu population generally has little confidence in the processes and perceive them as exemplars of victor's justice. Even victims of the genocide remain deeply ambivalent about the country's transitional justice processes.

Many survivors of the genocide perceive Gacaca in particular as disguised amnesty, of which they disapprove. Reconciliation remains an aspiration yet to be achieved. Rwandan society remains as deeply divided along ethnic lines, and some Rwandans and scholars of Rwanda share the opinion that the prospect of fresh violent conflict is very real (Waldorf 2004: p. 138; Haile 2008: p. 50; Silva-Leander 2008: p. 1616; Kayumba et al., 2010). Rwanda's transitional justice processes indicate that criminal prosecutions of mass atrocity can be politically destabilizing and socially divisive (Office of the President of the Republic of Rwanda 1995).

The post-genocide government has been criticized by advocates of restorative justice for not having opted for a restorative justice approach to the legacy of the genocide (Drumbl 2000a, 2000b). Critics of Rwanda's reliance on criminal justice processes in its attempts to reckon with the genocide's legacy do not realize the intensity of yearnings for justice in the aftermath of the mass atrocity (African Rights 2000: p. 91; Oomen 2006: p. 13). Rwanda's experience demonstrates that unless perpetrators of atrocity remain in power or retain strong political influence, the transitional justice processes of a society that has experienced mass atrocity must ideally involve the investigation and prosecution of at least the perpetrators who bear the greatest responsibility and, if possible, other perpetrators. In such situations, accountability for atrocity is not just a fulfilment of legal obligations, it is also a social and political imperative, regardless of the legal and material constraints. Exclusive reliance on processes that do not promise the trial and punishment of perpetrators is not a viable option in such situations. Accountability mechanisms such as a truth commission, which some urged Rwanda to consider as an alternative to criminal prosecutions (Sarkin 2000, 2001), are not alone adequate for meeting the demands for justice of traumatized victims of atrocities. Retributive justice is an indispensable part of responses to legacies of atrocity.

However, the experience of Rwanda's accountability processes also suggests that the application of conventional transitional justice and human rights orthodoxy, which argues that all serious human rights violations have to be investigated, prosecuted and punished in a court of law, must be questioned where the situation involves mass atrocity with large-scale popular participation. Rwanda's transitional justice experience has demonstrated the limits of a maximal approach to accountability for mass atrocity that seeks to identify, try and punish all. Even critics of Rwanda's transitional justice processes agree that no government could possibly render justice for mass atrocity on the scale of the Rwandan genocide (Waldorf 2006b: p. 30). While the existing transitional justice practice framework provides guidance for policy making on how societies that have experienced grave human rights violations can reckon with the violence of their past, situations of mass atrocity involving large-scale popular participation require a unique approach. Criminal prosecutions alone are not an adequate or appropriate response to mass atrocity, especially mass atrocity involving large-scale popular participation. No judicial system is designed to handle mass atrocity in which large numbers of people have participated (Sarkin 1999a; Drumbl 2000a: p. 291). No judicial system, let alone a judicial system of a poor country recovering from the devastation of war and years of repression and authoritarian rule, would ever be able to handle litigation relating to mass atrocity in which large numbers of citizens have participated.

Rwanda's transitional justice processes have shown that attempts to achieve universal accountability for mass atrocity involving large-scale popular participation through criminal trials (by ordinary courts or alternative mechanisms such as Gacaca) may in fact hinder rather than advance attainment of the long-term goals of transitional justice, including building a culture of respect for human rights, reconciliation, stability and peace. Some argue that such prosecutions may exacerbate existing divisions and destabilize a fragile society even further (Tiemessen 2004). An attempt to try and punish all persons who have participated in mass atrocity in which large numbers of people have taken part will almost inevitably result in widespread human rights abuses (Le Mon 2007: p. 17). Unfair trials deepen cleavages rather than promote prospects for reconciliation between parties in conflict and are detrimental to peace building. Attempts to investigate, prosecute and punish every crime committed in the course of mass atrocity may enhance social polarization rather than social harmony, healing or peace, as Rwanda's experience has demonstrated.

Rwanda's transitional justice processes point to the need for societies that have experienced mass atrocity involving large-scale popular participation to proceed with caution in determining the extent to which they should rely on criminal prosecutions to address legacies of past violence. Since it may not be possible, or even advisable or desirable, to respond to mass atrocity by prosecuting all perpetrators, societies which have experienced mass atrocity (particularly atrocity in which large numbers of people have participated) must necessarily make difficult choices as to what proportion of perpetrators should be prosecuted and what proportion should be dealt with by alternative processes of accountability (Wolters 2005a; Le Mon 2007: p. 16).

Rwanda's experience of domestic prosecutions and trials by Gacaca also strongly suggests that post-conflict societies reckoning with legacies of large-scale popular participation in atrocities should endeavour to respect universal human rights norms. Such societies should undertake criminal prosecutions of perpetrators only to the extent that prosecutions safeguard the rights of both the accused and victims. The response to the challenge of accountability for mass atrocity should never be to disregard the rights of persons suspected of being perpetrators. Such disregard for human rights only leads to a cycle of human rights abuses that further undermine the legitimacy of transitional justice processes and the attainment of goals such as eradicating impunity, establishing the rule of law, promoting reconciliation and ensuring peace and stability. Ideally, a prosecutorial strategy should prioritize prosecutions of those most responsible for mass atrocities, firstly, because they bear greater responsibility for planning, inciting and directing the atrocities and, secondly, because they are few in number and cases can be investigated and tried in a timely and fair manner.

10.3.2 Non-prosecutorial mechanisms of accountability for atrocity

Prosecutions can serve certain important functions: they can set standards, implement principles, create precedents and stigmatize misfeasors (Drumbl 2002b: p. 6). It is often argued that prosecutions of gross human rights abuses may be useful in discouraging future human rights abuses, curtailing vigilantism and fostering respect for the rule of law and the new democratic order (Scharf and Rodley 2002: pp. 89–90). Prosecutions respond to the duty of states under international law to prosecute and punish or to extradite persons responsible for atrocity. However, as indicated in the preceding section, fair prosecutions aiming at universal accountability for crimes of mass atrocity involving large-scale popular participation are neither practically feasible nor likely to achieve the goals of transitional justice.

One of the lessons learned from the experience of Rwanda's transitional justice processes is that universal accountability for mass atrocity involving large scale popular participation is neither feasible nor helpful in promoting the long-term goals of transitional justice. The implication of this lesson is that the most appropriate policy response to such a legacy is a blend of responses from within and beyond criminal justice. Societies which have experienced mass atrocity (particularly mass atrocity in which large numbers of citizens have participated) need to devise non-prosecutorial mechanisms to complement criminal prosecutions (Drumbl 2002b: pp. 9–10; Strain and Keyes 2003: p. 132; Fink 2005). These non-prosecutorial mechanisms may include, but are not limited to, truth commissions, public inquiries, traditional justice mechanisms, reparations, amnesties, purges, lustration and mediation (Drumbl 2002b: pp. 9–10). In considering possible responses to situations of mass atrocity involving large-scale popular participation, alternatives to criminal prosecutions are not an option, but an absolute necessity. Ideally, these alternative mechanisms should aim to be restorative in nature (Drumbl 2002b: pp. 9–10).

Traditional justice and mass atrocity

Rwanda's Gacaca have provided an opportunity for transitional justice to explore the potential of traditional justice institutions as mechanisms of accountability for gross human rights abuses. Rwanda's implementation of Gacaca has shown that traditional justice mechanisms have both strengths and weaknesses. Gacaca has demonstrated that tradition-based practices as tools of transitional justice enhance access to justice. They have potential to contribute positively to establishing the truth. They provide a degree of accountability. They may, subject to certain conditions, contribute to reconciliation.

However, Gacaca has also shown that traditional justice systems also have certain disadvantages and carry certain risks as mechanisms of accountability for atrocity, especially atrocity involving large-scale popular participation. The conditions that make traditional justice mechanisms effective in their natural setting, such as a sense of community, social cohesion and the existence of governance systems that enjoy broad community support, may no longer exist after violent conflict (Waldorf 2006b: p. 31). War, genocide and oppression have a devastating impact on social capital, on community relations and on the legitimacy of traditional leaders and their capacities to perform justice and reconciliation rituals (Huyse 2008: p. 189). Traditional justice mechanisms are as likely to protect certain crimes or certain perpetrators from accountability and reparations as the formal justice system does, as Gacaca's lack of authority to deal with abuses alleged to have been committed by the RPA has demonstrated (Huyse 2008: p. 184). Where traditional justice mechanisms have a retributive justice element (such as the power to impose sentences of imprisonment for many years), they may not be very effective in unearthing the truth. They may also lead to even more intense social polarization andendanger the safety of victims and witnesses. Traditional justice mechanisms also run the risk of capture and manipulation by state and bureaucrats, which reduces their legitimacy. The above and other shortcomings limit thecapacity of traditional justice mechanisms to promote some of the major goals of transitional justice, such as the healing of survivors, promoting social harmony, advancing reconciliation and preventing new conflict. Traditional accountability processes are ideally suited to serving as instruments of restorative justice, complementing the ordinary criminal justice system, and other accountability processes that might be adopted. They are unlikely to be satisfactory as stand-alone accountability processes for mass atrocity as Gacaca has demonstrated.

Traditional justice systems are, by their nature, designed to deal with small numbers of cases of wrongdoing. They, like the formal justice system, are not effective in situations where large numbers of citizens have participated in committing atrocities. Traditional systems of justice do not meet basic human rights standards relating to fair trial. They lack effective regulation and supervision and have few effective safeguards against abuses (Grenfell 2006: p. 320). They are thus likely to lead to serious human rights violations when they are granted the extensive powers that ordinary criminal courts have, as has been the case in Rwanda.

Rwanda's Gacaca have generated a very heated debate about whether transitional justice processes based on customary law or traditional practices should, in exercising functions of a judicial nature, be required to comply with universal human rights norms. Rwanda's transitional justice experiences have demonstrated that the argument of scholars and commentators such as Clark (2010) that traditional or neo-traditional mechanisms of conflict resolution such as Gacaca can exercise functions of a judicial nature, judging crimes involving very serious violations of human rights, and still be exempt from compliance with universal human standards is inconsistent with scholarship on transitional justice, human rights and peace building and at variance with the needs of post-conflict societies. While restorative justice mechanisms have a legitimate role in transitional justice, they should not be attributed criminal justice functions where it is not possible to ensure respect for human rights norms, especially the right to fair trial. Unfair trials undermine post-conflict peacebuilding in general and transitional justice in particular.

I recognize that Gacaca could never have been able to comply fully with all the legal requirements of the right to a fair trial. I also acknowledge that Gacaca had the potential to play a useful role in advancing the goals of transitional justice in the aftermath of the violence that Rwanda experienced. However, I believe that it was not appropriate to give Gacaca the full range of powers that criminal justice courts have. Gacaca should, in my opinion, have served as a kind of decentralized truth commission without the powers of criminal courts to sentence suspects to long terms of imprisonment. The powers of prosecution and punishment should have been left to the ordinary courts, that would try only as many cases (mainly of persons who bore great responsibility for the crimes that were committed) as they could try fairly. Gacaca should only have had jurisdiction for crimes that were committed by the rank and file and its jurisdiction should have been limited to the power to award reparations or community service. The decisions of Gacaca courts should also have been open to review by the ordinary courts.

Reparation

The processes of accountability undertaken by Rwanda have highlighted the complexity of and raised difficult questions about the question of reparations in the context of mass atrocity. What reparation programmes are appropriate in situations of mass atrocity where the numbers of victims, survivors and perpetrators are very large? What is the right balance between meeting reparation obligations and development programming? How does a society manage the unavoidable conflict that arises when victims pursue claims for compensation for abuses in which so many of their fellow citizens have participated? How does a society avoid or mitigate such tensions? What role should the state have in facilitating resolution of the conflicts?

Rwanda's transitional justice experiences have demonstrated the complexity of the challenges of designing reparation policies to address legacies of mass atrocity.

The Rwanda government adamantly refuses to acknowledge the suffering of victims of crimes attributed to the RPA. In failing to acknowledge the occurrence of these crimes, the government has denied justice, including reparation, to a significant proportion of the population. As a result of the large-scale popular participation in the genocide, the numbers of victims and survivors has been very large. While the government acknowledges legal responsibility for the genocide, it has (due to financial constraints) disavowed its obligation to pay compensation to its victims, agreeing only to provide assistance to the needy survivors of the genocide. The government's failure to provide reparation in material form, namely restitution and compensation, to both victims of the genocide and of the crimes attributed to the victors has undermined the legitimacy of the accountability processes the country has undertaken and their effectiveness in promoting the healing of victims and the restoration of sound relations between victims and perpetrators and their families. Meanwhile, genocide victims' pursuit of compensation from individual perpetrators has become politicized. Opponents of the government argue that awards made by Gacaca courts (to compensate victims for material losses) are a deliberate attempt by the government to render the Hutu community destitute.[1] Rwanda has failed to find a blend of reparation policies and programmes that satisfy the material and psychological needs of all victims of the violence of the 1990s (Rombouts and Vandegiste 2005; Waldorf 2009; REDRESS/African Rights 2011). The Rwanda government's policies on reparations have contributed significantly to disillusionment on the part of genocide survivors and resentment on the part of the Hutu community towards all of Rwanda's transitional justice processes.

The experience of Rwanda's accountability mechanisms strongly suggest that reparation ought to be a critical component of every process of reckoning with the violence of the past. Rwanda is the first situation where transitional justice mechanisms have had to grapple with the complex issues relating to reparation for mass atrocity involving large-scale popular participation. The design of reparation programmes that satisfy the grievances of all victims in a situation of mass atrocity is an extremely difficult challenge. The lessons from Rwanda's experience suggest that reparation in such contexts is both extremely delicate and complex. While reparation can play a critical role in promoting the healing of victims, the application of laws on torts to mass atrocity in which there has been large-scale popular participation has the potential to renew or deepen cleavages between individuals, groups and communities that have previously been in conflict. Societies that have experienced mass violence need to place the issue of reparation at the centre of the design of their transitional justice processes (De Greiff 2006). In order to reduce or avoid tensions between individuals and communities that have been in conflict over reparations, the state should ideally assume responsibility for compensation due to all victims of mass atrocity. Assets of perpetrators that are necessary for their livelihood such as farming land and homes should not be subject to attachment, except where the perpetrators are wealthy individuals. As compensation by the state for human rights violations committed in the context of mass atrocity will inevitably always be limited by lack of resources, reparation programmes should give priority to meeting the needs of the most vulnerable among victims, such as children, widows and the poor. While some symbolic compensation to survivors is desirable, reparation programs addressing legacies of mass atrocity should prioritize community wide, instead of individual needs.

10.3.3 International criminal justice

The field of international criminal justice as we know it today was in its infancy at the time of the Rwanda genocide (Schabas 2005a: p. 89). The RPF called for the establishment of an international criminal court to try the organizers of the genocide while the genocide was still underway. The government that assumed power at the end of the genocide reiterated the call (albeit under pressure from the international community) after it assumed office in July 1994. However, no one (in Rwanda or elsewhere) had any idea as to how this new experiment in international criminal justice would work out over time. Indeed, the general sentiment about prospects of both the Rwanda and former Yugoslavia tribunals was one of scepticism (Zacklin 2004). Expectations within the Rwanda government about the potential of the proposed tribunal were modest (United Nations 1994j: Statement of the Permanent Representative of Rwanda).

The United Nations ad hoc tribunals are nearing the very end of their respective mandates and debate about the legacies of the two institutions is already underway. The two tribunals have been the subjects of severe criticism (Schabas 2006: pp. 30–1). International criminal justice has often been derided by some as tokenism, as processes undertaken to cover up for the failures of the international community to prevent or stop atrocity (Mutua 2002; Zacklin 2004). In Africa, international criminal justice is now widely criticized as a form of judicial imperialism, and portrayed as a hegemonic tool of Western powers that is invoked in a selective and discriminatory manner to target leaders of governments (du Plessis 2010).

The above criticism notwithstanding, it can be argued that the ad hoc United Nations tribunals have substantially performed their respective mandates. In the case of Rwanda, the ICTR has successfully apprehended, prosecuted and punished many of the leaders who bore the greatest responsibility for planning and/or directing the genocide through trials that are generally regarded as credible. The ICTR has established a historical record of the Rwanda genocide that is far less contested than one that domestic courts could ever have hoped to establish.

The ICTR, along with its Yugoslav counterpart, has contributed to the emergence of international criminal justice as a major component of the strategies and mechanisms that the international community has developed for the purpose of fighting impunity, promoting respect for human rights and promoting global peace and security. International criminal justice may, in some situations, provide the only opportunity to bring perpetrators of atrocity to justice. In deeply divided societies, international criminal justice is preferable to trials by national institutions because foreign judges are better positioned to judge cases impartially and without bias (Cassese 1998). The two tribunals have demonstrated that international human rights law and international humanitarian law are not just a set of abstract legal principles, but bodies of laws that are capable of effective enforcement and viable tools in the fight against impunity. Whereas the ideal response to gross human rights abuses committed during conflict should be to investigate, prosecute and punish the abuses in national courts, the ICTR and ICTY have demonstrated that international criminal justice can play a critical role in ensuring accountability for gross human rights abuses that would otherwise almost certainly have gone unpunished. The work of the two tribunals offers lessons about the potential of international criminal justice to contribute to fighting impunity in the years and decades ahead.

However, the experiences of the ICTR and ICTY have also demonstrated the inherent shortcomings of the system of international criminal justice that the international community has devised to deal with legacies of violent conflict across the world. The experience of the two tribunals has taught us that international criminal justice mechanisms do not afford a sense of ownership of their processes to the societies that they are established to help. They depend unduly on state cooperation, and are impotent in the face of recalcitrant governments. These mechanisms are eager to take action against weak parties to or losers of armed conflicts, but are unlikely to pursue perpetrators of atrocity who come to or remain in power after conflict in the absence of strong diplomatic support from the major powers of the West. These judicial institutions are vulnerable to external manipulation, and are often driven to make selective and partisan decisions and choices, depending on how the major Western powers that fund and control them choose to use their power and influence to shape their agendas. Until the establishment of the ICC, the management of international criminal courts was not accountable to any outside body or subject to any independent oversight, with the result that there was no mechanism for seeking redress when these institutions make politically motivated choices and decisions, as the ICTR prosecutor has done in relation to crimes attributed to the RPA.

Of the states that the jurisdiction of the ad hoc United Nations tribunals covered, Rwanda was undoubtedly the most vocal in its criticism of international criminal justice mechanisms. Aspects of Rwanda's criticism of the system of international criminal justice as it was during the late 1990s (such as the lack of national ownership and the absence of a framework for including victims in the tribunal's work) were directly addressed during the formulation of the Rome Treaty of the ICC. However, other shortcomings of international criminal justice that the work of the ad hoc tribunals exposed are yet to be adequately addressed. The most critical of these residual shortcomings especially include the question of dealing with the crimes of perpetrators of international crimes who come to or remain in power after the end of armed conflict.

10.3.4 Addressing human rights violations attributable to the victors

The RPF has dominated Rwanda's political system since its ascension to power in 1994. The rationale for the RPF's claim of political legitimacy and entitlement to domination of political power has largely been founded on the heroic role that the RPA played in stopping the genocide. However, it is contended that the RPA was itself responsible for serious human rights violations during and after the genocide. Rwanda's domestic justice system has not seriously addressed allegations of human rights violations attributed to the RPA. Neither Gacaca nor the ordinary civilian justice system have jurisdiction to investigate and prosecute the alleged offences. Jurisdiction for crimes committed by members of the military is exclusively reserved to the military justice system.[2] Rwanda's military justice system has failed to investigate and prosecute the rights violations alleged to have been committed by members of the RPA during and after 1994 (Human Rights Watch 2008).

Rwanda's accountability processes have demonstrated the complexity of the problem of addressing human rights violations attributable to perpetrators who remain or come to power at the end of conflict. Ensuring such accountability poses challenges for both national as well as international justice mechanisms. The approach of the Rwanda government to the issue of accountability for human rights abuses attributable to the RPA is neither unique nor unexpected. Governments the world over, including in established democracies, go to great lengths to protect their military from the risk of criminal prosecutions for human rights abuses committed during conflict.[3] Rwanda's transitional justice experience demonstrates that national mechanisms of accountability (whether formal or informal) are unlikely to ever be effective in addressing the crimes of the victors. Accountability mechanisms in situations where perpetrators have come to (or retain power) as a result of military victory (or a negotiated settlement) are more likely than not to focus exclusively on the crimes of the losers and invariably end up as victor's justice. The weaknesses of national judicial mechanisms in addressing the crimes of the victors make a compelling case for international criminal justice to try such crimes where the states whose officers are responsible for the crimes are unable or unwilling to act against the perpetrators in good faith.

The experience of the United Nations ad hoc tribunals in general, and of the ICTR in particular, suggests that the architecture of international criminal justice mechanisms that the community of nations has crafted to ensure accountability for egregious human rights abuses weak capacity to investigate and prosecute human rights abuses that were committed by perpetrators who remain or come to power after conflict (Peskin 2008). International criminal justice institutions rely on state cooperation and support for their effective functioning. These tribunals are often powerless to undertake investigations and prosecutions contested by successor regimes in the absence of strong diplomatic support from the major (usually Western) powers. This dependence on state cooperation and diplomatic support sometimes constrains the independence of the institutions, as the ICTR's decision to forego the investigation and prosecution of allegations of human rights abuses that are alleged to have been committed by the RPA clearly demonstrates.

The Office of the Prosecutor failed in its obligations to investigate and prosecute human rights violations attributed to the victors. The claims by successive prosecutors of the ICTR that they could only investigate the crimes attributed to the RPA with the help of the Rwanda government is both absurd and factually incorrect. The rationale for the exercise of international jurisdiction is that the sitting government is unable or unwilling to investigate and prosecute crimes attributed to its members in good faith. The lesson to be drawn from the ICTR's handling of the crimes attributed to the RPA is that international criminal tribunals are unlikely to secure the smooth cooperation of states required to investigate and prosecute crimes of perpetrators who remain in power. It is likely that the victors in a post-conflict context will only be brought to justice where international tribunals benefit from the concerted support of major powers, and the regime under scrutiny has compelling reasons (economic, security, diplomatic or other) to cooperate with the international community in bringing some of its own members to justice.

Because of their weak capacity to take on cases against the victors, international criminal tribunals may in some cases help sitting governments to consolidate their power and to stigmatize political opponents, while shielding their own illiberal practices from scrutiny, as has been the case in Rwanda (Drumbl 2009). The weak capacity of international criminal justice mechanisms to pursue abuses by perpetrators who remain in power will be the principal challenge of the permanent International Criminal Court. Strategies are required to enhance the effectiveness of international criminal justice mechanisms against perpetrators who remain in power. In practice, most governments are loath to openly support, let alone actively facilitate, measures to hold perpetrators who remain in power accountable for their crimes. The emerging system of international criminal justice will have to rely on advocacy by civil society to pressure governments to provide the support and assistance that international criminal tribunals need to investigate and prosecute crimes by perpetrators who remain in power.

10.3.5 External stakeholders: what role for foreign governments and transitional justice in post-conflict societies?

The experience of Rwanda's accountability processes has provided some insight into the factors that shape and determine the effectiveness of transitional justice mechanisms. One of the factors that have emerged as a significant contributor to the effectiveness (or weaknesses) of transitional justice mechanisms is the policies of foreign stakeholders, particularly the governments of the major world powers. There is a link between international relations and transitional justice processes. Foreign governments have the power to, and often do, influence (negatively or in a positive manner) the course of transitional justice processes of at least some of the states emerging from conflict or authoritarian rule. The choices that foreign governments make as to whether or not to support improvements in human rights practices or political reforms, in general, in a particular post-conflict setting may have a strong bearing on whether societies in trasition stay on an old and familiar path (of unaccountable government, repression and authoritarian rule) or make a break with the past and opt for genuine democracy, the rule of law and respect for human rights. Policies of foreign governments may also determine the extent to which international criminal justice institutions are able to perform some aspects of their mandates effectively. International tribunals depend on states for financing and for cooperation to enable them to carry out investigations, to get access to witnesses and evidence, and to secure custody of suspects. Governments heavily influence the functioning of the international criminal justice system through funding arrangements, calibrating the provision or withholding of cooperation, and through the exercise of diplomacy behind the scenes to promote their strategic interests.

Rwanda's history before, during and after the genocide illustrates these strong links between international relations and domestic human rights practices and accountability processes. Rwanda has a long history of impunity for gross human rights violations. Needless to say, primary responsibility for this impunity lies with the leadership of the country's successive governments. However, foreign powers, organizations and individuals have contributed to the development of this phenomenon as well. The origins of the impunity can be traced to the 1959 'revolution'. The 'revolution' was orchestrated by the Belgian colonial administration (Harroy 1984) and actively supported by foreign clergy of the Catholic Church (Lemarchand 1970). The 'revolution' led to the overthrow of the Tutsi aristocracy and the installation regime was responsible for widespread human rights abuses directed against the Tutsi community. These events may have claimed around twenty thousand lives and drove hundreds of thousands more into exile (Lemarchand 1970).

Armed attacks against the Kayibanda government by Tutsi insurgents based in neighbouring countries often led to vicious reprisals that claimed the lives of thousands of innocent Tutsis who had remained in the country. When General Juvenal Habyarimana took over power in 1973, the new government promptly arrested, imprisoned without trial and subsequently executed dozens of the leadership of the previous government (Prunier 1995). The Habyarimana regime was also responsible for widespread human rights abuses against members of the Tutsi community, particularly during the 1990–94 war (Africa Watch 1992; Human Rights Watch 1992: Des Forges 1999).

None of the perpetrators of the gross human rights abuses that were committed during the Kayibanda and Habyarimana regimes were ever brought to justice (Ngoga 2009). The atrocities were widely reported in the international media. However, the reporting largely fell on deaf ears in Africa and further afield (Lemarchand 1970). The gross human rights abuses for which the two governments were responsible occurred in the context of the

Cold War. Rwanda was allied to the West and the West generally chose to turn a blind eye to these abuses. Rwanda's 'development partners' in the West chose to go on with business as usual, instead of calling on the government to hold the perpetrators of the atrocities to account. Donors adopted what Uvin has called a policy of voluntary blindness to the politics of prejudice, injustice, exclusion and human rights violations in Rwanda (Uvin 1998: pp. 154–9, 228–34). The human rights record and repressive nature of Rwanda's governments notwithstanding, Rwanda acquired a reputation as a model recipient of international aid (Silva-Leander 2008: p. 1603). Development assistance to Rwanda dramatically increased (Uvin 1998). Rwanda's government and leadership enjoyed very cordial relations with governments of most Western countries, especially France, Belgium and Switzerland. France provided military assistance as well, and even continued to provide such assistance during the war and genocide.

The indifference of the international community to the grave human rights situation in Rwanda continued even after the genocide began. Representatives of the regime responsible for the genocide were welcomed to world capitals. Several countries including France, South Africa, Egypt and China continued to ship arms to the regime even at the height of the genocide (Melvern 2000a).[4] The government was allowed to participate in meetings of international organizations, including the Organisation of African Unity, the United Nations Commission on Human Rights and the UN Security Council, even as the genocide raged. The United Nations Security Council allowed Rwanda's representative to remain on the Council, even as the Council discussed how to respond to the genocide for which the government he represented was responsible. The major powers of the world individually, and the United Nations Security Council collectively, watched as the genocide unfolded and chose to do nothing to stop it or to provide support to its victims. The government of the United States bears particular responsibility for the failure of the international community to provide assistance and prosecutions to those who were threatened by genocide in 1994. The government of the United States not only failed to provide leadership in responding to the genocide, it actively impeded efforts by other countries to find a suitable response to the genocide (Power 2001).

The human rights practices of Rwanda's governments, past and present, have been heavily influenced by the policies, actions and omissions of the governments of Rwanda's major bilateral and multilateral partners. The failure of governments and international organizations to hold successive governments of Rwanda accountable for human rights violations under their watch contributed to the entrenchment of impunity. The failure of the international community to respond to the human rights abuses by regimes that ruled Rwanda prior to 1994 heavily influenced the policies, actions and decisions of the organizers of the genocide. The organizers of the genocide conceived and carried out their plans, confidently believing (on the basis of historical experience) that the international community did not have the political will to intervene to stop the genocide (Power 2001). The decision of the United Nations Security Council to withdraw the United Nations peacekeeping forces from Rwanda at the beginning of the genocide and that of the US government to obstruct any redeployment of United Nations peacekeepers to Rwanda during the genocide, confirmed to the genocide's organizers that the international community would indeed do nothing to stop it. The failure of the international community to prevent or stop the genocide and to disarm and disable those responsible for the genocide from continuing to threaten the security of Rwanda after they were driven to exile has, in turn, heavily influenced the conduct of the military and security forces of Rwanda's post-genocide government.

The leadership of Rwanda's military strongly believes that the international community has neither the moral right nor the political will to hold it or the members of the forces under its command accountable for rights abuses, past or present. This leadership has all along been convinced that if the international community could not mobilize the political will to take action against the organizers of the genocide, it can never summon the political will to confront the RPA and to investigate, prosecute and punish allegations of human rights abuses attributed to it.[5] Policy makers, governments and international institutions with which Rwanda has significant relations have largely avoided confronting the government of Rwanda over domestic repression, exclusion, inequality and other human rights abuses (Straus and Waldorf 2011b: pp. 12, 15). It has been claimed that failure of some major Western countries which have strong influence on Rwanda's government (particularly the United Kingdom and the United States) to hold the leadership of Rwanda's military accountable for human rights violations that were committed by members of the RPA has undermined the effectiveness of both national and international processes of accountability for atrocity (Del Ponte and Sudetic 2009; Reyntjens 2011). As I have elaborated in Chapter 4, there is a sound basis for this claim.

Political reform in societies in transition must necessarily be nationally owned and driven to succeed. However, the international community can play a positive role in supporting and promoting political change. Genocide, mass atrocity and other gross human rights abuses happen by design, as the handiwork of persons who believe that they are above the law for even highly egregious human rights abuses. Policies of foreign governments, in respect to countries going through political transition after violent conflict or authoritarian rule, matter. How the international community relates to the government of a state in transition has implications for the country's human rights practices. Governments in transition after conflict care about the policies of major foreign powers on their human rights practices. The manner in which the international community engages political actors in countries undergoing or recovering from violent conflict involving gross human rights abuses or authoritarian rule sends signals to those actors, signals that either promote greater respect for human rights or encourage continuation of a culture of impunity. The international community (and in particular the governments of the major global powers and economies) have capacity to make a more effective contribution to fighting impunity for gross human rights violations and promoting greater respect for human rights through their diplomacy and other policies (Zorbas 2004: pp. 51–2). The silence of international actors on human rights practices of states prone to human rights abuses, some even argue, can lead to complicity (Oomen 2005: p. 907).

The policies of foreign governments also affect the functioning of the international criminal justice system. For the most part, states have played a positive role in supporting the work of the ad hoc United Nations tribunals. The Rwanda tribunal would, for example, never have been able to investigate and try the large number of important cases that it has tried without the support of the international community in general and the US in particular.[6] Countries such as Kenya, Cameroon and the Democratic Republic of Congo only began to surrender suspects wanted by the tribunal after intense diplomatic pressure. On the other hand, states may and occasionally do (by action or omission) undermine some aspects of the work of the tribunals. For example, the UK and the US have undermined the ICTR's plans to pursue cases against the RPA.[7] The roles that foreign states and international organizations have played explains the differences in the records of the Rwanda and the Yugoslav tribunals in investigating and prosecuting human rights violations that were committed by members of the victorious parties in the Rwanda and Balkan conflicts. The Rwanda tribunal has failed to issue even a single indictment against members of the RPA (Peskin 2008). The Yugoslav tribunal has, on the other hand, succeeded in trying and punishing persons from top echelons of the leadership from all the countries of the former Yugoslavia. What accounts for this difference is that whereas the Yugoslav tribunal has enjoyed the strong backing of the European Union for its actions, the Rwanda tribunal's attempt to investigate and prosecute allegations against the RPA have been undermined by some of the major world powers (Peskin 2005). The role that international relations play in the operation of the international criminal justice system has strong implications for the future of the International Criminal Court.

10.3.6 Accountability for past human rights abuses and political transition

Rwanda has implemented what is in all likelihood the most comprehensive process of accountability for atrocity that any society has ever undertaken. The country's accountability mechanisms have achieved certain important results. As yet it is unclear, however, whether they have helped to secure the ultimate goals of transitional justice: the healing of survivors, social harmony and long-term peace (Huyse 2008: p. 181). In terms of institutional and economic development, Rwanda has made an almost phenomenal recovery from the consequences of war and genocide. Its progress in social and economic reconstruction and development is generally regarded as impressive (Oomen 2005: p. 900; Gahima 2006: pp. 101–4; McDoom 2011). However, Rwanda has failed to transition to a democratic system of government (Nifosi 2005). The government seeks to perpetuate its hold on power through political repression and denying its opponents any opportunity for political participation (Waldorf 2006b: p. 28). Issues that have driven the country's conflict during the past (among them, questions relating to political representation, access to power, access to resources, respect for individual human rights, identity and legitimacy of government) remain unresolved (Oomen 2005: p. 906). The country remains deeply divided along ethnic lines (Sarkin 1999a: p. 800). Accountability processes, including the Rwanda tribunal's trials, are perceived by many as victor's justice (Huyse and Vandegiste 1999; Borocan 2004: p. 370; Tiemessen 2004; Zorbas 2004). The government is adamantly opposed to any kind of negotiation with the opposition on modalities for resolving existing conflict. Rwanda has made relatively little progress towards strengthening democratic political participation since 1994. The absence of democracy has implications for future human rights practices and prospects for peace and stability. Prospects for sectarian violence in the future remain very high (Sarkin 2001: p. 171; Waldorf 2004; Haile 2008: p. 50; Silva-Leander 2008: p. 1616; Kayumba et al., 2010). Consequently, the transitional justice goals of achieving healing and social harmony and deterring new conflict remain elusive.

An evaluation of Rwanda's accountability processes points to links between the fate of political transition and the effectiveness of transitional justice processes. Accountability mechanisms are not an end in themselves. The prosecution and punishment of perpetrators of atrocity does not by itself enhance prospects for the rule of law, reconciliation or durable peace. The experience of Rwanda's accountability mechanisms suggests that transitional justice processes in any post-conflict situation can only succeed in healing victims, achieving reconciliation and improving human rights practices if they are part of a successor regime's wider political agenda for addressing and resolving the fundamental causes of conflict. The potential of transitional justice to promote sustainable peace depends on how well a particular society is able to manage the process of developing policy responses that address the core causes of conflict in a comprehensive manner. Mechanisms of accountability for atrocity have little prospect of helping a post-conflict country to achieve the objectives of transitional justice if they are not part of a wider process of reform that address the fundamental causes of conflict (Huyse 2008: p. 195). Transitional justice instruments and broader governance and democratization challenges are intimately linked (Huyse 2008: p. 194). Progress in building a culture of respect for human rights depends on the degree to which such a society is able to embrace the rule of law. Building a genuinely democratic culture offers the only long-term solution to the challenge of protecting human rights, preventing conflict and sustaining peace.

Democracy, at least in the sense of governance arrangements that are inclusive and fair (Huyse and Vandegiste 1999) and the rule of law are prerequisites for genuine national reconciliation (Sarkin 2001: p. 822). A society cannot deal with the legacy of its violent past in a comprehensive manner in the absence of democracy (Sarkin 1999a: p. 822, 2000: p. 116). Rwanda still has some way to go in meeting that test.

*10.3.7 **Responsibility to protect***

> There ... are not many ideas that have the potential to matter for more good, not only in theory but practice, than that of the responsibility to protect. (Evans 2008: p. 7)

The Rwanda genocide will always represent a singular failure on the part of international institutions and mechanisms responsible for protecting human rights and maintaining international peace and security (United Nations 1999a; Melvern 2000a). As Huyse has remarked, when an authoritarian regime collapses, large sections of the population cry out loudly for severe punishment of those who bear responsibility for the crimes of the past (Huyse 1995: p. 123). As Elizabeth Neuffer wrote before her untimely passing, 'there is an innate human need for some kind of reckoning, an accounting' (2001: p. xiv). Justice aims to right the wrongs that have been done against victims. Justice, the theory goes, leads to closure and healing. Assuming it were practically possible and politically expedient to investigate, prosecute and punish each and every crime committed in a campaign of genocide or other mass atrocity, could accountability processes be adequate to meet the needs of victims? Could justice ever come anywhere close to restoring victims of genocide and mass atrocity to the situation that they would have been in but for the events of their victimization? Can justice ever put right the harm that victims of atrocities have been subjected to? Is it possible for individuals and societies who experienced genocide and other atrocities to reach closure and healing as a result of judicial processes? Of how much value can justice be, when it comes too late to make a difference for populations under threat, as it did for the victims of genocide in Rwanda?

One of the major shortcomings of processes of accountability as tools for promoting respect for human rights and combating impunity is that the processes only become available long after violence has taken its toll and caused irreparable damage. My own personal experience in dealing with victims of genocide during the course of investigations and prosecutions of genocide cases has left little doubt that no form of justice can ever be adequate to make up for the suffering and loss of such victims. Accountability mechanisms are not futile but can never undo or sufficiently compensate the harm that is visited upon victims of mass atrocity. Justice comes too late for innocent lives forever obliterated from existence. For survivors, living with the memory of their experiences involves pain neither time nor justice can heal. That much, at least, I have come to learn from my contact with the survivors I met and worked with in the course of my work as a war prosecutor. How would justice bring closure to a lone survivor, three or four generations of whose relatives have perished? How meaningful can justice be for victims who survive but are condemned to physical and psychological wounds that last for the rest of their lives? What kind of justice would be sufficient to satisfy victims of sexual violence who have been infected with HIV/AIDS as a result of rape, and are condemned to a slow and painful death, daily reliving the pain, humiliation and dehumanization to which they were subjected?

It is doubtful, if not obvious, that justice cannot ever completely heal the pain, or ever bring a sense of real satisfaction to the lives of genocide victims (Burnet 2009: p. 182). Justice, in whatever form, remains wanting when we come face to face with the impact of genocide and mass atrocity on individual lives. Victims of genocide may have an acute thirst for justice, but it is a thirst that can never be quenched (Sosnov 2008: p. 144). Healing and closure may be an illusion that only exists in the imagination of strangers who did not experience the suffering that the victims have experienced.

Not only are criminal prosecutions after the fact hardly of much consolation to victims; there is little evidence as yet that they have any impact on deterring fresh atrocities (Rodman 2008). Remnants of the army and militia groups that spearheaded the Rwanda genocide have continued to commit gross human rights abuses against unarmed civilians from their bases in the Democratic Republic of Congo. Members of Rwanda's current military and security forces are still able to commit human rights abuses with impunity. The accountability mechanisms (national as well as international) that Rwanda has experimented with have not had any influence on the status of human rights in surrounding countries either. Neither the work of the Rwanda tribunal nor Rwanda's own domestic trials have had any significant impact on deterring widespread human rights violations in the Great Lakes region or other parts of Africa (Barria and Roper 2005: p. 358). On the contrary, violent conflicts involving horrendous human rights abuses have ravaged the region even as the Rwanda tribunal calmly proceeded with its work. There is no indication that the conduct of national armies and other armed groups involved in the conflicts underway in Rwanda, Burundi, the Democratic Republic of Congo, Uganda, the Central African Republic or Sudan's Darfur region has in any significant way been affected by consideration of prospects for accountability before national or international courts. Experience in the Great Lakes region of Central Africa during the period since the genocide indicates that the benefits of the accountability processes that the international community had in mind in establishing the Rwanda tribunal (including combating impunity and deterring conflict and atrocity) will at best be achieved only gradually, if at all, and the impact, if any, of international criminal justice will only be felt in the very long term.

In Rwanda, the victims of the genocide question whether the suffering they endured was inevitable or unavoidable. Did the genocide have to happen? Could it have been stopped or prevented? If so, why was nothing done? Which individuals and institutions bear responsibility for failing to take action to prevent or stop the genocide? Survivors of the genocide believe that the international community should have acted to protect or rescue them. They know that their compatriots and the rest of the world failed them. The views of survivors are widely shared by many other Rwandans and foreigners, who all believe that the international community could, and should have acted to stop or prevent the genocide, that the genocide was not unavoidable. The genocide in Rwanda has been named 'The Preventable Genocide' (Organisation of African Unity 2000). Not only was it preventable, it could have been stopped before it claimed hundreds of thousands of lives (Dallaire 2005; Feil 2009). The RPA, without the military equipment, intelligence assets and diplomatic muscle that world powers have at their disposal, was able to stop the genocide and to drive its organizers from power in a period of only three months. Former US President Bill Clinton has admitted that his failure to send troops to Rwanda was one of the most significant regrets of his presidency, and that he believes that sending about 20,000 US troops could have saved 250,000–400,000 of an estimated 800,000 victims (Associated Press 2009).

The failure of the international community to protect civilians at risk of atrocity has enduring consequences. By failing to act to prevent or stop mass atrocity, the international community sends the message that it lacks the will to protect communities under threat. Potential perpetrators perceive this unwillingness to act to protect civilians at risk as unspoken licence, and the perpetrators of the Rwanda genocide perceived it as such. Failing to act to protect communities at risk of atrocity perpetuates impunity. It hampers prospects for post-conflict reconciliation. It provides justification for authoritarian rule. The international community's failure to prevent or stop the Rwanda genocide partly accounts for Rwanda's failure to transition to democracy. The Tutsi minority emerged out of the experience of the genocide with a determination never to leave the fate of their community in the hands of the international community. They feel threatened by majority rule. They are determined to use repression if necessary to preserve their hold on power. Rwanda's history might easily have turned out differently (and changed for the better) had the international community acted to prevent or stop the genocide.

The international community's failure to prevent or stop the Rwanda genocide has shaped Rwandans' views about the usefulness or relevance of international criminal justice. No one argues that criminal prosecutions (by national as well as international criminal tribunals) are futile or undesirable. However, victims of genocide and Rwandans, in general, still primarily view international criminal justice as a self-serving act of atonement to cover up the international community's failure to come to their rescue. Accountability mechanisms that are not part of a wider and more effective system to provide protection for communities threatened with atrocity are not an effective deterrent to potential perpetrators; neither do they have much credibility with victims. The responsibility to protect should, if anything, be prioritized over reliance on criminal prosecutions as tools for combating impunity for mass atrocity. The international community cannot afford to rely exclusively, or even principally, on post-conflict justice mechanisms to deter future atrocity. A new approach to international criminal justice (linking accountability with prevention and protection) is necessary, if the evolving system of processes of accountability for mass atrocity is to have any practical relevance or to be credible in the eyes of the victims that it is intended to serve. The handling of the conflict in Kosovo demonstrated that international cooperation in protecting societies, communities and individuals, threatened by deadly conflict, can be effective. The question is whether the political will to protect can be generated when communities outside of Europe, particularly in Africa, are threatened by atrocity (Welsh 2009).

11 Conclusion

Rwanda experienced horrendous violence, including genocide, during the 1990s. Reckoning with the violence of that period has been an important and critical part of Rwanda's reconstruction. The issues of accountability for past human rights violations and advancement of the rule of law that post-genocide Rwanda has confronted are not unique. They frequently arise as part of the discourse on national reconstruction in societies emerging from periods of violent conflict involving gross human rights violations. The genocide in Rwanda was unique, however, among incidents of mass atrocity of modern times in the extent to which large numbers of citizens who were not officials of the state participated in committing atrocities. Rwanda has undertaken what is, in all probability, the most ambitious attempt any society has ever undertaken to ensure accountability for atrocity. In formulating policies on accountability for atrocity in the context of the country's extraordinary circumstances, the post-genocide government of Rwanda sought to achieve certain worthy objectives, common to transitional justice of most post-conflict situations, including providing justice to victims, establishing a culture of respect for human rights, ending impunity, promoting the rule of law, facilitating reconciliation and enhancing social cohesion and sustainable peace within Rwandan society.

Rwanda's reckoning with the legacy of the violence of the 1990s has been shaped by both the popular character of the violence, evidenced by the widespread social participation, as well as the circumstances in which the Rwandan conflict was brought to an end. The policy choices made by the government in pursuit of its transitional justice objectives were unprecedented. Rwanda opted to pursue a maximal approach to accountability that aimed to identify and hold accountable each and every person who had participated in mass atrocity and became the first state to attempt to achieve universal accountability for mass atrocity in which large numbers of citizens had participated. No justice system had ever been designed to deal with violence on the scale of the Rwandan genocide. In order to carry out the policy of indiscriminate investigations, trials and punishment of all perpetrators of genocide, Rwanda eventually had to resort to a unique variation of a traditional Rwandan conflict resolution mechanism, the Gacaca.

From a human rights perspective, full accountability is the ideal response to atrocity. The accountability processes that Rwanda has tried to carry out were a fulfilment of both the state's legal obligations and moral imperatives. The accountability processes pursued were a constructive contribution towards the country's reconstruction in the aftermath of the genocide and have, to varying degrees, succeeded in some of their short-term objectives.

Processes of accountability for atrocity, Rwanda's own included, are shaped by the political environment that prevails in the wake of violent conflict. The effectiveness of accountability processes is frequently constrained by the immediate requirements of post-conflict politics. Because of these limitations, few, if any, post-conflict societies that have experienced gross human rights violations have succeed in designing transitional justice processes that perfectly match the demands of human rights activists. Transitional justice processes that comply with what may be considered 'best practices' according to international law or even domestic laws are the exception rather than the norm. The mechanisms of accountability implemented by Rwanda have, not unexpectedly given the exceptional challenges faced, manifested some serious shortcomings, including abuses of human rights in the administration of justice, lack of impartiality and failure to address some of the fundamental causes of conflict in Rwandan society. As a result of these and other shortcomings, Rwanda's accountability processes have not been able to adequately facilitate the healing of victims, mending of fractured relationships, building of cohesion and promotion of constructive collaboration between parties to the conflict.

Rwanda's transitional justice processes remain a work in progress; there remains much unfinished business. The high hopes that Rwanda's accountability processes initially promised have not been realized. Divisions and conflicts, rooted in the country's violent past, have not been overcome by the transitional justice processes pursued to date. Far from expressing remorse and seeking the forgiveness of the victims, most of the perpetrators of the genocide remain in denial. Genocide victims remain, at best, ambivalent about the accountability processes pursued. Rwandan society is yet to openly acknowledge and address the violence that victims in the Hutu community experienced during the conflicts of the 1990s. The Hutu community largely perceives the transitional justice processes undertaken as no more than exemplars of victor's justice. Rwandan society remains deeply divided along ethnic lines. The reparations that Rwanda's accountability processes have provided are considered inadequate by survivors of the genocide, and have left out Hutu victims of violence altogether.

More ominously, Rwanda has not carried out the institutional reforms that are necessary to guarantee sustainable peace and stability for its people. The potential of the accountability processes Rwanda has undertaken to advance reconciliation has been constrained by the lack of progress in reform of political governance systems. Many of the problems of discrimination in access to political representation, to power and to resources and of lack or the failure of the state to ensure respect of the fundamental human rights of citizens that have previously driven conflict in Rwandan society are yet to be adequately addressed. The risk of new conflict remains very real. Rwanda must at some point in the future revisit the above outstanding issues, including political participation, discrimination and inequality, before they can be finally laid to rest.

The shortcomings of Rwanda's accountability processes do not negate the worth of pursuing justice. Rather, these shortcomings stress the complexity of the challenges involved in rebuilding post-conflict societies in the aftermath of mass atrocity, especially mass atrocity in which a large number of citizens have taken an active part. Rwanda's experience of transitional justice has demonstrated not just the potential but also the limits of justice as an instrument of social change, political reform and peace-building in the aftermath of violent conflict, particularly conflict linked to questions of identity, 'race' and ethnicity.

Mass atrocity inflicts injury and harm on individuals as well as society at large. Its impact is, if not eternal, certainly very long lasting. Peacebuilding in the wake of such atrocity is a delicate and long-term process. The challenge of crafting appropriate responses to legacies of past violence, and particularly violence involving genocide or mass atrocity, is the work of not one, but many generations. The transitional justice processes that Rwanda has undertaken ought to be viewed as the beginning and not the end of an ongoing process of coming to terms with the legacy of extreme violence. Future generations, leaders and governments of Rwanda will, without doubt, find it necessary to revisit the violence of the 1990s. The aspects of that violence that Rwanda will inevitably have to reconsider include the question of reparations for all victims, accountability for human rights abuses attributable to the victors and the need to establish a more inclusive complete historical record of the Rwanda conflict, which addresses the concerns and experiences of all segments of Rwandan society.

The current government of Rwanda considers the closure of Gacaca as the final chapter of the process of reckoning with the violence of the past. The truth of the matter is that Rwandan society still has some way to go before it can claim to be ready for closure in relation to the violence experienced during the 1990s. The country will, in future, still have to undertake new transitional justice processes as part of a necessary process of reckoning with the legacies of the violence of the 1990s. These processes could include prosecutions of the crimes that current mechanisms have not addressed, a future truth and reconciliation commission, provision of reparations to victims, reforms of the political system to enhance the opportunity for political participation and inclusion or even negotiations between the current government and its opponents with a view to reaching a comprehensive strategy for peace and reconciliation (Borocan 2004: p. 367).

Transformation of war-torn, deeply divided societies with histories of gross human rights abuses into democratic, peaceful and stable states is a process fraught with many difficult challenges. Accountability for past atrocities is a critical component of strategies to facilitate such transformation. The potential to bring those responsible for atrocity to justice (through national as well as international mechanisms) is widening, albeit slowly (Graybill and Lanegran 2004: p. 2). Criminal prosecutions, by national courts and international criminal tribunals, have begun to play a critical role in the rebuilding of societies' recovery from violent conflict. Judging from Rwanda's experience, however, it may be that restorative justice mechanisms are a more suitable response to mass atrocity, especially atrocity in which large numbers of civilians have taken part, than strictly retributive justice processes (Minow 1998: pp. 50–1; Sarkin 2001: pp. 170–2; Drumbl 2002b; Graybill 2004: p. 1128; Tiemessen 2004; Fierens 2005). However, justice, whatever its form, is by itself inadequate for ensuring successful transition to democracy, the rule of law or peace and stability. National policy makers, diplomats, development workers and peace-building practitioners, scholars and human rights activists need to acknowledge the significant limits of accountability processes as tools for promoting social change or political transformation (Minow 1998; Drumbl 2002b: p. 18; Graybill and Lanegran 2004: p. 11). Reform of political governance systems may ultimately be more essential to the process of building more cohesive, peaceful and stable societies in the aftermath of mass atrocity (Sarkin 2001; Vandegiste 2001a; Haile 2008). Transitional justice processes are unlikely to achieve their intended objectives if they are not part of a wider process that addresses the root causes of a country's conflict (Mamdani 2001; Sarkin 2001; Vandegiste 2001a; Kamatali 2003; Haile 2008). This is a principle that is relevant to the future and perhaps the very survival of Rwanda.

Notes

Introduction

1 The tribunal was established by UN Security Council Res. 827 (1993), 25 May 1993, UN Doc. S/RES/827.
2 National prosecutions have been organized in accordance with Organic Law No. 08/96 of 30 August 1996 on the Organization of Prosecutions for Offences Constituting the Crime of Genocide or Crimes Against Humanity between 1 October 1990 and 31 December 1994 as amended to date. Gacaca courts were initially established by Organic Law No. 40/2000 of 26/01/2001 setting up '*Gacaca* jurisdictions' and organizing prosecutions for offences constituting the crime of genocide or crimes against humanity committed between 1 October 1990 and 31 December 1994. This law has since been amended several times. The ICTR was set up pursuant to Security Council Resolution 955 (8 November 1994) UN Doc. S/RES/955(1994).

1 Theoretical Framework of Transitional Justice

1 General Assembly Resolution 897(IX) (1954).
2 Situations of mass atrocity that went unaccounted for during the post-World War II period included the following: Russia (1924–53), China (1949–76), Sudan (1955–72, 1983–2005), Indochina (1960–75), East Pakistan/Bangladesh (1971), Uganda (1971–79), Burundi (1972), East Timor (1974–99), Cambodia (1975–79). (See Drumbl (2007).)
3 *Chorzow Factory Case (Ger. v. Pol.)* (1928) P.C.I.J., Sr. A, No.17, Judgment of 13 September 1928, Permanent Court of Arbitration.
4 Sixteen cases in seven situations have been brought before the International Criminal Court. Source: www.icc-cpi.int/Menus/ICC/Situations+and+Cases/ (accessed 25 July 2012.)
5 Exceptions: the Special Tribunal for Lebanon and the Charles Taylor case: *Prosecutor* v. *Taylor*, Case No. SCSL-03-1-T, Judgment of 26 April 2012. The charges against Charles Taylor related to his alleged support for Revolutionary United Front (RUF) rebels fighting in Sierra Leone. The RUF were alleged to have committed horrendous atrocities, including unlawful killings, sexual violence, physical violence, looting, conscription and use of child soldiers, abduction, terrorism and other atrocities. Due to concerns that a trial in Sierra Leone could destabilize both Sierra Leone and Liberia, the trial was transferred to the Hague.
6 The drive for 'ownership' of a judicial process can go too far: the United Nations and the government of Cambodia engaged in an acrimonious debate about the ratio of international to national judges in the Extraordinary Chambers, and the Iraqi Special Tribunal has been criticized for its insistence upon using only Iraqi judges and prosecutors (see Gersh 2004).
7 Quoted in Christie, Kenneth (2000). *The South African Truth Commission*. New York: St. Martin's Press, p. 61.

8 Article 35 of the Draft Articles on Responsibility of States for Internationally Wrongful Acts.

9 Human Rights Committee: Concluding Observations on Peru, 15 November 2000, CCPR/CO/70/PER, para. 11 (b); *Sarma* v. *Sri Lanka*, Communication No.950/2000, Views of 31 July 2003, CCPR/C/78/D/950/2000, Human Rights Committee, para. 11; *Casafranca de Gómez* v. *Peru*, Views of 20 August 2000, CCPR/C/78/D/981/2001, para. 9; *Assanidze* v. *Georgia*, Application No. 71503/01, Judgment of 8 April 2004, ECtHR, paras 202–203; *Ilascu et al.* v. *Moldova and Russia*, Application No. 48787/99, Judgment of 8 July 2004, ECtHR, para. 490; *Loayza Tamayo* v. *Peru*, Judgment of 17 September 1997, Series C No. 33, I/ACtHR, operative paragraph 5; *Constitutional Rights Project and Civil Liberties Organisation* v. *Nigeria*, Communication 102/93, Decision, 24th Ordinary Session, October 1998, AfrCmHPR; *Centre for Free Speech* v. *Nigeria*, Communication 206/97, Decision, 26th Ordinary Session, 15 November 1999, AfrCmHPR.

10 *Malawi African Association et al.* v. *Mauritania*, Communications 54/91, 61/91, 98/93, 164/97, 196/97, 210/98, Decision, May 2000, 27th Ordinary Session, AfrCmHPR; *John K. Modise* v. *Botswana*, Communication 97/93, Decision, November 2000, 28th Ordinary Session, AfrCmHPR; Working Group on Enforced or Involuntary Disappearances General Comments on Article 19 of the Declaration on the Protection of All Persons from Enforced Disappearance, 12 January 1998, E/CN.1/1998/43, para. 75.

11 *Malawi African Association et al.* v. *Mauritania*, supra note 10.

12 *Jiménez Vaca* v. *Colombia*, Communication No. 859/1999, Views of 15 April 2002, CCPR/C/74/D/859/1999, Human Rights Committee, para. 9; see also Working Group on Enforced or Involuntary Disappearances, General Comments on Article 19 of the Declaration on the Protection of All Persons from Enforced Disappearance, 12 January 1998, E/CN.1/1998/43, para. 75.

13 *Busyo* v. *Democratic Republic of Congo*, Communication No 933/2000, Views of 9 August 2003, CCPR/C/78/D/933/2000, Human Rights Committee, para. 6.2; *Nyekuma Kopita Toro Gedumbe* v. *Democratic Republic of the Congo*, Communications No. 641/1995, Views of 1 August 1997, CCPR/C/75/D/641/1995, Human Rights Committee, para. 6.2.

14 *Hentrich* v. *France*, Application No. 13616/88, Judgment of 22 September 1994, Series A No. 296-A, ECtHR, para. 71; see also *Papamichalopoulos and Others* v. *Greece* (Article 50), Application No. 14556/89, Judgment of 31 October 1995, Series A No. 330-B, ECtHR, para. 38; *Brumarescu* v. *Romania* [GC], Application No. 28342/95, Judgment of 23 January 2001, Reports 2001-I, ECtHR

15 Article 36, Draft Articles on Responsibility of States for Internationally Wrongful Acts.

16 Commentary to the Draft Articles on Responsibility of States for Internationally Wrongful Acts; Report of the International Law Commission on its Fifty-third Session, GA, Supplement No. 10 (A/56/10); cph. IV.E.

17 See, for example, ruling of the Inter-American Court of Human Rights in the Velásquez Rodríguez Case, Serial C, No. 4 (1989), para. 174. See also *Papamichalopoulos* v. *Greece* (Art. 50) Serial A, supra note 14.

18 Article 9 (5), International Covenant on Civil and Political Rights; Article 14, Convention Against Torture; Article 5 (5), European Convention on Human Rights; Articles 16 (4) and (5), Indigenous and Tribal Peoples Convention 1989 (No. 169); Article 75 (1), Rome Statute of the International Criminal Court; Article 19, Declaration on the Protection of all Persons from Enforced Disappearance; Principle 12, Declaration of Basic Principles of Justice for Victims of Crime and Abuse of Power; Article 9 (2), Declaration on the Right and Responsibility of Individuals, Groups and Organs of Society to Promote and Protect Universally Recognized Human Rights and Fundamental Freedoms, adopted by United Nations General Assembly resolution 53/144 of 8 March 1999. In the regional instruments: Article 63 (1) ACHR; Article 9, Inter-American Convention to Prevent and Punish Torture; Article 288 (2), Treaty of the European Community; Article 41 (3), Charter of Fundamental Rights of the European Union; Article 21 (2), AfrCHPR; Article 27 (1), Protocol to the African Charter on Human and Peoples' Rights on the Establishment of an African Court on

Human and Peoples' Rights; Article 9 (5) ICCPR; Article 5 (5), ECHR; Article 10, ACHR; Article 16, Arab Charter on Human Rights; Article 85, Rome Statute of the International Criminal Court; Article 91, First Additional Protocol to the Geneva Conventions; Article 68, Third Geneva Convention relative to the Treatment of Prisoners of War.

19 *Chorzow Factory Case (Ger. v. Pol.)* (Claim for Indemnity) (The Merits), supra note 3.

20 Concluding Observations on the Libyan Arab Jamahiriya, 6 November 1998, CCPR/C/79/Add.101, para. 7; Concluding Observations on Mexico, 27 July 1999, CCPR/C/79/Add.109, para. 6; Concluding Observations on Guatemala, 27 August 2001, CCPR/CO/72/GTM, para. 12; *Bleier* v. *Uruguay,* Views of 23 May 1978, CCPR/C/15/D/30/1978, para. 5.

21 Resolution E/CN.4/2003/32 (torture), 23 April 2003, para. 10.

22 Report of the Special Rapporteur on cultural practices in the family that are violent towards women, E/CN.4/2002/83, 31 January 2002, paras 116, 119; Report of the Special Rapporteur on torture, E/CN.4/2003/68, 17 December 2002, para. 26 (l).

23 Principle 20.

24 *Busyo* v. *Democratic Republic of Congo*, Communication No. 933/2000, Views of 9 August 2003, CCPR/C/78/D/933/2000, Human Rights Committee, para. 6.2; *Nyekuma Kopita Toro Gedumbe* v. *Democratic Republic of the Congo*, Communications No. 641/1995, Views of 1 August 1997, CCPR/C/75/D/641/1995, Human Rights Committee; *Çakici* v. *Turkey*, Application No. 23657/94, Judgment of 8 July 1999, Reports 1999-IV, ECtHR23657/94, para. 127; *Selçuk and Asker* v. *Turkey*, Applications 12/1997/796/998-999, Judgment of 24 April 1998, Reports 1998-II, ECtHR, para. 112; *Orhan* v. *Turkey*, Application No. 25656/94, Judgment of 18 June 2002, ECtHR, para. 430. See also *Aktas* v. *Turkey*, Application No. 24351/94, Judgment of 24 April 2003 and *Ipek* v. *Turkey*, Application No. 25760/94, Judgment of 17 February 2004, CPR/C/75/D/641/1995, ECtHR, para. 6.2.

25 The European Court of Human Rights has awarded compensation for such material damages as loss of house and other property (*Selçuk and Asker* v. *Turkey*, Applications 12/1997/796/998-999, Judgment of 24 April 1998, Reports 1998-II, ECtHR, para. 106; *Bilgin* v. *Turkey*, Application No. 23819/94, Judgment of 16 November 2000, ECtHR, paras 138–152); loss of livestock (*Ipek* v. *Turkey*, Application 13972/88, Judgment of 24 November 1993, Series A No. 275, ECtHR, paras 228, 229); additional expenditures (Case *Ipek* v. *Turkey*, paras 232, 233); costs of alternative housing (*Selçuk and Asker* v. *Turkey*, paras 104–115); costs of removals or higher living costs in a new residence resulting from human rights violations (*Orhan* v. *Turkey*, Application No. 25656/94, Judgment of 18 June 2002, ECtHR, para. 438); and reimbursement of legal costs and expenses for the proceedings, in so far as they are necessary, reasonable and actually incurred (*Selçuk and Asker* v. *Turkey*, paras 120–122).

26 *Aloeboetoe et al.* v. *Suriname* (Reparations), Judgment of 10 September, 1993, Series C No. 15, I/ACtHR, para. 96. The Inter-American Court of Human Rights ordered that the heirs of the victims must receive compensation to be able to study. But it also considered that it was not sufficient to just grant compensation; rather, there also had to be a school available for the children; consequently, it ordered that the state should reopen the local school and staff it with teachers and administrative personnel.

27 *Coronel et al.* v. *Colombia*, Communication No. 778/1997, Views of 29 November 2002, CCPR/C/76/D/778/1997, Human Rights Committee, para. 10; Opinion in the Lusitania Cases, 1 November 1923, Report of International Arbitral Awards, Volume VII, p. 36.

28 *Chorzow Factory Case (Ger. v. Pol.)*, (1928) P.C.I.J., Sr. A, No.17, Judgment of 13 September 1928, Permanent Court of Arbitration, p. 47.

29 The Africa Commission on Human and Peoples Rights considered a case, *The Social and Economic Rights Action Center and the Center for Economic and Social Rights* v. *Nigeria*, Communication 155/96, Decision, October 2001, 30th Ordinary Session, AfrCmHPR, involving claims on behalf of a community. The Commission found multiple violations of the rights of the Ogoni Communities in Nigeria by oil companies with the acquiescence of the government, particularly of Article 21, AfrCHPR, which guarantees the right of peoples to freely dispose of their wealth and natural resources. It appealed to the government 'to

ensure protection of the environment, health and livelihood of the people of Ogoniland' by, amongst others, 'stopping all attacks on Ogoni communities and leaders [...]', 'ensuring adequate compensation to victims of the human rights violations [...] and undertaking a comprehensive cleanup of lands and rivers damaged by oil operations.'

30 Article 14 (1) CAT; Article 39, CRC.
31 Principle 21.
32 Principle 22.
33 See Droege 2006: p.145 on right to remedy and reparation; *Golder* v. *United Kingdom*, Application 4451/70, Judgment of 21 February 1975, Series A No. 18, ECtHR, para. 46; *Oçalan* v. *Turkey*, Application No. 46221/99, Judgment of 12 March 2003, ECtHR, para. 250; *Cesti Hurtado* v. *Peru* (Reparations), Judgment of 31 May 2001, Series C No. 78, I/ACtHR, para. 59.
34 *Sarma* v. *Sri Lanka*, Communication No.950/2000, Views of 31 July 2003, CCPR/C/78/D/950/2000, Human Rights Committee, para. 12; *Busyo* v. *Democratic Republic of Congo*, Communication No. 933/2000, Views of 9 August 2003, CCPR/C/78/D/933/2000, Human Rights Committee, para. 6.3; *Nyekuma Kopita Toro Gedumbe* v. *Democratic Republic of Congo*, Communications No. 641/1995, Views of 1 August 1997, CCPR/C/75/D/641/1995, Human Rights Committee, para. 6.3.
35 *Trujillo-Oroza* v. *Bolivia* (Reparations), Judgment of 27 February 2002, Series C No. 92, I/ACtHR, para. 119; *Barrios Alos* v. *Peru* (Reparations), Judgment of 30 November 2001, Series C No. 87, I/ACtHR, para. 44 (d); *Cantoral Benavides* v. *Peru* (Reparations), Judgment of 3 December 2001, Series C No. 88, I/ACtHR, para. 79; *Durand and Ugarte* v. *Peru* (Reparations), Judgment of 3 December 2001, Series C No. 89, I/ACtHR, para. 39 (a) and operative para. 3 (a); *Bámaca Velásquez* v. *Guatemala* (Reparations), Judgment of 22 February 2002, Series C No. 91, I/ACtHR, para. 84; *Caracazo* v. *Venezuela* (Reparations), Judgment of 29 August 2002, Series C No. 95, I/ACtHR, para. 128; *Juan Humberto Sánchez* v. *Honduras*, Judgment of 7 June 2003, Series C No. 102, I/ACtHR, para. 188.
36 *El Amparo* v. *Venezuela* (Reparations), Judgment of 14 September 1996, Series C No. 28, I/ACtHR, para. 35; *Neira Alegría et al.* v. *Peru* (Reparations), Judgment of 19 September 1996, Series C No. 29, I/ACtHR, para. 56; *Castillo Páez* v. *Peru* (Reparations), Judgment of 27 November 1998, Series C No. 43, I/ACtHR, para. 84; *Blake* v. *Guatemala* (Reparations), Judgment of 22 January 1999, I/ACtHR, para. 55.
37 *Villagrán Morales et al.* v. *Guatemala* (The 'Street Children' Case) (Reparations), Judgment of 26 May 2001, Series C No. 77, I/ACtHR, para. 88; *The Mayagna (Sumo) Awas Tingni Community* v. *Nicaragua*, Judgment of 31 August 2001, Series C No. 79, I/ACtHR, para. 166; *Cantoral Benavides* v. *Peru* (Reparations), Judgment of 3 December 2001, Series C No. 88, I/ACtHR, para. 79.
38 Principle 23.

2 A Decade of Atrocities

1 The organizations were: International Federation for Human Rights, Africa Watch, Inter-African Union of Human and Peoples' Rights and the International Centre for Human Rights and Democratic Development.
2 See the Protocol between the Government of Rwanda and the RPF signed on 18 September 1992.
3 See the Protocols between the Government of Rwanda and the RPF signed on 30 October 1992 and 18 September 1992.
4 See the Protocol between the Government of Rwanda and the RPF signed on 9 June 1993.
5 See the Protocol between the Government of Rwanda and the RPF signed on 3 August 1993.
6 See the Protocol between the Government of Rwanda and the RPF signed on 3 August 1993.
7 *The Prosecutor* v. *Theoneste Bagosora et al.*, Case No. ICTR-98-41-T, Judgment and Sentence of 18 December 2008, Trial Chamber.

8 *The Prosecutor* v. *Jean Kambanda*, Case No. ICTR 97-23-S, Judgment of 19 October 2000, Appeals Chamber.

9 See *The Prosecutor* v. *Jean Kambanda*, supra note 8, para. 39(vi). The training was conducted by both serving army and retired members of the military. The training was conducted at military complexes such as Gabiro, Bigowe, Nyungwe and other places. The training comprised both short training on the use of arms and ideological indoctrination with anti-Tutsi teachings.

10 The arms that were being purchased included massive quantities of implements such as machetes that had no military application and could only have been intended to arm the civilian population. The local company that manufactured machetes sold 'an unusually high number of machetes' between August and December 1993 (Des Forges 1999: pp. 127–8). Huge quantities of machetes were imported from abroad as well (Melvern 2004: p. 56).

11 The paper's editor, Hassan Ngeze, was convicted of genocide by the International Criminal Tribunal for Rwanda. See *The Prosecutor* v. *Hassan Ngeze*, Case No. ICTR-99-52-R, Judgment of 27 November 2007.

12 *The Prosecutor* v. *Theoneste Bagosora et al.*, supra note 7.

13 *The Prosecutor* v. *Jean Kambanda*, supra note 8; *Prosecutor* v. *Theoneste Bagosora et al.*, supra note 7.

14 *The Prosecutor* v. *Jean Kambanda*, supra note 8.

15 *The Prosecutor* v. *Jean Kambanda*, supra note 8, para. 39(xi).

16 The Head of the Interim Government, President Sindikubwabo, held meetings in Butare at which he berated the local community for not joining the Hutu community and the rest of the country in killing the Tutsi.

17 Jean Kambanda, Prime Minister of the Interim Government, participated in public distributions of weapons. *The Prosecutor* v. *Jean Kambanda,* supra note 8, para. 39.

18 Source of information: Fidele Uwizeye, Prefect of Gitarama during part of the period of the genocide (interviewed in 1997).

3 Accountability for Mass Atrocity: Challenges, Choices and Goals of Transitional Justice in Post-Genocide Rwanda

1 Due to the tight control that the government exercises over debates surrounding the genocide, it has not been possible to make an accurate and independent assessment of the number of the victims of the genocide and other violence that Rwanda experienced during the period. Other estimates: Prunier 1995: 800,000–850,000; Des Forges 1999: 500,000.

2 The mission was approved by Security Council Resolution 929 (1994) UN Doc. S/RES/929 (1994).

3 See more on the subject of the objectives of the ICTR's establishment in the next chapter.

4 Preamble, Security Council Resolution 955 establishing the ICTR (8 November 1994) UN Doc. S/RES/955(1994).

5 Organic Law No. 8/96 on the organization of genocide prosecutions created four categories of genocide suspects. Article 2 provides as follows:

> Persons accused of offences set out in Article I of this organic law and committed during the period between 1 October 1990 and 31 December 1994 shall, on the basis of their acts of participation, be classified into one of the following categories:
>
> **Category 1:**
>
> a) persons whose criminal acts or whose acts of criminal participation place them among the planners, organizers, instigators, supervisors and leaders of the crime of genocide or of a crime against humanity;
>
> b) persons who acted in positions of authority at the national, prefectoral, communal, sector or cell level, or in a political party, the army, religious organizations or in a militia and who perpetrated or fostered such crimes;

c) notorious murderers who by virtue of the zeal or excessive malice with which they committed atrocities, distinguished themselves in their areas of residence or where they passed;
d) persons who committed acts of sexual torture.

Category 2: persons whose criminal acts or whose acts of criminal participation place them among perpetrators, conspirators or accomplices of intentional homicide or of serious assault against the person causing death;

Category 3: persons whose criminal acts or whose acts of criminal participation make them guilty of other serious assaults against the person;

Category 4: persons who committed offences against property.

6 Organic Law 8/96 of 30 August 1996 on the organisation of prosecutions for offences constituting the crime of genocide or crimes against humanity committed since 1 October 1990. Published in the *Gazette of the Republic of Rwanda*, 35th year, no.17, 1 September 1996. (Hereinafter, referred to only as Organic Law 8/1996.)
7 See contribution of President Bizimungu in the Report on the Reflection Meetings (Office of the President, Republic of Rwanda 1999: p. 4).
8 Mouvement Démocratique Républicain (MDR), Parti Socialiste Démocrate (PSD), Parti Libéral (PL), Parti Démocrate Chrétien (PDC), Parti Démocratique Islamique (PDI), Union Démocratique du Peuple Rwandais (UDPR) and Parti Socialiste Rwandais (PSR), in addition to the Rwandese Patriotic Front which was the organization in power.
9 I was appointed to the office of Prosecutor General in August 1998.
10 Organic Law No. 40/2000 of 26/01/2000 setting up 'Gacaca jurisdictions' and organising prosecutions for offences constituting the crime of genocide or crimes against humanity committed between 1 October 1990 and 31 December 1994. (Hereinafter, referred to only as Organic Law 40/2000.)
11 See Basic Principles and Guidelines on the Right to Reparations for Victims of Gross Violations of Human Rights and Humanitarian Law (UN Doc. E/CN.4/sub.2/1996/17 annex).
12 Riddell (2005) cites figures in F. Digneffe and J. Fierens (eds), *Justice et Gacaca: L'expérience rwandaise et le génocide* (Presses Universitaires de Namur, 2003) to the effect that 1,240 persons of all ethnicities were prosecuted for the 1959 massacres.

4 Accountability, Justice and the Role of the International Criminal Tribunal for Rwanda

1 *Nydia Erika Bautista de Arellana* v. *Colombia*, Decision of 13 November 1995, Communication 563/1993, United Nations document CCPR/C/55/D/563/1993, Human Rights Committee, para 8.2; *Vicente et al.* v. *Colombia*, Decision of 29 July 1997, Communication 612/1995, UN Doc. CCPR/C/60/D/612/1995, Human Rights Committee, para. 8.2.
2 See International Covenant on Civil and Political Rights; International Convention on the Suppression and Punishment of the Crime of *Apartheid*, G. A. res. 3068 (xxviii), 28 UN GAOR Supp. (No. 30) at 75, UN Doc. A/9030 (1974), 1015 U.N.T.S. 243, *entered in force* 18 July 1976. Convention against Torture and Other Cruel, Inhuman or Degrading Treatment or Punishment (Articles 4 and 5); International Convention for the Protection of All Persons from Enforced Disappearance adopted by the General Assembly 20 December 2006; the Geneva Conventions of 1949; Additional Protocol No. I to the Geneva Conventions and Additional Protocol No. II to the Geneva Conventions; Optional Protocol to the Convention on the Rights of the Child on the sale of children, child prostitution and child pornography (Articles 3–5); Optional Protocol to the Convention on the Rights of the Child on the involvement of children in armed conflict (Article 4); Convention on the Prevention and Punishment of the Crime of Genocide (Articles IV, V and VI);

Inter-American Convention to Prevent and Punish Torture (Articles 1 and 6); Inter-American Convention on the Prevention, Punishment and Eradication of Violence against Women (Article 7); Inter-American Convention on Forced Disappearance of Persons (Articles I and IV); Convention on the Non-Applicability of Statutory Limitations to War Crimes and Crimes Against Humanity; European Convention on the Non-Applicability of Statutory Limitation to Crimes against Humanity and War Crimes.

3 Article 4 (c) and (d), Declaration on the Elimination of Violence against Women; Article 4, Declaration on the Protection of All Persons from Enforced Disappearance; Article 18, UN Principles on Extra-legal Executions; Principle 7, Basic Principles on the Use of Force and Firearms by Law Enforcement Officials; Principle 5, Principles of international cooperation in the detection, arrest, extradition and punishment of persons guilty of war crimes and crimes against humanity; Paras 60 and 62, Vienna Declaration and Programme of Action; Paras 84–89, Programme of Action of the World Conference against Racism, Racial Discrimination, Xenophobia and Related Intolerance.

4 *Aksoy* v. *Turkey*, Application No. 21987/93, Judgment of 18 December 1996, Reports 1996-VI, ECtHR, para. 98; *Aydin* v. *Turkey*, Application No. 23178/94, Judgment of 25 September 1997, Reports 1997-VI, ECtHR, para. 103; *Kaya* v. *Turkey*, Application No. 22729/93, Judgment of 19 February 1998, Reports 1998-I, ECtHR, paras 106–107; *Orhan* v. *Turkey*, Application No. 25656/94, Judgment of 18 June 2002, ECtHR, para. 384.

5 See Convention on the Non-Applicability of Statutory Limitations to War Crimes and Crimes Against Humanity; Principles of international cooperation in the detection, arrest, extradition and punishment of persons guilty of war crimes and crimes against humanity; Draft Code of Crimes against Peace and Security of Mankind of 1996 of the International Law Commission (ILC Report on its 48th Session (1996), A/51/10, 1996, Chapter II(2), paras 46–48).

6 See Reservations to the Convention on the Prevention and Punishment of the Crime of Genocide, Advisory Opinion of 28 May 1951, I.C.J. Reports 1951, p. 15; Articles IV, V and VI, Convention on the Prevention and Punishment of the Crime of Genocide.

7 Article 5, Protocol to Prevent, Suppress and Punish Trafficking in Persons, especially Women and Children.

8 Articles 3, 4 and 5, Optional Protocol to the Convention on the Rights of the Child on the sale of children, child prostitution and child pornography.

9 Article 4 (a), International Convention on the Elimination of All Forms of Racial Discrimination (CERD); Concluding Observations on Italy, UN Doc. CERD/C/304/Add.68, 7 April 1999, paras 9 and 14. See also Concluding Observations on Germany, UN Doc. CERD/C/304/Add.115, 27 April 2001, para. 14(c); Concluding Observations on France, UN Doc. CERD/C/304/Add.91, 19 April 2000, para. 11; Concluding Observations on Czech Republic, UN Doc. CERD/C/63/CO/4, 10 December 2003, para. 15.

10 According to Madeleine Albright, the former US Secretary of State and Permanent Representative to the United Nations, the High Commissioner undertook the mission at her request. (Source: Author's meeting with Ambassador Albright, May 1994.) Other sources credit the initiative to ask the High Commissioner to undertake the mission to the Government of Canada.

11 After losing power in mid-July, the remnants of the Rwandan regime that had presided over the genocide issued a call for the creation of an international tribunal, adding that its jurisdiction should cover human rights violations in Rwanda since October 1990, when the civil war had begun.

12 These provisions were adopted as Articles 8, 11 and 12 (3) of the Statute of the ICTR, 8 November 1994, UN Doc. S/RES/955(1994).

13 Article 15 of the draft of the statute provided that the Prosecutor of the ICTY would also serve as the Prosecutor of the ICTR. Article 16 of the statute of the ICTY provided that its Prosecutor would be appointed by the Security Council on nomination by the Secretary General.

14 The provision was adopted as Article 16 (3) of the Statute of the ICTR.
15 Ibid., Article 27.
16 Former US President Bill Clinton, in a speech in Kigali in March 1998, said: 'We come here today partly in recognition of the fact that we in the United States and the world community did not do as much as we could have and should have done to try to limit what occurred in Rwanda' (Power 2001).
17 Article 1, Statute of the ICTR, supra note 12.
18 The state of Zaire was renamed The Democratic Republic of Congo in May 1997.
19 The indictment related to the Kibuye case, in which Clement Kayishema, Charles Sikubwabo, Aloys Ndimbati, Ignace Bagilishama, Vincent Rutaganira, Muhimana Mika, Obed Ruzindana and Ryandikayo were charged. *The Prosecutor* v. *Clément Kayishema and Obed Ruzindana*, Case No. ICTR-95-1-A, Judgment of 21 May 1999, Trial Chamber, Reasons for Judgment, 1 June 2001, Appeals Chamber.
20 Ibid. Georges Anderson Rutaganda and Jean-Paul Akayesu appeared before the First Trial Chamber, presided over by Judge Kama and composed of Judges Aspegren and Pillay (ICTR 1996a: paras 38–39).
21 In *The Prosecutor* v. *Theoneste Bagosora et al.*, Case No. ICTR-98-41-T, Judgment and Sentence of 18 December 2008, Trial Chamber, a motion was submitted on behalf of Bagosora contending that his pre-trial detention of five years was excessive so as to warrant his release. The Trial Chamber denied the motion, ruling that: 'The Chamber notes that in certain circumstances, six years of pre-trial detention may be a factor in the consideration of exceptional circumstances warranting the release of an accused. However, the length of the current or potential future detention of the Accused cannot be considered material in these circumstances because it does not mitigate in any way that the Accused, who is charged with the grave offences coming under the subject matter jurisdiction of this Tribunal, which offences carry maximum term of imprisonment of life, may be a flight risk or may pose a threat to witnesses or to the community if he were to be released.'
22 For example, only four trials (including two guilty pleas) were completed during the period 1 July 1998–30 June 1999. Three trials (including two in which there were guilty pleas) were completed during the period 1 July 1999–30 June 2000. Only one trial was completed during the 1 July 2000–30 June 2001 reporting period. See ICTR Third Annual Report, 1998, UN Doc. A/53/429-S/1998/857, paras 33–38; Fourth Annual Report, 1999, UN Doc. A/54/315-S/1999/943; Fifth Annual Report, 2000, UN Doc. A/55/435-S/2000/927; Sixth Annual Report, 2001, UN Doc A/56/351-S/2001/863.
23 *The Prosecutor* v. *Jean-Bosco Barayagwiza*, Case No. ICTR-97, Decision on Appeal against Trial Chamber's Decision on the Extremely Urgent Motion by the Defence for Orders to Review and Nullify the Arrest and Provisional Detention of the Suspect, 3 November 1999, Appeals Chamber.
24 *The Prosecutor* v. *Jean-Bosco Barayagwiza*, Case No. ICTR-97-19-AR72, Decision (Prosecutor's request for review or reconsideration), Judgment of 31 March 2000, Appeals Chamber.
25 An example is the case of *The Prosecutor* v. *Nzabirinda*, Case No. ICTR-2001-77-T, Judgment of 27 February 2009. The defence investigator who was indicted in this case pleaded guilty to genocide-related charges.
26 The Office of Internal Oversight Services (OIOS) assists the Secretary General in fulfilling their oversight responsibilities in respect of the resources and staff of the organization through internal audit, monitoring, inspection, evaluation and investigation services.
27 Article 16, Statute of the ICTR, supra note 12.
28 Article 11, United Nations Security Council Resolution 1503 (28 August 2003), UN Doc. S/RES/1503.
29 Barayagwiza (ICTR-97-19-AR72), Decision, 3 November 1999.
30 The single exception was Frodouald Karamira, a genocide suspect who was arrested in Addis Ababa, Ethiopia after being deported from India. Even in this case, however, the suspect's transfer was only possible after the tribunal's prosecutor had voluntarily agreed to

withdraw the tribunal's request for transfer of the suspect to the tribunal. I was personally involved in the negotiations for Karamira's transfer. There is no basis whatsoever to the claims by some commentators (Cruvellier 2010) that the Rwanda government ever had any confrontation with Prosecutor Goldstone over the custody of Karamira.

31 *The Prosecutor* v. *Jean-Bosco Barayagwiza*, supra note 22.

32 I appeared *amicus curiae* and argued these issues before the review panel of the Appeals Chamber that heard an application by the prosecutor for the review of the decision.

33 *The Prosecutor* v. *Jean-Bosco Barayagwiza*, supra note 23.

34 *The Prosecutor* v. *Jean-Bosco Barayagwiza*, supra note 22; *The Prosecutor* v. *Andre Ntagerura, Emmanuel Bagambiki, Samuel Imanishimwe*, ICTR-99-46-A, Judgment of 7 July 2006, Appeals Chamber.

35 There have been incidents where persons who have been witnesses for the prosecution have returned to Rwanda only to die in mysterious circumstances. Although no conclusive evidence links these deaths to the testimony of the witnesses, the tribunal was often widely criticized by survivors for failing to protect these and other witnesses.

36 Witnesses who were taken to Arusha were kept under surveillance in safe houses under conditions which deprived them of their freedom. They were not allowed to drink alcohol. The witnesses found the conditions under which they were kept similar to prison. They also found the treatment they received to be patronizing. Even judges were insensitive on occasion. In one case, the judges laughed at a witness who was testifying about her rape in *The Prosecutor* v. *Arsene Shalom Ntaholbali*, Case No. ICTR-97-21-T, Decision on Ntahobali's Motion for Certification to Appeal the Decision on Ntahobali's Motion for Admission of Two Rwandan Judgments Involving Prosecution Witness TQ, 14 January 2009.

37 These standards are based on international human rights instruments that most states have ratified. They are set out in guiding documents which include: Standard Minimum Rules for the Treatment of Prisoners; Body of Principles for the Protection of All Persons under Any Form of Detention or Imprisonment.

38 Article 23, Statute of the ICTR, supra note 12.

39 See: Law No. 13/2004 of 17/5/2004 relating to the Code of Criminal Procedure (O.G. special No. of 30/07/2004), Article 131.

40 After seven years and expenditure totalling more than US$400 million, both the ICTY and the ICTR had completed only 15 trials (United Nations 1999c).

41 Security Council Resolution 1966 (2010), adopted by the Council at its 6463th meeting on 22 December 2010.

42 Article 3, Statute of the International Residual Mechanism for Criminal Tribunals

43 Ibid., Article 3.

44 Ibid., Article 4.

45 As of June 2012, there were nine fugitives in the case of the ICTR: Pheneas Munyarugarama, Ladislas Ntaganzwa, Aloys Ndimbati, Charles Ryandikayo, Charles Sikubwabo, Augustin Bizimana, Félicien Kabuga, Protais Mpiranya and Fulgence Kayishema.

46 Ibid., Article 27.

47 Ibid., Article 4 (1).

48 Ibid., Articles 5 and 6.

49 Ibid., Article 11.

50 Ibid., Article 6.

51 Source: Correspondence, interviews and discussions between the author and refugees, including some accused of genocide, in Europe and North America (2010–12).

5 National Prosecutions

1 Organic Law No. 8/96 of 30th August 1996 on the organisation of prosecutions for offences constituting the crime of genocide or crimes against humanity committed since 1 October 1990.

2 At the Gitarama prison, 877 prisoners died between December 1994 and June 1995.
3 See Basic Principles on the Role of Lawyers. See also Article 14(3)(d), International Covenant on Civil and Political Rights.
4 Law 3/97 of 19 March 1997 relating to the establishment of the Bar in Rwanda.
5 The recruitment of new personnel for the justice sector was overseen by Hutu Ministers of Justice (Alphone Nkubito and Martha Mukamurenzi) and carried by foreign NGOs supporting the justice sector.
6 Article 2, Organic Law 8/96 of 30 August 1996, supra note 1.
7 Ibid., Article 5.
8 Ibid., Article 6.
9 The Government took the decision to release minors less than 14 years of age (the age of criminal liability) in May 1996.
10 Organic Law No. 13/2008 of 19/5/2008 modifying and complementing Organic Law No. 16/2004 of 19 June 2004 establishing the organisation, competence and functioning of Gacaca Courts charged with prosecuting and trying the perpetrators of the crime of genocide and other crimes against humanity, committed between 1 October 1990 and 31 December 1994.
11 This is a reference to the Rules of Procedure and Evidence of the ICTR, which entered into force 29 June 1995. The rules have been amended many times since.
12 See for further details: www.interpol.int/Public/Wanted/images/rwanda.pdf.
13 Organic Law No. 31/2007 of 25/07/2007 relating to the abolition of the death penalty.
14 See Law No. 20/2006 of 22 April 2006 modifying and complementing Organic Law No. 13/2004 of 17/5/2004 relating to the Code of Criminal Procedure; Organic Law No. 56/2007 of 13/12/2007 modifying and complementing Organic Law No. 07/2004 of 25/04/2004 determining the organization, functioning and jurisdiction of courts; Organic Law No. 15/2006 of 24/3/2006 modifying and complementing Organic Law No. 3/2004 of 20/03/2004 determining the organization, powers and functioning of the prosecution service; Law No. 09/2004 of 29 April 2004 relating to code of ethics for the judiciary.
15 See Organic Law No. 11/2007 of 16/03/2007 concerning transfer of cases to the Republic of Rwanda from the International Criminal Tribunal for Rwanda and from Other States; Organic Law No. 03/2009/OL of 26/05/2009 modifying and complementing Organic Law No. 11/2007 of 16/03/2007 concerning the transfer of cases to the Republic of Rwanda from the International Criminal Tribunal for Rwanda and from Other States; Organic Law No. 31/2007 of 25/07/2007 relating to the abolition of the death penalty.
16 *The Prosecutor* v. *Wenceslas Munyeshyaka*, Case No. ICTR-05-87-I, Decision on the Prosecutor's Request for the Referral of Wenceslas Munyeshyaka's Indictment to France, 20 November 2007; and *The Prosecutor* v. *Laurent Bucyibaruta*, Case No. ICTR-05-85-I, Indictment, 16 June 2005.
17 *The Prosecutor* v. *Michel Bagaragaza*, Case No. ICTR-05-86-AR11 bis, Decision on Prosecutor's Appeal against Trial Chamber's Decision on Rule 11 bis Application to Refer Case to Norway, 30 August 2006.
18 *The Prosecutor* v. *Munyakazi*, Case No. ICTR-97-36-R11 bis, Decision of the Trial Chamber on the Prosecutor's Request for Referral of Case to the Republic of Rwanda, 28 May 2008; *The Prosecutor* v. *Kanyarukiga*, Case No. ICTR-2002-78-R11 bis, Decision on the Prosecutor's Request for Referral, Judgment of 6 June 2008; *The Prosecutor* v. *Hategikimana*, Case No. 2000-55-R11 bis, Decision on the Prosecutor's Request for Referral of Case to the Republic of Rwanda, 19 June 2008; *The Prosecutor* v. *Gatete*, Case No. ICTR-2000-61-R11 bis, Decision on the Prosecutor's Request for Referral to the Republic of Rwanda, 17 November 2008; and *The Prosecutor* v. *Kayishema et al.*, Case No. ICTR-95-R11 bis, Decision on the Prosecutor's Request for Referral of Case to the Republic of Rwanda, 16 December 2008.
19 Supra note 18.
20 Ibid.
21 Organic Law No. 03/2009/OL of 26/05/2009 modifying and completing Organic Law No. 11/2007 of 16/03/2007 concerning the transfer of cases to the Republic of Rwanda from the International Criminal Tribunal for Rwanda and from Other States.

22 *Uwikindi Prosecutor* v. *Charles Sikubwabwo*, Case No. ICTR-2001-75-R11 bis, Decision on the Prosecutor's Request for Referral of the Case to the Republic of Rwanda, 28 June 2011.

23 *The Prosecutor* v. *Charles Sikubwabwo*, Case No. ICTR-95-1D-R11 bis, Decision on the Prosecutor's Request for Referral of the Case to the Republic of Rwanda, 26 March 2012; *The Prosecutor* v. *Fulgence Kayishema*, Case No. ICTR-01-67-R11 bis, Decision on the Prosecutor's Request for Referral of the Case to the Republic of Rwanda, 22 February 2012; *The Prosecutor* v. *Bernard Munyagishari*, Case No. ICTR-2005-89-R11 bis, Decision on the Prosecutor's Request for Referral of the Case to the Republic of Rwanda, 6 June 2012; *The Prosecutor* v. *Ladislas Ntaganzwa*, Case No. ICTR-96-9-R11 bis, Decision on the Prosecutor's Request for Referral of the Case to the Republic of Rwanda, 8 May 2012. The Prosecutor v. Ryankikayo, Case No. ICTR-95-1E-R11 bis, Decision on the Prosecutor's Request for Referral of the Case to the Republic of Rwanda 20 June 2012; The Prosecutor v. Aloys Ndimbati, Case No. ICTR-1F-R11 bis, Decision on the Prosecutor's request for the Referral of the Case of Aloys Ndimbati to Rwanda, 25 June 2012; The Prosecutor v. Munyarugerero, Case Number ICTR-02-79-R11 bis, Decision on the Prosecutor's Request for Referral of Case to the Republic of Rwanda, 28 June 2012.

24 Examples: François Bazaramba (Finland), Sylvere Ahorugeze (Denmark), Agathe Habyarimana (the widow of assassinated President Juvenal Habyarimana), Laurent Bucyibaruta, Laurent Serubuga, Cyprian Kayumba, Fabien Neretse, Fabien Nsabimana, Rwamucyo Eugene, Dominique Ntawukuriryayo, Stanislas Mbonampeka, Kamali Isaac, Kamana Claver, Col. Bivugabagabo Marcel, Simbikangwa Pascal, Tegera Pierre, Twagira Charles, Ngenzi Octavien, Habyarimana Joseph, Camy (Kanyamihigo) Paul, Barahira Tito, Bwigenzare Manasse, Nyombayire Venuste, Nsengiyumva Hyacinthe Rafiki, Wenceslas Munyashyaka, Dr Sosthene Munyamana and Venuste Nyombayire (France), Onesphore Rwabukombe (Germany), Vincent Bajinya aka Brown, Celestine Ugirashebuya, Charles Munyanesa and Emmanuel Nteziryayo (United Kingdom).

25 Bandora, Extraditions Proceedings No. 10/28-C-01 8911236, Oslo District Court, Norway.

26 See details in Chapter 7, which discusses trials of cases relating to the Rwanda genocide on the basis of the principle of universal jurisdiction.

27 *Mugesera* v. *Canada (Minister of Citizenship and Immigration)*, [2005] S.C.J. No. 39 (SCC).

28 *Ahorugeze* v. *Sweden*, Application No. 37075/09, Judgment of 27 October 2011, ECtHR.

29 Ibid. The Judgment became final on 4 June 2012.

30 The above information relating to the ruling party's control of the judiciary (as well as other organs of the state) is derived from knowledge acquired during the author's decade of public service in Rwanda.

31 An example is the case of Col. Diogene Mudenge. The accused was granted bail pending trial. The military authorities refused to release him from custody.

32 In the same case of Col. Diogene Mudenge, the accused was then tried and acquitted by a military court after a long period of illegal detention. The accused was re-arrested after acquittal and sent back to prison. The judges who had acquitted the accused, including Brigadier General Steven Karyango and Lt. Col. Marc Sebaganji were suspended from office as judges of the military court and from their functions in the military.

33 Opposition politicians who have been victims of politically motivated prosecutions include Pasteur Bizimungu (Former President); Charles Ntakirutinka (Former Minister and founder member PDR Ubuyanja Party); Victoire Ingabire (President, FDU-Inkingi Party); Bernard Ntaganda (President, PS Imberakuri Party); Deo Mushayidi (President, PDP Imanzi Party); Dr Niyitegeka (Former Presidential candidate) and journalists Nkusi Uwimana Agnes and Mukakibibi Saidate of Umurabyo Newspaper. Human rights organizations, including Amnesty International, have condemned the trials of these and critics of the government.

34 For example, Col. Patrick Karegeya was arrested in 2005 and detained without charge in a secret location for six months. In 2010, Lt. Col. Rugigana Ngabo was arrested and held without charge in a secret location for a period of six months. See Judgment of the East African Court of Justice. Relatives of Col. Rugigana filed an application (*Placeda Rugumba* v. *The Secretary General of the East African Community and Attorney General of the Republic of*

Rwanda, Reference No. 8 of 2010) before the East African Court of Justice challenging his detention by the authorities of the state of Rwanda. In a judgment dated 1 December 2010, the East African Court of Justice ruled in the applicant's favour, declaring:

> A declaration is hereby issued that the detention of the Subject, Lieutenant Colonel Seveline Rugigana Ngabo by the agents of the Government of the Republic of Rwanda from 20th August 2010 to 28th January 2011 was in breach of the fundamental and operational principles of the East African Community as enunciated in Articles 6(d) and 7(2) of the Treaty which demands that Partner States shall be bound by principles of *inter alia*, good governance and the rule of Law. (p. 31)

35 See the decision in *United States* v. *Francois Karake et al.*, Criminal Action No. 2-0256 (ESH), Judgment of 17 August 2006, District Court, District of Columbia.

36 Prominent personalities who have been victims of enforced disappearances include Major Alex Ruzindana, Judge Augustine Cyiza and Member of Parliament Dr Leonard Hitimana.

37 In 2010, the United Kingdom Metropolitan Police Service took the extraordinary step of warning some members of an opposition Rwanda group living in the United Kingdom of an imminent attack against them by agents of the Rwanda government. The notification of the Metropolitan Police Service reads, in part:

> Reliable intelligence states that the Rwanda Government poses an imminent threat to your life. The threat could come in any form ... You should be aware of other high profile cases where action such as this has been conducted in the past. Conventional and unconventional means have been used. (Source: Rene Claude Mugenzi and Jonathan Musonera, both resident in London. Copies of notices issued to them available on file.)

38 An attempt was made against the life of General Kayumba Nyamwasa in South Africa in 2010. The trial of the persons suspected of involvement in the attempted assassination of General Kayumba is in progress at the time of writing. The evidence that has been uncovered in the investigation of the case would appear to implicate a considerable number of senior military and intelligence officers of the Rwanda government. Charles Ingabire, a journalist, was assassinated in Uganda in 2011.

39 Law on the Court of Bosnia and Herzegovina, Official Gazette of Bosnia and Herzegovina, Nos. 29/00, 15/02, 16/02, 24/02, 3/03, 37/03, 61/04 and 32/07, Article 13(1).

6 Seeking Alternative Accountability Mechanisms: The Gacaca Courts

1 The full title of the law is Organic Law No. 40/2000 of 26/01/2000 setting up 'Gacaca jurisdictions' and organising prosecutions for offences constituting the crime of genocide or crimes against humanity committed between 1 October 1990 and 31 December 994.

2 The most recent change in categorization of suspects under the Gacaca system was introduced by Organic Law No. 13/2008 of 19/05/2008 modifying and complementing Organic Law No. 16/2004 of 19/6/2004 establishing the organisation, competence and functioning of Gacaca Courts charged with prosecuting and trying the perpetrators of the crime of genocide and other crimes against humanity, committed between 1 October 1990 and 31 December 1994. Article 9 provides as follows:

> Article 51 of Organic Law No. 16/2004 of 19/6/2004 establishing the organisation, competence and functioning of Gacaca Courts charged with prosecuting and trying the perpetrators of the crime of genocide and other crimes against humanity, committed between October 1, 1990 and December 31, 1994 as amended to date is hereby amended as follows:
>
> Commission of offences in article 1 of Organic Law No. 16/2004 of 19/6/2004 establishing the organisation, competence and functioning of Gacaca Courts charged

with prosecuting and trying the perpetrators of the crime of genocide and other crimes against humanity, committed between October 1, 1990 and December 31, 1994 as amended to date, an accused may be put in one of the following categories:

First Category:

1. any person who committed or was an accomplice in the commission of an offence that puts him or her in the category of planners or organisers of the genocide or crimes against humanity.
2. any person who was at a national leadership level and that of the prefecture level: public administration, political parties, army, gendarmerie, religious denominations or in militia group, and committed crimes of genocide or crimes against humanity or encouraged others to participate in such crimes, together with his or her accomplice;
3. any person who committed or was an accomplice in the commission of an offence that puts him or her among the category of people who incited, supervised and ringleaders of the genocide or crimes against humanity;
4. any person who was at the leadership level at the Sub-Prefecture and Commune: public administration, political parties, army, gendarmerie, communal police, religious denominations or in militia, who committed any crimes of genocide or other crimes against humanity or encouraged others to commit similar offences, together with his or her accomplice;
5. any person who committed the offence of rape or sexual torture, together with his or her accomplice.

The Prosecutor General of the Republic shall publish at least twice a year, a list of offenders in the first category forwarded by the Gacaca Cell Courts.

Second Category:

1. a notorious murderer who distinguished himself or herself in his or her location or wherever he or she passed due to the zeal and cruelty employed, together with his or her accomplice;
2. any person who tortured another even though such torture did not result into death, together with his or her accomplice;
3. any person who committed a dehumanising act on a dead body, together with his or her accomplice;
4. any person who committed or is an accomplice in the commission of an offence that puts him or her on the list of people who killed or attacked others resulting into death, together with his or her accomplice;
5. any person who injured or attacked another with the intention to kill but such intention was not fulfilled, together with his or her accomplice;
6. any person who committed or aided another to commit an offence against another without intention to kill, together with his or her accomplice.

Third Category:

A person who only committed an offence related to property. However, when the offender and the victim come to a settlement by themselves, settle the matter before the authorities or before the witnesses before commencement of this law, the offender shall not be prosecuted.

3 Ibid., Article 2.

4 Ibid., Article 46.

5 Article 143, Constitution of the Republic of Rwanda (adopted 26 May 2003).

6 Rwanda is administratively divided into provinces, which are themselves divided into districts. Districts are divided into sectors, which are in turn divided into cells, the cell being the lowest administrative organ in Rwanda. At the time when Gacaca courts were first established, Rwanda was divided into 10 provinces, 100 districts, 1,545 sectors and 9,011 cells and a corresponding number of Gacaca courts was established at each of the above levels of public administration. Currently, Rwanda is organised into 5 provinces

(*Intara*) and 30 districts (*Akarere* (singular) and *Uturere* (plural)). The cell unit has been renamed *Akagari*. The sector is now called *Umurenge*. See Organic Law No. 29/2005 of 31/12/2005 determining the administrative entities of the Republic of Rwanda. See Penal Reform International 2010b: p. 24 for a description of Rwanda's territorial organization.

7 Article 3, Organic Law No. 40/2000, supra note 1. Law No. 47/2000 of 19 December 2000 modifying and completing Law No. of 15 April 1963 relating to the administrative organization of the territory of the Republic of Rwanda as modified and completed to date; Law 11/2003 of 20 May 2003 modifying and completing Law No. 47/2000 of 19 December 2000 modifying and completing law of 15 April 1963 relating to the administrative organization of the territory of the Republic of Rwanda as modified and completed to date.

8 The full title of the law is Organic Law No. 16/2004 of 19/6/2004 establishing the organisation, competence and functioning of Gacaca Courts charged with prosecuting and trying the perpetrators of the crime of genocide and other crimes against humanity committed between 1 October 1990 and 31 December 1994.

9 Ibid., Articles 3 and 105.

10 Ibid., Articles 88 and 89.

11 Ibid., Article 5.

12 Article 6, Organic Law No. 16/2004, supra note 8; Article 3, Organic Law No. 13/2008, supra note 2.

13 Article 14, Organic Law No. 16/2004, supra note 8; Article 3, Organic Law No. 10/2007 of 01/03/2007 modifying and complementing Organic Law No. 16/2004 of 19/06/2004 establishing the organisation, competence and functioning of Gacaca Courts charged with prosecuting and trying the perpetrators of the crime of genocide and other crimes against humanity, committed between 1 October 1990 and 31 December 1994. The addition of genocide ideology as a disqualification for participation in the organs of Gacaca was part of a wider government crackdown on what the government said was a worrying resurgence of political activities by individuals and groups of citizens who still espouse the hope of resuming the genocide against the Tutsi.

14 Article 11, Organic Law No. 40/2000, supra note 1.

15 Article 15, Organic Law No. 16/2004, supra note 8.

16 Ibid., Article 16.

17 Ibid., Article 11.

18 Article 34 (10), Organic Law No. 16/2004, supra note 8; Article 23, Organic Law No. 13/2008, supra note 2.

19 Articles 34 and 36, Organic Law No. 16/2004, supra note 8.

20 Ibid., Article 39.

21 Instruction No. 04/2005 of 16/02/2005 from the Executive Secretary of the National Service for Gacaca Courts Related to Conditions Required from Observers, Researchers and Journalists in the Gacaca Process.

22 Article 21, Organic Law No. 16/2004, supra note 8.

23 Organic Law No. 40/2000, supra note 1; Organic Law No. 16/2004, supra note 8; Organic Law No. 10/2007, supra note 13; and Organic Law No. 13/2008, supra note 2.

24 Article 29, Organic Law No. 16/2004, supra note 8.

25 Ibid.

26 Ibid., Article 70.

27 Ibid., Article 98.

28 Article 22, Organic Law No. 13/2008, supra note 2.

29 Article 73, Organic Law No. 40/2000, supra note 1; Article 73, Article 13, Organic Law No. 10/2007, supra note 13; Article 17, Organic Law No. 13/2008, supra note 12.

30 Article 15, Organic Law No. 10/2007, supra note 13.

31 Articles 68–75, Organic Law No. 40/2000, supra note 1; Articles 72–81, Organic Law No. 16/2004, supra note 8; Articles 13–14, Organic Law No. 10/2007, supra note 13; Article 17, Organic Law No. 13/2008, supra note 12.

32 Article 68, Organic Law No. 40/2000, supra note 1; Article 13, Organic Law No. 10/2007, supra note 13; Article 17, Organic Law No. 13/2008, supra note 2. As opposed to the situation under Organic Law 8/96 of 30 August 1996 on the organisation of prosecutions for offences constituting the crime of genocide or crimes against humanity committed since 1 October 1990, under which Category 1 suspects were not eligible to join the Guilty Plea and Confession Programme, the legislation regulating Gacaca has permitted all perpetrators, including Category 1 accused, to participate in the Guilty Plea and Confession Programme and to be eligible for associated reductions in their sentences.

33 Article 54, Organic Law No. 40/2000, supra note 1 and Organic Law No. 16/2004, supra note 8.

34 Article 69, Organic Law No. 40/2000, supra note 1; Article 73, Organic Law No. 16/2004, supra note 8; Article 14, Organic Law No. 10/2007, supra note 13.

35 Article 74, Organic Law 40/2000, supra note 1; Article 79, Organic Law No. 16/2004, supra note 8; Article 16, Organic Law No. 10/2007, supra note 13; Article 20, Organic Law No. 13/2008, supra note 12.

36 Article 71, Organic Law No. 40/2000, supra note 1; Article 75, Organic Law No. 16/2004, supra note 8; Article 16, Organic Law No. 10/2007, supra note 13; Article 20, Organic Law No. 13/2008, supra note 2.

37 Article 21, Organic Law No. 13/2008, supra note 2.

38 In the second half of 2006 alone, at least 40 Gacaca witnesses were victims of murder or attempted murder. See Le Mon (2007).

39 Articles 2 and 42, Organic Law No. 16/2004, supra note 8.

40 Ibid., Article 51.

41 Ibid., Article 13.

42 See Supreme Court of Rwanda (u.d.).

43 Guidelines available on the website of the National Service for Gacaca Jurisdictions: http://www.inkiko-Gacaca.gov.rw.

44 Gacaca have reportedly handled approximately two million cases in less than three years. The formal justice system has concluded trials of slightly over 10,000 cases over a period of 15 years.

45 Civil law systems allow victims of crime to civil parties to criminal proceedings for the purpose of pursuing claims for damages during the criminal case, instead of filing a separate civil case.

7 Trials Based on the Principle of Universal Jurisdiction

1 Article 49, First Geneva Convention for the Amelioration of the Condition of the Wounded and Sick in Armed Forces in the Field, 1864; Article 50, Second Geneva Convention for the Amelioration of the Condition of the Wounded, Sick and Shipwrecked Members of Armed Forces at Sea, 1906; Article 129, Third Geneva Convention relative to the Treatment of Prisoners of War, 1929; Article 146, Fourth Geneva Convention relative to the Protection of Civilian Persons in Time of War, 1949.

2 Article 9 (2).

3 Restatement Third of Foreign Relations Law of the United States (1988), para. § 404.

4 Suggested in the Tadic case, where the court suggests that customary international law imposes criminal liability for serious violations of Common Article 3 of the Geneva Conventions, which apply to internal armed conflict. See *The Prosecutor* v. *Dusko Tadic*, Case No. IT-94-1-AR72, Decision on the Defence Motion for Interlocutory Appeal on Jurisdiction, 2 October 1995, Appeals Chamber, ICTY.

5 The countries that established specialized units included Germany (1958), the United States (1979), Canada (1985), Australia (1987), the United Kingdom (1991) and Poland (1998).

6 The case is discussed at length in Reydams (2002).

7 *The Prosecutor* v. *Fulgence Niyonteze*, Judgment of 30 April 1999, Military Tribunal Division 2, Lausanne.

8 *Fulgence Niyonteze* v. *The Prosecutor*, Judgment of 26 May 2000, Appellate Military Tribunal, Geneva.
9 *Fulgence Niyonteze* v. *The Prosecutor*, Judgment of 27 April 2001, Military Court of Cassation, Yverdon-les-Bains, ILDC, 349 (CH 2001).
10 Law of 16 June 1993 relating to the repression of grave violations of International Conventions of Geneva of 12 August 1949 and Additional Protocols I and II of 8 June 1977 to these Conventions, as amended by Law of 10 February 1999.
11 *Le ministère public c. « les quatre de Butare »*, Cour d'Assises, Brussels, 8 June 2001. The case is discussed in Reydams (2003b).
12 Supra note 10.
13 Law of 5 August 2003 relating to grave breaches of international humanitarian law.
14 *Nzabonima and Ndashyokirwa*, Judgment of 29 June 2005, Cour d'Assises de L'Arrondissement Administratif de Bruxelles-Capital.
15 *Ntuyahaga Bernard*, Judgment of 5 July 2007, Cour d'Assises de L'Arrondissement Administratif de Bruxelles-Capital. See Ponthus (2007).
16 *Nkezabera*, Judgment of 1 December 2009, Cour d'Assises de L'Arrondissement Administratif de Bruxelles-Capital.
17 Criminal Law in Wartime Act (Wet Oorlogsstrafrecht) Stb. 408 (1952); Law implementing the UN Torture Convention (Uitvoeringswet Folterverdrag), Stb. 478 (1988).
18 *The Prosecutor* v. *Joseph Mpambara*, The Hague District Court, LJN: BI2444, 09/750009-06 and 09/750007-07, Judgment of 7 July 2011.
19 *The Prosecutor* v. *Joseph Mpambara*, The Hague District Court, LJN: BB0494, 09/750009-06 + 09/750007-07, Decision on Jurisdiction, 24 July 2007.
20 *Mpambara*, The Hague Court of Appeal, LJN: BR0686, Gerechtshof's-Gravenhage, 22-002613-09, Judgment of 7 July 2011.
21 Information received by the author from the trial attorney involved in the Bagaragaza Case, November 2007.
22 *The Prosecutor* v. *Michel Bagaragaza*, ICTR-2005-86-R11bis, Decision on the Prosecution Motion for Referral to the Kingdom of Norway, 19 May 2006, para. 1.
23 Email addressed to the author by the accused's attorney, Victor Koppe. Message on file with the author. The Prosecutor v. Ntacyobatara Basebya, The Hague District Court, LJN: 09/748000-09.
24 Article 689-1, Code of Criminal Procedure.
25 *Wenceslas Munyeshyaka*, Court of Appeal of Nîmes, Decision of 20 March 1996; *Wenceslas Munyeshyaka*, Cour de Cassation, Criminal Jurisdiction Chamber, Application No.: 96-82491, Decision on Jurisdiction, 6 January 1998, published in *Revue Générale de Droit International Public*, vol. 102, 1998, p. 825.
26 Act No. 95-1 of 2 January 1995: United Nations Security Council resolution 827 of 25 May 1993 establishing an international tribunal for the purpose of prosecuting persons responsible for serious violations of international humanitarian law committed in the territory of the former Yugoslavia after 1 January 1991; and Act No. 96-432 of 22 May 1996: United Nations Security Council resolution 955 of 8 November 1994 establishing an international tribunal for the purpose of prosecuting persons responsible for genocide and other serious violations of international humanitarian law committed in the territory of Rwanda and Rwandan citizens responsible for genocide and other such violations committed in the territory of neighbouring States, between 1 January 1994 and 31 December 1994.
27 Interviews with three of the suspects conducted 22–23 November 2010 (Paris), 15 February 2011 (Brussels), 25 April 2012 (via Skype).
28 *Bazaramba, François*, Case No. R 09/404, District Court of Ita-Uusima, Division 1, Finland, Judgment of 11 June 2010.
29 *Mbarushimana, Emmanuel*, County Court of Roskilde, Denmark, Judgment of 31 May 2011.
30 *Mbarushimana, Emmanuel*, Court of Appeal, Copenhagen, Judgment of 26 October 2011.
31 Law No. 132 of 29 April 1955.
32 Judicial Power Organization Act No. 6/1985 of 1 July 1985 (Official Gazette No. 157 of 2 July 1985).

33 Article 23.4 of Act No. 6/1985, Judicial Power Organization Act No. 6/1985 of 1 July 1985.
34 Organization Act No. 18/2003 of 10 December on cooperation with the International Criminal Court (Official Gazette No. 296 of 11 December 2003).
35 Organization Act No. 3/2005 of 8 July amending Judicial Power Organization Act No. 6/1985 of 1 July on extraterritorial prosecution for female genital mutilation (Official Gazette No. 163 of 9 July 2005).
36 Organization Act No. 13/2007 of 19 November, on extraterritorial prosecution for human trafficking or smuggling of persons (Official Gazette No. 278 of 20 November 2007).
37 Organization Act No. 1/2009 of 3 November, supplementing the procedural reform law for the introduction of the new Judicial Office, which amended Judicial Power Organization Act No. 6/1985 of 1 July (Official Gazette No. 266 of 4 November 2009).
38 See Anonymous (2008) 'The Spanish Indictments of High Ranking Rwandan Officials', *Journal of International Criminal Justice*, vol. 5, pp. 1003–11.
39 Audencia Nacional, Auto del Juzgado Central de Instrucción No. 4, 6 February 2008, pp. 151–7.
40 See Central Investigations Tribunal No. 5 of the National High Court, Preliminary Proceedings, Brief Proceeding 399/2006 V, Decision of 16 October 2008, Facts, RJ primero.
41 National High Court, Central Investigations Tribunal No. 5, Preliminary Proceedings, Brief Proceeding 399/2006 V, Decision of October 2008, Facts.
42 See Special Case 3/20048/2009, Second Chamber of the Supreme Court, Action, 26 January 2009; Special Case No. 3/20048/2009, Second Chamber of the Supreme Court, Action, 26 March 2009.
43 Law No. 46/1977 of 15 October 1977 relating to Amnesty (Spain).
44 See Special Case 3/20048/2009, Second Chamber of the Supreme Court, Defense Writing, 17 June 2010.
45 Garzon, Special Case No. 20048/2009, Judgment No. 101/2012 of 27 February 2012, Supreme Court, Madrid.
46 *Public Prosecutor* v. *Mirsad Repak*, Case No. 08-018985med-otir/08, Oslo District Court, Judgment of 2 December 2008.
47 *Mirsad Repak*, Supreme Court of the Kingdom of Norway, Case No. LB-2009-24039, Judgment of 14 April 2011.
48 The Prosecutor v. Sadi Bugingo, Case No. 07/63-I-04 8910621, Oslo District Court, Norway.
49 Eugene Nkuranyabahizi, Investigation Case No. 07/61-C-06 8910830, Norwegian National Authority for Prosecution of Organized and Other Serious Crimes, Olso, Norway.
50 See comments on trials of genocide suspects in the Netherlands, Section 5.3 above.
51 Geneva Conventions Act 1957.
52 Section 134, Criminal Justice Act 1988; *R.* v. *Bow Street Stipendiary Magistrate and others, ex parte Pinochet Ugarte* [1999] 2 All ER 97–192.
53 *R.* v. *Zardad (Faryadi Sarwar)* [2007] EWCA Crim 279.
54 *Bajinja, Munyaneza, Nteziryayo and Ugirashebuja* v. *Government of Rwanda and the Secretary of State for the Home Department*, Judgment, 8 April 2009, High Court of Justice, Divisional Court [EWHC] 2009 770.
55 Article 70.
56 Interview with Dr Vincent Bajinya, alias Brown, 15 February 2012.
57 *Regina* v. *Imre Finta*, Court of Appeal for Ontario, Judgment of 10 July 1989, 69 O.R. (2nd),1989, p. 557.
58 *Regina* v. *Imre Finta*, Supreme Court, Judgment on Appeal from the Court of Appeal for Ontario, including dissenting opinion, 24 March 1994, [1994] 1 S.C.R. 701 and D.L.R. (4th), vol. 112, p. 513.
59 *Mugesera et al.* v. *Minister of Citizenship and Immigration*, IMM-5946-98, 10 May 2001, (T.D.) [2001] 4 F.C. 421.
60 *Mugesera et al.* v. *Canada (Minister of Citizenship and Immigration)*, Federal Court of Appeal, Judgment of 8 September 2003, 2003 FCA 325.

61 *Mugesera et al.* v. *Canada (Minister of Citizenship and Immigration)*, Supreme Court, Canada, Judgment of 28 June 2005, [2005] 2 S.C.R. 100, 2005 SCC 40.
62 Case No. 500-73-002500-052, Superior Court, 22 May 2009.
63 18 U.S.C. § 1091 (2008).
64 18 U.S.C. § 1091(d)(1).
65 18 U.S.C. § 1091(d)(2).
66 18 U.S.C. §§ 2340 and 2340A.
67 18 U.S.C. § 2340A(b).
68 Pub. L. No. 110-151; 121 Stat 1821.
69 U.S.C. § 1091(d)(3)–(5) (2008).
70 See Indictment, *United States* v. *Charles McArthur Emmanuel (a.k.a. 'Chuckie Taylor')*, No. 06-20263 (S.D. Fla., 28 April 2006).
71 *United States* v. *Mudahinyuka*, 04 CR 471 (N.D. Ill), Judgment of 14 June 2005, United District Court, for the Northern District of Illinois Eastern Division.
72 *Mudahinyuka* v. *Holder*, Petition No. 09-3255, United States Court of Appeals, Seventh Circuit, 10 August 2010.
73 Immigration and Naturalization Service, Alien Number No. A79-O51-835.
74 Section 212(a)(3)(E)(ii) of the Immigration and Nationality Act, 8 USC 1227(a)(4)(D).
75 *United States* v. *Prudence Kantengwa*, Case 1:08-cr-10385-RGS, United States District Court, District of Massachusetts.
76 *United States* v. *Munyenyezi*, Criminal Case No. 10-CR-085-SM, United States District Court, New Hampshire.
77 *United States* v. *Lazare Kobagaya*, Case No. 09-10005-01-MLB, United States District Court for the District of Kansas.
78 Desire Munyaneza (Canada), Joseph Mpambara (Netherlands), Charles Bandora (Norway), Charles Munyaneza (United Kingdom), Enos Kagaba (United States).
79 *United States* v. *Prudence Kantengwa*, supra note 64.
80 Canada spends around $15 million per year on its war crimes investigations and trials. The United States repotedly spends several million dollars on each of its prosecutions of genocide suspects. In cases where there are hung juries, decisions as to whether to seek retrial are heavily influenced by financial considerations.
81 *The Prosecutor* v. *Joseph Mpambara*, supra note 18.
82 Bandora, Extraditions Proceedings No. 10/28-C-01 8911236, Oslo District Court, Norway.
83 Wenceslas Munyeshyaka, supra note 25.
84 Emmanuel Mbarushimana, supra notes 29 and 30.
85 *The Prosecutor* v. *Mirsad Repak*, supra note 47.
86 Author's interviews with Rwandan refugees, including three genocide suspects based in France and Belgium (2010–11).
87 Author's interviews with Hutu opposition leaders living in exile and some of the genocide suspects who have been the subject of investigations in France, Belgium and the United Kingdom, supra note 27.

8 Untold Story, Unfinished Business: Confronting the Crimes of the Victors

1 Article 1, Organic Law No. 40/2000 of 26/01/2000 setting up 'Gacaca jurisdictions' and organizing prosecutions for offences constituting the crime of genocide or crimes against humanity committed between 1 October 1990 and 31 December 1994.
2 The President's speech was broadcast live on national radio, Radio Rwanda, 3 October 2001.
3 Article 1, Organic Law No. 16/04 of 19/6/2004 establishing the organization, competence, and functioning of Gacaca Courts charged with prosecuting and trying the perpetrators of the crime of genocide and other crimes against humanity, committed between 1 October 1990 and 31 December 994.
4 Ibid.

5 Article 3, Amendment of the Fundamental Law of 18 January 1996 (Official Gazette, 1996, No. 3, 1 February 1996) provides:

> The first part of Article 49 of the Arusha Peace Agreement, in its protocol relating to the integration of the armed forces of the two sides, is amended and complemented in the following manner:
>
> > Military courts have jurisdiction to try members of the national armed forces, as well as civilians who are accomplices in the crimes that have been committed by members of the armed forces as they are established in criminal law. Military courts may simultaneously adjudicate claims for damages during the course of a criminal trial.

The 2003 Constitution of Rwanda and Organic Law No. 07/2004 of 25/04/2004 determining the organization, functioning and jurisdiction of courts are both silent on the jurisdiction of military courts. In practice, Rwanda's military courts continue to exercise criminal jurisdiction over civilians who are alleged to be accomplices of defendants who are military personnel.

6 See Articles 3 and 4, Statute of the International Criminal Tribunal for Rwanda.

7 *The Prosecutor* v. *General Gumisiriza et al.*, Case No. RP 0151/08/TM, Judgment of 24 October 2008, Military Tribunal, Kigali; *Gumisiriza* v. *Prosecutor*, No. RPA 0062/08/HCM, Judgment of 25 February 2009, High Military Court, Kigali. See Waldorf (2011a) for detailed discussion of the case. It is very important in the Rwanda conflict because of the influence that the Catholic Church enjoys and the status that bishops of the Church enjoy in predominantly Catholic Rwanda. According to a Tutsi witness and survivor of the massacre whom I have spoken to, the Tutsi priests were killed because their attackers believed the priests would later tell the truth about the massacres of the bishops if they were spared. The indictment that Rwanda's military justice system issued in this case did not include the officers who ordered the killings. Of the persons who were indicted for the massacre, two junior officers (Captains John Butera and Dieudonne Rukeba) were convicted on their own guilty pleas. The senior officers, including a general and a major in the RPA (Brigadier General Wilson Gumisiriza and Major Wilson Ukwishaka) were acquitted. The prosecution lost an appeal against the first instance decision. The captains' appeal against conviction was dismissed but the appellate court reduced their sentences from eight to five years imprisonment. Human Rights Watch has indicated that it is of the strong view that the case was not tried in good faith. See letter dated 14 August 2009 addressed to Hassan Jallow, Prosecutor of the ICTR, by Kenneth Roth, Executive Director, Human Rights Watch (Roth 2009b).

8 Article 8, Universal Declaration of Human Rights; Basic Principles and Guidelines on the Right to a Remedy and Reparation for Victims of Gross Violations of International Human Rights Law and Serious Violations of International Humanitarian Law, adopted and proclaimed by General Assembly resolution 60/147 of 16 December 2005.

9 Assessing the Impact and Legacy of Rwanda's Mechanisms of Accountability for Atrocity

1 See Article 8, Universal Declaration of Human Rights; Articles 2 (3), 9 (5) and 14 (6), International Covenant on Civil and Political Rights; Article 6, International Convention on the Elimination of All Forms of Racial Discrimination; Articles 13 and 14, Convention against Torture and Other Cruel, Inhuman or Degrading Treatment or Punishment; Articles 9 and 13, International Convention for the Protection of All Persons from Enforced Disappearance; and Article 75, Rome Statute of the International Criminal Court.

2 See Articles 5 (5), 13, 41 and 50, European Convention on Human Rights; Article 47, Charter of Fundamental Rights of the European Union; Articles 25, 68 and 63 (1), Inter-American Convention on Human Rights; Articles 7 (1) (a) and 21 (2), African Charter on Human and Peoples' Rights; Article III (1), Inter-American Convention on Forced

Disappearance of Persons; Article 8 (1), Inter-American Convention to Prevent and Punish Torture; Article 9, Arab Charter on Human Rights; and Articles 7 (1) (a) and 25, American Convention on Human Rights.

3 Basic Principles and Guidelines on the Right to a Remedy and Reparation for Victims of Gross Violations of International Human Rights Law and Serious Violations of International Humanitarian Law; Article 19, Declaration on the Protection of All Persons from Enforced Disappearance; UN General Assembly resolution 47/133 of 18 December 1992; Principle 20, Principles on the Effective Prevention and Investigation of Extra-legal, Arbitrary and Summary Executions, recommended by Economic and Social Council resolution 1989/65 of 24 May 1989; Declaration on the Elimination of Violence against Women; Article XVIII, American Declaration of the Rights and Duties of Man; Principles 4 and 16, United Nations Principles on Extra-legal Executions; Principles 4–7, Declaration of Basic Principles of Justice for Victims of Crime and Abuse of Power; Article 27, Vienna Declaration and Programme of Action; Articles 13, 160–162, 165, Programme of Action of the World Conference against Racism, Racial Discrimination, Xenophobia and Related Intolerance; and Article 9, Declaration on Human Rights Defenders.

4 HRC: General Comment No. 31 on the Nature of the General Legal Obligation Imposed on States Parties to the Covenant, 26 May 2004, CCPR/C/21/Rev.1/Add.13, para. 15; I/ACtHR: Advisory Opinion OC-9/87, Judicial Guarantees in States of Emergency, 6 October 1987, Series A No. 9, para. 24; AfrCmHPR, Principles and Guidelines on the Right to a Fair Trial and Legal Assistance in Africa, Principle C, African Union Doc. DOC/OS (XXX) 247; *The Social and Economic Rights Action Center and the Center for Economic and Social Rights* v. *Nigeria,* Communication 155/96 (30th Ordinary Session, October 2001), para. 61, in which the Commission considered that the State had to ensure 'legal remedies'; ECHR: *Airey* v. *Ireland*, Judgment of 9 October 1979, Series A No. 32, para. 33.

5 United Nations Human Rights Committee, General Comment No. 31 on the Nature of the General Legal Obligation Imposed on States Parties to the Covenant, 26 May 2004, CCPR/C/21/Rev.1/Add.13, para. 15; *L.K.* v. *the Netherlands,* Communication No. 4/1991, Views of 16 March 1993, CERD/C/42/D/4/1991, CERD Committee, para. 6.9; *Habassi* v. *Denmark*, Communication No. 10/1997, Views of 6 April 1999, CERD/C/54/D/10/1997, CERD Committee, paras 9.3–10; *Blake* v. *Guatemala*, Judgment of 24 January 1998, Series C No 36, I/ACtHR, para. 97; *Villagrán Morales et al.* v. *Guatemala* (The 'Street Children' Case), Judgment of 19 November 1999, I/ACtHR, para. 225; *Castillo Páez* v. *Peru*, Judgment of 3 November 1997, Series C No. 34, I/ACtHR, para. 90; I/ACmHR: *Extrajudicial Executions and Forced Disappearances* v. *Peru*, Case 10.247 *et al.,* Report No. 101/01, Inter-Am. C.H.R., OEA/Ser./L/V/II.114 Doc. 5 rev. at 563 (2001), para. 243; see also *Riofrío Massacre (Colombia)*, Case 11.654, Report No. 62/01, Inter-Am. C.H.R., OEA/Ser.L/V/II.111 Doc. 20 rev. at 758 (2000), para 74; *Aksoy* v. *Turkey*, Application No. 21987/93, Judgment of 18 December 1996, Reports 1996-VI, ECtHR, paras 95–100.

6 See Article 7 of the African Charter on Human and Peoples' Rights.

7 See Chapter 6.

8 24,000 prisoners were released in 2003 in response to the Presidential Decree of 1 January 2001. A further 4,000 prisoners were released in 2004 and 40,000 were released in 2005. See Mibenge (2004: pp. 417–18).

9 *Parada Cea et al.* v. *El Salvador*, Case 10.480, Report No. 1/99, I/ACtHR, para. 150.

10 *Hugo Rodríguez* v. *Uruguay*, Communication No. 322/1988, Decision of 19 July 1994, I/ACtHR, paras 12 (3) and 14.

11 *Ignacio Ellacuría S.J. et al.* (El Salvador), Report No. 136/99, Case 10.488, 22 December 1999, Inter-American Commission on Human Rights, para. 229 et seq.

12 *Bámaca Velásquez* v. *Guatemala* (Reparations), Judgment of 22 February 2002, Series C No 91, I/ACtHR, para. 77; *Caracazo* v. *Venezuela* (Reparations), Judgment of 29 August 2002, Series C No. 95, I/ACtHR, para. 118.

13 *Myrna Mack Chang* v. *Guatemala*, Judgment of 23 November 2003, vol. 101, Series C, No. 101, I/ACtHR, paras 274–275.

14 See discussion on objectives of Rwanda's transitional justice processes in Chapter 3.

15 *The Prosecutor* v. *Karemera et al.*, Case No. ICTR 98-44-AR73(C), Decision on Prosecutor's Interlocutory Appeal of Decision on Judicial Notice, 16 June 2006, para. 38.

16 Ibid.

17 Project by Harvard University, 'Through a Glass Darkly: Genocide Memorials in Rwanda 1994– Present' at http://genocidememorials.cga.harvard.edu/data.html.

18 Law No. 147/1997 of 2 December 1997 relating to the creation of the National Fund for the Assistance of Needy Victims of the Genocide and Massacres that were committed in Rwanda between 1 October 1990 and 31 December 1994. Law No. 11/1998 of 2 November 1998 modifying and completing law 02/98 relating to the creation of the National Fund for the Assistance of Needy Victims of the Genocide and Massacres that were committed in Rwanda between 1 October 1990 and 31 December 1994. Law No. 69/2008 of 30/12/2008 relating to the establishment of the Fund for the support of and assistance to the survivors of the Tutsi genocide and other crimes against humanity committed between 1 October 1990 and 31 December 1994, and determining its organization, powers and functioning.

19 Ibid., Article 22.

20 Ibid., Article 3. The beneficiaries of the fund are defined as 'survivors of the Genocide against the Tutsi and other crimes against humanity committed between 1 October 1990 and 31 December 1994'.

21 Organic Law No. 40/2000 Setting up 'Gacaca jurisdictions' and organizing prosecutions for offences constituting the crime of genocide or crimes against humanity committed between 1 October 1990 and 31 December 1994, Article 91.

22 Ibid., Articles 64 and 65.

23 Ibid., Article 90.

24 Organic Law No. 40/2000, supra note 21, Article 90; a subsequent reform of Organic Law No. 40/2000 in 2004 provided that 'other forms of compensation for victims are to be determined by a particular law', thereby opening up the possibility for survivors to claim for non-pecuniary damages, subject to the adoption of a particular law. See Article 75 of Organic Law No. 16/2004 of 19/6/2004 establishing the organization, competence and functioning of Gacaca Courts charged with prosecuting and trying the perpetrators of the crime of genocide and other crimes against humanity, committed between 1 October 1990 and 31 December 1994.

25 Supra note 18.

26 Author's interviews with Hutu refugees living in Europe and North America (2010–12).

27 Law No. 47/2001 of 18/12/2001 instituting punishment for offences of discrimination and sectarianism.

28 Established by Law No. 03/99 of 12/02/1999 relating to the creating of the National Unity and Reconciliation Commission.

29 Law 04/99 of 12 February 1999 relating to the creating of National Human Rights Commission.

30 See Section 4, Chapter 3 dealing with the objectives of Rwanda's accountability processes.

31 Ibid.

32 See Constitution of the Republic of Rwanda (2003); Organic Law No. 03/2004 of 20/03/2004 determining the organization, powers and functioning of the Prosecution Service; Law 06 bis/2004 establishing the Statute governing Judges and other judicial personnel; Organic Law No. 07/2004 of 25/04/2004 determining the organization, functioning and jurisdiction of courts; Law No. 09/2004 of 29 April 2004 relating to code of ethics for the judiciary; Law No. 13/2004 of 17/5/2004 establishing the code of criminal procedure; Law No. 13/2004 of 17/5/2004 relating to the Code of Criminal Procedure (O.G special No of 30/07/2004); Organic Law No. 29/2005 of 23 December 2005 determining the administrative entities of the Republic of Rwanda; Organic law 12/2006 of 21/3/2006 modifying and complementing Organic Law 22/2004 of 13/8/2004 on the Statute of Public Prosecutors and Personnel of the Public Prosecution Service; Organic law 13/2006 of 0/3/2006 modifying and complementing Organic Law 01/2004 of 13/8/2004 establishing the organization, functioning and jurisdiction of the Supreme Court; Organic Law no. 14/2006 modifying and complementing Organic law 07/2004 of 25/4/2004 on the organization, functioning and jurisdiction of courts; Organic Law No. 15/2006

of 24/3/2006 modifying and complementing Organic Law No. 3/2004 determining the organization, powers and functioning of the prosecution service; See Law No. 20/2006 of 22/04/2006 modifying and complementing Law No. 13/2004 of 17/5/2004 relating to the Code of Criminal Procedure; Organic Law 56/2007 of 13/12/2007 modifying and complementing Organic Law No. 07/04/2004 determining the organization, functioning and jurisdiction of courts; Organic Law 58/2007 of 16/12/2004 modifying and complementing Organic Law No. 01/2004 of 29/01/2004 establishing the organization, functioning and jurisdiction of the Supreme Court.

33 The constitution grants the President power to appoint more than a third of the members of the Senate (Article 82). The President is able to influence the appointment of all the remaining members. The Senate has extensive powers, especially in legislative matters and the appointment of a vast number of public offices, including the judiciary. Most of the bills passed by the lower house require the approval of the Senate to become law. The Senate has powers of supervision of the conduct of political parties. Through the control of the Senate, the President is able to control the lower house, the Chamber of Deputies. The President is also able to control the judiciary through the power of the Senate to appoint and remove the judges of the Supreme Court. Parliament and the judiciary are not independent of the executive. There is no real separation of powers under Rwanda's constitution. See Jordaan (2006: p. 346). A new round of arrests, detentions and extrajudicial killings preceded the 2009 presidential elections (Amnesty International 2011).

34 See also the judgment in *Bajinja, Munyaneza, Nteziryayo and Ugirashebuja* v. *Government of Rwanda and the Secretary of State for the Home Department*, Judgment, 8 April 2009, High Court of Justice, Divisional Court [EWHC] 2009 770, para. 67.

35 See section 2.9 'Promoting sustainable peace and stability' below.

36 The President made the speech at Bwisige in northern Rwanda, 31 March 2003.

37 Pierre Gakwandi, the Secretary General of the opposition MDR Party, was arrested and imprisoned in January 2002 on charges of inciting ethnic divisions and defaming the government in press interviews. Pasteur Bizimungu, the former president of Rwanda, Charles Ntakirutinka, and other members of the PDR Ubuyanja Party were arrested on 19 April 2002 on charges of inciting ethnic strife and organizing an armed rebellion against the state. Bizimungu was pardoned, but remains under house arrest. Other political prisoners languishing in detention on politically motivated criminal charges at the time of writing include Victoire Ingabire, President of the FDU-Inkingi Party; Bernard Ntaganda, President of the PS Imberakuri Party; Deo Mushayidi, President of the PDP Imanzi Party; and Dr Niyitegeka, a former presidential candidate.

38 During the period of particularly intense repression that preceded the presidential and parliamentary elections of 2003, several individuals who were considered opponents of the regime disappeared in still unexplained circumstances. The most prominent of these individuals were Dr Leonard Hitimana, a member of the National Assembly who had been identified by the parliamentary commission on the MDR Party as one of the party's members who shared the genocide ideology, and Judge Augustine Cyiza, a former army officer, Supreme Court judge and human rights activist. The disappearance of Judge Cyiza has been linked to the command of the Department of Military Intelligence of the Rwanda army. See Guichaoua *et al.* (2004: pp. 209–14).

39 Seth Sendashonga, who resigned in August 1995 in protest over massacres of Hutu civilians by the RPF, was assassinated in Nairobi, Kenya in 1998. Theoneste Lizinde, an army officer, was assassinated in Nairobi, Kenya in 1997. General Kayumba Nyamwasa, a former army chief, has survived several assassination attempts in South Africa since 2010. Charles Ingabire, journalist, was murdered in Kampala, Uganda in December 2011.

40 Law No. 47/2001 of 18/12/2001 instituting punishment for offences of discrimination and sectarianism.

41 See Articles 52–56 of the Constitution and Organic Law No. 16/2003 of 27/6/2003 on the organization of political parties for details of legal and constitutional restrictions on political representation and participation.

42 Former President Pasteur Bizimungu was charged with inciting genocide on the basis of this statement in an interview conducted by journalist Valérie Thorin (2001). On 7 June 2004 he was sentenced to 15 years in prison for attempting to form a militia, inciting violence and embezzlement. He was released on 6 April 2007, having been pardoned by President Kagame. See Associated Press (2007).

43 See Chapter 5 for detailed discussions of the challenges, weaknesses and shortcomings of the ICTR.

44 *The Prosecutor* v. *Jean Paul Akayesu*, Case No. ICTR-96-4-T, Judgment of 2 September 1998, Trial Chamber.

45 Ibid.

46 Ibid., para. 687.

47 Ibid., para. 688.

48 Ibid., para. 688.

49 *The Prosecutor* v. *Nahimana, Barayagwiza and Ngeze*, Case No. ICTR-99-52-T, Judgment of 3 December 2003, Trial Chamber.

50 *The Prosecutor* v. *George Anderson Rutaganda*, Case No. ICTR-96-3-T, Judgment and Sentence of 6 December 1999, Trial Chamber, Judgment of 24 April 2003, Appeals Chamber.

51 *The Prosecutor* v. *Laurent Semanza*, Case No. ICTR-97-20-T, Judgment and Sentence of 15 May 2003, Trial Chamber, Judgment of 20 May 2005, Appeals Chamber.

52 *The Prosecutor* v. Alfred Musema, Case No. ICTR-96-13-T, Judgment and Sentence, 27 January 2000, Trial Chamber, 16 November 2001, Appeals Chamber.

53 *The Prosecutor* v. *Eliezer Niyitegeka*, Case No. ICTR-96-14-I, Judgment and Sentence of 16 May 2003, Trial Chamber, Judgment of 9 July 2004, Appeals Chamber.

54 *The Prosecutor* v. *Kambanda*, Case No. ICTR 97-23-S, Judgment and Sentence of 4 September 1998, Trial Chamber, Judgment of 19 October 2000, Appeals Chamber.

10 Tentative Lessons from Rwanda's Mechanisms of Accountability for Atrocity

1 See Chapter 9, Section 2.6 on Reparation.

2 See Decree-La No. 002/94 of 1 December 1994 relating to the modification of Decree-Law No. 09/80 of 7 July 1980 establishing the Code on the organisation and jurisdiction of the military justice system; Law No. 08/95 of 6 December 1995 relating to the modification of decree-law No. 09/80 relating to the establishment of the Code on the organisation and jurisdiction of the military justice system; Organic Law No. 5/99 of 8 January 1999 modifying and completing Organic Law 8/95 of December 1995 modifying Decree-law No. 09/80 of July 1980 instituting the code on the organization and jurisdiction of the military justice system and Organic Law No. 11/2000 of 19 April 2000 modifying Decree- Law 8/95 of 6 December 1995 instituting the code on the organization and jurisdiction of the military justice system as modified by Organic law 5/99 of January 1999.

3 The US has concluded bilateral immunity agreements, otherwise referred to as Article 98 agreements, with more than 100 nations. 'Article 98' is a reference to Article 98 of the Rome Treaty establishing the International Criminal Court that provides:

> The Court may not proceed with a request for surrender which would require the requested State to act inconsistently with its obligations under international agreements pursuant to which the consent of a sending State is required to surrender a person of that State to the Court, unless the Court can first obtain the cooperation of the sending State for the giving of consent for the surrender.

The agreements prohibit states that are party to the ICC from surrendering any US personnel, including past and present US service members, nationals or employees and contractors of the US government to the court. In 2002, Congress passed the American Service Members'

Protection Act or ASPA (P.L. 107-206, title II, 116 Stat. 889 (2002), codified at 22 U.S.C. §§ 7421 *et seq.*), which prohibits military assistance to countries that are party to the ICC and that do not have Article 98 agreements. The Nethercutt Amendment to the FY2005 Consolidated Appropriations Act (H.R. 4818/P.L. 1082006-447) and FY2006 Appropriations Act (H.R. 3057/P.L. 109-102) prohibited some economic assistance to the governments of those same countries that do not have Article 98 agreements. Under the ASPA, countries that belong to the ICC would no longer be eligible for US military assistance unless they are explicitly exempted in the ASPA legislation, the President waives the requirement for national security reasons, or the President waives the requirement because the countries have concluded a bilateral immunity agreement with the US. Under the Nethercutt Amendment, countries that belong to the ICC would not be eligible for US economic support funds unless they are statutorily exempted, the President waives the requirement for national security reasons, or the President waives the requirement because the countries have concluded a bilateral agreement with the US. The agreements remain in force, although the anti-ICC sanctions on countries refusing the agreements have been repealed.

4 The author has seen bank documents relating to the transactions. See also Melvern (2000a).

5 Alone and together with the then Representative of Rwanda to the ICTR (current Prosecutor General of Rwanda), I had the opportunity at various times during my tenure as Prosecutor General to discuss the issue of Rwanda's cooperation with the tribunal's investigations of human rights abuses attributable to the RPA with Paul Kagame and his senior military officers. Kagame was always of the view that he did not believe the West had the political will to seek or support indictments against members of the RPA.

6 Kenya, Cameroon and the Democratic Republic of Congo are prime examples.

7 See discussion on the impact of policies of the US and UK governments on the effectiveness of the ICTR in Chapter 6.

Bibliography

Abu-Nimer, M. (ed.) (2001) *Reconciliation, Justice, and Coexistence: Theory and Practice*, Lanham, MD: Lexington Books.

ACCT, Agence de Coopération Culturelle et Technique (1994) *Mission Francophone D'Évaluation des Besoins Prioritaires dans le Domaine de L'État de Droit et des Droits de L'Homme au Rwanda du 17 au 21 novembre 1994*, Paris: Agence de Coopération Culturelle et Technique. www.grandslacs.net/doc/2072.pdf (accessed 2 August 2012).

Adelman, H. (2003) 'The Use and Abuse of Refugees in Zaire (April 1996 – March 1997)' in Stedman, S.J. and Tanner, F. (eds) *Refugee Manipulation: War, Politics, and the Abuse of Human Suffering*, Washington, DC: Brookings Institution.

Adelman, H. and Suhrke, A. (eds) (1999) *The Path of Genocide: The Rwanda Crisis from Uganda to Zaire*, New Brunswick, NJ and London: Transaction Publishers.

Africa Watch (1992) *Rwanda: Talking Peace and Waging War: The Human Rights Situation Since the October 1990 Invasion*, vol. IV, no. 3, New York: Human Rights Watch.

African Commission on Human and Peoples' Rights (1999a) *Dakar Resolution on Fair Trial and Judicial Assistance in Africa*, Banjul: African Commission on Human and Peoples' Rights.

— (1999b) *Dakar Declaration on the Right to Fair Trial*, Banjul: African Commission on Human and Peoples' Rights. www.chr.up.ac.za/test/images/files/documents/ahrdd/theme17/fair_trial_dakar_declaration_1999.pdf (accessed 30 August 2012).

— (2001) *The Principles and Guidelines on the Right to a Fair Trial and Legal Assistance in Africa*, DOC/OS(XXX)247, Banjul: African Commission on Human and Peoples' Rights. www.achpr.org/instruments/fair-trial/ (accessed 30 August 2012).

African Rights (1996) *Rwanda, Killing the Evidence: Murder, Attacks, Arrests, and Intimidation of Survivors and Witnesses*, London: African Rights.

— (2000) *Rwanda: Death, Despair and Defiance*, London: African Rights.

— (2003) *Gacaca: A Shared Responsibility*, Kigali: African Rights.

— (2004) *Rwanda, Broken Bodies, Torn Spirits: Living with Genocide, Rape and HIV/AIDS*, London: African Rights.

Aggernaes, L.S. (2006) *Development as Peace-building: A Study of Paradigm Shifts and Donor Policies towards Post-genocide Rwanda*, Master of Arts thesis, Department of Political Science, University of Copenhagen.

Akhavan, P. (1996) 'The International Criminal Tribunal for Rwanda: The Politics and Pragmatics of Punishment', *American Journal of International Law*, vol. 90, pp. 501–10.

— (1997) 'Justice and Reconciliation in the Great Lakes Region of Africa: The Contribution of the International Criminal Tribunal for Rwanda', *Duke Journal of Comparative and International Law*, vol. 7, no. 2, pp. 325–48.

— (2001) 'Beyond Impunity: Can International Criminal Justice Prevent Atrocities?', *American Journal of International Law*, vol. 95, no. 1, pp. 7–31.

Algard, A. (2005) *Does the Gacaca System in Rwanda Provide an Effective Remedy in Compliance with International Norms and Standards?*, Master of Arts thesis, Faculty of Law, University of Lund.

Ambos, K., Large, J. and Wierda, M. (eds) (2009) *Building a Future of Peace and Justice, Studies on Transitional Justice, Peace and Development: The Nuremberg Declaration on Peace and Justice*, Berlin and Heidelberg: Springer.

Amnesty International (1994) *Rwanda: Reports of Killings and Abductions by the Rwandese Patriotic Army, April–August 1994*, AI Index AFR 47/16/94, London: Amnesty International.

— (1995a) *Rwanda and Burundi. A Call for Action by the International Community*, AI Index AFR 47/05/95, London: Amnesty International.

— (1995b) *Rwanda: Crying Out for Justice*, AI Index AFR 47/05/95, London: Amnesty International.

— (1995c) *Rwanda: Human Rights May Be the Main Casualty of Tensions in the Rwandese Government*, AI Index AFR 47/18/95, London: Amnesty International.

— (1996a) *Two Years After the Genocide: Human Rights in the Balance, an Open Letter to President Pasteur Bizimungu*, AI Index AFR/47/02/96, London: Amnesty International.

— (1996b) *Rwanda: Arming the Perpetrators of the Genocide*, AI Index AFR 02/14/95, London: Amnesty International.

— (1997a) *Rwanda: Ending the Silence*, AI Index AFR/032/1997, London: Amnesty International.

— (1997b) *Rwanda, Unfair Trials: Justice Denied*, AI Index AFR/47/008/1997, London: Amnesty International.

— (1997c) *Rwanda: Civilians Trapped in Armed Conflict: The Dead Can No Longer Be Counted*, AI Index AFR 47/044/1997, London: Amnesty International.

— (1997d) *Democratic Republic of Congo: Deadly Alliances in Congolese Forests*, London: Amnesty International.

— (1998) *International Criminal Tribunal for Rwanda: Trials and Tribulations*, AI Index IOR 40/003/1998, London: Amnesty International.

— (2000) *Rwanda: The Troubled Course of Justice*, AI Index AFR 47/11/00, London: Amnesty International.

— (2002a) *Gacaca Tribunals Must Conform with International Fair Trial Standards*, AI Index AFR 47/005/2002, London: Amnesty International.

— (2002b) *Gacaca: A Question of Justice*, AI Index AFR, London: Amnesty International.

— (2002c) *Rwanda: Gacaca – Gambling with Justice*, AI Index AFR 47/003/2002, London: Amnesty International.

— (2004) *Rwanda: The Enduring Legacy of the Genocide*, AI Index: AFR 47/008/2004, London: Amnesty International.

— (2005) *Country Report: Rwanda 2005*, London: Amnesty International.

— (2010) *Universal Jurisdiction: A Preliminary Survey of Legislation Around the World*, London: Amnesty International.

— (2011) *Unsafe to Speak Out: Restrictions on Freedom of Expression in Rwanda*, AI Index AFR 47/002/2001, London: Amnesty International.

Amstutz, M. (2006) 'Is Reconciliation Possible After Genocide? The Case of Rwanda', *Journal of Church and State*, vol. 48, no. 3, pp. 541–65.

Andersen, R. (2000) 'How Multilateral Development Assistance Triggered the Conflict in Rwanda', *Third World Quarterly*, vol. 21, no. 3, pp. 441–56.

Anonymous (2008) 'The Spanish Indictments of High Ranking Rwandan Officials', *Journal of International Criminal Justice*, vol. 5, pp. 1003–11.

Aptel, C. (1997) 'The International Criminal Tribunal for Rwanda', *International Review of the Red Cross*, no. 321, pp. 675–83.

— (2008) 'Closing the UN International Criminal Tribunal for Rwanda: Completion Strategy and Residual Issues', *New England Journal of International and Comparative Law*, vol. 14, no. 2, pp. 169–89.

Arenhovel, M. (2008) 'Democratization and Transitional Justice', *Democratization*, vol. 15, no. 3 (June), pp. 570–87.

Arriaza, L. and Roht-Arriaza, N. (2002) 'Social Reconstruction as a Local Process', *International Journal of Transitional Justice*, vol. 2, no. 3, pp. 152–72.

Article 19 (2009) *Commentary on the Law Relating to the Crime of Genocide Ideology in Rwanda*, London: Article 19.

Associated Press (2007) 'Libération de l'ancien président Pasteur Bizimungu', Associated Press report, 6 April.

— (2009) 'Bush and Clinton share Canadian stage for more agreement than debate', Associated Press report, 29 May.

Atterbury, M.C. (1970) *Revolution in Rwanda*, Madison, WI: University of Wisconsin Press.

Aukerman, M.J. (2002) 'Extraordinary Evil, Ordinary Crime: A Framework for Understanding Transitional Justice', *Harvard Human Rights Journal*, vol. 15, pp. 39–98.

Austin, K. (1994) 'Rwanda readies for another bloodbath', *The Providence Journal*, 25 November, p. A19.

Avocats Sans Frontières (ASF) (2008) *Monitoring des juridictions gacaca*, Kigali: Avocats Sans Frontières.

Bababola, J., Karambizi, J., Boubacar, S. and Ruzibuka, J.B. (2003) 'Evaluation of the Gacaca Promotional Campaign in Rwanda', Kigali: John Hopkins University. http://pdf.usaid.gov/pdf_docs/PNACT554.pdf (accessed 15 October 2011).

Ball, H. (1999) *Prosecuting War Crimes and Genocide: The Twentieth Century Experience*, Lawrence, KS: Kansas University Press.

Banks, A. (2004) 'Carla Del Ponte: Her Retrospective of Four Years in The Hague', Conference Report, *International Law Forum*, vol. 6, no. 1 (February), pp. 37–42.

Barayagwiza, J.B. (2000) 'The International Criminal Tribunal for Rwanda (ICTR): Impossible Justice'. http://membres.multimania.fr/barayagwiza/filescommunications/impossiblejustice.pdf (accessed 1 September 2001).

Barnett, M. (2002) *Eyewitness to Genocide: The United Nations and Rwanda*, Ithaca, NY and London: Cornell University Press.

Barria, L.A. and Roper, S.D. (2005) 'How Effective Are International Criminal Tribunals? An Analysis of the ICTY and the ICTR', *International Journal of Human Rights*, vol. 9, no. 3 (September), pp. 349–68.

Barry, H. (ed.) (2008) *Peace Building in Traumatized Societies*, Lanham, MD: University Press of America.

Bass, G.J. (2000) *Stay the Hand of Vengeance: The Politics of War Crimes Tribunals*, Princeton, NJ: Princeton University Press.

Bassiouni, M.C. (2001) 'Universal Jurisdiction for International Crimes: Historical Perspectives and Contemporary Practice', *Virginia Journal of International Law*, vol. 42, no. 81, pp. 81–162.

— (ed.) (2002a) *Post-Conflict Justice*, Ardsley, NJ: Transnational Publishers.

— (2002b) 'Universal Jurisdiction for International Crimes: Historical Perspectives and Contemporary Practice', in Bassiouni, M.C. (ed.) (2002a) *Post-Conflict Justice,* Ardsley, NJ: Transnational Publishers.

Benomar, J. (1993) 'Confronting the Past: Justice in Transitions', *Journal of Democracy*, vol. 4, no. 1, pp. 3–14.

Berry, J.A. and Berry, C.P. (1999) *Genocide in Rwanda, A Collective Memory*, Washington, DC: Howard University Press.

Beswick, D. (2010) 'Managing Dissent in a Post-Genocide Environment: The Challenge of Political Space in Rwanda', *Development and Change*, vol. 41, no. 2, pp. 225–51.

— (2011) 'Aiding State Building and Sacrificing Peace Building? The Rwanda–UK Relationship 1994–2011', *Third World Quarterly*, vol. 32, no. 10, pp. 1911–30.

— (2012) 'The Role of the Military in Contemporary Rwanda', in Campioni, M. and Noack, P. (eds) *Rwanda Fast Forward: Social, Economic, Military and Reconciliation Prospects*, London: Palgrave Macmillan.

Biggar, N. (ed.) (2003) *Burying the Past: Making Peace and Doing Justice after Civil Conflict*, Washington, DC: Georgetown University Press.

Bloomfield, D., Barnes, T. and Huyse, L. (2003) *Reconciliation after Violent Conflict: A Handbook*, Stockholm: International Institute for Democracy and Electoral Assistance.

Bonner, R. (1994) 'Inadequate U.N. Effort Seen Against Killers In Rwanda', *New York Times*, 4 September.

Booth, D. and Golooba-Mutebi, F. (2012) 'Developmental Patrimonialism? The Case of Rwanda', *African Affairs*, vol. 111, no. 444, 23 July, pp. 379–403.

Borland, R.M. (2003) 'The Gacaca Tribunals and Rwanda After the Genocide: Effective Restorative Community Justice or Further Abuse of Human Rights', *Swords & Ploughshares. Journal of International Affairs*, vol. 13, no. 2 (Fall).

Bornkamm, P.C. (2012) *Rwanda's Gacaca Courts: Between Retribution and Reparation*, Oxford: Oxford University Press.

Borocan, M.G. (2004) 'Rwandan Gacaca: An Experiment in Transitional Justice', *Journal of Dispute Resolution*, vol. 2, pp. 357–400.

Bosch, W.J. (1970) *Judgement at Nuremberg*, Chapel Hill, NC: University of North Carolina Press.

Boutros-Ghali, B. (1992) *An Agenda for Peace: Preventive Diplomacy, Peacemaking and Peace-keeping*, UN Document A/47/277 – S/241111, New York: Department of Public Information, United Nations.

— (1995) *Supplement to An Agenda for Peace: Position Paper of the Secretary General on the Occasion of the Fiftieth Anniversary of the United Nations Document A/50/60 – S/1995/1*, New York: Department of Public Information, United Nations.

Bouvier, O.L., Gasasira, E., Hakizimfura, E., Mukayiranga, L., Nkubito, A.M. and Ntagozera, C. (1992) *La Place de la justice et le rôle du magistrat dans l'édification d'un état démocratique*, Kigali: Ministry of Justice.

Bowden, B., Charlesworth, H. and Farall, J. (eds) (2009) *The Role of International Law in Rebuilding Societies After Conflict: Great Expectations*, Cambridge and New York: Cambridge University Press.

Bradley, E. (1998) 'In Search for Justice – A Truth and Reconciliation for Rwanda?', *Journal of International Law and Practice*, vol. 7, no. 2, pp. 129–58. www.restorativejustice.org/articlesdb/articles/6085/?searchterm=rwanda (accessed 30 August 2012).

Bradol, J.H. and Guibert, A. (1997) 'Le temps des assassins et l'espace humanitaire', *Hérodote*, no. 86/87.

Braley, M.B. (2004) 'Rooting, Reforming, Restoring: A Framework for Justice in Rwanda', *Journal of Lutheran Ethics*, vol. 4, no. 3. www.restorativejustice.org/articlesdb/articles/6085/?searchterm=rwanda (accessed 1 September 2012).

Brannigan, A. and Jones, A. (2009) 'Genocide and the Legal Process in Rwanda: From Genocide Amnesty to the New Rule of Law', *International Criminal Justice Review*, vol. 19, pp. 192–207.

Brouneus, K. (2008) 'Truth-telling as Talking Cure? Insecurity and Re-traumatisation in the Rwandan Gacaca Courts', *Security Dialogue*, vol. 39, no. 1, pp. 55–76.

Buckley-Zistel, S. (2006) 'Dividing and Uniting: The Use of "Citizenship" in Conflict and Reconciliation in Rwanda', *Global Society*, vol. 20, no. 1, pp. 125–44.

— (2009) 'We Are Pretending Peace: Local Memory and the Absence of Social Transformation and Reconciliation in Rwanda', in Clark, P. and Kaufman, Z.D. (eds) *After Genocide: Transitional Justice, Post-Conflict Reconstruction, and Reconciliation in Rwanda and Beyond*, New York: Columbia University Press and London: C. Hurst & Co.

Burnet, J.E. (2007) *Countries at the Crossroads: Rwanda*, Washington, DC: Freedom House.

— (2008) 'The Injustice of Local Justice: Truth, Reconciliation, and Revenge in Rwanda', *Genocide Studies and Prevention*, vol. 3, no. 2, pp. 173–93.

— (2009) 'Whose Genocide? Whose Truth? Representations of Victim and Perpetrator in Rwanda', in Hinton, A.L. and O'Neil, K.L. (eds) *Genocide: Truth, Memory and Reconciliation*, Durham, NC: Duke University Press.

Busingye, J. (2006) 'Realities and Challenges of Judicial Reconstruction in Rwanda', Paper presented at CILC Seminar on 'Legal and Judicial Reform in Post-Conflict Situations and the Role of the International Community', The Hague, 7 December.

Buyse, A. (2008) 'Lost and Regained? Restitution as a Remedy for Human Rights Violations in the Context of International Law', *ZaöRV*, vol. 68, pp. 129–53.

Call, C.T. (2004) 'Is Transitional Justice Really Just?' *Brown Journal of World Affairs,* vol. 11, no. 1 (Fall 2004), pp. 101–13.

Cannon, P. (2005) 'Elusive Quest? The Political Economy of Reconciliation in Rwanda', Paper presented at the 14th Annual Africa/Diaspora Conference, Sacramento State Center for African Peace and Conflict Resolution. www.csus.edu/org/capcr/documents/archives/2005/ConferenceProceedings/Cannon-1.pdf (accessed 2 September 2012).

Caplan, G. (2011) *Gacaca Courts, Justice, Reconciliation: Challenges of Rwanda*. www.pambazuka.org/en/category/features/72786 (accessed 30 March 2012).

Caritas International (2002) *Peacebuilding: A Caritas training manual.* www.caritas.org/upload/pea/peacebil-ing.pdf

Carnegie Commission on Preventing Deadly Conflict (1997) *Preventing Deadly Conflict: Final Report*, New York: Carnegie Corporation of New York.

Carroll, C. (2000) 'An Assessment of the Role and Effectiveness of the International Criminal Tribunal for Rwanda and the Rwandan National Justice System in Dealing with the Mass Atrocities of 1994', *Boston University International Law Journal*, vol. 18, no. 2 (Fall), pp. 163–200.

Cassese, A. (1998) 'Reflections on International Criminal Justice', *Modern Law Review*, vol. 61, no. 1 (January), pp. 1–10.

Chakravarty, A. (2006a) 'State Power, Human Rights and the Rule of Law in Post-genocide Rwanda: An Ethnographic Analysis of a Grassroots Judicial Process', Paper presented at the American Political Science Association, Philadelphia, 29 August.

— (2006b) 'Gacaca Courts in Rwanda: Explaining Divisions within the Human Rights Community', *Yale Journal of International Affairs*, vol. 1, no. 2, pp. 132–48.

Chrétien, J.P. (ed.) (1995) *Rwanda: les medias du genocide*, Paris: Editions Karthala.

Christian Aid (2004) *It's Time to Open Up: Ten Years After the Genocide in Rwanda: A Christian Aid Report on Government Accountability, Human Rights and Freedom of Speech*, London: Christian Aid.

Clark, P. (2006) 'Interviews with Key Figures in Debates over Post Genocide Justice and Reconciliation in Rwanda and Uganda', *Oxford International Review, 2005–2006.*

— (2007) 'Hybridity, Holism and Traditional Justice: The Case of the Gacaca in Courts in Post-Genocide Rwanda', *George Washington International Law Review*, vol. 39, no. 4, pp. 765–83.

— (2009a) 'The Rules and Politics of Engagement: The Gacaca Courts and Post-genocide Justice, Healing and Reconciliation in Rwanda', in Clark, P. and Kaufman, Z. (eds), *After Genocide: Transitional Justice, Post-conflict Reconstruction and Reconciliation in Rwanda*, New York: Columbia University Press.

— (2009b) 'Establishing a Conceptual Framework: Six Key Transitional Justice Themes', in Clark, P. and Kaufman, Z. (eds) *After Genocide: Transitional Justice, Post-conflict Reconstruction and Reconciliation in Rwanda*, New York: Columbia University Press.

— (2009c) 'Grappling in the Great Lakes: the Challenges of International Justice in Rwanda, the Democratic Republic of Congo and Uganda', in Bowden, B., Charlesworth, H. and Farrell, J. (eds) *The Role of International Law in Rebuilding Societies After Conflict*, Cambridge: Cambridge University Press.

— (2010) *The Gacaca Courts, Post-Genocide Justice and Reconciliation in Rwanda: Justice without Lawyers*, Cambridge and New York: Cambridge University Press.

— (2012) *How Rwanda Judged Its Genocide*, London: Africa Research Institute.

Cobban, H. (2007) *Amnesty after Atrocity? Healing Nations after Genocide and War Crimes*, Boulder, CO: Paradigm.

Cobián, R.A. and Reátegui, F. (2009) 'Toward Systemic Social Transformation: Truth Commissions and Development', in De Greiff, P. and Duthie, R. (eds) *Transitional Justice and Development: Making Connections*, New York: Social Research Council.

Cohen, D. (2002) *Seeking Justice on the Cheap: Is the East Timor Tribunal Really a Model for the Future?* Analysis from the East-West Center, no. 61. www.eastwestcenter.org/fileadmin/stored/pdfs/api061.pdf (accessed 15 June 2012).

Commission Nationale des Droits de L'homme, Rwanda (2003) *Raporo y'ubutumwa mu ntara ya Gikongoro*, Kigali: Government of Rwanda.

Commission Nationale sur l'Unité et la Réconciliation (2004) *Rapport sur le IIIème Sommet national sur l'unité et la réconciliation*, Kigali: Commission Nationale sur l'Unité et la Réconciliation, République Rwandaise.

Cooke, J.G. (2011) *Rwanda: Assessing Risks to Stability*, Washington, DC: Centre for Strategic and International Studies.

Corey, A. and Joireman, S. (2000) 'Retributive Justice: The Gacaca Courts in Rwanda', *African Affairs*, vol. 103, no. 410, pp. 73–89.

Coser, L.A. (1956) *The Functions of Social Conflict*. New York: Free Press.

Cousineau, M. (1996) 'L'établissement de l'État de Droit au Rwanda: un but irréalisable', *Ottawa Law Review*, vol. 28, pp. 171–90.

Crocker, D.A. (1998) 'Transitional Justice and International Civil Society: Toward a Normative Framework', *Constellations: An International Journal of Critical & Democratic Theory*, vol. 5, no. 4, pp. 492–517.

— (1999) 'Reckoning with Past Wrongs: a Normative Framework', *Ethics & International Affairs*, vol. 13, pp. 43–64.

Cruvellier, T. (2010) *Court of Remorse: Inside the International Criminal Tribunal for Rwanda*, trans. Charles Voss, Madison, WI: University of Wisconsin Press.

Dallaire, R. (2005) *Shake Hands with the Devil: The Failure of Humanity in Rwanda*, London: Arrow Books.

Daley, P. (2006) 'Challenges to Peace: Conflict Resolution in the Great Lakes Region of Africa', *Third World Quarterly*, vol. 27, no. 2, pp. 303–19.

Daly, E. (2002a) 'Between Punitive and Reconstructive Justice: The Gacaca Process in Rwanda', *New York University Journal of International Law and Policy*, vol. 34, pp. 355–96.

— (2002b) 'Transformative Justice: Charting a Path to Reconciliation', *International Legal Perspectives*, vol. 12, pp. 73–183.

— (2006) 'Reconciliation in Divided Societies: Finding Common Ground', with Foreword by Archbishop Desmond Tutu, Philadelphia, PA: University of Pennsylvania Press.

Daly, E. and Sarkin, J. (2004) 'Too Many Questions, Too Few Answers: Reconciliation in Divided Societies', *Columbia Human Rights Law Review*, vol. 35, pp. 101–68.

Danish Centre for Human Rights (2000) *Mid-Term Evaluation of the Danish Centre for Human Rights Project 'Judicial Defenders in Rwanda'*, Copenhagen: Danish Centre for Human Rights.

— (2004) *Legal Aid in Rwanda: A Report on Legal Assistance Available in Rwanda*, Copenhagen: Danish Centre for Human Rights.

Darcy, S. and Schabas, W. (2004) *Truth Commissions and Courts: The Tension Between Criminal Justice and the Search for Truth*, Dordrecht: Kluwer Academic.

De Greiff, P. (2009) 'Articulating the Links Between Transitional Justice and Development: Justice and Social Integration', in de Greiff, P. and Duthie, R. (eds) *Transitional Justice and Development: Making Connections*, New York: Social Research Council.

— (ed.) (2006) *The Handbook of Reparations*, Oxford and New York: Oxford University Press.

De Greiff, P. and Duthie, R. (eds) (2009) *Transitional Justice and Development: Making Connections*, New York: Social Research Council.

De Ycaza, C. (2010) 'Performative Functions of Genocide Trials in Rwanda: Reconciliation Through Restorative Justice?', *African Journal of Conflict Resolution*, vol. 10, no. 3, pp. 9–28.

De Zeeuw, J. and Kumar, K. (eds) (2006) *Promoting Democracy in Post-Conflict Societies*, Boulder, CO: Lynne Rienner.

Del Ponte, C. and Sudetic, C. (2009) *Madam Prosecutor: Confrontations with Humanity's Worst Criminals and the Culture of Impunity*, New York: Other Press LLC.

Des Forges, A. (1999) *Leave None to Tell the Story: Genocide in Rwanda*, New York: Human Rights Watch and Paris: International Federation for Human Rights.

Des Forges, A. and Longman, T. (2004) 'Legal Responses to Genocide in Rwanda', in Weinstein, H. and Stover, E. (eds) *My Neighbour, My Enemy: Justice and Social Reconstruction in Rwanda and the Former Yugoslavia*, Cambridge: Cambridge University Press.

Department for International Development (2010) *Building Peaceful States and Societies: A DFID Practice Paper*. London: Department for International Development.

Department of State (2005) *Country Reports on Human Rights Practices*, Washington, DC: Department of State.

— (2009) *Country Reports on Human Rights Practices*, Washington, DC: Department of State.

Desrosiers, M. and Thomson, S. (2011) 'Rhetorical Legacies of Leadership: Projections of "Benevolent Leadership" in Pre- and Post-Genocide Rwanda', *Journal of Modern African Studies*, vol. 49, no. 3, pp. 429–53.

Destexhe A. (1994) *Rwanda and Genocide in the Twentieth Century*, London: Pluto Press.

Dialogue (1997) 'Le Refugies Rwandais: Le Drame Persiste', Special Issue, no. 198 (May–June).

Dickinson, L.A. (2003) 'Notes and Comments: The Promise of Hybrid Courts', *American Journal of International Law*, vol. 97, pp. 295–310.

Digneffe, F. and Fierens, J. (eds) (2003) *Justice et Gacaca: L'expérience rwandaise et le génocide*, Namur: Presses Universitaires de Namur.

Dorsey, M. (2000) 'Violence and Power-Building in Post-Genocide Rwanda', in Droege, C. (2006) *The Right to a Remedy and to Reparation, A Practitioner's Guide*, Geneva: International Commission of Jurists.

Doughty, K.C. (2011) 'Contesting Community: Legalized Reconciliation Efforts in the Aftermath of Genocide in Rwanda', Publicly Accessible Penn Dissertations, Paper 333, http://repository.upenn.edu/edissertations/333 (accessed 6 June 2012).

Drumbl, M. (1998) 'Rule of Law Amid Lawlessness: Counselling the Accused in Rwanda's Domestic Genocide Trials', *Columbia Human Rights Law Review*, vol. 29, pp. 543–647.

— (1999) 'Sobriety in a Post-Genocidal Society: Good Neighbourliness Among Victims and Aggressors in Rwanda?', *Journal of Genocide Research*, vol. 1, no. 1, pp. 25–41.

— (2000a) 'Sclerosis: Retributive Justice and the Rwanda Genocide', *Punishment and Society: The International Journal of Penology*, vol. 2, no. 3, pp. 287–308.

— (2000b) 'Punishment, Post Genocide: From Guilt to Shame to Civis in Rwanda', *New York University Law Review*, vol. 75, p. 1221–326.

— (2001) 'The (Al)lure of the Genocide Trial: Justice, Reconciliation, and Reconstruction in Rwanda', in Barnhizer, D. (ed.) *Effective Strategies for Protecting Human Rights*, Dartmouth: Ashgate.

— (2002a) 'Lessons for International Criminal Justice from Rwanda', *Washington & Lee Public Law Research*, Paper No. 02–13.

— (2002b) 'Restorative Justice and Collective Responsibility: Lessons from the Rwandan Genocide', *Contemporary Justice Review*, vol. 5, no. 1, pp. 5–22.

— (2004) 'Law and Atrocity: Settling Accounts in Rwanda', *Ohio Northern University Law Review*, vol. 31, pp. 41–74.

— (2005) 'The ICTR and Justice for Rwandan Women', *New England Journal of International Comparative Law*, vol. 12, pp. 105–17.

— (2007) *Atrocity, Punishment and International Law*, Cambridge: Cambridge University Press.

— (2009) 'International Law: Taking Stock of a Busy Decade', Issue 1, *Melbourne Journal of International Law*, vol. 10, pp. 38–46.

— (2010) 'Prosecution of Genocide v. the Fair Trial Principle: Comments on *Brown and Others* v. *The Government of Rwanda and the United Kingdom Secretary of State for the Home Department*', *Journal of International Criminal Justice*, vol. 8, pp. 289–309.

Dugard, J. (2000) 'Dealing with Crime of a Past Regime: Is Amnesty Still an Option?', *Journal of International Law*, vol. 12, pp. 1001–105.

Du Plessis, M. (2010) *The International Criminal Court that Africa Wants*, Pretoria: Institute of Security Studies.

du Toit, F. (2011) *Reconciliation and Transitional Justice: The Case of Rwanda's Gacaca Courts*, Capetown: Institute for Justice and Reconciliation.

East African (2006) 'Rwanda: Why no one would dare oppose Kagame in Rwanda', *East African*, 4 December.

Eltringham, N. (2004) *Accounting for Horror: Genocide Debate in Rwanda*, London: Pluto Press.

Emizet, K.N.F. (2000) 'The Massacre of Refugees in Congo: A Case of UN Peacekeeping Failure and International Law', *Journal of Modern African Studies*, vol. 38, no. 2, pp. 163–202.

Erlanger, S. and Gall, C. (2000) 'As Election Nears, Yugoslavia's Main Rivals Lash Out', *New York Times*, 21 September.

European Union (2003) 'Council Decision 2003/335/JHA of 8 May 2003 on the investigation and prosecution of genocide, crimes against humanity and war crimes', Brussels: European Union.

Evans G. (2008) *The Responsibility to Protect, Ending Mass Atrocity Once and For All*, Washington, DC: Brookings Institution Press.

FDU-Inkingi (2009) *Political Program*. www.fdu-rwanda.com/wp-content/uploads/2011/09/PLEASE-READ-THE-COMPLETE-PROGRAM-HERE.pdf (accessed 12 May 2012). Brussels: FDU-Inkingi.

— (2012) 'Gacaca Courts, Made Up Legacy and a More Divided Rwanda', Press statement, 14 June, Kigali: FDU-Inkingi.

Fédération Internationale des Ligues des Droits de l'Homme *et al.* (1993) *Rapport de Commission Internationale D'Enquete Sur Les Violations de Droits de L'Homme au Rwanda Depuis 1er Octobre 1990. Rapport Finale.* Paris: Fédération Internationale des Droits de l'Homme; New York: Africa Watch; Ouagadougou: Union Inter-Africaine des Droits de l'Homme et des Peuples; Montréal: Centre Internationale des Droits de la Personne et du Développement Démocratique. www.usip.org/publications/commission-inquiry-rwanda-93 (accessed 28 July 2012).

Feil, S.R. (2009) *Preventing Genocide: How the Early Use of Force Might Have Succeeded in Rwanda*, New York: Carnegie Corporation of New York.

Fierens, J. (2005) 'The Gacaca Courts: Between Fantasy and Reality', *Journal of International Criminal Justice*, vol. 3 no. 4 (September), pp. 896–919.

Fink, J.B. (2005) 'Deontological Retributivisms and the Legal Practice of International Jurisprudence: The Case of the International Criminal Tribunal for Rwanda', *Journal of African Law*, vol. 49, no. 2, pp. 101–31.

Fisher, J. (2005) 'The Role of NGOs in Institution-Building in Rwanda', in Richmond, O.P. and Carey, H.F. (eds) *Subcontracting Peace: The Challenges of NGO Peace Building*, Aldershot: Ashgate.

Freedom House (2003) *Country Report – Rwanda (2000)*, Washington, DC: Freedom House.

Freeman, M. and Hayner, P. (2003) 'Truth Telling', in Bloomfield, D., Barnes, T. and Huyse, L. (eds) *Reconciliation after Violent Conflict: A Handbook*, Stockholm: International Institute for Democracy and Electoral Assistance (International IDEA).

Gabisirege, S. and Babalola, S. (2001) *Perceptions About the Gacaca Law in Rwanda: Evidence from a Multi-Method Study*, Special Publication No. 19, Kigali: Université Nationale du Rwanda Centre de Gestion des Conflits, Kigali: Ministry of Justice and Institutional Relations and Baltimore, MD: Johns Hopkins University School of Public Health, Center for Communication Programs.

Gahima, G. (2002) 'Re-establishing the Rule of Law and Encouraging Good Governance', Paper presented at 55th United Nations Department of Public Information and NGO Conference, 9 September, New York.

— (2006) 'In the Aftermath of Genocide: The US Role in Rwanda', *Mediterranean Quarterly*, vol. 17, no. 3, pp. 101–4.

Gersh, D. (2004) 'Poor Judgment: Why the Iraqi Special Tribunal is the Wrong Mechanism for Trying Saddam Hussein on Charges of Genocide, Human Rights Abuses, and Other Violations of International Law', *Georgia Journal of International and Comparative Law*, vol. 33, pp. 273–302.

Ghai, Y. (2009) *Rwanda's Application for Membership of the Commonwealth: Report and Recommendations of the Commonwealth Human Rights Initiative*, New Delhi: Commonwealth Human Rights Initiative.

Goldstone, R. (2000) *For Humanity: Reflections of a War Crimes Investigator*, New Haven, CT: Yale University Press.

Gourevitch, P. (1998) *We Wish to Inform You That Tomorrow We Will Be Killed With Our Families: Stories from Rwanda*, New York: Farrar, Straus, & Giroux.

— (2009) 'The Life After: Fifteen Years after the Genocide in Rwanda, the Reconciliation Defies Expectations', *New Yorker*, 4 May.

Gowing, N. (1998) 'New Challenges and Problems for Information Management in Complex Emergencies: Ominous Lessons from the Great Lakes and Eastern Zaire in Late 1996 and Early 1997', Paper presented at Dispatches from Disaster Zones Conference, Oxford, 28 May.

Graybill, L.S. (2001) 'To Punish or to Pardon: A Comparison of the International Criminal Tribunal for Rwanda and the South African Truth and Reconciliation Commission', *Human Rights Review*, vol. 2, no. 4, pp. 3–18.

— (2004) 'Pardon, Punishment and Amnesia: Three African Post-Conflict Methods', *Third World Quarterly*, vol. 25, no. 6, pp. 1117–30.

Graybill, L.S. and Lanegran, K. (2004) 'Truth, Justice and Reconciliation in Africa: Issues and Cases', *African Studies Quarterly*, vol. 8, no. 1, pp. 1–18.

Gready, P. (2011) 'Beyond "You're with Us or Against Us": Civil Society and Policymaking in Post-genocide Rwanda', in Straus, S. and Waldorf, L. (eds) *Remaking Rwanda: State Building and Human Rights after Mass Violence*. Madison, WI: The University of Wisconsin Press.

Green, L.L. (2002) 'Propaganda and Sexual Violence in the Rwandan Genocide: an Argument for Intersectionality in International Law', *Columbia Human Rights Law Review*, vol. 33, pp. 733–76.

Greenhouse, S. (1994) 'US, Having Won Changes, Is Set to Sign Law of the Sea', *New York Times*, 4 September, quoted in Schabas, W. (2006) *The UN International Criminal Tribunals: The Former Yugoslavia, Rwanda and Sierra Leone*, Cambridge: Cambridge University Press.

Grenfell, L. (2006) 'Legal Pluralism and the Rule of Law in Timor-Leste', *Leiden Journal of International Law*, no. 19, pp. 305–37.

Guichaoua, A., Twagiramungu, N. and Vidal, C. (2004) 'Le 23 April 2003', in Cruvellier, T. and Cyiza, A. *Un Homme Libre au Rwanda*, Paris: Karthala.

Habimana, A. (2009) *What Does International Justice Look Like in Post-Genocide Rwanda*, New York: Carnegie Council for Ethics in International Affairs. www.carnegiecouncil.org/resources/publications/dialogue/2_02/articles/615.html (accessed 15 December 2011).

Haile, D. (2008) 'Rwanda's Experiment in People's Courts (Gacaca) and the Tragedy of Unexamined Humanitarianism: Normative/Ethical Perspective', Discussion Paper No. 2008.01, Antwerp: Institute of Development Policy and Management, University of Antwerp.

Hall, C.K. (2010) 'The Role of Universal Jurisdiction in the International Criminal Court Complementarity System', in Bergsmo, M. (ed.) *Complementarity and the Exercise of Universal Jurisdiction for Core International Crimes*, Oslo: Torkel Opsahl Academic Epublisher.

Halvorsen, K. (1999) 'Protection and Humanitarian Assistance in the Refugee Camps in Zaire: The Problem of Security', in Adelman H. and Suhrke A. (eds) *The Path of a Genocide: The Rwanda Crisis from Uganda to Zaire*, New Brunswick, NJ: Transaction Publishers.

Hamber, G. (2000) 'Repairing the Irreparable: Dealing with Double-Binds of Making Reparations for Crimes of the Past', *Ethnicity and Health*, vol. 5, nos 3 and 4, pp. 215–26. www.csvr.org.za/docs/trc/repairingtheirreparable.pdf (accessed 1 September 2012).

Harrell, P.E. (2003) *Rwanda's Gamble: Gacaca and a New Model of Transitional Justice*, New York: Writers Club Press.

Harroy, J.P. (1984) *Rwanda: de la féodalité a la démocratie (1955–1962)*, Brussels: Hayes.

Hatzfeld, J. (2000) *Life Laid Bare: The Survivors in Rwanda Speak*, Paris: Seuil.

— (2003) *Machete Season: The Rwandan Genocide: The Killers Speak*, Paris: Seuil.

— (2008) *A Time for Machetes: The Rwandan Genocide – The Killers Speak*, London: Profile Books.

Hayman, R. (2008a) 'Rwanda: Milking the Cow: Creating Policy Space in Spite of Aid Dependency', in Whitfield, L. (ed.) *The Politics of Aid: African Strategies for Dealing with Donors*, Oxford: Oxford University Press.

— (2008b) 'Evaluating International Influences on Democratic Development (Volume 2: Post-Conflict Countries) – Rwanda', in *External Democracy Promotion in Post-Conflict Zones: Evidence from Case Studies*, Berlin: Freie Universität Berlin.

— (2011) 'Funding Fraud: Donors and Democracy in Rwanda', in Straus, S. and Waldorf, L. (eds) *Remaking Rwanda: State Building and Human Rights after Mass Violence*, Madison, WI: University of Wisconsin Press.

Hayner, P.B. (2001) *Unspeakable Truths: Confronting State Terror and Atrocity*, New York: Routledge.

Hazan, P. (2006) 'Measuring the Impact of Punishment and Forgiveness: A Framework for Evaluating Transitional Justice', *International Review of the Red Cross*, vol. 88, no. 861, pp. 19–47.

— (2010) *Judging War, Judging History: Behind Truth and Reconciliation*, Stanford, CA: Stanford University Press.

Heberer, P. and Matthäus, J. (2008) *Atrocities on Trial: Historical Perspectives on the Politics of Prosecuting War Crimes*, Lincoln, NB and London: University of Nebraska Press.

Henkin, A.H. (ed.) (2002) *The Legacy of Abuse: Confronting the Past, Facing the Future*, New York: Aspen Institute.

Hilker, L.M. (2011) 'The Role of Education in Driving Conflict and Building Peace: The Case of Rwanda', *Quarterly Review of Comparative Education*, vol. 41, no. 2, pp. 267–82.

Hinton, A.L. (2010) *Transitional Justice: Global Mechanisms and Local Realities after Genocide and Mass Violence*, New Brunswick, NJ: Rutgers University Press.

Hirondelle News Agency (2008) 'Ibuka Report: 167 genocide survivors murdered since 1995', 15 July.

— (2009) 'More than one third of genocide survivors are impoverished', 13 January.

— (2009) 'Ibuka accuses ICTR of negating genocide', 15 December.

Honeyman, C., Hudani, S., Tiruneh, A., Hierta, J., Chirayath, L., Hiff, A. and Meierhenrich, J. (2004) 'Establishing Collective Norms: Potentials for Participatory Justice in Rwanda', *Peace and Conflict: Journal of Peace Psychology*, vol. 10, pp. 1–24.

Hubbard, J.A. (2007) *Breaking the Silence: Women's Experiences with Sexual Violence During the 1994 Rwandan Genocide*, Master of Science thesis, Virginia Polytechnic Institute and State University.

Hughes, E., Schabas, W. and Thakur, R. (eds) (2007) *Atrocities and International Accountability: Beyond Transitional Justice*, Tokyo, New York and Paris: United Nations University Press.

Human Rights First Report (1997) *Prosecuting Genocide in Rwanda: A Human Rights First Report on the ICTR and National Trials*, New York: Human Rights First.

Human Rights Watch (1992) 'Rwanda: Talking Peace and Waging War, Human Rights since the October 1990 Invasion', *Africa Watch*, vol. 4, no. 3, New York: Human Rights Watch.

— (1993) *Beyond the Rhetoric: Continuing Human Rights Abuses in Rwanda*, publication vol. 5, no. 7, New York: Africa Watch.

— (1994a) *Arming Rwanda: The Arms Trade and Human Rights Abuses in the Rwanda War*, publication HRW Index no. A601, New York: Human Rights Watch.

— (1994b) *Genocide in Rwanda April – May 1994*, publication vol. 6, no. 4 (A), New York: Human Rights Watch.

— (1994c) *Rwanda: A New Catastrophe? Increased International Efforts Required to Punish Genocide and to Prevent Further Bloodshed*, publication vol. 6, no. 12, New York: Human Rights Watch.

— (1995) *Re-arming with Impunity: International Support for the Perpetrators of the Rwandan Genocide*, publication vol. 7, no. 4, New York: Human Rights Watch.

— (1996) *Shattered Lives: Sexual Violence during the Rwandan Genocide and Its Aftermath*, publication HRW Index no. 2084, New York: Human Rights Watch.

— (1997) *What is Kabila Hiding: Civilian Killings and Impunity in Congo*, New York: Human Rights Watch.

— (2003) *Lasting Wounds: Consequences of Genocide and War on Rwanda's Children*, publication vol. 15, no. 6(A), New York: Human Rights Watch.

— (2005) *Arms Project, Rearming Former Rwanda Regime*, New York: Human Rights Watch.

— (2006a) *World Report 2006*, New York: Human Rights Watch.

— (2006b) *The Rwanda Genocide: How It Was Prepared, A Human Rights Watch Briefing Paper*, New York: Human Rights Watch.

— (2006c) *Universal Jurisdiction in Europe: The State of the Art*, publication vol. 18, no. 5(D), New York: Human Rights Watch.

— (2007) *There Will Be No Trial*, publication vol. 19, no. 10(A), New York: Human Rights Watch.

— (2008) *Law and Reality Progress in Judicial Reform in Rwanda*, New York: Human Rights Watch.

— (2009) *Rwanda: Tribunal's Work Incomplete*, New York: Human Rights Watch.

— (2011) *Justice Compromised: the Legacy of Rwanda's Community-based Courts*, New York: Human Rights Watch.

Huyse, L. (1995) 'A Devil's Choice: Dilemmas of Backward-Looking Justice', *European Journal of Crime, Criminal Law and Criminal Practice*, vol. 2, no. 2, pp. 120–40.

— (2005) 'The Process of Reconciliation' in Bloomfield, D., Barnes, T. and Huyse L. (eds) *Reconciliation after Violent Conflict*, Stockholm: International Institute for Democracy and Electoral Assistance (IDEA).

— (2008) 'Conclusions and Recommendations', in Huyse, L. and Salter, M. (eds) *Traditional Justice and Reconciliation After Violent Conflict: Learning from African Experiences*, Stockholm: International Institute for Democracy and Electoral Assistance (IDEA).

Huyse, L. and Salter, M. (eds) (2008) *Traditional Justice and Reconciliation After Violent Conflict: Learning from African Experiences*, Stockholm: International Institute for Democracy and Electoral Assistance (IDEA).

Huyse, L. and Vandegiste, S. (1999) 'Approches consociatives dans le contexte du Rwanda', in Marysse, S. and Reyntjens, F. (eds) *L'Afrique des Grands Lacs: Dix Ans de Transitions Conflictuelles, Annuaire 2005–2006*, Paris: L'Harmattan.

ICCO *et al.* (2003) *Tell Our Government It Is OK to Be Criticised*, Rwanda Monitoring Group Project Report 2003, Kigali, Rwanda and the Netherlands: ICCO/Kerkinactie Global Ministries, NOVIB, CORDAID, Pax Christi Netherlands.

ICTR, International Criminal Tribunal for Rwanda (1995) International Criminal Tribunal for Rwanda, Rules of Procedure and Evidence, entered into force 29 June 1995. As amended.

— (1996a) First Annual Report, UN Doc. A/51/399-S/1996/778.

— (1996b) Rules of Procedure and Evidence, United Nations International Criminal Tribunal for Rwanda, UN Doc. ITR/3/REV.1 (1995).

— (1997) Second Annual Report, UN Doc. A52/582-s/1997/868.

— (1998) Third Annual Report, UN Doc. A/53/429-S/1998/857.

— (1999) Fourth Annual Report, UN Doc. A/54/315 S/1999/943.

— (2000a) Fifth Annual Report, UN Doc. A/55/435-S/2000/927.

— (2000b) Letter dated 9 November 2000 from the President of the International Criminal Tribunal for Rwanda addressed to the Secretary General, UN Doc. S/2000/1198, annex.

— (2000c) Letter dated 12 October 2000 from the President of the International Tribunal for the Former Yugoslavia addressed to the Secretary General, UN Doc. S/2000/1063.

— (2001) Sixth Annual Report, UN Doc. A/56/351-S/2001/863.

— (2002) Seventh Annual Report, UN Doc. A/57/163-S/2002/733.

— (2003a) Eighth Annual Report, UN Doc. A/58/140-s/2003/707.

— (2003b) First Completion Strategy Report, UN Doc. S/2003/946.

— (2004a) Ninth Annual Report, UN Doc. A/59/183-S/2004/601.

— (2004b) Second Completion Strategy Report, UN Doc. S/ 2004/341.

— (2004c) Third Completion Strategy Report, UN Doc. S/2004/921.

— (2005a) Tenth Annual Report, UN Doc. A/60/229-S/2005/534.

— (2005b) Fourth Completion Strategy Report, UN Doc. S/2005/336.

— (2005c) Fifth Completion Strategy Report, UN Doc. S/2005/782.

— (2006a) Eleventh Annual Report, UN Doc. A/61/265-S/2006/658.

— (2006b) Sixth Completion Strategy Report, UN Doc. S/2006/358.

— (2006c) Seventh Completion Strategy Report, UN Doc. S/2006/951.

— (2006d) Letter of 29 May 2006, UN Doc. S/2006/358, from the President of the ICTR addressed to the President of the Security Council.

— (2007a) Twelfth Annual Report, UN Doc. A/62/284-S/2007/502.

— (2007b) Eighth Completion Strategy Report, UN Doc. S/2003/2007/323.

— (2007c) Ninth Completion Strategy Report, UN Doc. S/2007/6762.

— (2008a) Thirteenth Annual Report, UN Doc A/63/209-S/2008514.

— (2008b) Tenth Completion Strategy Report, UN Doc. S/2008/322.

— (2008c) Eleventh Completion Strategy Report, UN Doc. S/2008/726.

— (2009a) Twelfth Completion Strategy Report, UN Doc. S/2009/247.

— (2009b) International Criminal Tribunal for Rwanda, Letter dated 22 June 2009 from Hassan Jallow, the Prosecutor of the ICTR, addressed to Kenneth Roth, Executive Director, Human Rights Watch.

— (2010a) Report on Completion Strategy of the International Criminal Tribunal for Rwanda (as of 25 May 2010), UN Doc. S/2010/259.

— (2010b) Report on Completion Strategy of the International Criminal Tribunal for Rwanda (as of 1 November 2010), UN Doc. S/2010/574.

— (2011a) Report on Completion Strategy of the International Criminal Tribunal for Rwanda (as of 12 May 2011), UN Doc. S/2011/317.

— (2011b) Report on Completion Strategy of the International Criminal Tribunal for Rwanda (as of 4 November 2011), UN Doc. S/2011/731.

ILC (International Law Commission) (1957) 'Principles of International Law Recognized in the Charter of the Nürnberg Tribunal and in the Judgment of the Tribunal, with Commentaries', *Yearbook of the International Law Commission*, 1950, vol. II, UN Doc. A/CN. 4/SER.A/1950/Add. 1, New York: United Nations.

— (1996) 'Draft Code of Crimes against the Peace and Security of Mankind, adopted by the International Law Commission', *Yearbook of the International Law Commission*, vol. II(2), UN Doc. ILC(XLVIII)/DC/CRD.3, New York: United Nations.

— (2008a) 'Draft Articles on Responsibility of States for Internationally Wrongful Acts', *Yearbook of International Law* Commission, vol. II, UN Doc. A/CN.4/SER.A/2001/Add.1, New York: United Nations.

— (2008b) *Commentary to the Draft Articles on State Responsibility for Internationally Wrongful Acts: Report of the International Law Commission on its Fifty-third Session*, GA, Supplement No. 10 (A/56/10); cph. IV.E., New York: United Nations.

International Crisis Group (1999) *Five Years After the Genocide: Justice in Question. Report on Rwanda*, ICG Report Rwanda No. 1, Brussels: International Crisis Group.

— (2001a) *International Criminal Tribunal for Rwanda: Justice Delayed*, Africa Report No. 30, Brussels: International Crisis Group.

— (2001b) *'Consensual democracy' in Post-Genocide Rwanda: Evaluating the March 2001 District Elections*, Brussels: International Crisis Group.

— (2002a) *International Criminal Tribunal for Rwanda: The Countdown*, Africa Report No. 50, Brussels: International Crisis Group.

— (2002b) *Rwanda at the End of the Transition: A Necessary Political Liberalisation*, Africa Report No. 53, Brussels: International Crisis Group.

Ingelaere, B. (2006) 'Changing Lenses and Contextualising the Rwandan (Post-Genocide)', in Reyntjens F. and Marysse, S. (eds) *L'Afrique des Grands Lacs: Dix Ans de Transitions Conflictuelles, Annuaire 2005–2006*, Paris: L'Harmattan.

— (2008) 'The Gacaca Courts in Rwanda', in Huyse L. and Salter M. (eds) *Traditional Justice and Reconciliation After Violent Conflict*, Stockholm: International Institute for Democracy and Electoral Assistance (IDEA).

— (2009a) 'Does the Truth Pass through the Fire without Burning? Locating the Short Circuit in Rwanda's Gacaca courts', *Journal of Modern African Studies*, vol. 47, pp. 507–28.

— (2009b) 'Living the Transition: Inside Rwanda's Conflict Cycle at the Grassroots', *Journal of East African Studies*, vol. 3, no. 3, pp. 438–63.

— (2010) 'Do We Understand Life After Genocide? Center and Periphery in the Construction of Knowledge in Post-Genocide Rwanda', *African Studies Review*, vol. 53, no. 1, pp. 41–59.

Ingabire, V.U. (2012) 'Gacaca Was Utterly in Vain, and It Divided the People of Rwanda'. www.facebook.com/note.php?note_id=10150924813753423 (accessed 17 August 2012).

Inter-American Commission on Human Rights (1986) *Annual Report 1985–1986*, OEA/Ser.L/V/II.68, Doc. 8, rev. 1, 28 September, Chapter V.

International Centre for Human Rights and Democratic Development (1998) *International Non-Governmental Commission of Inquiry into the Massive Violations of Human Rights in the Democratic Republic of Congo (Former Zaire 1996–1997)*, Montreal: International Centre for Human Rights and Democratic Development.

International Legal Assistance Consortium (2007) *Justice in Rwanda: An Assessment*, Stockholm: International Legal Assistance Consortium.

IRDP, Institute of Research and Dialogue for Peace (2003) *Sustaining Peace in Rwanda: Voice of the People*, Kigali: Institute of Research and Dialogue for Peace. www.irdp.rw/docs/democracy.pdf (accessed 12 November 2011).

— (2005) *Democracy in Rwanda*, Kigali: Institute of Research and Dialogue for Peace. www.irdp.rw/docs/democracy.pdf (accessed 12 November 2011).

— (2006) *Rwandan Tutsi Genocide: Causes, Implementation and Memory*, Kigali: Institute of Research and Dialogue for Peace. www.irdp.rw/docs/democracy.pdf (accessed 12 November 2011).

Ironside, P. (2002) 'Rwandan Gacaca: Seeking Alternative Means to Justice, Peace, and Reconciliation', *New York International Law Review*, vol. 15, no. 31, pp. 1–26.

Jallow, H. (2009) 'The Contribution of United Nations International Criminal Tribunal for Rwanda to the Development of International Criminal Law', in Clark, P. and Kaufman, Z. (eds) *After Genocide: Transitional Justice, Post-conflict Reconstruction and Reconciliation in Rwanda*, New York: Columbia University Press.

Joint Committee on Human Rights (2009) *Closing the Impunity Gap: UK Law on Genocide (and Related Crimes) and Redress for Torture Victims, Twenty-fourth Report of Session 2008–09*, London: House of Commons/House of Lords.

Jones, B.D. (1999) 'The Arusha Peace Process', in Adelman, H. and Suhrke, A. (eds) *The Path of a Genocide: The Rwanda Crisis from Uganda to Zaire*, New Brunswick, NJ: Transaction Press.

— (2000) *Peacemaking in Rwanda: The Dynamics of Failure*, Boulder, CO: Lynne Reinner.

Jones, N.A. (2010) *The Courts of Genocide: Politics and the Rule of Law in Rwanda and Arusha*, Oxford and New York: Routledge.

Jordaan, E. (2006) 'Inadequately Self-Critical: Rwanda's Self Assessment for the African Peer Review Mechanism', *African Affairs*, vol. 105/420, pp. 333–51.

Justino, P. and Verwimp, P. (2006) 'Poverty Dynamics, Violent Conflict and Convergence in Rwanda', HiCN Working Paper 16, Brighton: University of Sussex.

Kagame, P. (2009) 'Preface', in Clark, P. and Kaufman, Z. (eds) *After Genocide: Transitional Justice, Post-conflict Reconstruction and Reconciliation in Rwanda*, New York: Columbia University Press.

— (2010) 'The Challenge of Nation Building in Africa; The Case of Rwanda', Speech delivered at the International Institute for Strategic Studies, London, 16 September.

— (2011) 'Keynote address to the High Level Meeting on Post-Conflict Building: Rwanda's Experience', Kigali: Office of the President. www.presidency.gov.rw/speeches (accessed 28 December 2011).

Kakwenzire, J. and Kamukama, D. (1999) 'The Development and Consolidation of Extremist Forces in Rwanda', in Adelman, H. and Suhrke, A. (eds) *The Path of a Genocide: The Rwanda Crisis from Uganda to Zaire*, New Brunswick, NJ: Transaction Press.

Kamatali, J.M. (2003) 'The Challenges of Linking International Criminal Justice and National Reconciliation: The Case of the ICTR', *Leiden Journal of International Law*, vol. 16, pp. 115–33.

Kamminga, M.T., Oomen, B.M., Borren, S., van Boven, T.C., Fernhout, R., Meindersma, C.F., Verrijn Stuart, H.M., Bos, A., Nollkaemper, P.A., de Wet, E. and Parmentier, S. (2009) *Transitional Justice: Justice and Peace in Times of Transition*, Report No. 65, AIV/No. 19, CAVV April 2009, The Hague: Advisory Council on International Affairs & Advisory Committee on Issues of Public International Law.

Karekezi, A.U., Nshimiyimana, A. and Mutamba B. (2004) 'Localising Justice: Gacaca Courts in Post-Genocide Rwanda', in Stover E. and Weinstein H.M. (eds) *My Neighbour, My Enemy: Justice and Community in the Aftermath of Mass Atrocity*, Cambridge: Cambridge University Press.

Kaufman, D. (2001) *Misrule of Law: Does the Evidence Challenge Conventions in Judiciary and Legal Reforms?*, Washington, DC: World Bank. http://siteresources.worldbanak.org/INTBIGOVANTCOR/Resources/misruleoflaw'pdf (accessed 21 August 2012).

Kaufman, Z. and Clark, P. (eds) (2009) *After Genocide: Transitional Justice, Post-Conflict Reconstruction and Reconciliation in Rwanda and Beyond*, New York: Columbia University Press.

Kayumba, N., Karegeya, P., Rudasingwa, T. and Gahima, G. (2010) *Rwanda Briefing*. http://rwandabriefing (accessed 5 January 2012).

Kiernan, B. (2007) *Blood and Soil: A World History of Genocide and Extermination from Sparta to Darfur*, New Haven, CT and London: Yale University Press.

Kievelitz, U., Kruk, G. and Frieters, N. (2003) *Joint Utstein Study of Peace Building*, Eschborn: Deutsche Gesellschaft für Technische Zusammenarbeit (GTZ) GmbH.

Kim, H. and Skkink, K. (2010) Explaining the Deterence Effect of Human Rights Prosecutions for Transitional Countries, *International Studies Quarterly*, vol. 54, no. 4, pp. 939–63.

King, E. (2005) 'Educating for Conflict or Peace: Challenges and Dilemmas in Post-Conflict Rwanda', *International Journal*, vol. LX, no. 4, pp. 904–18.

— (2006) 'The Human Security Impact of Education in Rwanda', CCHS Human Security Fellowship Policy Brief. www.humansecurity.info/sites/cchs/files/pdfs/Fellow%20Papers/Policy_brief/Elisabeth_King_Policy_Brief.pdf (accessed 21 August 2012).

— (2009) 'From Data Problems to Data Points: Challenges and Opportunities of Research in Post-Genocide Rwanda', *African Studies Review*, vol. 52, no. 3, pp. 127–48.

— (2010a) 'Memory Controversies in Post-Genocide Rwanda: Implications for Peace Building', *Genocide Studies and Prevention*, vol. 5, no. 3, pp. 293–309.

— (2010b) 'Interventions to Promote Social Cohesion in Sub-Saharan Africa', *Journal of Development Effectiveness*, vol. 2, no. 3, pp. 336–72. (with C. Samii and B. Snilstveit).

Kirby, C. (2006) 'Rwanda's Gacaca Courts: A Preliminary Critique', *Journal of African Law*, vol. 50, no. 2, pp. 94–117.

Klein-Ahlbrandt, S.T. (2004) *The Protection Gap in International Protection of Internally Displaced Persons: The Case of Rwanda*, Paper No. 04/01, Working Papers, Geneva: Graduate Institute of International Studies.

Kritz, N. (1996a) 'Coming to Terms with Atrocities: A Review of Accountability Mechanisms for Mass Violations of Human Rights', *Law & Contemporary Problems*, vol. 59, no. 4, pp. 127–52.

— (1996b) 'War Crimes on Trial', *Issues of Democracy*, vol. 1, no. 3, pp. 20–8.

— (1996c) 'The Rule of Law in the Post-Conflict Phase' in Crocker, C.A., Hampson, F.O. and Aall, P. (eds) *Managing Global Chaos: Sources of and Responses to International Conflict*, Washington, DC: United States Institute of Peace Press.

— (1997) 'War Crimes and Truth Commissions: Some Thoughts on Accountability Mechanisms for Mass Violations of Human Rights', Paper presented at USAID Conference, *Promoting Democracy, Human Rights, and Reintegration in Post-conflict Societies*, Washington, DC, 30–31 October. http://pdf.usaid.gov/pdf_docs/PNACD090.pdf (accessed 21 December 2011).

— (2002a) 'Where We Are and How We Got Here: An Overview of Developments in the Search for Justice and Reconciliation', in Henkin, A.H. (ed.) *The Legacy of Abuse: Confronting the Past, Facing the Future*, Washington, DC: Aspen Institute.

— (2002b) 'Progress and Humility: The Ongoing Search for Post Conflict Justice', in Bassiouni, C. (ed.) *Post-Conflict Justice*, Ardsley NJ: Transnational Publishers.

Kritz, N. (ed.) (1995) *Transitional Justice: How Emerging Democracies Reckon with Former Regimes* (Volumes I, II and III), Washington, DC: United States Institute of Peace.

Lahiri, K. (2009) 'Rwanda's "Gacaca" Courts: A Possible Model for Local Justice in International Crime?', *International Criminal Law Review*, vol. 9, no. 2, pp. 321–32.

Lambourne, W. (2001a) 'Justice and Reconciliation: Post-conflict Peace-building in Cambodia and Rwanda', in Abu-Nimer, M. (ed.) *Reconciliation, Justice and Coexistence: Theory and Practice*, Lanham, MD: Lexington Books, pp. 311–37.

— (2001b) 'Responding to Genocide in Rwanda and East Timor: Prevention and Prosecution', in Evans-Kent, B. and Bleiker, R. (eds) *Rethinking Humanitarianism Conference Proceedings*, St Lucia, Qld: University of Queensland, pp. 63–81.

— (2004) 'Post-Conflict Peace Building: Meeting Human Needs for Justice and Reconciliation', *Peace, Conflict and Development*, vol. 4, April, pp. 1–24.

— (2005) 'Reconciliation in Rwanda: Applying Gacaca Community Justice to Genocide', *Peace Writes*, no. 2005–02, December, pp. 4–5.

— (2006) 'Justice in the Aftermath of Mass Crimes: International Law and Peace Building', in Dolgopol, U. and Gardam, J. (eds) *The Challenge of Conflict: International Law Responds*, Leiden: Martinus Nijhoff.

— (2009) 'Transitional Justice and Peace Building After Mass Violence', *International Journal of Transitional Justice*, vol. 3, no. 1, pp. 28–48.

— (2010) 'Transitional Justice After Mass Violence: Reconciling Retributive and Restorative Justice', in Irving, H., Mowbray, J. and Walton, K. (eds) *Julius Stone: A Study in Influence*, Sydney: Federation Press.

Lanegran, K. and Graybill, L.S. (2004) 'Truth, Justice and Reconciliation in Africa: Issues and Cases', *African Studies Quarterly*, vol. 8, no. 1 (Fall), pp. 1–18.

Lawyers Committee for Human Rights (2002) *What Is a Fair Trial? A Basic Guide to Legal Guides and Practice* (March 2000), New York: Lawyers Committee for Human Rights.

Lederach, J.P. (1998) *Building Peace: Sustainable Reconciliation in Divided Societies*, Washington, DC: United States Institute of Peace.

Lemarchand, R. (1970) *Rwanda and Burundi*, New York: Praeger.

— (1995) 'Rwanda: The Rationality of the Genocide', *Issue: A Journal of Opinion*, vol. 23, no. 2, pp. 8–11.

— (1997) 'The Rwanda Genocide', in Totten, S., Parsons, W. and Charny, I. (eds) *Century of Genocide: Eyewitness Accounts and Critical Views*, New York: Garland.

— (2000) 'Exclusion, Marginalization, and Political Mobilization: The Road to Hell in the Great Lakes', in Wimmer, A., Goldstone, R., Horowitz, D., Joras, U. and Schetter, C. (eds) *Facing Ethnic Conflicts: Toward a New Realism*. Boulder, CO: Rowman & Littlefield.

— (2002a) 'Disconnecting the Threads: Rwanda and The Holocaust Reconsidered', *Journal of Genocide Research*, vol. 4, no. 4, pp. 499–518.

— (2002b) 'A History of Genocide in Rwanda: Review of Mahmood Mamdani, When Victims Become Killers', *Journal of African History*, vol. 43, pp. 307–11.

— (2009) *The Dynamics of Violence in Central Africa*, Philadelphia: University of Pennsylvania Press.

Lemarchand, R. and Niwese, N. (2007) 'Mass Murder, the Politics of Memory and Post-Genocide Reconstruction: The Cases of Rwanda and Burundi', in Pouligny, M., Chesterman, S. and Schnabel, A. (eds) *After Mass Crime: Rebuilding States and Communities*, Tokyo: United Nations University Press.

Le Mon, C. (2007) 'Rwanda's Troubled Gacaca Courts', *Human Rights Brief*, vol. 14, no. 2, pp. 16–20.

Lenzen, M. (2009) 'Roads Less Traveled? Conceptual Pathways (and Stumbling Blocks) for Development and Transitional Justice', in De Greiff, P. and Duthie, R. (eds), *Transitional Justice and Development: Making Connections*, New York: Social Research Council.

Leopold, E. (1994) 'UN Council Creates New War Crimes Commission', Reuters, 1 July.

Lewis, P. (1994) 'Rwanda agrees to a UN War Crimes Tribunal', *New York Times*, August.

Longman, T. (1996) 'Democracy and Disorder: Violence and Political Reform', in Gardinier, D. and Clark, J. (eds) *Political Reform in Francophone Africa*, Boulder, CO: Westview Press.

— (1997) 'Rwanda: Chaos from Above', in Villalon, L. and Huxtable, P. (eds) *Critical Juncture: The African State in Transition*, Boulder, CO: Lynne Rienner.

— (2004a) 'Obstacles to Peace Building in Rwanda', in Matthews, R. and Ali, T.M. (eds) *Durable Peace: Peace Building in Africa*, Toronto: University of Toronto Press.

— (2004b) 'Memory, Identity and Community in Rwanda', in Stover, E. and Weistein, H.M. (eds) *My Neighbour, My Enemy: Justice and Community in the Aftermath of Mass Atrocity*, Cambridge: Cambridge University Press.

— (2004c) 'The Domestic Impact of the International Criminal Tribunal for Rwanda', in Ratner, S.R. and Bischoff, J.L. (eds) *International War Crimes Trials: Making a Difference?*, Austin, TX: University of Texas Law School.

— (2005) 'Rwanda: Achieving Equality or Serving an Authoritarian State?', in Bauer, G. and Britton, H. (eds) *Women in African Parliaments*, Boulder, CO: Lynne Rienner.

— (2006a) 'Gacaca Trials in Rwanda: Justice at the Grassroots', in Roht-Arriaza, N. and Mariezcurrena, J. (eds) *Beyond Truth Versus Justice: Transitional Justice in the New Millenium*, Cambridge: Cambridge University Press.

— (2006b) 'Justice at the Grassroots? Gacaca Trials in Rwanda', in Roht-Arriaza, N. *et al.*, *Transitional Justice in the Twenty First Century*, Cambridge: Cambridge University Press.

— (2009) 'An Assessment of Rwanda's Gacaca Courts', *Peace Review*, vol. 21, no. 3, pp. 304–12.

— (2010) 'Trying Times for Rwanda: Re-evaluation of Gacaca Courts in Post-Genocide Reconciliation', *Harvard International Review*, vol. 32. http://hir.harvard.edu/law-of-the-land/trying-times-for-rwanda (accessed 1 September 2012).

— (2011) 'Limitations to Political Reform: The Undemocratic Nature of Transition in Rwanda', in Straus, S. and Waldorf, L. (eds) *Remaking Rwanda: State Building and Human Rights after Mass Violence*. Madison, WI: University of Wisconsin Press.

Longman, T., Pham, P., Weinstein, W. and Karekezi, A. (2004) 'Connecting Justice to Human Experience: Attitudes Toward Accountability and Reconciliation in Rwanda', in Weinstein, H. and Stover, E. (eds) *My Neighbor, My Enemy: Justice and Social Reconstruction in Rwanda and the Former Yugoslavia*, Cambridge: Cambridge University Press.

Longman, T. and Rutagengwa, T. (2006) 'Memory and Violence in Post-Genocide Rwanda', in Bay, E.G. and Donham, D.L. (eds) *States of Violence: Politics, Youth, and Memory in Contemporary Africa*, Charlottesville, VA: University of Virginia Press.

Lutz, E.L. (1995) 'After the Elections: Compensating Victims of Human Rights Abuses', in Neil J. and Kritz, N.J. (eds) *Transitional Justice: How Emerging Democracies Reckon with Former Regimes*, vol. 1, General Considerations, Herndon, VA: United States Institute of Peace Press.

Magnarella, P. (2000) *Justice in Africa: Rwanda's Genocide, Its Courts, and the U.N. Criminal Tribunal*, Aldershot: Ashgate.

Mahoro, Z. (2012) 'Impamvu 77 zerekana ukuntu gacaca ari igikoresho cyo kurimbura abahutu' ('77 explanations demonstrating that gacaca is an instrument for the extermination of the Hutu'). www.leprophete.fr/2012/02/26/ingingo-77-zerekana-ukuntu-inkiko-gacaca-ari-igikoresho-cyo-kurimbura-abahutu-zelote-mahoro/#permalink (accessed 31 March 2012).

Mamdani, M. (1996) 'Reconciliation Without Justice', *Southern African Review of Books*, Nov./Dec., pp. 3–5.

— (2001) *When Victims Become Killers: Colonialism, Nativism and the Genocide in Rwanda*, Princeton, NJ: Princeton University Press.

Management Systems International (2002) *Rwanda Conflict Vulnerability Assessment, Greater Horn of Africa Peace Building Project* (Revised October 2002), Washington, DC: Management Systems International.

Marchak, M.P. (2008) *No Easy Fix: Global Responses to Internal Wars and Crimes Against Humanity*, Montreal: McGill-Queens University Press.

Marysse, S. and Reyntjens, F. (eds) (2005) *The Political Economy of the Great Lakes Region in Africa: The Pitfalls of Enforced Democracy and Globalization*, Basingstoke and New York: Palgrave Macmillan.

— (2006) 'Changing Lenses and Contextualizing the Rwandan (Post) Genocide', in Marysse, S. and Reyntjens, F. (eds) *L'Afrique des Grands Lacs: Dix Ans de Transitions Conflictuelles, Annuaire 2005–2006*, Paris: L'Harmattan.

Mayer-Rieckh, A. (2006) 'Vetting, Institutional Reform and Transitional Justice', in Bleeker, M. (ed.) *Dealing with the Past and Transitional Justice: Creating Conditional for Peace and Rule of Law*, Berne: Federal Department of Foreign Affairs, Swiss Confederation.

Mbonimana, G. (1998) 'Ingingo zagize uruhare muri politiki y'u Rwanda kuva mu mwaka wa 1952 kugeza 1962', Kigali: Nyakanga. Réseau Documentaire International sur la Région des Grands Lacs Africains. http://129.194.252.80/catfiles/1601.pdf (accessed 1 September 2012).

McDonough, D. (2008) 'From Guerrillas to Government: Post-Conflict Stability in Liberia, Uganda and Rwanda', *Third World Quarterly*, vol. 29, no. 2, pp. 357–74.

McDoom, S. (2011) *Rwanda's Exit from Pathway from Violence: A Strategic Assessment, Background Case Study for the World Development Report 2011*, Washington, DC: World Bank.

McGoldrick, D. (1994) *The Human Rights Committee, Its Role in the Development of the International Covenant on Civil and Political Rights*, Oxford: Clarendon Press.

McLean, H.L. (2010) 'The Role of Education in Driving Conflict and Building Peace: The Case of Rwanda', *Quarterly Review of Comparative Education*, vol. 41, no. 2, pp. 267–82.

MDR (Mouvement Démocratique Républicain) (1994) 'Position du Parti MDR sur les grand problèmes actuel du Rwanda'. www.grandslacs.net/doc/0668.pdf (Réseau Documentaire International sur la Région des Grands Lacs Africains) (accessed 15 December 2011).

Megwalu, A. (2006) *Looking Back, Moving Forward: The Gacaca Courts in Rwanda*. Bachelor of Arts research paper, Princeton, NJ: Princeton University Woodrow Wilson School of Public and International Affairs.

Megwalu, A. and Loizides, N. (2010) 'Dilemmas of Justice and Reconciliation: Rwandans and the Gacaca Courts', *African Journal of International and Comparative Law*, vol. 18, no. 1, pp. 1–23.

Meierhenrich, J. (2011) 'Typographies of Remembering and Forgetting: The Transformation of Lieux de Memoire in Rwanda', in Straus, S. and Waldorf, L. (eds) *Remaking Rwanda: State Building and Human Rights After Mass Violence*, Madison, WI: University of Wisconsin Press.

Melvern L. (2000a) *A People Betrayed: The Role of the West in Rwanda's Genocide*, London: Zed Books.

— (2000b) 'Behind Closed Doors: UN Security Council', *World Today*, vol. 56, no. 8, pp. 9–11.

— (2004) *Conspiracy to Murder: Planning the Rwanda Genocide*, London: Verso Books.

Melvin, J. (2012) *Beyond the Veneer of Reconciliation: Human Rights and Democracy in Rwanda*, London: Commonwealth Advisory Bureau.

Méndez, J.E. (1997) 'Accountability for Past Abuses', *Human Rights Quarterly*, vol. 19, pp. 255–82.

Meyerstein, A. (2007) 'Between Law and Culture: Rwanda's Gacaca and Postcolonial Legality', *Law and Social Inquiry*, vol. 32, no. 2, pp. 467–508.

Mibenge C. (2004) 'Enforcing International Humanitarian Law at the National Level: The Gacaca Courts of Rwanda', *Yearbook of International Humanitarian Law*, vol. 7, pp. 410–24.

Miller, Z. (2007) 'Constructing Sustainable Reconciliation: Land, Power, and Transitional Justice', in *Post-Genocide Rwanda*, Cape Town: Institute for Justice and Reconciliation.

Ministère de l'Administration Local, de l'Information et des Affaires Sociales (2002) *Dénombrement des Victimes du Génocide, Rapport Finale*, Kigali: Government of Rwanda.

Ministère de Finance (1996) 'Conférence de Table Ronde 1996: Justice et Sécurité de Personnes et des Biens', Document de travail, Ministère de la Défense National, Ministère du Plan, Ministère de l'Intérieur et du Développement Communal, Ministère de la Justice, 31 mai, Kigali: Ministère de Finance, Rwanda.

Ministry of Finance and Economic Planning (1999) *Social Sector Review: Objectives and Expenditures Scenarios*, Kigali: Ministry of Finance and Economic Planning. www.wds.worldbank.org/external/default/WDSContentServer/WDSP/IB/2012/06/13/000333037_20120613014257/Rendered/PDF/698870ESW0P0570EVIEW00February01999.pdf (accessed 31 August 2012).

Ministère de la Justice (1992) *Rwanda, La Place de la Justice et le Rôle du Magistrat dans l'Édification d'un État Démocratique*, Kigali: Government of Rwanda.

Ministry of Justice (u.d.) *Position of the Government of Rwanda on the International Criminal Tribunal for Rwanda*, Kigali: Ministry of Justice. www.grandslacs.net/doc/0608.pdf (accessed 20 May 2012).

Ministry of Justice, Helsinki (2009) Press Stament on the Case of Bazaramba François, 20 February, Helsinki: Ministry of Justice. http://government.fi/ajankohtaista/tiedotteet/tiedote/en.jsp?oid=254185 (accessed 30 August 2012).

Minow, M. (1998) *Between Vengeance and Forgiveness: Facing History After Genocide and Mass Violence*, Boston: Beacon Press.

Minow, M. and Roseblum, N.L. (2002) *Breaking Cycles of Hatred: Memory, Law and Repair*, Princeton, NJ: Princeton University Press.

Moghalu, K. (2002) 'Image or Reality of War Crimes Justice: External Perceptions of the International Criminal Tribunal for Rwanda', *Fletcher Forum of World Affairs*, vol. 26, no. 2, pp. 21–46.

— (2005) *Rwanda's Genocide: The Politics of Global Justice*, New York: Palgrave Macmillan.

— (2008) *Global Justice: The Politics of War Crimes Trials*, Stanford, CA: Stanford University Press.

Molenaar, A. (2005) *Gacaca: Grassroots Justice After Genocide, the Key to Reconciliation in Rwanda?*, Research Report 77/2005, Leiden: African Studies Centre.

Morris, M. (1997) 'Justice in the Wake of Genocide: The Case of Rwanda', *ILSA Journal of International Law*, vol. 3, p. 689.

Morris, V. and Scharf, M. (1998) *The International Criminal Tribunal for Rwanda*, Irvington-on-Hudson, NY: Transnational Publishers.

Morrison, H., Gon Kwon, O., Murphy, P., Harmon, M.B., Pocar, F., Mose, E., Cassese, A., Roth, K., Dama-ka, M.R., Weigend, T., Cayley, A., Gaeta, P. and Schabas, W. (2008) 'Discussion of the Completion Strategies of the Ad Hoc Tribunals', *Journal of International Criminal Justice*, vol. 6, no. 4, pp. 681–709.

Møse, E. (2005) 'The ICTR: Experiences and Challenges', *New England Journal of International and Comparative Law*, vol. 12, no. 1, pp. 1–16.

— (2008) 'The ICTR's Completion Strategy: Challenges and Possible Solutions', *Journal of International Criminal Justice*, vol. 6, pp. 667–79.

Moussalli, M. (1998) *Report on the Situation of Human Rights in Rwanda Prepared by the Special Representative of the Commission on Human Rights Pursuant to Economic and Social Council Decision 1998/266 of 30 July 1998*, UN Doc. A 53/402, Geneva: United Nations Commission on Human Rights.

Mucyo, J.D. *et al.* (2008) *Report of Independent National Commission of the Inquiry Charged with the Assembly of Evidence Indicating the Implication of State of France in the Preparation and Execution of the Genocide that was Perpetrated in Rwanda in 1994*, Kigali: Ministry of Justice. http://cec.rwanda.free.fr/documents/doc/Rapport_Rwanda/RapportRwanda-2008-08.pdf (accessed 13 August 2012).

Musoni, E. (2012) 'The Legacy of Gacaca', *New Times*, 10 April. www.newtimes.co.rw/news/index.php?i=14958&a=52323 (accessed 25 January 2012).

Mutara, E. (2009) '156 Genocide Survivors and Witnesses Killed', *New Times*, 7 March.

Mutisi, M. (2009) 'Gacaca Courts in Rwanda: An Endogenous Approach to Post-Conflict Justice and Reconciliation', *Africa Peace and Conflict Journal*, vol. 2, no. 1, pp. 17–26.

Mutua, M. (1997) 'Never Again: Questioning the Yugoslav and Rwanda Tribunals', *Temple International and Comparative Law Journal*, vol. 11, pp. 167–87.

— (2000) 'From Nuremberg to the Rwanda Tribunal: Justice or Retribution?', *Buffalo Human Rights Law Review*, vol. 6, pp. 77–91.

Naftalin, M. (2011) 'A New Rwanda?', *World Today*, vol. 67, no. 7, pp. 22–4.

Nagy, R. (2008) 'Transitional Justice as a Global Project: Critical Reflections', *Third World Quarterly*, vol. 29, no. 2, pp. 275–89.

National Democratic Institute (2003) *Assessment of Rwanda's Pre-Election Political Environment and the Role of Political Parties*, Washington, DC: National Democratic Institute.

National Service for Gacaca Jurisdictions (2005a) *Instruction No. 04/2005 of 16/02/2005 from the Executive Secretary of the National Service for Gacaca Courts Related to Conditions Required from Observers, Researchers and Journalists in the Gacaca Process*, Kigali: National Service for Gacaca Jurisdictions.

— (2005b) *Instruction No. 06/2005 of 20/7/2005 of the Executive Secretary of the National Service of Gacaca Courts on Dismissal of the Judge Inyangamugayo from the Gacaca Court Bench, Dissolution of a Gacaca Bench and Replacement of the Judges Inyangamugayo*, Kigali: National Service for Gacaca Jurisdictions.

— (n.d.) *Gacaca Jurisdictions: Achievements, Problems and Future Prospects*, Kigali: National Service for Gacaca Jurisdictions.

National Unity and Reconciliation Commission (2001) *Report on the Evaluation of National Unity and Reconciliation*, 23 November, Kigali: National Unity and Reconciliation Commission.

Ndaruhutse, S. (2011) *State Building, Peace Building and Service Delivery in Fragile and Conflicted Affected States, Case Study: Rwanda*, London: DFID.

Ndori, F. (2012) 'Gacaca: Mission Accomplished', *New Times*, 13 June. http://www.newtimes.co.rw/news/index.php?i=15022&a=54756 (accessed on 13 June 2012).

Neher, L., Linares, A.M., Rose, L. and Mathieu, P. (1995) *Rwanda Rule of Law Design: Four-week Interim Report, Introduction and Technical Reports*, Washington, DC: Associates in Rural Development, Inc. in Association with Management Systems International.

Neier, A. (1998) *War Crimes: Brutality, Genocide, Terror and the Struggle for Justice*, New York: Random House.

NEPAD, New Partnership for Africa's Development (2006) *Country Review Report of the Republic of Rwanda*, Midrand: NEPAD.

Neuffer, E. (2001) *The Key to My Neighbor's House: Seeking Justice in Rwanda and Bosnia*, New York: Picador.

Newbury, C. (1978) 'Ethnicity in Rwanda: The Case of Kinyaga', *Africa Journal of the International African Institute*, vol. 48, no. 1, pp. 17–29.

— (1988) *The Cohesion of Oppression, Clientship and Ethnicity in Rwanda, 1860–1960*, New York: Columbia University Press.

— (1995a) 'Background to Genocide: Rwanda', *Journal of Opinion*, vol. 23, no. 2, pp. 12–17.

— (1995b) 'Identity, Genocide and Reconstruction in Rwanda', Paper presented at the conference on Les Racines de Violance dans la Region des Grands Lacs, European Parliament (12–13 January).

— (1998) 'Ethnicity and the Politics of History in Rwanda', *Africa Today*, vol. 45, no. 1, pp. 1–11.

Ngoga, M. (2009) 'The Institutionalisation of Impunity: A Judicial Perspective of the Rwanda Genocide', in Clark, P. and Kaufman, Z. (eds) *After Genocide: Transitional Justice, Post-Conflict Reconstruction and Reconciliation in Rwanda and Beyond*, New York: Columbia University Press.

Nifosi, I. (2005) 'A New Conceptual Framework on Political Transitions: A Case Study on Rwanda', in Marysse, S. and Reyntjens, F. (eds) *L'Afrique des Grands Lacs: Dix Ans de Transitions Conflictuelles, Annuaire 2005–2006*, Paris: L'Harmattan.

Norwegian Helsinki Committee (2002) *Prosecuting Genocide in Rwanda: The Gacaca System and the International Criminal Tribunal for Rwanda, Report 2/2002*. www.donika.com/prosecuting_genocide_in_rwanda.htm (accessed 16 December 2011).

Nowak, M. (1993) *UN Covenant on Civil and Political Rights, CCPR Commentary*, Arlington, VA: N.P. Engel.

Nowrojee, B. (2005) *'Your Justice Is Too Slow': Will the ICTR Fail Rwanda's Victims?*, Geneva: United Nations Research for Social Development.

Ntamabyariro, A. (1999) 'The Rwandan People Accuse', in Berry, J.A. and Berry, C.P. (eds) *Genocide in Rwanda, A Collective Memory*, Washington, DC: Howard University Press.

O'Donnell, G. and Schmitter, C. (eds) (1986) *Transitions from Authoritarian Rule: Tentative Conclusions about Uncertain Democracies*, Baltimore, MD: Johns Hopkins University Press.

OECD (2011) *The DAC guidelines. Helping prevent conflict.* Paris: Development Assistance Committee, OECD.

Office of the President of the Republic of Rwanda (1995) 'Recommendations of the Conference held in Kigali from November 1st to 5th, 1995' on Genocide, Impunity and Accountability: Dialogue for a National and International Response, Kigali: Rwanda.

— (1999) *Report on the Reflection Meetings held in the Office of the President from May 1998 to March 1999*, Kigali: Office of the President.

Oko, O. (2007) 'The Challenges of International Criminal Prosecutions in Africa', *Fordham International Law Journal*, vol. 31, no. 2, pp. 343–414.

— (2009) 'Justice Mechanisms and the Question of Legitimacy: The Example of Rwanda's Multi-Layered Justice Mechanisms', in Ambos, K., Large, J. and Wierda, M. (eds) *Building a Future of Peace and Justice, Studies on Transitional Justice, Peace and Development: The Nuremberg Declaration on Peace and Justice*, Berlin and Heidelberg: Springer.

Oomen, B. (2005) 'Donor-Driven Justice and its Discontents: the Case of Rwanda', *Development and Change*, vol. 36, no. 5, pp. 887–910.

— (2006) 'Rwanda's Gacaca: Objectives, Merits and their Relation to Supranational Criminal Law', in Haveman, R. and Olusanya, O. (eds) *Sentencing and Sanctioning in Supranational Criminal Law*, The Hague: Intersentia.

— (2009) 'Justice Mechanisms and the Question of Legitimacy: The Example of Rwanda's Multi-Layered Justice Mechanisms', in Ambos K., Large, J. and Wierda, M. (eds) *Building a Future of Peace and Justice, Studies on Transitional Justice, Peace and Development: The Nuremberg Declaration on Peace and Justice*, Berlin and Heidelberg: Springer.

Oosthuize, G. and Schaeffer, R. (2008) 'Complete Justice: Residual Functions and Potential Residual Mechanisms of the ICTY, ICTR and SCSL', *Hague Justice Journal*, vol. 3, no. 1, pp. 48–67.

Orentlicher, D. (1991) 'Settling Accounts: The Duty to Prosecute Human Rights Violations of a Prior Regime', *Yale Law Journal*, vol. 100, pp. 2537–615.

— (2005) *Updated Set of Principles for the Protection and Promotion of Human Rights Through Action to Combat Impunity*, UN Doc. E/CN.4/2005/102/Add. 1 Feb. 8, 2005.

Organisation of African Unity (2000) *Rwanda: The Preventable Genocide*, Report of the International Panel of Eminent Personalities to Investigate the 1994 Genocide in Rwanda and the Surrounding Events. Addis Ababa: Organisation for African Unity.

Otunnu, O. (1999) 'An Historical Analysis of the Invasion of the Rwandese Patriotic Army (RPA)', in Adelman, H. and Suhrke, A. (eds) *The Path of a Genocide: The Rwanda Crisis from Uganda to Zaire*, New Brunswick, NJ: Transaction Publishers.

Osiel, M. (1997) *Mass Atrocity, Collective Memory, and the Law*, New Brunswick, NJ: Transaction Publishers.

Pall, Z. (2010) 'Light Shining Darkly: Comparing Post-conflict Constitutional Structures Concerning Speech and Association in Germany and Rwanda', *Columbia Human Rights Review*, vol. 42, no. 1, pp. 5–54.

Pankhurst, D. (1999) 'Issues of Justice and Reconciliation in Complex Political Emergencies: Conceptualizing Reconciliation, Justice and Peace', *Third World Quarterly*, vol. 20, no. 1, pp. 239–56.

Parent, G. (2010) 'Reconciliation and Justice After Genocide: A Theoretical Exploration', *Genocide Studies and Prevention*, vol. 5, no. 3 (Winter), pp. 277–92.

PDR Ihumure, Party for Democracy in Rwanda (2012) *Equitable Justice at the Service of Peace and Reconciliation*, Brussels: PDR Ihumure. www.ihumure.org/?page_id=46 (accessed 15 May 2012).

Parliament, Rwanda (2004) *Rapport de la commission parlementaire extraordinaire mise en place le 20 janvier 2004, chargée d'examiner les massacres commis Gikongoro et analyser l'idéologie du génocide et ceux qui la propagent partout dans le pays*, Kigali: Parliament, Republic of Rwanda.

Penal Reform International (2000) *Access to Justice in Sub-Saharan Africa: The Role of Traditional and Informal Justice Systems*, London: Penal Reform International. www.gsdrc.org/docs/open/SSAJ4.pdf (accessed 15 August 2011).

— (2002a) *Gacaca Report No. 1: Gacaca Jurisdictions and Its Preparations*, Kigali: Penal Reform International.

— (2002b) *Gacaca Research Report III: Jurisdictions in the Pilot Phase* (June 2002), Kigali: Penal Reform International.

— (2003a) *Gacaca and Reconciliation, Kibuye Case Study*, Kigali: Penal Reform International.

— (2003b) *Research Report on the Gacaca. Report IV: The Guilty Plea Procedure, Cornerstone of the Rwandan Justice System*, Kigali: Penal Reform International.

— (2003c) *Gacaca Research Report V: Cell-level Preparations*, Kigali: Penal Reform International.

— (2006) *Research Report on the Gacaca Courts: Information Gathering During the National Phase*, Kigali: Penal Reform International.

— (2010a) *The Contribution of the Gacaca Jurisdictions to Resolving Cases Arising from the Genocide: Contributions, Limitations, and Expectations of the Post Gacaca Phase*, Final monitoring and research report on the Gacaca process, Kigali: Penal Reform International.

— (2010b) *Eight Years On, A Record of Gacaca Monitoring in Rwanda*, Kigali: Penal Reform International.

Permanent Mission of the United Kingdom to the United Nations (2011) *Scope and Application of the Principle of Universal Jurisdiction*, New York: Permanent Mission of the United Kingdom.

Peskin, V. (2005) 'Beyond Victor's Justice? The Challenge of Prosecuting the Winners at the International Criminal Tribunal for the Former Yugoslavia and Rwanda', *Journal of Human Rights*, vol. 4, no. 2, pp. 213–31.

— (2008) *International Justice in Rwanda and the Balkans: Virtual Trials and the Struggle for State Cooperation*, Cambridge: Cambridge University Press.

— (2011) 'Victor's Justice Revisited: Rwandan Patriotic Front Crimes and the Prosecutorial Endgame at the ICTR', in Straus, S. and Waldorf, L. (eds) *Remaking Rwanda: State Building and Human Rights after Mass Violence*, Madison, WI: University of Wisconsin Press.

Peter, C.M. (1997) 'The International Criminal Tribunal for Rwanda: Bringing the Killers to Book', *International Review of the Red Cross*, no. 321, pp. 695–704.

Physicians for Human Rights (1997) *Investigation in Eastern Congo and Western Rwanda: A Report for Physicians for Human Rights*, Boston: National Office, Physicians for Human Rights.

Pillay, N., Kritz, N., Muna, B. and Rudasingwa, T. (1998) 'The Rwanda Tribunal and Its Relationship to National Trials in Rwanda', *American University International Law Review*, vol. 13, pp. 1469–93.

Pitsch, A.M. (2003) 'The Gacaca Law of Rwanda: Possibilities and Problems in Adjudicating Genocide Suspects', Working paper NUR–UMD Partnership, Centre for International

Development and Conflict Management, University of Maryland. www.cidcm.umd.edu/ICT/papers/gacaca_assessment_journal.pdf (accessed 13 October 2006).

Pomfret, J. (1997) 'Rwandans Led Revolt in Congo; Defence Minister Says Arms, Troops Supplied for Anti-Mobutu Drive', *Washington Post*, 9 July 1997.

Ponthus, J. (2007) 'Rwandan Gets 20 Years in Genocide Trial', Reuters, 5 July. www.reuters.com/article/worldNews/idUSL05127632007070 5.

Porter, N. (2003) *The Elusive Quest: Reconciliation in Northern Ireland*, Belfast: The Blackstaff Press. p. 108.

Pottier, J. (2002) *Re-Imagining Rwanda: Conflict, Survival and Disinformation in the Late Twentieth Century*, Cambridge: Cambridge University Press.

Pouligny, B. (2002) 'Building Peace in Situations of Post-Mass Crimes', *International Peacekeeping*, vol. 9, no. 2, pp. 201–20.

Pouligny, B., Chesterman, S. and Schnabel, A. (eds) (2007) *After Mass Crime: Rebuilding States and Communities*, New York: United Nations University Press.

Power, S. (2001) 'Bystanders to Genocide: Why the US Let the Rwanda Tragedy Happen', *Atlantic Magazine*, September.

Prendergast, J. and Smock, D. (1999) *Post Genocide Reconstruction: Building Peace in Rwanda and Burundi*, Special Report No. 53, Washington, DC: United States Institute of Peace.

Prunier, G. (1995) *The Rwanda Crisis: History of a Genocide*, New York: Columbia University Press.

Purdekova, A. (2011) '"Even if I am not here, there are so many eyes": Surveillance and State Reach in Rwanda', *Journal of Modern African Studies*, vol. 49, no. 3, pp. 475–97.

Rafti, M. (2008) 'A Perilous Path to Democracy: Political Transition and Authoritarian Consolidation in Rwanda', Discussion Paper /2008.03, Antwerp: Institute of Development Policy and Management, University of Antwerp.

Raper, J. (2005) 'The Gacaca Experiment: Rwanda's Restorative Dispute Resolution Response to the 1994 Genocide', *Pepperdine Dispute Resolution Law Journal*, vol. 5, no. 1, pp. 1–56.

Ratner, S.R., Abrams, J.S. and Bischoff, J.L. (2009) *Accountability for Human Rights Atrocities in International Law: Beyond the Nuremberg Legacy*, 3rd edn, Oxford: Oxford University Press.

Raub, L. (2009) 'Positioning Hybrid Tribunals in International Criminal Justice', *International Law and Politics*, vol. 41, pp. 1012–53.

Rawson, D. (2001) 'Coping with Chaos while Acting Justly: Lessons from Rwanda', in Barnhizer, D. (ed.) *Effective Strategies for Protecting Human Rights*, London: Ashgate, pp. 125–34.

RDR, Rally for the Return of Refugees and Democracy in Rwanda (2000) 'The Troubling Course of One-sided Justice at the International Criminal Tribunal for Rwanda', Press Release No. 7/2000, 8 November.

REDRESS/FIDH (2009) *The Unfinished Business of the UN International Criminal Tribunals of the Former Yugoslavia (ICTY) and Rwanda (ICTR): The Future Role of the EU and Member States*, London: REDRESS Trust and Paris: FIDH.

— (2010) *Strategies for the Effective Investigation and Prosecution of Serious International Crimes: The Practice of Specialized War Crimes Units*, London: REDRESS Trust and Paris: FIDH.

REDRESS/African Rights (2008a) 'Extraditing Genocide Suspects from Europe to Rwanda: Issues and Challenges', A Report of a Conference Organized by REDRESS and African Rights at the Belgian Parliament, 1 July 2008.

— (2008b) *Survivors and Post-genocide Justice in Rwanda: Their Experiences, Perspectives and Hopes*, London: REDRESS Trust and Kigali: African Rights.

— (2011) *Access to Reparation for Survivors of the 1994 Genocide in Rwanda*, London: REDRESS Trust and Kigali: African Rights.

Reed, W.C. (1995) 'The Rwanda Patriotic Front: Politics and Development in Rwanda', *Journal of Opinion*, vol. XXIII/2, pp. 48–53.

— (1996) 'Exile, Reform, and the Rise of the Rwandan Patriotic Front', *Journal of Modern African Studies*, vol. 34, no. 3, pp. 479–501.

Rettig, M. (2008) 'Gacaca: Truth, Justice, and Reconciliation in Post Conflict Rwanda?', *African Studies Review*, vol. 51, no. 3, pp. 25–50.

— (2011) 'The Sovu Trials: The Impact of Genocide Justice on One Community', in Straus, S. and Waldorf, L. (eds) *Remaking Rwanda: State Building and Human Rights after Mass Violence*, Madison, WI: University of Wisconsin Press.

Reuchamps, M. (2006) *What Justice for Rwanda? Gacaca versus Truth Commission?* http://orbi.ulg.ac.be/handle/2268/464 (accessed 18 December 2011).

Reydams, L. (2002) 'Niyonteze v. Public Prosecutor', *American Journal of International Law*, vol. 96, p. 231.

— (2003a) *Universal Jurisdiction: International and Municipal Legal Perspectives*, Oxford: Oxford University Press.

— (2003b) 'Belgium's First Application of Universal Jurisdiction: The Butare Four Case', *Journal of International Criminal Justice*, vol. 1, p. 428.

Reyntjens, F. (1995) 'Subjects of Concern: Rwanda, October 1994', *Journal of Opinion*, vol. 23, no. 2, pp. 39–43.

— (1996) 'Rwanda: Genocide and Beyond', *Journal of Refugee Studies*, vol. 9, no. 3, pp. 240–51.

— (2004) 'Rwanda, Ten Years On: From Genocide to Dictatorship', *African Affairs*, vol. 103, pp. 177–210.

— (2006) 'Post-1994 Politics in Rwanda: Problematising "liberation" and "democratisation"', *Third World Quarterly*, vol. 27, no. 6, pp. 1103–17.

— (2011) 'Constructing the Truth, Dealing with Dissent, Domesticating the World: Governance in Post-Genocide Rwanda', *African Affairs*, vol. 110, no. 438, pp. 1–34.

Richters, A., Dekker, C. and de Jonge, K. (2005) 'Reconciliation in the aftermath of violent conflict in Rwanda', *Intervention*, vol. 3, no. 3, pp. 203–21.

Riddell, J.G. (2005) 'Addressing Crimes Against International Law: Rwanda's Gacaca in Practice', Master of Law thesis, Aberdeen: University of Aberdeen. www.restorativejustice.org/10fulltext/ridelljennifer (accessed 9 December 2011).

Rigby, A. (2001) *Justice and Reconciliation: After the Violence*, London: Lynne Rienner.

RNC (Rwanda National Congress) (2012) *Statement on Extraditions and Transfers to Rwanda*, Washington, DC: Rwanda National Congress.

Roberts, D. (2008) 'Post-Conflict State Building and State Legitimacy: From Negative to Positive Peace?', *Development and Change*, vol. 39, no. 4, pp. 537–55.

Rodman, K.A. (2008) 'Darfur and the Limits of Legal Deterrence', *Human Rights Quarterly*, vol. 30, no. 3, pp. 529–60.

Roht-Arriaza, N. (2004) 'Reparations Decisions and Dilemmas', *Hastings International & Comparative Law Review*, vol. 27, no. 2, pp. 157–219.

— (ed.) (1995) *Impunity and Human Rights in International Law and Practice*, New York and Oxford: Oxford University Press.

— (2006) *Transitional Justice in the Twenty-First Century: Beyond Truth versus Justice*, Cambridge and New York: Cambridge University Press.

Rombouts, H. and Vandegiste, S. (2005) 'Reparations for Victims in Rwanda: Caught Between Theory and Practice', in De Feyter, K., Parmentier, S., Bossuyt, M. and Lemmens P. (eds) *Out of the Ashes: Reparation for Victims of Gross and Systematic Human Rights Violations*, Antwerp and Oxford: Intersentia.

Rosenbaum, E.M. (2007) Statement of Director, Office of Special Investigations, Criminal Division, Department of Justice, Before the Subcommittee on Crime, Terrorism and Homeland Security Committee on the Judiciary, United States House of Representatives Concerning Genocide and the Rule of Law, 23 October, Washington, DC.

Rotberg, R.I. (2000) 'Truth Commissions and the Provision of Truth, Justice, and Reconciliation', in Rotberg, R.I. and Thompson, D. (eds) *Truth v. Justice: The Morality of Truth Commissions*, Princeton, NJ: Princeton University Press.

Roth, K. (2009a) 'The Power of Horror in Rwanda', *Los Angeles Times*, 11 April.

— (2009b) Letter addressed to Hassan Jallow, Prosecutor of the ICTR, 14 August 2009.

Rothe, D.L. and Mullins, C.W. (2010) *State Crime: Current Perspectives*, New Brunswick, NJ: Rutgers University Press.

RPF (Rwandese Patriotic Front) (1994) *RPF Declaration relating to the Putting in Place of Institutions*, 17 July, Kigali, Rwanda.

Rudasingwa, T. (1994) *Rwanda: Background to Genocide*, Dar Es Salaam: Thackers Publishers.

— (1996) 'The Balance between the Necessity for Justice and Imperatives of National Unity, Reconciliation and Democratization', Paper presented at the International Conference on Genocide, Impunity and Accountability: A Dialogue for a National and International Response, Kigali, 1–5 November 1995. Dar es Salaam: Thackers Publishers.

Rugege, S. (2005) 'Judicial Independence in Rwanda', Paper presented at the conference, Judicial Independence and Legal Infrastructure: Essential Partners for Economic Development, University of the Pacific, McGeorge School of Law, Sacramento, CA, 28 October.

Rwanda Parliament (2004) *Rapport de la commission parlementaire extraordinaire mise en place le 20 janvier 2004, chargée d'examiner les massacres commis Gikongoro et analyser l'idéologie du génocide et ceux qui la propagent partout dans le pays*, Kigali: Rwanda Parliament.

Ryngaert, C. (2007) 'Universal Jurisdiction over Genocide and Wartime Torture in Dutch Courts: An Appraisal of the Afghan and Rwandan cases', *Hague Justice Journal*, vol. 2, no. 2, pp. 13–36.

Salter, M. and Huyse, L. (eds) (2008) *Traditional Justice After Violent Conflict: Learning from African Experiences*, Stockholm: International Institute for Democracy and Electoral Assistance.

Sarkin, J. (1999) 'The Necessity and Challenges of Establishing a Truth and Reconciliation Commission in Rwanda', *Human Rights Quarterly*, vol. 21, no. 3, pp. 767–823.

— (2000) 'Promoting Justice, Truth and Reconciliation in Transitional Societies: Evaluating Rwanda's Approach in the New Millennium of Using Community-Based Gacaca Tribunals to Deal with the Past', *International Law Forum*, vol. 2, pp. 112–21.

— (2001) 'The Tension Between Justice and Reconciliation in Rwanda: Politics, Human Rights, Due Process and the Role of Gacaca in Dealing with the Genocide', *Journal of African Law*, vol. 45, no. 2, pp. 143–72.

Sarkin, J. and Daly, E. (2004) 'Too Many Questions, Too Few Answers: Reconciliation in Transitional Societies', *Columbia Human Rights Law Review*, vol. 35, no. 3, pp. 101–68.

Sasaki, K. (2009) 'Beyond Dichotomies: The Quest for Justice and Reconciliation and the Politics of National Identity Building in Post-genocide Rwanda'. PhD thesis, Department of Peace Studies, University of Bradford.

Schabas, W. (1997) 'Justice, Democracy and Impunity in Post-Genocide Rwanda: Searching for Solutions to Impossible Problems', *Criminal Law Forum*, vol. 8, pp. 523–60.

— (2001) 'International Criminal Tribunal for Rwanda', in *The Global Community: Yearbook of International Law and Jurisprudence*, vol. I, New York: Oceana Publications, pp. 617–32.

— (2002) *The Abolition of the Death Penalty in International Law*, 3rd edn, Cambridge: Cambridge University Press.

— (2003a) 'Barayagwiza v. Prosecutor, Commentary', in Klip A. and Sluiter, G. (eds) *Annotated Leading Cases of International Criminal Tribunals, The Criminal Tribunal for Rwanda 2000–2001*, vol. 6, pp. 261–66.

— (2003b) 'Relevant Lessons from the ad hoc Tribunals', *Palestine Yearbook of International Law*, vol. 12, pp. 5–26.

— (2003c) 'National Courts Finally Begin to Prosecute Genocide, the Crime of Crimes', *Journal of International Criminal Justice*, vol. 1, no. 1, pp. 39–63.

— (2004a) 'International Criminal Tribunal for Rwanda' in *The Global Community: Yearbook of International Law and Jurisprudence 2004*, vol. II, Dobbs Ferry, NY: Oceania Publications, pp. 977–87.

— (2004b) 'Ethnic Cleansing and Genocide: Similarities and Distinctions', *European Yearbook of Minority Issues, 2003/4*, vol. 3, pp. 109–28.

— (2004c) 'Internationalised Courts and Their Relationship with Alternative Accountability Mechanisms: The Case of Sierra Leone', in Romano, C.P.R., Nollkaemper, A. and Kleffner, J.K. (eds) *Internationalised Criminal Courts and Tribunals, Sierra Leone, East Timor, Kosovo and Cambodia*, Oxford: Oxford University Press.

— (2005) 'Rwandan Courts in Quest of Accountability: Genocide Trials and Gacaca Courts', *Journal of International Criminal Justice*, vol. 3, no. 4, pp. 879–95.

— (2006) *The UN International Criminal Tribunals: The Former Yugoslavia, Rwanda and Sierra Leone*, Cambridge: Cambridge University Press.

— (2007a) *Introduction to the International Criminal Court*, 3rd edn, Cambridge: Cambridge University Press.

— (2007b) 'International Criminal Tribunal for Rwanda' in *The Global Community: Yearbook of International Law and Jurisprudence, 2006*, vol. I, Dobbs Ferry, NY: Oceana Publications, pp. 641–54.

— (2009a) *Genocide in International Law*, 2nd edn, Cambridge: Cambridge University Press.

— (2009b) 'International Tribunals', in Krause, C. and Scheinin, M. (eds) *International Protection of Human Rights: A Textbook*, Turkü/Abo: Abo Akademi University Institute for Human Rights, pp. 637–63.

— (2009c) 'Anti-Complementarity: Referral to National Jurisdictions by the UN International Criminal Tribunal for Rwanda', *Max Planck Yearbook of United National Law*, vol. 13, pp. 29–60.

— (2010) *The Rome Statute of the International Criminal Court: A Commentary*, Oxford: Oxford University Press.

Schabas, W., Carbonare, J., Degni-Segui, R., Des Forges, A., Dodinval, P., Gillet, E., Odink, R., Quedraogo, H., Paradis, A. and Dahinden, P. (1993) *Report of the International Commission Concerning Human Rights Violations in Rwanda Since 1 October 1990*, Paris, Toronto and New York: Africa Watch, Fédération Internationale des Droits de l'Homme (FIDH), International Centre for Human Rights and Democratic Development (Rights & Democracy), and the Union Interafricaine des Droits de l'Homme et des Peuples (UIDH).

Schabas, W. and Lapachelle, J. (1994) *For A System of Justice in Rwanda, Report Report of an Exploratory Mission on the Needs of the Judicial System in Rwanda*, Montreal: International Centre for Human Rights and Democratic Development.

Scharf, P.M. (1995) 'Have We Really Learned the Lessons of Nuremberg'. Conference paper, Nuremberg and Rule of Law: A Fifty-Year Verdict, Charlottesville, Virginia, 17–18 November.

— (1996) 'The Letter of Law: The Scope of the International Obligation to Prosecute Human Rights Crimes, Law and Contemporary Problems', vol. 59, no. 4, pp. 41–62.

— (1999) 'Responding to Rwanda: Accountability Mechanisms in the Aftermath of Genocide', *Journal of International Affairs*, vol. 52, pp. 621–38.

Scharf, M. and Rodley, N. (2002) 'International Law Principles on Accountability', in Bassiouni, M.C. (ed.) *Post-Conflict Justice, International and Comparative Criminal Law Series*, Ardsley, NJ: Transnational Publishers.

Schirch, L. (2008) 'Strategic Peace Building: State of the Field Peace Prints', *South Asian Journal of Peace Building*, vol. 1, no. 1, pp. 1–17.

Schlutter, B. (2010) *Developments in Customary International Law: Theory and Practice of the International Court of Justice and the International ad hoc Tribunals for Rwanda and Yugoslavia*, Leiden and Boston: Martinus Nijhoff Publishers.

Sebastian, M. (2010) 'Justice Sector Reform in Rwanda: A Space of Contention or Consensus?', ISP Collection, Paper 887. http://digitalcollections.sit.edu/isp_collection/887 (accessed 18 December 2011).

Secretariat, Conference of Catholic Church Bishops (2002) 'Ibaruwa y' abepiskopi Gatolika igenewe Abakirisitu mu gihe cy' inkiko gacaca: ubutabera bwunga', 13 Kamena 2002, Kigali: Secretariat, Conference of Catholic Church.

Sendashonga, S. (1995) Letter of Resignation from Council of Ministers, Kigali Rwanda. See www.grandslacs.net/doc/0186.pdf (accessed 12 August 2012).

Shattuck, J. (2006) 'The Legacy of Nuremberg: Confronting Genocide and Terror through the Rule of Law', *Gonzaga Journal of International Law*, vol. 10, pp. 6–16.

Shaw, R. and Waldorf, L. (2010) *Localizing Transitional Justice: Interventions and Priorities after Mass Violence*, Stanford, CA: Stanford University Press.

Sikkink, K. (2011) *The Justice Cascade: How Human Rights Prosecutions Are Changing World Politics*. New York: W.W. Norton.

Silva-Leander, S. (2008) 'On the Danger and Necessity of Democratisation: Trade-Offs between Short-Term Stability and Long-Term Peace in Post-Genocide Rwanda', *Third World Quarterly*, vol. 29, no. 8, pp. 1601–20.

— (2011) *Structural Violence and Conflict: Vertical and Horizontal Inequality in Post-Genocide Rwanda*, conference publication, CRISE, Palgrave: London.

Skaar, E. (2011) 'Understanding the Impact of Transitional Justice on Peace and Democracy', Paper presented at ECPR conference, 25–27 August, Reykjavik.

Smith, D. (2003) *Getting Their Act Together: Towards a Strategic Framework for Peacebuilding*, Oslo: International Peace Research Institute.

Snyder, J. and Leslie, V. (2003) Trial and Errors: Principle and Pragmatism in Strategies of International Justice, *International Security,* vol. 28, no. 3, pp. 5–44.

Soerensen, M.J. (2007) *Truth, Justice and Security in Rwanda – Gacaca Courts as a Post-Genocide Reconciliation Effort*, Lund: Transnational Foundation for Peace and Future Research.

Sooka, Y. (2006) 'Dealing with the Past and Transitional Justice: Building Peace through Accountability', *International Review of the Red Cross*, vol. 88, no. 862, pp. 311–25.

Sosnov, M. (2008) 'The Adjudication of Genocide: Gacaca and the Road to Reconciliation in Rwanda', *Denver Journal of International Law and Policy*, vol. 36, pp. 125–53.

Southern Africa Litigation Centre (SALC) / REDRESS (2012) *Closing the Impunity Gap: Southern Africa's Role in Ensuring Justice for the 1994 Genocide in Rwanda – Moving Beyond the Tribunal Completion Strategy and Residual Mechanisms*, Johannesburg: Southern Africa Litigation Centre and London: REDRESS.

Spears, I. (2000) 'Understanding Inclusive Peace Agreements in Africa: The Problems of Sharing Power', *Third World Quarterly*, vol. 21, no. 1, pp. 105–18.

Sriram, C.K., Martin-Ortega, O. and Herman, J. (2009) *Evaluating and Comparing Strategies of Peacebuilding and Transitional Justice*, JAD-PbP Working Paper Series No. 1, Just and Durable Peace by Piece Project, London: Centre on Human Rights in Conflict, University of East London. www.lu.se/upload/LUPDF/Samhallsvetenskap/Just_and_Durable_Peace/Workingpaper1.pdf (accessed 15 March 2012).

Staub, E. (2003) 'Preventing Violence and Generating Humane Values: Healing and Reconciliation in Rwanda', *International Review of the Red Cross*, vol. 85, no. 852, pp. 791–806. www.icrc.org/eng/resources/documents/misc/5wnjcf.htm (accessed 21 August 2012).

Stover, E. and Weinstein, H.M. (eds) (2004) *My Neighbor, My Enemy: Justice and Community in the Aftermath of Mass Atrocity*, Cambridge: Cambridge University Press.

Strain, J. and Keyes, E. (2003) 'Accountability in the Aftermath of Rwanda's Genocide', in Stromseth, J. (ed.) *Accountability for Atrocities: National and International Responses*, Ardsley, NY: Transnational Publishers.

Straus, S. (2004) 'How Many Perpetrators Were There in the Rwandan Genocide? An Estimate', *Journal of Genocide Research*, vol. 6, no. 1, pp. 85–98.

— (2007a) *The Order of Genocide: Race, Power and War in Rwanda*, Ithaca, NY and London: Cornell University Press.

— (2007b) 'Origins and Aftermaths: The Dynamics of Genocide in Rwanda and Their Post-Crime Implications', in Chesterman, S., Pouligny, B. and Schnabel, A. (eds) *Mass Crimes and Post-Conflict Peace-Building*, Tokyo: United Nations University Press.

Straus, S. and Waldorf L. (eds) (2011a) *Remaking Rwanda: State Building and Human Rights after Mass Violence,* Madison, WI: The University of Wisconsin Press.

Straus, S. and Waldorf, L. (2011b) 'Introduction: Seeing Like a Post-Conflict State', in *Remaking Rwanda: State Building and Human Rights after Mass Violence*, Madison, WI: University of Wisconsin Press.

Stroh, A. (2009) 'The Effects of Electoral Institutions in Rwanda: Why Proportional Representation in Rwanda Supports the Authoritarian Regime', no. 105, GIGA Working Papers, Hamburg: German Institute of Global and Area Studies.

Stromseth, J. (ed.) (2003) *Accountability for Atrocities: National and International Responses*, Ardsley, NJ: Transnational Publishers.

Supreme Court of Rwanda (u.d.) *Manuel Explicatif sur la Loi Organique portent Creation des Jurisdictions Gacaca*, Kigali: Gacaca Jurisdictions Department, Supreme Court of Rwanda.

Takeuchi, S. (2011) *Gacaca and DDR: The Disputable Record of State Building in Rwanda*, Tokyo: JICA Research Institute.

Teitel, R. (2003a) 'Transitional Justice Genealogy', *Harvard Human Rights Journal*, vol. 16 (Spring), pp. 69–94.

— (2003b) 'Transitional Justice in a New Era', *Fordham International Law Journal*, vol. 26, no. 4, pp. 893–906.

— (2010) 'Global Transitional Justice', Paper No. 8, Project on Human Rights, Global Justice and Democracy, Fairfax, VA: Center for Global Studies, George Mason University.

Thakur, R. (ed.) (2004) *From Sovereignty to International Accountability: The Search for Justice in a World of States*, Tokyo, New York and Paris: United Nations University Press.

Theissen, G. (2004) 'Supporting Justice, Co-Existence and Reconciliation After Armed Conflict: Strategies for Dealing With the Past', Berghof Research Center for Constructive Conflict Management. www.berghof-handbook.net/articles/theissen_handbook.pdf (accessed 12 August 2010).

Thompson, A. (2008) 'Rwanda', in Mehler, A., Melber, H. and van Walrave, K. (eds) *Africa Yearbook 5: Politics, Economy and Society South of the Sahara, 2008*, Leiden: Brill.

— (ed.) (2006) *The Media and the Rwanda Genocide*, London: Pluto Press.

Thoms, O.N.T. (2010) 'State-Level Effects of Transitional Justice: What Do We Know?', *International Journal of Transitional Justice*, vol. 4, no. 3, pp. 329–54.

Thoms, O.N.T. and Ron, J. (2007) 'Do Human Rights Violations Cause Internal Conflict?', *Human Rights Quarterly*, vol. 29, no. 3, pp. 674–705.

Thoms, O.N.T., Ron, J. and Paris, R. (2008) 'The Effects of Transitional Justice Mechanisms: A Summary of Empirical Research Findings and Implications for Analysts and Practitioners', Working Paper, Ottawa: University of Ottawa.

Thomson, M.S. (1999) 'Why the International Criminal Tribunal for Rwanda is Doing Nothing to Promote Sustainable Peace in Rwanda', *Scientific Journal of Law*, vol. 56, no. 3 (August), pp. 127–49.

— (2009) *Resisting Reconciliation: State Power and Everyday Life in Post-genocide Rwanda*, PhD thesis, Halifax: Dalhousie University.

— (2010) 'Getting Close to Rwandans since the Genocide: Studying Everyday Life in Highly Politicized Research Settings', *African Studies Review*, vol. 53, no. 3, pp. 19–34.

— (2011a) 'Whispering Truth to Power: The Every Day Resistance of Rwandan Peasants to Post-genocide Reconciliation', *African Affairs*, June, pp. 1–18.

— (2011b) 'The Darker Side of Transitional Justice: The Power Dynamics Behind Rwanda's Gacaca Courts', *Africa*, vol. 81, no. 3, pp. 373–90.

— (2011c) 'Rhetorical Legacies of Leadership: Projections of "Benevolent Leadership" in Pre- and Post Genocide Rwanda' (with Marie-Eve Desrosiers), *Journal of Modern African Studies*, vol. 49, no. 3, September.

Thomson, M.S. and Nagy, R. (2011) 'Law, Power and Justice: What Legalism Fails to Address in the Functioning of Rwanda's Gacaca Courts', *International Journal of Transitional Justice*, vol. 5, pp. 11–30.

Thorin, V. (2001) 'Interview with Former President Pasteur Bizimungu', *Jeune Afrique*, no. 2112, 3–9 July.

Tiemessen A.E. (2004) 'After Arusha: Gacaca Justice in Post Genocide Rwanda', *African Studies Quarterly*, vol. 8, no. 1, p. 57.

Truth and Reconciliation Commission (1998) *Truth and Reconciliation Commission of South Africa Report*, vol. I. www.justice.gov.za/trc/report/finalreport/Volume%201.pdf (accessed 25 July 2012).

Tully, D. (2003) 'Human Rights Compliance and the Gacaca Jurisdictions in Rwanda', *Boston College International and Comparative Law Review*, vol. 26, no. 2, pp. 385–414.

Twagiramungu, F. (1995) Letter of Resignation from office of Prime Minister, Kigali, Rwanda. See www.grandslacs.net/doc/0186.pdf (accessed 17 June 2005).

Umugwaneza, G. (2005) 'Gacaca Courts in Rwanda: Avenues for Justice and Reconciliation?', Master of Law thesis, Cambridge, MA: Harvard Law School.

United Nations (1952) Report of the Committee on International Criminal Jurisdiction, UN Doc. A/2135 (1952), New York: United Nations.

— (1954) Report of the Committee on International Criminal Jurisdiction, UN Doc. A/2645 (1954), New York: United Nations.

— (1966) International Covenant on Civil and Political Rights, Adopted and opened for signature, ratification and accession by General Assembly Resolution 2200A (XXI) of 16 December 1966.

— (1988) United Nations General Assembly Resolution 43/173, *Body of Principles for the Protection of All Persons under Any Form of Detention or Imprisonment: resolution/adopted by the General Assembly*, 9 December 1988, UN Doc. A/RES/43/173. www.unhcr.org/refworld/docid/3b00f219c.html (accessed 3 August 2012).

— (1992) United Nations General Assembly Resolution 47/133 of 18 December 1992.

— (1993a) Report of Bacre Wale Ndiaye, Special Rapporteur, Extrajudicial, Summary or Arbitrary Executions, submitted pursuant to Commission of Human Rights Resolution 1993/71. UN Doc. E/CN.4/1994/7/Add.1, New York: United Nations.

— (1993b) United Nations Security Council Resolution 827 (25 May 1993), UN Doc. S-RES-827(1993).

— (1994a) Report of the Secretary General on the situation in Rwanda, UN Doc. S/1994/640, New York: United Nations.

— (1994b) Security Council, Provisional Verbatim Record of the 3371st meeting, held on 30 April 1994 (S/PV.3371), New York: United Nations.

— (1994c) Minutes, United Nations Security Council, 3377th Meeting (16 May 1994), UN Doc. S/PV.3377.

— (1994d) United Nations Security Council Resolution 918 (17 May 1994), UN Doc. S/RES/918, para 18.

— (1994e) Minutes, United Nations Security Council 3388th Meeting (8 June 1994), UN Doc. S/PV.3388.

— (1994f) Report of the Secretary General on the establishment of a Commission of Experts pursuant to paragraph 1 of Security Council Resolution 935 (1994) of 1 July 1994, UN Doc. S/1994/879, New York: United Nations.

— (1994g) United Nations Security Council Resolution 935 (1 July 1994), UN Doc. S/RES/935(1994).

— (1994h) Report to the Secretary General on the Situation in Rwanda, UN Doc. s/1994/640, 31 May 1994.

— (1994i) Security Council, Statement dated 28 September 1994 on the question of refugees and security in Rwanda, UN Doc. S/1994/1115, New York: United Nations.

— (1994j) Preliminary Report of the Independent Commission of Experts established pursuant to Security Council Resolution 935 (1994), UN Doc. S/1994/1125 4, New York: United Nations.

— (1994k) Final Report of the Independent Commission of Experts established pursuant to Security Council Resolution 935 (1994), UN Doc. S/1994/1405, New York: United Nations.

— (1994l) United Nations Security Council 3453rd Meeting (8 November 1994), UN Doc. S/PV.3453, New York: United Nations.

— (1994m) United Nations Security Council Resolution 955 (8 November 1994), UN Doc. S/RES/955(1994), New York: United Nations.

— (1994n) Concluding Observations: El Salvador, 18 April 1994, CCPR/C/79/Add.34, Human Rights Committee, New York: United Nations.

— (1995) Conclusions and Recommendations: Chile, 26 June 1995, UN Doc. A/50/44, Committee Against Torture, New York: United Nations.

— (1996a) Report of the Joint Mission charged with investigating allegations of massacres and other human rights violations occurring in eastern Zaire (now Democratic Republic of Congo since September 1996), UN Doc. A/51/942, New York: United Nations.

— (1996b) Concluding Observations on Guatemala, Human Rights Committee, 3 April 1996, UN Doc. CCPR/C/79/Add.63, New York: United Nations.

— (1997) Report of the Office of Internal Oversight Services on the Audit and Investigation of the International Criminal Tribunal for Rwanda, UN Doc. A/51/789, New York: United Nations.

— (1998a) Report of the Secretary General's Investigative Team charged with investigating serious violations of human rights and international humanitarian law in the Democratic Republic of Congo, UN Doc. S/1998/581, New York: United Nations.

— (1998b) Report on the situation of human rights in Rwanda prepared by the Special Representative of the Commission on Human Rights pursuant to Economic and Social Council decision 1998/266, UN Doc. A 53/402, New York: United Nations.

— (1998c) Report of the Working Group on Enforced or Involuntary Disappearances, General Comments on Article 19 of the Declaration on the Protection of All Persons from Enforced Disappearance, 12 January 1998, UN Doc. E/CN.1/1998/43, New York: United Nations.

— (1999a) Report of the Independent Inquiry into the United Nation's Actions during the 1994 Rwanda Genocide (The Carlson Report), 15 December 1999, UN Doc. S/1999/1257, New York: United Nations.
— (1999b) Minutes of 4063rd meeting of United Nations Security Council (10 November 1999), UN Doc. S/PV.4063.
— (1999c) Report of the Expert Group to Conduct a Review of the Effective Operation and Functioning of the International Criminal Tribunal for the Former Yugoslavia and the International Criminal Tribunal for Rwanda, UN Doc. A/54/634, New York: United Nations.
— (1999d) Concluding Observations on Italy, 7 April 1999, UN Doc. CERD/C/304/Add.68, Committee on the Elimination of Racial Discrimination (CERD), New York: United Nations.
— (1999e) Concluding Observations on Romania, 28 July 1999, CCPR/C/79/Add.111, Human Rights Committee, New York: United Nations.
— (1999f) Concluding Observations on Lesotho, 8 April 1999, CCPR/C/79/Add. 106, Human Rights Committee, New York: United Nations.
— (2000a) Minutes of 4150th meeting of the Security Council, UN Doc. S/PV.4150 (2 June 2000).
— (2000b) Concluding Observations on France, 19 April 2000, CERD/C/304/Add.91, Committee on the Elimination of Racial Discrimination (CERD).
— (2001a) Report of the Office of Internal Oversight Services on the Investigation into possible fee-splitting arrangements between defence counsel and indigent detainees at the International Criminal for Rwanda and the International Criminal Tribunal for the Former Yugoslavia, UN Doc. A/55/759, New York: United Nations.
— (2001b) Minutes of 4429th meeting of the Security Council, UN Doc. S/PV.442 (27 November 2001).
— (2001c) Report of the Special Representative on Human Rights Defenders, UN Doc. A/56/341, 10 September 2001.
— (2001d) Concluding Observations on Germany, 27 April 2001, CERD/C/304/Add.115, Committee on the Elimination of Racial Discrimination (CERD).
— (2002) Report on the Follow-up Investigation into possible fee-splitting arrangements between defence counsel and indigent detainees at the International Criminal Tribunal for Rwanda and the International Criminal Tribunal for the Former Yugoslavia (26 February 2002), UN Doc. A/56/836, New York: United Nations.
— (2003a) United Nations Security Council Resolution 1503 (28 August 2003), UN Doc. S/RES/1503.
— (2003b) 'The Security Council Appoints Separate Prosecutors for the Two Ad Hoc UN Tribunals', Press Release, ICTR/INFO-9-2-359.EN Arusha, 4 September 2003.
— (2003c) United Nations Security Council Resolution 1504 (4 September 2003) UN Doc. S/RES/1504.
— (2003d) United Nations Security Council Resolution 1505 (4 September 2003) UN Doc. S/RES/1505 (2003).
— (2003e) Minutes of 4838th meeting of United Nations Security Council, UN Doc. S/PV.4838.
— (2003f) United Nations Security Council Resolution 1512 (2003) (27 October 2003) UN Doc. S/RES/1512 (2003).
— (2003g) Concluding Observations on Czech Republic, 10 December 2003, CERD/C/63/CO/4, Committee on the Elimination of Racial Discrimination (CERD), New York: United Nations.

— (2004a) Report of the Secretary General on the Rule of Law and Transitional Justice, UN Doc. S/2004/616, New York: United Nations.

— (2004b) Security Council Resolution 1534 (26 March 2004), UN Doc. S/RES/1534 (2004).

— (2005a) Minutes of 5199th meeting of United Nations Security Council (13 June 2005), UN Doc. S/PV.5199.

— (2005b) Minutes of 5328th meeting of United Nations Security Council (15 December 2005), UN Doc. S/PV.5199.

— (2006) Basic Principles and Guidelines on the Right to a Remedy and Reparation for Victims of Gross Violations of International Human Rights Law and Serious Violations of International Humanitarian Law, adopted by Resolution A/RES/60/147 of the General Assembly, 21 March 2006. UN Doc. E/CN.4/sub.2/1996/17 annex. www.unhcr.org/refworld/docid/4721cb942.html (accessed 17 June 2012).

— (2008a) Securing Peace and Development: The Role of the United Nations in Supporting Security Sector Reform, UN Doc. A/62/659 – S/2008/39, New York: United Nations.

— (2008b) Minutes of 5904th Meeting of United Nations Security Council (4 June 2008), UN Doc. S/PV.5904.

— (2009a) Minutes of 6134th Meeting of United Nations Security Council (4 June 2009), UN Doc. S/PV.6134.

— (2009b) Minutes of 6228th Meeting of United Nations Security Council (3 December 2009), UN Doc, S/PV.6228.

— (2009c) Report of the Secretary General on the administrative and budgetary aspects of the options for possible locations for the archives of the International Tribunal for the Former Yugoslavia and the International Criminal Tribunal for Rwanda and the seat of the Residual Mechanism(s) for the tribunals, UN Doc, S/2009/258, New York: United Nations.

— (2010) United Nations Security Council Resolution 1966 (22 December 2010), UN Doc. S/RES/1966 (2010).

UNCHR (United Nations Commission on Human Rights) (1993a) Final report submitted by Mr Theo van Boven, Special Rapporteur, Study concerning the right to restitution, compensation and rehabilitation for victims of gross violations of human rights and fundamental freedoms, UN Doc. E/CN.4/Sub.2/1993/, Geneva: United Nations Commission on Human Rights.

— (1993b) Report of the Special Rapporteur, Bacre Ndiaye, on mission to Rwanda from 8 to 17 April 1993. Corrigendum: Extrajudicial, summary or arbitrary executions, UN Doc. E/CN.4/1994/7/Corr.1, Geneva: United Nations Commission on Human Rights.

— (1994a) First Report on the situation of human rights in Rwanda submitted by Mr Rene Degni-Segui, Special Rapporteur of the Commission on Human Rights, under paragraph 20 of resolution S-31 of 25 May 1994 (Date of Report: 28 June 1994), UN Doc. E/CN.4/1995/7, Geneva: United Nations Commission on Human Rights.

— (1994b) Second Report on the situation of human rights in Rwanda submitted by Mr Rene Degni-Segui, Special Rapporteur of the Commission on Human Rights, under paragraph 20 of resolution S-31 of 25 May 1994 (Date of Report: 12 August 1994), UN Doc. E/CN.4/1995/12, Geneva: United Nations Commission on Human Rights.

— (1994c) Third Report on the situation of human rights in Rwanda submitted by Mr Rene Degni-Segui, Special Rapporteur of the Commission on Human Rights, under paragraph 20 of resolution S-31 of 25 May 1994 (Date of Report: 11 November 1994), UN Doc. A/49/508, S/1994/1157, Geneva: United Nations Commission on Human Rights.

— (1994d) Fourth Report on the situation of human rights in Zaire, prepared by the Special Rapporteur, Mr Roberto Garreton, in accordance with Commission Resolution 1994/87, UN Doc. E/CN.4/1995/67, Geneva: United Nations Commission on Human Rights.

— (1994e) Report on the situation of human rights in Zaire, prepared by the Special Rapporteur, Mr Roberto Garreton, in accordance with Commission Resolution 1994/87 (23 December 1994), UN Doc. E/CN.4/1995/67, Geneva: United Nations Commission on Human Rights.

— (1995) Report on the situation of human rights in Rwanda submitted by Mr Rene Degni-Segui, Special Rapporteur of the Commission on Human Rights, under paragraph 20 of resolution S-31 of 25 May 1994 (Date of Report: 17 January 1995), UN Doc. E/CN.4/1995/71, Geneva: United Nations Commission on Human Rights.

— (1996) Report on the situation of human rights in Rwanda submitted by Mr Rene Degni-Segui, Special Rapporteur of the Commission on Human Rights (1996), UN Doc. E/CN.4/1996/68, Geneva: United Nations Commission on Human Rights.

— (1997) Situation of human rights in Rwanda: Report of the situation of human rights in Rwanda prepared by the Special Representative of the Commission on Human Rights pursuant to Economic and Social Council Resolution 1997/66 and Social Council Decision 1997/274, UN Doc. A/52/522, Geneva: United Nations Commission on Human Rights.

— (1998a) Report of the Working Group on Enforced or Involuntary Disappearances, UN Doc. E/CN.4/1998/43, Geneva: United Nations Commission on Human Rights.

— (1998b) Situation of human rights in Rwanda: Report of the situation of human rights in Rwanda prepared by the Special Representative of the Commission on Human Rights pursuant to Economic and Social Council Resolution 1998/266 of 30 July 1998, UN Doc. A/53/402, Geneva: United Nations Commission on Human Rights.

— (1999) Situation of human rights in Rwanda: Report of the situation of human rights in Rwanda prepared by the Special Representative of the Commission on Human Rights pursuant to Economic and Social Council decision 1999/288 of 30 July 1999, UN Doc. A/54/359; Section XI, Geneva: United Nations Commission on Human Rights.

UNDP (United Nations Development Program), Rwanda (2007) *Turning 2020 Vision into Reality: From Recovery to Sustainable Human Development*, Kigali: National Human Development Report.

United Nations Human Rights Committee (1992) CCPR General Comment No. 20: Article 7 (Prohibition of Torture, or Other Cruel, Inhuman or Degrading Treatment or Punishment), 10 March 1992. www.unhcr.org/refworld/docid/453883fb0.html (accessed 30 July 2012).

— (2004) General Comment No. 31 on the Nature of the General Legal Obligation Imposed on States Parties to the Covenant, 26 May 2004, CCPR/C/21/Rev.1/Add.13.

UNOHCHR (United Nations Office of the United Nations High Commissioner for Human Rights) (1984) General Comment 13: Equality before the courts and the right to a fair and public hearing by an independent court established by law (Article 14, ICCPR), para. 4.

— (1987) Views of the Human Rights Committee under Article 5, paragraph 4 of the Optional Protocol to the ICCPR, Communication No. 263/1987, para. 5.2.

— (1994) Report of the United Nations High Commissioner for Human Rights on his Mission to Rwanda of 11–12 May 1994, UN Doc. E/CN.4/S-3, Geneva: Office of the United Nations High Commissioner for Human Rights.

— (1996) The Administration of Justice in Post-Genocide Rwanda, Report of Human Rights Field Operation Mission in Rwanda, June 1996, Doc. HRFOR/Justice/June 1996/E, Kigali, Rwanda.

— (2001) General Comment 29 on States of Emergency (Art. 4) of the United Nations Human Rights Committee, UN Doc. CCPR/C/21/Rev.1/Add.11, 31 August 2000.

— (2004) General Comment No. 31 on the Nature of the General Legal Obligation Imposed on States Parties to the Covenant, Human Rights Committee, 26 May 2004, CCPR/C/21/Rev.1/Add.13.

— (2006a) Rule-of-Law Tools for Post-Conflict States: Truth Commissions, Geneva and New York: United Nations.
— (2006b) Study on the right to truth, Summary, Report of the Office of the United Nations High Commissioner for Human Rights, UN Doc. E/CN.4/2006/91, Geneva: Office of the United Nations High Commissioner for Human Rights.
— (2006c) Rule-of-Law Tools for Post-Conflict States – Vetting: An Operational Framework, Geneva and New York: United Nations.
— (2008) Rule-of-Law Tools for Post-Conflict States: Reparations Programmes, Geneva: Office of the United Nations High Commissioner for Human Rights.
— (2010) Report of the Mapping Exercise documenting the most serious violations of human rights and international humanitarian law committed within the territory of the Democratic Republic of the Congo between March 1993 and June 2003, Geneva: Office of the United Nations High Commissioner for Human Rights.
United States Institute of Peace (2008) *Transitional Justice: Information Handbook*, Washington, DC: United States Institute of Peace. www.usip.org (accessed on 15 February 2012).
Uvin, P. (1996) *Development, Aid and Conflict: Reflections from the Case of rwanda*, Research for Action 24, Helsinki: United Nations University Press/World Institute for Development Economic Research.
— (1997) 'Prejudices, Crisis and Genocide', *African Studies Review*, vol. 40, no. 2, pp. 91–115.
— (1998) *Aiding Violence: The Development Enterprise in Rwanda*, West Hartford: Kumarian Press.
— (2000) 'The Introduction of a Modernised Gacaca for Judging Suspects of Participation in the Genocide and Massacres' (A Discussion Paper). http://fletcher.archive.tusm-oit.org/faculty/uvin/pdfs/reports/Boutmans.pdf (accessed 28 July 2012).
— (2001) 'Difficult Choices in the New Post-Conflict Agenda: The International Community in Rwanda After the Genocide', *Third World Quarterly*, vol. 22, no. 2, pp. 177–89.
— (2003a) 'The Gacaca Tribunals in Rwanda: A Case Study', in Bloomfield, D., Barnes, T. and Huyse, L. (eds), *Reconciliation After Violent Conflict: A Handbook*, Stockholm: International IDEA.
— (2003b) 'Wake Up! Some personal reflections and policy proposals'. http://ui04e.moit.tufts.edu/faculty/uvin/pdfs/reports/wakeup.pdf (accessed 12 February 2012).
Uvin, P. and Mironko, C. (2003) 'Western and Local Approaches to Justice in Rwanda', *Global Governance*, vol. 9, pp. 219–31.
Valji, N. (2009) 'Trials and Truth Commissions: Seeking Accountability in the Aftermath of Violence', in Hinze, D. (ed.) *Handbook on Human Rights Activities*, Bonn and Berlin: Friedrich-Ebert-Stiftung.
van Boven, T. (1995) 'United Nations Commission on Human Rights: Study Concerning the Right to Restitution, Compensation, and Rehabilitation for Victims of Gross Violations of Human Rights', in Kritz, N.J. (ed.) *Transitional Justice: How Emerging Democracies Reckon with Former Regimes*, vol. 1, General Considerations, Herndon, VA.: United States Institute of Peace Press.
Van den Herik, L.J. (2005) *The Contribution of the Rwanda Tribunal to the Development of International Law*, Leiden: Martinus Nijhoff Publishers.
Van der Merwe, H., Baxter, V. and Chapman R.A. (eds) (2009) *Assessing the Impact of Transitional Justice: Challenges for Empirical Research*, Washington, DC: United States Institute of Peace.
Van Lierop, R.F. (1997) 'Rwanda Evaluation: Report and Recommendations', *International Lawyer*, vol. 31, no. 3, pp. 887–910.

van Zyl, P. (u.d). *How transitional justice processes can contribute to peacebuilding*, Oslo: Ministry of Foreign Affairs. www.regjeringen.no/nb/dep/ud/kampanjer/refleks/innspill/menneskerettigheter/zyl_justice.html?id=534731 (accessed 29 August 2012).

Vandegiste, S. (1997) *Justice for Rwanda and International Cooperation*, Antwerp: University of Antwerp.

— (1999a) 'Approches consociatives dans le contexte du Rwanda', in Marysse, S. and Reyntjens, F. (eds) *L'Afrique des Grands Lacs: Dix Ans de Transitions Conflictuelles, Annuaire 2005–2006*, Paris: L'Harmattan.

— (1999b) 'Justice, Reconciliation and Reparation after Genocide and Crimes against Humanity: The Proposed Establishment of Popular Gacaca Tribunals in Rwanda', Paper presented at the All-Africa Conference on African Principles of Conflict Resolution and Reconciliation, Addis Ababa, 8–12 November 1999. www.grandslacs.net/doc/3666.pdf (accessed 15 August 2008.)

— (2001a) 'Rwanda: Dealing with Genocide and Crimes against Humanity in the Context of Armed Conflict and Failed Political Transition', in Biggar, N. (ed.) *Burying the Past. Making Peace and Doing Justice after Civil Conflict*, Washington, DC: Georgetown University Press.

— (2001b) 'Reparation pour les victimes de genocide, de crimes contre l'humanité et de crimes de guerre au Rwanda', in Marysse, S. and Reyntjens, F. (eds) *L'Afrique des Grands Lacs: Dix Ans de Transitions Conflictuelles, Annuaire 2005–2006*, Paris: L'Harmattan.

— (2003a) 'Reparation', in Bloomfield, D., Barnes, T. and Huyse, L. (eds) *Reconciliation after Violent Conflict: A Handbook*, Stockholm: International Institute for Democracy and Electoral Assistance (International IDEA).

— (2003b) 'Victims of Genocide, Crimes against Humanity, and War Crimes in Rwanda: The Legal and Institutional Framework of their Right to Reparation', in Torpey, J. (ed.) *Politics and the Past: On Repairing Historical Injustices*, Lanham, MD and Oxford: Rowman & Littlefield.

— (2004) 'Justice for Rwanda, Ten Years After: Some Lessons Learned for Transitional Justice, in Marysse, S. and Reyntjens, F. (eds) *L'Afrique des Grands Lacs: Dix Ans de Transitions Conflictuelles, Annuaire 2005–2006*, Paris: L'Harmattan.

— (2009) 'Law as a Source and Instrument of Transitional Justice in Burundi', PhD thesis, Belgium: University of Antwerp.

— (2010) *Stones Left Unturned. Law and Transitional Justice in Burundi*, Mortsel, Belgium: Intersentia.

Venter, C.M. (2007) 'Elimination of Fear Through Recreating Community: The Role of the Gacaca Courts', *Texas Wesleyan Law Review*, vol. 13, pp. 577–99.

Verwimp, P. (2003) 'Testing the Double Genocide Thesis for Central and Southern Rwanda', *Journal of Conflict Resolution*, vol. 47, no. 4, pp. 423–42.

Villa-Vicencio, C. (2003) 'Reconciliation as Politics', *Reconciliation Barometer*, vol. 1, no. 1, pp. 1–3.

Villa-Vicencio, C., Nantulya, P. and Savage, T. (2006) *Building Nations: Transitional Justice in the African Great Lakes Region*, Cape Town: Institute for Justice and Reconciliation.

Villa-Vicencio, C. and Savage, T. (eds) (2001) *Rwanda and South Africa in Dialogue: Addressing the Legacies of Genocide and a Crime Against Humanity*, South Africa: Institute for Justice and Reconciliation.

Villa-Vicencio, C. and Verwoerd, W. (2000) *Looking Back, Reaching Forward: Reflections on the Truth and Reconciliation Commission of South Africa*, Cape Town: University of Cape Town Press.

Waldorf, L. (2004) 'Views from the Field', *Fletcher Journal of International Development*, vol. XIX, pp. 137–41.

— (2006a) 'Rwanda's Failing Experiment in Restorative Justice', in Sullivan, D. and Tifft, L. (eds) *Handbook of Restorative Justice: A Global Perspective*, London and New York: Routledge Taylor & Francis.

— (2006b) 'Mass Justice for Mass Atrocity: Rethinking Local Justice as Transitional Justice', *Temple Law Review*, vol. 79, no. 1, pp. 1–87.

— (2009) 'Goats and Graves: Reparations in Rwanda's Community Courts', in Ferstman, C., Goetz, M. and Stephens, A. (eds) *Reparations for Victims of Genocide, Crimes against Humanity and War Crimes*, Leiden: Martinus Nijhoff Publishers.

— (2011a) 'A Mere Pretence of Justice: Complementarity, Sham Trials, and Victor's Justice at the Rwanda Tribunal', *Fordham International Law Journal*, vol. 33, no. 4, pp. 1220–77.

— (2011b) 'Instrumentalizing Genocide: The RPF's Campaign Against Genocide Ideology', in Straus, S. and Waldorf, L. (eds) *Remaking Rwanda: State Building and Human Rights after Mass Violence*. Madison, WI: University of Wisconsin Press.

Wallace, I. (2005) *Post-conflict Reconstruction: Experiences in Rwanda*, Teddington, UK: Tearfund International Learning Zone. http://tilz.tearfund.org/Publications/Footsteps%2031-40/Footsteps%2036/Post%20conflict+reconstruction+experiences+in+Rwanda.htm (accessed 1 September 2012).

Watson, C. (1991) *Exile from Rwanda: Background to an Invasion*, Washington, DC: US Committee for Refugees.

Welsh, J.M. (2006) 'Mass Justice for Mass Atrocity: Rethinking Local Justice as Transitional Justice', *Temple Law Review*, vol. 79, no. 1, pp. 1–87.

— (2009) 'The Rwanda Effect: Development and Endorsement of the 'Responsibility to Protect', in Clark, P. and Kaufman, Z. (eds) *After Genocide: Transitional Justice, Post-Conflict Reconstruction and Reconciliation in Rwanda and Beyond*, New York: Columbia University Press.

Werchick, L. (2001) 'Prospects for Justice in Rwanda's Citizen Tribunals', *Human Rights Brief*, vol. 8, no. 3, pp. 15–17.

Wierzynska, A. (2004) 'Consolidating Democracy through Transitional Justice: Rwanda's Gacaca Courts', *New York University Law Review*, vol. 79, pp. 1934–69.

Willum, B. (2001) 'Foreign Aid to Rwanda: Purely Beneficial or Contributing to War?', PhD thesis, Institute of Political Science, University of Copenhagen.

Wilson, R.A. (2011) *Writing History in International Criminal Tribunals*, Cambridge and New York: Cambridge University Press.

Wolters, S. (2005a) 'The Gacaca Process', *Africa Security Review*, vol. 14, no. 3, pp. 67–8.

— (2005b) *The Gacaca Process: Eradicating the Culture of Impunity in Rwanda*, Pretoria: Institute of Security Studies.

World Bank (1998) *Rwanda Poverty Note. Rebuilding an Equitable Society: Poverty and Poverty Reduction after the Genocide*, Report No. 17792, Washington, DC: World Bank.

— (2008) *Country Assistance Strategy for the Republic of Rwanda: FY09-FY12*, Washington, DC: World Bank.

— (2011) *Rwanda: Country Brief*, Washington, DC: World Bank. http://web.worldbank.org/WBSITE/EXTERNAL/COUNTRIES/AFRICAEXT/RWANDAEXTN/0,,menuPK:368714~pagePK:141132~piPK:141107~theSitePK:368651,00.html (accessed 16 August 2012).

Zacklin R. (2004) 'The Failings of the Ad Hoc International Tribunals', *Journal of International Criminal Justice*, vol. 2, pp. 541–5.

Zalaquett, J. (1990) 'Confronting Human Rights Violations Committed by Former Governments: Principles Applicable and Political Constraints' in *State Crimes: Punishment and Pardon*, New York: Aspen Institute, 1989. Reprinted in *Hamline Law Review*, 1990, vol. 13, p. 623–60.

Zorbas, E. (2004) 'Reconciliation in Post Genocide Rwanda', *African Journal of Legal Studies*, vol. 1, pp. 29–52.

— (2011) 'Aid Dependence and Policy Independence: Explaining the Rwanda Paradox' in Straus, S. and Waldorf, L. (eds) (2011) *Remaking Rwanda: State Building and Human Rights after Mass Violence*, Madison, WI: University of Wisconsin Press.

Index